DISTRIBUTED SYSTEMS
CONCEPTS AND DESIGN

Second Edition

George Coulouris, Jean Dollimore and Tim Kindberg

INTERNATIONAL COMPUTER SCIENCE SERIES

Consulting Editor **A D McGettrick University of Strathclyde**

SELECTED TITLES IN THE SERIES

High-Level Languages and Their Compilers *D Watson*

Interactive Computer Graphics: Functional, Procedural and Device-Level Methods
  P Burger and D Gillies

Real Time Systems and Their Programming Languages *A Burns and A Wellings*

Prolog Programming for Artifical Intelligence (2nd edn) *I Bratko*

Introduction to Expert Systems (2nd edn) *P Jackson*

Logic for Computer Science *S Reeves and M Clarke*

Computer Architecture *M De Blasi*

The Programming Process: an Introduction using VDM and Pascal *J T Latham,
  V J Bush and D Cottam*

Analysis of Algorithms and Data Structures *L Banachowski, A Kreczmar and W Rytter*

Handbook of Algorithms and Data Structures in Pascal and C (2nd edn) *G Gonnet and
  R Baeza-Yates*

Algorithms and Data Structures *J H Kingston*

Principles of Expert Systems *P Lucas and L van der Gaag*

Discrete Mathematics for Computer Scientists *J K Truss*

Software Engineering (4th edn) *I Sommerville*

Distributed Database Systems *D Bell and J Grimson*

Software Development with Z *J BWordsworth*

Program Verification *N Francez*

Performance Modelling of Communication Networks *P Harrison and N Patel*

Concurrent Systems: An Integrated Approach to Operating Systems, Database, and
Distributed Systems *J Bacon*

Concurrent Programming *A Burns and G L Davies*

Comparative Programming Languages (2nd Edn) *L Wilson and R Clark*

Programming in Ada: Plus an Overview of Ada 9X (4th Edn) *J Barnes*

Programming Language Essentials *H E Bal and D Grune*

Human-Computer Interaction *J Preece, Y Rogers, H Sharp, D Benyon, S Holland and
  T Carey*

Fortran 90 Programming *T M R Ellis, I Philips and T Lahey*

DISTRIBUTED SYSTEMS

CONCEPTS AND DESIGN

second edition

GEORGE COULOURIS
JEAN DOLLIMORE
TIM KINDBERG

Queen Mary and Westfield College
University of London

ADDISON-WESLEY PUBLISHING COMPANY

Harlow, England • Reading, Massachusetts • Menlo Park, California
New York • Don Mills, Ontario • Amsterdam • Bonn • Sydney • Singapore
Tokyo • Madrid • San Juan • Milan • Paris • Mexico City • Seoul • Taipei

Cover designed by Hybert Design and Type, Maidenhead
Printed in the United States of America

1st and 2nd impressions 1994
3rd and 4th impressions 1995

ISBN 0–201–62433–8

British Library Cataloguing-in-Publication Data

A catalogue record for this book is available from the British Library.

Library of Congress Cataloging-in-Publication Data is available

FOREWORD

DISTRIBUTED SYSTEMS:
THE CHALLENGE OF ENTERPRISE COMPUTING

by Kenneth P. Birman
Associate Professor of Computer Science, Cornell University

I find it curious that although I have worked in Distributed Computing for almost 20 years now, there is a sense in which the field has even more open problems today than it did when I first began to learn about it. At that time, the first questions about how to approach distributed computing were still being posed. Researchers were proposing all sorts of approaches to writing and reasoning about distributed software, and the most important experimental projects were just getting under way. By now, a huge number of approaches have been explored. Satisfactory solutions have been nailed down in many areas, standards have emerged, and there are many impressive success stories confirming that distributed computing systems really can be made to work well, bringing the full power of modern computing technology to the desktop, the factory floor, the communications-switch, or whatever.

Yet, in 1994, the field is apparently about to reinvent itself! Just as we thought we understood distributed computing, ATM networks and novel presentations of computing threaten a 100-fold scaling up of the numbers of components in distributed systems, the performance demands, and the complexity of typical software solutions. The US government is constructing an ambitious national data highway: distributed computing systems will be the key to exploiting this astonishingly high performance, pervasive technology.

This new, much-revised and expanded edition of *Distributed Systems: Concepts and Design*, by Coulouris, Dollimore and Kindberg, is an impressive testimony to the state-of-the-art today. For many years, I have found it difficult to teach distributed computing to students new to the field. There has been little middle ground between general-purpose operating systems textbooks and advanced research papers. For the first time, the basic principles underlying state-of-the-art distributed computing have been pulled together in a form intended to be approachable by advanced undergraduate students and graduate students.

It would be hard to imagine a situation in which knowledge of distributed computing would be of greater importance to students than it is today. Organizations are moving to exploit computing systems more effectively, and this is giving rise to a new class of large-scale distributed applications. These *enterprise computing systems* offer highly integrated, highly reliable computing to users who may be physically separated by large distances and interacting with a multiplicity of computing devices. They combine large numbers of independently executing programs into an (apparently) seamless whole, and often provide services critical to the organization. The development of software for such systems poses difficult challenges, particularly because of the need to respond dynamically to failures and recoveries. This is further complicated by the constraint that the system behave consistently regardless of where it is accessed.

Enterprise computing systems differ in significant ways from the types of distributed computing that have been common during the 1970s and 1980s. During this period, a move has occurred from mainframe systems to networked *personal computing systems*, with network software providing such functionality as shared data storage and electronic mail. Despite the interconnectivity of such systems, they remain largely independent: each user runs his or her own applications (word-processing, spreadsheets, engineering design tools, and so on), and any interactions between systems are through shared files and mail. Client-server computing has also become common: in such systems, a number of client systems are configured as a sort of ring around a centralized server, which provides database functionality, file management, or other support. Again, the client systems interact indirectly, through shared servers.

Enterprise computing systems, in contrast, are characterized by a close, direct coupling of application programs running on multiple platforms in a networked environment. The programs involved will generally coordinate their actions to present a consistent image of the system to users. Indeed, it is common for a such a system to mimic a single highly reliable program, despite the decentralized nature of the underlying software. Within the book, Chapters 11 through 15 discuss exactly this issue of reliability, reviewing several of most important and widely used approaches. Other chapters, such as 4, 5 and 10, discuss fundamental technologies on which current systems are based.

The need for close coupling of distributed programs arises in many settings. Telecommunications systems that provide services to mobile users are an obvious example. The software involved in providing services to such a user must worry about the hand-off of a call from switching node to switching node without disruption of service, and thus the subsystems providing services are enterprise computing systems. Moreover, the trend is to allow easy customization of services and the introduction of new services, suggesting that this problem may need to be solved repeatedly in each of a large number of applications.

Enterprise computing issues are also seen in banking and brokerage settings, and indeed any commercial setting where the trend towards a paperless, information-flow commerce requires coordinated actions at multiple points in a distributed system. Banks and brokerages, for example, are rapidly moving to develop electronic stock and bond trading markets. Moreover, individual institutions must increasingly coordinate trading in multiple markets to hedge against currency fluctuations, manage financial risk associated with the institution's overall position, and to respond to trends in a globalized trading environment. To give just one example, it is common to limit the percentage of financial assets invested in any one currency or trading instrument. In an international firm, this means that trading activity in, say, Tokyo may have important immediate implications for trading in New York or Zurich. The software used to inform traders of the current limits must run close to where they trade – otherwise, a communication outage could cripple trading, since the traders would hesitate to trade at the risk of exceeding a legal limit or company policy. It follows that a collection of programs running locally to each trading centre must somehow coordinate the advice that they are giving to traders, and in a way that is always safe, but that also maximizes the chances of riding out a short communication outage or failure without disruption. This is a typical enterprise computing problem, and instances of similar problems are seen throughout modern trading systems.

The list of settings in which enterprise computing issues arise is growing rapidly. Scientific computer users seek ways of sharing supercomputers over a network. The enterprise here is the shared facility, and the computing problems include resource allocation, facilities for monitoring executions and mechanisms for dynamically recovering from failures. The same questions also arise within applications, for example when a weather simulation is developed by glueing together an atmospheric model specialized to a vector processor with a massively parallel ocean model and displaying the result on a graphics supercomputer – a system being developed by the Los Alamos Advanced Computing Laboratory. Data collection in devices like the new CERN particle accelerator raises similar questions. Semiconductor manufacturers seek to increase efficiency and flexibility by automating entire VLSI fabrication lines, linking dozens of specialized computers and devices to a network which may in turn be connected to hundreds of workstations used for engineering design, administration, and other functions. Here, the enterprise revolves around software for coordinating the fabrication process in the presence of dynamic demands. Hospitals look to increased computing support as a way of cutting costs and improving efficiency, and also seek to dedicate substantial computing resources to each patient in order to support real-time monitoring functions.

To function effectively as a technology developer in distributed systems, knowledge of the basic techniques available in this area has become vital. Through study of the material brought together in this book, an undergraduate or graduate student can rapidly come up to speed, learning what is known, what works and when, and how the basic techniques have been applied in prior projects.

On the other hand, we are still far from knowing the full story. While the student who masters the material in this text will be well prepared to attack the great majority of distributed problems encountered in research and industry, there are many problems on which further progress is needed. I consider reliability to be the one area most in need of additional study (others might argue that privacy and security are at least as critical, but to me these are just parts of an overriding concern). Although this topic goes slightly beyond the book, I want to comment on it briefly because I view distributing computing as being so critically important in many settings. To me, it is imperative that we engineer these systems to the highest possible standards of reliability, and that we pursue programs of research that will advance the frontiers beyond the limitations of current technology.

As organizations move to depend more and more heavily on their distributed computing applications and systems, the reliability of these becomes increasingly critical to the economic viability of the entire organization. For this reason, a key issue to ask about this emerging class of software concerns the degree of reliability that systems of this sort can achieve. Strong arguments can be advanced against placing extreme confidence in the reliability of isolated programs. Thus, one must anticipate that both software and hardware failures will occur while an enterprise computing application is running. However, since these are multi-component systems, the question remains whether redundancy can somehow be exploited to enable the overall system to ride out and recover from all but the most extreme failures. Reliability is an imprecise term in the context of computing settings. One would expect a reliable distributed system to behave in a predictable, consistent manner regardless of the point(s) through which it is accessed: there should be no contradiction between the actions and state of the system at different locations, the system as a whole should do only what it was designed to do, and the system should operate or 'manage' itself, with minimal human intervention.

Beyond consistency, reliability connotes additional properties such as self-management, real-time responsiveness, data recoverability (the ability to restore data that were being manipulated at the time of a crash), security, privacy, and the ability of the system to tolerate incorrect input (e.g. from sensors or users). However, these problems are well known from non-distributed computing systems, and adequate solutions have existed for many years. Were it not for the need to tolerate failures, existing technologies could be used to obtain highly reliable distributed software, much as it is possible to develop acceptably reliable non-distributed software using systematic programming techniques and careful testing. Such software may not be perfectly reliable, but extremely high levels of reliability are routinely achieved.

Thus, the core technical problem concerns consistency and fault tolerance. Clearly, it is impossible to build a system that reacts to failures in a timely manner, while never making mistakes by classifying an operational component as faulty. (This is because it is impossible to distinguish a process that is faulty from one that is merely having communication problems). Yet, an erroneous failure classification can throw a multi-component system into a chaotic state, in which different components have inconsistent views of the status (operational or faulty) of other components of the system, and hence behave in inconsistent ways. It is only very recently that techniques for tolerating failures and recoveries while maintaining consistent behavior have been developed. I think that it would be hard to over-stress the importance of seeing the solutions in this area move from the laboratory into widespread use.

This raises a second but closely related concern. Even where techniques for making systems reliable are already well understood, distributed computing systems have often failed to exploit them. Many readers will recall that in 1987, a highly publicized attack on the Internet that links tens of thousands of research computers caused some six thousand machines to crash. The Internet Worm responsible for this exploited relatively simple security loopholes that could easily have been plugged. Worse, several of these loopholes were well known and scheduled for repair in future releases of vendor operating systems. The success of the Internet Worm was primarily illustrative of the relatively low importance that reliability has received in modern computing systems, not of any technical problem. Fortunately, this class of obstacle to reliability is diminishing through public awareness of the issue, which has created a competitive advantage for vendors able to offer a more reliable computing platform. In the future, non-intrinsic limitations to reliability should continue to fade away.

In contrast, during the same period (1989-91) there were several major failures of the nationwide telephone system. These problems were tracked to relatively obscure software bugs in the programs used to balance load among the components of a recently introduced switching system, called SS-7. One bug involved a fairly subtle synchronization problem that was triggered when a switching node was upgraded to a new software release, while a different bug was caused by a minor coding error. In both cases, the problem rippled through the network of telecommunication switching nodes, shutting down large parts of it. In effect, the system was unable to contain and (correctly) reconfigure itself after certain types of failures occurred.

Problems of this sort are more basic: they stem from the technical complexity of building distributed software that maintains consistency and dynamically reconfigures itself in the presence of failures and other events. If this issue can be addressed, other aspects of reliability (such as security) follow; lacking adequate solutions to this basic problem, there would be little hope for developing acceptable enterprise computing software.

In light of the tremendous potential of reliable enterprise distributed computing systems, it is remarkable that relatively little attention has been paid to developing better reliability technologies and marketing them. The existing technology base, with its many obstacles to reliability, stands as a significant culprit: if a computing system cannot be relied upon, or compels a trade-off between reliability and performance, organizations will not use computers in settings where reliability is an issue. For more than a decade, operating systems and network development has pursued simplicity and performance at the expense of consistency and fault tolerance.

An awesome resource has been created by the computing and telecommunications industries, but it is still largely untapped. However, as reliability technologies become increasingly standard, and they surely will, this will inevitably change.

Arguably, distributed computing systems are already as critical to society as bridges, airplanes and medical devices. Through the study of fundamental issues, diligent design and further research, we can make these systems reliable enough to justify the trust that is being placed in them – and in us, as their developers! And, given distributed software systems that can be relied upon, and that can tolerate the sorts of disruptions and transient outages that any large system experiences, the future holds the promise of a distributed computing technology revolution, every bit as far reaching as the computer revolution has been during its first three decades.

Ken Birman, 1994

To Anna, Jason, Julian, Rachel, Susan
Alice and Gene

PREFACE

The second edition of our textbook appears almost six years after publication of the first edition. In the interval distributed systems have become a major topic in computer science teaching and research, and their development and use has become a key activity in many companies.

This edition constitutes a comprehensive revision and expansion of the book, bringing it up-to-date and encompassing a wider range of topics. There is now a substantial body of knowledge on the sound design and construction of general-purpose distributed systems and their applications. The development of the field has been so rapid that it has necessitated a major re-write. Virtually every chapter has been re-written and with the help of an extra author seven chapters have been added, to produce a book almost twice the size of the previous edition.

Like the first edition, this book is intended to provide knowledge of the principles and practice of distributed system design. We have set out to convey this knowledge in sufficient depth to allow readers to evaluate existing systems and design new ones. We have retained the approach of the first edition, using case studies to illustrate the design concepts related to each major topic.

The book reflects the openness of distributed systems, which are largely constructed from open services built around a standard communication framework. In the first chapter we introduce distributed systems through a set of simple exemplars and a discussion of the basic underlying concepts. We identify design issues and motivate the study of their solutions in the second chapter. In the following pair of chapters we describe remote procedure calling and multicast communication between groups of processes, the most important communication methods needed for open systems. We then build upon these foundations a thorough and, as far as possible, orthogonal coverage of each of the sub-fields of distributed computing, from kernel facilities to open services such as file management, naming and clock synchronization. We include transactional services for shared data, and advanced operating system services such as distributed shared memory. In addition, we cover techniques for enhancing services, including security and replication.

Purposes and readership

The book is intended as a text for undergraduate and postgraduate study. It can equally be used for self-study. We assume that readers have a knowledge of programming and elementary computer architecture, together with a familiarity with basic operating system concepts. We cover the field with sufficient depth and breadth to enable readers to tackle most non-theoretical research papers in distributed systems.

Programs are written either in Modula-2 or, where more appropriate in the light of actual implementations, ANSI C. Only a small and self-explanatory subset of each language is used. The reader need not be familiar with networks, since the book provides sufficient coverage of the most important aspects of networking relevant to distributed systems, including local area network technology and internetworks.

How to use the book

The following diagram is intended to provide a guide to the book's structure, indicating navigation routes for teachers wishing to provide, or readers wishing to achieve, an understanding in various subfields of distributed system design. The diagram is organized under seven main topic areas that group chapters or subsections of chapters:

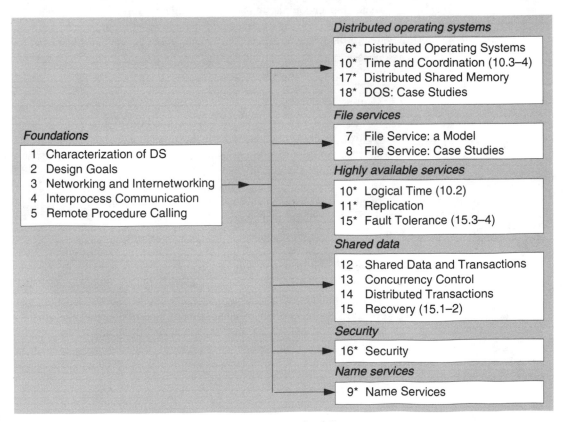

The chapters that are new or have been substantially re-written since the first edition are indicated by asterisks in the diagram. In addition, nearly all the case studies have been replaced by a wider range of more up-to-date systems.

Undergraduate and postgraduate courses may be based on one or more of the topic areas shown in the diagram. At Queen Mary and Westfield College, we use the material in this book for an undergraduate course taken in the second or third year, which has as a prerequisite an introductory course on concurrency and basic computer resource management in operating systems. We also use a larger part of the book for a one-year course at masters level, in which students apply their knowledge in a substantial practical project. We use the material as follows:

Undergraduate teaching □ (25 hours lectures)

Foundations: Chapters 1, 2 and parts of 5.

File services: Chapter 7 and Sun NFS case study from Chapter 8.

Distributed operating systems: parts of Chapter 6 and 10 and a case study from Chapter 18 (e.g. Mach).

Shared data: Chapter 12 and Section 13.1(on locking).

Postgraduate teaching □ We give courses on distributed operating systems and on distributed data, preceded by a foundation course, all taught in seminar style.

Foundations (20 hours):
A thorough study of all the material in Chapters 1–5.

Distributed Operating Systems (30 hours):
DOS principles: Chapters 6 and 10; case studies from Chapter 18 (e.g. Mach, UNIX Emulation and Clouds); Chapters 9, 11, 16 and 17, covering name services, replication, security and distributed shared memory.

Distributed Data and Algorithms (30 hours):
File services: Chapter 7 and case studies on Sun NFS, Andrew File System and Coda from Chapter 8; shared data and transactions: Chapters 12-15.

The book supports the seminar style of teaching with extensive illustrations and exercises designed for class discussion. In our courses, students are asked to prepare and present short discussions based around their solutions to selected exercises. Page numbers appended to the exercises refer the reader to the context in which they are set.

Individual study □ Readers who have studied Chapters 1 and 2 should be able to pursue individual study in a several ways. For example, they could then proceed to study any of the following topics:

Internetworking: Read Chapter 3.

File services: Read Chapter 7 followed by an appropriate case study from Chapter 8, using Chapters 4 and 5 as reference material.

Mach, Chorus or Amoeba: Read the relevant case study from Chapter 18, using Chapters 4– 6 as reference material.

Name services: Read Chapter 9, using Chapter 5 as reference material.

Security: Read Chapter 16.

Support for instructors and readers   (this section updated 1995)

Instructor's guide □ An Instructor's Guide is available, giving presentation notes on each chapter, solutions to the end-of-chapter exercises, viewgraph transparency masters and a set of laboratory exercises. The Instructor's Guide is available in hardcopy form from the publishers and in electronic form as detailed below. The solutions are available only to *bona-fide* teachers.

Internet access □ You can access the Instructor's Guide, a list of corrections and other recent material relating to the book via the World Wide Web or by anonymous FTP.

URL for the book's home page:	Anonymous FTP address:	
http://www.dcs.qmw.ac.uk/research/ *distrib/book.html*	*host:*	*ftp.dcs.qmw.ac.uk*
	directory:	*distrib/dsbook*

Mailing lists □ Two network mailing lists are available for readers to use:

DSBookAuthors@qmw.ac.uk is an alias for the authors' email addresses.

DSBookReaders@qmw.ac.uk is an open subscription list. You should subscribe to *DSBookReaders* if you want to be informed about corrections, updates and additional material available for FTP. Readers can also use the list to communicate with other readers. To subscribe to it send a message to:

listserv@qmw.ac.uk

containing the line:

subscribe DSBookReaders <your name>

For documentation about using the list, send a message to *listserv@qmw.ac.uk* with a body containing the word *help*.

Acknowledgements

We are grateful to several classes of students studying for the MSc in Distributed and Parallel Systems at Queen Mary and Westfield College who have studied from earlier drafts of this edition of the book. Their efforts to present the material in seminar classes have helped us to produce what is, we hope, a useful textbook.

We are particularly grateful to Jean Bacon, who has reviewed both editions of the book with great energy and provided us many constructive comments and suggestions. We are also grateful to her for kind permission to include Figures 1.3 and 9.14.

We should like to thank the following, all of whom gave us input or feedback and comments on specific parts of the book: Tom Berson, Ken Birman, Richard Bornat, Flaviu Cristian, Kurt Jensen, Daniel Julin, Steve Kille, Roger Needham, David Pick, David Mosberger, Harry Porter, Stephen Sedley, David Steer.

Finally, we should like to thank Simon Plumtree of Addison-Wesley, the anonymous reviewers, and the cohort of teachers using the first edition of the book who provided us with their comments through Addison-Wesley's survey.

George Coulouris
Jean Dollimore
Tim Kindberg
London, February 1994.

CONTENTS

CHARACTERIZATION OF DISTRIBUTED SYSTEMS

We define a distributed system as a collection of autonomous computers linked by a network, with software designed to produce an integrated computing facility.

Distributed systems are implemented on hardware platforms that vary in a size from a few workstations interconnected by a single local area network to the Internet – a world-wide interconnected collection of local and wide area networks linking thousands or even millions of computers.

Applications of distributed systems range from the provision of general-purpose computing facilities for groups of users to automated banking and multimedia communication systems, and they embrace almost all commercial and technical applications of computers.

The key characteristics of distributed systems are: support for resource sharing, openness, concurrency, scalability, fault tolerance and transparency. We define these and indicate their implications for the design of distributed system software.

The history of distributed systems has its origins in the development of multi-user computers and computer networks in the 1960s and was stimulated by the development of low-cost personal workstations, local area networks and the UNIX operating system in the 1970s. We outline these and other historical factors in the development of distributed systems.

1.1 Introduction

A **distributed system** consists of a collection of autonomous computers linked by a computer network and equipped with distributed system software. Distributed system software enables computers to coordinate their activities and to share the resources of the system – hardware, software and data. Users of a well-designed distributed system should perceive a single, integrated computing facility even though it may be implemented by many computers in different locations.

The development of distributed systems followed the emergence of high-speed local area computer networks at the beginning of the 1970s. More recently, the availability of high-performance personal computers, workstations and server computers has resulted in a major shift towards distributed systems and away from centralized and multi-user computers. This trend has been accelerated by the development of distributed system software, designed to support the development of distributed applications.

Much research and development work has been done on the design of distributed systems and their underlying principles. Section 1.4 provides an overview of the historical background and identifies some of the more important developments. The work continues, but there are already many effective practical implementations of distributed systems and a substantial body of theoretical and empirical knowledge about their design.

This book aims to present the current state of knowledge about the design and construction of distributed systems and to elucidate the concepts and techniques that underlie them. As in many other fields of computer science, the development of distributed systems has progressed by the formulation of abstract models for systems that meet a range of general requirements, followed by the design and implementation of systems that support those models. Our method of description follows the same pattern. For each of the major topics that the book deals with we define the requirements,

Figure 1.1   A simple distributed system.

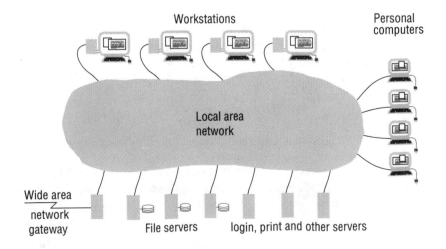

Figure 1.2   A centralized multi-user system.

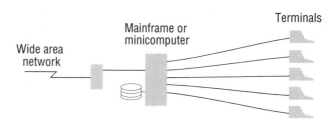

describe the most important models that have been developed to meet them and illustrate the use of the models by the description of specific systems as case studies.

This chapter serves as an introduction to the subject and defines the scope of the book. In Section 1.2 we illustrate the range of distributed systems and applications. In Section 1.3 we describe their special characteristics and advantages.

1.2 Examples

In this section we outline some typical distributed systems and applications. We introduce these examples at this stage in order to illustrate the wide range of requirements and design problems that can arise in distributed systems.

Distributed UNIX □ Figure 1.1 shows the components of a distributed system based on a local network. Such a system, equipped with appropriate software can support the computing needs of a substantial population of users, fulfilling a similar role to the centralized multi-user mainframe and minicomputer systems that preceded the advent of distributed systems (Figure 1.2).

Multi-user systems were constructed around a single time shared computer, with an operating system that allocates and manages the hardware resources, such as the central processor and memory, in order to share them between the users. UNIX [Ritchie and Thompson 1974] is perhaps the best-known example of a multi-user operating system. Since it was already in widespread use and easily available when distributed systems were being developed, many distributed system researchers and developers adopted the model provided by the original UNIX as their goal. They aimed to produce implementations of the UNIX model that could exploit the resources of many computers, offering facilities and performance that exceeded those of the single multi-user system that they replaced. The improvements were not just in performance, but in reliability, extensibility and support for applications that involve communication; we shall discuss these further in Section 1.3.

These developments began with the extension of the original UNIX system design to include support for interprocess communication. This was achieved in the 4BSD versions of UNIX developed at the University of California at Berkeley in the late 1970s. Subsequently, these communication facilities were extended and exploited as a basis for the development of full distributed systems, and the necessary components for systems that follow the structure illustrated in Figure 1.1 were constructed. The BSD

UNIX interprocess communication facilities are described in outline in Chapter 4 and in great detail by Leffler *et al.* [1989].

In Figure 1.1 there is no shared central computer. Instead, each user is provided with a computer sufficiently powerful to run the programs that they wish to use, and there are **servers** that provide access to a variety of shared system facilities and resources. These include filing, printing, wide-area communication and user authentication. The programs running on users' workstations act as **clients** of the servers, obtaining whatever access they require to the servers' resources. Servers may be multiplied as required to support the workload. For example, several file servers are often included, even in quite small distributed systems, because the frequency of access to files by client programs would swamp the processing capacity of a single server computer. This simple client-server model has been the basis for much of the distributed system development undertaken to date and the techniques that underlie it are a major theme of this book.

The distributed UNIX model outlined here has been implemented in several forms. The most widely used implementation is that developed by Sun Microsystems, a workstation manufacturer that took the Berkeley BSD UNIX as the starting point for an extensive software effort, which led to the development of the well known Network File System (NFS). This software component and its associated Remote Procedure Calling (RPC) and Network Information Service (NIS) components are now offered by almost every workstation vendor (under licence from Sun Microsystems) and are used as the basis for most current distributed UNIX implementations. Other distributed UNIX implementations have been undertaken as applied research efforts aimed at removing some of the limitations and difficulties associated with the original UNIX definition and at achieving systems on scales well beyond those possible with multi-user UNIX systems. Examples of these include three of the distributed operating systems that are described in Chapter 18: the Amoeba system, developed at the Vrije University, Amsterdam, the Mach and Chorus distributed operating systems and some distributed system components that were designed as extensions of UNIX. These include the Andrew distributed file system from Carnegie-Mellon University (described in Chapter 8) and the Kerberos system for security in distributed systems developed at MIT (described in Chapter 16).

Although the development of distributed UNIX systems offers obvious commercial and technical advantages, UNIX was originally designed to meet a restricted range of requirements in an era when the limitations of computer hardware restricted the scope of designers' ambitions. A new generation of distributed operating systems whose design goals go beyond the aims of UNIX is now emerging. An important attribute of distributed operating systems is their **openness** – a characteristic that enables systems to be extended to meet new application requirements and user needs. We shall define openness in Section 1.3. See the accompanying box for a definition of distributed operating systems. The goals and design features of distributed operating systems are the subject of Chapter 6 and several examples are described in detail in Chapter 18.

Commercial applications □ Many commercial data processing and information systems involve data communication. Examples include the systems used by airlines for seat reservation and ticketing, the networks operated by banks to support their branches

Figure 1.3 An automatic teller machine network.

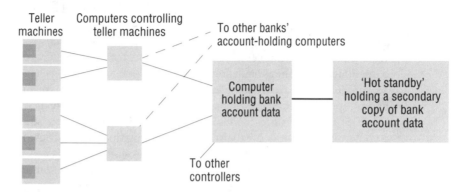

and to operate their automatic teller (cash dispensing) machines and the systems operated by supermarket and other retail chains to coordinate their stock control, delivery and sales check-out.

The requirements of such applications include a high level of reliability, security against external interference and privacy of the information that the system holds. They must provide for concurrent access to databases by many users, guaranteed response times, service access points that are geographically widely distributed, potential for system growth to accommodate business expansion and scope for the integration of systems used by different companies and user organizations.

Most current implementations of such commercial applications are based on dedicated hardware, software and communication networks. Their software is designed to support a system structure in which the database for each application is centralized, and the performance of the system is optimized by delegating some functions to computers that are remote from the database machine.

Figure 1.3 illustrates the structure of a typical automatic teller machine network. The main function of automatic teller machines is to provide a service for cash withdrawal from customers' accounts. Security and reliability are prime requirements.

Distributed operating systems: An important goal of recent research and development in distributed system design has been to develop *distributed operating systems*. We can define the goals of distributed operating systems by comparison with those of conventional operating systems such as UNIX. Like a conventional operating system, a distributed operating system is a collection of software components that simplifies the task of programming and supports the widest possible range of applications. Unlike conventional operating systems, distributed operating systems are modular and extensible. New components may be added to distributed operating systems in response to new application needs. The modularity of distributed operating systems is based on the support that they provide for communication between modules. Because they are extensible, it is fruitless to attempt to specify a fixed list of software components that defines a distributed operating system. Some components fall in the borderline between operating system and application software.

The user's identity must be carefully validated before any transaction can occur. Withdrawals must not be permitted unless the user has sufficient funds in their bank account. When a withdrawal occurs the user's account record must be updated to show the withdrawal. The user's identification details (card code and PIN number) must not be compromised at any point in the processing of a transaction. All of these requirements must be met with a very high degree of reliability, even in the face of communication failures and computer failures.

Bacon [1993] gives a useful summary of a typical design for such a system. It is a highly specific solution, requiring the development of many levels of application-specific software support. This approach has been employed successfully in many commercial applications, but it suffers from limitations that restrict the scope for system growth, reliability and security.

Although for historical reasons most implementations of large-scale commercial applications such as those mentioned above do not currently exploit general-purpose distributed system techniques, all of the requirements that we have mentioned above are in areas for which distributed solutions have been developed. In this book we describe the relevant methods for achieving reliability (Chapter 15), security and privacy (Chapter 16) concurrent access to data (Chapter 13), resource allocation and performance optimization (Chapter 6), replication of data for performance and availability (Chapter 11), and the extension and integration of application domains (Chapter 9).

Wide area network applications □ The significance of wide area networks has increased as the population of computers connected to them and the range of software supporting their use has grown.

The Internet is discussed in detail in Chapter 3. It is a world-wide interconnected collection of local and wide area networks that has emerged from the development of national computer networks in the 1970s. The software technology of the Internet is derived directly from the ARPAnet, the first wide-area computer network, developed in the US. A key design goal for the Internet was that it should be **scalable**, enabling the network and the applications that run on it to expand by several orders of magnitude. In 1980 there were approximately 100 computers connected to the Internet, in 1990 there were 100,000 and at the time of writing the number exceeds a million. The design of the underlying communication software has not had to be changed in the intervening period and most of the distributed applications that run on it have survived without major modification.

Despite the restricted speeds of the data transmission lines on which the Internet is currently based, it supports several applications that are distributed in character; their design has been successful in coping with the dramatic changes in scale that have occurred.

The best-known of these applications is electronic mail. This relatively simple distributed application faces a substantial problem in locating the host computers of the users to whom mail is addressed. The problem is that of translating a name attached to an email message, such as *John.Davison@dcs.qmw.ac.uk* or *President@whitehouse.gov*, which carries no network routing information, to an address that can be used to route the message to the host computer that holds the electronic mailbox of the intended recipient. This is an example of the general problem of *name resolution* in distributed systems. The

Internet solution is based on the hierarchical structure embedded in Internet names (such as *dcs.qmw.ac.uk*), but the design of a system that scales to handle the many millions of messages delivered in the Internet each day, allowing names to be added, modified and deleted without interrupting the operation of the system was a challenging problem. Internetworking techniques and Internet naming, addressing and routing are described in Chapter 3. Name resolution in the Internet and the general problem of name resolution for distributed systems are discussed in detail in Chapter 9.

The Internet has spawned several other distributed applications including the well-known *netnews* service, which distributes electronic messages to users organized in thousands of electronic newsgroups, similar to bulletin boards. Netnews has millions of users at sites throughout the Internet. Another example is the Gopher distributed information retrieval system that supports 'information browsing' in a web of electronic documents containing text and other media. The documents are located in computers throughout the Internet with indexes containing links to them. The links are resolved and documents retrieved in a few seconds, enabling users to 'browse' through a set of documents stored on computers at different points in the network as though they were on her desk.

The examples of wide-area distributed applications outlined above demonstrate the feasibility of using wide area networks in distributed applications. But high-speed local area networks have been the main breeding ground for distributed systems because

This illustration shows another Internet information service: World Wide Web (WWW) – a network-based hypermedia information system. WWW client programs provide interactive facilities for browsing hypermedia documents. The documents are stored as structured text with embedded references (called *links*) to other documents, pictures, sounds and video sequences that are held on the WWW servers in the Internet. There are many WWW servers, each holding a range of documents and information in other media on diverse topics.

Links

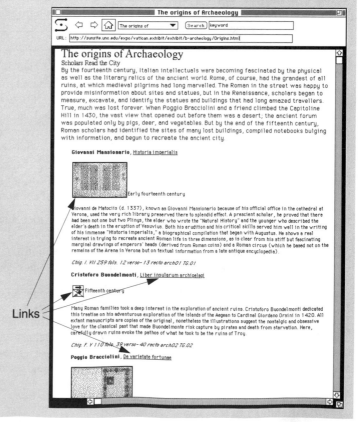

their performance enables a much wider range of distributed systems and applications to be developed in a transparent manner, exploiting the speed of the network to hide the effect of the physical distribution of hardware and information. We use the term *transparent* here to refer to the concealment from users and programs of the distribution of resources; see page 20 for a fuller definition. The current performance of wide-area networks does not offer the same potential for transparency. The range of distributed applications that they can support is restricted and many applications have to be carefully designed to circumvent their performance limitations. In Chapter 3 we shall see that wide area networking technologies now under development will provide transmission speeds comparable to, or better than current local networks. The wide area networks of the immediate future are likely to combine the scale of the Internet with the performance of local area networks.

Multimedia information access and conferencing applications □ Multimedia applications employ digital representations of photographic images, audio and video sequences to support users performing tasks ranging from computer-aided learning, remote conferencing or cooperative design work to game playing and shopping. The storage, transmission and presentation of digital representations of audio and video sequences derived from recordings, on-line video cameras, computer-synthesized animations and simulations plays a prominent role in multimedia applications.

Many multimedia applications depend upon an underlying distributed system to enable several users to interact with each other or to share resources. We are concerned here with the special requirements that they bring to the design of distributed systems. They include:

1. Digital audio and video are continuous media. They are sometimes referred to as *time-based data* because they are generated and must be reproduced at some fixed rate. If sound is not reproduced at the rate at which it was originally generated, it quickly becomes incomprehensible. If the timing of video sequences is not maintained, they become distorted and the synchronization between sound and pictures is lost. For applications of the types mentioned above, video information is usually generated and reproduced at a rate of 16 frames per second, each frame comprising an array of up to 512×512 16-bit pixels, resulting in a data rate of about 100 megabits per second. With current image compression techniques, that figure can be reduced to an average of about one megabit per second.

2. In interactive applications such as video phone and conferencing, there is an additional requirement: the delay between the initiation of a conversational interaction at one site and its reproduction at another should be less than about 100 milliseconds, otherwise the delay becomes perceptible as a hesitation before each interaction in a video conversation.

The services used to store and transmit time-based data must provide guarantees that the data can be stored, read and transmitted at the required rates and with specified maximum delays in order to maintain adequate quality in the resulting sound and pictures. This implies a minimum data transfer rate and a maximum delay requirement on the servers used to store time-based data and the networks used to transmit them. The operating systems used in client and server computers must also meet relevant real-time constraints.

Figure 1.4   The Pandora system.

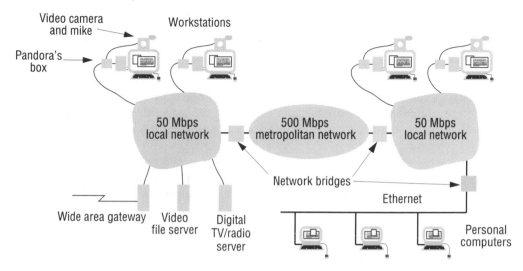

The development of multimedia applications and the provision of appropriate hardware, software and communication support for them is at an early stage. Most current examples are in experimental systems and their capabilities are restricted by the performance of the networking technologies that they use. We outline one such system here to indicate the potential of multimedia and the demands that it will place on distributed systems.

Figure 1.4 shows the main components of the Pandora multimedia distributed system developed at the Olivetti Research Laboratory, Cambridge, England [Jones and Hopper 1993]. The system is designed to support a range of experimental applications of multimedia, including video conferencing, video phone and mail applications and the storage and retrieval of audio and video sequences.

The workstations shown in Figure 1.4 are conventional workstations equipped with a video camera, a microphone and a hardware unit known as a *Pandora's box*. A Pandora's box contains components suitable for capturing and compressing audio and video signals in digital form, displaying video in windows on the workstation's screen and switching audio and video between the camera, the network interface and the display system. In principle, all of these functions could be performed by software, but the real-time constraints of time-based data lead to the need to construct a dedicated unit to perform them. Some personal computers are attached to the Pandora system but these are not equipped with Pandora's boxes, and they offer more restricted multimedia functionality based on a software implementation of the Pandora's box operations.

The communication bandwidths required to support multimedia applications are at least an order of magnitude greater than in other applications. The video frame size is restricted in the Pandora system so that video streams require a maximum communication bandwidth of about one megabit per second including the associated audio stream or sound-track. In an application such as video conferencing several separate video/audio streams can be displayed at each workstation (originating from other workstation cameras or from stored video). A conference may involve several workstations, and the relevant video streams must be transmitted to each of them. Several video conferences, video phone calls and other applications can proceed simultaneously. When overloads occur in Pandora, the transmission of speech data is given priority over other tasks, including the transmission of video, because speech quickly becomes incomprehensible if it is not played back at the rate at which it was uttered.

The constraints of time-based data impose a real-time requirement on network hardware and software and on workstation operating systems. Network software and operating systems must allocate network bandwidth and workstation processing capacity in small discrete quantities so that they can be multiplexed between the tasks associated with several audio and video channels without loss of quality.

The control of the quality of service to meet the requirements of time-based data handling is an important feature of systems designed to support multimedia applications. When overloading occurs the priorities must be carefully determined. The term *quality of service* has been adopted from telecommunications engineering to refer to resource allocation methods that can be tailored to meet the requirements of specific applications.

The requirements of multimedia applications for high-speed data communication and control over the quality of service supplied to each application have led to the recent development of networks based on the Asynchronous Transfer Mode (ATM) method of communication, and to work on the design of real-time distributed operating systems, clients and servers to meet the required criteria for the synchronization and continuity of multimedia data transmission. The Pandora system exploits two different ATM networking technologies to achieve the required bandwidth within single sites and over a wider area encompassing several sites and up to 50 workstations in the town of Cambridge, England. Its client and server software are designed to degrade gracefully when an overload occurs within a workstation or across the network. We shall discuss ATM networking techniques in Chapter 3 and methods for meeting the requirements of multimedia in distributed operating systems in Chapter 6. Work on the design of servers for the storage of time-based data is the subject of current research at Cambridge University [Bacon *et al.* 1991] and elsewhere [Anderson *et al.* 1992].

1.3   Key characteristics

Six key characteristics are primarily responsible for the usefulness of distributed systems. These are *resource sharing*, *openness*, *concurrency*, *scalability*, *fault tolerance* and *transparency*. In this section we define and elaborate on each of them. It should be noted that they are not automatic consequences of distribution; system and application software must be carefully designed in order to ensure that they are attained.

Resource sharing □ The term 'resource' is a rather abstract one, but it best characterizes the range of things that can be shared usefully in a distributed system. The range extends from hardware components such as disks and printers to software-defined entities such as files, windows, databases and other data objects.

Users of both centralized and distributed computer systems are so accustomed to the benefits of resource sharing that they may easily overlook their significance. The benefits of shared access to a single filing system containing databases, programs, documentation and other information were first recognized with the emergence of multi-user or time-sharing systems in the early 1960s, and multi-user UNIX systems in the 1970s.

- Hardware devices such as printers, large disk drives and other peripherals are shared for convenience and to reduce costs.

- Data sharing is an essential requirement in many computer applications.

  - Software developers working as a team may need access to each other's work and can share the same development tools, requiring only a single copy of compilers, procedure libraries, editors and debugging aids; whenever a new development tool or a new release of a compiler is installed, all users immediately obtain access to it.

  - Many commercial applications such as those outlined in Section 1.2 enable users to access shared data objects in a single active database.

  - A rapidly-expanding area of application for networks and distributed systems is the use of computers in support of groups of users working cooperatively – project work, team management, remote teaching and many other cooperative tasks can benefit from such support. *Computer supported cooperative working* (CSCW, also known as *groupware*) depends heavily on the sharing of data objects between programs running on different workstations.

The resources of a multi-user computer are normally shared between all of its users, but the users of networked single-user workstations and personal computers do not automatically obtain the benefits of resource sharing. Resources in a distributed system are physically encapsulated within one of the computers and can only be accessed from other computers by communication. For effective sharing each resource must be managed by a program that offers a communication interface enabling the resource to be accessed, manipulated and updated reliably and consistently.

The generic term **resource manager** is sometimes used to denote a software module that manages a set of resources of a particular type. Each type of resource requires some separate management policies and methods, but there are also common requirements. These include the provision of a naming scheme for each class of resource, enabling individual resources to be accessed from any location; the mapping of resource names to communication addresses and the coordination of concurrent accesses that change the state of shared resources on order to ensure their consistency.

Figure 1.5 illustrates an abstract view of a distributed system composed of a set of resource managers and a set of resource using programs. The resource users communicate with the resource managers to access the shared resources of the system. We can develop this perspective to yield two very interesting models for distributed systems, the client-server model and the object-based model.

> *The client-server model*: Figure 1.6 illustrates this model. It is currently the best-known and most widely-adopted system model for distributed systems and was introduced in the preceding section in connection with distributed UNIX systems (Figure 1.1). There is a set of server processes, each acting as a resource manager for a collection of resources of a given type, and a collection of client processes,

Figure 1.5   Resource managers and resource users.

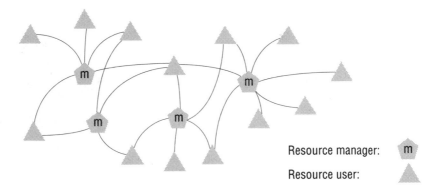

each performing a task that requires access to some shared hardware and software resources. Resource managers may themselves need to access shared resources managed by another process, so some processes are both client and server processes. In the client-server model, all shared resources are held and managed by server processes. Client processes issue requests to servers whenever they need to access one of their resources. If the request is a valid one, then the server performs the requested action and sends a reply to the client process.

We use the term *process* here in the sense normally understood in the field of operating systems. A process is a running program. It consists of an environment for execution together with at least one thread of control. The UNIX process construct is an adequate example. In Chapter 6 we go in to the definition of models for processes and threads in greater detail.

The client-server model provides an effective general-purpose approach to the sharing of information and resources in distributed systems. The model can be implemented in a variety of different hardware and software environments. The

Figure 1.6   Client and server processes.

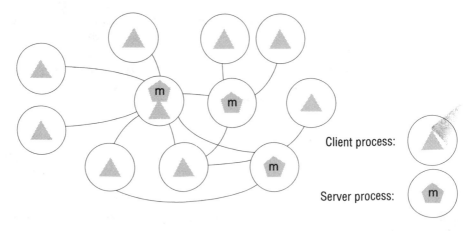

computers used to run the client and server processes can be of many types and there is no need to distinguish between them; both client and server processes can be run on the same computer – and indeed, a server process may use the services of another server, appearing as a client to the latter.

In this simple view of the client-server model each server process might be seen as a centralized provider of the resources that it manages. Centralized resource provision is undesirable in distributed systems for a number of reasons that will become apparent as we proceed.

It is for this reason that a distinction is made between the *services* that are provided to clients and the *servers* that provide them. A service is considered to be an abstract entity that may be provided by several server processes running on separate computers and cooperating via the network.

The client-server model has been very effectively deployed in current systems with services managing many different types of shared resource – electronic mail and news messages, files, network-wide synchronized clocks, disk storage, printers, wide-area communication and even the windowed display space on the screens of networked computers. But it isn't possible for all of the resources that exist in a distributed system to be managed and shared in this way; for efficient operation some types of resource must remain local to each computer – random access memory, central processors and the local network interface are usually regarded as the minimum set of such resources. These key resources are separately managed by an operating system in each computer; they may be shared only between processes located in the same computer.

We shall see in later chapters that the client-server model does not meet all requirements – some applications require more direct cooperation between clients than it can provide, but it is adequate for most current applications and provides an effective basis for general-purpose distributed operating systems.

The object-based model: This second model is not unlike the traditional object-oriented programming model in which every entity in a running program is viewed as an object with a message-handling interface providing access to its operations [Wegner 1984; Myer 1988]. In the object-based model for distributed systems, each shared resource is viewed as an object. Objects are uniquely identified and may be moved anywhere in the network without changing their identities. Whenever a resource-using program requires access to a resource it sends a message containing a request to the corresponding object. The message is dispatched to the appropriate procedure or process which performs the requested operation and sends a reply message to the requesting process if required.

This pure object model is illustrated in Figure 1.7. It is attractive in its simplicity and flexibility. It enables *all* shared resources to be viewed in a uniform way by resource users. As in the client-server model, objects can act both as resource users and resource managers. In the client-server model, the naming scheme used for resources varies depending upon the service that manages them. But in the object-oriented model, resource users can refer to all resources in a uniform manner.

We shall use the term **object manager** to refer to the collection of procedures and data values that together characterize a class of objects. There is a

Figure 1.7   Objects and managers.

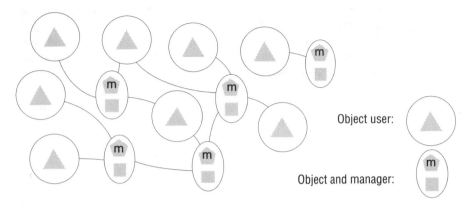

Object user:

Object and manager:

correspondence between these and the resource managers of the client-server model.

The implementation of the object-based model raises some difficult problems. It requires an object manager of the relevant type to be located wherever an object is located, because objects contain a representation of their state, and a manager must be co-located with an object in order to access its state. This is straightforward when objects cannot be moved, and several distributed systems designed to support uniform object addressing have been constructed. Examples include Argus [Liskov 1988], Amoeba and Mach (which are described in Chapter 18). To date, the more general distributed object model in which objects can migrate freely has been implemented only in experimental systems such Arjuna [Shrivastava *et al.* 1989], Clouds (described in Chapter 18) and Emerald [Black *et al.* 1987]). In those implementations objects are located with one of a set of object managers of the relevant type, and the relevant object manager must be replicated at the new site whenever an object moves.

Openness □ The openness of a computer system is the characteristic that determines whether the system can be extended in various ways. A system can be open or closed with respect to hardware extensions – for example, the addition of peripherals, memory or communication interfaces – or with respect to software extensions – the addition of operating system features, communication protocols and resource-sharing services. The openness of distributed systems is determined primarily by the degree to which new resource-sharing services can be added without disruption to or duplication of existing services.

Openness is achieved by specifying and documenting the key software interfaces of a system and making them available to software developers. In a word, the key interfaces are *published*. This process is akin to the standardization of interfaces, but it often bypasses official standardization procedures which are cumbersome and slow-moving.

Historically, computer systems were largely closed. They executed programs in a range of programming languages but they did not allow application developers to extend the semantics of the languages to exploit new hardware or operating system features.

UNIX was an early example of a more open system design. It includes a programming language, C, that allows programmers to access all of the facilities (resources) managed by the operating system. C is a high-level language, enabling programs to be compiled and executed on a wide range of different computers.

The resources of the UNIX operating system are accessed through a set of procedures (called *system calls*) that are fully documented and available to programs written in C and other languages that support conventional procedure calling facilities. When a new type of peripheral device is installed in a UNIX system, the operating system can be extended to enable application programs to access it by adding new system calls or more commonly, by implementing some additional parameter values for existing system calls. The openness of UNIX is limited by the inextensible nature of its system calls. See the box below for a discussion of ways in which this limitation has been overcome in subsequent UNIX development.

Thus UNIX is more open than the systems that preceded it:

for application developers: because they have access to the *entire* range of facilities that the system offers;

for hardware vendors and system managers: because the operating system can be extended relatively easily to add new peripheral devices or network controllers;

for software vendors and users: because it is hardware-independent. Software developers can produce programs that will run without modification on many different manufacturers' computers. (This statement is only correct in so far as computer manufacturers have reached agreement about exactly what version of UNIX they will supply.)

The set of system calls that an operating system supports defines a set of resources and facilities available to the programs that run on the system. They are implemented by a program called the **kernel** that is loaded when the computer starts up. The kernel manages and controls the hardware of the computer to provide the facilities and

Openness through communication: The resource types originally supported by the UNIX kernel are primarily *files* and *processes*. Files together with the associated file naming structure provide a useful programming abstraction for the use of non-volatile storage (for example, magnetic disks) and are also used for direct access to some other types of peripheral. Processes provide a mechanism for the concurrent execution of programs.

In the early 1980s UNIX was extended to include a set of system calls to support *interprocess communication*. These extensions, developed at the University of California at Berkeley and introduced in the version of UNIX known as BSD UNIX, provide a uniform set of facilities that enable processes running in UNIX systems to communicate with each other. The communicating processes may be located in the same computer or in different computers that are connected by a network. The system calls are the same in both cases, enabling programs to be written without regard to the location of the processes. At about the same time, interprocess communication facilities were added to other operating systems, and in some cases, these were designed to conform to standards, enabling processes to communicate even when they run in different computers with different operating systems.

resources that are accessed by other programs through system calls. Thus the design of the kernel determines the range of resource types available to other programs.

The availability of interprocess communication in BSD UNIX and other operating systems and of standard protocols for communication dramatically increased the scope for achieving openness in computer system design. It became possible for server processes running on any computer and any operating system to offer facilities for accessing their resources to other processes (clients) running in computers on the same network. The range of system resources and facilities available to an application program was no longer restricted by the system calls supported in the local operating system. This is the essential foundation on which current distributed systems have been developed.

Systems that are designed to support resource sharing in this way are termed *open distributed systems* to emphasise the fact that they are extensible. They may be extended at the hardware level by the addition of computers to the network and at the software level by the introduction of new services, enabling application programs to share resources. A further benefit that is often cited for open systems is their independence from individual vendors.

To summarize:

- Open systems are characterized by the fact that their key interfaces are published.

- Open distributed systems are based on the provision of a uniform interprocess communication mechanism and published interfaces for access to shared resources.

- Open distributed systems can be constructed from heterogeneous hardware and software, possibly from different vendors. But the conformance of each component to the published standard must be carefully tested and certified if users are to be protected from responsibility for resolving system integration problems.

Concurrency □ When several processes exist in a single computer we say that they are executed concurrently. (Since each process only exists for the duration of a program execution, coexistence implies concurrency of execution.) If the computer is equipped with only a single central processor, this is achieved by interleaving the execution of portions of each process. If the computer has N processors, then up to N processes can be executed simultaneously (that is, in parallel), achieving an N-fold improvement in computational throughput.

In distributed systems there are many computers, each with one or more central processors. If there are M computers in a distributed system with one central processor each, then up to M processes can run in parallel, provided that the processes are located in different computers.

In a distributed system that is based on the resource-sharing model described above, opportunities for parallel execution occur for two reasons (Figure 1.8):

1. Many users simultaneously invoke commands or interact with application programs.

2. Many server processes run concurrently, each responding to different requests from client processes.

Figure 1.8   Opportunities for concurrency in a distributed system.

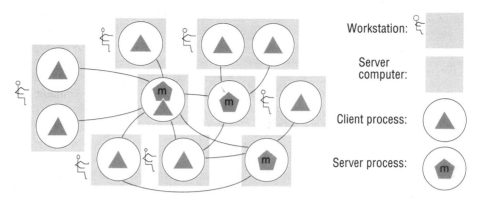

Case 1 arises from one or more application processes running on behalf of each active user. In most distributed system architectures, application processes run in a user's workstation and they do not conflict for processing resources with the application processes of other users. If the workstation has only a single processor and there is more than one application process running on the workstation, they are executed in an interleaved manner. Workstations with multiple processors enable users to perform several computations in parallel or to execute application programs that exploit more than one processor.

Case 2 arises from the existence of one or more server processes for each type of resource. These normally run in additional computers, enabling each server process to proceed in parallel with other servers and with the processes running on workstations. Multi-processor computers are particularly effective for the implementation of heavily-used servers, since an *N* processor server has the potential to handle up to *N* requests from clients without delay. Requests for access to resources in a given server are queued at the server and processed in sequence or several may be processed concurrently by multiple instances of the resource manager process. When several resource-using programs access the same resource concurrently, the server process must synchronize their actions to ensure that they do not conflict. The synchronization must be carefully planned to ensure that the benefits of concurrency are not lost. Several methods for the control of concurrency when accessing shared resources are described in Chapter 13.

To summarize, concurrency and parallel execution arise naturally in distributed systems from the separate activities of users, the independence of resources and the location of server processes in separate computers. The separation of these activities enables processing to proceed in parallel in separate computers. Concurrent accesses and updates to shared resources must be synchronized.

Scalability   □   Distributed systems operate effectively and efficiently at many different scales. The smallest practicable distributed system probably consists of two workstations and a file server, whereas a distributed system constructed around a single local-area network may contain several hundred workstations and many file servers, print servers and other special-purpose servers. Several local-area networks are often interconnected to form **internetworks**, and these may contain many thousands of computers that form a single distributed system, enabling resources to be shared between all of them.

The system and application software should not need to change when the scale of the system increases. This characteristic is achieved to a significant extent in most current distributed systems and components, but it is an area in which further research is required and in progress to accommodate the very large-scale systems and applications that are likely to emerge as internetworking increases and high-performance networks appear.

An example of lack of scalability was recently experienced by users of the London telephone system. Dialled locally, London numbers have seven digits, and these used to be prefixed by the code 01- when dialled from outside London. However, even these ten million numbers were not enough and the telephone company decided to split London into two regions, with prefixes 071- and 081-, with telephones retaining their seven-digit numbers inside the regions. This of course doubled the capacity. If eight-digit phone numbers had been assigned in the first place, then no disruption need have occurred and the numbering system would have been more coherent. However, to be fair to the telephone company, there is no correct solution to this problem. It is difficult to predict the demand that will be placed upon a system years ahead (note that an accurate projection would have had to predict the advent and large-scale usage of facsimile machines). Moreover, overcompensating for future growth may be worse than adapting to a change when we are forced to – after all, we could have been assigned twenty-digit numbers, just to be on the safe side.

The need for scalability is not just a problem of hardware or network performance. We shall see that the issue permeates almost every aspect of distributed system design. In centralized computer systems certain shared resources – memory, processors, input-output channels – are in limited supply and cannot be replicated indefinitely. In distributed systems, the limitation on the supply of some of those resources is automatically removed – we have already noted that there can be a potentially unlimited number of computers, each with memory, one or more central processors and input-output channels. But other limitations may remain if the design of the system does not explicitly recognize the need for scalability.

The demand for scalability in distributed systems has led to a design philosophy in which no single resource – hardware or software – is assumed to be in restricted supply. Rather, as the demand for a resource grows, it should be possible to extend the system to meet it. For example, the frequency with which files are accessed is likely to grow as the number of users and workstations in a distributed system increases. It must be possible to add server computers to avoid the performance bottleneck that would arise if a single file server had to handle all file access requests. Some files may be accessed so frequently that the processing of requests for access to a single file or a small group of files becomes a performance bottleneck. In that case, those files must be replicated in several servers and the system must be designed so that when replicated files are updated the updates are applied to all of the replicas.

As the size and complexity of computer networks grows, it is a major challenge to design distributed system software that will remain effective for such network configurations. The Internet already embraces more than one million computers. The requirement is to design distributed services that continue to operate effectively with thousands or millions of clients. The work involved in processing any single request to access a shared resource should be nearly independent of the size of the network.

The issue of scale has been a dominant theme of the past decade of development in distributed systems. The techniques that have been successful in coping with large-scale applications are discussed extensively in this book. They include the use of *replicated data* (Chapters 8 and 11), the associated technique of *caching* (Chapters 2 and 7) and the deployment of multiple servers to handle commonly performed tasks enabling several similar tasks to be performed concurrently.

Fault tolerance ☐ Computer systems sometimes fail. When faults occur in hardware or software, programs may produce incorrect results or they may stop before they have completed the intended computation. We shall discuss a range of possible fault types and methods for detecting and recovering from them in Chapter 15.

The design of fault-tolerant computer systems is based on two approaches, both of which must be deployed to handle each fault:

> *hardware redundancy*: the use of redundant components;
>
> *software recovery*: the design of programs to recover from faults.

To produce systems that are tolerant of hardware failures, two interconnected computers are often employed for a single application, one of them acting as a standby machine for the other. The *hot standby* machine in our Automatic Teller Machine example (Figure 1.3) is an example of this. This is a costly solution – the cost of the hardware is doubled to produce two-fold redundancy in hardware provision.

In distributed systems, redundancy can be planned at a finer grain – individual servers that are essential to the continued operation of critical applications can be replicated.

The allocation of redundant hardware required for fault tolerance can be designed so that the hardware is exploited for non-critical activities when no faults are present. For example, a database may be replicated in several servers to ensure that the data remains accessible after the failure of any single server. The servers can be designed to detect faults in their peers; when a fault is detected in one server, clients are redirected to the remaining servers. By techniques such of this, tolerance to some types of hardware fault can be provided in distributed systems at a relatively low cost.

Software recovery involves the design of software so that the state of permanent data can be recovered or 'rolled back' when a fault is detected. In general, the computations performed by some programs will be incomplete when a fault occurs, and the permanent data that they update (files and other material stored in permanent storage) may not be in a consistent state. Mechanisms are described in Chapter 15 that enable files and other persistent data to be restored to the state they were in before the failed program began its execution.

Distributed systems also provide a high degree of **availability** in the face of hardware faults. The availability of a system is a measure of the proportion of time that it is available for use. A single failure in a multi-user computer almost always results in the non-availability of the system to all of its users. When one of the components in a distributed system fails, only the work that was using the failed component is affected. A user may move to another workstation if the one that they were using fails; a server process can be restarted on another computer.

The networks on which distributed systems are based are not normally redundant. Failure of the network causes programs that use the network to hang until communication is restored, and the service to users will be interrupted. Overloading of the network degrades the performance and responsiveness of the system to users. Much effort has gone into the design of reliable and fault-tolerant networks.

Other software organizations are often needed to exploit concurrency fully and to obtain a higher degree of tolerance to faults than can be achieved with client-server systems. A useful paradigm for the construction of concurrent programs involving replication that has been developed as a result of recent research is the **process group**. This is a construct that enables a number of concurrent processes to cooperate by sharing a single communication mechanism – a sort of 'virtual network of computers' composed of a collection of processes that can be created, extended or diminished in size on demand. We shall introduce the communication and other mechanisms needed to support process groups in Chapter 4.

Transparency □ Transparency is defined as the concealment from the user and the application programmer of the separation of components in a distributed system, so that the system is perceived as a whole rather than as a collection of independent components. The implications of transparency are a major influence on the design of the system software.

The separation of components is an inherent property of distributed systems. Its consequences include the need for communication and for explicit system management and integration techniques. Separation allows the truly parallel execution of programs, the containment of component faults and recovery from faults without disruption of the whole system, the use of isolation and control of communication channels as a method for enforcing security and protection policies, and the incremental growth or contraction of the system through the addition or subtraction of components.

The ANSA Reference Manual [ANSA 1989] and the International Standards Organization's Reference Model for Open Distributed Processing (RM-ODP) [ISO 1992] identify eight forms of transparency. These provide a useful summary of the motivation and goals for distributed systems. We have paraphrased the original ANSA definitions, employing the term 'information object' to denote the entities to which distribution transparency is applied:

Access transparency enables local and remote information objects to be accessed using identical operations.

Location transparency enables information objects to be accessed without knowledge of their location.

Concurrency transparency enables several processes to operate concurrently using shared information objects without interference between them.

Replication transparency enables multiple instances of information objects to be used to increase reliability and performance without knowledge of the replicas by users or application programs.

Failure transparency enables the concealment of faults, allowing users and application programs to complete their tasks despite the failure of hardware or software components.

Migration transparency allows the movement of information objects within a system without affecting the operation of users or application programs.

Performance transparency allows the system to be reconfigured to improve performance as loads vary.

Scaling transparency allows the system and applications to expand in scale without change to the system structure or the application algorithms.

The two most important transparencies are access and location transparency; their presence or absence most strongly affects the utilization of distributed resources. They are sometimes referred to together as *network transparency*. Network transparency provides a similar degree of anonymity for resources to that found in centralized computer systems.

As an illustration of the absence of network transparency, consider the familiar UNIX command *rlogin*. The *rlogin* command allows a user only to log on to a named machine, and so it does not provide location transparency. Moreover, the procedure that a user follows to use *rlogin* is different from that used for logging on to a local machine: in the latter case, the login program is automatically run, and does not have to be invoked explicitly, so the use of *rlogin* does not provide access transparency. It might to be possible in a more transparent system to log on to a *domain* of a distributed system rather than to an individual machine. Users would then be authorized to access all of the services within that domain.

On the other hand, as an illustration of the presence of network transparency, consider the use of an Internet electronic mail address such as *Fred.Flintstone@stoneit.co*. The address consists of a user's name and a domain name. Domains are defined and allocated names on the basis of organizational structures. Users are allocated a mail name within a domain. Sending mail to such a user does not involve knowing their physical or network location. Nor does the procedure to send a mail message depend upon the location of the recipient. Thus electronic mail within the Internet provides both location and access transparency (that is, network transparency).

Transparency hides and renders anonymous the resources that are not of direct relevance to the task-in-hand from users and application programmers. This may not always be what is required. For example, it is generally desirable for similar hardware resources to be interchangeably allocated to perform a task – the identity of a processor used to execute a process is generally hidden from the user and remains anonymous. But when a document is printed, it is normal to arrange for it to be printed at a particular, named printer: usually one that is near to the user. Also, to a programmer developing parallel programs, not all processors are anonymous. He or she may be interested in the processors used to execute a parallel program, at least to the extent of their number and interconnection topology.

1.4 Historical background

In this section we present a schematic view of the major steps in computer system design that led to the development of distributed systems. In Figure 1.9 we give a perspective on the interplay between experience and the formulation of requirements, portraying

Figure 1.9   Conceptual developments in system design leading to distributed systems.

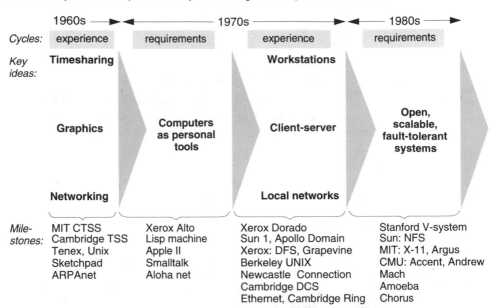

them as a cycle in which experience in the development and use of systems leads to the formation of concepts and requirements for new systems, which leads in turn to further experience. Major milestone systems are listed in Figure 1.9. These are placed in their chronological context in Figure 1.10. Figure 1.11 gives further details about some major distributed system milestones and cites sources of further information on them. (Dates shown in Figure 1.11 are those at which systems were first operational.) Further information on many of the workstations and systems mentioned in this section can be found in the proceedings of the 1986 ACM Conference on the History of Personal Workstations [Goldberg 1988], or in the historical survey of computer architectures edited by Siewiorek, Bell and Newell [Siewiorek *et al.*1981].

The potential for distributed systems first became apparent in the early 1970s, a few years after the emergence of minicomputers. The use of minicomputers as single-user graphical workstations and their effectiveness for software development and other interactive tasks were important influences, pointing the way for the provision of a more effective environment for interactive computing than could be achieved with multi-user timesharing systems. But the necessary hardware and software to make single-user computers fully effective and the communication facilities to enable them to be used in a cooperative fashion were absent.

The earliest and some of the most significant developments aimed at filling those gaps were made by a team of researchers working at the Xerox Palo Alto Research Center (known as Xerox PARC) in the period 1971–80. These included the development of the first single-user workstations, file and print servers, the first high-speed local network (the Ethernet) and several experimental distributed systems. The first workstation developed at Xerox PARC was the *Alto*. It had a high-resolution monochrome display, a mouse, 128 kilobytes of main memory, a 2.5 megabyte hard

Figure 1.10   Chronology of relevant systems.

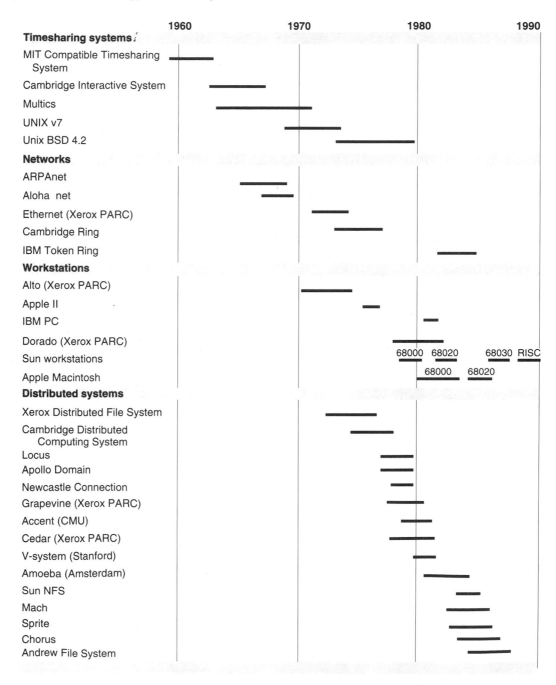

Note: bars represent the periods over which the designs were formulated and implemented.

Figure 1.11   Milestones in distributed systems.

System	Organization	Network	Computers	Date	References; notes
Xerox DFS	Xerox PARC	Ethernet and Internet	Xerox Alto	1977	[Mitchell and Dion 1982, Mitchell 1985]; a very early file server design; see Cedar below for subsequent development.
Cambridge DCS	Cambridge University	Cambridge Ring	LSI-4, M68000	1979	[Needham and Herbert 1982]; based on the Processor Pool architecture, see Chapter 2.
Locus	UCLA	Ethernet	VAX, IBM PC	1980	[Popek and Walker 1985]; an advanced distributed operating system that emulates UNIX.
Apollo Domain	Apollo Computers	Token Ring	Apollo	1980	[Leach et al. 1983]; a commercial distributed system, largest configuration: 1800 workstations
Newcastle Connection	Newcastle University	various	various	1980	[Brownbridge et al. 1982]; precursor to the Sun NFS file system.
Grapevine	Xerox PARC	Ethernet	Xerox Alto	1981	[Birrell et al. 1982]; a distributed, replicated application-oriented database service.
Cedar	Xerox PARC	Ethernet	Xerox Dorado and Dandelion	1982	[Teitelman 1984, Donahue 1985]; a research environment for the development of office and personal systems.
V system	Stanford University	Ethernet	VAX, Sun	1982	[Cheriton 1984, Cheriton and Zwaenpoel 1985]; an experimental distributed operating system that interworks with UNIX.
Argus	MIT	—	—	1983	[Liskov and Scheifler 1982]; a research project to develop an integrated programming language and system based on the language CLU.
Accent	Carnegie-Mellon University	Ethernet	PERQ, VAX, Sun	1982	[Rashid 1986]; a distributed OS based on message passing. Precursor of Mach including many of the same features.
Amoeba	Vrije University, Amsterdam	Ethernet	VAX, M68000 + others	1984	See Chapter 18; a research project on the use of *capabilities* in distributed systems. Interworks with UNIX.
UNIX BSD 4.2 + Sun NFS	Sun Microsystems	Ethernet	VAX, Sun + others	1985	See Chapter 8; a widely used distributed UNIX system.
Mach	CMU	Ethernet	VAX, Sun + others	1986	See Chapter 18; an operating system kernel for distributed systems. Runs UNIX. Successor to CMU Accent system.
Chorus	Chorus Systèmes	Ethernet	Sun + others	1988	See Chapter 18; an operating system kernel to support distributed and real-time systems.

disk and a microprogrammed central processor that executed machine-level instructions at speeds of 2–6 microseconds. The Altos were linked by the Ethernet. They were exploited both as personal workstations and as server platforms and were used in a wide range of experimental services and applications including the Xerox Distributed File Server, and the Grapevine and Cedar systems (Figure 1.11).

Other research done before 1980 that had an important impact on subsequent developments include the Cambridge Distributed Computing System (CDCS), the Apollo Domain system, the Newcastle Connection and the Locus distributed operating system (Figure 1.11). From the start of the 1980s there was a rapid expansion of research and development in distributed systems, for example the Accent, Mach, Amoeba, Argus, V-system and Chorus research projects and the Sun NFS-based product development. All of these systems are discussed later in the book.

1.5   Summary

Distributed systems have become the norm for the organization of computing facilities. They can be used to implement general-purpose interactive computing systems in the style of UNIX and to support a wide range of commercial and industrial applications of computers. They are increasingly being used as the basis for new applications in areas such as networked information services and multimedia applications, where communication is a basic requirement.

In all of these roles, distributed systems are capable of offering substantial benefits to their users. We have identified their key characteristics under the following headings: resource sharing, openness, concurrency, scalability, fault tolerance and transparency. The benefits that they bring are not achieved automatically, they depend upon the careful design of system components. Methods for the achievement of this form the main topic for the next chapter.

Resource sharing is the fundamental characteristic of distributed systems; it underpins the other characteristics discussed in this chapter and it strongly affects the software architectures that are available in distributed systems. Resources may be items of data, software or hardware components. Resources are distinguished from data items managed within individual processes by the need for several processes to share them. This leads to the need for them to be managed externally to the processes that use them. In client-server systems this takes the form of a server process, or more generally a service supplied by several cooperating processes. Object-based systems may provide a more flexible model for the management of shared resources, but the best form of design for such a model remains the subject of research.

Openness has both a technical aspect and a commercial one. We are concerned primarily with the technical aspect which takes the form of a requirement for the availability of well-defined interfaces to resource managers. In distributed systems, the interfaces are accessed by interprocess communication. In an open system, the interfaces are published and they must be general-purpose to avoid the need to duplicate resources and resource managers for different applications.

Concurrency brings the benefit of higher performance. In general-purpose distributed systems we can exploit concurrency between client processes and between server processes, but we cannot exploit concurrency within a single application unless the application program has been constructed as a system of concurrent processes.

Scalability has been a dominant concern in distributed system design during the last decade, and its importance continues. The replication of data and the distribution of load between servers are the key techniques that are used to address it.

Fault tolerance can be addressed more efficiently in distributed systems than in more centralized system architectures. Hardware redundancy can be exploited to ensure that essential tasks are re-allocated to another computer when one fails. But recovery from hardware and software failures without loss of data requires careful design.

Transparency addresses the needs of users and application programmers to perceive a collection of networked computers as an integrated system, hiding the distributed nature of the resources used to perform the user's task.

The current state of knowledge about distributed systems has emerged from a wealth of research and development. Many fascinating and exciting research projects have been completed in the last twenty years. We have listed and provided a schematic view of some of the more important ones in the preceding section.

EXERCISES

1.1   What are the main characteristics of the 'UNIX model' for computer systems which has been adopted as a goal for many distributed system developments?

page 3

1.2   What new features of BSD UNIX made it more suitable as a basis for the implementation of distributed systems and applications than previous versions of UNIX?

page 3

1.3   Discuss which distributed services would be required in a fully distributed implementation of UNIX.

page 4

1.4   What are the arguments for duplicating servers of the same type in a distributed system?

page 4

1.5   Discuss the distributed implementation of any commercial data processing application with which you are familiar. What services would be required? What problems might arise? What limitations would there be on the scale of the resulting system?

page 4

1.6   If you are familiar with the Internet *netnews* application suggest two alternative models for its implementation and compare them.

page 6

1.7   What are the special requirements of time-based data? Distinguish between the requirements with respect to network transmission delay and bandwidth.

page 8

1.8   What is 'information browsing'? What requirements does the implementation of it impose on a distributed system?

page 8

1.9   What facilities might a digital video conferencing system, based on networked workstations, usefully provide.

page 9

1.10 Discuss the concept of *shared resources* in a distributed system. Give examples of resources that might be shared. Say what the implications of resource sharing are for (a) the types of application that can be supported; (b) hardware costs in a distributed system.

page 10

1.11 What is a resource manager?

page 11

1.12 What are the characteristics of object identifiers in an object-based distributed system?

page 13

1.13 What is openness?

page 14

1.14 What characteristics of UNIX made it more open than the systems that preceded it?

page 15

1.15 What feature of UNIX restricted its openness and how do distributed systems overcome the restriction?

page 15

1.16 Define concurrency and parallelism. What opportunities for parallelism arise in distributed client-server systems (for example a distributed UNIX system)?

page 16

1.17 How can the design of a distributed system ensure that it will be scalable?

page 17

1.18 Define fault tolerance.

page 19

1.19 Two processes operate concurrently upon shared information objects. Give an example of what might happen in the absence of concurrency transparency, that is of 'interference' between the operations of the two processes.

page 20

1.20 A service is implemented by several servers. Explain why resources might be transferred between them. Would it be satisfactory for clients to multicast all requests to the group of servers as a way of achieving migration transparency?

page 20

1.21   What technical factors led to the displacement of multi-user minicomputers and mainframes?

page 22

1.22   A department has a multi-user computer, a few workstations and a number of terminals and is planning to extend its computing resources. Make the case for installing a distributed system rather than another multi-user computer and terminals.

1.23   Discuss some of the consequences that might arise when one computer in a distributed system fails and the rest continue to run:

i)   if the failed computer is a workstation;

ii)   if the failed computer is a file server.

1.24   A student laboratory contains a number of networked workstations for use by various groups of students. Any particular student comes to the laboratory from time to time and does not necessarily always expect to use the same workstation. How do you suggest that the students files should be stored:

i)   if the workstation has a small hard disk (for example 80 megabytes);

ii)   if the workstation has a floppy disk drive, but no hard disk?

2

DESIGN GOALS

The design of distributed systems aims to achieve high performance, reliability, scalability, consistency and security. In this chapter we outline the technical issues affecting the achievement of these goals, thereby introducing many of the topics that form the subject matter of the remainder of the book.

We review users' requirements concerning the functionality, reconfigurability and quality of service provided by distributed systems.

2.1   Introduction

In keeping with its title, this book aims to convey both conceptual and design knowledge. In this chapter, we outline key problems that the designer of a distributed system or application is likely to face and indicate the nature of the solutions. We assume that the key characteristics of distributed systems defined in Chapter 1 – namely *resource sharing*, *openness*, *concurrency*, *scalability*, *fault tolerance* and *transparency* are generic design requirements for distributed systems. In this chapter we focus on the system architectures and components that are used to meet those requirements and the technical issues that must be addressed in their design. The technical solutions are not elaborated here – they form the subject matter of the bulk of the remainder of the book.

The design, as well as the implementation, of distributed systems is open. The development of distributed applications frequently results in a need to add new services. Those services should be designed to work satisfactorily in conjunction with existing services and to meet similar standards with respect to key design goals (Figure 2.1). In this sense, the development of each new distributed application involves design decisions that address the same concerns as the initial design of the underlying system – thus design knowledge is indispensable, not only in the initial design of distributed systems, but also for the development of distributed applications.

What does the design of a distributed service involve? Specific goals can be identified with respect to each of the categories listed in Figure 2.1 and possibly other, service-specific categories. These goals may be expressed in the form of *guarantees*: formal statements about the behaviour of a system, such as: 'the service will continue to be available after the failure of any single server process' that can be verified either by analysis of the design or by testing. The achievement of such goals is a measure of the success of a design.

In Section 2.2 we outline the main technical problems and pitfalls that must be overcome in the achievement of design goals. But good design is more than the solution of technical problems and the avoidance of pitfalls; it should be directed towards goals that are rooted at least as much in users' and software developers' needs as they are in the underlying technology. The specific needs of both of these classes of user are notoriously difficult to identify, but in Section 2.3 we aim to outline generic user requirements for distributed systems.

The Grapevine distributed mail transfer and name translation service [Birrell *et al.* 1982] is an early example of a distributed system designed to meet specific goals and to offer guarantees of the systems' behaviour. It provides guarantees concerning the reliability of the service in the face of client program errors, hardware failures and

Figure 2.1   Key design goals.

Categories of design goal for distributed services:	Performance
	Reliability
	Scalability
	Consistency
	Security

network failures. It promises to maintain the security of users' data against eavesdropping or alteration and it defines a specific target for the range of system sizes over which it will scale.

An examination of Lampson's collection of hints for computer system designers [Lampson 1983] is recommended to readers interested in a more general view of techniques for the design of computer systems. It is one of the few published discussions on the topic and the author is the designer of several successful computer systems and an important contributor to the development of distributed systems. Saltzer *et al.* [1984] provide a classic discussion of design issues for communication protocols.

2.2 Basic design issues

Although the designer of a distributed system or application must consider issues that are largely unrelated to its distribution – such as software engineering techniques, human–computer interaction and algorithm design – we shall restrict our discussion to design issues that arise specifically from the distributed nature of systems. Under this heading we include:

Naming: Distributed systems are based on the sharing of resources and on the transparency of their distribution. The names assigned to resources or objects must have global meanings that are independent of the locations of the object, and they must be supported by a name interpretation system that can translate names in order to enable programs to access named resources. A design issue is to design naming schemes that will scale to an appropriate degree and in which names are translated efficiently to meet appropriate goals for performance.

Communication: The performance and reliability of the communication techniques used for the implementation of distributed systems are critical to their performance. We shall see in Chapter 3 that very high transmission speeds can now be achieved in both local and wide area networks, but even with high-speed networks, communication can be time-consuming because of the number and complexity of the software layers involved. A design issue is to optimize the implementation of communication in distributed systems while retaining a high-level programming model for its use.

Software structure: Openness is achieved through the design and construction of software components with well-defined interfaces. Data abstraction is an important design technique for distributed systems. Services can be viewed as the managers of objects of a given data type; the interface to a service can be viewed as a set of operations. A design issue is to structure a system so that new services can be introduced that will interwork fully with existing services without duplicating existing service elements.

Workload allocation: Good performance is a requirement of most engineered products, and is a major concern for most programmers and system designers. The design issue for distributed systems is how to deploy the processing and communication and resources in a network to optimum effect in the processing of a changing workload.

Consistency maintenance: Under this heading we introduce several problems of consistency that can arise in distributed systems. Their significance for design is in their impact on the performance of distributed systems and applications. The maintenance of consistency at reasonable cost is perhaps the most difficult problem encountered in the design of distributed systems.

Naming

A process that requires access to a resource which it does not manage must possess a name or an identifier for it. We shall use the term *name* to refer to names that can be interpreted by users *or* by programs and the term *identifier* to refer to names that are interpreted or used *only* by programs.

We say that a name is *resolved* when it is translated into a form in which it can be used to invoke an action on the resource or object to which it refers. In distributed systems, a resolved name is generally a **communication identifier** together with other attributes that may be useful for communication. The form of a communication identifier depends on the kinds of identifier interpretation provided in the communication system that is in use. For example, in Internet communication a communication identifier must contain two parts: a *host identifier* (also called an *IP address*; this is the four-part numeric address of a computer, for example, 192.135.231.4) and a *port number* (a small integer) identifying a particular communication port among those located at that host. In the Mach distributed operating system a communication identifier is simply an identifier for a communication port – a primitive construct in the Mach system. Since Mach ports can migrate between computers, port identifiers are managed by the Mach communication subsystem in each computer and it is responsible for mapping the identifiers to network addresses in order for communication to occur.

The resolution of names may involve several translation steps. At each step, a name or identifier is mapped to a lower-level identifier that can be used to specify a resource when communicating with some software component. At some stage in this sequence of translations a communication identifier is produced that is acceptable to the communication subsystem that is in use, and this can be used to transmit a request to a resource manager. The communication subsystem may have to perform further translations to produce network addresses and routing information that are acceptable to lower-level network software layers.

Naming in distributed systems involves the following design considerations:

1. The choice of an appropriate name space for each type of resource. A name space may be finite or it may be potentially infinite, and it may be structured or flat. These distinctions are discussed below. All of the resources managed by a given type of resource manager should have different names, no matter where they are located. In object-based systems, all objects are uniformly named – they occupy a single name space.

2. Resource names must be resolvable to communication identifiers. In general this is done by holding copies of names and their translations in a **name service**. Some types of resource, such as files, are accessed so frequently that name resolution is best left to the resource manager. A local cache of recently-used names and their

resolved identifiers is often held in the client environment in order to avoid unnecessary communication with resource managers or name servers.

Names are always resolved relative to some context. For example, the name John Smith doesn't have much meaning unless we provide some contextual information – the name of the organization in which John Smith works or the street where he lives. In computer systems, contexts are represented by name tables or databases. In the case of file systems, each directory represents a context. To resolve a name, we must supply the context and the name. A name service accepts requests for the translation of names or identifiers in one name space to identifiers in some other space. A name service also handles requests to register new names or identifiers with their corresponding translations and to delete existing entries. Thus a name service manages a database for each context, providing a view that is as up-to-date as possible of the names or identifiers of a given type existing in a distributed system and their translations in some other name space. Name services are a key component of distributed systems, especially in large-scale systems. The design of efficient name services for large-scale systems is a challenging problem. We describe the principles involved and some examples in Chapter 9.

There are many forms of names and identifiers, each serving to support the purposes to which it is put. Some names are designed to be 'human readable' so that users can read, recall and re-use them. File names (such as */etc/passwd*) and high-level network names (such as Internet domain names, for example, *qmw.ac.uk*) are usually of this sort. Others are designed to have compact representations in memory or to provide some clues as to the locations of the objects that they name. The latter is liable to interfere with transparency and is generally to be avoided except in layers of software that deal with resolved names in a transient manner. Names may have an internal structure that represents their position in a hierarchic name space, as in the UNIX file system, or in an organizational hierarchy, as is the case for Internet domain names, or they may be chosen from a flat set of numeric or symbolic identifiers.

The most important advantage of hierarchic name spaces is that each part of a name is resolved relative to a separate context, and the same name may be used with different meanings in different contexts. Thus */etc/passwd* is a hierarchic name with two parts. The first part, '*etc*', is resolved relative to the context '*/*' or root, and the second part '*passwd*' is relative to the context '*etc*'. The name */oldetc/passwd* can have a different meaning because its second part is resolved in a different context. Hierarchic name spaces are potentially infinite, so they enable a system to grow indefinitely. Flat name spaces are usually finite; their size is determined by fixing a maximum permissible length on names. If no limit is set on the length of the names in a flat name space, then it also is potentially infinite.

Naming schemes can be designed to protect the resources that they identify from unauthorized access. Each identifier is chosen so that it is computationally difficult for any process that does not already hold the identifier to reproduce it without assistance from a naming service, and the naming service checks the authority of its clients to hold the identifiers that they request. Identifiers that fulfil this requirement are known as *capabilities*. We shall discuss the use of capabilities to identify resources in greater detail in Chapters 6 and 7.

The embedding of network addresses or other location information in names and identifiers conflicts with the transparency requirements discussed in Chapter 1. Needham [1993], makes the distinction between a *pure* name and other names. Pure names are simply bit patterns carrying no interpretation – they must be resolved by reference to stored lists of names with the corresponding communication identifiers. Other names contain information about the location of the object that they name, or about the permissible uses of the object – they can be resolved by performing some algorithm that extracts a communication identifier from the name. Names that contain embedded information about the locations of the resources they identify become invalid if the resource to which they refer changes its location; if they are stored, care must be taken to maintain an up-to-date database of valid names, and old names must not be re-assigned to new resources.

Communication

The components of a distributed system are both logically and physically separate; they must communicate in order to interact. Distributed systems and applications are composed of separate software components that interact in order to perform tasks. We shall assume that all of the components that require or provide access to resources in distributed systems are implemented as processes. This is true for the client-server model outlined in Chapter 1; the object-oriented model that was defined there can also be implemented in that form. In client-server systems a client process must interact with a server process whenever it requires access to a resource that it does not control – hardware, software or data.

Communication between a pair of processes involves operations in the sending and receiving processes that together result in:

a) the *transfer of data* from the environment of the sending process to the environment of the receiving process;

b) in some communication operations, the *synchronization* of the receiving activity with the sending activity, so that the sending or receiving process is prevented from continuing until the other process makes an action that frees it.

For (a) to occur, the communicating processes must share a communication channel – a means for data to be transferred between them whereas (b) is implicit in the operation of all programming primitives for communication.

The basic programming constructs take the form of programming primitives *send* and *receive*. Together, these primitives perform **message-passing** actions between a pair of processes. Each message-passing action involves the transmission by the sending process of a set of data values (a message) through a specified communication mechanism (a channel or port) and the acceptance by the receiving process of the message. The mechanism may be *synchronous* or *blocking*, meaning that the sender waits after transmitting a message until the receiver has performed a receive operation or it may be *asynchronous* or *non-blocking* meaning that the message is placed in a queue of messages waiting for the receiver to accept them and the sending process can proceed immediately. *Receive* normally blocks the receiving process when no message is currently available.

This basic communication model follows Hoare's Communication Sequential Processes model (CSP) [Hoare 1978] – an abstract formulation that uses blocking, and does not assume the physical separation of the sender and the receiver – and the Distributed Processes model of Brinch Hansen [1978]. A variety of abstractions have been defined to fulfil the role of the communication mechanisms in message passing, under names such as *channels*, *sockets* and *ports*. They vary in the methods by which connections are established between processes and in the degree to which buffering of messages occurs between sender and receiver, but all share the basic characteristics identified above. The range of such constructs is well-described in several texts on concurrent programming, including Ben-Ari [1990], Andrews [1991] and Bacon [1993].

The practical implementation of message passing between processes located in different computers requires the use of a communication network for the transmission of data and for communication of synchronization signals. In Chapter 3 we consider the provision of physical communication mechanisms for distributed systems and the network software that supports their use.

Distributed systems can be designed entirely in terms of message-passing, but there are certain patterns of communication that occur so frequently and are so useful that they can be regarded as an essential part of the support for the design and construction of distributed systems.

Here we introduce the two patterns of communication most commonly used in the construction of distributed systems. These are the **client-server** communication model for communication between pairs of processes and the **group multicast** communication model for communication between groups of cooperating processes. In an accompanying box we introduce *function shipping* – an interesting variation of the client-server model that offers great flexibility. In Chapters 4 and 5 we shall consider the design and implementation of message passing and of these higher-level patterns of interprocess communication.

The performance of distributed systems depends critically on the performance of the communication subsystems used for interprocess communication. This is not just a question of 'raw' network performance, nor is it simply a matter of optimization in the lower layers of network software. High-performance distributed systems require optimized implementations of the patterns of communication described below. In particular, the performance of the software that implements these patterns of communication has a critical impact on the latency (delay) of interprocess communication.

Client-server communication □ The client-server communication model is oriented towards service provision. An exchange consists of:

1. transmission of a request from a client process to a server process;

2. execution of the request by the server;

3. transmission of a reply to the client.

This pattern of communication involves the transmission of two messages (Figure 2.2) and a specific form of synchronization of the client and the server. The server process must become aware of the request message sent in Step 1 as soon as it arrives, and the

Figure 2.2   Client-server communication.

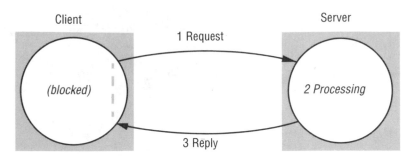

activity issuing the request in the client process must be suspended (*blocked*), causing it to wait after Step 1 until the reply has been received in Step 3.

The client-server pattern of communication can be implemented in terms of the basic message-passing operations, *send* and *receive* outlined above, but it is commonly presented at the language level as a **remote procedure calling** (RPC) construct that conceals the communication operations behind the familiar procedure-calling abstraction and is implemented in terms of a *request-reply protocol*, for which the underlying communication operations are optimized to the purpose at hand.

In its lifetime a server process serves many clients and it need have no prior knowledge of them. Each request contains a communication identifier that is used to

Function shipping: In the client-server pattern of communication the contents of messages passed between clients and servers are purely data, even though a part of the first message specifies which action (procedure) the server is to execute to satisfy the request. An extension of this model allows function shipping, in which procedure definitions – that is, the instructions making up procedures – are passed from client to server. In the function-shipping model, the server acts as an execution environment and interpreter for programs in some specified programming language, and clients transmit sequences of instructions for interpretation. Some sequences of instructions are definitions of named procedures to be stored by the server for later execution and others are procedure calls, invoking the procedures that have been previously shipped to the server or procedures built-in to the server's interpreter.

This approach is very flexible – it enables clients to extend the repertoire of actions that can be performed in the server – but it must be implemented in terms of a specific programming language that is interpreted by the server, and clients must issue their requests in that language. The environment in which the programs are interpreted on the server requires careful design to ensure that the interactions between clients are properly controlled.

Because of these constraints, there are few examples of the practical application of function shipping, but there is one outstandingly successful one: the use of PostScript language for communication with laser printers and window systems. This approach is used in a very wide range of laser printers, but has appeared to date in only two window systems: the Sun NeWS window system [Sun 1987b] and the NeXTStep system from NeXT Computer Inc.

Figure 2.3   Multicasting to a process group.

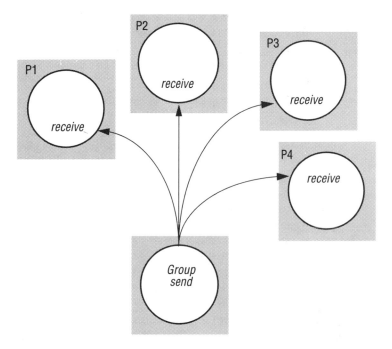

transmit the reply to the client. In an open system clients cannot be initialized to hold the communication identifiers of all of the server processes managing the resources that they may wish to use. Some form of *dynamic binding* must take place. Typically, when a server process starts up it registers itself with a naming service, stating its network address and a well known name for the service that it provides. Clients obtain its network address by interrogating the naming service using the same well known service name and so are able to communicate with it. Note that a process is a client or a server only for the purposes of a particular exchange or series of exchanges. A server can request the services of another server, and so can be a client of other processes, and similarly a client can be a server to other processes.

Group multicast ☐ In the group multicast pattern of communication, processes interact by message passing, but in this case the target of a message is not a single process but a group of processes. To a single group *send* operation there corresponds a *receive* performed by each member of a process group, as illustrated in Figure 2.3. Sending a message to the members of a specified group of processes is known as **multicasting**. (The term *broadcasting* is used in this book only to refer to a facility for sending messages to all of the computers in a given network environment – a technique that is often used in local area networks, but does not scale well and should therefore be used sparingly in distributed systems.)

Group multicast communication can be motivated by the following examples:

Locating an object: a client multicasts a message containing the name of a file directory to a group of file server processes. Only the one which holds the relevant directory replies to the request.

Fault tolerance: a client multicasts its requests to a group of server processes, all of which process the requests identically and one or more of which reply to them. A group of two or more servers can continuously provide the service, even if one of their members fails.

Multiple update: an event such as 'the time is 18:01' can be multicast to a group of interested processes.

There may or may not be hardware support for multicast communication in the underlying network. Without this support, a multicast message has to be sent sequentially by the communication system to the members of a process group; with it, it can be sent in parallel. The importance of communication with process groups is as a structuring concept for distributed systems and is independent of the existence of hardware support for multicasting.

An important issue is whether the membership of a group is transparent to the processes that send to it. An example of the implementation of process groups is the ISIS programming environment which is described in Chapter 11. In the ISIS model group membership is normally transparent. As well as group *send* and *receive* operations, this model provides for dynamically manipulating the membership of any particular group by *groupCreate*, *groupDelete*, *groupJoin* and *groupLeave* operations that create an empty group, delete a group, cause a process to join an existing group or leave it, respectively. On joining or leaving a group, a process is included in or removed from the corresponding list of recipients of multicast messages. Multicast communication and its application are further examined in Chapters 4 and 11.

Software structure

The design of operating systems for centralized computer systems is often referred to as 'monolithic' because the set of abstractions that they provide for use in application programs is determined by a single immutable interface – such as the system call interface in UNIX. In contrast, the design of a distributed system need not be monolithic because application programs can access many different services, each providing its own procedural interface for accessing resources. The resources provided to application programs can be extended by adding new services. This distinction reflects the key characteristic of distributed systems called openness introduced in Chapter 1.

Figure 2.4 shows the four main hardware and software layers in a centralized computer system: applications, run-time support for programming languages (for example, interpreters and libraries), the operating system and hardware components. Each layer uses facilities in the layer below it. Note that several alternative system standards can be substituted within each of the bottom layers: programming languages (for example, C or Smalltalk), operating systems (for example, UNIX or OS/2) and hardware (for example, Motorola 68040 or Intel 80486).

Figure 2.4   Layers in centralized computer systems.

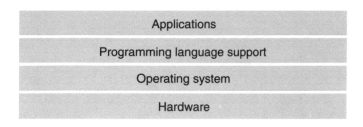

In centralized computers the operating system is the main system software layer. It manages all of the basic resources in the system and provides essential services to application programs and users. These include:

- Basic resource management:
  - memory allocation and protection;
  - process creation and processor scheduling;
  - peripheral device handling.
- User and application services:
  - user authentication and access control (for example, login facilities);
  - file management and file access facilities;
  - clock facilities.

All of these services are performed primarily by the operating system kernel in centralized systems.

In distributed systems, we must provide these and other services to application programs in a manner that enables new services to be conveniently added. To do so, we restrict the role of the kernel to basic resource management:

- memory allocation and protection;
- process creation and processor scheduling;
- interprocess communication;
- peripheral device handling;

and we introduce a new class of software components called open services to provide all other shared resources and services. The task of a kernel is then to present a set of universal problem-oriented programming abstractions such as processes to users and applications, shielding them from the underlying details of the processor and other hardware. In addition, kernels protect both their own code and data and the hardware from unwanted accesses by users and applications. Kernels are not designed to be modified routinely. Any services that do not require privileged access to the kernel's code and data or the hardware of the computer need not be included in the kernel. They are implemented by processes that appear at the same level as application processes.

Figure 2.5   The main categories of software in a distributed system and their dependencies.

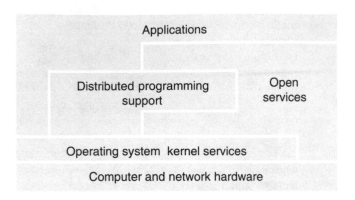

Openness means that distributed systems can be configured to the particular needs of a given community of users or set of applications. System managers configure the services available in a system and users select and use applications that depend upon them. Redundant system components can be avoided, and advantage can be taken of new machines or software. In principle, as open systems evolve, computers with different architectures and operating system kernels can be integrated, and new applications run alongside and in cooperation with one another.

Apart from the technical aspects of openness, systems are also sometimes called open when hardware or software components supplied by different companies can work together in the system. The phrase 'open system' is often used with this commercial connotation, rather than the technical meaning given above.

Figure 2.5 illustrates the main categories of software that exist in distributed systems and their interdependencies. In that figure and other similar figures throughout the book, a shared horizontal line signifies that services provided by the box below the line are directly used by the components above it. For example, application programs may use OS kernel services, distributed programming support and open services.

The categories shown in Figure 2.5 correspond to different levels of abstraction of the distributed system, each of which offers a different degree of transparency to its users. For example, a user running only a spreadsheet program might have little concept of the system at all; a distributed applications programmer sets up programs running at a collection of machines, but deals with the function of the programs rather than the specific characteristics of the underlying machines; he or she might write in a distributed programming language, and use knowledge of the services available; a system programmer or system administrator uses knowledge of the different roles of different machines in the system.

Each box in the figure is implemented by a *set* of hardware or software components, which may differ in their interfaces and their construction. Apart from the application and hardware layers, we can distinguish three main categories of software that support the execution of applications. They may be considered as the components of a distributed operating system. Their roles are outlined below:

Operating system kernel services: There must be a software kernel in each computer, responsible for providing the most basic set of resources and services while protecting the basic hardware components from inadmissible access. This might be a conventional Unix kernel extended to provide network communication services, as in 4.BSD UNIX. But many of the services provided by UNIX can also be supplied by open services. This can result in an awkward duplication of functions and is undesirable since the services provided by the kernel are immutable.

This has led to the development of **microkernels**; these are kernels that provided the smallest possible set of services and resources on which the remaining services required can be built. Typically this basic set of services includes a process abstraction and a basic communication service. The maximum degree of openness is achieved with this approach. We shall describe the design features of a typical microkernel in Chapter 6 and we present three examples (Mach, Amoeba and Chorus) in Chapter 18. Note that computers running different kernels can be used in a distributed system provided that the communication services are standardized. A single distributed system can contain some computers with UNIX kernels together with other computers with different microkernels optimized to the needs of particular applications or services.

Open services: It is these that bring the programming facilities of a distributed system up to the level required for application programming. New services can be developed and installed as required, enabling distributed systems to be adapted to the needs of many different types of application. These services range from basic resources such as a file service to facilities not normally considered part of the operating system such as an electronic mail delivery service. Most systems are provided initially with at least the set of services needed for a conventional distributed UNIX implementation. Server processes and application programs are indistinguishable to the kernels or microkernels of the computers on which they run – the kernel's role is simply to provide them with basic processing and communication facilities.

The distinction between kernel services and open services is made because kernels cannot be open, they must enforce their own protection against run-time modification. Their role is to provide a stable interface to low-level resources.

Support for distributed programming: Distributed programming support includes run-time support for language facilities that allow programs written in conventional languages to work together, such as remote procedure calling and group multicast communication. Some programming languages have been developed specifically for distributed applications. These require more extensive run-time support. Language support components that are not related to distribution, such as language interpreters and libraries are omitted from Figure 2.5 for the sake of clarity.

Workload allocation

In a centralized computer system all of the processor and memory resources are available for allocation by the operating system in any manner required by the current workload. In the simple architectural model of distributed systems introduced in Figure 1.1, the processor performance and memory capacity of a workstation determines the size of the largest task that can be performed on behalf of its user. We shall refer to this simple architectural model as the **workstation-server** model. As we shall see when we consider the requirement for user interface consistency later in this chapter, there are substantial advantages for users in 'putting the processor cycles near the users', especially in highly interactive applications, and this is achieved very effectively in the workstation-server model. But it is self-evident that the simple workstation-server model does not optimize the use of processing and memory resources, nor does it enable a single user with a computing task that has large processing and memory requirements to obtain additional resources.

We shall discuss two modifications of the workstation-server model that have been developed to meet these requirements. One, the **processor pool model**, involves a modification of the workstation-server architecture to include processors that can be allocated to users' tasks dynamically. The other is a software extension of the workstation-server model that enables tasks to be allocated to idle or under-utilized workstations. Finally, we shall introduce **shared-memory multiprocessor** computers and note that they can be applied effectively in both models, especially for large computing loads that can be handled by several separate processors, such as heavily loaded servers.

The processor pool model ☐ In the processor pool model processors are allocated to processes for their lifetimes, resulting in the sharing of processors at the grain of whole processes. A user who performs a task involving several processes is able to access more computing power than a single workstation can offer. A commonly-cited example of such a task is the compilation of a multi-segment program in a language such as C, in which each of the segments can be compiled independently to produce separate relocatable object code files. In a processor pool system a program with n segments can be compiled using n processors producing a potential n-fold speed-up of that phase of the task (assuming that the separate compilation processes do not conflict for any other resources, such as disk access or network bandwidth).

A distributed system that supports the processor pool model (Figure 2.6) consists of a workstation-server system in which one or more processor pools have been integrated. A processor pool consists of a collection of low-cost computers, each consisting of little more than a processor, memory and network interface. Each pool processor has an independent network connection, as do the workstations and servers. The computers in a pool usually consist of single circuit boards that are rack-mounted so as to be physically compact and to share power supply units. The processors do not have to be homogeneous in architecture; a system might, for example, include both Motorola and Intel chip sets in the pool, in order to broaden the range of software that can be run.

For users, the processor pool model differs from the workstation-server model in that the user can do useful work on a computer with only meagre hardware resources, or even on a networked terminal such as the *X terminals* shown in Figure 2.6 and discussed in the accompanying box on *window systems*. The user's workstation or terminal simply provides a means to access the computing resources of the system; the user's computing work can be performed partly or entirely on the pool processors. Whenever the user

Figure 2.6   The processor pool model.

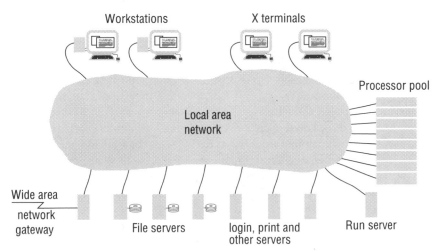

initiates a task, for example by typing a UNIX command, a pool processor is allocated and the task is initiated on it. If the user initiates more than one task, or a task spawns some subtasks, pool processors can be allocated to each of them, and they can all run in parallel.

Window systems: In modern workstations, a window system handles input from interactive devices such as a keyboard and a mouse, and manages the display screen, performing updates to the display screen in response to requests to do so from programs that the user is currently interacting with.

The most popular window system for workstations is X-11. X-11 is organized as a client-server system. An X-11 server manages the interactive devices and the display screen. This always runs on the workstation whose display it manages. The clients of the X-11 server are the application programs that the user is currently interacting with. They handle commands and other input from the user and generate information for display. The client programs communicate with the server by invoking procedures, just as in other client-server systems, and X-11 provides an extensive library of procedures for creating windows, displaying and modifying graphical objects in windows. The clients need not be located in the same workstation as the server, since the server procedures are always invoked using an RPC mechanism. In the processor pool model, clients of the window server are almost always located in a different node.

An *X terminal* is a networked computer without disk storage, dedicated to run as an X-11 server only. A user can access the system and do useful work from an X terminal only by causing client programs to run on a pool processor or on some other user's workstation. An X terminal with a dedicated pool processor can be expected to be as responsive as a workstation only as long as not too much communication – of graphical data, for example – has to occur between the two. We shall examine this issue later in this chapter under the heading of user interface consistency.

The Amoeba system, developed by Tanenbaum and his colleagues at the Vrije University, Amsterdam is described in detail in Chapter 18. It is an example of a system that supports the processor pool model. Users can use interactive or graphical application programs when working from workstations or X terminals. A variety of pool processors is available. In addition to running programs for users of X terminals, they can be used to run programs for workstation users when the workstation is not suitable or to perform tasks that exceed the workstation's processing capacity. Server processes, such as name servers, that do not require direct access to peripherals can also be run in pool processors.

Processes are created from executable binary files (*executables*), several of which may be compiled from the same program source code, corresponding to the different machine architectures in the Amoeba system. The use of the pool processors is organized by a *run server*. Pool processors are allocated dynamically: when a client program such as a command interpreter needs to run a program the run server is contacted. This server matches the available executables for the program to the available architectures in the pool processors it manages. For example, executables for the chosen program may exist for both a Motorola 68030 and an Intel 80486. From the processors available it chooses one on the basis of current processing and memory loads and the program's memory requirements.

Other recent designs that have incorporated processor pools include Plan 9 [Pike *et al.* 1990] and the Clouds system which is described in Chapter 18. The first distributed system based on the processor pool model was the Cambridge Distributed Computing System developed in the Computer Laboratory at Cambridge University, England [Needham and Herbert 1982]. There were no workstations in the original implementation of that system. Users were provided with simple terminals and were allocated processors from a heterogeneous processor pool. Networked window systems had not been developed at that time and its use was therefore restricted to non-graphical applications.

Use of idle workstations ☐ A further interesting variation on the workstation-server model is the use of idle or under-utilized workstations as a fluctuating pool of extra computers which can be used similarly to pool processors in the processor pool model. At any one time – and especially overnight – a significant proportion of workstations on a network may either be unused or be used for lightweight activities such as document editing. These workstations have spare processing capacity, and can be used to run jobs for users who are logged on at other workstations and do not have sufficient capacity at their machine.

Several examples exist of systems that have been developed to utilize idle workstations. This includes early work on so-called *worm programs* done at Xerox PARC [Shoch and Hupp1982] and many recent developments [Nichols 1987]. Worm programs are in this context a positive way of putting computer resources to use – as opposed to the maliciously contrived programs which are known by the same name (discussed in Chapter 16). The name worm program derives from its ability to continue to operate on a changing set of machines, as users log off and log on to their workstations – that is, to survive even when pieces of it are lost. For example, the Xerox worm programs performed computations for animated graphics in parallel, and ran a telephone-based alarm service. To avoid competition for processing resources on a

Figure 2.7   A shared-memory multiprocessor.

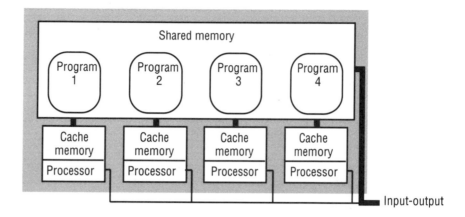

workstation, a program component or *segment* of a worm was not allowed to co-exist with interactive programs running on the same machine – it would be destroyed when a user logged on to the machine.

More recently, the Sprite operating system for distributed systems [Ousterhout *et al.* 1988] has provided a facility for users to run individual commands at idle or under-utilized workstations. The target workstation is chosen transparently by the system, just as a pool processor is chosen transparently in the Amoeba system. Sprite includes a facility for *process migration* – the re-location of an executing program from one machine to another. This means that a remotely executing program can be migrated safely back to its 'home' machine where it can continue with its execution, when a user logs on or starts using its workstation more heavily.

Shared-memory multiprocessors □ Figure 2.7 illustrates the processor and memory architecture of a shared-memory multiprocessor computer. This is one of a number of types of parallel computer that is now available. It is not the purpose of this book to discuss the design of those parallel computers whose purpose is to provide large quantities of processing power for use in the solution of large-scale numerical and other computational problems. However, shared-memory multiprocessor computers are commonly used as server machines in open distributed systems because of the performance advantages that this architecture brings for relatively low hardware and software costs.

A shared-memory multiprocessor contains several independent processors, each able to execute a separate program. Each processor is comparable in power to a processor used in a conventional, single-processor computer – and in many cases is exactly such a processor. The number of processors that can be deployed is in the range 2–64; this limit being determined by the engineering costs and performance overheads involved in the provision of efficient interfaces to the shared memory, which involves the provision of a substantial cache memory with each processor.

Support for shared-memory multiprocessors can be integrated into a distributed operating system in a relatively straightforward manner, exploiting the shared memory as a high-speed mechanism for interprocess communication and allocating the processors to system and user tasks as required. When used to support server processes, a multiprocessor computer can service several client requests in parallel, reducing the potential for the provision of key services to become a bottleneck in distributed system. Multiprocessor workstations are also now widely available and their processing capacity is particularly in demand for applications in areas such as virtual reality and multimedia.

Consistency maintenance

Consistency issues frequently arise from the separation of processing resources and the concurrency in distributed systems. We define several important types of consistency here. Further discussion of them and of techniques for their resolution will be found throughout the remainder of the book.

Update consistency □ Consistency issues arise when several processes access and update data concurrently. The activity of changing a related set of data values cannot be performed instantaneously, but the desired effect is that the updates should appear to be atomic – a related set of changes made by a given process should appear to all other processes as though it was instantaneous. This problem is not unique to distributed systems; it arises in many applications that involve the use of shared data, including most database applications, but it is of particular significance in distributed systems (a) because there are likely to be many users accessing shared data, and (b) because the operation of the system itself depends on the consistency of certain databases, such as the file directories managed by file services or the naming databases managed by name servers. This important topic is discussed extensively in Chapter 13.

Caching in distributed systems: When a resource (for example, a file or a name table) is accessed by a client, copies of some or all of the data values representing the resource are likely to be transferred to the client environment. The term *caching* refers to a mechanism, implemented by software in the client computer, for the retention in the client's environment of a copy of the data values for subsequent re-use, avoiding the need to request them again when the same resource is accessed subsequently. Since the storage available for caching in a client's environment is likely to be more limited than that available to the relevant resource manager, only a fraction of the data held by the resource manager can be retained in the client environment. The usefulness of caching therefore depends upon the hypothesis of *locality* in the pattern of references to data values – that data values from resources that have been accessed in the recent past are likely to be accessed again in the immediate future.

Caching is a powerful and transparent technique for optimizing the performance of client-server interactions. It can be implemented by an independent software module in the client environment without modification to the servers whose data are cached. We shall see in later chapters that locality of reference is a common phenomenon in distributed systems and caching is a key technique for designing distributed systems with satisfactory performance; it is applied in file services, name services and many other areas of distributed system design.

Replication consistency □ If data that are derived from a single source have been copied to several computers and subsequently modified at one or more of them, then the possibility of inconsistencies arises between the values of data items at different machines. Consider, for example, a multi-user computer game in which players using networked personal computers or workstations move creatures around in a maze, and in which information about the positions and actions of the creatures is replicated at the workstation of each player. The replication of each move might be implemented by sending (multicasting) a similar message from that player's computer to each of the other players' computers. But another player may be moving concurrently and the messages reporting the moves of the two players may arrive in different orders at other players' computers. In the absence of measures to ensure that the messages are received and replicas are updated in the same sequence at each computer, it is possible for different players to see the creatures' movements in different orders, which may even make it appear that the game's rules have been broken.

Another, more commonplace example of replication inconsistency arises in the Internet *netnews* system in which messages posted to newsgroups appear in an inconsistent order at some sites – the answers to questions often appearing before the question has appeared. Techniques for the maintenance of replication consistency can be found in Chapter 11.

Cache consistency □ See the accompanying boxes for a definition of caching as it is used in distributed systems and a discussion of its benefits. Cache consistency refers to the problem that arises when data values that have been cached by one client are updated by another. This can happen, for example, when the same blocks of a file stored in a file server are requested and cached at several workstations. When a block is updated by a client at one of the workstations, the version held in the file server and those held in caches at other workstations are said to be *stale*. The updated block may be sent by the client to the resource manager (the file server) responsible for the file, but the other workstations will retain the out-of-date version unless they are notified by the server that it is stale.

The performance benefits of caching: Consider a client program that reads data from a file one byte at a time. A request-reply message exchange to fetch 1 byte of data from another computer takes about 2 milliseconds over a 10 megabits per second Ethernet local area network, using a reasonably efficient operating system. To fetch 1 kilobyte, the request message is of the same length, and the reply message contains about 1000 extra bytes. The corresponding request-reply exchange takes about 3 ms using the same network and operating system. Thus it is about 700 times less costly in time to fetch the data in blocks of 1000 bytes than by 1000 separate requests for one byte. Once a block has been fetched and cached at the client, the client program can access the data without further network communication.

Furthermore, it is to our advantage to retain data in the cache for as long as possible. If the same client, or another client in the same environment (for example, another client running at the same workstation), accesses the data again while it is in the cache, no further network communication will be required.

The problem of cache consistency is a special case of the replication consistency problem outlined above, and can be addressed by similar techniques. In addition, some special techniques for maintaining cache consistency are discussed in Chapters 7 and 8.

Failure consistency ☐ When a centralized computer system fails, all of the programs that are running on it fail simultaneously – there is a single mode of failure. In a distributed system when one component fails, the others, including any with which it was cooperating, will normally continue to run. But if they depend on the continued operation of the failed computer or program then they may fail later. This is the problem of multiple **failure modes** in distributed systems. Each of the cooperating components involved in a failed computation may have reached a different point in its program. To ensure that the permanent data stored by all of the components remains consistent, recovery procedures are needed to cause the data to be 'rolled back' to a known state after a failure. Approaches to this are discussed in Chapter 15.

Clock consistency ☐ Many of the algorithms used in both application and system software depend on the use of *timestamps* – stored data values that represent the time at which some event has occurred. In distributed systems, a timestamp generated at one computer may well be passed in messages to other computers, where they may be compared with locally-generated timestamps. But the notion of physical time is a problem in distributed systems. This is not due to the effects of Special Relativity, which are negligible or non-existent for normal computers (unless one counts computers travelling in rocket ships!); the problem is based on a similar limitation concerning our ability to pass information from one computer to another. This is that the clocks belonging to different computers can only be synchronized, at least in the majority of cases, by network communication. Message passing is limited by virtue of the speed at which it can transfer information, but this in itself would not be a problem if we knew how long message transmission took. The problem is that sending a message through a network normally takes an unpredictable amount of time, rendering it difficult or impossible to design protocols that will synchronize clocks precisely.

Fortunately, the requirement in distributed system design is often not for an absolute measure of time but for an ordering on some events such as the updates to a file. In Chapter 10 we discuss techniques for the approximate synchronization of physical clocks and introduce *logical clocks*, which are used to define an order on events without measuring the physical time at which they occurred.

User interface consistency ☐ There are many issues to be considered in the design of user interfaces for interactive programs; most are outside the scope of this book, but we shall consider here the effect of distributed resources and possible communication delays on the responsiveness of interactive programs. This is an issue of consistency: whenever a user performs an input action such as a key depression or a mouse click in an interactive program the screen becomes temporarily inconsistent with the user's model of the program's state. The program then processes the user's input and performs the necessary operations to update the screen. Unless the input is processed and the changes are transmitted to the screen quickly enough to give the user the impression of an instantaneous change the user becomes aware of the screen inconsistency. Ergonomic measurements show that a delay of not more that 0.1 second must be achieved in order to produce this impression when interacting using modern graphical user interfaces. We have already mentioned this in connection with multimedia applications in Chapter 1.

The interactive delay is the sum of:

- the time required to receive and process the user's input and compute the changes needed to the screen image, and

- the time required to transmit the changes to the window system and to alter the screen image.

The time required to transmit changes from the application program space to the window system managing the user's display screen is of particular interest in distributed systems. Since the ergonomic requirement for interactive response is independent of the volume of data transmitted for each screen update, there can be a problem in achieving adequate performance in highly interactive applications, animations and the display of photographic images. Caching of the data used by interactive programs is often used to address this problem. See the accompanying box for a historical perspective on the requirement for consistency of user interface response. We shall discuss the transfer rates and latency characteristics of networks and their bearing on this in Chapter 3.

2.3   User requirements

The designers of systems must consider the needs of their potential users. Given that most distributed systems are designed to provide general-purpose computing facilities, it would be beyond the scope of this book to provide a comprehensive review of user requirements. In this section we aim to highlight some of the more important requirements that arise in practical systems.

A historical perspective on interactive delays: In centralized systems the response to user interaction is slow and irregular, depending on the total load caused by all of the users, whereas for users of workstations and personal computers it is generally fast and regular. This is one of the factors that drove the transition to personal computing, and distributed systems should aim to maintain the improvement. In a distributed system a separate computer can be allocated to each user to execute all of his or her tasks in order to produce a faster and more regular response to user interaction.

This characteristic of distributed systems has been described very well by James Morris of the University of California at Berkeley in the epithet: 'The nicest thing about workstations is that they don't run faster at night'. However, this leaves aside the question of how remote data and resource accesses affect the performance of applications and system software. The time cost of a remote access is normally greater than that of the same operation performed locally, because of the communications costs involved. An application running on a workstation in a distributed system can suffer from irregular response when application programs make remote accesses to overloaded servers.

We shall structure our discussion under these headings:

Functionality: what the system should do for users.

Quality of service: embracing issues of performance, reliability and security.

Reconfigurability: the need for a system to accommodate changes without causing disruption to existing service provision.

Functionality

What services can users and application writers expect from a distributed computer system? What applications can users run? We have seen that key benefits of a distributed computer system are (a) the economy and convenience that comes from sharing hardware resources and information, and (b) the potential improvement in performance and reliability that can come from exploiting the separation of software components so that they can be executed in separate computers.

The minimal requirement for a distributed system is that the functionality provided by a distributed system should be not less than the user could expect from any single computer by itself – one that would reasonably be used to provide the same user's computing facilities. We shall turn shortly to the question of whether this functionality should be identical to or merely comparable with what users are used to from a non-distributed system.

The stronger requirement is that a distributed system should bring an improvement over the services provided by any single computer by itself – aside from information sharing – through one or both of the following enhancements:

- Sharing across a network can bring access to a richer variety of resources than could be provided by any single computer. This includes specialized processors and peripherals attached to machines that become accessible over a network.

- Utilization of the advantages of distribution can be made possible at the level of the application programming interface, so that applications that carry out explicit sharing and fault-tolerant or parallel applications can be programmed.

Most users are mainly interested in the question of what applications they can run. On the one hand, new functionalities – ones that have no counterpart in a non-distributed computer system – can be provided in a distributed system. For example, physically distributed users based in different organizations can cooperate in editing the same diagram or text. (Such applications belong to the field known as Computer-Supported Cooperative Working – CSCW.)

On the other hand, a great deal of software already exists which runs on non-distributed computer systems. Much effort and financial investment has gone into the production and maintenance of this software. From an individual or organization who has invested in such software there will come the question: will it still work in the transition to a new distributed computer system? Some software has to be superseded in a transition to a system that exploits the advantages of distribution.

There are three options open when considering a migration path from multi-user centralized computing or single-user PC-based computing to distributed computing:

1. *Adapt existing operating systems*: Continue to use existing operating system software that has been adapted for networking, such as UNIX; add services as applications on top of UNIX wherever possible, but modify the kernel in some important cases to provide transparently a distributed implementation of an existing facility – for example, the Sun Network File System (described in Chapter 8).

2. *Move to an entirely new operating system designed specifically for distributed systems*: To take full advantage of distribution the designers should not be constrained by the characteristics of older systems. All operating system services can be open and distributed in this option. Existing software becomes unusable.

3. *Emulation*: Move to a new operating system designed for distributed systems, but one that can emulate one or more existing operating systems. That way, existing software will continue to run, but new software can be written using the new operating system's system call interface, to take full advantage of distribution. Both types of software can run side-by-side.

We shall see in later chapters that option 1 is rather limited in the possibilities for new functionalities that it offers. Option 2 represents an ideal from the designers' point of view but would leave a great many current users dissatisfied. Option 3, if practical, seems preferable to either of the other two. Considerable research and development work has been applied towards the emulation of UNIX on operating system kernels designed for distributed systems. The Mach and Chorus designs are notable in this respect. We shall examine these designs in Chapter 18. They have demonstrated considerable success in producing systems that provide binary emulation of UNIX, although questions remain about the performance of their emulations, and it is not possible to reproduce UNIX failure semantics – the behaviour of programs when faults occur — exactly in a distributed system.

Reconfigurability

The scalability of a distributed system design and its ability to accommodate heterogeneity are relevant both when the design is to be implemented in separate installations of different sizes or machine mixes, and when a particular installation expands. In the latter case, the change itself should occur without disrupting the system – something that didn't happen when the prefixes changed in the London telephone system, as described in Chapter 1. It is not practical to interrupt the work of five hundred users when adding a workstation to the system for the five-hundred-and-first user, nor when adding a file server to expand the capacity of the file service.

There are two timescales in distributed computer systems on which changes are potential causes for disruption that should be addressed in the design of system software:

Short-term changes: Distributed system software may be designed to handle the following short-term changes in run-time conditions:

- a failed process, computer or network component is replaced by another, working counterpart;

- computational load is shifted from over-loaded to less-loaded machines, so as to increase the total throughput of the distributed system;

- network communications are minimized by transferring activities or data between machines in such a way as to make an activity's data locally accessible, and so avoiding network communication.

Medium-to-long-term evolution: In addition to the changes due to the expansion in scale and the need to accommodate heterogeneous components that occur as part of a distributed system's normal development, existing machines are sometimes assigned new roles, or one-off purchases of new machines made. For example, the file service could be upgraded by transferring its data to a more powerful type of machine.

The ability to accommodate changes on either of these timescales is called *reconfigurability*, and the individual changes themselves are called reconfigurations. The requirement to effect reconfigurations without disruption amounts to that of making them transparently.

Quality of service

Once users are provided with the functionality that they require of a service such as the file service in a distributed system, we can go on to ask about the quality of service provision, and whether there is any added value arising from distribution. We shall discuss the quality of service under three areas. A distributed system must give adequate *performance*, in terms of the response times experienced by its users. Some applications are such that failure can lead to highly inconvenient or disastrous results, and we can ask whether a service can continue to be provided or can be brought to a safe halt when failures occur – that is, we can ask about its *reliability* and *availability*. Lastly, we can ask whether a distributed service provision is *secure* against unauthorized access.

Performance: We have already considered the users' requirement for a fast and consistent response to interaction and the impact of communication to and from the screen on it. Interactive client programs often perform accesses to shared resources.

When a service is accessed, the speed at which the response is generated is determined by the performance of all of the software components that are involved – the operating systems' communication services and distributed programming support (the remote procedure calling software, for example) as well as the software that implements the service. The designer must seek to optimize the use of communication at all of these levels.

Reliability and availability: In Chapter 1 we introduced fault tolerance as a key characteristic of distributed systems. We indicated there that its achievement is not automatic; the design of distributed system software has a strong influence on it.

From the users' point of view, reliability is often a requirement. Any user would opt for high reliability given a chance – imagine a world in which you could keep on editing and saving an important document, even though a file server used for storing the document has crashed. However, highly reliable services in distributed systems often give worse response times than those without these features. The distinction between whether reliability is a convenience or an absolute requirement is thus an important one.

Certain applications are such that a disruption or malfunction in their processing is highly inconvenient or even dangerous to life. Examples of this include software controlling financial transactions and air traffic control software. A computer system's *reliability* is a measure of how small is the likelihood of it deviating from behaving as it was designed to do – that is, according to a specification of its correct behaviour. This includes the case of the system stopping, without having taken any individual incorrect actions. Reliability can be enhanced by designing the system so that deviations – known as failures – can be detected and recovered from. The hardware or software cause of a failure is called a fault. A **fault-tolerant system** is one which can detect a fault and either fail gracefully (that is, predictably) or mask the fault so that no failure is perceived by users of the system. We shall discuss the design of fault-tolerant systems fully in Chapter 15.

Distributed systems offer some resilience against hardware failure as an automatic consequence of their architecture. The failure of a single workstation interrupts the work of a single user but does not affect the service provided to other users. Even the failure of a server computer may not have a critical impact on the service to users if there are several instances of the same service running in the system, as is sometimes the case for the most common services, such as printing and filing. In the case of filing, files must be replicated in a number of servers to gain this sort of advantage; replication is discussed in Chapter 11.

Security: Centralized computer systems achieve a reasonable degree of security applied to the data stored and transmitted within the system, and continuous service provision in the face of possible attempts to disrupt this. Although there are known weaknesses in the security provisions of some widely used centralized operating systems, distributed systems bring about a new set of security problems, which make them fundamentally less secure unless special precautions are taken.

The security problem stems from two main threats that are consequences of distribution itself. The first of these threats is against the privacy and integrity of users' data as it travels over the network. It is very hard – often impossible, in practice – to secure a network against tampering aimed at copying or interfering with data as it passes over it. Interference can be achieved either by tampering with the network cable itself, or by connecting a machine which is either set up to read all network data packets or used to inject maliciously synthesized data packets. The second main reason for poor security in distributed systems is their openness to interference with system software: not all machines on a network can in general be made physically secure, and any software can be run on vulnerable machines. As an extreme example, a networked computer could in principle be set up to act as a bogus file server which provides incorrect data in response to read requests and throws away data when it is 'written' by unwitting clients.

These threats arise from the exposure to attack by potential intruders of the channels of communication and the software interfaces between system components of distributed systems. These characteristics are an essential consequence of their geographic distribution and their openness. The requirement of most users of a distributed computer system is, clearly, that these security weaknesses are dealt with adequately. Techniques available for achieving this are dealt with in Chapter 16.

2.4 Summary

The design of distributed systems involves the development or selection of solutions to the technical issues discussed in this chapter. The choice of technical solutions determines the extent to which the key characteristics introduced in Chapter 1 and the design goals listed in Figure 2.1 are achieved. The technical issues introduced in this chapter are *naming*, *communication*, *software structuring*, *workload allocation* and several types of *consistency maintenance*. The design of solutions to each of these is discussed in detail in the remaining chapters of the book.

The provision of general-purpose schemes for the *naming* of resources is a necessary consequence of resource sharing. Naming schemes must be designed to support scalability and location transparency. Name services maintain the information needed to resolve names and provide a name resolution service to clients. Their design impacts the performance, scalability and security of distributed systems.

The design of *communication* subsystems, particularly the communication patterns for which they are optimized, impacts the performance and the openness of distributed systems. We have described two main patterns of communication – *client-server* and *group multicast*. These two patterns have emerged as the most effective ones for the construction of open distributed systems and their efficient implementation is a key design requirement.

Software structuring methods are required to enable the benefits of openness to be realized. The choices to be made in this area fall in the domain of operating system design – the methods by which the basic resources required by all applications will be provided and the extent to which they can be configured and optimized to meet user requirements.

Workload allocation has received less attention to date than other design issues. It impacts the effectiveness with which the hardware resources of a distributed system are used, and hence the overall performance of the system. We defined the basic workstation-server model for the distribution of hardware resources an alternative known as the processor pool model. We have also introduced shared-memory multiprocessor computers which are often used for processor-intensive tasks in distributed systems, and we have outlined an approach to the construction of software for the use of idle workstations to perform long-running computational tasks.

Consistency maintenance has many aspects and many of them are significant for distributed systems. We have outlined the need for consistency when shared data or resources are updated by several independent processes and the need to maintain consistency between replicated copies of data, including the important case in which copies of resources or parts of resources are *cached* in client computers. Failure consistency, clock consistency and user interface consistency were also introduced as design issues for distributed systems.

Finally, we have outlined some user requirements under the headings of functionality, quality of service and reconfigurability. These enable users and application programs to exploit the special features of distributed systems without compromising the key characteristics and design goals already identified.

EXERCISES

2.1 Discuss suitable design goals for a file service such as Sun NFS with respect to each of the following: performance, reliability, scalability, consistency, security.

page 30

2.2 What is a resolved name?

page 32

2.3 What operations should a general-purpose distributed name service provide?

page 33

2.4 What would be a reasonable size for an object identifier space to be used in a distributed object-based system that may be used in the Internet.

page 32

2.5 Distinguish between flat and hierarchic naming schemes. Under what circumstances is each most useful?

page 33

2.6 Design a simple message protocol that might be used to implement remote procedure calling. (List the types of messages needed and their formats, and give an example showing how a procedure call with parameters would be passed to a server and how the result of the procedure would be delivered to the client.)

page 35

2.7 In your protocol (Exercise 2.6), discuss how the client would behave (a) if the server fails while processing a procedure call; (b) if the computation requested requires several minutes of computation in the server.

page 35

2.8 How does the client discover the identity (the communication identifier or network address) of the server?

page 35

2.9 Explain the difference between monolithic and open operating systems.

page 38

2.10 A design goal for microkernels is to provide the minimal set of basic services that is sufficient to support all of the other services that are required. Discuss the composition of the set of basic services, with arguments for your choices.

page 41

2.11   Discuss the efficiency of use of the processor and memory resources in a distributed system based on a simple workstation-server architecture. What techniques can be used to improve it?

page 42

2.12   Give reasons for and against equipping workstations with local disks.

page 42

2.13   A system contains X terminals and a processor pool. What determines the number of processors there should be in the pool? What will happen under conditions of heavy load?

page 42

2.14   Three source files normally take 10 seconds, 18 seconds and 30 seconds respectively to compile by themselves on one processor in a processor pool. How long should it take to compile all the files using two processors? Explain what is liable to limit the time attainable for a parallel compilation, especially as the number of compilations increases.

page 44

2.15   Should the location of processes be fully transparent in a system that utilizes the processing capacity of idle workstations?

page 44

2.16   Outline a design for a system to utilize the processing capacity of idle workstations. Consider how your design will affect the availability of a user's workstation when s/he returns from a coffee break.

page 44

2.17   Are shared memory multiprocessors distributed systems?

page 45

2.18   Contrast the problems of implementing process migration between workstations and between processors within a shared memory multiprocessor.

page 45

2.19   Explain why some *netnews* messages appear to contain answers to questions that have not yet been put.

page 47

2.20   Distinguish between buffering and caching.

page 47

2.21   Suggest a design for a protocol to synchronize the clocks of two computers and say how well it will work.

page 48

2.22   It is required to emulate an operating system (say 4.3BSD) upon another operating system kernel such as Mach. What is required for binary emulation? Compare and contrast this with emulation at the source code level. Assume that all software runs on the same machine architecture.

page 50

2.23   Recent research has found that the cost of communication within a computer can be a more significant performance parameter than that of communication between computers. Why should this be? (Hint: microkernels.)

page 52

2.24   Why are distributed systems intrinsically less secure than centralized
       computer systems?

page 53

2.25   In some NFS implementations, the relevant user and group identifier is
       included in every request to a UNIX-based NFS server. Is this secure?

page 53

2.26   Would it be possible in your local system for Dr. Allysia P. Cracker to set
       up her workstation as a bogus file server?

page 53

3

NETWORKING AND
INTERNETWORKING

Computer networks provide the necessary means for communication between the components of a distributed system. In this chapter we discuss the communication requirements of distributed systems and how they affect the design of networking hardware and software.

Distributed systems can be implemented over local area networks and over internetworks. We outline the characteristics of local and wide area networks and discuss their integration in internetworks. We summarize the principles of protocols and protocol layering and show how they can be used to provide a uniform method for communication between processes in a distributed system.

Network and internetwork design and implementation are illustrated with several case studies; two local network technologies: Ethernet and Token Ring; the Asynchronous Transfer Mode (ATM) switching method for high-bandwidth networks and two internetwork protocol suites.

3.1 Introduction

This chapter provides an introductory overview of computer networking with reference to the communication requirements of distributed systems. Readers who are not familiar with computer networking should regard it as an underpinning for the remainder of the book while those who are already familiar with the topic will find that this chapter offers an extended summary of those aspects of computer networking that are particularly relevant for distributed systems.

The networking facilities used in distributed systems are implemented by a variety of hardware components including communication circuits, switches and interfaces, and software components such as protocol managers and communication handlers, some of which are normally considered as part of the operating system, or even part of the application software running in the computers connected to the network. The resulting functionality and performance is determined by all of these components and not simply by the networking hardware and the lower layers of the software. We shall refer to the collection of hardware and software components that provide the communication facilities for a distributed system as a *communication subsystem*.

The design of a communication subsystem is strongly influenced by the characteristics of the operating systems used in the computers of which the distributed system is composed as well as the networks that interconnect them. In this chapter, we consider the impact of network technologies on the communication subsystem; the operating system issues are discussed in Chapter 6.

Performance parameters ☐ The network performance parameters that are of primary interest for our purposes are those affecting the speed with which individual messages can be transferred between two interconnected computers. These are the latency and the point-to-point data transfer rate.

> *Latency* can be defined as the time required to transfer an empty message between the relevant computers. It is a measure of the software delays involved in accessing the network at the sender and at the receiver, the delays incurred in obtaining access to the network and those incurred within the network itself.

> *Data transfer rate* is the speed at which data can be transferred between two computers in the network, once transmission has begun, quoted in bits per second.

Following from these definitions, the time required for a network to transfer a message containing *length* bits between two computers is:

$$Message\ transfer\ time = latency + length/data\ transfer\ rate$$

The transfer rate of a network is determined primarily by its physical characteristics, whereas the latency is determined primarily by software overheads, routing delays and by a load-dependent statistical element arising from conflicting demands for access to transmission channels. Many of the messages transferred between processes in distributed systems are small in size and latency is therefore often of equal or greater significance than transfer rate in determining performance.

The *total system bandwidth* of a network is a measure of throughput – the total volume of traffic that can be transferred across the network in a given time. In many local area network technologies including the Ethernet, the full transmission capacity of the network is used for every transmission and the system bandwidth is the same as the data transfer rate. But in most wide area networks messages can be transferred on several different channels simultaneously and the total system bandwidth bears no direct relationship to the transfer rate. The performance of networks deteriorates in conditions of overload – when there are too many messages in the network at the same time. The precise effect of overload on the latency, data transfer rate and total system bandwidth of a network depends strongly on the network technology.

Performance requirements □ Consider the use of client-server communication to access an item of data in a persistent shared resource such as a shared file. We should aim to achieve performance comparable to file access in a centralized architecture. The speed of file access operations is generally limited by the performance of disk storage. Access to a single data item or a single block is completed typically in a few milliseconds: 10–20 milliseconds is a typical figure. In the case of a client-server system, the time to perform a file access includes the time to send a request message to a file server and to receive a reply. These messages will be relatively short. To perform a file *read* the request occupies a few tens of bytes and the reply about one kilobyte for typical applications.

The time to transmit a request message and receive a reply message should be no longer than the time required to access a disk – the transfer time for each message should certainly be less than 10 milliseconds. To achieve such performance, the latency for message transmission should be less than 5 milliseconds and the transfer rate greater than 200 kilobytes per second, including software overheads.

There is a large gulf between the internal speeds of processors and the input-output performance of both disks and networks. The use of persistent shared resources necessarily incurs the cost of bridging that gulf, whether they are stored locally on a disk in a centralized system or remotely in a distributed file system. For comparison, when a program accesses private data the time required is simply that needed to execute a conventional procedure call. A 10 MIPS processor requires only one or two microseconds to execute a procedure call without arguments and perhaps 100 microseconds for a call involving 1000 bytes of arguments and results.

Reliability requirements □ Guarantees of reliability are required for most, but not all, applications of distributed systems. The reliability of communication is very high in most transmission media. When errors occur they are often due to timing failures in the software at the sender and receiver (for example failure by the receiving computer to accept a packet) than in the network. The detection of errors and their correction is often performed by application-level software.

Types of network □ Computer networks can be divided into two broad classes:

Local area networks (LANs): carry messages at relatively high speeds between any of the computers connected to a communication medium, such as a fibre-optic or coaxial cable, that traverses a single building or campus. No routing of messages is required, since the medium provides direct connections between all of the computers in the network. Latency is low in local area networks except when message traffic is very high.

There is a very large installed base of local area networks, encompassing virtually all working environments that contain more than one or two personal computers or workstations. The transfer rates offered by current local network technologies is in the range 0.2 to 100 megabits per second. These transfer rates are adequate for the implementation of distributed systems, but some multimedia applications demand higher bandwidths. Some examples of the local area network technologies currently available are tabulated below, with their transfer rates:

Network type	Standard	Data transfer rate (megabits per second)
Ethernet	IEEE 803.2	10
FDDI	FDDI-I	100
IBM token ring	IEEE 803.5	4 or 16
Apple LocalTalk	–	0.23

Wide area networks (WANs): carry messages at lower speeds between computers that are separated by large distances. The computers that are interconnected by a wide area network are called *host* computers. They may be located in different cities, countries or continents. The communication medium is a set of communication circuits linking a set of dedicated computers called *packet switches* that manage the network. The host computers are connected to the network through the packet switches and messages or packets are routed to their destinations by the packet switches. The routing operations introduce a delay at each point in the route, and the total transmission time for a message depends on the route that it follows. The current performance of wide area networks does not fully meet the requirements of distributed systems. Typical latencies are in the range 0.1 to 0.5 seconds. The circuits used in current wide area networks have data transfer rates in the range 20–500 kilobits per second.

The emergence of ISDN and B-ISDN telecommunication networks is expected to have a major impact on the development of wide area computer networking. ISDN stands for 'Integrated Services Digital Network', and refers to telecommunication networks that transfer voice and other types of information, including computer data, in digital form throughout the network with transfer rates that are multiples of a basic channel speed of 64 kilobits per second. B-ISDN stands for 'Broadband ISDN' and refers to ISDN networks with point-to-point transmission speeds sufficient to carry high-bandwidth services such as high-quality video and bulk data as well as voice and packetized data at transfer rates of 150 megabits per second and above.

The performance of wide area digital networks will be dramatically changed by the projected introduction of Broadband ISDN (B-ISDN) networks to provide an integrated communication infrastructure for voice, video and data transmission, and the adoption of ATM (Asynchronous Transfer Mode) switching techniques. ATM networks use a transmission method known as *cell-relay* that is designed to exploit the high-speed and reliability of fibre-optic and satellite transmission links. ATM networks offer data transfer rates up to 600 megabits per second with much lower latencies than current packet-switching networks. They are described further in Section 3.4. The expected widespread installation of B-ISDN networks using ATM protocols should ensure that the performance of wide area networks and internetworks will be adequate for the construction of distributed systems and the implementation of a wide range of distributed applications.

A third class of network is emerging, but is not yet in sufficiently widespread use to justify its detailed consideration in this book:

> *Metropolitan area networks (MANs)*: This class of network is based on the fibre-optic cabling of towns and cities for the transmission of video, voice and other data over distances of up to 50 kilometres. The data transmission facilities of such networks can be exploited to provide data transfer rates that are compatible with the requirements of distributed systems. Their data transfer rates are similar to B-ISDN networks and they are likely to use ATM switching techniques. Message routing and other delays are much shorter than for wide area networks, producing typical latencies of less than one millisecond. MAN networks meet needs similar to those currently met by local area networks while spanning greater distances.

Whereas the focus has been on local area networks for the provision of the necessary communications infrastructure for distributed systems, the advent of B-ISDN and ATM switching techniques will radically alter this situation, offering communication mechanisms compatible with the needs of distributed systems that are independent of geographical distance.

Packets □ In most applications of computer networks the requirement is for the transmission of logical units of information or **messages** – sequences of data items of arbitrary length. But before a message can be transmitted it must be subdivided into **packets**. The simplest form of packet is a sequence of binary data elements (for example, an array of bits or bytes) of restricted length, together with addressing information sufficient to identify the sending and receiving computers. Packets of restricted length are used:

* so that each computer in the network can allocate sufficient buffer storage to hold the largest possible incoming packet, and

* to avoid the undue delays that would occur in waiting for communication channels to become free if long messages were transmitted without subdivision.

Internetworks □ A key characteristic of distributed systems is their extensibility, and this leads to a need for distributed systems to contain more computers than can be connected to a single local area network. The requirement for openness in distributed systems (Chapter 2) also implies a need to integrate computer networks supplied by different vendors and based on different networking standards. To meet these needs, networks are linked together to form internetworks. An internetwork is a communication subsystem in which several networks are linked together to provide common data communication facilities that conceal the technologies and protocols of the individual component networks and the methods used for their interconnection.

Internetworks are needed for the development of extensible, open distributed systems. The openness characteristic of distributed systems implies that the networks used in distributed systems should be extensible to very large numbers of computers, whereas individual networks have restricted address spaces and some have performance limitations that are incompatible with their large-scale use. In internetworks a variety of local and wide area network technologies, possibly supplied by different vendors, can be integrated providing the networking capacity needed by each group of users. Thus internetworks bring many of the benefits of open systems for the provision of communication in distributed systems.

Internetworks are implemented by linking component networks with dedicated packet routing computers called *routers* or by general-purpose computers called *gateways*, and adding protocols that support the addressing and transmission of data to computers throughout the internetwork. The resulting internetwork can be thought of as a 'virtual network' constructed by overlaying a set of internetwork protocols over a communication medium that consists of the underlying networks, routers and gateways.

A router is used to link two or more networks, which may be of different types. Routers pass packets from one network to another, using a strategy that enables messages to reach their correct destinations anywhere in the internetwork. To make this possible, routers must hold tables describing part of the structure of the internetwork beyond the networks to which they are directly connected. Their method of operation is based on the use of routing tables in a manner analogous to that of the PSEs used in wide area networks (see Section 3.2). Gateways have a similar function to routers, but since they are normally used to link only two networks their routing tables are simpler and the workload involved in acting as a gateway is small enough to permit the computer to act as a host for other work.

Many wide area and local area networks can be combined to produce a single internetwork – a communication system that interconnects large collections of geographically dispersed computers. Such wide area internetworks are subject to performance limitations due to the cost and the physical constraints of long-distance communication channels; and additional security and system management problems arise because of the multiplicity of administrative domains that they interconnect – the component networks are owned and managed by many different administrative authorities. These administrative and system management issues have been the subject of much recent research. Some of the resulting methods for the management of large name spaces and security in distributed systems are described in Chapters 9 and 16.

Internetworks can also be constructed on a single site such as an office building, a factory or a university campus, to achieve interconnection between several local area networks on the site. Figure 3.1 illustrates a local internetwork with connections to a wide area network. Such local internetworks are relatively simple to implement, especially when the interconnected networks are all based on a single local area network technology, and their end-to-end performance is similar to that of the individual component networks. *Bridges* are used to connect networks of the same type; their use to interconnect Ethernets is described in a later section. Some aspects of their implementation are discussed in the Section 3.2. The performance of local internetworks is adequate to support the construction of distributed systems, but some additional addressing and system management issues must be resolved to enable them to be used for this purpose.

The *connected Internet* (henceforth referred to as *the Internet*, with a capital 'I') is a particular instance of a wide area internetwork; it is a single world-wide collection of interconnected networks that share a uniform scheme for addressing host computers

Figure 3.1   A typical campus internetwork.

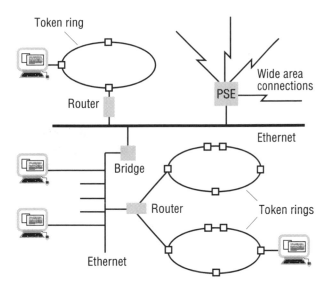

and a suite of agreed protocols. At the time of writing (1993) it connects approximately 1.3 million computers, 8,000 networks and 10 million users and is still growing fast.

The Internet has emerged from two decades of research and development work on wide area networking in the US, commencing in the early 1970s with the ARPANET – the first large-scale computer network development. An important part of that research was the development of the TCP/IP protocol suite. TCP stands for Transmission Control Protocol; IP stands for Internet Protocol. The widespread adoption of the TCP/IP and Internet application protocols in national research networks, and more recently in commercial networks in many countries has enabled the national networks to be integrated into a single internetwork that has grown extremely rapidly to its present size of more than one million computers. Many application services now exist that are based on TCP/IP, such as remote login, file transfer and electronic mail and more recently there has been a growth in the development and use of TCP/IP based information services such as Gopher [Martin 1993] and World Wide Web [Berners-Lee *et al.* 1992a, Berners-Lee *et al.* 1992b].

The reader is referred to Douglas Comer's excellent book on the topic [Comer 1991] for a review of these developments and a detailed description of the Internet technology. We shall outline the characteristics of TCP/IP protocols and discuss their limitations when used in distributed systems in Section 3.5.

Although the Internet (TCP/IP) protocols were developed primarily to support applications such as remote login, file transfer and electronic mail, involving communication with relatively long latencies between many geographically dispersed computers, they are quite efficient and have been used extensively for the implementation of distributed applications on local networks, and to a limited extent on wide area networks.

The Internet protocols (TCP/IP) have some drawbacks: they do not support migration transparency for client and server processes in a distributed system, they have no integrated support for secure communication, and they require substantial system management effort in the allocation of Internet addresses. Several other experimental internetwork protocols have been developed that are explicitly designed to support the construction of distributed systems over interconnected local area networks. These include the VMTP protocol suite developed as a part of the V System project at Stanford University [Cheriton 1986] and the FLIP protocol suite developed at the Vrije University, Amsterdam [Kaashoek *et al.* 1993]. We shall describe the FLIP protocol suite and discuss its design aims in Section 3.5.

To summarize, internetworking techniques are important because they provide a communication infrastructure for scalable distributed systems, allowing very large numbers of computers to operate as a single distributed system. They introduce additional design problems because of the administrative and system management problems arising from networks that span many administrative domains. A wide area internetwork is not yet a suitable basis for a distributed system because of the relatively low performance of the long-distance links.

3.2   Network technologies

Wide area networks □   The first computer networks were wide area networks. These are designed to provide communication between computers that are separated by large distances and usually located in separate organisations.

A wide area network consists of a collection of communication channels linking special-purpose computers, known as **packet switches** or *packet-switching exchanges* (PSEs), first introduced in the ARPA network with the name Interface Message Processors (IMPs). A PSE is located at each node in the network (Figure 3.2). PSEs are dedicated to the task of data communication. They send and receive packets of data through the network on behalf of other computers.

The PSEs operate the network by forwarding packets from one PSE to another along a route from the sender to the recipient. They are responsible for defining the route taken by each packet. This mode of network operation is referred to as *store-and-*

Figure 3.2   A wide area network.

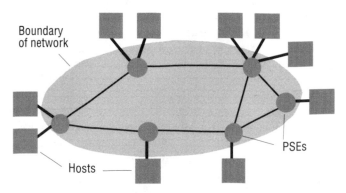

Boundary
of network

PSEs

Hosts

forward communication, because every packet of data is stored temporarily by each PSE along its route before it is forwarded to another PSE. Store-and-forward network systems can be used for computer-to-computer communication over any distance where circuits exist to carry the packets.

Computers that use a network to send and receive data are called *hosts*. Hosts are normally located close to a PSE and connected directly to it. They pass packets of data to the PSEs for transmission through the network to other hosts and receive packets from the PSEs that are addressed to them.

Early wide area networks and most current ones operate at transmission rates in the range 20–500 kilobits per second, giving minimum transmission times for a 1000 byte message across a single circuit in the range 16–400 milliseconds. But the packet-switching method involves additional delays of the order of a few milliseconds at each PSE in the transmission path. As a consequence, message transmission times are relatively long and may depend upon the route taken by each message. Short messages are transmitted in 100–200 milliseconds in typical wide area networks. Satellite transmission necessarily involves an additional latency because the *time of flight* of an electronic signal to an orbiting synchronous satellite and back to ground is in the order of 200 milliseconds. If satellite channels are used or the route is complex, involving many PSEs, the transmission time for a short message may be as long as 500 milliseconds. ATM-based wide area networks are expected to offer transfer rates in the region of 150 megabits per second with latencies below one millisecond for the transmission of packets once a connection has been established.

Local area networks □ Local area networks were developed in response to the same needs that led to the development of distributed systems – they were designed to enable computer users working on dedicated personal computers and workstations to share resources.

Local networks are structured either as buses or rings (Figure 3.3 and Figure 3.4) with dedicated communication circuits, normally on a single site and extending at most over a few kilometres. Messages are transmitted directly from the source computer to the destination computer without intermediate storage or processing. There are no PSEs in local networks; instead, the host computers are responsible collectively for the management of traffic on the network using special-purpose hardware interfaces to transmit and receive the data on the network circuits. The mode of operation is based on **broadcast communication** rather than the store-and-forward mode used in wide area networks. That is, each packet is transmitted to all of the computers in the network and each computer is responsible for identifying and receiving the packets that are addressed to it.

With all broadcast-mode communication the network is a shared channel, and only one sender at a time can use it to transmit data. This leads to conflicts between senders that must be resolved within the network hardware or software and if communication traffic is heavy it means that the effective transmission rate seen by an individual host is reduced because the network is not always available for transmission. Fortunately, the traffic that is typically generated in distributed systems does not impose a high or continuous load on local networks. In lightly-loaded conditions latency is low and the effective transmission rate is comparable to the total network bandwidth.

Figure 3.3   Bus topologies.

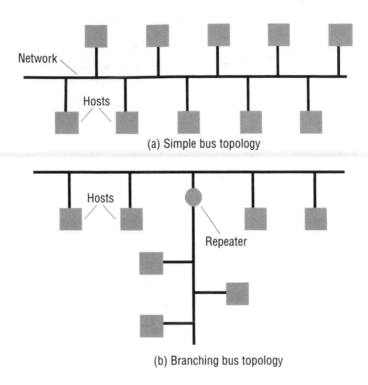

(a) Simple bus topology

(b) Branching bus topology

Figure 3.4   Ring topology.

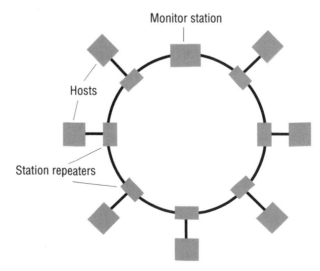

Communication in local networks is achieved without the need for specialized computers dedicated to communication tasks. The host computers are connected directly to a communication channel by relatively simple interface hardware. The interface hardware and network driver software in each host can send and receive data at high speeds with low error rates and without switching delays, implementing the physical layer, the datalink layer and the network layer with a single protocol.

It is possible to provide relatively simple software in each computer that can perform the entire task of transmitting or receiving messages. These important characteristics of local networks give considerable advantages in cost, speed and reliability in comparison with wide area networks.

The circuits used in local networks may be pairs of twisted wires, coaxial cables or optical fibres, capable of data transmission speeds ranging from 0.2 to 100 megabits per second. Since all local networks are designed to provide direct communication between any two hosts, the topology used (ring, bus or branching bus) has relatively little influence on the behaviour as seen by the user.

3.3 Protocols

The term **protocol** is used to refer to a well-known set of rules and formats to be used for communication between processes in order to perform a given task. The definition of a protocol has two important parts to it:

- A specification of the sequence of messages that must be exchanged.

- A specification of the format of the data in the messages.

Protocol definitions are a good example of the standardization and publication of interfaces that were identified in Chapter 2 as an important prerequisite for open systems. The existence of well-known protocols enables the separate software components of distributed systems to be developed independently and implemented in different programming language on computers that may have different order codes and data representations.

A protocol is implemented by a pair of software modules located in the sending and receiving computers. For example, a *transport protocol* transmits messages of any length from a sending process to a receiving process. A process wishing to transmit a message to a another process issues a call to a transport protocol module, passing it a message in the specified format. The transport software then concerns itself with the transmission of the message to its destination, subdividing it into packets of some specified size and format that can be transmitted to the destination via the *network protocol* – another, lower-level protocol. The corresponding transport protocol module in the receiving computer receives the packet and performs inverse transformations to regenerate the message before passing it to a receiving process.

Protocol layers ☐ Network software is arranged in a hierarchy of layers. Each layer presents an interface to the layers above it that extends and generalizes some of the properties of the underlying communication system. A layer is represented by a module in every computer connected to the network. Figure 3.5 illustrates the structure and the flow of data when a message is transmitted using a layered protocol. Each module appears to communicate directly with a module at the same level in another computer in the network. But in reality data is not transmitted directly between the protocol modules at each level. Instead, each layer of network software communicates by local procedure calls with the layers above and below. On the sending side, each layer (except the topmost, or *application layer*) accepts items of data in a specified format from the layer above it and applies transformations to encapsulate the data in the format specified for that layer before passing it to the layer below for further processing. On the receiving side the converse transformations are applied to data items received from the layer below before they are passed to the layer above.

Thus each layer provides a service to the layer above it and extends the service provided by the layer below it. At the bottom is a *physical layer*. This is implemented by the communication medium (copper or fibre-optic cables, satellite communication channels or radio transmission) and by the analogue circuits in each computer that transmit signals through the communication medium. At the destination, data items are received and passed upwards through the hierarchy of software modules, transformed at each stage until they are in a form that can be passed to the intended recipient process.

Protocol suites □ A complete set of protocol layers is referred to as a **protocol suite** (or sometimes as a **protocol stack**, reflecting the layered structure). The choice of a protocol suite for use in a communication subsystem is an important design issue. Many have been developed and some have been adopted as standards.

Figure 3.6 shows a protocol stack that conforms to the seven-layer Reference Model for *open systems interconnection (OSI)* adopted by the International Standards Organisation (ISO). The OSI Reference Model was adopted in order to encourage the development of protocol standards that would meet the requirements of open systems.

The purpose of each level in the OSI Reference Model is summarized in Figure 3.7. As its name implies, it is a framework for the definition of protocols and not a definition for specific suite of protocols. Protocol suites that conform to the OSI model must include at least one specific protocol at each of the seven levels that the model defines.

Internetwork protocol suites include an application layer, a transport layer and an *internetwork layer*. The internetwork layer is a 'virtual' network layer that is responsible for transmitting internetwork packets to a destination computer. An *internetwork packet* is the unit of data transmitted over an internetwork.

Figure 3.5   Conceptual layering of protocol software.

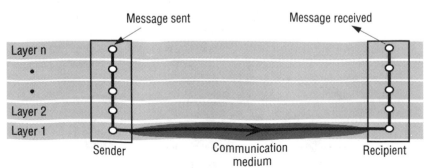

Figure 3.6   Protocol layers in the ISO *Open Systems Interconnection (OSI)* protocol model.

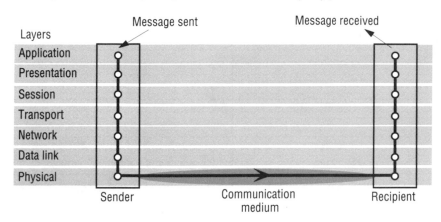

Figure 3.7   OSI protocol summary.

Layer	Description	Examples
Application	Protocols that are designed to meet the communication requirements of specific applications, often defining the interface to a service.	FTP, Telnet, SMTP, X400, X500
Presentation	Protocols at this level transmit data in a network representation that is independent of the representations used in individual computers, which may differ. Encryption is also performed in this layer, if required.	XDR, ASN.1, encryption
Session	At this level communication between processes is established and error recovery is performed. It is not required for connectionless communication.	
Transport	This is the lowest level at which messages (rather than packets) are handled. Messages are addressed to communication ports, Protocols in this layer may be connection-oriented or connectionless.	TCP, UDP
Network	Transfers data packets between computers in a specific network. In a WAN or an internetwork this involves the generation of a route passing through PSEs or routers. In a single LAN no routing is required.	X25, IP
Data link	Responsible for error-free transmission of packets between computers that are directly connected. In a WAN the connections are between pairs of PSEs and PSEs and hosts. In a LAN they are pairs of hosts.	HDLC Ethernet: CSMA/CD
Physical	The circuits and hardware that drives the network. It transmits sequences of binary data by analogue signalling, using amplitude or frequency modulation of electrical signals (on cable circuits), light signals (on fibre-optic circuits) or electromagnetic signals (on radio and microwave circuits).	X.21 Ethernet: baseband signalling

Figure 3.8   Internetwork layers.

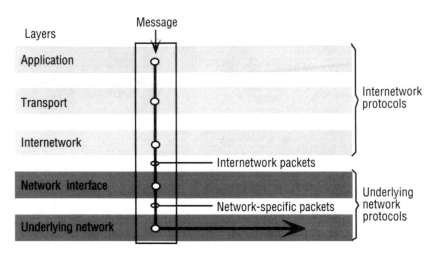

Internetwork protocols are overlaid on underlying networks as illustrated in Figure 3.8. The *network interface* layer accepts internetwork packets and converts them into packets suitable for transmission by the transport layer of a specific underlying network. The underlying network consists of the transport, network, data link and physical layers of all of the *real* networks that constitute the internetwork.

Packet assembly ☐ The task of dividing messages into packets before transmission and reassembling them at the receiving computer is performed in the transport layer. The transport layer must be used, directly or indirectly, by all programs wishing to transmit or receive messages.

In most network technologies, the network layer protocol transfers packets consisting of a **header** and a **data field**. The data field is variable in length, but with a limit called the **maximum transfer unit** (MTU). For example, for Ethernets the MTU is 1500 – not more than 1500 bytes of data can be transmitted in a single Ethernet packet. If the length of a message exceeds the MTU the transport layer splits it into several packets before transmission and reconstruct it at the destination.

In the Internet suite of protocols, the IP protocol is a 'network layer' protocol. The MTU for IP packets is unusually large – 64 kilobytes including the packet header as well as the data field. This large size means that UDP transport layer datagrams seldom need to be sub-divided before being put into IP packets, although the latter may need to be sub-divided by the network interface layer, for example to fit into Ethernet packets.

However, the size of TCP streams is unlimited, so the TCP transport layer protocol must decompose the stream of data supplied to it by application programs into chunks of data and construct IP packets that are not more than 64 kilobytes in length.

Addressing ☐ The transport layer's task is to provide a network-independent message transport service between pairs of network **ports**. These ports are local to a particular host and should not be confused with the logical or location independent ports provided by Mach and other distributed operating systems that will be introduced in Chapter 4. Ports are software-definable destination points for communication within a host computer. The transport layer is responsible for delivering messages to destinations with **transport addresses** that are composed of the network address of a host computer and a *port number*.

In TCP/IP networks there are typically several ports at each host computer with well-known numbers, each allocated to a given Internet service such as *telnet* or *ftp* and to UNIX services such as *rlogin* and *rcp*. The well-known port number and service definitions are registered with a central authority. To access a service at a given host, a request is sent to the relevant port at the host. The service then allocates a new port (with a private number) and sends the number of the new port to the client. Further requests to the service are then directed to the new port.

Additional port numbers are available for general use, for example by new services. A distributed system generally has a multiplicity of servers which differs from one time to another and from one organization to another. Clearly the allocation of fixed hosts or fixed port numbers to these services is not feasible. The solution to the problem of clients locating arbitrary servers in a distributed system is discussed in the subsection on binding in Section 5.2.

Connection-oriented and connectionless communication □ Two types of data transport service can be provided:

> *connection-oriented*: in which a 'virtual connection' is set up between a sending and a receiving process and is used for the transmission of a **stream** of data;

> *connectionless*: in which individual messages, known as **datagrams**, are transmitted to specified destinations.

The virtual connection on which connection-oriented services are based is a logical channel between a pair of communicating processes. It must be set up before any data is transmitted and it is closed when no longer needed. Once a connection has been opened, it can be used for transmitting a stream of data items to the receiving process. The data items are usually bytes, and the stream may be of any length – this form of communication corresponds to the stream construct that is found in the input-output systems of many high-level programming languages. The transport-layer software is responsible for subdividing the stream of data for transmission and delivering it reliably and in the correct sequence to the receiving process.

The datagrams transmitted by connectionless services are similar to packets. They are addressed to processes whereas the packets that are transmitted by the network layer are addressed only to host computers. Connectionless services may be unreliable, leaving the application-layer software to detect lost or out-of-order datagrams and to take remedial action.

The provision of one of these two types of communication service is logically sufficient for the implementation of any desired communication pattern and each type of service can be implemented in terms of the other, but since each offers performance and programming benefits for some classes of application, both are generally provided is a network protocol suite.

For example, the Internet protocol suite provides two types of transport-layer service:

> *TCP* is a connection-oriented service that transmits streams of bytes across a pre-established connection, and

UDP is a connectionless service that transmits messages of up to 64 kilobytes to a specified destination (an Internet address and a port number).

Both of them are implemented over the IP 'network layer' packet delivery service.

Connection-oriented communication is useful for implementing network services such as remote login and bulk file transfer, which require streams of data of indefinite length to be transferred. Connectionless services are less complex and incur fewer overheads. They are often used for the implementation of client-server communication in distributed systems built over local area networks, since the establishment of a connection constitutes a substantial overhead when client-server interactions may entail the exchange of only a single pair of messages.

In the network layer, the distinction between connection-oriented and connectionless communication is mirrored by the distinction between network services that deliver packets using virtual circuits and those using datagram delivery. These are described below.

It is important to note that there is no essential dependency between a connection-oriented transport service and a virtual-circuit based network layer. Each type of transport service can be implemented by either type of network-layer service.

Virtual circuit packet delivery ☐ Virtual circuits correspond to the 'virtual connections' that were described as the basis for connection-oriented transport services. Some network-level services (for example, the ISO X25 protocol) implement packet transmission in a connection-oriented manner. The establishment of a virtual circuit involves the identification of a route from the source (the sending computer) to the destination (the receiving computer), passing through a number of packet switches. At each switch on the route a table entry is made, indicating which link should be used for the next stage of the route.

Each network-layer packet contains a virtual circuit number. It need not contain the address of the destination, since the circuit number serves to identify the destination. Packets are routed at each switch by reference to the circuit number. The packets are also checked and acknowledged at each step along the route. On arrival at the destination, they are passed to the transport layer in a format that includes a channel identifier in the case of a connection-oriented service or the sender's address in the case of a connectionless service.

Virtual circuits are an important feature of the OSI protocol suite, reflecting its origins as a comprehensive suite of protocols for use in potentially-unreliable wide area networks. There is little need for such techniques in local internetworks and the more reliable wide area networks that are now in common use.

In the TCP/IP suite, IP is the network-level protocol. Its method of packet delivery is based upon datagram packet delivery. Thus the TCP protocol, although connection-oriented, does not depend upon the use of virtual circuits.

Datagram packet delivery ☐ Each network-level packet contains the network address of the source computer and the destination computer. At the source computer, and at each switch along the route to the destination, the destination address is used to determine the next step along the route, using pre-defined routing tables that are held in each switch. The routing tables are subject to modification as a result of network faults or changes in loading, so different packets may follow different routes to the same destination.

Comparisons □ We now compare the two methods of packet delivery when used for the implementation of connection-oriented and connectionless transport protocols.

In both cases the transport layer must pass packets to the network layer in a form acceptable to it. In the case of a connection-oriented protocol this includes the segmentation of the data stream into packets and the attachment of network-level (source and destination) addresses, sequence number and checksum. In the case of a connectionless protocol, the transport-level datagrams are encapsulated in 'envelopes' containing the source and destination addresses and a checksum. On receipt of each packet, the transport layer checks its validity.

In the connection-oriented case the transport layer uses the sequence number to insert each packet in its correct position in the data stream, waiting for any unarrived packets with lower sequence numbers before doing so. It acknowledges packets, deletes any duplicate packets and the transport layer at the source resends any unacknowledged packets.

When a connection-oriented protocol is implemented over a virtual circuit network layer, packet sequencing, error checking and acknowledgement are applied by the network layer, and are repeated for each stage in the route.

When a local area network is used, no packet switches or routing are required and packets cannot be delivered out of sequence, so much less work is done in the transport layer.

In the case of a connectionless transport layer protocol, neither the transport layer nor the network layer is required to perform any sequencing or acknowledgement of packets. The application layer takes responsibility for this when it is needed. For example, when a datagram service is used to implement remote procedure calling, the RPC software must deal with the possibility of lost messages, as we shall describe in Section 4.3. When a datagram service is implemented over a local area network, datagrams will arrive in the sequence in which they are sent.

To summarize, the lowest latencies are likely to be achieved in communication services for distributed systems when a connectionless transport protocol is implemented over datagram service in a local area network. Connection-oriented protocols can also be implemented with adequate performance in the same environment. TCP is an example of such a transport service, implemented over the IP datagram service. In Section 3.5 we shall describe the methods by which IP is implemented over a variety local and wide area networks.

3.4 Technology case studies: Ethernet, Token Ring and ATM

We have introduced the topologies and transmission media used in wide area and local networks in Section 3.2. Here we describe the principles of operation of two important local area network technologies and of the emerging ATM technology for broadband ISDN networks. First, we discuss the general principles of operation of bus and ring-based local networks.

In networks with a simple or branching bus topology there is a circuit composed of a single cable or a set of connected cables passing near all of the hosts on the network. When more than one cable is used the connections can be made by *repeaters* – simple amplifying and connecting units that have no effects on the timing or logical behaviour of the network. The cable is passive, and each host has a *drop cable* connected to the main cable by a T-connection or *tap*. Data is transmitted by 'broadcasting' a signal on the cable as a single sequence of pulses. This form of signalling is analogous in some ways to the data bus systems that were originally developed to connect the parts of conventional computer systems together. The major difference between bus networks and the system buses used inside computer systems is that the latter are parallel buses allowing the transmission of 16 or 32 bits simultaneously and the transmission of data on them is scheduled by a central arbitration unit, whereas in bus-like local networks there are no centralized components and the use of the cable is scheduled by a distributed method of control involving co-operation between all the computers connected to the network. This has led to the description of such networks as **contention buses**, because all of the host computers needing to send a message at any time contend for the use of the cable.

In networks with a ring-like topology the cable is made up of separate links connecting adjacent stations. Data is transmitted in one direction around the ring by signalling between stations. Each node applies the signal it receives to the next section of cable. The data circulates around the ring until some station removes it from the circuit; the receiving station does this in some ring systems, but in others the data is allowed to complete a circular journey and is removed by the sending station. In most ring systems a *monitor station* is included to ensure that data does not circulate indefinitely (for example, in case the sending station or the receiving station fails) and to perform other 'housekeeping' functions. Ring networks fall into several subclasses: slotted, register insertion, contention and token rings.

Local networks have been the subject of much development work since the early 1970s and a number of network technologies have emerged with adequate performance to support distributed systems. Standardization work by the Institute of Electrical and Electronic Engineers resulted in the adoption of four different local network technologies as American National Standards [IEEE 1990], partially unified by the use of common address and data field formats [IEEE 1985c].

The Ethernet, originally developed at Xerox PARC in the early 1970s, has been adopted as IEEE/ISO Standard 802.3 [IEEE 1985a] and is the most widely used local network technology for distributed systems. It is based on broadcasting over a simple passive circuit, with a single high-speed cable linking all of the computers using the network. The Cambridge Ring developed at Cambridge University in the mid-1970s exemplifies another class of local network, known as a **slotted ring**, in which all of the computers in the network are linked in a ring structure and data is transmitted in small fixed-size packets by passing it from station to station around the ring. Another ring network technology, known as a **token ring**, can accommodate larger, variable-size packets, and has been adopted as IEEE Standard 802.5 and by IBM and some other manufacturers for linking personal computer and workstation products [IEEE 1985b]. We describe the main attributes and the implementation of the Ethernet and Token Ring in Section 3.4.

Current local networks are able to transmit data at rates in the range 0.2–10 megabits per second, with some recent networks running at speeds of up to 200 megabits per second. These transmission rates do not take conflicting communication traffic or any protocol or software overheads into account, but they give some indication of the potential performance of lightly-loaded local networks, giving basic transmission times for a 1000 byte message in the range 4 milliseconds down to 40 microseconds in the fastest networks.

The topologies used in local networks mean that there are no storage or switching delays and the latency in most lightly-loaded local networks is small (less than one millisecond), although the software in the sending and receiving hosts may add delays of up to 10 milliseconds if they have operating systems that are not optimized for interprocess communication (Chapter 6).

Local networks with transmission speeds above one megabit per second should offer acceptable performance for use in lightly-loaded distributed systems and that 10 megabits per second offers a reasonable capacity to support systems that generate substantial traffic. Experience with local area networks in distributed systems supports this conjecture.

Ethernet

The Ethernet was developed at Xerox PARC in 1973 [Metcalfe and Boggs 1976; Shoch *et al.* 1982; 1985] as a part of the intensive programme of research carried out there on personal workstations and distributed systems. The pilot Ethernet was the first high-speed local network, demonstrating the feasibility usefulness of high-speed local networks linking computers on a single site, allowing them to communicate at high transmission speeds with low error rates and without switching delays.

We shall describe the Ethernet as specified in IEEE/ISO Standard 802.3 [IEEE 1985a]. It operates at a transmission rate of 10 megabits per second using low-loss coaxial cable and high-speed drivers in the computers connected to it; the original prototype Ethernet ran at 3 megabits per second and many proprietary networks have been implemented using the same basic method of operation with cost/performance characteristics suitable for a variety of applications. At the lowest cost level the same principles of operation are used to connect low-cost microcomputers with transmission speeds of 100–200 kilobits per second.

The Ethernet is a simple or branching bus-like network using a circuit consisting of several continuous segments of low-loss coaxial cable linked by repeaters. It is a contention bus and is a member of the class of networks described by the phrase 'carrier sensing, multiple access with collision detection' (abbreviated: CSMA/CD).

Packet broadcasting □ The basic method of communication in CSMA/CD networks is by broadcasting packets of data on a cable that is accessible to all of the stations on the network. All stations are continually 'listening' to the cable for packets that are addressed to them. Any station wishing to transmit a message broadcasts one or more packets (called *frames* in the Ethernet Specification) on the cable. Each packet contains the address of the destination station, the address of the sending station and a variable-length sequence of bits representing the message to be transmitted. Data transmission proceeds at 10 million bits per second and packets vary in length between 64 and 1518 bytes, so the time to transmit a packet on the Ethernet ranges from 50–1200 microseconds depending on its length. (Although 1518 bytes is set as the MTU in the IEEE 802.3 Standard [IEEE 1985a], there is no technical reason for any fixed limit except buffer capacity, to hold incoming packets.)

The address of the destination station normally refers to a single network interface. Each station receives a copy of every packet, but ignores packets for other computers and passes on to its host only those that are addressed to it. The address of the destination station may also specify a broadcast or a multicast address. Ordinary addresses are distinguished from broadcast and multicast addresses by their higher order bit (0 and 1 respectively). An address consisting of all 1s is reserved for use as a broadcast address and is used when a message is to be received by all of the stations on the network. Any station that receives a packet with a broadcast address will pass it on to its host. A multicast address specifies a limited form of broadcast which is received by a group of stations whose network interfaces have been configured to receive packets with that multicast address. Not all implementations of Ethernet network interfaces can recognize multicast addresses.

The Ethernet network protocol (providing for the transmission of Ethernet packets between pairs of hosts) is implemented in the Ethernet hardware interface, so protocol software is required for the transport layer and those above it.

Ethernet packet layout □ The packets (or frames) transmitted by stations on the Ethernet have the following layout:

6 bytes	6 bytes	2 bytes	46 bytes ≤ length ≤ 1500 bytes	4 bytes
Destination address	Source address	Type	Data for transmission	Frame check sequence

Apart from the destination and source addresses already mentioned, packets contain a type field, a data field and a frame check sequence. Note that the length of the packet is not transmitted. Instead, receiving stations detect the end of transmission (there is a mandatory interval of 9.6 microseconds between packets) and it is assumed that the last 4 bytes received constitute the frame check sequence. (In the IEEE 802.3 Standard the length of the data field *is* transmitted in place of the type field, but the type information is important in internetworks since it allows multiple transport protocols to be transmitted without interference and it has been retained in most Ethernet implementations.)

The type field is used by the upper layers of protocol to distinguish packets of various types. The specification does not allow more than 1024 stations in a single Ethernet, but addresses occupy 6 bytes, and every Ethernet hardware interface is given a unique address by the manufacturer, in order to allow all of the stations in a set of interconnected Ethernets to have unique addresses. The US Institute of Electrical and Electronic Engineers (IEEE) acts as an allocation authority for Ethernet addresses, allocating separate ranges of 48-bit addresses to the manufacturers of Ethernet hardware interfaces.

The data field contains all or part (if the message length exceeds 1500 bytes) of the message that is being transmitted. It is the only field whose length may vary between defined limits. The lower bound of 64 bytes on the packet length is necessary to ensure that collisions can be detected by all stations on the network.

The frame check sequence is a checksum generated and inserted by the sender and used to validate packets by the receiver. Packets with incorrect checksums are simply dropped by the datalink layer in the receiving station. This is an example of the potential unreliability of the simple datagram protocols used in local networks; to guarantee the transmission of a message, the application layer must use a protocol that acknowledges receipt of each packet and retransmits any unacknowledged packets. The incidence of data corruption in local networks is so small that the use of this method of recovery when guaranteed delivery is required is perfectly acceptable.

Packet collisions □ Even in the relatively short time that it takes to transmit packets there is a finite probability that two stations on the network will attempt to transmit messages simultaneously. If a station attempts to transmit a packet without checking whether the cable is in use by other stations, a collision may occur.

The Ethernet has three mechanisms to deal with this possibility. The first is called *carrier sensing*; the interface hardware in each station listens for the presence of a signal (known as the *carrier* by analogy with radio broadcasting) in the cable. When a station wishes to transmit a packet, it waits until no signal is present in the cable and then begins to transmit.

Unfortunately, carrier sensing does not prevent all collisions. The possibility of collision remains due to the finite time τ taken for a signal inserted at a point in the cable (travelling at electronic speed: approximately 2×10^8 metres per second) to reach all other points. Consider two stations A and B that are ready to transmit packets at almost the same time. If A begins to transmit first, B can check and find no signal in the cable at any time $t < \tau$ after A has begun to transmit. B then begins to transmit, *interfering* with A's transmission. Both A's packet and B's packet will be damaged by the interference.

The technique used to recover from such interference is called *collision detection*. Whenever a station is transmitting a packet through its hardware output port, it also listens on its input port and the two signals are compared. If they differ, then a collision has occurred. When this happens the station stops transmitting and produces a *jamming signal* on the cable to ensure that all stations recognize the collision. As we have already noted, a minimum packet length is necessary to ensure that collisions are always detected. If two stations transmit approximately simultaneously from opposite ends of the network, they will not become aware of the collision for 2τ seconds (because the first sender must be still transmitting when it receives the second signal). If the packets that they transmit take less than τ to be broadcast, the collision will not be noticed, since each sending station would not see the other packet until after it has finished transmitting its own, whereas stations at intermediate points would receive both packets simultaneously, resulting in data corruption.

After the jamming signal, all transmitting and listening stations cancel the current packet. The transmitting stations then have to try to transmit their packets again. A further difficulty now arises. If the stations involved in the collision all attempt to retransmit their packets immediately after the jamming signal another collision will probably occur. To avoid this, a technique known as *back-off* is used. Each of the stations involved in a collision chooses to wait a time $n\tau$ before retransmitting. The value of n is a random integer chosen separately at each station and bounded by a constant L defined in the network software. If a further collision occurs, the value of L is doubled and the process is repeated if necessary for up to ten attempts.

Finally, the interface hardware at the receiving station computes the check sequence and compares it with the check sum transmitted in the packet. If the comparison fails the packet is rejected (that is, it is not transmitted). Using all of these techniques, the stations connected to the Ethernet are able to manage the use of the cable without any centralized control or synchronisation.

Ethernet efficiency □ The efficiency of an Ethernet is the ratio of the number of packets transmitted successfully as a proportion of the theoretical maximum number that could be transmitted without collisions. It is affected by the value of τ, since the interval of 2τ seconds after a packet transmission starts is the 'window of opportunity' for collisions – no collision can occur later than 2τ seconds after a packet starts to be transmitted. It is also affected by the number of stations on the network and their level of activity.

For a one kilometre cable the value of τ is less than 5 microseconds and the probability of collisions is small enough to ensure a high efficiency. The Ethernet can achieve a channel utilization of between 80 and 95 per cent, although the delays due to contention become noticeable when 50 per cent utilization is exceeded. Because the loading is variable, it is impossible to *guarantee* the delivery of a given message within any fixed time, since the network might be fully loaded when the message is ready for transmission. But the *probability* of transferring the message with a given delay is as good as, or better than, other network technologies.

Empirical measurements of the performance of an Ethernet at Xerox PARC and reported by Shoch and Hupp [1980] confirm this analysis. In practice, Ethernets used in distributed systems are relatively lightly loaded. They operate for most of the time with no stations waiting to transmit and a channel utilization close to one.

Interconnected Ethernets □ Since the addresses allocated to all Ethernet interfaces are unique, two or more Ethernets can be interconnected, allowing the computers on the interconnected networks to communicate without fear of duplicate addresses. There are two types of connections at this level: repeaters and bridges. Whereas a repeater is an analogue electronic device that simply relays the electrical signals that it receives, a bridge is a computer that passes network packets between the networks that it interconnects. Bridges have many advantages; because they operate digitally and at the packet level they do not replicate noise or distortion and they eliminate the problem of end-to-end delay: any number of Ethernets of any length can be interconnected using bridges. But the resulting network is not an internetwork in the sense that we have defined it, since the interconnected networks can be of only one type.

Most bridges can do something better than just taking all the packets received on the interface to one Ethernet and retransmitting them on the interface to the other Ethernet. They can for example keep a list of the addresses on each of the Ethernets and retransmit only those packets that are destined to a different Ethernet. A bridge may also be programmed to filter out messages to particular destinations.

Token ring

Token rings were explored early in the development of local network technologies [Farmer and Newhall 1969, Farber and Larson 1972, Pierce 1972] but their exploitation has been slower than that of the other local network technologies. Nevertheless, they have been used in several commercial products and IBM has adopted a token ring that conforms to the IEEE/ISO 802.5 Standard [IEEE 1985b] as a basis for distributed system products. Messages of almost any length can be transmitted as single packets. This is achieved with the help of a single permanently-circulating *token packet* that has a distinguished format.

An analogy with the transport of freight by train may be helpful in understanding the operation of token rings. The analogy has the token packet as a locomotive that is everlastingly circulating around a looped track (like a circular shuttle service) and the data packets as freight wagons. The locomotive is marked as 'busy' or 'free'. When there are no wagons attached it is free, otherwise it is busy. Wagons containing data can be attached to the locomotive whenever it passes a station and it is not busy. When wagons are attached the locomotive is marked as busy and the destination address of wagons is marked on the locomotive. The destination station must detach the wagons as they pass and mark the locomotive as free.

A single token is used in most token rings. It circulates continuously and there is a monitor station that injects a free token if it is missing (to initialize the network and to guard against loss of the token when a station fails). In the IEEE Token Ring the token occupies 3 bytes and a single bit in the token is used to indicate whether it is busy or free. When the token is free, no other data circulates in the ring. When it is busy, the token is followed by a sequence of address and data field bytes. The formats of packets and tokens are shown below.

3 bytes	*6 bytes*	*6 bytes*	*≤ 5000 bytes*	*4 bytes*	*1 byte*	*1 byte*
Token	Destination address	Source address	Data for transmission	Frame check seq.	End delimiter	Frame status

A token has the following format:

1 byte	*1 byte*	*1 byte*
Starting delimiter	Access control	Frame control

The *starting delimiter* byte has a fixed bit pattern that enables stations to recognize the start of a frame and synchronize to the data transmission rate. The 8 bits in the *access control* field are used to distinguish between busy and free tokens, to identify the priority of the frame that is being transmitted (3 bits) and to reserve the next free frame with a given priority (3 bits). The monitor station uses the eighth bit to help it to check that the ring is functioning correctly.

The operation of the token ring follows the pattern defined in our 'freight train' analogy. A station wishing to send a message checks the access control field and sets the busy bit if it is free. The source and destination address fields are inserted by the sending station, and the message data is appended to them, followed by the frame check sequence and the end delimiter. The destination station sets the access control field to free and removes all of the trailing fields from the token.

We will not detail the use of the priority and reservation bits in the access control field; their purpose is to enable a variety of regimes for sharing of the channel capacity among the stations on the network. One important consequence is that they can be used to ensure a fair distribution of the channel capacity among stations waiting to transmit messages, preventing the hogging of the available bandwidth by one or two stations.

The token ring does not suffer from the drawbacks of small or fixed-size packets (the packets may in principle be of almost any length; the limitation to 5000 bytes is a default value for a parameter that can be configured on a per-installation basis). The requirement for a monitor station is the most severe remaining drawback.

Asynchronous Transfer Mode

ATM has been designed to carry a wide variety of data including multimedia data such as voice and video. It is a fast packet-switching network based on a method of packet routing known as *cell relay* that can operate much faster than conventional packet switching. It achieves its speed by avoiding flow control and error checking at the intermediate nodes in a transmission. The transmission links and nodes must therefore have a low likelihood of corrupting data. Another factor affecting the performance is the small, fixed-length units of data transmitted, which reduces buffer size and complexity and queuing delay at intermediate nodes. ATM operates in a connected mode, but a connection can only be set up if sufficient resources are available. Once a connection is established, its quality (that is, its bandwidth and latency characteristics) can be guaranteed.

It is intended to be layered over B-ISDN, to conform to the CCITT I.150 standard [CCITT 1990], but it can also be implemented directly as a pure (also called *native mode*) ATM switching network. In both cases, an optical fibre transmission medium is intended to be used, allowing bandwidths of up to several gigabits per second with current fibre technology. B-ISDN has been designed to support a large range of services with varying speeds. These include voice (32 kilobits per second), fax, distributed systems services, video, high definition television (100–150 megabits per second). For ATM implemented over B-ISDN, the Standard has selected a data transfer rate of 155 megabits per second, but a future rate of 622 megabits per second is also recommended.

The ATM service can be viewed in three layers as shown in Figure 3.9. The *ATM adaptation layer* is intended to be used to provide existing higher-level protocols such as TCP/IP and X25 over the ATM layer. This layer should be able to provide a variety of different adaptation functions to suit the requirements of different organizations. It will include some common functions such as packet assembly and disassembly for use in building specific higher layer protocols.

The *ATM layer* provides a connection-oriented service that transmits fixed length packets called *cells*. A connection consists of a sequence of virtual channels within virtual paths. A *virtual channel (VC)* is a logical unidirectional association between two end-points of a link in the physical path from source to destination. A *virtual path (VP)* is a bundle of virtual channels that are associated with a physical path between two switching nodes. Virtual paths are intended to be used to support semi-permanent

Figure 3.9   ATM protocol layers.

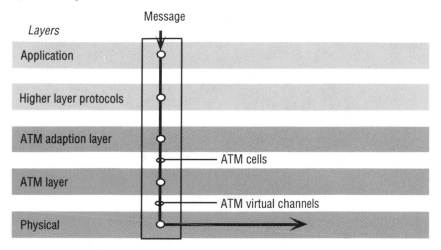

connections between pairs of endpoints. Virtual channels are allocated dynamically when connections are set up.

The nodes in an ATM network can play three distinct roles:

- *hosts* that send and receive messages;

- *VP switches* that hold tables showing the correspondence between incoming and outgoing virtual paths;

- *VP/VC switches* that hold similar tables for both virtual paths and virtual channels.

An ATM cell has a 5 byte header and a 48 byte data field (Figure 3.10). The full data field is always sent even when it is only partially filled with data. The header contains an identifier for a virtual channel and an identifier for a virtual path which together provide the information required to route the cell across the network. The virtual path identifier refers to a particular virtual path on the physical link on which the cell is transmitted. The virtual channel identifier refers to one specific virtual channel inside the virtual path. Other header fields are used to indicate the type of cell, its cell loss priority and the cell boundary.

When a cell arrives at a VP switch, the virtual path identifier in the header is looked up in its routing table to work out the corresponding virtual path identifier for the outgoing physical path; see Figure 3.11. It puts the new virtual path identifier in the header and then transmits the cell on the outgoing physical path. A VP/VC switch can perform similar routing based on both virtual path identifier and virtual channel identifier.

Figure 3.10   ATM cell layout.

Virtual path id	Virtual channel id	Flags	Data

Header: 5 bytes

53 bytes

Figure 3.11   Switching virtual paths in an ATM network.

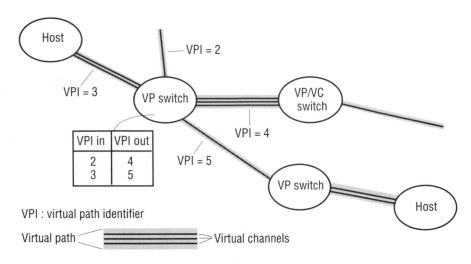

Note that the virtual path and virtual channel identifiers are defined locally. This scheme has the advantage that there is no need for global network-wide identifiers, which would need to be very large numbers. A global addressing scheme would introduce administrative overheads and would require cell headers and the tables in switches to hold more information.

ATM provides a service with low latency – the switching delay will be about 25 microseconds per switch, giving for example, a latency of 250 microseconds when a message passes through ten switches. This compares well with our estimated performance requirements for distributed systems (Section 3.1), suggesting that an ATM communication service will support interprocess communication and client-server interactions with a performance similar to that now available from local area networks. Very high bandwidth channels with guaranteed quality of service, suitable for transmitting streams of multimedia data at speeds up to 600 megabits second will also be available. Gigabits per second will be attainable in pure ATM networks.

3.5   Protocol case studies: Internet protocols and FLIP

The TCP/IP Internet protocols

The TCP/IP family of protocols was developed for use in the Internet and other applications that use interconnected networks. The protocols are layered, but do not conform precisely to the ISO 7-layer model. There are three internetwork protocol layers in the TCP/IP protocol stack, and these must be supported by one, two or more conventional network protocol layers as illustrated in Figure 3.12. The Internet transport layer provides two transport protocols – TCP (Transport Control Protocol) and UDP (User Datagram Protocol). TCP is a reliable connection-oriented protocol and UDP is a

Figure 3.12   TCP/IP layers.

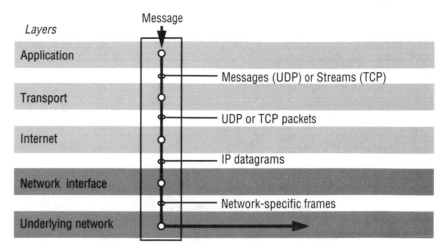

datagram protocol that does not guarantee reliable transmission. The Internet Protocol (IP) is the underlying 'network' protocol of the Internet virtual network – that is, IP datagrams provide the basic transmission mechanism for the Internet and other TCP/IP networks.

The TCP/IP specifications [Postel 1981a; 1981b] do not specify the layers below the Internet datagram layer – IP packets in the Internet layer are transformed into packets for transmission over almost any combination of underlying networks or data links.

For example, IP ran initially over the ARPANET which consisted of hosts and PSEs connected by long distance data links. IP also runs over local area networks such as Ethernets and token ring networks connected by IP routers. When used with networks that support OSI-conformant protocols such as X25, TCP/IP protocols are implemented by a technique known as *tunnelling* in which the TCP/IP protocols are implemented by transporting IP packets over X25 connections. IP has even been implemented over serial lines and telephone circuits, via the SLIP [Romkey 1988] protocol or the PPP [Parker 1992] protocol, enabling it to be used for communication over modem connections.

The success of the TCP/IP protocols is based on their independence of the underlying transmission technology, enabling internetworks to be built up from many heterogeneous networks and data links. Users and application programs perceive a single virtual network supporting TCP and UDP protocols and TCP and UDP implementors see a single virtual IP network, hiding the diversity of the underlying transmission media. Figure 3.13 illustrates this view. TCP is used in most of the well-known Internet services such as file transfer (FTP), Telnet, mail delivery (SMTP), Domain Name System (DNS) and Netnews (NNTP). UDP is often used for experimental or small-scale distributed applications and where the reliability of communication is ensured at the application level. Examples include the *rwho* service, network monitoring, time service and a simplified file transfer service (TFTP).

Many RPC implementations can be configured to use either TCP or UDP. When UDP is used, the RPC layer takes responsibility for the reliability of communication. Section 4.5 describes the UNIX *socket* programming interface to UDP and TCP.

Ports □ The IP layer delivers packets to a specified host computer anywhere in the Internet. IP packets contain the IP addresses of the destination host and the sending host. In the TCP and UDP protocols, *port numbers* are used for addressing messages to processes within a particular computer and are valid only within that computer. A port number is a 16-bit integer. Once an IP packet has been delivered to the destination host, the TCP or UDP layer despatches it to a specific port at that host.

Naming, addressing and routing □ Perhaps the most challenging aspect of the design of the Internet protocols was the construction of the schemes for naming and addressing hosts and for routing IP packets to their destinations.

> *Naming*: The Internet supports a scheme for the allocation and use of symbolic names for hosts and networks, such as *binkley.cs.mcgill.ca* or *essex.ac.uk*. The named entities are organized into a naming hierarchy. The named entities are called *domains* and the symbolic names are called *domain names*. Domains are organized in a hierarchy that is intended to reflect their organizational structure. The naming hierarchy is entirely independent of the physical layout of the networks that constitute the Internet. Domain names are convenient for human users, but they must be translated to Internet (IP) addresses before they can be used as communication identifiers. This is the responsibility of a specific service, the Domain Name System (DNS). We describe the design and implementation of DNS in Chapter 9.

> *Addressing*: In the Internet, hosts are allocated IP addresses – 32-bit numeric identifiers containing a network identifier which uniquely identifies one of the subnets in the Internet and a host identifier which uniquely identifies the host's interface to that network. It is these that are used to route IP packets to their destinations.

> *Routing*: The IP layer routes packets from their source to their destination. Each router in the Internet contains an IP layer that implements a routing algorithm that moves IP packets to their destinations in a number of hops. Packets addressed to hosts on the same network as the sender are transmitted to the destination host in a single hop, using the host identifier part of the address to obtain the address of the destination host on the underlying network. For a destination on another network the packet must be routed to its destination in several hops and the routing process is itself distributed. Each hop involves the transmission of the packet to an IP router that is 'closer' to the destination, and each router searches in its routing tables for the network identifier portion of the destination address. The routing tables contain sufficient information to determine the next hop.

Figure 3.13   The programmer's conceptual view of a TCP/IP Internet.

Application		Application
TCP		UDP
IP		

Figure 3.14   Internet address structure.

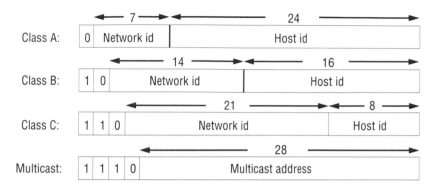

Host addresses □ The addresses used to address IP packets to their destinations are known as Internet or IP addresses. The scheme used for assigning host addresses to networks and the computers connected to them must satisfy the following requirements:

- It must be *universal* – every host must be able to send packets to any host on the Internet.

- It must be efficient in its use of the address space – it is impossible to predict the ultimate size of the Internet and the number of network and host addresses likely to be required. The address space must be carefully partitioned to ensure that addresses will not run out.

- The addressing scheme must lend itself to the development of a flexible and efficient routing scheme, but the addresses themselves cannot contain very much of the information needed to route a packet to its destination.

The design adopted for Internet addresses is shown in Figure 3.14. There are three classes of internet address – A, B and C, plus a provision for Internet multicast communication which is currently implemented only some Internet hosts and routers. Internet multicast communication is of increasing importance for group work applications and a group of user organizations have established a multicast network called MBONE (multicast backbone) that is implemented as a subset of the routers in the Internet.

Network identifiers are allocated by the Internet Network Information Center (NIC) to organizations with networks connected to the Internet. Host identifiers for the computers on each network connected to the Internet are assigned by the manager of the relevant network.

Since host addresses include a network identifier, any computer that is connected to more than one network must have separate addresses on each, and whenever a computer is moved to a different network, its Internet address must change. These requirements can lead to substantial administrative overheads, for example in the case of portable computers.

The three classes of address are designed to meet the requirements of different types of organizations. Thus class A addresses are reserved for very large networks such as the ARPANET and other national wide area networks. Class B addresses are

Figure 3.15   Decimal representation of Internet Addresses.

	octet 1	octet 2	octet 3	octet 4
	Network id		Host id	
Class A:	1 to 127	0 to 255	0 to 255	0 to 255
	Network id		Host id	
Class B:	128 to 191	0 to 255	0 to 255	0 to 255
		Network id		Host id
Class C:	192 to 233	0 to 255	0 to 255	1 to 254
		Multicast address		
Multicast:	234 to 255	0 to 255	0 to 255	1 to 254

allocated to organizations that operate networks likely to contain more than 255 computers and Class C addresses are allocated to all other network operators.

The resulting 32-bit Internet addresses containing a network identifier and host identifier are usually written as a sequence of four decimal numbers separated by dots. Each decimal number represents one of the four bytes, or *octets* of the IP address. The permissible values for each class of network address are shown in Figure 3.15.

Internet addresses with host identifiers 0 and all 1's (binary) are used for special purposes. Addresses with host identifier set to 0 are used to refer to 'this host' and a host identifier that is all 1's is used to address a broadcast message to all of the hosts connected to the network specified in the network identifier part of the address.

IP datagram protocol □ The Internet Protocol layer (IP) transmits datagrams from one host to another, if necessary via intermediate routers. The full IP packet format is rather complex, but Figure 3.17 shows the main components. The remaining header fields are used by the transmission and routing algorithms.

IP provides a delivery service that is described as offering *unreliable* or *best-effort* delivery semantics, because there is no guarantee of delivery. Packets can be lost, duplicated, delayed, or delivered out of order, but these errors arise only when the

Internet example: Figure 3.16 shows part of the network with some of the host computers at Queen Mary and Westfield College, University of London (domain name: *qmw.ac.uk*; domain names are discussed below). The campus 'backbone' is a fast FDDI Ring backed-up in case of failure by an Ethernet, both of which have class B addresses and link four high-speed routers. The routers are 'Cisco BRouters' (BRouter = bridge+router) used to connect departmental Ethernets to the campus backbone. As well as performing Internet routing, they act as Ethernet bridges.

The figure shows two sub-domains of *qmw.ac.uk*; *maths.qmw.ac.uk* (the School of Mathematics) and *dcs.qmw.ac.uk* (the Department of Computer Science). There are two Class C address spaces (for IP addresses 192.135.231.x and 192.135.233.x) in the *dcs.qmw.ac.uk* domain. These are used to assign addresses to computers connected to two Ethernets with an interconnecting gateway called *jugula*. For example, *it024* is connected to the second and has an IP address of 192.135.233.24.

Figure 3.16   Part of the QMW network.

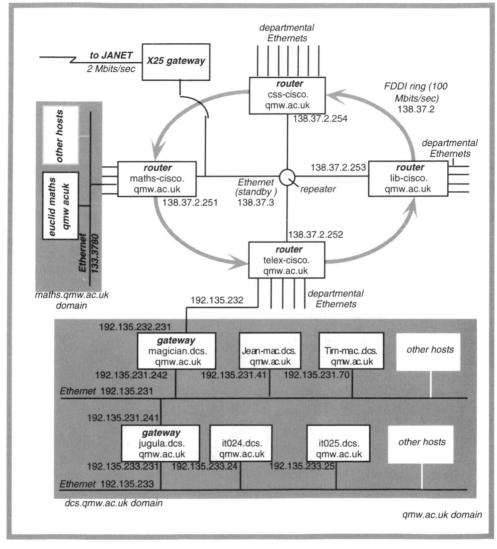

underlying networks fail or the buffers are full. The only checksum in IP is a header checksum, which is inexpensive to calculate. There is no data checksum, which avoid overheads when crossing routers, but leaves the higher-level protocols to provide their own checksums.

Figure 3.17   IP packet layout.

The IP layer puts IP datagrams into the physical packets of the underlying network. When an IP datagram is longer than the MTU of the underlying network (for example, Ethernet), it is broken into smaller packets at the source and reassembled at its final destination. Packets can be further broken up during the journey from source to destination. (Each packet has a fragment identifier to enable out-of-order fragments to be collected.)

The IP layer must also supply the 'physical' network address of the message destination to the underlying network. It obtains this from the address resolution module in the Internet Network Interface layer.

Address resolution □ The address resolution module is responsible for converting Internet addresses to network addresses (sometimes called physical addresses) for a specific underlying network. For example, if the underlying network is an Ethernet, the Address Resolution module converts 32-bit Internet addresses to 48-bit Ethernet addresses.

This translation is network technology-dependent:

- some hosts are connected directly to Internet packet switches; IP packets can be routed to them without address translation;

- some local area networks allow network addresses to be assigned to hosts dynamically, and the addresses can be conveniently chosen to match the host identifier portion of the Internet address – translation is simply a matter of extracting the host identifier from the IP address;

- for Ethernets and some other local networks the network address of each computer is hard-wired into its network interface hardware and bears no direct relation to its Internet address – translation depends upon knowledge of the correspondence between IP addresses and Ethernet addresses for the hosts on the local Ethernet.

We now outline the method used for the resolution of IP addresses in Ethernets. To enable IP packets to be delivered on an Ethernet, each computer connected to the Ethernet must implement the Address Resolution Protocol (ARP). Consider first the case in which a host computer connected to an Ethernet uses IP to transmit a message to another computer on the same Ethernet. The IP software module on the sending computer must translate the recipient's Internet address that it finds in the IP packet to an Ethernet address before the packet can be delivered. It invokes the ARP module on the sending computer to do so.

The ARP module on each host maintains a cache of *(IP address, Ethernet address)* pairs that it has previously obtained. If the required IP address is in the cache, then the query is answered immediately. If not, then ARP transmits an Ethernet broadcast packet (an ARP request packet) on the local Ethernet containing the desired IP address. Each of the computers on the local Ethernet receives the ARP request packet and checks the IP address in it to see whether it matches its own IP address. If it does, an ARP reply packet is sent to the originator of the ARP request containing the sender's Ethernet address; otherwise the ARP request packet is ignored. The originating ARP module adds the new *IP address → Ethernet address* mapping to its local cache of *(IP address, Ethernet address)* pairs so that it can respond to similar requests in future without broadcasting an ARP request. Over a period of time, the ARP cache at each computer will contain an *(IP address, Ethernet address)* pair for all of the computers that IP packets are sent to. Thus ARP broadcasts will be needed only when a computer is newly connected to the local Ethernet.

IP routing □ Routing is very simple if the sender and recipient of an IP packet are connected to the same network. The IP layer simply uses ARP to get the network address of the destination and then uses the underlying network to transmit the packets.

If the IP layer in the sending computer discovers that the destination is on a different network, it must send the message to a local router. It uses ARP to get the network address of the gateway or router and then uses the underlying network to transmit the packet to it. As gateways and routers are connected to two or more networks, they have several Internet addresses, one for each network to which they are attached. For example, in Figure 3.16 *jugula* is a gateway between two Ethernets and has addresses on each of them. When a message arrives at a gateway or router, the IP layer inspects the destination IP address and then (unless the message is for the router itself) decides where to send it next. For example, when *jugula* receives a packet addressed to *192.135.231.41* and sent by a host in the *192.135.233* network it uses ARP to get the equivalent network address and transmits an Ethernet packet with the resulting destination address on the network *192.135.231*.

Each computer has information to enable it to make routing decisions. The IP routing information on a host (a non-router computer) is always kept as simple as possible: hosts generally just know the 'nearest' routers or gateways. For example, in Figure 3.16, the routers on the network *192.135.231* are *magician* and *jugula*. All messages from that network to *192.135.233* are directed to *jugula* and those to all other networks are directed to *magician*.

Routers generally have more complex routing information than hosts. Some organizations choose to use general-purpose computers as gateways linking pairs of networks. In our example, *jugula* is a Sun workstation that plays other roles such as file serving and contains very simple routing tables: the tables in *jugula* enable it to select one of the two networks *192.135.231* or *192.135.233*.

Each organization generally operates at least one router with more complex tables enabling it to make decisions between several destination networks. In our example, the computers labelled *router* play this role.

Domain names □ Application programs such as Telnet, file transfer and electronic mail handlers can accept Internet addresses (in their decimal form) to identify the computers to which connections are to be established. Numeric identifiers are generally too cumbersome for human beings to remember and use, so a separate symbolic naming scheme, based on the idea of naming domains has been developed for identifying hosts and other entities in the Internet at the application level.

The use of user-level symbolic names for computers has been common since organizations began to have several computers. These names are called hostnames in UNIX environments. Figure 3.16 shows some examples of hostnames, for example, *magician*, *Jean-mac* and *it024*. Names like this are suitable for use by a single organization with a single network, but the Internet consists of multiple interconnected networks belonging to a variety of organizations world-wide. A hierarchic naming scheme is more suitable. It can be extended to accommodate any number of computers, authority for allocating names within any portion of the hierarchy can be delegated without danger of clashing with the names in other parts of the hierarchy, the names are

Figure 3.18   Domain name hierarchy.

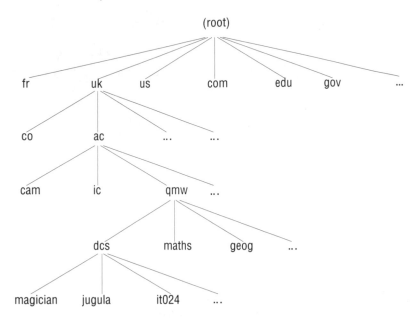

likely to be more memorable and the services that resolve the names can base their searching strategies on the name structure.

Internet *domain names* refer to countries, groups of organisations, individual organisations and host computers within them. Domains are hierarchically structured; domains may contain further domains. The hierarchic structuring of domain names is reflected in their syntax. Thus *uk* is the identifier for the domain that embraces the portions of the Internet that are located in the United Kingdom. Within that, the academic portions are identified as *ac.uk*, and each academic institution has a domain name, so Queen Mary and Westfield College is *qmw.ac.uk*, and the Department of Computer Science is *dcs.qmw.ac.uk*. At the bottom of the hierarchy are named computers, thus in the Department of Computer Science at QMW, we find computers with names such *redstar*, *magician* and *jugula* and their domain names are *redstar.dcs.qmw.ac.uk, magician.dcs.qmw.ac.uk* and *jugula.dcs.qmw.ac.uk*. See Figure 3.18.

For historic reasons, country identifiers such as *uk* are not the only identifiers found in the top-most or *root* domain. The naming scheme was developed at a time when the Internet was almost wholly located in the US, and the first-level domain names were allocated on that assumption. So domains such as *com, edu* and *gov* are still in use to refer to companies, educational institutions and government organizations within the US.

Domain names are accepted as parameters by application programs such as Telnet and electronic mail, but they must be resolved to Internet addresses before they can be used in communication operations. The translation of domain names to Internet addresses is the responsibility of a separate service, the *Domain Name System (DNS)*.

Application programs pass requests to the DNS to convert the domain names that users specify into Internet addresses.

The implementation of the DNS is described in detail in Chapter 9. It is implemented as a server process that can be run on host computers anywhere in the Internet. There are at least two DNS servers in each domain and often more. The servers in each domain hold a partial map of the domain name tree below their domain. They must hold at least the portion consisting of all of the domain and host names within their domain, but they often contain a larger portion of the tree. DNS servers handle requests for the translation of domain names outside their portion of the tree by issuing requests to DNS servers in the relevant domains, proceeding recursively from left to right resolving the name in segments. The resulting translation is then cached at the server handling the original request so that future requests for the resolution of names referring to the same domain will be resolved without reference to other servers. The DNS would not be workable without the extensive use of caching, since the 'root' name servers would be consulted in almost every case, creating a service access bottleneck.

Fast Local Internet Protocol – FLIP

Kaashoek *at al.* [1993] point out that there are several requirements not met by protocols such as TCP/IP that should be taken into account for large-scale distributed systems when the communication subsystem is composed of several component networks connected by high-speed direct links. These include:

Transparency: The patterns of communication introduced in Chapter 2 call for communication between processes in a distributed system. This implies that the communication subsystem should transmit messages to processes, or to communication ports that are attached to processes, rather than to the host computers (as in IP) or ports with fixed identifiers attached to the host computers (as in UDP). Communication ports are discussed in Chapter 4. For full transparency, the communication subsystem ought to maintain communication when processes or communication ports are migrated between computers in the network.

Security: For applications that require secure communication, messages should be encrypted unless the network is known to be entirely trustworthy (Chapter 16). In an internetwork, some of the component networks may be trustworthy but not others. Only messages that pass over untrusted portions of the network must be encrypted, but the communication subsystem can offer much better performance for secure communication if it supports this notion of trustworthiness for the component networks in an internetwork.

Ease of network management: In internetworks with many computers and component networks, computers and networks are frequently added to or removed from the network. The allocation of new addresses is performed manually in the Internet. There is a requirement that the allocation of addresses to computers and networks should be done entirely automatically, without interrupting the use of the communication subsystem.

Figure 3.19   Correspondence between Internet and FLIP layers.

Layer	Internet protocols	FLIP
Application	Ftp, telnet, smtp, etc.	User-defined
Session	–	RPC and process group communication
Transport	TCP, UDP	(FLIP is UDP-like)
Internetwork	IP	FLIP

These goals are difficult to attain in a widely-dispersed internetwork because of performance limitations and the multiplicity of administrative domains that occur in such internetworks, but Tanenbaum and his co-workers at Vrije University have designed and built a suite of internetwork protocols that meet the above requirements called FLIP (Fast Local Internet Protocol), for use in a more limited internetwork environment with several interconnected Ethernets and computers running the Amoeba distributed operating system [Kaashoek *et al.* 1993]. We outline FLIP below. The Amoeba operating system is described in Chapter 18.

The FLIP protocol provides an unreliable datagram service. The correspondence between the layers of the Internet and FLIP protocols is shown in Figure 3.19. FLIP is intended primarily as a basis for the implementation of a fast and general-purpose remote procedure-calling protocol and a group multicast protocol. It does not include a byte-stream protocol analogous to TCP, although one could easily be provided. The implementation of FLIP and the relationship between FLIP, RPC and the Amoeba group communication protocol is discussed in Section 18.5.

FLIP provides basic internetwork communication – it is at the same level as IP, but whereas IP delivers packets to computers, the source and destination points for FLIP packets are Amoeba processes. This together with the fact that FLIP messages can be of any size up to 4 gigabytes, means that there is no need for a transport level datagram protocol such as UDP.

Amoeba processes have FLIP ports with 64-bit FLIP identifiers. A new unique port identifier is generated automatically whenever a port is created. These identifiers are in fact location-independent addresses (see Chapter 4). This means that a message addressed to a port with a given FLIP identifier will be delivered to that port even if the process moves from one computer to another, or even to another network.

FLIP identifiers can also refer to groups of ports (and hence they can be used to address groups of processes) with the effect that a message addressed to a group of ports with a given FLIP identifier will be delivered to some or all of those ports. A request to multicast a message specifies the number of destinations that it should be delivered to.

A FLIP broadcast message is delivered to all the computers on the local network and can also be delivered to a number of adjacent networks up to a specified 'distance' in terms of the number of networks crossed.

Each computer in a FLIP internetwork is connected to the physical networks by means of a 'FLIP box' which may be implemented in hardware or (more usually) software and contains the following components:

Packet switch: passes packets between hosts and networks and from one network to another. It uses routing tables to choose the network on which to transmit each packet. These tables vary dynamically as processes move from one computer to another. FLIP identifiers are if necessary located by means of broadcast messages over gradually increasing 'distances'.

Host interface: provides interfaces to the FLIP protocols for sending and receiving unicast, multicast and broadcast messages. The messages are put into packets for transmission by the packet switch. The host interface also allows processes (for example, servers) to register their FLIP identifiers for receiving messages. Processes may, if necessary register their FLIP identifiers in a secure manner, using a one-way encryption function. (See the section on put ports and get ports in Section 18.5 for an explanation.)

Network interfaces: a host has a single interface and a router has several interfaces to different networks. The network interface has a similar role to the one in the Internet protocols.

The main differences between FLIP and the Internet protocols are:

- FLIP provides location transparency based on location-independent message destinations, whereas IP message destinations are port numbers in computers.

- Port identifiers are generated and allocated automatically, reducing administration costs.

- Group communication is supported by FLIP, because messages may be addressed to groups of processes.

- FLIP messages can be an order of magnitude larger than IP messages, supporting a wider variety of application types with datagram communication.

- FLIP supports secure communication without incurring the overheads of encryption for transmission on networks that are known to be secure.

- FLIP is intended for use in internetworks based on small, reliable collections of WANs and LANs.

3.6 Summary

We have focused on the networking concepts and designs that are needed as a basis for distributed systems and have approached them from the point of view of a distributed system designer. Packet networks and layered protocols provide the basis for communication in distributed systems. Local area networks are based on packet broadcasting, exploiting the bus- or ring-structured circuits found in such networks. wide area networks are based on packet switching to route packets to their destinations through a partially-connected network. Metropolitan area networks are expected to emerge based on the recently-developed broadband networks that exploit ATM techniques over synchronous (ISDN) or asynchronous (native ATM) circuits.

Internetworks are constructed by layering a 'virtual' internetwork protocol over collections of networks linked together by routers. For example, the Internet TCP/IP protocols enable computers in the Internet to communicate with one another in a uniform manner, irrespective of whether they are on the same local area network or in different countries.

Most currently available local area networks provide adequate data transfer rates and sufficiently low latency to enable effective distributed system software to be constructed over them. Current wide area networks do not provide the performance required for distributed systems, but faster wide area networks with low latencies are expected to arrive shortly based on ATM switching. The Internet standards include many application-level protocols that are suitable for use in wide area distributed applications.

The last section compares the Internet protocols whose use is well established in world-wide internetworks with the FLIP protocol. The latter has been designed as an infrastructure for distributed systems, relates well to RPC and group communication and provides location transparency. Although it is designed for relatively small WANs and has only been used with the Amoeba operating system, we feel that it demonstrates well the approach required for distributed operating systems in internetworks.

EXERCISES

3.1   A client sends a 200 byte request message to a service, which produces a response containing 5000 bytes. Estimate the total time to complete the request in each of the following cases, with the performance assumptions listed below:

i)   Using connectionless (datagram) communication (for example, UDP);

ii)   Using connection-oriented communication (for example, TCP);

iii)   The server process is in the same machine as the client.

> [Latency per packet (local or remote,
> incurred on both send and receive):   5 milliseconds
> Connection setup time (TCP only):   5 milliseconds
> Data transfer rate: 10 megabits per second
> MTU: 1000 bytes
> Server request processing time: 2 milliseconds
> Assume that the network is lightly loaded.]

pages 60, 69

3.2   What is the task of an Internet router? What tables must it maintain?

page 63

3.3   What is the task of an Ethernet bridge? What tables must it maintain?

page 64

3.4   Describe the work done by the software in each protocol layer when the ISO Reference Model is implemented over an Ethernet.

pages 70, 77

3.5   Compare the layers in a 'native mode' Internet implementation with those in the ISO reference model.

pages 70, 84

3.6 What are the most important differences between connectionless and connection-oriented communication?

page 73

3.7 Compare connectionless and connection-oriented communication for the implementation of each of the following application-level or presentation-level protocols:

i) virtual terminal access (for example, Telnet);

ii) file transfer (for example, FTP);

iii) user location (for example, rwho, finger);

iv) information browsing (for example, Gopher);

v) remote procedure call.

page 73

3.8 Explain how it is possible for a sequence of packets transmitted through a wide area network to arrive at their destination in an order that differs from that in which they were sent. Why can't this happen in a local network? Can it happen in an ATM network?

pages 72, 77, 82

3.9 What is the main drawback of satellite communication channels when used in computer networks?

page 67

3.10 What are the limitations of Ethernet communication for multimedia applications? Compare the suitability of token rings and Ethernets for multimedia applications.

pages 77, 81

3.11 How can we be sure that no two computers in the Internet have the same addresses?

page 87

3.12 Explain the relationship between domain names and Internet addresses (IP addresses) in the Internet.

page 87

3.13 Can two computers connected to different local networks in the Internet have the same (local) network address?

page 90

3.14 What limitations does Internet communication impose on distributed system implementations?

page 93

3.15 The FLIP protocol aims to support secure communication. Why should this be considered a responsibility of the transport level protocol?

page 93

3.16 What problems would arise if FLIP were implemented over a large wide area network?

page 95

3.17   A specific problem that must be solved in remote terminal access protocols such as Telnet is the need to transmit exceptional events such as 'kill signals' from the 'terminal' to the host in advance of previously-transmitted data. Discuss the solution of this problem with connection-oriented and connectionless protocols.

3.18   What are the disadvantages of using hardware-supported broadcasting to locate resources

    i)   in a single local network;

    ii)   in a local internetwork? How does Ethernet multicast avoid the disadvantages of broadcasting?

3.19   How might multicasting be efficiently implemented in an internetwork?

4

INTERPROCESS COMMUNICATION

This chapter discusses the requirements for communication and synchronization between co-operating processes in distributed systems and the implementation of protocols to support them.

We discuss the building blocks for interprocess communication protocols. The basic building block is simple message passing, but location-independent identifiers for message destinations are important for location transparency.

We discuss the construction of protocols to support the two communication patterns that are most commonly used in distributed programs:

- client-server communication – in which request and reply messages provide the basis for communication between clients and servers;
- group communication – in which the same message is sent to several processes.

Interprocess communication in UNIX is dealt with as a case study.

4.1   Introduction

In Chapter 2 we introduced two main patterns of communication: client-server and group multicast. In both of these, the communicating entities are *processes* – the activities performed when programs are executed. Distributed systems and applications are composed of collections of processes that play specific roles determined by the nature of the tasks that they perform. The roles played by the various processes determines the patterns of communication that occur between them.

Software tools are needed to support the construction of distributed systems and applications. An important element of this support is the provision of useful high-level protocols to support the main patterns of communication that occur in distributed software, together with facilities for the naming and location of processes.

Chapter 3 discussed the protocols for computer networks without discussing how application programs could use these protocols. In particular, two transport level protocols, UDP and TCP, were discussed.

The last section of this chapter presents the BSD UNIX socket interface to UDP and TCP as a case study of an application interface to transport level protocols.

The application program interface to TCP provides the abstraction of a two-way *stream* between sender and recipient. The information communicated consists of a stream of data items with no message boundaries. Stream communication is supported by buffering which enables the sender to get ahead of the recipient. Stream communication is used to implement some services such as remote login and file-transfer in UNIX-based and other networked environments. These will be discussed in Section 4.5 below. Streams provide a building block for producer–consumer communication [Bacon 1993] which has limited applicability in distributed systems in general, but has been widely used in some specific multiprocess and networked applications. A producer and a consumer form a pair of processes in which the role of the first is to produce data items and the role of the second is to consume them. The data items sent by the producer to the consumer are queued on arrival until the consumer is ready to receive them. The consumer must wait when there are no data items available. The producer must wait if the storage used to hold the queued data items is exhausted.

The application program interface to UDP provides a *message passing* abstraction – the simplest form of interprocess communication. This enables a sending process to transmit a single message to a receiving process. In UNIX, the sending process specifies the destination as a socket which is an indirect reference to a particular port used by the destination process at a destination computer. We have seen in Chapter 3 that FLIP provides the ability to transmit a message to a location-independent message destination.

The first section of this chapter is concerned with the building blocks of interprocess communication. The data structures in application programs must be translated into a form suitable for sending in messages to computers that may use different representations for data items. Message passing is the basic building block from which most other patterns of communication are constructed. However, its semantics vary from one implementation to another. The main differences relate to whether it provides location transparency, whether it is synchronous or asynchronous and how reliable it is.

The second and third sections of this chapter deal with the design of suitable protocols for client-server communication and process group multicast communication. Request-reply protocols are designed to support client-server communication. Multicast protocols are designed to support group communication. Message-passing operations can be used to construct protocols to support particular process roles and communication patterns; as for example client-server interchanges. By examining the roles and communication patterns, it is possible to design suitable communication primitives and their supporting protocols based on the actual exchanges and avoid redundancy. In particular, these specialized protocols should not include redundant acknowledgements. For example, in a request-reply communication, it is generally considered redundant to acknowledge the request message because the reply message serves as an acknowledgement. If a more specialized protocol requires sender acknowledgement or any other particular characteristics, these are supplied with the specialized operations. The idea is to add specialized functions only where they are needed with a view to achieving protocols that use a minimum of message exchanges.

When we are designing protocols we have to consider not only how to avoid redundant messages, but also what semantics they will provide. For example, in client-server communication, where the reply is the only acknowledgement, we must consider the case when the reply is lost – how should client proceed? There are several possibilities:

- the request message was never received by the server;

- the server failed during its task or is still working on it;

- the server received the request and performed the operation, but the reply went astray.

This leads on to another question as to whether it would be correct to repeat the operation. We return to this issue in Section 4.3.

4.2   Building blocks

Mapping data structures and data items to messages □   The data items in programs are represented as data structures whereas the information in messages is sequential. Irrespective of the form of communication used, the data structures must be flattened before transmission, and rebuilt on arrival. The information transmitted in messages can be data values of many different types and not all computers store even simple values such as integers and sequences of characters in the same order. In order for any two computers to exchange data values:

- the values are converted to an agreed external data form before transmission and converted to the local form on receipt;

- for communication between computers of the same type, the conversion to external data form may be omitted. When connection-oriented communication is used, pairs of computers may negotiate as to whether to use an external data representation;

Figure 4.1   XDR message.

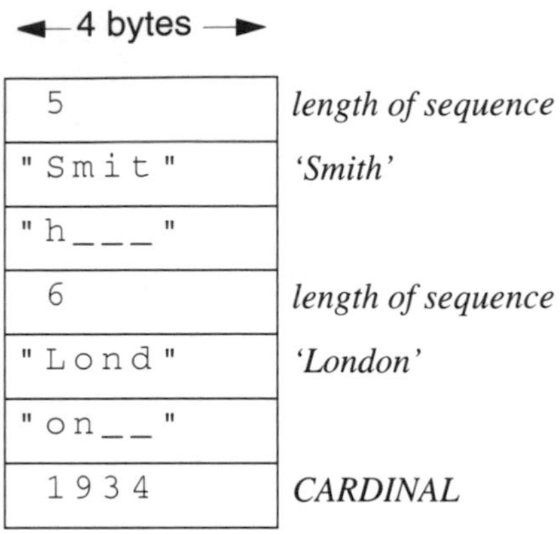

◄— 4 bytes —►

5	*length of sequence*
" S m i t "	*'Smith'*
" h _ _ _ "	
6	*length of sequence*
" L o n d "	*'London'*
" o n _ _ "	
1 9 3 4	*CARDINAL*

The message is: 'Smith', 'London', 1934

• an alternative to using an external data representation is to transmit data values in their native form together with an architecture identifier – and recipients convert the data if necessary.

External data representation □ Sun XDR (External Data Representation) [Santifaller 1991; Sun 1990] and Courier [Xerox 1981] are examples of standards defining a representation for the commonly used simple and structured data types including strings, arrays, sequences and records. The Sun XDR standard was developed by Sun for use in the messages exchanged between clients and servers in Sun NFS (see Chapter 8).The Courier standard was developed by Xerox and is used in the ANSA testbench (Chapter 5).

The type of a data item is not given with the data representation in the message in either of these standards. In contrast, the ASN.1 (Abstract Syntax Notation) standard [CCITT 1985] provides a notation for defining the type as part of the representation of each item. The Mach distributed operating system (Chapter 18) 'tags' each item of data in a message with its type. However, it is not necessary to label message items with their types when messages are used in a context in which sender and recipient have common knowledge of the order and types of the items in a message.

Figure 4.1 shows a message in the Sun XDR external data representation in which the entire message consists of a sequence of 4-byte objects using a convention that a cardinal or integer occupies one object and that strings of four characters also occupy an object. Arrays, structures and strings of characters are represented as sequences of bytes with the length specified. Characters are in ASCII code. A further convention defines which end of each object is the most significant and, when characters are packed, which of the four bytes comes first. The use of a fixed size for each object in a message reduces computational load at the expense of bandwidth.

Marshalling □ Marshalling is the process of taking a collection of data items and assembling them into a form suitable for transmission in a message. Unmarshalling is the process of disassembling them on arrival to produce an equivalent collection of data items at the destination. We see that marshalling consists of both the flattening of structured data items into a sequence of basic data items and the translation of those data items into an external data representation. Similarly, unmarshalling consists of the translation from the external data representation to the local one and the unflattening of the data items. Marshalling may be done 'by hand' – meaning that the sending program explicitly converts each of the items into the external data representation format and writes them in sequence into an array of bytes which is transmitted and the recipient does the opposite to unmarshal it.

Marshalling operations can be generated automatically from the specification of the types of data items to be transmitted in a message. This requires that the types of the data structures and the types of the basic data items are described in a suitable notation. Both Sun XDR and Courier provide a notation for describing the types of the data structures in a message. For example, in the Courier notation, we might describe our message as:

> *Person : TYPE = RECORD [*
> *name, place : SEQUENCE OF CHAR;*
> *year : CARDINAL*
> *]*

The type specifications accompany a program in a programming language (generally C). Any source program containing type specifications for messages will be pre-processed so as to insert the appropriate marshalling operations for messages to be transmitted and unmarshalling operations for messages to be received. The sending and receiving processes must use the same type definitions for messages exchanged. In the next chapter, we discuss how an interface compiler generates appropriate marshalling

---

Marshalling by hand: A simple way of marshalling by hand is to convert the items to an array of ASCII characters before transmission. For example, the marshalled message corresponding to Figure 4.1 might contain the following sequence of characters:

```
5 Smith 6 London 1934
```

In C programs, *sprintf* may be used to convert data items to an array of characters and *sscanf* may be used to retrieve the data items form an array of characters. For example, the sending program might include:

> *char *name = "Smith", place = "London"; int year = 1934;*
> *sprintf(message, "%d %s %d %s %d",*
> *strlen(name), name, strlen(place), place, year);*

The receiving program will then convert the characters in the incoming message into values for name, place and year. This method of marshalling is wasteful of bandwidth.

Figure 4.2   Definition of message-passing operations

```
DEFINITION MODULE Message;
EXPORT QUALIFIED Message, ErrorReport, PortId, Send, Receive;
TYPE
      PortId = (* global port identifier, represented for example by 128 bits *)
      Message = RECORD
          dataItems:(* sequence of bytes *);
      END;
      ErrorType = (NONE, TIMEOUT);
VAR  ErrorReport: ErrorType; (* used when Receive times out *)
PROCEDURE Send(p:PortId; m:Message);
      (* Basic send - does not guarantee to deliver the message -
      it therefore does not produce any error reports *)
PROCEDURE Receive( p:PortId; VAR m:Message);
      (* Basic receive produces an error report when it times out *)
END Message.
```

operations for the arguments and results of remote procedures from the definitions of signatures specifying the types of parameters and results of procedures.

Send and Receive operations

Single message passing can be supported by two message communication operations: *Send* and *Receive*, defined in terms of destinations and messages. In order for one process to communicate with another, one process sends a message (a sequence of data items) to a destination and another process at the destination receives the message. This activity involves the communication of data from the sending process to the receiving process and may involve the synchronization of the two processes.

Figure 4.2 shows an interface in the form of a Modula-2 definition module for the *Send* and *Receive* operations using ports. The interface also defines types for *PortId* and *Message*. A message contains a sequence of bytes which may represent data items in a flattened form. Each port has a unique identifier that is valid throughout a distributed system (see page 105). These ports should not be confused with the port numbers introduced in Chapter 3 which are valid only within a particular computer.

Synchronous and asynchronous communication

A queue is associated with each message destination. Sending processes add messages to queues and receiving processes remove messages from queues. Communication between the sending and receiving process may be either synchronous or asynchronous. In the **synchronous** form of communication, the sending and receiving processes synchronize at every message. In this case, both the *Send* and *Receive* are **blocking** operations. Whenever a *Send* is issued the sending process is blocked until the corresponding *Receive* is issued. Whenever a *Receive* is issued the process blocks until a message arrives.

The following table shows the variations of synchronous and asynchronous communication with examples of languages and distributed operating systems that use them:

Communication type	Blocking Send	Blocking Receive	Languages and systems
Synchronous	Yes	Yes	occam
Asynchronous	No	Yes	Mach, Chorus, BSD 4.x UNIX
Asynchronous	No	No	Charlotte

In the **asynchronous** form of communication, the use of the *Send* operation is **non-blocking** in that the sending process is allowed to proceed as soon as the message has been copied to a local buffer and the transmission of the message proceeds in parallel with the sending process.

In the asynchronous form of communication the *Receive* operation can have blocking and non-blocking variants. In the non-blocking variant, the receiving process proceeds with its program after issuing a *Receive* operation which provides a buffer to be filled in the background, but it must separately receive notification that its buffer has been filled, by polling or interrupt.

In a system environment that supports multiple threads in a single process (see Chapter 6), the blocking *Receive* has few disadvantages, for it can be issued by one thread while other threads in the process remain active, and the simplicity of synchronizing the receiving threads with the incoming message is a substantial advantage. Non-blocking communication appears to be more efficient, but it involves extra complexity in the receiving process associated with the need to acquire the incoming message out of its flow of control.

A simple blocking *Receive* could wait for ever for the arrival of a message; but for many purposes a timeout is required. A **timeout** specifies an interval of time after which the operation will give up its action. The blocking form of *Receive* is suitable for use in servers that have nothing else to do when waiting for request messages from clients. But in some programs, it is not appropriate that a process that has used a *Receive* operation should wait indefinitely, in situations where the potential sending process has crashed or the expected message has been lost. One solution is to associate a timeout with *Receive* operations on certain ports, for example when a new port is created. Choosing an appropriate timeout interval is difficult, but it should be fairly large in comparison to the time required to transmit a message.

Message destinations

One of the arguments of the *Send* operation specifies an identifier denoting a message destination such as a port. The identifier of a message destination must therefore be known to any potential sending process; for example, in the context of the simple client-

Figure 4.3   Message destinations.

Message destinations	Operating systems and distributed programming environments	Location-independent?
Processes	V	yes
Ports	Mach, Chorus and Amoeba	yes
Sockets	BSD 4.x UNIX (see Section 4.5)	no
Groups of processes	V, Amoeba	yes
Groups of ports	Chorus	yes
Objects	Clouds, Emerald	yes

server model, potential clients need to know an identifier for communicating with a server.

Location-independent identifiers for destinations □ In the Internet protocols, destination addresses for messages are specified as a port number used by a process and the Internet address of the computer on which it runs. This has the effect that a service must always run on the same computer for its address to remain valid. One of the primary design aims of distributed operating systems is to provide location transparency. A key step in the provision of location transparency is to provide location-independent identifiers for message destinations such as those in the FLIP protocol described in Chapter 3.

When the destination in the *Send* operation is specified as a location-independent identifier, this is mapped onto a lower-level address in order to deliver a message. This mapping is carried out by routing software when the message is sent and takes into account the current location of the destination. In distributed operating systems that use location-independent identifiers for message destinations, services can be relocated without having to inform clients about their new locations.

Types of message destination □ Figure 4.3 indicates the variety of message destinations used in current distributed operating systems. Most operating systems have chosen to use either processes or ports as message destinations. A **port** is one of several alternative points of entry to a receiving process. We have noted that it is very useful to be able to deliver the same message to the members of a set of processes. Grouping can be applied to the naming of destinations as well as to the delivery of messages. Some IPC systems provide the ability to send messages to groups of destinations – either processes or ports. In both cases, the destination address is specified as a group identifier that is mapped onto a set of destinations for the message. As group identifiers require mapping onto lower-level destination addresses, they are always a location-independent form of address. Figure 4.3 shows the sorts of entities used as message destinations and some examples of operating systems that use them.

A port is a message destination that has exactly one receiver, but can have many senders. Ports are sometimes called *mailboxes* – a mailbox always has a message queue, whereas a port may or may not have one. The name port is used to describe one of several alternative points of communication to a receiving process – processes can use multiple ports from which to receive their messages (see Figure 4.4). Any process that

Figure 4.4   Ports as message destinations.

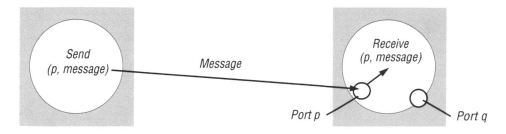

knows the identifier of a port can send a message to it. Servers generally publicize their port identifiers for use by clients.

The Mach, Chorus and Amoeba operating systems provide dynamically created ports with location-independent identifiers. The operating system in the sender maps these onto their current location. This provides location transparency and allows services to be relocated (see Chapter 18). In Mach or Chorus a port can be bound to a process and moved from process to process.

Reliability

The term *unreliable message* is used to refer to a single message transmitted from sender to recipient, without acknowledgement or retries. UDP is an example of a protocol that is suitable for an unreliable message service. The system does not guarantee that all messages sent are actually received at the destination. However it makes its 'best effort' to deliver each message. Processes using unreliable messages are left to provide their own checks to achieve the quality of reliable communication they require. In an internetwork, messages may be lost, duplicated, delivered out of order or delayed.

In a local area network, messages may occasionally be dropped, either because of a checksum error or because there is no available buffer space at the source or destination. There will be no duplicates and messages will arrive in the same order as they were sent. The use of a checksum ensures that all messages received are uncorrupted.

A reliable delivery service may be constructed from an unreliable one by the use of acknowledgements. Positive acknowledgements are used in client-server communication. Negative acknowledgements can be useful in group multicast.

For some applications, perfectly reliable communication is not needed and may cause unnecessary overhead. There are three main sources of overhead: (i) the need to store state information at source and destination, and (ii) to transmit extra messages and (iii) possible latency for sender or recipient.

Message identifiers □ Any scheme that involves the management of messages to provide additional properties such as reliable message delivery or request-reply communication requires that each message should have a unique message identifier by which it may be referenced. A message identifier consists of two parts: (i) a *requestId* which is taken from an increasing sequence of integers by the sending process and (ii) an identifier for the sender process, for example the port on which it may receive replies.

Figure 4.5   Request-reply communication.

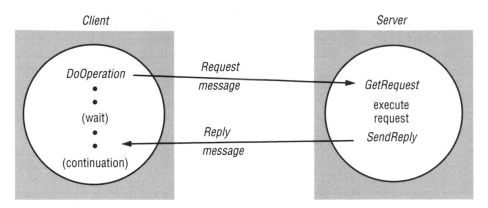

The first part makes the identifier unique to the sender and the second part makes it unique in the distributed system. When the value of the message identifier reaches the maximum value of an unsigned integer (for example, $2^{32} - 1$) it is reset to zero. The only restriction here is that the lifetime of a message identifier should be much less than the time taken to exhaust the values in the sequence of integers.

4.3   Client-server communication

This form of communication is designed to support the roles and message exchanges in typical client-server interaction. In the normal case, request-reply communication is synchronous because the client process blocks until the reply arrives from the server. It can also be reliable because the reply from the server is effectively an acknowledgement to the client.

Asynchronous request-reply communication is an alternative that may be useful in situations where clients can afford to retrieve replies later.

When a client-server exchange is performed using *Send* and *Receive*, four operations are required: two *Send* and two *Receive* operations. Each message-passing operation involves a system call.

Request-reply protocols ☐ The Amoeba, Chorus, Mach and V distributing operating systems have protocols designed to support this pattern of communication more directly and hence to reduce the overheads, by introducing a trio of message communication primitives: *DoOperation*, *GetRequest* and *SendReply* as shown in Figure 4.5. The communication costs are reduced because there are only three system calls instead of four.

This specially designed request-reply protocol uses the server reply message as an acknowledgement of the client request message. It may be designed to provide certain delivery guarantees. If the basic *Send* and *Receive* operations are used, the matching of replies to requests, and the delivery guarantees must be provided by software at a level above the basic *Send* and *Receive* operations.

Figure 4.6   Request-reply message structure.

messageType	*(Request, Reply)*
requestId	*CARDINAL*
procedureId	*CARDINAL*
arguments	*(* flattened list*)*

DoOperation is used by clients to invoke remote operations. Its arguments specify the identifier of the server port together with the request message and a buffer for receiving a reply message. The request message specifies which server operation to use, together with additional information (arguments) required by the operation.

PROCEDURE DoOperation (serverPort:PortId; request:Message;
  VAR reply: Message);
  send request message, *request* to server at port *serverPort* and receive reply *reply*.

The *DoOperation* operation could be implemented by using a *Send* operation containing the request message followed by a *Receive* operation. When *DoOperation* is used by a client the process is blocked until the server performs the requested operation and transmits a reply message to the client process.

PROCEDURE GetRequest (serverPort:PortId; VAR request:Message);
  acquire a client request, *request* via server port *serverPort*.

PROCEDURE SendReply (clientPort:PortId; reply:Message);
  send reply message, *reply* to client at its port *clientPort*.

GetRequest is used by a server process to acquire service requests as shown in Figure 4.5. When the server has executed the operation indicated in the request message, it uses *SendReply* to send the reply message to the client. When the reply message is received by the client the original *DoOperation* is unblocked, and execution of the client program continues.

The information to be transmitted in a request message or a reply message is shown in Figure 4.6. A *DoOperation* in the client generates a *requestId* for each request message and the server copies them into the corresponding reply messages. This enables *DoOperation* to check that a reply message is the result of the current request, not from a delayed earlier call. The procedure identifier *procedureId* refers to the server procedure that implements the operation requested by the client. Chapter 5 describes the RPC software that manages procedure identifiers and the marshalling of arguments in a manner than is transparent to the client and server programs.

Figure 4.7   RPC protocols.

Name	Messages sent by		
	Client	Server	Client
R	Request		
RR	Request	Reply	
RRA	Request	Reply	Acknowledge reply

Delivery failures □ The following assumptions are made about failures in the environment in which the above remote procedure calling primitives are used:

- Messages are occasionally dropped by senders, receivers and network gateways.

- Networks may become partitioned. That is, one or more nodes of a network may become detached from the remainder of the network.

- Processes may sometimes fail. In general, it is impossible for a sender to distinguish between a process failure and a communication failure. When a process does not reply after some agreed number, N of attempts to communicate with it, it is assumed to be unavailable. The choice of N is difficult – if it is too small, a process may mistakenly be considered to have failed – but, if N is too large, the time to detect a failure will be excessive.

- No corruption of data. Messages that are received are correct – this is ensured by error-checking mechanisms at the network level.

To allow for occasions when a server has failed or a request or reply message is dropped, *DoOperation* should use a timeout when it is waiting to get the server's reply message. The action taken when a timeout occurs depends upon the type of RPC exchange protocol in use, as discussed below.

RPC exchange protocols □ Three protocols, with differing semantics in the presence of communication failures, are used for implementing various types of RPC. They were originally identified by Spector [1982]:

- the **request (R)** protocol

- the **request-reply (RR)** protocol;

- the **request-reply-acknowledge reply (RRA)** protocol.

The messages passed in these protocols are summarized in Figure 4.7.

The R protocol may be used when there is no value to be returned from the procedure and the client requires no confirmation that the procedure has been executed. The client may proceed immediately after the request message is sent as there is no need to wait for a reply message.

The RR protocol is useful for most client-server exchanges because it is based on the request-reply protocol. Special acknowledgement messages are not required because a server's reply message is regarded as an acknowledgement of the client's request message. Similarly, a subsequent call from a client may be regarded as an acknowledgement of a server's reply message.

The RRA protocol is based on the exchange of three messages: request-reply-acknowledge reply. The acknowledge reply message contains the *requestId* from the reply message being acknowledged. The arrival of a *requestId* in an acknowledgement message will be interpreted as acknowledging the receipt of all reply messages with lower *requestId*s, so the loss of an acknowledgement message is harmless. Although the exchange involves an additional message, it need not block the client as the acknowledgement may be transmitted after the reply has been given to the client, but it does use processing and network resources. Exercise 4.18 suggests an optimization to the RRA protocol.

Timeouts □ There are various options as to what *DoOperation* can do after a timeout. The simplest option is to return immediately from *DoOperation* with an indication to the client that the *DoOperation* has failed. This is not the usual approach – the timeout may have been due to the request or reply message getting lost – and in the latter case, the operation will have been performed. To compensate for the possibility of lost messages, *DoOperation* sends the request message repeatedly until either it succeeds or else it is reasonably sure that the delay is due to lack of response from the server rather than to lost messages. Eventually when *DoOperation* returns it will indicate to the client that the server has probably failed.

Discarding duplicate request messages □ In cases when the request message is retransmitted, the server may receive it more than once. For example, the server may receive the first request message, but take longer than the client's timeout to execute the command and return the reply. This can lead to the server executing an operation more than once for the same request. To avoid this, the protocol is designed to recognize successive messages (from the same client) with the same message identifier and to filter out duplicates. If the server has not yet sent the reply, it need take no special action – it will transmit the reply when it has finished executing the operation.

Lost reply messages □ If the server has already sent the reply when it receives the duplicate request it may need to execute the operation again to obtain the result. This will be the case when the loss of a reply message is the reason for the retransmission of the request message. Some servers can execute their operations more than once and obtain the same results each time. An **idempotent operation** is an operation that can be performed repeatedly with the same effect as if it had been performed exactly once. For example, an operation to add an element to a set is an idempotent operation because it will always have the same effect on the set each time it is performed; whereas an operation to append an item to a sequence is not an idempotent operation because it extends the sequence each time it is performed. A server whose operations are all idempotent need not take special measures to avoid executing its operations more than once.

History □ For servers that require retransmission of replies without re-execution of operations, a history may be used. The term history is used to refer to a structure that contains a record of (reply) messages that have been transmitted. An entry in a history contains a message identifier, a message and an identifier of the client to which it was sent. Its purpose is to allow the server to retransmit reply messages when client processes request them. A problem associated with the use of a history is its memory cost. A history will become very large unless the server can tell when the messages will no longer be needed for retransmission.

As clients can make only one request at a time, the server can interpret each request as an acknowledgement of its previous reply. Therefore the history need contain only the last reply message sent to each client. However, the volume of reply messages in a server's history may be a problem when it has a large number of clients. In particular, when a client process terminates, it does not acknowledge the last reply it has received – messages in the history are therefore normally discarded after a limited period of time. An alternative is to use the RRA protocol in which clients acknowledge the receipt of each reply to enable the server to discard entries from its history.

Multipacket messages □ The message-passing protocols used in local networks generally provide datagrams with limited length, often as large as 8 kilobytes, but this may not be regarded as adequate for use in transparent RPC systems since the arguments or results of procedures may be of any size. A solution is to design a protocol on top of the message-passing operations for passing multipacket request and reply messages.

The term multipacket is used by Spector [1982] to refer to a message made up of a sequence of datagrams. Requests and replies that do not fit within a single datagram can be transmitted as multipackets. In order to interleave multipackets with normal datagrams, each packet has an element that indicates whether it is part of a multipacket and a sequence number. The recipient re-assembles the parts of a multipacket.

Multipackets may be implemented by transmitting the component request packets in sequence without acknowledgement or retransmission. The server acknowledges the entire request message by replying to the request when all of the packets have been received. If anything goes wrong, either the client retransmits all of the packets after a time out or the protocol allows the server to request selected missing packets.

An alternative is for the server to acknowledge each request packet and the client to retransmit packets after timeouts. The last packet is acknowledged by the reply to the request. This alternative has the advantage that it imposes a flow control mechanism which prevents a sender from overrunning a receiver, so that packets are not dropped because, for example, of lack of buffer space at the receiver. The same considerations apply to reply messages.

Flow control and multipackets can be taken into account in the design of a request-reply protocol. We shall examine these issues in more detail in Section 18.5, when we consider the Amoeba FLIP protocol as a case study, and compare it with another protocol, VMTP.

4.4 Group communication

The exchange of single messages is not the best model for communication from one process to a group of other processes, as for example when a service is implemented as a number of different processes in different computers, perhaps to provide fault tolerance or to enhance availability. A **multicast message** is more appropriate – this is a message that is sent by one process to the members of a group of processes. Multicast messages provide a useful infrastructure for providing fault tolerance in distributed applications. There is a range of possibilities in the desired behaviour of a multicast. The simplest is an unreliable multicast which provides no guarantees about message delivery or ordering.

Multicast messages are a very useful tool for constructing distributed systems with the following characteristics:

1. *Fault tolerance based on replicated services*: A replicated service consists of a group of servers. Client requests are multicast to all the members of the group, each of which performs an identical operation. Even when some of the members fail, clients can still be served.

2. *Locating objects in distributed services*: Multicast messages can be used for locating objects within a distributed service, such as files within a distributed file service. In the V system [Cheriton and Zwaenpoel 1985] clients locate files with given names by multicasting a name query to the servers – only the appropriate server responds. In the V system, the frequency of multicast queries is reduced to less than one per cent of accesses by the use of a file name prefix cache. Chapter 7 discusses alternative ways of locating files.

3. *Better performance through replicated data*: data are replicated to increase the performance of a service – in some cases replicas of the data are placed in users' workstations. Each time the data changes, the new value is multicast to the processes managing the replicas. See Figure 4.9 for an example.

4. *Multiple update*: multicast to a group may be used to notify processes when something happens, for example, a news system might notify interested users when a new message has been posted on a particular news group.

From these uses for group communication we can derive some useful properties for group communication protocols.

Atomicity

In case (1) we require that each server receives all requests, so that all the servers have done the same as one another and are in the same state at any time. This requires atomic multicast:

Atomic multicast: A message transmitted by **atomic multicast** is either received by all of the processes that are members of the receiving group or else it is received by none of them. We define the membership of groups so that failed processes cannot remain as members of any groups.

Atomic multicast is not always necessary. For example, since the receipt of a single reply is often sufficient when making queries to a set of servers with the same replicated data, there is no need to ensure that all of the processes holding replicas receive the request. Reliable multicast will do for such queries.

Reliable multicast: is a message transmission method that makes a best effort to deliver to all members of a group but does not guarantee to do so. An unreliable multicast just transmits the multicast message once, for example, in Chorus (see Chapter 18).

In case (2) the data is partitioned between several servers and we require that each server receives a request to be sure that we include the one that knows the answer. Reliable multicast is sufficient for this purpose because it can be repeated in the (infrequent) cases when there is no reply.

Ordering

Both atomic and reliable multicast provide FIFO ordering between pairs of processes. In FIFO ordering, the messages from any one client to a particular server are delivered in the order sent. This is simple to achieve by attaching sequence numbers to messages.

In case (1) we require that all the servers execute their operations in the same order, under conditions in which the multicast requests are transmitted by different clients.

Without a mechanism to ensure ordered delivery of messages, when two originators multicast to a group at about the same time, their messages may not arrive in the same relative order at members of the group. For example, this may happen if one of the messages is dropped by one of the recipients and has to be retransmitted to it. This is illustrated in Figure 4.8.

The strongest form of ordering is **totally-ordered multicast**:

Totally-ordered multicast: when several messages are transmitted to a group by totally-ordered multicast the messages reach all of the members of the group in the same order.

Total ordering applies to all the messages sent to a group from all senders. Total ordering is potentially expensive in its use of communication. Causal ordering is an ordering property that is less restrictive than total ordering but meets most application requirements. It is based on the notion of causality, which is introduced in Chapter 10.

Figure 4.8   Multicasts without ordering constraints.

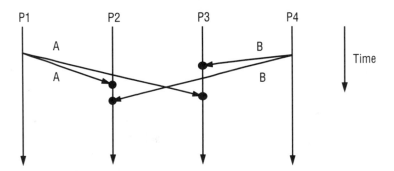

Multicasts from different processes may arrive in different orders. P1 multicasts message A and P4 multicasts B to P2 and P3 at about the same time. A arrives first at P2 and B arrives first at P3.

We will return to the use of atomic, totally-ordered and causally-ordered multicasts in Chapter 11.

Implementation of group communication

The simplest form of multicast is an *unreliable multicast* in which a single message is sent to each destination. A simple but inefficient implementation based on simple message sending to ports might take the form:

```
PROCEDURE multicast(destinations: ARRAY OF PortId; m:Message);
(* potentially unreliable multicast - uses basic Send which is potentially unreliable*)
VAR  i : CARDINAL;
BEGIN
        FOR i := 0 TO HIGH(destinations) DO Send(destinations(i) , m) END;
END;
```

This implementation assumes that group membership is managed by a separate module, and that the array parameter *destinations* has been instantiated by making a request to the membership module.

The multicast procedure simply sends the message to each port in an array of ports. This is both unreliable and inefficient. The reliability can be dealt with by the introduction of mechanisms for atomicity and ordering. These are discussed below.

Efficiency ☐ The efficiency of multicast communication can be improved in most local networks. For example, recall from Chapter 3 that the Ethernet provides a facility to broadcast a packet to all of the computers on the local network. It can also provide a facility to multicast a message to a group of computers (not processes).

Where the members of a process group are all located in a single local network, a single broadcast message on the network will suffice to transmit a message to all of the members of the group.

Broadcast facilities at the local network level are helpful, but they do not address the whole problem. A general-purpose group multicast facility should support multicast communication with arbitrary groups of processes. On the one hand there may be several processes in a single network node, and on the other hand the processes may be at nodes that are located in several different local networks. A fully-optimized multicast mechanism should exploit multicast addressing at the network level where it is available, but must provide a general-purpose service that spans multiple local networks and addresses processes wherever they may be located.

Reliability ☐ The simple implementation of multicast outlined above is potentially unreliable in the sense that the message may not arrive at all of the destination ports. There are two reasons why a message may arrive at some, but not all of the ports:

- one of the messages may be dropped;

- the originating process may fail after transmitting some, but not all of the messages.

Neither of these outcomes is acceptable for applications that require atomic or totally ordered multicast. We discuss the implementation of these now.

Monitoring ☐ When a process is waiting for a reply from another group member, it monitors the latter to see whether it fails. The monitoring may include retransmission of the message requiring a reply. Eventually either the member receives the reply or detects that the other process has failed. As before, a process is deemed to have failed if it does not reply after some agreed number of attempts to communicate with it. The monitoring function forms part of the group membership service. Processes that are deemed to have failed are removed from all groups. Subsequent messages from 'failed' processes are discarded. Monitoring is an essential part of atomic multicast protocols.

A reliable and atomic multicast ☐ A way to implement a reliable multicast is for the sender to send the message to each member of the destination group, and then await an acknowledgement from each. When all the acknowledgements have been received, the sender has completed the multicast – it can confirm to the caller that the message has reached all members of the group.

If some acknowledgements are not received after a timeout interval, the originator retransmits the original message until an acknowledgement is received, or if no acknowledgement arrives after a number of retransmissions, it assumes that the relevant member process has failed and removes it from the group.

But consider the case where the originator fails during the above process, in which case it will not be atomic. To make it atomic, the protocol must ensure that one of the recipients will take over from the originator, so that any multicast which was partially completed will be completed after the failure. Each member of the group that receives a message returns an acknowledgement to the originator and then monitors the originator to see whether it fails or whether it confirms that the multicast is complete. When a member detects that the originator has failed, it takes over the multicast protocol.

The issue is: how do the members of the group know when a multicast is complete? This will require notification from the originator which would be equivalent to doing another atomic multicast. A way to reduce the costs is: that an originator does not start another atomic multicast until the previous one is completed. Members use each message received as an acknowledgement of the completion of the multicast of the previous message from the same originator.

This atomic multicast protocol performs poorly even in the normal case in which messages are not lost. Its main drawback is the total number of messages exchanged due to the large numbers of acknowledgement messages. There is also a degree of originator delay due to the rule that a reliable multicast must be completed before the next is started.

Two techniques are widely used to overcome problems in the implementation of ordered and atomic multicasts. They are *hold-back* and *negative acknowledgement*. We have coined the term hold-back to describe a technique that is quite widely used, but for which we can find no previously-used label.

Hold-back ☐ To meet the requirements of atomicity and ordering for messages, it is often necessary to delay the final delivery of a multicast message that has been received by the communication handler at a network node until some other message has been received. In this case the message is retained by the communication handler and is released to the final destination (for example, an application) once the ordering and atomicity requirements have been met.

Negative acknowledgement □ Negative acknowledgement is a method of achieving higher performance by reducing the number of messages involved. Each sender maintains a count of the messages it has sent. The count is appended to all the messages it sends, acting as a message sequence number. Recipients send no acknowledgement messages unless the sequence numbers on the messages from a particular sender indicate that a message has been missed, in which case the missing message is requested from that sender. As in the request-reply protocol each sender must keep copies of the messages it has transmitted in a history list in case of requests for their retransmission.

In the basic atomic multicast mechanism outlined above, we have stipulated that other members must be able to take over when an originator has failed before all the members have received its messages. This requires that members must have a history containing copies of all the messages they have received in case they need to take over. As in the previous examples of the use of a history, the main concern is to prevent the history from becoming too large.

Solutions to the problem are generally based on the use of occasional positive acknowledgements by members. These positive acknowledgements describe the highest message identifier seen from each member of the group. They are generally piggy-backed on other messages.

Totally ordered atomic multicast □ Totally ordered and atomic multicast are generally combined in a single protocol. This can be achieved by assigning unique totally sequenced message identifiers to all messages. A message is regarded as **stable at a member** [Schneider 1990] if no further message with a lower message identifier is expected to arrive. Members pass on to their application only the stable messages, taking the one with the lowest message identifier first.

It would be simple to design an ordered multicast protocol if the originators could assign message identifiers with a common global ordering. We will discuss the protocol under this assumption. The members save all incoming messages in a queue for delivery to the application processes for which they are intended. Messages in the queue can be delivered immediately unless there is a gap in the message identifiers, in which case messages after the gap cannot be delivered until the ones in the gap have arrived. This ensures that all multicast messages are delivered at all members in the same order.

The problem here is to generate the next message identifier in a sequence for attaching to a message. We require that the originator of any ordered multicast should be able to take the message identifier from a shared sequence of identifiers available to the members of the group. There are several approaches to the provision of a shared sequence of identifiers.

1. Use timestamps obtained from logical or physical clocks. See Chapter 10.

2. Use a **sequencer** – a process to which all messages are sent before being multicast. The sequencer attaches an identifier to each message and then multicasts it. See the Kaashoek protocol in Chapter 18.

3. Use a protocol amongst the members to generate the identifiers. See the ABCAST protocol in Chapter 11.

The latter two approaches are preferable to the first because they integrate the generation of the sequence of identifiers with the transmission of multicast messages.

The implementation and use of ordered atomic multicasts, including both total ordering and causal ordering, is a topic of much current research. It is discussed further in Chapter 11.

Application of group communication: an example

We will use an example application to illustrate the use of replicated data in users' workstations:

Simple dealing room system □ We consider a simple dealing room system whose task is to allow dealers using workstations to see the latest information about the market prices of the stocks they deal in. The market prices for a single named stock are represented as a record with several fields. The information arrives in the dealing room from several different external sources in the form of records or updates to fields of records and is collected by processes we call information providers. Dealers are typically interested only in their specialist stocks. A dealing room system could be modelled by the use of processes with two different tasks:

- An information provider process continuously receives new trading information from a single external source and forwards each record or field to all dealers who have registered interest in the corresponding stock. There will be a separate information provider process for each external source.

Figure 4.9   Dealing room system.

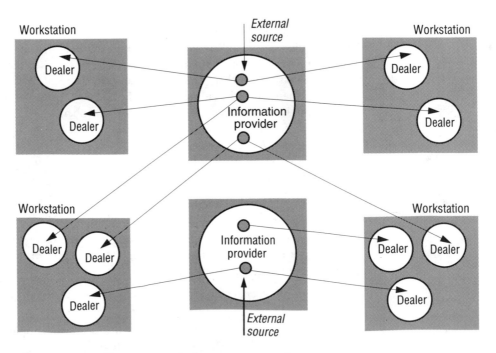

The origin of a multicast message is shown as a grey circle.

- A dealer process is created when a user requests the display of a named stock. The dealer process registers the interest with the relevant information provider. It then receives all the information sent to it and displays it to the user. There will be a separate dealer process for each of the stocks required by a particular user.

The communication between these processes is shown in Figure 4.9. An information provider process must send each record or field update to each of the dealer processes that have registered interest in a stock. To be fair to the dealers interested in a particular stock, atomic and ordered multicast is required to ensure that all dealer processes for the same stock receive the same information and in the same sequence.

If we assume that the external sources deal with different stocks, then we require only that the messages from an information provider arrive at all the dealers in the order in which they were sent. This is FIFO ordering. But note that with FIFO ordering, the information about a pair of different stocks coming from different external sources will not necessarily arrive in the same order at all of the dealers' workstations.

If however, information about the same stock could arrive from either of the external sources, then the dealer processes must register interest with both the information providers. In this case, a totally-ordered multicast would be required.

4.5   Case study: interprocess communication in UNIX

UNIX pre-dates the development of distributed systems, as it was originally developed in the period 1969–74 [Ritchie and Thompson 1974]. Early versions of UNIX provided facilities for communication between concurrent processes within a single computer – user-level programs running concurrently in separate address spaces. But originally the only form of communication between processes was the *pipe* – an unnamed, unidirectional stream of bytes – and there was no support for networked communication. Pipes were designed as a method for linking chains of simple data-transforming programs (called filters) to make pipelines to perform more complex data transformations. The processes in a pipeline are created by a single parent process which also creates all of the pipes needed to connect them – no separate binding operation is required, so pipes are not globally named. The communication between the filter processes that make up a pipeline is a classic producer-consumer situation, so pipes are defined as input/output streams without any explicit synchronization between the sending and receiving process. Even if pipes are extended to operate across a network they are not suitable for request-reply communication and other distributed uses because delayed binding of processes to pipes is not possible.

BSD 4.x UNIX

The IPC primitives in BSD 4.x versions of UNIX are provided as system calls which are implemented as a layer over the Internet TCP and UDP protocols. Message destinations are specified as **socket addresses** – a socket address is a communication identifier that consists of a local port number and an Internet address. Communication identifiers are introduced in the subsection on naming in Section 2.2. Internet addresses and port numbers are introduced in Chapter 3.

The interprocess communication operations are based on **socket** pairs, one belonging to each of a pair of communicating processes [Leffler *et al.* 1989]. Interprocess communication consists of an exchange of some information by transmitting it in a message between a socket in one process and a socket in another process. Messages are queued at the sending socket until the networking protocol has transmitted them, and until an acknowledgement arrives, if the protocol requires one. When messages arrive, they are queued at the receiving socket until the receiving process makes an appropriate system call to receive them.

Any process can create a socket for use in communication with another process. This is done by invoking the *socket* system call, whose arguments specify the communication domain (normally the Internet), the type (datagram or stream) and sometimes a particular protocol. The protocol (for example, TCP/IP or UDP/IP) is usually selected by the system according to whether the communication is datagram or stream.

The socket call returns a descriptor by which the socket may be referenced in subsequent system calls. The socket lasts until it is *closed* or until every process with the descriptor exits. A pair of sockets may be used for communication in both or either direction between processes in the same or different computers.

Before a pair of processes can communicate, the recipient must **bind** its socket descriptor to a socket address. The sender must also bind its socket descriptor to a socket address if it requires a reply. The bind system call is used for this purpose; its arguments are a socket descriptor and a reference to a structure containing the socket address to which the socket is to be bound. Once a socket has been bound, its address cannot be changed.

It might seem more reasonable to have one system call for both socket creation and binding a name to a socket. The advantage of having two separate calls is that sockets can be useful without names.

Socket addresses are public in the sense that they can be used by any process. After a remote process has bound its socket to a socket address, the socket may be addressed indirectly by another process referring to the appropriate socket address. Any process, for example a server that plans to receive messages via its socket, must first bind that socket to a socket address and make the socket address known to potential clients.

Datagram communication

In order to send datagrams, a socket pair is identified each time a communication is made. This is achieved by the sending process using its local socket descriptor and the socket address of the receiving socket each time it sends a message.

This is illustrated in Figure 4.10 in which the details of the arguments are simplified.

- Both processes use the *socket* call to create a socket and get a descriptor for it. The first argument of *socket* specifies the communication domain as the Internet domain and the second argument indicates that datagram communication is required. The last argument to the socket call may be used to specify a particular protocol, but setting it to zero causes the system to select a suitable protocol.

Figure 4.10   Sockets used for datagrams

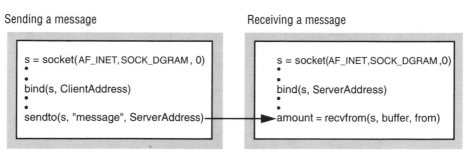

Sending a message

```
s = socket(AF_INET,SOCK_DGRAM, 0)
•
•
bind(s, ClientAddress)
•
•
sendto(s, "message", ServerAddress)
```

Receiving a message

```
s = socket(AF_INET,SOCK_DGRAM,0)
•
•
bind(s, ServerAddress)
•
•
amount = recvfrom(s, buffer, from)
```

ServerAddress and *ClientAddress* are sockets consisting of internet address and port number

- Both processes then use the *bind* call to bind their sockets to socket addresses. The sending process binds its socket to a socket address referring to any available local port number. The receiving process binds its socket to a socket address which must be made known to the sender.

- The sending process uses the *sendto* call with arguments specifying the socket through which the message is to be sent, (a reference to a structure containing) the socket address of the destination and the message itself. The *sendto* call hands the message to the underlying UDP and IP protocols and returns the actual number of characters sent. As we have requested datagram service, the message is transmitted to its destination without an acknowledgement. If the message is too long to be sent, there is an error return (and the message is not transmitted).

- The receiving process uses the *recvfrom* call with arguments specifying the local socket on which to receive a message and memory locations in which to store the message and (a reference to a structure containing) the socket address of the sending socket. The *recvfrom* call collects the first message in the queue at the socket, or if the queue is empty it will wait until a message arrives.

Communication occurs only when a *sendto* in one process and a *recvfrom* in another use the same pair of sockets. In client-server communication, there is no need for servers to have prior knowledge of clients' socket addresses because the *recvfrom* operation supplies the sender's address with each message it delivers.

Broadcast datagrams □   When the underlying network – for example, an Ethernet – supports the transmission of broadcast messages, processes can send them. A broadcast message will be received by any process that has executed a *recvfrom* on the appropriate local port. To address a broadcast message, the sender sets the host part of the destination socket address to the value for an Internet broadcast.

Stream communication

In order to use the stream protocol, two processes must first establish a connection between their pair of sockets. The arrangement is asymmetric because one of the sockets

Figure 4.11   Sockets used for streams.

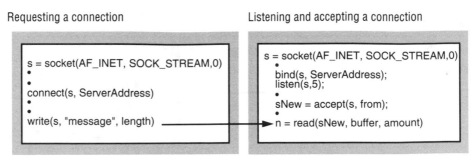

ServerAddress is a socket consisting of Internet address and port number

will be listening for a request for a connection and the other will be asking for a connection. Once a pair of sockets has been connected, they may be used for transmitting data in both or either direction. That is, they behave like streams in that any available data is read immediately in the same order as it was written and there is no indication of boundaries of messages. However, there is a bounded queue at the receiving socket and the receiver blocks if the queue is empty, the sender blocks if it is full.

For communication between clients and servers, clients request connections and a listening server accepts them. When a connection is accepted, UNIX automatically creates a new socket and pairs it with the client's socket so that the server may continue listening for other clients' connection requests through the original socket. A connected pair of stream sockets can be used in subsequent stream communication until the connection is closed.

Stream communication is illustrated in Figure 4.11 in which the details of the arguments are simplified. The figure does not shows the server closing the socket on which it listens. Normally a server would first listen and accept a connection and then fork a new process to communicate with the client. Meanwhile it will continue to listen in the original process.

- The server or listening process first uses the *socket* operation to create a stream socket and the *bind* operation to bind its socket to a socket address. The second argument to the *socket* system call is given as SOCK_STREAM, to indicate that stream communication is required. If the third argument is left as zero, the TCP/IP protocol will be selected automatically. It uses the *listen* operation to listen on its socket for client requests for connections. The second argument to the *listen* system call specifies the maximum number of requests for connections that can be queued at this socket

- The server uses the *accept* system call to accept a connection requested by a client and obtain a new socket for communication with that client. The original socket may still be used to accept further connections with other clients.

- The client process uses the *socket* operation to create a stream socket and then uses the *connect* system call to request a connection via the socket address of the listening process. As the *connect* call automatically binds a socket name to the caller's socket, prior binding is unnecessary.

• After a connection has been established, client and server may then use the *write* and *read* operations on their respective sockets to send and receive sequences of bytes via the connection. The *write* operation is similar to the write operation for files. It specifies a message to be sent to a socket. It hands the message to the underlying TCP/IP protocol and returns the actual number of characters sent. The *read* operation receives some characters in its buffer and returns the number of characters received. The connection behaves like a stream – any available data is read immediately, in the same sequence as it was written by the corresponding write operations. There is no indication of message boundaries.

Stream applications – rlogin, rsh, rcp □   When BSD UNIX was extended to include sockets, remote versions of login, shell, copy and other utilities were provided as applications of streams. The remote login, remote shell and remote copy commands are named *rlogin*, *rsh* and *rcp* respectively. In all of these requests, the name of the remote computer is supplied as an argument. Any computer that can accept such remote requests acts as a server for each of these requests – by listening for clients' requests for connections on sockets bound to addresses containing reserved TCP/IP port numbers. Remote login allows a user to login on a remote computer. Rsh is not a remote shell, but simply executes a single command on a remote computer with the standard input and output connected via TCP/IP streams to local processes. The facility for connecting processes into pipelines is thereby extended to include remote processes. Remote copy allows files or even whole directories and their sub-trees of files to be copied from one computer to another, together with their access rights. For further details of the remote applications, see Santifaller [1991] which provides a wealth of practical details regarding UNIX network programming.

For further detail on the interprocess communication mechanisms in current UNIX systems, readers are referred to the book by Leffler *et al.* [1989] on the design of the 4.3BSD UNIX system.

4.6   Summary

Effective special-purpose protocols for distributed systems are based on a potentially unreliable message protocol that transmits a single message from an originating process to a destination process.

The required degree of reliability and the style of communication varies from one application to another. It is a good idea to build protocols to suit different classes of applications rather than to build a single ultra-reliable protocol for general use because the latter would perform poorly in the normal case, in which faults seldom occur.

There is a variety of different types of message destinations (for example, ports, processes or objects). But irrespective of the type used, location-independent destination addresses are particularly useful because they provide location transparency.

Acknowledgement messages, message identifiers and message retransmission may be used to build the degree of reliability required by a particular application.

Protocols for a local area network should be designed to perform well in the normal case in which messages arrive safely.

The use of a history reduces the need for acknowledgements in multicast protocols and avoids the need to re-execute procedures in the request-reply protocol, but it has an associated storage penalty. The manager of a history needs to know when messages are no longer needed, so that it may reclaim the space they occupy. To provide such knowledge, some degree of acknowledgement is required.

In the request-reply protocol, the reply message forms an acknowledgement for the request message, thus enabling the request message to reach the server reliably without any additional overhead. Another aspect of this protocol is the need to be able to retransmit server replies. In applications in which the operation in a call should be executed once only, a history may be used to hold reply messages in case they need to be retransmitted.

Multicast messages are used in communication between the members of a group of processes. An atomic multicast is received by all the members of a process group. A totally ordered multicast is an atomic multicast that is received in the same order by all the members. In multicast protocols, the use of a hardware multicast reduces the number of messages and the time taken by the originator to transmit the message.

EXERCISES

4.1   Compare sending a message with sending data over a stream.

page 100

4.2   One way of managing the conversion of data types is for computers always to convert data into a standard form before transmission. Explain why this may be inefficient, and describe an alternative. Which of the alternatives should be used?

page 101

4.3   When is it necessary to include type information in messages?

page 102

4.4   Suggest a method of marshalling (i) an array, (ii) a linked list, (iii) a tree.

page 103

4.5   What are the advantages of a non-blocking form of *Send*?

page 104

4.6   What are the advantages of a blocking form of *Send*?

page 104

4.7   If *Send* blocks, how can a sender nonetheless be made to execute asynchronously from the receiver?

page 104

4.8   Suggest two possible semantics for a non-blocking *Receive*. (Hint: *Receive* supplies a buffer to be filled with an arrived message.)

page 104

4.9   Explain why a process might need to have several ports.

page 106

4.10   How would you emulate ports, given a communication system that uses processes as destinations?

page 106

4.11   Is it conceivably useful for a port to have several receivers?

page 106

4.12   A server creates a port which it uses to receive requests from clients. Discuss the design issues concerning the relationship between the name of this port and the names used by clients. Compare this to a system in which processes or groups of processes or ports are used as message destinations.

page 106

4.13   What are the advantages of *DoOperation-GetRequest-SendReply* over *Send-Receive* for request-reply communication?

page 108

4.14   Describe a scenario in which a client receives a reply from an earlier call.

page 108

4.15   Might a client know that a request was not received because of: (i) a server *process* failure, rather than a communication failure? (ii) a communication failure rather than a server failure?

page 109

4.16   Discuss whether the following operations are idempotent:

•   Pressing a lift (elevator) request button;

•   Writing data to a file;

•   Appending data to a file.

Is a necessary condition for idempotence that the operation should not be associated with any state?

page 111

4.17   Explain the design choices that are relevant to minimizing the amount of reply data held in a server's history. Compare the storage requirements when the RR and RRA protocols are used.

page 110

4.18   A client receives a reply and immediately crashes. How long should servers retain unacknowledged reply data? Should servers repeatedly send the reply in an attempt to receive an acknowledgement?

page 110

4.19   Why might the number of messages exchanged in a protocol be more significant to performance than the total amount of data sent? Design a variant of the RRA protocol in which the acknowledgement is piggy-backed on (that is, transmitted in the same message as the next request) where appropriate, and otherwise sent as a separate message. (Hint: use an extra timer in the client.)

page 110

4.20   Discuss whether it might be useful to use TCP to transmit each of the request and reply in the RR protocol.

page 110

4.21   The OSF's Distributed Computing Environment allows for bidirectional pipes (that is, connected sockets) to be used between clients and servers, in addition to and between a request and a reply. Suggest a use for this.

pages 110, 121

4.22   Give a list of the main design issues and options for the design of group communication.

page 112

4.23   Give an example in which the ordering of multicasts sent by two clients is not important. Give an example in which it is important.

page 114

4.24   Devise a scenario in which multicasts sent by different clients are delivered in different orders at two group members. Explain the need for hold-back in a protocol to achieve total ordering.

pages 114, 116

4.25   Give an example to show the importance of multicast atomicity. Explain why a reliable multicast might fail to be atomic.

page 113

4.26   In the atomic multicast protocol outlined in the chapter, what should a group member do when it discovers that a message originator has failed? What should happen if several group members discover this?

page 117

4.27   In terms of group communication semantics, what is it to register an interest in a particular type of financial information?

page 118

4.28   Would totally ordered multicast be necessary in a dealing room system?

page 118

4.29   Define the semantics for and design a protocol for a group form of request-reply interaction. It need not be atomic or totally ordered.

pages 108, 112

5

REMOTE PROCEDURE CALLING

In this chapter we introduce remote procedure calling (RPC), describing the similarities and differences between RPC and conventional procedure calling and the effects that these have on its design and use.

The implementation of RPC requires an interface language processor, a communication handler and a binding service. We describe approaches to the design and implementation of each of these.

The case studies describe Sun RPC and ANSA testbench as illustrations of RPC systems.

We describe an extension of RPC to deal with asynchronous communication, which allows client and server to improve their combined performance by executing in parallel.

5.1 Introduction

A distributed program can be viewed as a set of software components running in a number of computers in a network. In the client-server pattern of communication (Chapter 2), users interact with application programs which may be clients of any of the services available in the network. The service programs may themselves be clients of other service programs. Each service provides a set of operations that may be invoked by clients. Communication between clients and servers is based on the request-reply communication protocol introduced in Chapter 4. Clients invoke service operations by sending request messages to the servers. Servers perform the requested operation and send a reply message back to the client. The client always waits for the reply message before continuing its execution, even when no result is expected from the operation, since there may be an error to report.

Remote procedure calling mechanisms integrate this arrangement with conventional procedural programming languages in a convenient manner, enabling clients to communicate with servers by calling procedures in a similar way to the conventional use of procedure calls in high-level languages. The remote procedure call is modelled on the local procedure call, but the called procedure is executed in a different process and usually a different computer from the caller.

In general, a service manages a set of resources (for example, data items) on behalf of its clients. Clients can access them only by calling the procedures supplied by the service. The servers providing a service wait for requests from clients and execute the requested procedures, possibly changing the values of the data items. A server's resources are shared, so a client is aware of the effects of other clients' operations.

At the RPC level a service may be viewed as a module with an interface that exports a set of procedures appropriate for operating on some data abstraction or resource. For example, a file service provides a set of procedures for operating on the file data abstraction. An authentication service provides procedures for validating users' names and passwords. The ability to combine a group of procedures and variables in a module and to export only selected procedure names was introduced in programming languages such as Modula-2 and Ada as a method for structuring programs. The procedures exported by a module are generally defined to provide a complete set of operations on a given type of resource.

From the perspective of client programs a service provides the same facilities as a software module – enabling clients to import its procedures. A server process that executes remote procedure calls has a lifetime that is distinct from that of its clients. Normally, a server process runs indefinitely and its operations may be invoked by many clients. This enables the resources that it manages to be shared between clients.

Features of remote procedure calls □ The aim of a remote procedure calling mechanism is to maintain as far as is possible the semantics of conventional procedure calls in an implementation environment that differs radically from that of conventional procedure calling.

We outline the main aspects of the semantics of RPC:

- The definition of a remote procedure specifies *input* and *output* parameters. Input parameters are passed to the server by sending the values of the arguments in the request message and copying them into variables that are passed as parameters to a procedure in the server's execution environment. Output parameters are returned to the client in the reply message and they are used to replace the values of the corresponding variables in the calling environment. When a parameter is used for both input and output, the value must be transmitted in both the request and the reply message.

- Input parameters provide a direct equivalent to parameters passed by value in conventional procedure calls. But to implement parameter passing by reference in languages such as Modula-2 (or the use of pointers to variables as arguments in languages such as C), further information is needed, indicating for each such parameter whether it is used for input, for output or for both input and output. The need to specify these alternatives is one of the reasons why an interface definition language is an essential component of any RPC system.

- A remote procedure is executed in a different execution environment from its caller and therefore cannot access variables in the calling environment, such as the global variables declared by the caller.

- It is meaningless for a process to pass addresses of memory locations or their equivalent in messages to other processes. Thus the arguments and results of remote procedures cannot include data structures that contain pointers to memory locations.

The last restriction is less serious than it might appear to be. Programmers generally use pointers either to refer to individual data items or to build dynamic data structures such as lists, graphs and trees. But if a server is viewed as a shared module that manages a collection of resources then the internal structure of such resources should be hidden from the client for reasons of program modularity. Instead of returning pointers, servers may return opaque references – an opaque reference is a reference to a resource that can be passed by the client as an argument in a subsequent remote procedure call to the same service, but cannot be interpreted in the client's environment.

There is generally no need to transmit complex data structures in their entirety between servers and clients. If the need does arise to transmit data structures containing pointers the structures must be 'flattened' before they can be transmitted in messages. The process that manages a particular data structure is responsible for flattening and unflattening it. Thus a tree-structured list might be flattened by converting it to a bracketed expression.

User package □ A service is accessed by means of calls to the remote procedures that it offers. In some RPC systems, calls to remote procedures are written in a special notation. Because of the differences between local and remote procedures and because a service should be defined at a level appropriate for the widest possible use, the RPC interface is not necessarily the most convenient for client programs.

For these reasons, and because there are some tasks, such as the location of a suitable server, that must be performed by the client, the use of services by application programs is often supported by a **user package**; this is a library of conventional procedures that can be used in application programs. Figure 5.1 shows the relationship between a client program, a user package and the software below the RPC interface (which is described in Section 5.3).

Figure 5.1   Levels in the client software.

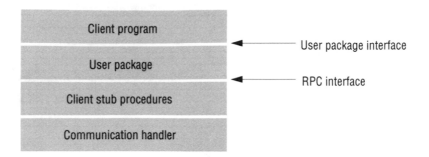

The user package is a library of conventional procedures that presents a convenient procedural interface for use by application programs. The actual remote procedure calls to servers are embedded within the user package. Because remote calls are concealed from application programs, the use of a user package has the additional advantage that the application programmer can be insulated from the need to work in an interface definition language.

It may sometimes improve the performance or reduce the complexity of the remote service to put some of the functionality of the service in the user package. For example, the implementation of a cache containing values of data items retrieved can improve performance. But the procedures in the user package must only perform activities that can be safely handled outside the server without compromising the reliability or security of the service as seen by other clients. As we shall see in Chapter 16, when considering the security of a service in a distributed system it is useful to distinguish between trusted and untrusted software. In this sense, software such as the user package that runs in workstations is untrusted, since it may be intentionally or inadvertently modified.

The two-level interface model that results from the use of a user package is analogous to the application programming interface to system calls in UNIX, where input/output is done through a standard input/output library that supplies a convenient and comprehensive range of input-output functions based on the more limited set of system calls that the UNIX kernel makes available.

5.2   Design issues

Classes of RPC system □   In a classic paper, Birrell and Nelson [1984] describe the RPC mechanism they built for the Cedar programming environment, using datagram communication over the Xerox Internet. They based their RPCs on the Mesa language [Mitchell *et al*. 1979] and aimed to make RPC as simple to use as ordinary procedure calls.

This work was preceded by the publication of Xerox Courier RPC [Xerox 1981], a standard intended to be used for building remote applications in internetworks.

Many RPC systems have been built since then. They fall into two classes:

- In the first class, the RPC mechanism is integrated with a particular programming language that includes a notation for defining interfaces.

- In the second class, a special-purpose interface definition language is used for describing the interfaces between clients and servers.

The first class includes Cedar, Argus and Arjuna [Shrivastava *et al*. 1989]. The language integration that it achieves has the advantage that the particular requirements of remote procedures can be dealt with by language constructs such as exceptions. The Argus language developed at MIT by Liskov [Liskov 1988] is designed for the construction of distributed programs and remote procedure calls are integrated into the language. The Argus language is based on the CLU language developed earlier at MIT to support data abstraction. Argus provides *guardians* – these are modules that may be used to provide services and they are intended to be accessed by remote procedure call. The procedures in a guardian are called *handlers* and a call to a handler is automatically treated as a remote call.

The second class includes Sun RPC, on which the Sun Network File System is based and ANSA Testbench, both of which are described in case studies later in this chapter. Other examples are the Matchmaker interface language [Jones and Rashid 1986] that can be used with C, Pascal and Lisp and later MIG – The Mach Interface Generator [Draves *et al*. 1989], both of which were developed for use in conjunction with the Mach operating system. The separate interface language approach has the advantage that it is not tied to a particular language environment, although in practice, almost all examples of this approach are used in a C programming environment.

Interface definition language □ An RPC interface definition specifies those characteristics of the procedures provided by a server that are visible to the server's clients. The characteristics that must be defined include the names of the procedures and the types of their parameters. Each parameter should also be defined as input, output or in some cases both, to enable the RPC system to identify which values should be marshalled into the request and reply messages.

An interface contains a list of procedure *signatures* – that is, their names, together with the types of their input and output arguments. Interface compilers can be designed to process interfaces for use with different languages enabling clients and servers written in different languages to communicate by using remote procedure calls. For an example of an interface definition see Figure 5.7. An interface specifies a service name that is used by clients and servers to refer to the service that is offered by the collection of procedures.

Exception handling □ Any remote procedure call may fail because it may not be able to contact a server, probably because the server has failed or is too busy to reply. Therefore remote procedure calls must be able to report error types such as time-outs that are due to distribution as well as those that relate to problems encountered in executing the procedure. As an example of the latter, a client of a file service might quote an invalid file identifier, or attempt to read beyond the end of a file. Because any RPC may fail, an RPC system requires an effective exception handling mechanism for reporting such failures to the caller. The same mechanism may be used to report errors discovered by procedures.

Some recent programming languages including ADA, CLU [Liskov *et al.* 1981] and Modula-3 [Nelson 1991, Harbison 1992] provide language constructs for exception handling in which the expected result of a procedure is either a normal result or an exception consisting of a name describing the exception and sometimes some results. The exception handling mechanism consists of two parts, the *raising of exceptions* and their *handling procedures*. When an error occurs in a procedure, an exception is raised and the appropriate handling procedure is automatically executed in the caller's environment. As this book does not include a full explanation of exception handling in programming languages, the reader is referred to Liskov and Guttag [1986] for further information.

A similar facility may be provided in an RPC system to deal with both failures of communication and errors reported in reply messages from servers. An exception will be raised in both cases, causing the exception handling procedure to be called. Exception handling is provided in both Argus and Cedar – the former is based on CLU's and the latter on Mesa's facilities for notifying exceptions. Exception handling can be provided as part of the interface language in language independent RPC systems.

The Xerox Courier RPC protocol defines an extension to conventional procedure semantics that enables an error report to be passed explicitly to the caller, instead of a result, as the response to the calling instruction. When a procedure is defined, input and output parameter types are specified and in addition an error report specification is given, containing the names used to identify the various types of error that may occur.

Many RPC systems are designed for use with existing programming languages that have no exception handling mechanisms. In the absence of an exception handling mechanism, RPC systems generally resort to the method used in UNIX and other conventional operating systems, in which the system functions deliver a well-known value to indicate failure and further information about the type of error is reported in a variable in the environment of the calling program. In the case of an RPC, a return value indicating an error is used both for errors due to failure to communicate with the server and errors reported in the reply message from the server. Further information about the type of error is stored in a global variable in the client program. This method has the disadvantage that it requires the caller to test every return value.

Delivery guarantees ☐   Request-reply protocols were discussed in Section 4.3 where we showed that *DoOperation* can be implemented in different ways to provide different delivery guarantees. The main choices are:

Retry request message: whether to retransmit the request message until either a reply is received or the server is assumed to have failed;

Duplicate filtering: when retransmissions are used, whether to filter out duplicates at the server;

Retransmission of replies: whether to keep a history of reply messages to enable lost replies to be retransmitted without re-executing the server operations.

Delivery guarantees			RPC call semantics
Retry request message	Duplicate filtering	Re-execute procedure or retransmit reply	
No	Not applicable	Not applicable	Maybe
Yes	No	Re-execute procedure	At-least-once
Yes	Yes	Retransmit reply	At-most-once

The combinations of these choices leads to a variety of possible semantics for the reliability of remote procedure calls as seen by the caller. The choices of interest are shown in the table above, with corresponding names for the call semantics that they produce.

The semantics are as follows:

Maybe call semantics: No fault tolerance measures. If the reply message has not been received after a time-out and there are no retries, it is uncertain whether the procedure has been executed. If the request message was lost or the server crashed, then the procedure will not have been executed. On the other hand, it may have been executed and the reply message lost. This is known as **maybe** call semantics, because clients cannot tell for sure whether remote procedures have been called or not. It is not generally acceptable.

At-least-once call semantics: Retransmission of request messages without filtering of duplicates. The caller is eventually either given a reply, or else is informed that the server is presumed to have failed. In cases when the request message is retransmitted, the server may receive and execute it more than once. Eventually, when the RPC is completed, the client will not know how many times it has been called. This is called **at-least-once** call semantics. If a server can be designed with idempotent operations in all of its remote procedures, then at-least-once call semantics may be acceptable.

At-most-once call semantics: Filtering of duplicates and retransmission of replies without re-executing operations. Some operations can have the wrong effect if they are performed more than once. For example, an operation to increase a bank balance by $10 should only be performed once; if it were to be repeated, the balance could grow and grow! To allow the use of such non-idempotent operations, RPCs should be designed to execute their operations exactly once. Birrell and Nelson guarantee in Cedar RPC that if the server does not crash and the client receives the result of a call, then the procedure has been executed exactly once. Otherwise, an exception is reported and the procedure will have been called either once or not at all. This is known as **at-most-once** call semantics and is the one usually chosen in RPC implementations.

Transparency □ Birrell and Nelson aimed to make remote procedure calls as much like local procedure calls as possible and there is no distinction in syntax between a local and a remote procedure call. Procedure definitions are used to define the names and parameter types of remote procedures and the Cedar RPC software automatically provides the necessary calls to marshalling and message passing procedures for the client. Although request messages are retransmitted after a timeout, this is transparent to the caller and the duration of remote calls is unlimited provided the server is still running – to make the semantics of remote procedure calls like local procedure calls.

RPCs are more vulnerable to failure than local calls, since they involve a network, another computer and another process. They consume much more time than local ones – the time taken to call a remote procedure is several orders of magnitude greater than for a local call. Therefore it can be argued that programs that make use of remote procedures must handle errors that cannot occur in local procedure calls. In Argus, calls to procedures in guardians can be distinguished from local calls. This is an example of an alternative philosophy that RPC syntax should not be transparent and the language should be extended to make remote operations explicit to the programmer.

The choice as to whether RPCs should be transparent is also available to the designers of interface languages. In the transparent case, the client calls remote procedures in the normal way for the language in use. In the non-transparent case, the client uses a special notation for calling remote procedures – with the advantage that this notation may provide the ability to express requirements for distributed programming, for example, to specify a call semantics or to handle exceptions. Sun RPC uses the former and the ANSA Testbench the latter approach.

Another motivation for distinguishing between remote and local calls is that they require different implementations. When calls are known to be local, they can be implemented as normal procedure calls. The designers of the Emerald system [Black *et al.* 1987] argue that although different implementations are required, they need not be visible to the programmer. Choosing the right mechanism requires that the programmer needs to know all future uses of an object.

In discussing the design of RPC in Argus, Liskov and Scheifler [1982] say that although the RPC system should hide low-level details of message passing from the user, the possibility of long delay or failure should not be hidden from the caller. The caller should be able to cope with failures according to the demands of the application, possibly by terminating an RPC, and in that case it should have no effect. If clients are allowed to abort RPCs, this can have implications for the design of the server; an aborted RPC should have no effect whatsoever. This implies that even if the server has partially executed a procedure it should be able to restore things to how they were before the procedure was called. These issues are discussed in Chapter 15.

5.3   Implementation

The software that supports remote procedure calling has three main tasks:

Figure 5.2   Stub procedures.

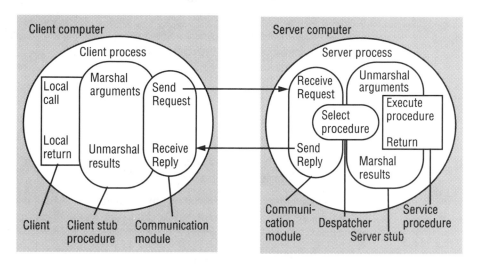

Interface processing: Integrating the RPC mechanism with client and server programs in conventional programming languages. This includes the marshalling and unmarshalling of arguments in the client and the server and the dispatching of request messages to the appropriate procedure in the server;

Communication handling: transmitting and receiving request and reply messages;

Binding: Locating an appropriate server for a particular service.

Interface processing □ An interface definition may be used as a basis on which to construct the extra software components of the client and server programs that enable remote procedure calling. These components are illustrated in Figure 5.2.

Both client and server assign the same unique procedure identifier to each procedure in an interface (they are usually numbered 0, 1, 2 ... in order) and the procedure identifier is included in request messages.

Building the client program: An RPC system will provide a means of building a 'complete client program' by providing a **stub procedure** to stand in for each remote procedure that is called by the client program. The purpose of a client stub procedure is to convert a local procedure call to a remote procedure call to the server. The types of the arguments and results in the client stub must conform to those expected by the remote procedure. This is achieved by the use of a common interface definition. The task of a client stub procedure is to marshal the arguments and to pack them up with the procedure identifier into a message, send the message to the server and then await the reply message, unmarshal it and return the results.

Building the server program: An RPC system will provide a **despatcher** and a set of server stub procedures. The despatcher uses the procedure identifier in the request message to select one of the server stub procedures and pass on the arguments. The task of a server stub procedure is to unmarshal the arguments, call the appropriate service procedure, and when it returns, to marshal the output arguments (or in the case of failure an error report), into a reply message.

An interface compiler processes interface definitions written in an interface definition language. Interface compilers are designed to produce components that can be combined with client and server programs, without making any changes to the existing compilers. An interface compiler normally performs the following tasks:

1. Generate a client stub procedure to correspond to each procedure signature in the interface. The stub procedures will be compiled and linked with the client program.

2. Generate a server stub procedure to correspond to each procedure signature in the interface. The despatcher and the server stub procedures will be compiled and linked with the server program.

3. Use the signatures of the procedures in the interface – which define the argument and result types – to generate appropriate marshalling and unmarshalling operations in each stub procedure.

4. Generate procedure headings for each procedure in the service from the interface definition. The programmer of the service supplies the bodies of these procedures.

The use of a common interface definition when generating the stub procedures for the client program and the headings for the procedures in the server programs ensures that the argument types and results used by clients conform to those defined in a server.

Communication handling □ The task of the communication handling module in both the client and the server programs is to deal with communication between them, generally by using a form of request-reply communication as described in Section 4.3. The communication handling module is provided in forms suitable for linking with client and server programs.

Binding

An interface definition specifies a textual service name for use by clients and servers to refer to a service. However, client request messages must be addressed to a server port.

Binding means specifying a mapping from a name to a particular object, usually identified by a communication identifier. The binding of a service name to the communication identifier specifying the server port (whether it be a port identifier, a port group identifier, or any other form of destination) – is evaluated each time a client program is run. The form of the communication identifier depends on the environment. For example, in a UNIX environment, it will be a socket address containing the internet address of a computer and a port number. In Mach, Chorus and Amoeba it will be a location independent port identifier.

Binding is essential when server port identifiers include host addresses, because it avoids the need to compile server port identifiers into client programs. If a client program does include the host address of a server, it will need to be altered and recompiled whenever the server is relocated.

In a distributed system, a **binder** is a separate service that maintains a table containing mappings from service names to server ports. A binder is an example of a

Figure 5.3   Binder Interface.

PROCEDURE Register (serviceName:String; serverPort:Port; version:integer)
   causes the binder to record the service name and server port of a service in its table, together with a version number.

PROCEDURE Withdraw (serviceName:String; serverPort:Port; version:integer)
   causes the binder to remove the service from its table.

PROCEDURE LookUp (serviceName:String; version:integer): Port
   the binder looks up the named service and returns its address(or set of addresses) if the version number agrees with the one stored in its table.

Name Service. The Domain Name service (introduced in Chapter 3) which maps domain names into Internet addresses is another example. Chapter 9 gives a general approach to the design and implementation of Name Services.

A binder is intended to be used by servers to make their port identifiers known to potential clients. A typical binder would include the procedures shown in Figure 5.3. *Register* and *Withdraw* are intended to be used by servers. *LookUp* is intended to be used by clients to obtain the addresses of servers.

When a server process starts executing, it sends a message to the binder requesting it to *Register* its service name and server port. If a server process terminates, it should send a message to the binder requesting it to *Withdraw* its entry from the mappings.

When a client process starts, it sends a message to the binder requesting it to *LookUp* the identifier of the server port of a named service. The client program sends all its request messages to this server port until the server fails to reply, at which point the client may contact the binder and attempt to get a new binding.

The purpose of the version number is to enable client and server programs to check that they are using the same version of the software. If the program of a server is altered in such a way that clients will no longer be able to communicate with it, for example, requiring an extra argument to a procedure, then it must update its version number and client programs will have to be brought up to date.

If location-independent port identifiers are in use, then servers may be relocated without informing the binder and clients are unaffected by the move. However, if port identifiers include host addresses, the binder must be informed whenever a server is relocated and clients find out when their request messages to the old location are ignored, in which case they will contact the binder and be given the identifier of the new server port.

A binder is the single service on which all other services depend. For this reason, binders are generally made fault-tolerant, for example by saving the tables in a file each time they are updated. After a failure, a binder can recover its state from the file. However, any distributed system that depends entirely on a single binder is not scalable – therefore the tables in a binding service would normally be partitioned and perhaps replicated among a set of binder servers.

Some services are represented by multiple servers each of which runs on a different computer. We refer to these servers as *instances* of a service. A binder must be able to register several instances of the same service. If the binder provides only a simple string mapping function, then the instances of a service must append suffices to the service name in order to differentiate between them. Exercise 5.15 discusses this issue.

In server programs the name of the interface is exported and in client programs the interface is imported. *Exporting* consists of registering the interface name and the port identifier of the server with a binder. *Importing* consists of asking a binder to look up the interface name and return the server port identifier.

Locating the binder □ All clients and servers need to use a binder, to import and export services. Therefore they need to know the port identifier of a binder before they can do anything useful. The following alternative approaches are commonly used in systems such as UNIX in which a port identifier includes a host address:

- Always run the binder on a computer with a well known host address and compile this host address into all client programs. All client and server programs must be recompiled if the binder ever needs to be relocated.

- Make the client and server operating systems responsible for supplying the current host address of the binder at run time, for example in UNIX it may be supplied via an environment variable. Users running client and server programs need to be informed whenever the binder is relocated. This method allows occasional relocation of the binder.

- When a client or server program starts executing, it uses a broadcast message to locate the binder. For example, in UNIX, the broadcast message will specify the port number of the binder and a binder receiving such a request will reply with its current host address. The binder can be run on any computer and can easily be relocated.

5.4   Case studies: Sun and ANSA

Several RPC systems have been developed for use in networked UNIX systems. In this section we discuss two examples: Sun RPC and ANSA Testbench.

Sun RPC

The best known of the UNIX RPC systems is Sun RPC [Sun 1990] which was originally designed for client-server communication in the Sun NFS network file system. Sun RPC is supplied as a part of the various Sun UNIX operating systems and is also available with other NFS installations. Implementers have the choice of using remote procedure calls over either UDP/IP or TCP/IP.

The Sun RPC system provides an interface language called XDR and an interface compiler called *rpcgen*.

Interface definition language □ The Sun XDR language which was originally designed for specifying external data representations has been extended to become an interface definition language. It may be used to specify a Sun RPC interface which contains a program number and a version number rather than an interface name, together

Figure 5.4   Files interface in Sun XDR.

```
/*
 * FileReadWrite service interface definition in file FileReadWrite.x
 */
const MAX = 1000;
typedef int FileIdentifier;
typedef int FilePointer;
typedef int Length;
struct Data {
      int length;
      char buffer[MAX];
};
struct writeargs {
      FileIdentifier f;
      FilePointer position;
      Data data;
};
struct readargs {
      FileIdentifier f;
      FilePointer position;
      Length length;
};

program FILEREADWRITE {
 version VERSION {
      void WRITE(writeargs)=1;
      Data READ(readargs)=2;
      }=2;
 } = 9999;
```

with procedure definitions and supporting type definitions. A procedure definition specifies a procedure signature and a procedure number. As only a single input parameter is allowed, procedures requiring multiple parameters must include them as components of a single structure. The output parameters of a procedure are returned via a single result. The procedure signature consists of the result type, the name of the procedure and the type of the input parameter. The type of both the result and the input parameter may specify either a single value or a structure containing several values.

For example, see the XDR definition in Figure 5.4 of an interface with a pair of procedures for writing and reading files. The program number is 9999 and the version number is 2. The *READ* procedure takes as input parameter a structure with three components specifying: a file identifier, a position in the file and the number of bytes required. Its result is a structure containing the number of bytes returned and the file data. The *WRITE* procedure has no result. The *WRITE* and *READ* procedures are given numbers 1 and 2. The number zero is reserved for a null procedure that is generated automatically and is intended to be used to test whether a server is available.

The interface definition language provides a notation for defining constants, typedefs, structures, enumerated types, unions and programs. Typedefs, structures and enumerated types have the same syntax as in C. The interface compiler *rpcgen* can be used to generate the following from an interface definition:

- client stub procedures;

- server *main* procedure, despatcher and server stub procedures. The despatcher can pass authentication information (user id and group id) to the server procedures;

- XDR marshalling and unmarshalling procedures for use by the despatcher and client and server stub procedures;

- a header file, for example *"FileReadWrite.h"*, containing definitions of common constants and types that may be used in client and server programs. The service procedure signatures are given as C function prototypes. The developer of the service provides implementations of these procedures that conform to the prototypes.

Client program □ A client program imports the appropriate service interface and calls the remote procedures, for example, *READ* and *WRITE*. It is supported by the client stub procedures and the marshalling and unmarshalling procedures generated by the interface compiler *rpcgen*.

Sun RPC does not have a network-wide binding service. Instead it provides a local binding service called the *port mapper* which runs on every computer. Each instance of a port mapper records the port in use by each service running locally. Therefore to import an interface, the client must specify the hostname of the server as well as the program number and version number. In Figure 5.5, the procedure *clnt_create* is used for this purpose. It returns a client 'handle' to use when remote procedures are called. The client handle contains the necessary information for communicating with the server port, such as the socket descriptor and socket address.

---

clnt_create → *clientHandle*
>   Gets a client handle. The arguments give the hostname of the server and the program and version numbers specified in the interface definition. The last argument specifies whether UDP or TCP should be used.

Several variants of *clnt_create* are available. These provide more control for the programmer such as specifying the service port. When UDP is used the time-out value between retries may be specified. When TCP is used the send and receive buffer sizes may be specified.

The remote server procedures are called in normal C language procedure call notation. The remote calls are made indirectly via calls to the client stub procedures. Remote procedures are called in the same way as local procedures with two arguments. The input arguments must be packed into a single structure which is passed as the first argument, and the 'handle' returned by *clnt_create* is passed as the second argument.

The return value may be a structure containing several results. The client stub procedure name is the name given in the interface definition, converted to lower case and with an underscore and the version number appended, for example, READ is converted to *read_2*.

Client stubs ☐ Each client stub procedure calls the procedure *clnt_call* which has a similar function to *DoOperation* in Chapter 4.

---

clnt_call
    Makes an RPC call to a server. The arguments specify: a client handle, a procedure identifier, the input arguments and a procedure to marshal them, a reference to a variable in which to store the output arguments, a procedure to unmarshal them and the total time in seconds to wait for a reply after several retries.

Clnt_call uses at-least-once call semantics. The time-out between retries has a default value which can be set when the 'handle' is obtained. The number of retries is the total time to wait divided by the time-out between retries. After it sends a request message, it

Figure 5.5   C program for client in Sun RPC.

```
/* File : C.c - Simple client of the FileReadWrite service. */

#include <stdio.h>
#include <rpc/rpc.h>
#include "FileReadWrite .h"

main(int argc, char ** argv)
{
      CLIENT *clientHandle;
      char *serverName = "coffee";
      readargs a;
      Data *data;

      clientHandle= clnt_create(serverName, FILEREADWRITE,
            VERSION, "udp");    /* creates socket and a client handle*/
      if (clientHandle==NULL){
            clnt_pcreateerror(serverName); /* unable to contact server */
            exit(1);
      }
      a.f = 10;
      a.position = 100;
      a.length = 1000;
      data = read_2(&a, clientHandle);/* call to remote read procedure */
      •••
      clnt_destroy(clientHandle);          /* closes socket */
```

Figure 5.6   C program for server procedures in Sun RPC.

```
/* File S.c - server procedures for the FileReadWrite service */
#include <stdio.h>
#include <rpc/rpc.h>
#include" FileReadWrite.h"

void * write_2(writeargs *a)
{
/* do the writing to the file */
}

Data * read_2(readargs * a)
{
        static Data result;     /* must be static */
        result.buffer = ...     /* do the reading from the file */
        result.length = ...     /* amount read from the file */
        return &result;
}
```

waits for a time-out period and if there is no reply, tries again several times. Eventually if it gets no answer, it returns an error value. If an RPC is successful it returns zero. The input arguments and the procedure to marshal them are each given in a single argument to *clnt_call*. If there are several input arguments, they must be grouped together into a structure and the marshalling procedure must be designed to flatten the entire structure. If several results are returned by the server, they will be unmarshalled and stored in a single structure. When Sun RPC is used with UDP, the length of request and reply messages is restricted to 8 kilobytes in length.

Server program □ The implementor uses the C function prototypes in the header file created by *rpcgen* as a basis for the implementation of the service as shown in Figure 5.6. The server procedure names are the names given in the interface definition converted to lower case and with an underscore and the version number appended. The argument of each server procedure is a pointer to a single argument or to a structure containing all the arguments. Similarly the value returned is a pointer to a single result or to a structure that contains the results. The latter must be declared as *static*.

The server program consists of the server procedures, supported by the *main*, the despatcher and the marshalling procedures, all of which are output by *rpcgen*. The *main* procedure of a server program creates a socket for receiving client request messages and then exports the service interface by informing the local port mapper of the program number, version number and the port identifier of the server.

When a server receives an RPC request message, the despatcher checks the program and version numbers, unmarshals the arguments and then calls the server procedure corresponding to the procedure number specified in the RPC request message. When the server procedure returns the results, it marshals them and transmits the reply message to the client.

Binding □ We have already noted that Sun RPC operates without a network-wide binding service. Therefore clients must specify the hostname of the server when they import a service interface. The port mapper enables clients to locate the port number part of the socket address used by a particular server. This is a local binding service – it runs at a well-known port number on every host and is used to record the mapping from program number and version number to port number of the services running on that host. When a server starts up it registers its program number, version number and port number with the local port mapper. When a client starts up, it finds out the server's port by making a remote request to the port mapper at the server's host, specifying the program number and version number. This means that servers need not run at well-known ports.

When a service has multiple instances running on different computers, the instances may use different port numbers for receiving client requests. Recall that broadcast datagrams are sent to the same port number on every computer and can be received by processes via that port number. If a client needs to multicast a request to all the instances of a service that are using different port numbers, it cannot use a direct broadcast message for this purpose. The solution is that clients make multicast remote procedure calls by broadcasting them to all the port mappers, specifying the program and version number. Each port mapper forwards all such calls to the appropriate local service program, if there is one.

Marshalling □ Sun RPC can pass arbitrary data structures as arguments and results. They are converted to External Data Representation (XDR). The marshalling and unmarshalling procedures specified in *clnt_call* may be built-in procedures supplied in a library or user-defined procedures defined in terms of the built-in procedures. The library procedures marshal integers of all sizes, characters, strings, reals and enumerated types.

Lower-level facilities □ The RPC facilities described above supply a set of defaults which are adequate for most purposes. The lower-level facilities provide additional control for the programmer who needs it. The main lower-level facilities are the following:

- tools for testing the implementation and running of services, such as null RPC calls, to test whether a server is running, checks for invalid procedure identifiers and pseudo RPC calls allowing client and server to be tested within a single process;

- management of dynamic memory allocation in marshalling procedures (which is not provided by the built-in XDR procedures);

- broadcast RPC. A client program may make an RPC to all instances of a service. This call is directed to the port mapper at all computers in the local network which passes it on to the local service registered with the given program name. The client picks up any replies one by one;

- batching of client calls that require no reply. The RPC calls can be buffered and then sent in a pipeline to the server over TCP/IP;

- call-back by the server to a client. This allows the client to become a server temporarily and to pass in an RPC call the information about its service;

- authentication: Sun RPC includes a mechanism allowing clients to pass authentication parameters that can be checked by the server. The default is that this mechanism does not operate. The client program may select a UNIX or a DES style of authentication. In the UNIX style, the *uid* and *gid* of the user running the client program are passed in every request message. The authentication information is made available to the server procedures via a second argument. The server program is responsible for enforcing access control by deciding whether to execute each procedure call according to the authentication information. Chapter 16 describes DES (Data Encryption Standard). DES authentication is secure in comparison with UNIX authentication.

ANSA Testbench

The ANSA Testbench includes an RPC toolkit. It is based on the ANSA distributed system architecture [ANSA 1989] developed by Architecture Project Management Ltd., Cambridge, England and runs with brands of UNIX that support sockets. It includes an interface language and its compiler, a binder (called a Trader) and a communication handling module in the form of a library of C procedures to be used in client and server programs.

The ANSA RPC toolkit is built with C as the base language, which makes it possible to re-use many existing applications in a distributed environment. But the C language provides no facilities to cope with the different error modes in distributed programs, for example by handling exceptions. ANSA therefore uses a non-transparent approach in which the deficiency of C is remedied by using a separate notation called PREPC (statements in PREPC are *Pre*-processed to produce C – hence the name) to express calls to remote procedures including the handling of exceptions. Client and server programs are written in C with embedded PREPC statements. The client and server programs are pre-processed to convert PREPC statements to C.

Interface definition language ☐ The ANSA interface definition language is called IDL (Interface Definition Language) and includes facilities to define types and procedure signatures. IDL is a modified version of the Courier Language [Xerox 1981].

Interface definitions may include type definitions for the parameters or results of the procedures defined in the interface. The interface compiler translates type definitions to *typedef*s in the C programs generated. This enables the type names in the interface to be used in both the server and the client programs.

An interface includes a signature for each of its procedures. A signature specifies the name of the procedure, a list of the names and types of its *input* arguments and a list of the names and types of its results.

The interface language allows basic data types together with the three special types *InterfaceRef*, *ObjectId* and *InterfaceId* which are introduced for use in a distributed environment. It also includes some constructors to enable user defined types to be built from the basic types. The user defined types include enumerated types, arrays, sequences and records.

Figure 5.7   Files interface in ANSA IDL.

```
FileReadWrite : INTERFACE =
BEGIN
      FileIdentifier, FilePointer, Length : TYPE = CARDINAL;
      Data: TYPE = SEQUENCE OF CHAR;

      Write: ANNOUNCEMENT OPERATION [
          f: FileIdentifier; position: FilePointer; data: Data
          ] RETURNS[ ];

      Read : OPERATION [
          f: FileIdentifier ; position :FilePointer ; length: Length
          ] RETURNS [ Data ];
END.
```

The type *InterfaceRef* or interface reference is used to refer to instances of interfaces. Client calls to remote procedures specify an interface reference and a procedure name. Clients and servers may pass interface references as arguments and results of calls and any program that has a reference to an interface can call the procedures in that interface. A server normally makes its interface reference available to potential clients by registering its service name and interface reference with the Trader.

Figure 5.7 shows the ANSA IDL definition for the operations of a server whose interface is named *FileReadWrite*. This includes an example of the declaration of an *announcement* operation for *Write*. The keyword *ANNOUNCEMENT* indicates that an operation is an asynchronous call in which the client does not require either results or confirmation from the server.

The interface compiler generates the following from an interface definition:

- client stub procedures for each procedure defined in the interface;

- server despatcher and stub procedures;

- marshalling and unmarshalling procedures;

- skeletons for server procedures which have the correct parameter types. The developer of the service provides the implementations of these procedures.

PREPC notation □ Remote procedure calls are denoted in PREPC. Statements in the PREPC notation may be recognized by the *!* at the start of the line. The syntax for an RPC in PREPC is:

    !   {results} <- Ref$op(arguments)

where *results* and *arguments* are comma separated lists. *Ref* is an interface reference to a service that can execute the remote procedure. For example, the following calls the remote procedure *Read* in a service via an interface reference *aFileServerRef*:

Figure 5.8   Explanation of PREPC statements

!	indicates a statement in PREPC
!USE	import an interface for example, *Trader*
!DECLARE	declare whether interface reference is client or server
$	*I$P* denotes procedure *P* in interface *I*
<-	assignment

> *!*   *{data} <- aFileServerRef$Read(f, position, length)*

The table in Figure 5.8 summarizes the PREPC statements used in our example programs:

Any client or server program may use the name *traderRef* as an interface reference to the Trader. The *Import* and *Export* operations are invoked like any other operation in a service and are translated to Trader calls such as *Register* and *LookUp*. In the case of *Export*, a reference to the new interface and its name are passed to the Trader by the *Register* procedure.

Client program □ A client program is illustrated in Figure 5.9. It starts by importing a service interface, by making an RPC to the Trader as follows:

> *!*   *{aFileServerRef } <– traderRef$Import ("FileReadWrite ", "/", "")*

The Trader looks up the service *FileReadWrite* and returns an interface reference.

The client program has a *body* instead of a *main* and includes calls to the remote procedures of a service, for example calls to the remote procedures *Read* and *Write*. The client program is supported by the client stub and marshalling procedures generated by

Figure 5.9   C program for client in ANSA testbench.

```
!    USE    FileReadWrite
!    DECLARE {aFileServerRef} : FileReadWrite CLIENT
void body (int argc, char **argv)
{
        InterfaceRef aFileServerRef;
        f: fileIdentifier ;
        position: filePointer ;
        length: CARDINAL;
        Data data;

!    {aFileServerRef } <- traderRef$Import ("FileReadWrite ", "/", "")
!    {data} <- aFileServerRef$Read(f, position, length)
    ...
```

Figure 5.10   Outline of C program for server in ANSA testbench.

```
!     USE     Trader
!     DECLARE { myRef } : FileReadWrite SERVER

void body (argc, argv, envp)
      int argc;
      char *argv[];
      char **envp;
{
      ansa_InterfaceRef myRef;
!     {myRef} <- traderRef$Export ("FileReadWrite ", "/ansa/testservices", "", 5)
      printf("FileReadWrite server started\n");
}

int FileReadWrite_Write (ansa_InterfaceAttr *_attr,FileIdentifier f,
      FilePointer position, Data data)
{
      ...   procedure body to perform file writing ...

}

int FileReadWrite_Read (ansa_InterfaceAttr *_attr, FileIdentifier f,
      FilePointer position, Length length, Data *data)
{
      ...   procedure body to perform file reading into data ...

}
```

the interface compiler. The *body* procedure is used instead of a *main* so that the RPC system can provide its own main and pass on information via the body provided.

Server program □ Server programs also include some statements written in PREPC. In particular, a server uses a RPC denoted in PREPC when it exports its interface to the Trader. The programmer of a service provides a *body* procedure and a definition of each procedure in the interface definition by using the skeleton procedures which were generated by the interface compiler.

For example, see the outline of the server program *FileReadWrite* in Figure 5.10 in which the *body* procedure exports its interface to the Trader. As well as specifying the name of the interface, the *Export* procedure can specify a context in the Trader database, the desired attributes of the service and the number of requests that may be queued at the service (five in our example). The server program also includes one C procedure for each of the procedures in the *FileReadWrite* interface. The names of the server procedures consist of the interface name followed by an underline and the name of the corresponding procedure in the interface definition. For example, the service procedures corresponding to *Write* and *Read* in Figure 5.7 are *FileReadWrite_Write* and *FileReadWrite_Read* as in Figure 5.10. The first attribute pointer parameter of each procedure (*_attr*) is not relevant to our simple server example. (Some services have several instances of the same interface and this parameter can be used to access information belonging to the particular one in use.) The rest of the parameters consist of one value parameter for each argument in the argument list in the signature, followed by one pointer parameter for each result in the results list in the signature. Each pointer parameter will be bound to the address of a variable that can receive the result. For example, the *FileReadWrite_Read* procedure has one result whose type is declared as *Data **.

Each server procedure uses the values in the arguments corresponding to the argument list and puts its results (if any) in the pointer arguments corresponding to the results list. If the execution succeeds, the procedure should return *SuccessfulInvocation*. If it fails, the procedure may return *UnsuccessfulInvocation*, in which case the results (if any) will not be sent back to the client – the client will instead be given a special status value *abnormalReturn*.

Binding ☐ The binding functions that are necessary for servers to register their services and for clients to discover the location of services are supplied in ANSA by the Trading Service.

The trading service is based on one or more servers known as traders, each of which contains a database of information about some of the services that are currently on offer. The information in a trader database contains the names and interface references of exported services. The database has a hierarchic structure within which a context may be described by the use of a pathname. Entries may also have attributes (or properties) associated with them. Chapter 9 explores the concept of an attribute based name service.

Whenever a client wants to use a service, it imports an interface, giving the name of the service and its context. The client may also specify the desired attributes (for example, *cost less than 25, name is 'Jones'*) as an additional criterion for selecting the most suitable offer of service.

Whenever a server exports the name and interface reference of its interface, an entry is added to a trader database. The server supplies the name of the service and the context (for example, a pathname). In addition the server may specify a list of names and values of attributes (such as numbers and strings) associated with this 'offer' to provide a service. In effect a trading service matches offers made by servers to provide a particular service with each client request for a service with particular attributes.

A trading service is based on a set of cooperating traders running in different computers. A context in one trader's database can be bound to a context name in another trader's database. This enables traders in separate organizations to form a federation by associating contexts in their databases to allow the clients in one organization to access services in another organization.

Clients' requests to look up services start in a local trader but can continue in another trader's database. Clients' requests requiring particular properties can be carried out in more than one trader.

A comparison of Sun RPC and ANSA

The potential user of an RPC system will be interested in issues including its interface definition language, the availability of concurrency in client and server, its binder, and the call semantics available. They may also be interested in transparency issues and the ability to handle exceptions. We compare Sun RPC and ANSA under those headings.

Interface definition language: ANSA interface definition language allows a completely general specification of procedure signatures whereas Sun RPC requires single arguments and single results. ANSA provides interface names, Sun RPC provides program and version numbers.

Concurrency in a service: The need for multi-threaded servers and synchronization operations is introduced in Chapter 6. ANSA provides a very simple means for requesting that a server has a fixed number of threads, allowing several client calls to be serviced concurrently. The concurrency of a server may also be increased dynamically. ANSA also provides a mechanism for synchronization between threads. Sun RPC does not include any integrated facility for threads in the server or client, although a separate threads package is available.

Binder: ANSA provides a scalable and fault-tolerant binding service. Sun RPC provides binding of ports to versions of services on each computer.

Call semantics: Sun RPC provides at-least-once call semantics. ANSA RPC provides at-most-once call semantics.

Limitations on size of arguments and results: In the UDP case, Sun RPC messages are restricted to 8 kilobytes in length. In ANSA RPC the length of request and reply messages is not restricted.

Transparency issues: Sun RPC has no location transparency because clients must specify the hostname of servers. Calls to remote procedures are written in C, but are not access-transparent because procedure names include version numbers and single arguments and 'handles' are required. ANSA provides location transparency (by means of the Trader) but not access transparency because it requires remote procedure calls to be written in a special notation which allows for some exception handling.

Marshalling: Sun RPC allows user-defined marshalling procedures, enabling any value to be passed as argument or returned as a result. In ANSA marshalling is not accessible to the application programmer. Although a wide variety of data values can be marshalled, some values such as linked lists containing pointers cannot.

5.5   Asynchronous RPC

Distributed window systems such as X-11 [Scheifler and Gettys 1986; Davison *et al.* 1992] use an asynchronous form of RPC mechanism. The X-11 window system is programmed as a server, and application programs wishing to display items of text or graphics in windows on a display screen are its clients.

To generate or update the information displayed in a window, a client normally sends many requests to the server, each containing a relatively small amount of information, such as a string, a request for a change of font or even a single character.

Figure 5.11   Times for synchronous and asynchronous RPC

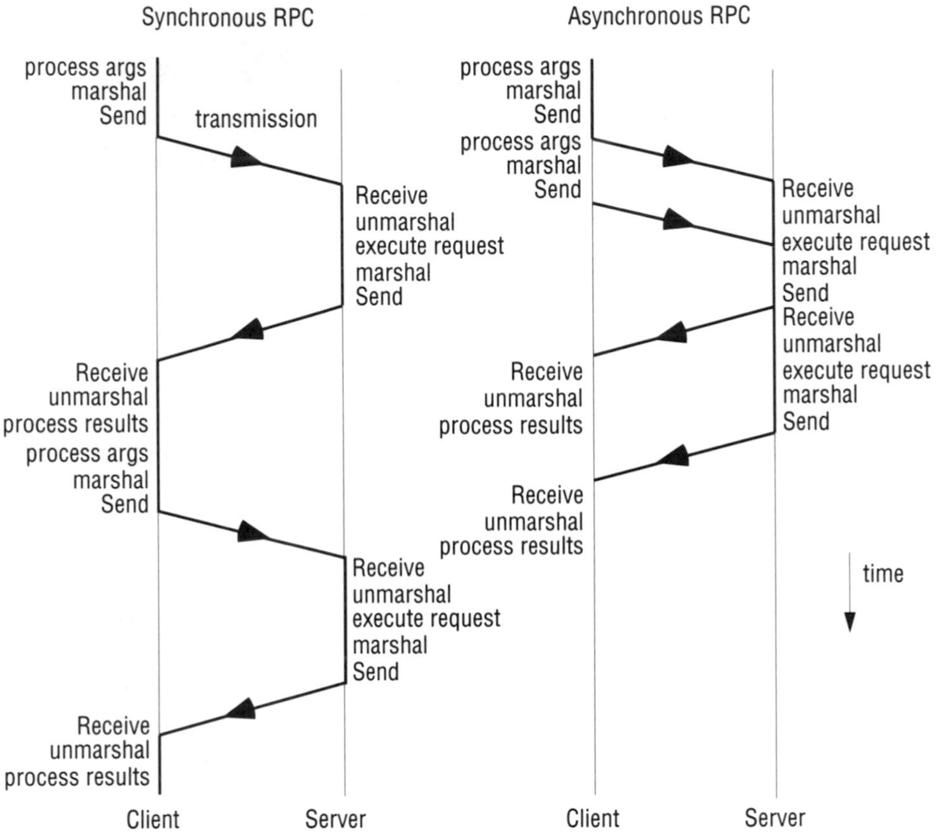

The client does not need a reply to each request and the combined performance of the client and the server can be enhanced if the client is not blocked, but allowed to make several requests without waiting for replies from the server. The client may need to perform quite intensive computations to calculate new items to be displayed, so there is a gain in the client's performance if it can do this work in parallel with the execution of previous calls in the server. The window server may need to handle requests from several clients as well as events from input devices. It can schedule its operations more efficiently if it does not have to generate replies to all requests. Remote procedure calls that do not receive replies are termed *asynchronous*. Many of the calls in the X-11 interface are asynchronous.

In an asynchronous RPC, the communication handler sends the request message and returns control to the client program immediately, instead of blocking the client.

Analysis of throughput for asynchronous RPC □ Figure 5.11 shows a comparison between consecutive synchronous and asynchronous RPC calls from a client to a server that is not currently serving any other clients. In the synchronous case, the client marshals the arguments, calls the *Send* operation and then waits until the reply from the server arrives – whereupon it *Receives*, unmarshals and then processes the results. After this it can make the second RPC call.

In the asynchronous case, the client marshals the arguments, calls the *Send* operation and then immediately makes the second call without waiting for a reply from the server. It then waits to receive the results of the two calls.

With asynchronous RPC, the client can send several consecutive messages without waiting for replies. The server and client work in parallel and if the client makes a large number of RPC calls, taking some time to process the arguments for each one, the replies may start arriving before the client has finished transmitting the requests. In this case, the client can receive the replies immediately after it has finished sending the requests.

If there are no reply messages, the time for an asynchronous call can be reduced, because the client does not need to collect the replies.

A further optimization that can be made in client communication with, for example, a window system is to buffer request messages at the client until a timeout elapses (since delays of a few milliseconds are imperceptible to human users) or until the client issues a request that requires a reply and then to send several requests together as a single communication. This reduces the time contribution due to the *Send* operation including network latency which can be substantial.

Parallel requests to several servers □ Consider a distributed implementation of a banking service in which there is one server for each branch. In order to calculate the total assets of the bank, a client has to send a request to each branch server to enquire about the total at that branch, collect the replies and calculate the sum.

With synchronous RPC, a client would have to wait for the reply from each request before making the next. However, asynchronous RPC would allow a client to send off all requests immediately and then collect the replies as they arrive. This arrangement will allow the servers to work in parallel.

Asynchronous RPC in the Mercury system □ The examples above illustrate the need for three asynchronous optimizations of the RPC paradigm:

- when no reply message is required, the client can make a remote procedure call and proceed without waiting for the server to complete the operation;

- when no reply message is required, several client request messages can be buffered and transmitted together;

- even when a reply message is required, a client may benefit if it is able make a remote procedure call that does not wait for the reply and the client claims the reply later.

The Mercury communication system was developed at MIT and is described in Liskov and Shrira [1988]. It combines synchronous and asynchronous RPCs with and without replies in one single communication facility called a **call-stream**. The different forms of communication are not visible to servers – they just receive calls and return replies. This enables servers to be designed according to the usual principles, without concern for the method of communication with their clients. This contrasts with other RPC systems in which the interface defines whether an operation returns a reply and consequently servers must be designed to reply or not reply accordingly.

Clients can choose whether to use normal (synchronous) RPC or one of the other forms of request in order to optimize their use of a server.

The Mercury call-stream provides a connection between a client and a server. The client can make requests to the server over the call-stream. The call-stream guarantees that the server receives the request messages in the order they were transmitted by the client, and that the client will receive reply messages in the same order as the corresponding request messages. In addition, each request is delivered exactly once to the server and each reply is delivered exactly once to the client. All messages are guaranteed to be delivered without any corruption. If these guarantees cannot be kept; for example, when a client or server crashes, the stream breaks. The break occurs after several attempts to deliver the messages.

Three different sorts of requests are available to clients: (i) ordinary synchronous RPC, (ii) asynchronous requests without replies and (iii) asynchronous RPCs with replies. Synchronous RPCs and their replies are transmitted immediately. When the client makes a request and does not expect a reply, the call-stream does not send the server's reply back to the client. In addition, asynchronous requests without replies and asynchronous RPCs with replies are buffered, to reduce the overhead for kernel calls and communication delays. The question that arises is how to provide a language construct to deal with picking up delayed replies.

Promises □ Liskov and Shrira [1988] describe a new data type called a *promise* that is designed to support asynchronous RPCs. Promises allow clients to continue with other work during a call and subsequently to pick up the results and exceptions from the call. The promise is created at the time of the call and is given a type corresponding to the types of the results and exceptions of the remote procedure. When the results arrive they are stored in the appropriate promise. The caller can subsequently claim the results from the promise.

A promise is in one of two states: blocked or ready. When it is created it is put in the blocked state – it remains in this state until the call returns, whereupon it enters the ready state. A promise in the ready state holds the outcome of the call and from then on is immutable.

The caller uses the *claim* operation to obtain the results from the promise. The claim operation blocks until the promise is ready, whereupon it returns the results or exceptions from the call. The same promise can be claimed several times – with the same outcome. The *ready* operation is available for testing a promise without blocking – it returns true or false according to whether the promise is ready or blocked.

5.6 Summary

The advantages of using remote procedure calling to build distributed programs are mainly related to the fact that it is similar to conventional procedure calling, which is well understood and provides a powerful program-structuring paradigm. The benefits of data abstraction and software modularity can be achieved by the appropriate design and use of RPC interfaces.

In contrast to message-based communication between processes, RPC enables application programs to be constructed without consideration for several low-level concerns such as the mapping of client procedure names to server procedures, the synchronization of operations in clients and servers and the independent failure of clients and servers.

Whereas a local procedure is always called exactly once, the semantics of an RPC depends on the degree of fault tolerance provided by the underlying request-reply protocol. The use of at-least-once call semantics requires servers to have idempotent operations. When an RPC fails due to a processor crash or a lost message, the client needs to deal with exceptions that would not occur in a non-distributed program.

There are arguments for and against transparent RPC – transparent RPC enables existing program modules to be made into a distributed program; but it can be argued that RPCs should not be entirely transparent as their semantics and performance differ from those of local procedure calls.

Interface definitions are required in RPC systems. Some languages, such as Argus, include constructs for defining interfaces, but purpose-designed interface languages are used either with languages such as C, which are not adequate in this respect, or when the RPC is to be designed for interworking between a number of different language systems. An interface compiler produces client and server stub procedures and a server despatcher – shielding the programmer from the need to be concerned with the details of marshalling.

The client that makes an RPC uses a binder to locate a server that has previously registered the service with that binder. The calls to the binder may be supplied by the interface compiler.

Sun RPC and the ANSA Testbench are examples of RPC systems for use in a C and UNIX environment that include the facilities described above.

The Mercury system attempts to address the performance problems of RPCs that are caused by the lack of concurrency between client and server with the standard synchronous RPC. They provide the call stream, which integrates synchronous and asynchronous RPC with synchronous sends. They also suggest a mechanism for claiming outstanding results from asynchronous RPCs – the promise. Asynchronous RPCs allow client and server to run in parallel, thus enhancing their combined performance in some applications.

Although the RPC is a generally applicable programming mechanism, its usefulness is limited to distributed applications that can be modelled as clients and servers. Other programming models such as process groups must also be considered.

EXERCISES

5.1   The Election Service provides two remote procedures:

Vote: with two parameters through which the client supplies the name of a candidate (a string) and the 'voter's number' (a positive integer used to ensure that each user votes once only).

Result: with two parameters through which the server supplies the client with the name of a candidate and the number of votes for that candidate.

Which of the parameters of these two procedures are *input* and which are *output* parameters?

page 128

5.2   Give the C function prototypes for the procedures *Vote* and *Result*.

Can you tell from the function prototypes whether the parameters are *input* or *output* parameters?

page 128

5.3   Give a Modula-2 definition module for the procedures *Vote* and *Result*.

Can you tell from the procedure headings whether the parameters are *input* or *output* parameters?

page 128

5.4   Give an example of a procedure whose parameter is used for *both input* and *output*. Define its Modula-2 procedure heading. Can you tell that the parameter is intended to be used for *both input* and *output*? Do either of the interface definition languages (Sun XDR and ANSA IDL) allow us to define procedures with parameters that are used for *both input* and *output*?

pages 128, 138 and 144

5.5   In an implementation of the *Election* service (Exercise 5.1) over UNIX, there is no need to supply users with 'voter's numbers' because the users' UIDs can be used for this purpose. Explain how a *user package* can provide a simpler interface to *Vote* than the RPC interface.

page 129

5.6   Consider the integration of an RPC mechanism with a programming language that has a notation for defining interfaces (for example, Modula-2 or C++). Assume that a programmer already understands how to use independent modules. Specify the additional rules that must be adhered to when programming servers and clients.

pages 128 and 130

5.7   Using the language considered in Exercise 5.6, describe how exceptions could be reported to clients. Consider first exceptions due to distribution such as time-outs on RPCs. Then consider exceptions due to conditions that the server finds unacceptable (for example, attempting to vote for a non-existent candidate in the *Election* service).

page 131

5.8   Define the interface to the *Election* service in Sun XDR and in ANSA IDL. Compare the methods for specifying *input* and *output* arguments. Do either of these interface definition languages allow the name of the service to be specified?

pages 138 and 144

5.9   Explain how an interface definition language can allow a client written in one language to use a server written in another language. Illustrate your answer with the ANSA IDL interface definition of the *Election* service (Exercise 5.8).

Give an example of a language that would be difficult to map onto this interface definition.

page 131

5.10 The *Election* service runs as a single server UNIX process. What should happen if several clients vote at about the same time as one another and messages arrive while the server is processing a vote?

Will this happen if the *Request-Reply* protocol is implemented over UDP?

page 132

5.11 The *Election* service must ensure that a vote is recorded whenever any user thinks they have cast a vote.

Discuss the effect of *maybe* call semantics on the *Election* service.

Would *at-least-once* call semantics be acceptable for the *Election* service or would you recommend *at-most-once* call semantics?

page 132

5.12 Suppose that an RPC mechanism is integrated with a language (as in Exercise 5.6). A module that implements the operations of a service has been constructed. Describe the software components that must be added to the module to make it a server. A potential client program uses operations imported from the module. Describe the additional software components required by this client program.

page 134

5.13 Define one of the client stub procedures for the *Election* service using the language of Exercise 5.6. *DoOperation* (from Chapter 4) should be used.

page 134

5.14 Explain how client stub procedures may be generated automatically from an interface definition.

page 134

5.15 The binding service described in Figure 5.3 does not support the registering of multiple instances of the same service. Define new versions of the procedures *Register*, *Withdraw* and *LookUp* that can deal with multiple instances of the same service.

Suggest how your binding service could use the knowledge of service instances to allocate clients evenly to several servers.

page 136

5.16 Suppose that a client makes only one RPC (for example, to cast a vote). Describe the overheads associated with the use of a binder, (i) when the location of the binder is known by the client, and (ii) when it is not known.

Compare these overheads with the overheads in Sun RPC. Sun RPC provides a function *callrpc* that a client may use to call a remote procedure directly, without any prior binding. Do you think this is useful?

pages 136 and 138–142

5.17   A client makes remote procedure calls to a server. The client takes 5 milliseconds to compute the arguments for each request, and the server takes 10 milliseconds to process each request. The local operating system processing time for each send or receive operation is 0.5 milliseconds, and the network time to transmit each request or reply message is 3 milliseconds. Marshalling or unmarshalling takes 0.5 milliseconds per message.

Calculate the time taken by the client to generate and return from two requests(i) if it is single-threaded, and (ii) if it has two threads which can make requests concurrently on a single processor. You can ignore context-switching times.

Is there a need for asynchronous RPC if processes are multi-threaded?

page 149

5.18   A client is written in C but uses a set of stubs compiled from a service interface definition module. Identify all the mechanisms by which the client call and the server procedure are correctly matched. You should include details of the binding interface involved, and two ways of implementing the binding service.

page 134-138

6

DISTRIBUTED OPERATING SYSTEMS

This chapter describes the fundamental issues and abstractions encountered in the design of distributed operating systems. A distributed operating system supports the encapsulation and protection of resources inside servers; and it supports mechanisms required to access these resources, including naming, communication and scheduling.

The chapter examines the system kernel, whose role is to support higher-level system services. In particular, the model of a microkernel is discussed, as a minimal kernel upon which all other services can be built.

The chapter examines how the traditional operating system concept of process has been superseded by multi-threaded processes with large address spaces; it discusses communication services and the invocation of operations upon local and remote resources; finally, it examines the impact of distribution on virtual memory support.

6.1   Introduction

The concept of a distributed operating system was introduced in Chapter 1, and its role
in an open distributed system was taken up again in Chapter 2. We can summarize those
discussions by the following broad characterization of a distributed operating system:

- Its task is to enable a distributed system to be conveniently programmed, so that
  it can be used to implement the widest possible range of applications.

- It does this by presenting applications with general, problem-oriented abstractions
  of the resources in a distributed system. Examples of such abstractions are
  communication channels and processes – instead of networks and processors.

- In an open distributed system, the distributed operating system is implemented by
  a collection of kernels and servers (server processes). There is no clear dividing
  line between the distributed operating system (or rather, its open services) and
  applications that run on top of it. Most would count the file service as belonging
  with the operating system, but does electronic mail?

There have been several efforts to design and implement distributed operating systems.
Most of them have started and ended life as research projects. Mach and Chorus are two
examples of kernels for distributed operating systems. They are notable for the fact that
they are each the result of several phases of continuous research over the 1980s and early
1990s, and that each has achieved a significant level of commercial as well as technical
interest. They have both attained a high degree of technical development. Amoeba,
Clouds and the V system are three other examples of distributed operating system
designs and implementations, which are of interest mainly for their technical
contributions (none has been accepted into general use). All five projects employ a
minimal kernel or *microkernel* as the basis of their designs.

   This chapter focuses on the part of a distributed operating system that acts as an
infrastructure for general, network-transparent resource management. The infrastructure
manages low-level resources – processors, memory, network interfaces and other
peripheral devices – to provide a platform for the construction of higher-level resources
such as spreadsheets, electronic mail messages and windows. These higher-level
resources may themselves be managed and offered to clients by system services.

   As we explained in Chapter 2, it is essential that clients can access resources in a
network-transparent way – that is, that resources can be accessed using location-
independent identifiers and using the same operations, regardless of their locations. A
distributed operating system provides this transparency at the lowest possible level, to
save having to provide it in each service. A collection of UNIX kernels does not
constitute a distributed operating system, because the boundaries between computers are
clearly visible. UNIX can manage files but not, for example, processes in a network-
transparent manner.

   A distributed operating system must provide facilities for encapsulating resources
in a modular and protected fashion, while providing clients with network-wide access to
them. Kernels and servers are both resource managers. They contain resources, and as
such we require the following of them:

Encapsulation: They should provide a useful service interface to their resources – that is, a set of operations that meet their clients' needs. The details of management of memory and devices used to implement resources should be hidden from clients, even when they are local.

Concurrent processing: Clients may share resources and access them concurrently. Resource managers are responsible for achieving concurrency transparency.

Protection: Resources require protection from illegitimate accesses – for example, files are protected from being read by users without read permissions, and device registers are protected from application processes.

Clients access resources by identifying them in arguments to operations – for example, remote procedure calls to a server, or system calls to a kernel. We call an access to an encapsulated resource an **invocation**, however it is implemented. A combination of client libraries, kernels and servers may be called upon to perform the following invocation-related tasks:

Name resolution: The server (or kernel) that manages a resource has to be located, from the resource's identifier.

Communication: Operation parameters and results have to be passed to and from resource managers, over a network or within a computer.

Scheduling: This is related to concurrency: when an operation is invoked, its processing must be scheduled within the kernel or server.

This chapter discusses each of the tasks just mentioned, primarily in the context of microkernels. A microkernel provides the most basic mechanisms upon which the general resource management tasks must be carried out. The separation of fixed resource management *mechanisms* from resource management *policies* that vary from installation to installation has been a guiding principle in operating system design for some time [Wulf *et al*.1974]. Servers, which may be adapted and dynamically loaded as required, implement the required resource management policies.

None but a few research-based distributed systems can be said to be controlled by a single, homogeneous distributed operating system in which every computer runs the same kernel. A distributed operating system must currently interwork with conventional operating system kernels such as UNIX, which most workstations run and for which many applications exist. Microkernels are an attempt to design a common kernel that is purpose-built for distributed systems and that should ultimately displace traditional, monolithic kernels such as UNIX, but which support emulations of these established operating systems.

After further discussion of kernels in the next section, Section 6.3 goes on to examine the process, address space and thread abstractions, which are at the heart of the distributed operating system model. Here the main topics are concurrency, local resource management and protection, and scheduling. Section 6.4 examines the facilities needed for system-wide resource naming and protection. Section 6.5 covers communication and factors relevant to the performance of invocation mechanisms. Finally, Section 6.6 discusses virtual memory in a distributed system. The reader could skip Section 6.6 on a first reading, although an understanding of the principles of virtual memory is necessary to follow aspects of the Mach case study.

Chapter 18 describes the main features of Amoeba, Mach and Chorus, as well as Clouds, a distributed operating system that directly supports objects.

6.2 The kernel

In this section we discuss the function of a kernel suitable for a distributed system. The section begins with a discussion of what a kernel is, and then compares the monolithic and microkernel designs, which were first introduced in Chapter 2.

Kernels and protection □ The kernel is a program that is distinguished by the fact that its code is executed with complete access privileges for the physical resources on its host computer. In particular, it can control the memory management unit and set the processor registers so that no other code may access the machine's resources. However, it may allow other, server code to access physical resources.

The kernel can set up **address spaces** to protect processes from one another and to provide them with their required virtual memory layout. An address space is a collection of ranges of virtual memory locations, in each of which a specified combination of memory access rights applies, such as read-only or read-write. A process may not access memory outside its address space. Processes executing kernel code execute in the kernel's address space; application processes normally execute in distinct address spaces.

In addition to memory-based protection, many processors have a hardware mode register whose setting determines whether privileged instructions can be executed, such as those used to determine which protection tables are currently employed by the memory management unit. A kernel process executes with the processor in *supervisor* (privileged) mode; the kernel arranges that other processes execute in *user* (unprivileged) mode. The terms *user process* or *user-level process* are normally used to describe one that executes in user mode and has a user-level address space (that is, one with restricted memory access rights compared to the kernel's address space). But note that in some systems a process with a user-level address space may execute in supervisor mode, in order to control a device.

The invocation mechanism for resources managed by the kernel is known as a *system call trap*. This is implemented by a machine-level *TRAP* instruction, which puts the processor into supervisor mode and switches to the kernel address space. The hardware forces the processor to execute a kernel-supplied handler function when the *TRAP* instruction has been executed, so that no user process may gain control of the hardware.

Monolithic kernels and microkernels □ According to the definition of openness given in Chapter 1, an open distributed operating system should make it possible to:

- run only that system software at each computer that is necessary for it to carry out its particular role in the system architecture; system software requirements can vary between, for example, single-user workstations and dedicated server computers. Loading redundant modules wastes memory resources;

- allow the software (and the computer) implementing any particular system service to be changed independently of other facilities;

- allow for alternatives of the same system service to be provided, when this is required to suit different users or applications;

- introduce new services without prejudice to existing ones.

A degree of openness is obtained using traditional kernels such as UNIX, which can run servers and support protocols such as remote procedure call for distributed processing. For example, the Distributed Computing Environment of the Open Software Foundation [OSF 1990] is a standard software architecture for distributed computing that is designed to operate across a range of standard UNIX, VMS, OS/2 and other kernels. It includes standards for RPC, name (binding) services, time (synchronization) services, security services and threads services (see Section 6.3) – all sufficient for client-server computing across heterogeneous architectures.

What about the openness of services provided by kernels themselves? There are two main approaches to kernel design: the so-called *monolithic* and *microkernel* approaches. Where these designs differ primarily is in the decision as to what functionality belongs in the kernel, and what is to be left to server processes that run on top of it.

The UNIX operating system kernel has been called monolithic (see definition in the box below). This term is meant to suggest the facts that it is *massive*: it performs all basic operating system functions and takes up in the order of one megabyte of code and data, and that it is *undifferentiated*: it is coded in a non-modular way. The result is that to a large extent it is *intractable*: altering any individual software component to adapt it to changing requirements is difficult.

Another prominent example of a monolithic kernel is that of the Sprite operating system, which is designed for distributed systems [Ousterhout *et al.* 1988]. A monolithic kernel can contain some server processes that execute within it, including file servers and some networking. The code that these processes execute is part of the standard kernel configuration (see Figure 6.1).

In the case of a microkernel design, the kernel provides only the most basic abstractions, principally processes, memory and inter-process communication, and *all* other system services are provided by servers that are dynamically loaded at precisely those computers in the distributed system that are to provide those services (Figure 6.1). These system services are accessed by message-based invocation mechanisms, principally remote procedure call.

Some microkernels run servers only as user processes. Modularity is then hardware-enforced by giving each process its own address space. Where servers require direct access to hardware, special system calls can be provided for these privileged processes, which map device registers and buffers into their address spaces, and which

Monolithic: The Chambers 20th Century Dictionary gives the following definition of *monolith* and *monolithic*. '**monolith**, *n.* a pillar, or column, of a single stone: anything resembling a monolith in uniformity, massiveness or intractability. – *adj.* monolithic pertaining to or resembling a monolith: of a state, an organisation, etc., massive, and undifferentiated throughout: intractable for this reason.'

Figure 6.1   Monolithic kernel and microkernel.

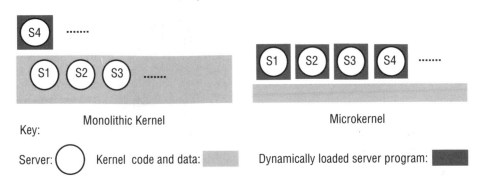

enable them to handle interrupts. The Chorus microkernel, on the other hand, allows servers to be loaded dynamically either into the kernel address space or into a user-level address space. This is discussed further in Chapter 18.

The place of the microkernel – in its most general form – in the overall distributed system design is shown in Figure 6.2. The microkernel appears as a layer between the hardware layer and a layer consisting of major system components called **subsystems**. Application processes or objects do not normally use the facilities of the microkernel directly (although they can). Rather, they use either the language support subsystem which is specific to a particular language; or, they use a higher-level operating system interface provided by an operating system emulation subsystem. Each of these, in turn, is implemented by a combination of library procedures linked into applications, and a set of servers running on top of the microkernel. Some microkernels support real-time processing, and so may be used, for example, in process control subsystems.

There can be more than one system call interface – more than one 'operating system' – presented to the programmer by the same underlying distributed operating system. This situation is reminiscent of the IBM 370 architecture, whose VM operating system can present several complete virtual machines to different programs running at the same (uniprocessor) computer. An example in the case of distributed systems is the

Figure 6.2   The role of the microkernel.

Open services and application processes/objects			
Language support subsystem	Language support subsystem	OS emulation subsystem	....
Microkernel			
Hardware			

The microkernel layer supports subsystems, open services and applications.

implementation of UNIX and OS/2 on top of the Mach distributed operating system kernel.

Comparison □ The chief advantages of a microkernel-based distributed operating system, then, are its openness and its ability to enforce modularity behind memory protection boundaries. In addition, a relatively small kernel is more likely to be free of bugs than one that is larger and more complex. Recent microkernel implementations have been prototyped and brought to a working state by just a few individuals working closely together, each of whom can be said to grasp a major portion, if not the totality, of the design.

The lack of structure in monolithic designs can be avoided by the use of software engineering techniques such as layering (used in MULTICS [Organick 1972]), or object-oriented design, used for example in Choices [Campbell *et al.* 1993]. But even a modularized monolithic kernel can be hard to maintain, and provides limited support for an open distributed system. As long as modules are executed within the same address space, using a language such as C or C++ that compiles to efficient code but permits arbitrary data accesses, it is possible for strict modularity to be broken by programmers seeking efficient implementations. Unless strict modularity is kept, it is impossible for any module to be extracted from the kernel so as to execute at a remote computer. In the absence of hardware protection between modules, a bug in one module can have an adverse effect upon the operation of another. Furthermore, re-implementing a module in a monolithic kernel implies rebuilding the kernel and re-starting it.

The advantage of a monolithic design is the relative efficiency with which operations can be invoked. As we shall see in the next section, changing the current address space can be an expensive operation. Invoking an operation in a microkernel-based system may involve passing the client's request to one or more server processes in separate address spaces (and perhaps in different computers). In a monolithic design, most request processing involves only kernels.

Attention has recently been focused on the problem of making invocations between address spaces faster, so that we can benefit from the software-engineering advantages of using microkernels, while maintaining satisfactory performance. This is discussed in Section 6.5.

Architecture of a microkernel

As we shall see in Chapter 18, there is no fixed definition of what functions are performed by a microkernel, but all include process management, memory management, and local message passing. Microkernels can vary in size from about ten kilobytes to several hundred kilobytes of executable code and static data.

The microkernel is designed to be portable between computer architectures. This means that the majority of it is coded in a high-level language such as C or C++, and that its facilities are layered so that machine-dependent components are reduced to a minimal bottom layer. These include procedures to manipulate the processor, memory management unit and floating point unit registers, and procedures for dispatching interrupts, traps and other exceptions.

Figure 6.3   Microkernel architecture.

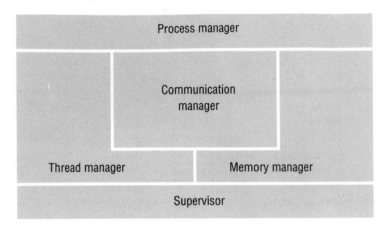

The architecture of a particular microkernel is shown in Figure 6.3. The figure shows dependencies between components by its horizontal divisions. The main components are the following:

Process manager: Handles the creation of and low-level operations upon processes. The facilities provided by this layer would normally be enhanced for applications by an intervening subsystem for language support or operating system emulation.

Thread manager: Thread creation, synchronization and scheduling. Threads are schedulable activities attached to processes, and are fully described in the next section. To take advantage of a multiprocessor, threads are scheduled across the available processors. Scheduling policy may be left to user-level modules.

Communication manager: Communication between threads attached to different local processes. In some designs, a level of support for communication between threads in remote processes is included in the kernel. In others, the kernel has no notion of other computers built into it, and an additional service is required for external communication. We shall discuss the communication design in Section 6.5.

Memory manager: Management of physical memory resources, memory management units and hardware caches. Section 6.6 will cover kernel support for virtual memory.

Supervisor: Dispatching of interrupts, system call traps and other exceptions. The reader is referred to Tanenbaum [1992] for a fuller description of the computer-dependent aspects of the kernel.

Most microkernels can execute on a shared memory multiprocessor. In the common *symmetric processing architecture*, each processor executes the same kernel and the processors play largely equivalent roles in managing the hardware. The processors share key data structures such as the queue of runnable processes, but some of their working data is private.

6.3   Processes and threads

The traditional UNIX-style notion of process was found in the 1980s to be unequal to the requirements of distributed systems – and also to those of more sophisticated single-computer applications that require internal concurrency. The problem, as we shall see, stems from the fact that UNIX associates just one processing activity with each process, even though the process is an expensive resource to create and manage. This makes sharing between related activities awkward and expensive.

The solution reached was to generalize the notion of process so that it could be associated with multiple activities. Henceforth, a process consists of an execution environment together with one or more threads. A **thread** is the operating system abstraction of an activity. The term derives from the phrase 'thread of execution'. An **execution environment** is the unit of resource management: a collection of local kernel-managed resources to which its threads have access. An execution environment primarily consists of:

- an address space;

- thread synchronization and communication resources such as semaphores and communication interfaces (for example ports).

Note that, in a microkernel architecture, higher-level resources such as open files and windows do not appear as part of the collection of resources of an execution environment. Higher-level resources are implemented by servers, and access to them is via the servers' ports.

Execution environments are normally expensive to create and manage, but several threads can share them – that is, they can share all resources accessible within them. Threads can be created and destroyed dynamically as needed. The central aim of having multiple threads of execution is to maximize the degree of concurrent execution between closely-related operations. This can be particularly helpful within servers, where concurrent processing of clients' requests can reduce the tendency for servers to become bottlenecks.

An execution environment provides protection, so that the data and other resources contained in it are by default inaccessible to threads residing in other execution environments. But certain kernels allow the controlled sharing of resources such as physical memory between execution environments residing at the same computer.

As many older operating systems allow only one thread per process, we shall sometimes use the term *multi-threaded process* for emphasis. Confusingly, in some programming models and operating system designs the term 'process' means what we have called a thread. The reader may encounter in the literature the terms *heavyweight process*, where an execution environment is taken to be included, and *lightweight process*, where it is not. See the box overleaf for an analogy describing threads and execution environments.

Figure 6.4 gives the names used in four major microkernel designs for the execution environment and thread abstractions. Despite the varied and conflicting terminology, these designs provide similar semantics for threads and execution environments. The above definitions are based on them.

Figure 6.4   Thread and process abstractions.

Distributed OS kernel	Thread name	Execution environment name
Amoeba	Thread	Process
Chorus	Thread	Actor
Mach	Thread	Task
V system	Process	Team

Address spaces

An address space, introduced in the previous section, is the most expensive component of an execution environment to create and manage. It is large (typically 2^{32} bytes) and consists of one or more **regions**, separated by inaccessible areas of virtual memory. A region (Figure 6.5) is an area of contiguous virtual memory that is accessible by the threads of the owning process. Regions do not overlap. Note that we distinguish between the regions and their contents. Each region is specified by the following properties:

- its extent (lowest virtual address and size);
- read/write/execute permissions for the process's threads;
- whether it can be grown upwards or downwards.

Note that this model is page-oriented rather than segment-oriented: regions, unlike segments, cannot be extended indefinitely because their address ranges would eventually overlap. Gaps are left between regions to allow for growth. This representation of an address space as a sparse set of disjoint regions is a generalization of the UNIX address space which has three regions: a fixed, unmodifiable text region containing program code; a heap, part of which is initialized by values stored in the program's binary file, and which is extensible towards higher virtual addresses; and a stack, which is extensible towards lower virtual addresses.

An analogy for threads and processes: The following memorable, if slightly unsavoury, way to think of the concepts of threads and execution environments was seen on the *comp.os.mach* USENET group, and is due to Chris Lloyd. An execution environment consists of a stoppered jar and the air and food within it. Initially there is one fly – a thread – in the jar. This fly can produce other flies and kill them, as can its progeny. Any fly can consume any resource (air or food) in the jar. Flies can be programmed to queue up in an orderly manner to consume resources. If they lack this discipline, they might bump into one another within the jar – that is, collide and produce unpredictable results when attempting to consume the same resources in an unconstrained manner. Flies can communicate with (send messages to) flies in other jars, but none may escape from the jar, and no fly from outside may enter it. In this view, a standard UNIX process is a single jar with a single sterile fly within it.

Figure 6.5   Address space.

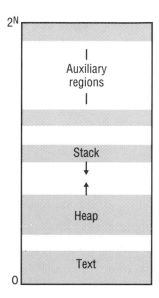

The provision of an indefinite number of regions is motivated by several factors. One of these is to enable files in general – and not just the text and data sections of binary files – to be mapped into the address space. A *mapped file* is one that is accessed as an array of bytes in memory. The virtual memory system ensures that accesses made in memory are reflected in the underlying file storage. This is discussed in Section 6.6 below.

Sharing between processes or between processes and the kernel in a single computer is another factor. A *shared memory region* (or *shared region* for short) is one that is backed by the same physical memory as one or more regions belonging to other address spaces. Processes therefore access identical memory contents in the regions that are shared. The uses of shared regions include the following:

Libraries: Library code can be very large, and would waste considerable memory if it was loaded separately into every process that used it. Instead, a single copy of the library code can be shared by being mapped as a region in the address spaces of processes that require it.

Kernel: Often the kernel code and data are mapped into every address space at the same location. When a process makes a system call or an exception occurs, there is no need to set up a new address space.

Data sharing and communication: Two processes, or a process and the kernel, might need to share data in order to cooperate on some task. It can be considerably more efficient for the data to be shared by being mapped as regions in both address spaces, than by being passed in messages between them. The use of region sharing for communication is described in Section 6.5.

An address space that is configured as an indefinite number of regions enables each thread within a process to be allocated its own stack region. This makes it possible to detect attempts to exceed the stack limits and control each stack's growth. The alternative is to allocate stacks for threads on the heap, but then it is difficult to detect when a thread has exceeded its stack limit.

Creation of a new process

The creation of a new process has traditionally been an indivisible operation provided by the operating system. For example, the UNIX *fork* system call creates a process with an execution environment copied from the caller (except for the return value from *fork*). The UNIX *exec* system call transforms the calling process into one executing the code of a named program. For a distributed operating system, the design of process creation has to take account of two new requirements. The first is the utilization of multiple computers; the second is the division of the process support infrastructure into separate system services.

The creation of a new process can be separated into three independent aspects:

- the choice of a target host,

- the creation of an execution environment, and

- the creation of a thread within it. The initial thread is created with a default stack pointer and program counter, in much the same way as a UNIX process is initialized.

Choice of target host □ The choice of computer at which the new process will reside is entirely a matter of policy. For example, the V system provides a command for users to execute a program at a particular computer, or at an idle workstation chosen by the operating system. In the Amoeba system, the *run server* (introduced in Chapter 2) chooses a host from the processor pool for each process, and the choice is transparent both to the programmer and the user. Those programming for explicit parallelism or fault tolerance, however, may require a means of specifying process location. In general, processor allocation policies range from localisation of processes to their originator's workstation to balancing the load between a set of shared computers. Tanenbaum [1992] discusses processor allocation schemes.

Creation of a new execution environment □ A process requires an execution environment consisting of an address space with initialized contents and an initial set of port capabilities for communicating with services. A kernel creates the new execution environment at the local computer. If necessary, a system service can request a remote server process to create an environment at a remote computer.

There are two approaches to defining and initializing the address space of a newly created process. The first approach is used where the address space is of statically defined format. For example, it could contain just a program text region, heap region and stack region. In this case, the address space regions are created from a list specifying their extent. Address space regions are initialized from an executable file or filled with zeroes as appropriate.

Figure 6.6 Copy-on-write.

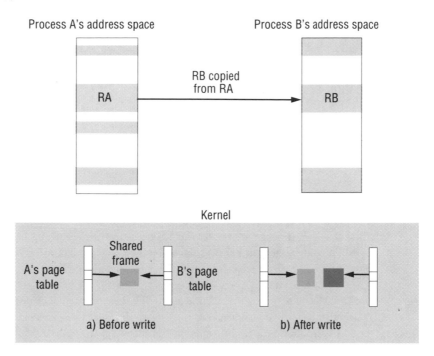

Alternatively, the address space can be defined with respect to an existing execution environment. In the case of UNIX *fork* semantics, for example, the newly created child process physically shares the parent's text region, and has heap and stack regions which are copies of the parent's in extent (as well as in initial contents). This scheme has been generalized so that each region of the parent process may be inherited by (or omitted from) the child process. An inherited region may either be shared with or logically copied from the parent's region. When parent and child share a region, the page frames (units of physical memory corresponding to virtual memory pages) belonging to the parent's region are mapped simultaneously into the corresponding child region.

Mach and Chorus apply an important optimization called **copy-on-write** when an inherited region is copied from the parent. The region is logically copied, but no physical copying takes place by default. The page frames that make up the inherited region are shared between the two address spaces. A page in the region is only physically copied when one or other process attempts to modify it.

Let us follow through an example of regions *RA* and *RB* whose memory is shared copy-on-write between two processes, *A* and *B* (Figure 6.6). For the sake of definiteness, let us assume that process *A* set region *RA* to be copy-inherited by its child, process *B*, and that the region *RB* was thus created in process *B*.

We assume, for the sake of simplicity, that the pages belonging to region A are resident in memory. Initially, all page frames associated with the regions are shared between the two processes' page tables. The pages are initially write-protected at the hardware level, even though they may belong to regions that are logically writable. If a thread in either process attempts to modify the data, a hardware exception called a *page*

Figure 6.7   Server with threads.

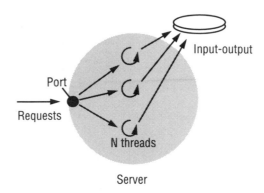

fault is taken. Let us say that process B attempted the write. The page fault handler allocates a new frame for process B, and copies the original frame's data into it byte-for-byte. The old frame number is replaced by the new frame number in one process's page table – it does not matter which – and the old frame number is left in the other page table. The two corresponding pages in processes A and B are then each made writable once more at the hardware level. After all of this has taken place, process B's modifying instruction is allowed to proceed.

Inheritance is a less promising option when it comes to determining the initial ports held by a new process. The sharing of the same port by two or more processes is normally ruled out. This is because it is easier to design a program under the assumption that no other process can consume messages from the same stream. However, each new process comes equipped with a standard set of 'bootstrap' port identifiers to communicate with binders. It uses these to obtain other service port identifiers as it requires them, and to register identifiers of its own ports.

Threads

Consider the server shown in Figure 6.7. It has one or more threads, each of which receives request messages from a port and applies the same procedure to process them. Let us assume that each request takes, on average, 2 milliseconds of processing and 8 milliseconds of input-output delay when the server reads from a device on behalf of the client (there is no caching). Let us further assume for the moment that the server executes at a single-processor computer.

Consider the *maximum* server throughput, measured in client requests handled per second, for different numbers of threads. If a single thread has to perform all processing, then the turnaround time for handling any request is on average $2 + 8 = 10$ milliseconds, and so this server can handle 100 client requests per second. Any new request messages that arrive while the server is handling a request are queued at the server port.

Now consider what happens if the server has two threads. We assume that threads are independently schedulable – that is, one thread can be scheduled when another becomes blocked for input-output. Then thread number two can process a second request, while thread number one is blocked, and vice versa. This increases the server

Figure 6.8   Client with threads.

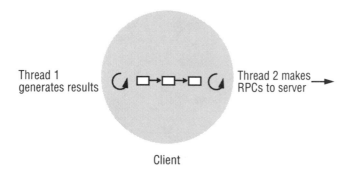

Thread 1
generates results

Thread 2 makes
RPCs to server

Client

throughput. Unfortunately, the input-output operations requested by the threads belonging to a server are unlikely to be performed in parallel, and the input-output device has a limiting effect on the rate at which requests can be processed. For example, the threads may become blocked behind a single disk drive. If all disk requests are serialized, and take 8 milliseconds each, then the maximum throughput is 1000/8 = 125 requests per second.

Suppose, now, that disk block caching is introduced. The server keeps data it reads in buffers in its address space; a server thread that is asked to retrieve data first examines the shared cache, and avoids accessing the disk if it finds it there. If a 75 per cent hit rate is achieved, the mean input-output time per request reduces to $(0.75 \times 8 + 0.25 \times 0) = 2$ milliseconds, and the maximum theoretical throughput increases to 500 requests per second. But if the average *processor* time for a request has been increased to 2.5 milliseconds per request as a result of caching (it takes time to search for cached data on every operation) then this figure cannot be reached. The processor can now handle at most 1000/2.5 = 400 requests per second.

The throughput can be increased by using a shared memory multiprocessor to remove the processor bottleneck. A multi-threaded process maps naturally onto a shared memory multiprocessor. The shared execution environment can be implemented in shared memory, and the multiple threads can be scheduled to run on the multiple processors. Consider now the case in which our example server executes at a multiprocessor with two processors. Given that threads can be independently scheduled to the different processors, then up to two threads can process requests in parallel. These two threads between them, bounded by the input-output time, can process 500 requests per second.

Threads can be useful for clients as well as servers. Figure 6.8 shows a client process with two threads. The first thread generates results to be passed to a server by remote procedure call, but does not require a reply. Unfortunately, conventional remote procedure calls block the caller, even when there is strictly no need to wait. This client process can incorporate a second thread, which performs the remote procedure calls and blocks while the first thread is able to continue computing further results. The first thread places its results in buffers which are emptied by the second thread. It is only blocked when the buffers are all full.

Figure 6.9   State associated with execution environments and threads.

Execution environment	Thread
Address space tables	Saved processor registers
Ports or other communication interfaces	Priority and execution state (such as *BLOCKED*)
Semaphores, other synchronization objects	Software interrupt handling information
List of thread identifiers	Execution environment identifier
Pages of address space resident in memory; hardware cache entries	

Threads versus multiple processes □ We can see from the above examples the utility of threads, which allow computation to be overlapped with input-output and, in the case of a multiprocessor, with other computation. The reader may have noted, however, that the same overlap could be achieved through the use of multiple single-threaded processes. Why, then, should the multi-threaded process model be preferred? The answer is twofold: threads are cheaper to create and manage than processes, and, resource sharing can be achieved more efficiently between threads than between processes because threads share an execution environment.

Figure 6.9 shows some of the main state components that must be maintained for execution environments and threads, respectively. An execution environment has an address space, communication interfaces such as ports, and thread synchronization objects such as semaphores; it also lists the threads associated with it. A thread has a scheduling priority, an execution state (such as *BLOCKED* or *RUNNABLE*), saved processor register values when the thread is *BLOCKED*, and state concerning the thread's *software interrupt* handling. A software interrupt is an event that causes a thread to be interrupted (similarly to the case of a hardware interrupt). If the thread has assigned a handler procedure, control is transferred to it. UNIX signals are examples of software interrupts.

The figure shows that an execution environment and the threads belonging to it are both associated with pages belonging to the address space held in main memory, and data and instructions held in hardware caches.

We can summarize a comparison of processes and threads as follows:

• Creating a new thread within an existing process is cheaper than creating a process.

• More importantly, switching to a different thread within the same process is cheaper than switching between threads belonging to different processes.

• Threads within a process may share data and other resources conveniently and efficiently compared to separate processes.

• But, by the same token, threads within a process are not protected from one another.

Consider the cost of creating a new thread in an existing execution environment. The main tasks are to allocate a region for its stack and to provide initial values of the processor registers and the thread's execution state (it may initially be *SUSPENDED* or *RUNNABLE*) and priority. Since the execution environment exists, only an identifier for this has to be placed in the thread's descriptor record (which contains data necessary to manage the thread's execution).

The overheads associated with creating a process are in general considerably greater than those of creating a new thread. A new execution environment must first be created, including address space tables and some initial ports. Anderson *et al.* [1991] quote a figure of about 11 milliseconds to create a new UNIX process, and about one millisecond to create a thread on the same CVAX processor architecture running the Topaz kernel; in each case the time measured includes the new entity simply calling a null procedure and then exiting. These figures are given as a rough guide only.

When the new entity performs some useful work rather than calling a null procedure, there are also long-term costs, which are liable to be greater for a new process than a new thread within an existing process. In a kernel supporting virtual memory, the new process will incur page faults as data and instructions are referenced for the first time; hardware caches will initially contain no data values for the new process, and it must acquire cache entries as it executes. In the case of thread creation, on the other hand, these long-term overheads may also occur, but they are liable to be less. When the thread accesses code and data that have recently been accessed by other threads within the process, it automatically takes advantage of any hardware or main memory caching that has taken place.

The second performance advantage of threads concerns switching between threads – that is, running one thread instead of another at a given processor. This cost is the most important because it may be incurred many times in the lifetime of a thread. Switching between threads sharing the same execution environment is considerably cheaper than switching between threads belonging to different processes. The overheads associated with thread switching are scheduling (choosing the next thread to run) and context switching.

A processor context comprises the values of the processor registers such as the program counter, and the current hardware protection environment: the address space and the processor protection mode (supervisor or user). A **context switch** is the transition between contexts that takes place when switching between threads, or when a single thread makes a system call. It involves the following:

- the saving of the original processor state, and the loading of the new state.

- when switching between execution environments, or to or from the kernel, a transfer has to be made to a new protection environment – this is known as a **domain transition**.

When switching between threads belonging to the same process on a kernel which supports threads directly, context switching only occurs to and from the kernel. If the kernel is mapped into the process's address space, the cost of this may be relatively low. When switching between threads belonging to different processes, however, there is also a context switch to a separate user-level execution environment. The box below explains the expensive implications of hardware caching for these domain transitions.

Longer-term costs of having to acquire hardware cache entries and main memory pages are more liable to apply when a domain transition occurs. Figures quoted by Anderson *et al.* [1991] are 1.8 milliseconds to switch between UNIX processes, and 0.4 milliseconds for the Topaz kernel to switch between threads belonging to a common execution environment. Even lower costs (0.04 milliseconds) can be achieved if threads are switched at user-level, as we shortly discuss. These figures are given as a rough guide only; they do not measure the longer-term caching costs.

In our example above of the client process with two threads, the first thread generates data and passes it to the second thread which makes an RPC. Since the threads share an address space, there is no need to use message passing to pass the data. Both threads may access the data via a pointer in a common variable. Herein lies both the advantage and the danger of using multi-threaded processes. The convenience and efficiency of access to shared data is an advantage. This is particularly so for servers, as the example of caching file data given above showed. However, threads that share an address space are not protected from one another. An errant thread can arbitrarily alter data used by another thread, causing a fault. If protection is required, it can be preferable to use multiple processes, instead of multiple threads.

Threads programming □ Threads programming is concurrent programming, as traditionally studied in the field of operating systems. This section refers to the following concurrent programming concepts, which are explained fully by Bacon [1993]: *race condition*, *critical section* (Bacon calls this a *critical region*), *condition variable*, *semaphore*.

Some languages provide direct support for threads. Modula-3 is a recent example [Harbison 1992]. However, much threads programming is done in a conventional language such as C, which has been augmented with a threads library. The C Threads package developed for the Mach operating system is an example of this [Cooper 1988], as is the SunOS Lightweight Processes (LWP) package. More recently, the Institute of Electrical and Electronic Engineers Computer Society has drafted a POSIX threads standard, to avoid incompatibilities between thread designs. This standard is known as *P Threads*. An implementation is available for the OSF/1 operating system, and the Free Software Foundation has developed an implementation, GNU Threads, which runs on SunOS. We shall describe part of the C Threads package here, because of its relatively

---

The aliasing problem: Memory management units usually include a hardware cache to speed up the translation between virtual and physical addresses, called a *translation lookaside buffer* (TLB). TLBs, and also virtually addressed data and instruction caches, suffer in general from the so-called *aliasing problem*. The same virtual address can be valid in two different address spaces, but in general it is supposed to refer to different physical data in the two spaces. Unless their entries are tagged with a context identifier, TLBs and virtually addressed caches are unaware of this and so might contain incorrect data. Therefore the TLB and cache contents have to be flushed on a switch to a different address space. Physically addressed caches do not suffer from the aliasing problem; but using virtual addresses for cache lookups is a common practice, largely because it allows the lookups to be overlapped with address translation.

Figure 6.10   Thread management calls in the C Threads Library.

---

cthread_fork(func, arg) → *threadId*
  Create a new thread that executes a given function *func* with a single argument *arg*; returns a thread identifier *threadId*, proceeds concurrently with the creating thread.

cthread_exit(result)
  Terminate the current thread.

cthread_join(threadId)
  A thread which has created another thread with identifier *threadId* can block until the latter terminates.

cthread_set_data(threadId, data)
  Associate global data exclusively with a thread whose identifier is *threadId*.

cthread_data(threadId)
  Return the data associated with a given thread.

cthread_yield( )
  Allow another thread to run.

---

straightforward interface. Boykin *et al.* [1993] describe both C Threads and P threads in the context of Mach.

In any threads implementation, calls are required for creating threads, destroying them and synchronizing them. The C Threads Library includes the calls listed in Figure 6.10.

Programming a multi-threaded process requires great care. The main difficult issues are the scope of variables and the techniques used for thread coordination and cooperation. Each thread has a private stack, therefore local variables in procedures are always private to the thread executing the procedure. However, threads are not, by default, given private heaps or private copies of static variables. (Note that, even if variables are private, they are still not *protected* against accesses by other threads.)

Consider, for example, an attempt to use the C standard input-output library, with a threads package. This library uses a single buffer for each input-output stream. If more than one thread attempted to use the same output stream to a terminal, let us say, then the characters output would be interleaved according to the scheduling pattern of the two threads – instead of being output in complete lines. Furthermore, since the library keeps a pointer to the position in the buffer where the next character is to be placed, a race condition could develop, wherein the two threads each read the value of this pointer and update it independently and inconsistently.

The input-output library either has to be modified, so that a different stream buffer is dynamically allocated for each thread and used exclusively by it; or, each stream buffer can be shared, but race conditions must be avoided by synchronizing accesses to the buffer's next-character-pointer. The calls *cthread_set_data* and *cthread_data* given in the table above can be used to associate data structures such as input-output buffers exclusively with a given thread.

Figure 6.11   Synchronization calls for the C Threads Library.

---

mutex_lock(mutexId)
   Blocks the thread if necessary until the mutex has been unlocked – then locks mutex;

mutex_unlock(mutexId)
   Unlock the mutex;

condition_wait(conditionId, mutexId)
   Unlocks the mutex and blocks the thread – queues it on the condition variable;

condition_signal(conditionId)
   If a thread is blocked on the condition variable, wake it.

The C Threads package provides resources called *mutexes* for the creation of *critical sections* of code – code in which only one thread at a time may execute, such as that necessary for accessing a shared stream buffer. A mutex behaves like a semaphore with an initial count of one. A thread wishing to enter a critical section calls *mutex_lock* and on leaving, it calls *mutex_unlock. Condition variables*, which are used by threads such as those in our two-threaded client example above to synchronize their accesses to shared data. These calls provide the usual semantics for condition variable *signal* and *wait* operations. *Semaphores* can be readily constructed from mutexes and condition variables. The C Threads synchronization calls are given in Figure 6.11.

Thread scheduling ☐ There are two main approaches to the scheduling of threads. In *preemptive scheduling*, a thread may be suspended to make way for another thread, even when it is otherwise runnable. In *non-preemptive scheduling* (sometimes called *coroutine scheduling*), a thread runs until it makes a call that causes it to be descheduled and another thread to be run. Both have been implemented for the C Threads package; the programmer chooses one or the other by linking in different libraries.

The advantage of non-preemptive scheduling is that any section of code that does not contain a call that might cause a rescheduling is automatically a critical section. Race conditions are thus conveniently avoided. On the other hand, non-preemptively-scheduled threads cannot take advantage of a multiprocessor, since they run exclusively. They are also unsuited to real-time applications, in which events are associated with absolute times by which they must be processed. Without preemption, a computationally intensive thread must explicitly make a call – *cthread_yield* – from time to time, to allow other threads to make progress.

C Threads does not allow individual threads to be given a priority. This renders it useless for any application in which certain events are deemed more urgent than others. This might arise in, for example, a server controlling processes in a factory, where a critical condition might arise such as a component overload. Ideally, urgent events would be notified in messages sent to a special port held by the server, and processed by a high-priority thread that receives messages from it. This thread would preempt all other processing when an urgent message arrived.

Static priorities by themselves are not sufficient for real-time processing. For example, in Chapter 1 we introduced multimedia applications and we noted that data such as voice and video have real-time requirements for both communication and processing (for example, filtering and compression) [Govindan and Anderson 1991]. Thread scheduling requirements are likely to be particular to each real-time application domain. It is therefore desirable for applications to implement their own scheduling policies. To consider this, we turn now to the implementation of threads.

Threads implementation □ Some conventional kernels have only a single-threaded process abstraction, but multi-threaded processes are implemented in a library of procedures linked with application programs. This is done, for example, by the SunOS 4.1 Lightweight Processes package. The kernel has no knowledge of lightweight processes, and therefore cannot schedule them independently. A threads run-time library organizes the scheduling of threads. A thread would block the process and therefore all threads within it if it made a blocking system call, so the asynchronous (non-blocking) input-output facilities of UNIX are used.

When no kernel support for multi-threaded processes is provided, a user-level threads implementation suffers from the following problems:

• the threads within a process cannot take advantage of a multiprocessor;

• threads within different processes cannot be scheduled according to a single scheme of relative prioritization.

User-level threads implementations, on the other hand, have significant advantages over kernel-level implementations:

• certain thread operations are significantly less costly. For example, switching between threads belonging to the same process does not necessarily involve a system call – that is, a relatively expensive trap to the kernel;

• given that the thread scheduling module is implemented outside the kernel, it can be customized or changed to suit particular application requirements. Variations in scheduling requirements occur largely because of application-specific considerations such as the real-time nature of multimedia processing;

• many more user-level threads can be supported than could reasonably be provided by default by a kernel.

It is possible to combine the advantages of user-level and kernel-level threads implementations, to some extent. One approach, applied, for example, to the Mach kernel [Black 1990], is to enable user-level code to provide scheduling hints to the kernel's thread scheduler. Another is to provide kernel support for user-level thread scheduling. The second approach has been adopted in work on so-called scheduler activations underlying the FastThreads package [Anderson *et al.* 1991], in the multimedia work of Govindan and Anderson [1991], and in the Psyche multiprocessor operating system [Marsh *et al.* 1991].

In the Psyche design, the kernel provides abstractions called *virtual processors*, which are resources belonging to processes. A virtual processor corresponds to an individual physical processor, and an application wishing to obtain parallelism would normally create one on each of several processors. The kernel schedules the virtual processors belonging to different processes on each processor. Virtual processors do not migrate between processors.

On top of the virtual processor abstraction, a user-level module provides threads. Information is transferred between the thread scheduler module and the kernel via a collection of data structures in a shared region mapped into the both the kernel's and the process's address space. This obviates the cost of system call traps, but use of this shared memory communication mechanism is restricted to cases where synchronization is not required between the kernel and the process.

The kernel can notify the user-level scheduler:

- when a virtual processor requires initialization (that is, it has become available to the process and should be assigned a thread to run);

- when a thread has blocked in a kernel call, and when it has completed a blocked call;

- when the kernel intends to preempt a particular virtual processor after a specified time.

Using this information, the scheduler can assign a new thread to a virtual processor, or it can re-assign a thread to a different virtual processor (bound to a different physical processor). The information is provided by the kernel in the shared data structures, but is normally conveyed via a software interrupt generated by the kernel and handled by a user-level handler.

This two-level scheduling scheme allows a user-level scheduler within a process to take advantage of multiple processors in a shared memory multiprocessor, while implementing its own scheduling policy between the threads belonging to the process. The kernel retains control over the allocation of processor time between processes, however.

6.4   Naming and protection

Section 2.2 introduced naming as a fundamental issue in distributed system design. It distinguished between human-readable textual names and system identifiers. Meaningful textual names such as '/project/status' are used by humans to refer to files and other resources. These names are resolved to lower-level identifiers which are recognized by the service that manages the resource. Identifiers are bit strings that can be efficiently stored and manipulated by the service.

Generally a service manages several resources, each of which can be accessed independently by its clients. To make this possible, a service provides an identifier for each of its resources. For example a file service provides file identifiers for each of the files it manages (Chapter 7). Services may be required to be reconfigurable – flexible as to which of a group of servers manages a particular resource, and as to the location of the servers. Clients require that the location of a resource is transparent. We shall explain how these requirements are reconciled by suitable naming schemes, and go on to examine the related problem of protecting resources against illegitimate accesses.

Clients access resources by making requests to the service that manages them, supplying the appropriate identifiers. For example, a client of a file service will supply the file identifier of a file to read or write. Client requests are directed to a communication identifier, which may be obtained from a binding service. In Mach,

Figure 6.12   Using a resource.

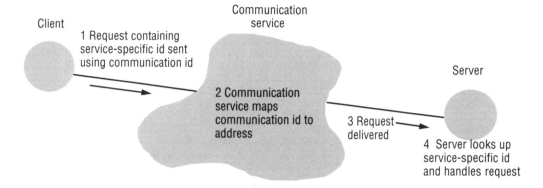

Chorus and Amoeba this communication identifier is that of a port, or a group of ports in the case of Chorus.

Thus, the identification of a resource in these systems requires a knowledge of:

- a port or port group to reach the server that manages the resource;

- a service-specific identifier for the resource (unless a unique port is associated with it).

The use of location-independent communication identifiers provides network transparency. The communication service implemented by the kernel, perhaps in conjunction with network servers, is responsible for looking up the corresponding physical server address (or addresses) and determining the message route for client request messages (Figure 6.12). The server (or group of servers) that receives the message looks up the service-specific identifier.

The format of identifiers used by a particular service can be chosen freely by the service implementor. It is usual for identifiers belonging to a particular type of resource not to vary in size, to simplify storage administration and marshalling. Identifiers should be large enough for the space of objects to be named, but should not be too large, in order to conserve memory and network bandwidth.

Identifiers should of course refer unambiguously to an individual resource, either in the context of a distributed system or at least within the service that manages the resource concerned. Amoeba identifiers (see Chapter 18) are unique within an entire distributed system. As we noted in Chapter 1, this is a distinguishing property of the object model of resource management. It allows an identifier to be mapped to a service, as well as a resource managed by that service; it has the advantage of allowing clients to use an identifier without knowing which service issued it. Amoeba furthermore saves looking up the service port by embedding a port identifier within each identifier.

How should identifiers be generated? Wherever possible, kernels and servers should be able to generate identifiers for new resources they create, without consulting their peers to avoid coining duplicate identifiers. A convenient way of generating identifiers that are guaranteed unique throughout a distributed system is to pre-allocate a large set of identifiers to each kernel or server in the system. An especially effective form of this idea is for every identifier to begin with the kernel's site identifier or server's identifier within a service, but without any requirement for the resource to remain at that physical location. Not all identifiers need be guaranteed to be unique indefinitely. Some system identifiers refer to volatile objects and are re-used on this basis: process identifiers in UNIX can name first one process, then another.

Reconfigurability □ Reconfigurability is the capacity of a distributed system to accommodate evolution and short-term changes in run-time conditions such as computer or network load, or failure of either of these, without disruption. Tolerance of failure is discussed in Chapter 15. Two other main forms of reconfigurability apply to servers:

> *Server relocation*: An instance of a service is moved from one server computer to another. This is achieved either by creating a new instance of a service at a new computer, or by migrating the server process intact to the new computer.

> *Resource mobility*: A resource or group of resources is moved from the management of one server to another implementing the same service, while the original server continues to manage other resources. For example, in *file migration* (see Chapter 7) a file or group of files is transferred between servers.

These reconfigurations lead to several complex design issues relating to the synchronization of the servers and transfer of state between them. The design of the communication system is crucial, since it affects the possibility of reconfiguration transparency [Kindberg 1990].

Whether changes are performed at run-time or are evolutionary, a degree of transparency is necessary so that the mapping of resource names to server addresses can be altered. The following levels of transparency, introduced in Chapter 2, can be achieved:

> *Location transparency*: the relocation of a resource between computers is transparent as long as the resource is not accessed while relocation takes place.

> *Migration transparency*: a resource continues to be uniformly accessible while relocation takes place (although there may be a performance degradation).

It is sometimes possible to reconfigure a service without clients noticing, simply by performing the change in a convenient interval such as night-time when the system is quiescent. If this is not possible, then the problem that must be faced is that of implementing the change transparently while the service is on-line to client processes.

A service is responsible for managing its internal tables so that service-specific resource identifiers remain valid despite any reconfiguration. Recall that a client also requires a port or port group identifier in order to communicate with the service. For transparency, clients should not experience communication failures when they attempt to access a resource using a port or port group that is supposed to be used to reach its service.

In the case of a service implemented by a single server, the current server should always listen on a port with the same identifier as that used by clients. It is then the communication subsystem's task to locate the port, despite its movement from computer to computer as the server's location changes. Chapter 18 describes the Amoeba and Mach port location service.

A service that is implemented by several servers may use a port group. Clients are asked to obey a convention of multicasting to the port group when requesting access to a resource, and supplying the service-specific identifier of the desired resource in the multicast request. The communication subsystem's task is to locate and deliver the request to all ports currently within the group. Whichever server currently manages the required resource then replies with a port to be used for accessing the resource. The port group facilities of Chorus are described in Chapter 18.

A service may allow a resource or group of resources to migrate between servers by associating a unique port with it. When the resource or group is moved, the new server begins to listen on the port, and the old server ceases to. Chorus and Mach support a port migration facility, whereby not only is the port moved between servers, but its message queue is also moved. This saves the old server from forwarding messages to its replacement. The client is unaware of the port's movement.

Resource protection

The aim of a protection scheme is to ensure that each process can access only those resources for which it has permission. The permission specifies which operations it may perform on the resource. Recall from Section 2.3 that protecting resources in a distributed system is complicated by the openness of networks and the susceptibility of unprotected computers to malicious changes to their system software.

As with other aspects of resource management, resource protection in a distributed operating system is largely service-specific. Kernels implement their own resource protection, and higher-level services do the same. Kernels employ hardware facilities such as memory management units to implement protection for themselves and the hardware they manage, as well as memory protection for the processes that they host. Servers, on the other hand, have to cope with the fact that they can be sent arbitrary messages from anywhere in the distributed system, and they have to rely on software techniques to protect their resources against maliciously contrived requests.

Protection domains □ In this chapter we consider processes to be the agents that can request operations to be performed (a more general definition of *principals* as agents is given in Chapter 16). A protection domain is a protection environment shared by a collection of processes: it is a set of <resource, rights> pairs, listing the resources that can be accessed by all processes executing within the domain, and specifying the operations permitted for each resource. For example, in UNIX, the protection domain of a process is determined by the associated user and group identifiers. Rights are specified in terms of allowed operations. For example, a file might be readable and writable by one process and readable by another.

A protection domain is only an abstraction. Two alternative implementations are commonly used in operating systems. These are capabilities and access control lists.

- *Capabilities*: a set of capabilities is held by each process according to the domain in which it is located. Capabilities are identifiers that contain additional random bits making them hard to forge. They were introduced in Chapter 2 and will be discussed in further detail in Chapter 7. Services only supply capabilities to clients when they authenticate them as belonging to the claimed protection domain.

Different capabilities are used for different combinations of access rights to the same resource.

- *Access control lists*: a list is stored with each resource, giving the domains that have access to the resource and the operations permitted in each domain.

Servers may be designed to use capabilities or access control lists:

- Client requests include a capability for the resource to be accessed, giving the server immediate proof that the client is authorized to access the resource identified by the capability with the operations specified by the capability.

- Client requests include an identifier for the resource to be accessed. The server authenticates the client and checks the access control list at each request. Authentication is generally achieved by communication between the client, the server and an authentication server.

The construction and use of capabilities in file systems is covered in Chapter 7, and their use in Amoeba is covered in Chapter 18. Chapter 16 discusses authentication protocols.

6.5   Communication and invocation

This section discusses the basic communication provision in distributed operating systems. Communication is not an end in itself, but is normally part of the implementation of what we have called an invocation – a construct, such as a remote procedure call, whose purpose is to bring about the processing of data in a different scope or execution environment.

Applications impose a variety of demands upon a communication system. These include producer-consumer, client-server and group communication. They vary as to the *quality of service* required, that is the delivery guarantees, bandwidth and latency, and security provided by the communication service. For example, video and voice data must be transmitted with very low latencies, whereas ordinary file transfer is much less demanding. Some applications require that data should be kept secret, despite the fact that they are passed over a physically insecure network. In addition, an application may require communication with a computer that happens to support only a particular protocol.

We can ask the following questions concerning the communication provision in a distributed operating system:

- What basic communication primitives are supplied?

- What quality of service guarantees are made?

- Which protocols are supported?

- How open is the communication implementation?

- What steps are taken to make communication as efficient as possible?

Communication primitives □ Distributed operating system kernels normally provide message passing in one or both of the forms given in Chapter 4: the *Send-Receive* combination and the *DoOperation-GetRequest-SendReply* combination. In some systems, however, *Send* is reliable. Where a system provides only one of the two models, it is on the grounds that it can be used to implement the other. For example, in Amoeba the asynchronous semantics of *Send* can be reproduced by (a) copying the contents of the given message into a dynamically allocated message buffer, so that the caller of *Send* can re-use its buffer; and (b) using an independent thread which executes *DoOperation* while the first thread proceeds.

Systems that provide both models do so on the basis that optimizations can be performed for each case. In the case of *DoOperation-GetRequest-SendReply*, the underlying transport protocol can be optimized to reflect the request-reply interchange of data packets. Other advantages are given in Chapter 4. In the case of *Send*, no thread manipulation is required to achieve asynchronous semantics.

In addition, group communication is provided in several distributed operating systems, including Amoeba, the V system and Chorus. The V system provides a multicast equivalent of *DoOperation*, which receives just one reply by default, even though each recipient can reply. Any further replies can be received by a separate call made by the client. Although receiving extra replies involves this extra call, a multicast version of *DoOperation* can be justified on the grounds that, in many cases, just one process in a group will reply – for example, when the multicast request is for a resource possessed by just one member of the group. Amoeba and Chorus provide only a *Send* operation to groups, on the basis that replies will be sent separately, as necessary.

Memory sharing □ Mach applies copy-on-write memory sharing to the transfer of large messages between local processes. A message may be constructed from an address space region, which consists of a set of entire pages (the programmer has to create a region for this purpose). When the message is passed to a local process, a region is created in its address space to hold the message, and this region is copied from the sent region in copy-on-write mode. (Copy-on-write sharing was introduced in Section 6.3.)

Shared regions (also introduced in Section 6.3) may be used for rapid communication between a user process and the kernel, or between user processes. Data are communicated by writing to and reading from the shared region. Data are thus passed efficiently, without copying them to and from the kernel's address space. System calls and software interrupts may be required for synchronization – such as when the user process has written data that should be transmitted, or when the kernel has written data for the user process to consume. Of course, a shared region is only justified if it is used sufficiently to offset the initial cost of setting it up.

Quality of service □ Even if the basic kernel communication primitives are unreliable, they are sufficient for the construction of a reliable version of *Send*, or a remote procedure call system with at-least-once or at-most-once semantics. Stream-oriented communication can also be implemented using them, with suitable buffering. High-level multicast communication semantics may be constructed, as described in Chapter 11. Security may be provided by passing data to a network server – or an in-client library – that encrypts the data before forwarding them to the destination (the distribution of encryption keys for this purpose is discussed in Chapter 16). All such enhancements of the basic communication facilities have been achieved.

Perhaps the central difficulty faced is that of achieving satisfactory latencies and bandwidths. As we have already pointed out, multimedia data are particularly demanding in this respect, because they impose real-time constraints. The required latency and bandwidth varies between the type of data (for example, video or voice), and the quality of presentation required. A professional audio application, for example, may be unable to function according to its specifications unless the operating system can guarantee a minimum bandwidth and maximum latency. Jeffay [1989] has suggested that the operating system should be able to manage its processing and communication resources so as either to guarantee a minimum quality of service specified by a client, or refuse to provide it and leave the client to try again later.

Some well-established operating system techniques have proved unequal or inappropriate in the case of multimedia data [Govindan and Anderson 1991]. The client-server communication model gives latencies that are typically too high. It is generally inappropriate to cache multimedia data, since it tends to be produced and consumed in streams because of its bulk and timeliness requirements. For example, video data might be read sequentially from a file server, uncompressed and displayed on-the-fly.

An example of the use of shared memory regions is the *memory mapped stream* of Govindan and Anderson, which is a shared circular buffer used for transferring multimedia data between a user process and the kernel. This has the advantages of shared memory communication mentioned above; in addition, the kernel knows that data within the region should not be cached, and so can immediately re-allocate used pages.

Protocols and openness □ Kernels differ in whether or not they support network communication directly. Some, notably Amoeba, the V system and Sprite, incorporate their own network protocols tuned to RPC interactions – Amoeba RPC [van Renesse *et al*. 1989], VMTP [Cheriton 1986] and Sprite RPC [Ousterhout *et al*. 1988], respectively. However, these protocols are not widely used beyond the research environments in which these distributed operating systems were designed.

Protocols such as TCP, UDP and IP, on the other hand, are widely used over LANs and WANs but do not directly support RPC interactions. Rather than design their own protocols, or commit the kernel to any particular established protocol, the designers of the Mach and Chorus kernels decided to make the communication design open. They support local message passing only, and leave network protocol processing to a server which runs on top of the kernel. Server processes that implement networking software are given direct access to the network hardware, for the sake of efficiency. See Chapter 18 for further detail.

The x-kernel [Peterson *et al*. 1990] is specifically designed for accessing Internet resources efficiently. It incorporates several protocols and is designed for further protocols to be incorporated. In order that the most efficient communication is provided, according to whether a resource is situated on the local LAN or over a WAN, protocols can be composed dynamically. A similar approach to protocol composition has also been followed in the design of the UNIX Streams facility [Ritchie 1984].

Invocation performance

Calling a local procedure, making a system call, sending a message, remote procedure calling and invoking a method in an object by sending a message to it, are all examples of invocation mechanisms. Each mechanism causes code to be executed out of scope of the calling procedure or object. Each involves, in general, the communication of

Figure 6.13   Invocations between address spaces.

(a) System call

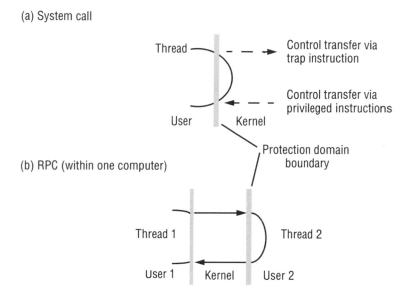

(b) RPC (within one computer)

(c) RPC (between computers)

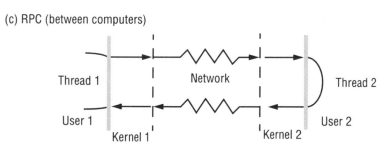

arguments to this code, and the return of data values to the caller. Invocation mechanisms can be either synchronous, as for example in the case of local and remote procedure calls, or they can be asynchronous, when for example an operation with no return values is invoked upon an object.

The important performance-related distinctions between invocation mechanisms, apart from whether or not they are synchronous, are: whether they involve a domain transition, whether they involve communication across a network, and whether they involve thread scheduling and switching. Figure 6.13 shows the particular cases of a system call, an RPC between processes hosted by the same computer, and an RPC between remote processes.

Much effort has been put into enhancing the performance of local and remote invocations across address space boundaries. In particular, RPC implementations have been the subject of considerable study because of the widespread acceptance of RPC for general-purpose client-server processing. Work has been carried out on RPCs [Schroeder and Burrows 1990, van Renesse *et al.* 1989, Hutchinson *et al.* 1989], and on the important special case of RPCs between processes hosted by the same computer

[Bershad *et al.* 1990, Bershad *et al.* 1991]. We describe some general performance considerations for RPCs between computers (Chapter 18 describes the Firefly RPC design in full), and then go on to the case of an RPC within a single computer.

RPC performance

A **null RPC** is defined as an RPC without parameters, that executes a null procedure, and returns no values. Its execution involves an exchange of messages carrying little system data and no user data. Currently, the best reported time for a null RPC between two user processes across a LAN is about one millisecond (by comparison, a null conventional procedure call takes a small fraction of a microsecond). Of the order of 100 bytes in total are passed across the network for a null RPC. With a raw bandwidth of 10 megabits per second, the total network transfer time for this amount of data is about 0.1 milliseconds. Clearly, much of the observed delay – the total RPC call time experienced by a client – has to be accounted for by the actions of the operating system and user-level RPC run-time code.

A typical RPC request or reply transfers a few small arguments. One study found that the most frequently occurring RPC calls, in a sample of 1.5 million calls, transferred fewer than 50 user bytes, and that a majority of all calls transferred fewer than 200 bytes [Bershad *et al.* 1990]. Data such as disk blocks transferred by RPC tend to be larger, of size 1–8 kilobytes. But the use of client caching has meant that such calls are made less frequently than might be imagined.

Most RPC request or reply messages fit into a single physical network packet, which is in the order of one kilobyte in size. Null RPC figures are important because they measure a fixed overhead. Of course, the cost of a call increases with the size of the arguments, but the fixed overhead is large compared with the remainder of the delay.

Consider an RPC that fetches a specified amount of data from a server. It has one integer request argument, specifying the size of data required. It has two reply arguments, an integer specifying success or failure (the client might have given an invalid size), and, when the call is successful, an array of bytes from the server.

Figure 6.14 shows client delay against requested data size. The delay is roughly proportional to the size until the size reaches a threshold at about network packet size. Beyond that threshold, at least one extra packet has to be sent, to carry the extra data. Depending on the protocol, a further packet might be used to acknowledge this extra packet. Jumps in the graph occur each time the number of packets increases.

Delay is not the only figure of interest for an RPC implementation: RPC bandwidth (or *throughput*) is also of concern when data have to be transferred in bulk. This is the rate at which data can be transferred between computers in a single RPC. If we examine Figure 6.14, we can see that the bandwidth is relatively low for small amounts of data, when the fixed processing overheads predominate. As the amount of data is increased, the bandwidth rises as those overheads become less significant. The maximum value is about 750 kilobytes per second in the fastest recent implementations [Hutchinson *et al.* 1989] using workstations over an Ethernet with a raw bandwidth of 10 megabits per second. Of course, RPC bandwidth for large amounts of data should rise considerably with the advent of networks rated at 100 megabits per second. But for small amounts of data, the fixed overheads still predominate. What are these overheads, and how can they be minimized?

Figure 6.14   RPC delay against parameter size.

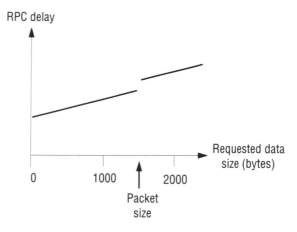

Recall that the steps in an RPC are as follows:

- a client stub marshals the call arguments into a message, sends the request message and receives and unmarshals the reply;

- at the server, a dispatcher thread receives the incoming request and calls the appropriate server stub;

- the server stub unmarshals the request message, calls the designated procedure, and marshals and sends the reply.

The following are the main components accounting for RPC delay, besides network transmission times:

Marshalling: Marshalling and unmarshalling, which involve copying and converting data, become a significant overhead as the amount of data grows.

Data copying: The processor in a present-day workstation can copy data from memory to memory at about 10 megabytes per second. This is about the same as the transfer rate that can be achieved on a 100 megabits-per-second network. Potentially, even after marshalling, message data is copied several times in the course of an RPC:

1. across the user-kernel boundary, between the client or server address space and kernel buffers;

2. across each protocol layer (for example, RPC/UDP/IP/Ethernet);

3. between the network interface and kernel buffers.

Transfers between the network interface and main memory are usually handled by direct memory access (DMA). The other copies have to be handled by the processor.

Packet initialization: This involves initializing protocol headers and trailers, including checksums. The cost is therefore proportional to the amount of data sent.

Thread scheduling and context switching: These may occur as follows:

1. several system calls (that is, context switches) are made during an RPC, as stubs invoke the kernel's communication operations;

2. a server thread is scheduled to call the remote procedure;

3. if the operating system employs a separate network manager process, then each *Send* involves a context switch to one of its threads.

Waiting for acknowledgements: The choice of RPC protocol may influence delay, particularly when large amounts of data are sent.

Several techniques for amortizing these costs are described in Chapter 18. The choice of protocol is discussed in the Amoeba case study, and other factors are addressed in the Firefly RPC design. In this chapter we have already described the use of shared regions and copy-on-write region copying to avoid physically copying data in the local case. We now turn to RPCs between local address spaces.

RPC within a computer

Bershad *et al.* [1990] report a study which showed that, in the installation examined, most cross-address-space invocation took place within a computer and not, as might be expected in a client-server installation, between computers. The trend towards the use of microkernels and operating system emulation by user-level servers at each computer means that more and more RPCs will be to a local process. This is especially so as caching is pursued aggressively, when the data needed by a client is liable to be held locally. The cost of an RPC within a computer is growing in importance as a system performance parameter. These considerations suggest that this local case should be optimized.

Figure 6.13 above suggests that an RPC is implemented in the local case exactly as in the remote case, except that the underlying message passing happens to be local. Indeed, this has largely been the model implemented. Bershad *et al.* [1990] developed a more efficient local invocation mechanism called *lightweight RPC (LRPC)* based on optimizations concerning data copying and thread scheduling.

First, they noted that it would be more efficient to use shared memory regions for client-server communication, with a different (private) region between the server and each of its local clients. Such a region contains one or more *A* (for argument) *stacks* (see Figure 6.15). Instead of RPC parameters being copied between the kernel and user address spaces involved, client and server are able to pass arguments and return values directly via an A stack. The same stack is used by the client and server stubs. In LRPC, arguments are copied once: when they are marshalled onto the A stack. In an equivalent RPC, they are copied four times: from the client stub's stack onto a message; from the message to a kernel buffer; from the kernel buffer to a server message; from the message to the server stub's stack. There may be several A stacks in a shared region, because several threads in the same client may call the server at the same time.

Figure 6.15   A lightweight remote procedure call.

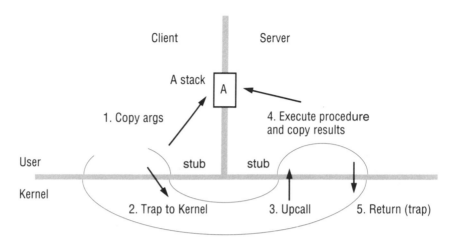

Bershad *et al.* also considered the cost of thread scheduling. Compare the model of system call and remote procedure calls in Figure 6.13. When a system call occurs, most kernels do not schedule a new thread to handle the call, but instead perform a context switch so that the calling thread handles the system call. In an RPC, a remote procedure may exist in a different computer from the client thread, so a different thread must be scheduled to execute it. In the local case, however, it may be more efficient for the client thread – which would otherwise be idle – to call the invoked procedure in the server's address space.

A server must be programmed differently in this case to the way we have described servers before. Instead of setting up one or more threads, which then listen on ports for invocation requests, the server exports a set of procedures that it is prepared to have called. Threads in local processes may enter the server's execution environment, as long as they start by calling one of the server's exported procedures. A client needing to invoke a server's operations must first bind to the server interface (not shown in the figure). It does this via the kernel, which notifies the server; when the server has responded to the kernel with a list of allowed procedure addresses, the kernel replies to the client with a capability for invoking the server's operations.

An invocation is shown in Figure 6.15. A client thread enters the server's execution environment by first trapping to the kernel and presenting it with a capability. The kernel checks this and only allows a context switch to a valid server procedure; if it is valid, the kernel switches the thread's context to call the procedure in the server's execution environment. Entering a body of code from a lower layer (the kernel) in this way is sometimes called an *upcall*. When the procedure in the server returns, the thread returns to the kernel, which switches the thread back to the client execution environment. Note that clients and servers employ stub procedures to hide the details just described from application writers.

Discussion of LRPC □   There is little doubt that LRPC is more efficient than RPC for local invocations, as long as enough invocations take place to offset the memory management costs. Bershad *et al.* record that LRPC delays are a factor of three smaller than those of RPC executed locally.

Location transparency is not sacrificed in Bershad's implementation. A client stub examines a bit set at bind time that records whether the server is local or remote, and proceeds to use LRPC or RPC respectively. The application is unaware of which is used. However, migration transparency might be hard to achieve when a resource is transferred from a local server to a remote server, or *vice versa*, because of the need to change invocation mechanisms.

In later work, Bershad *et al.* [1991] describe several performance improvements, which are addressed particularly to multiprocessor operation. The improvements largely concern avoiding traps to the kernel and scheduling processors in such a way as to avoid unnecessary domain transitions. For example, if a processor is idling in the server's memory management context at the time a client thread attempts to invoke a server procedure, then the thread should be transferred to that processor. This avoids a domain transition; at the same time, the client's processor may be re-used by another thread in the client. These enhancements involve an implementation of two-level (user and kernel) thread scheduling as described in Section 6.3.

6.6   Virtual memory

Virtual memory is the abstraction of single-level storage that is implemented, transparently, by a combination of primary memory, such as RAM chips, and backing storage, that is a high speed persistent storage mechanism such as a disk. Virtual memory is of considerable interest as an aspect of the design of distributed operating systems. First, a virtual memory implementation may need to use a backing store at a separate computer from the one that contains the primary memory. Secondly, it is possible to share data which is simultaneously mapped into the address spaces of processes residing at different computers in the form of distributed shared memory, which is described in Chapter 17.

Much of the implementation of virtual memory in a distributed system is common to that found in a conventional operating system. The main difference is that the backing store interface is to a server, instead of a local disk. For a full description of virtual memory and its implementation in conventional, uniprocessor operating systems, the reader is referred to Tanenbaum [1992]. This section outlines those general features of the virtual memory concept and implementation that are applicable to distributed systems.

A central aim of virtual memory systems is to be able to execute large programs, and combinations of programs, whose entire code and data are too large to be stored in main memory at any one time. In virtual memory systems, part of main memory is used as a cache of the contents of backing storage. By storing only those sections of code and data currently being accessed by processes, it is possible (a) to run programs whose associated code and data exceeds the capacity of main memory, (b) to increase the level of multiprogramming by increasing the number of processes whose working code and data can be stored in main memory simultaneously, and (c) to remove the concerns of physical memory limitations from programmers.

This idea was then generalized so that any open file (and not just sections of executable files) could be made to correspond with an address space region (see Section 6.3). A process reads or writes the data in mapped files by reading or writing the corresponding virtual memory locations. In a typical high-level language, the open file appears as an array of bytes. The underlying kernel is responsible for fetching data from secondary storage as the array is accessed, and for writing modified data to permanent store. MULTICS [Organick 1972] was the original operating system to include mapped files. A more recent example of an operating system which supports them is SunOS.

The most common implementation of virtual memory is called *demand paging*. Each page is fetched into primary memory upon demand: that is, when a process attempts to read or write data in a page which is not currently resident, it is fetched from backing store.

A virtual memory system is required to make decisions in two areas. First, its *frame allocation policy* is an algorithm for deciding how much main memory should be allocated to each running process. Secondly, a *page replacement policy* is used when a page must be fetched from secondary storage and there is no room in the main memory cache. A page is chosen to be replaced by the page to be brought in. The virtual memory system applies its policies at two points in the system's operation: (a) when a process attempts to reference a non-resident page, causing a page fault to be raised and handled by the kernel, and (b) periodically, upon measurement of page fault rates and/or each process's page reference patterns.

External pagers

In a distributed system, the computer running a process that incurs a page fault is not necessarily the same computer that manages the corresponding page data. For example, the first computer could be diskless. Even where a local disk is used for some paging, the pages of mapped files could be managed by a remote file server. The natural development for virtual memory implementation in distributed systems is for page data to be stored by a server, and not directly by the kernel using a local secondary storage device. These user-level servers are variously called **external pagers** or *external mappers* or *memory managers* (Figure 6.16).

Recall that a virtual address space is organized in regions. To consider a general model, we shall assume that any region in an address space is mapped to part or all of some underlying **memory object**. A memory object is a contiguous, addressable resource such as a file or a set of pages managed by an external pager. If the region is an execution stack, for example, then the underlying memory object is one which persists only as long as the process executes. In the case of a region into which a file has been mapped, the underlying memory object is the file itself. By using an external server for paging, instead of keeping this functionality in the kernel, customized paging schemes can be implemented. External pagers also provide an approach to the implementation of distributed shared memory.

To map a memory object into a region, the process sends a request to the external pager that manages the memory object (see Figure 6.16). After the mapping, messages pass between the kernel and the external server to deal with paging. The kernel fetches initial data values from the external pager, and pages data to it, just as a conventional

Figure 6.16   An external pager manages mapped memory objects.

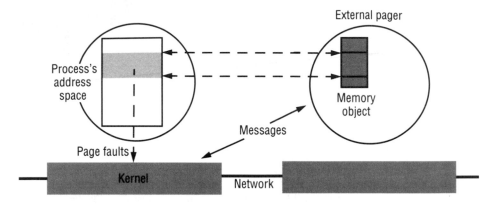

virtual memory operating system kernel pages in initial data values and pages out data to disk.

The kernel retains responsibility for handling page fault exceptions generated by local processes. It is responsible for main (physical) memory management, and therefore for implementing a frame allocation policy. The kernel is normally left to implement its own page replacement policy. The information necessary for applying the page replacement policy, such as bits set by the memory management unit when pages are referenced or modified, is local to the kernel.

The roles of the external pager are:

i) to receive and deal appropriately with data that have been purged by a kernel from its cache of pages, as part of the kernel's page replacement policy;

ii) to supply page data as required by a kernel to complete its page fault handling; and

iii)to impose consistency constraints determined by the underlying memory object abstraction, given that several kernels might attempt to cache modifiable pages of the object simultaneously.

Of these, (i) and (ii) are straightforward extensions of the conventional virtual memory subsystem that stores each page as a disk block and records its disk address, or which looks up the address of pages and fetches them from disk, respectively. The difference in the distributed case is that the kernel requires not a disk address but a capability for the memory object. It uses this to transmit or request page data in messages to the corresponding external pager. The kernel is unaware of the whereabouts of the external pager. Data are copied in messages, so there is no presumption of the pager being local.

The external pager's role number (iii), the maintenance of consistency, is relevant to mapped file access and distributed shared memory. See Chapter 17.

In summary, virtual memory is a framework for accessing any collection of memory objects that can be mapped to individual regions. The common requirement for any memory object abstraction is that it consists of contiguously addressable data items, which may be read and modified. A message passing protocol between the kernel and an external pager is discussed in the study of Mach in Chapter 18.

6.7   Summary

This chapter has developed a model of a minimal open distributed operating system as an infrastructure in which clients access resources managed by kernels and by dynamically loaded server processes. The distributed operating system provides a collection of mechanisms upon which varying resource management policies can be implemented – to meet local requirements, and to take advantage of technological improvements. This infrastructure allows servers to encapsulate and protect resources, while allowing clients to share them concurrently. It provides mechanisms necessary for clients to invoke operations upon resources. This involves name resolution, communication and scheduling.

There are two main approaches to kernel architecture: monolithic kernels and microkernels. The main difference between them lies in where the line is drawn between resource management by the kernel and resource management performed by dynamically-loaded (and usually user-level) servers. A microkernel must support at least a notion of process and inter-process communication. It supports operating system emulation subsystems as well as language support and other subsystems, such as those for real-time processing.

A process consists of an execution environment and threads: an execution environment consists of an address space, communication interfaces and other local resources such as semaphores; a thread is an activity abstraction that executes within an execution environment. Address spaces need to be large and sparse in order to support sharing and mapped access to objects such as files. New address spaces may be created with their regions inherited from parent processes. An important technique for copying regions is copy-on-write.

Processes can have multiple threads, which share the execution environment. Multi-threaded processes allow us to achieve relatively cheap concurrency, and to take advantage of multiprocessors for parallelism. They are useful for both clients and servers. Recent threads implementations allow for two-tier scheduling: the kernel provides access to multiple processors, while user-level code handles the details of scheduling policy.

Distributed operating systems support reconfigurability by providing mechanisms for port migration and location and multicast communication for the location of servers and resources. These mechanisms allow location and migration transparency to be achieved. The main software mechanisms for resource protection are capabilities and access control lists.

Distributed operating system kernels provide basic message passing primitives and mechanisms for communication via shared memory. Higher-level services provide a variety of quality of service options: delivery guarantees, bandwidth and latency, and security. Some microkernels include network communication as a basic facility, others provide only local communication and leave network communication to servers, which may implement a range of communication protocols. This is a trade-off of performance against flexibility.

We discussed remote RPCs and accounted for the difference between overheads due directly to network hardware, and overheads that are due to the execution of operating system code. We found the proportion of the total time due to software to be relatively large for a null RPC, but to decrease as a proportion of the total with the size of the RPC arguments. The chief overheads involved in an RPC that are candidates for optimization are marshalling, data copying, packet initialization, thread scheduling and context switching, and the flow control protocol used. RPC within a computer is an important special case, and we described the thread management and parameter passing techniques used in lightweight RPC.

Finally, we introduced some issues concerned with the implementation of virtual memory in a distributed system. We described the use of external pagers that manage the memory objects that back regions of processes' virtual address space. The kernels communicate with external pagers when page faults are taken and when data has to be purged to make room in the kernel's page cache.

Exercises

6.1   Discuss each of the tasks of encapsulation, concurrent processing, protection, name resolution, communication of parameters and results, and scheduling in the case of the UNIX file service (or that of another kernel that is familiar to you).

page 159

6.2   Explain what is security policy and what are the corresponding mechanisms in the case of a multi-user operating system such as UNIX.

page 159

6.3   Explain the program linkage requirements that must be met if a server is to be dynamically loaded into the kernel's address space, and how these differ from the case of executing a server at user-level.

page 161

6.4   How could an interrupt be communicated to a user-level server?

page 161

6.5   If UNIX is to be re-designed to include multi-threaded processes, should signal handlers belong to the process or to a thread?

page 165

6.6   Discuss the issue of naming applied to shared memory regions.

page 167

6.7   Smith decides that every thread in his processes ought to have its own *protected* stack – all other regions in a process would be fully shared. Does this make sense?

page 168

6.8   Suggest a scheme for balancing the load on a set of computers. You should discuss:

i)   what user or system requirements are met by such a scheme,

ii)   to what categories of applications it is suited,

iii)   how to measure load and with what accuracy, and

iv)   how to monitor load and choose the location for a new process. Assume that processes may not be migrated.

How would your design be affected if processes could be migrated between computers? Would you expect process migration to have a significant cost?

page 168

6.9   Explain the advantage of copy-on-write region copying for UNIX, where a call to *fork* is typically followed by a call to *exec*. What should happen if a region that has been copied using copy-on-write is itself copied?

page 169

6.10   Instead of a collection of threads that all receive messages from its port, some servers have a single 'master' thread that receives messages from the port and allocates processing to a set of 'worker' threads. Compare the two designs.

page 170

6.11   In the single-processor server example without caching, how many threads are needed to achieve the maximum sustainable rate of throughput? Is there any point in using more threads?

page 170

6.12   A spin lock (see Bacon [1993]) is a Boolean variable accessed via an atomic *test-and-set* instruction that is used to obtain mutual exclusion. Would you use a spin lock to obtain mutual exclusion between threads on a single-processor computer?

page 175

6.13   Do page faults present a problem for user-level threads implementations?

page 177

6.14   Explain the need for software interrupts in the Psyche threads design. Why should a threads package be interested in the events of a thread's becoming blocked or unblocked? Why should it be interested in the event of a virtual processor's impending preemption? (Hint: other virtual processors may continue to be allocated.)

page 177

6.15   Compare an object-based distributed operating system with one in which each service has its own resource identifiers.

page 178

6.16   Should a distributed operating system keep track of all processes that are able to send messages to each given port? Design a protocol to achieve migration transparency when ports are migrated.

page 180

6.17   What is the security problem raised by the distribution of capabilities over a network? What is the security problem raised by authentication over a network?

page 181

6.18   Explain how a shared region could be used for a process to read data written by the kernel. Include in your explanation what would be necessary for synchronization.

page 183

6.19   Network transmission time accounts for 20 per cent of a null RPC, and 80 per cent of an RPC that transmits 1024 user bytes (less than the size of a network packet). By what percentage will the times for these two operations improve if the network is upgraded from 10 megabits per second to 100 megabits per second?

page 186

6.20   Which factors identified in the cost of an RPC also feature in message passing?

page 187

6.21   i)   Can a server invoked by lightweight procedure calls control the degree of concurrency within it?

ii)   Explain why and how a client is prevented from calling arbitrary code within a server under lightweight RPC.

iii)   Does LRPC expose clients and servers to greater risks of mutual interference than conventional RPC (given the sharing of memory)?

page 188

6.22   Devise a protocol suitable for communication between a kernel and an external pager.

page 191

7

FILE SERVICE: A MODEL

The aim of this chapter is to introduce requirements, design issues and basic design solutions for one of the key components of current distributed systems – the file service. We describe a basic model for a distributed file service in terms of three separate components – a flat file service, a directory service and a client module.

We define an RPC interface for each component and show how they collectively achieve access and location transparency and support a hierarchic file system model.

The design and implementation of each of the basic file service components is discussed, emphasizing support for a minimum level of fault tolerance, file migration and security and the need for local caching of file and directory data to maintain the performance of remote file operations.

7.1 Introduction

Most applications of computers use files for the permanent storage of information or as a means for sharing information between different users and programs. The file is an abstraction of permanent storage. Since the introduction of disk storage in the 1960s, operating systems have included a **file system** component that is responsible for the organization, storage, retrieval, naming, sharing and protection of files. File systems provide a set of programming operations that characterize the file abstraction, freeing programmers from concern with the details of storage allocation and layout. File storage is implemented on magnetic disks and other non-volatile storage media.

In most file systems, a file is defined as a sequence of similar-sized data items (typically 8-bit bytes) and the file system provides functions to read and write sub-sequences of data items beginning at any point in the sequence. Here we shall consider only the design and implementation of file systems that support this basic file abstraction. Some file systems also provide facilities for accessing records and using keyword-based indexes for locating records, but such facilities fall more properly into the domain of database systems. In a well-constructed file system, they can be implemented at the application level.

File systems are designed to store and manage large numbers of files, with facilities for creating, naming and deleting the files. The naming of files is supported by the use of directories. A **directory** is a file, often of a special type, that provides a mapping from text names to internal file identifiers. In most file systems directories may include the names of other directories, leading to the familiar hierarchic file naming scheme and the multi-part *pathnames* for files used in UNIX and other operating systems. File systems also take responsibility for the control of access to files; restricting the access to files according to users' authorizations and the type of access requested (reading, updating, executing, and so on).

Figure 7.1 shows a typical layered module structure for the implementation of a file system as a component of a conventional operating system. Each layer depends only on the layers below it.

Distributed file service requirements ☐ A distributed **file service** is an essential component in distributed systems, fulfilling a function similar to the file system component in conventional operating systems. It can be used to support the sharing of persistent storage and of information; it enables user programs to access remote files

Figure 7.1   File system modules.

Directory module:	relates file names to file IDs
File module:	relates file IDs to particular files
Access control module:	checks permission for operation requested
File access module:	reads or writes file data or attributes
Block module:	accesses and allocates disk blocks
Device module:	disk I/O and buffering

without copying them to a local disk and it provides access to files from diskless nodes. Other services, such as the name service (binder), the user authentication service and the print service, can be more easily implemented when they can call upon the file service to meet their needs for persistent storage.

The file service is usually the most heavily-used service in a general-purpose distributed system, so its functionality and performance are critical. The design of the file service should support many of the transparency requirements for distributed systems identified in Section 1.3. The design must balance the flexibility and scalability that derive from transparency against software complexity and performance. The following forms of transparency are partially or wholly addressed by most current file services:

Access transparency: Client programs should be unaware of the distribution of files. A single set of operations is provided for access to local and remote files. Programs written to operate on local files are able to access remote files without modification.

Location transparency: Client programs should see a uniform file name space. Files or groups of files may be relocated without changing their pathnames, and user programs see the same name space wherever they are executed.

Concurrency transparency: Changes to a file by one client should not interfere with the operation of other clients simultaneously accessing or changing the same file. This is the well-known issue of concurrency control, discussed in detail in Chapter 13. The need for concurrency control for access to shared data in many applications is widely accepted and techniques are known for its implementation but they are costly. Most current file services follow modern UNIX standards in providing advisory or mandatory file- or record-level locking.

Failure transparency: The correct operation of servers after the failure of a client and the correct operation of client programs in the face of lost messages and temporary interruptions of the service are the main goals. For UNIX-like file services these can be achieved by the use of stateless servers and repeatable service operations. More sophisticated modes of fault tolerance are discussed in Chapter 15.

Performance transparency: Client programs should continue to perform satisfactorily while the load on the service varies within a specified a range.

There are two other important requirements that affect the usefulness of a distributed file service:

Hardware and operating system heterogeneity: The service interfaces should be defined so that client and server software can be implemented for different operating systems and computers. This requirement is an important aspect of *openness*.

Scalability: The service can be extended by incremental growth to deal with a wide range of loads and network sizes.

The following forms of transparency are also required if scalability is extended to include networks with very large numbers of active nodes. There is as yet no file service that achieves all of them fully, although most recently-developed file services address some of them.

Replication transparency: A file may be represented by several copies of its contents at different locations. This has two benefits – it enables multiple servers to share the load of providing a service to clients accessing the same set of files, enhancing the scalability of the service, and it enhances fault tolerance by enabling clients to locate another server that holds a copy of the file when one has failed.

Migration transparency: Neither client programs nor system administration tables in client nodes need to be changed when files are moved. This allows file mobility – files or, more commonly, sets or volumes of files may be moved, either by system administrators or automatically.

There are some features not found in current file services that will be important for the development of distributed applications in the future:

Support for fine-grained distribution of data: As the sophistication of distributed applications grows, the sharing of data in small units will become necessary. This is a reflection of the need to locate individual objects near the processes that are using them and to cache them individually in those locations. The file abstraction, which was developed as a model for permanent storage in centralised systems doesn't address this need well.

Tolerance to network partitioning and detached operation: Network partitions may be the result of faults, or they may occur deliberately, as for example when a portable workstation is taken away. When a file service includes the replication or caching of files, clients may be affected when a network partition occurs. For example, many replication algorithms require a majority of replicas to respond to request for the most up-to-date copy of a file. If there is a network partition, a majority may not be available, preventing the clients from proceeding.

In this chapter we describe a model for a basic file service that meets the requirements of access and location transparency and achieves a basic level of failure transparency and we discuss implementation techniques to achieve satisfactory performance, scalability and hardware and operating system heterogeneity. In the next chapter we describe several existing file systems that address many or all of the requirements identified above.

7.2   File service components

The scope for open, configurable systems is enhanced if the file service is structured as three components – a **flat file service**, a **directory service** and a **client module**. The relevant modules and their relationships are shown in Figure 7.2. The flat file service and the directory service each export an interface for use by client programs and their RPC interfaces, taken together, provide a comprehensive set of operations for access to

Figure 7.2   File service components.

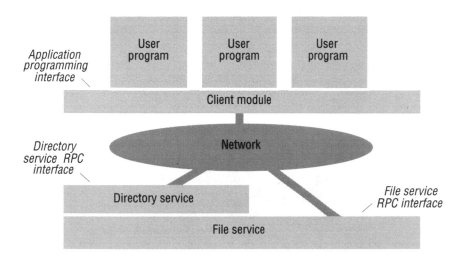

files. The client module integrates the flat file service and the directory service, providing a single programming interface with operations on files similar to those found in conventional file systems. The design is *open* in the sense that different directory services can be used with a single flat file service, supporting different naming rules and directory structures, and different client modules can be used to implement different programming interfaces, simulating the file operations of a variety of different operating systems and optimizing the performance to different workstation and server hardware configurations.

The division of responsibilities between the modules can be defined:

Flat file service □ The flat file service is concerned with implementing operations on the contents of files. **Unique file identifiers** (UFIDs) are used to refer to files in all requests for flat file service operations. The division of responsibilities between the file service and the directory service is based upon the use of UFIDs. UFIDs are long integers chosen so that each file has a UFID that is unique amongst all of the files in a distributed system. When the flat file service receives a request to create a file it generates a new UFID for it and returns the UFID to the requester.

Directory service □ The directory service provides a mapping between *text names* for files and their UFIDs. When a file is created, the client module must record the UFID of each file in a directory, together with a text name. When a text name for a file has been recorded in this way, clients may subsequently obtain the UFID of the file by quoting its text name to the directory service. The directory service provides the functions needed to generate and update directories and to obtain UFIDs from directories. It is a client of the flat file service; its directory files are stored in files of the flat file service. When a hierarchic file naming scheme is adopted, as in the UNIX, directories will hold references to other directories.

Client module □ The client module is an extension of the user package concept introduced in Chapter 5. A single client module runs in each client computer, integrating and extending the operations of the flat file service and the directory service under a single application programming interface that is available to user-level programs in client computers. For example, in UNIX hosts, a client module would be provided that simulates the full set of UNIX file operations, interpreting UNIX multi-part file names by iterative requests to the directory service. The client module also holds information about the network locations of the flat file server and directory server processes. Finally, the client module can play an important role in achieving satisfactory performance through the implementation of a cache of recently-used file blocks at the client.

7.3   Design issues

A distributed file service should offer facilities that are of at least the same power and generality as those found in conventional file systems and should achieve a comparable level of performance. Birrell and Needham [1980] expressed their design aims for the Cambridge File Server (CFS, see also Needham and Herbert [1982]) in these terms:

> We would wish to have a simple, low-level, file server in order to share an expensive resource, namely a disk, whilst leaving us free to design the filing system most appropriate to a particular client, but we would wish also to have available a high-level system shared between clients.

The changed economics of disk storage have reduced the significance of their first goal, but their perception of the need for a range of services addressing the requirements of clients with different goals remains and can best be addressed by a modular implementation of the type outlined above.

Flat file service □ Our flat file service model is designed to offer a simple, general-purpose set of operations. Files contain both *data* and *attributes*. The data consist of a sequence of data items, accessible by operations to read and write any portion of the sequence. The attributes are held as a single record containing information such as the length of the file, timestamps, file type, owner's identity and access control lists. A suitable attribute record structure is illustrated in Figure 7.3. Some of the attributes are maintained by the flat file service itself and the remainder are maintained by the directory service. The attributes that are maintained by the flat file service are shaded in Figure 7.3.

The remaining attributes, including the UserID of the file's owner and the access control list are maintained and accessed by the directory service; it would be unnecessarily costly for the flat file service to check users' authorizations before executing every request to access a file. That is the responsibility of the directory service, and is performed whenever the directory service processes a client's request for a UFID.

Fault tolerance □ The central role of the file service in distributed systems makes it essential that the service continue to operate in the face of client and server failures. Fortunately, a moderately fault-tolerant design is straightforward for simple servers. The RPC interfaces can be designed in terms of *idempotent* operations ensuring that duplicated requests do not result in invalid updates to files (see the subsection on lost reply messages in Section 4.3), and the servers can be *stateless*, so that they can be

Figure 7.3 Attribute record structure.

File length
Creation timestamp
Read timestamp
Write timestamp
Attribute timestamp
Reference count
Owner
File type
Access control list

restarted and the service restored after a failure without any need to recover previous state. These properties will be designed into each of the RPC interfaces of our model.

Directory service □ We shall define a basic directory service that creates and modifies entries in simple one-dimensional (non-hierarchic) directories, looks up text names in directories and returns the corresponding UFID after checking the user's authorization. Other levels of functionality will be constructed within the client module to parse multi-part pathnames, build directories into hierarchies or other structures and perform more complex searches.

The separation of the directory service from the file service enables a variety of directory services to be designed and offered for use with a single file service, each supporting a different name syntax and access control regime. Thus a UNIX directory service could be constructed and used with a file service to provide a precise emulation of the UNIX file system. The same file service could be used with a different directory service to emulate almost any other file naming scheme (such as that used in MS/DOS or in DEC's VMS) or to support some other novel or specialized file naming scheme.

The translation from file name to UFID performed by the directory service is a *stateless* substitute for the *open file* operation found in non-distributed systems. The directory service also takes responsibility for access control, and this requires that UFIDs take the role of *capabilities*. (Capabilities and access control are discussed further in Section 7.5.)

Client module □ The client module hides low-level constructs such as the UFIDs used in the RPC interfaces of the flat file service and the directory service from user-level programs, emulating a set of functions similar to the input-output functions of the host operating system in the client node. When files are located in several nodes, the client module is responsible for locating them, based on the identity of the file's group. (File groups are discussed further in Section 7.5.)

7.4   Interfaces

We describe service interfaces by listing their procedures, giving a brief explanation of the action of each procedure. We use the following notation for specifying the name of a procedure, its inputs and results, any error conditions (or exceptions) that may arise and a description of its operation:

ProcedureName(argument1, argument2, ...) → (result1, result2, ...) —
   REPORTS(error1, error2, ...)
   Description.

The input parameters are listed in brackets after the name of the operation, the names of parameters follow a set of naming conventions defined below. The results are listed after the input parameters, separated from them by an arrow and have names chosen according to the same convention. Any exceptions or error conditions that may arise in a procedure are identified by the names listed after the word REPORTS. The following names for parameters and results are used in this chapter:

File	the UFID of a file
i, n, l	integers
Data	a sequence of data items
Attr	a record containing the attributes of a file
Dir	a UFID referring to a directory
Name	a text name
AccessMode	a file service operation for which a UFID is required, for example, (*Read, Write, Delete, ...*) or a combination of these
Pattern	a regular expression
userID	an identifier enabling the directory service to identify a client
BadPosition	error: invalid position in file
NotFound	error: name absent from directory
NoAccess	error: caller does not have access permission
NameDuplicate	error: attempt to add name already in directory

For example, the procedure definition:

   Read (File, i, n) → Data — REPORTS (BadPosition)

defines the procedure *Read* with three input arguments – the UFID of a file and two integers – and returns a sequence of data items as its result. It will report a *BadPosition* error if the argument *i* is outside the bounds of the file.

Flat file service

Figure 7.4 contains a definition of the interface to the flat file service. This is the RPC interface used by client modules. It is not normally used directly by user-level programs. A UFID is invalid if the file that it refers to is not present in the server processing the request or if its access permissions are inappropriate for the operation requested. All of the procedures in the interface except *Create* report an error if the *File* argument contains an invalid UFID. These reports are omitted from the definition for clarity.

The most important operations are those for reading and writing. Both the *Read* and the *Write* operation require a parameter *i* specifying a position in the file. The *Read* operation copies the sequence of *n* data items beginning at item *i* from the specified file into *Data*, which is then returned to the client. The *Write* operation copies the sequence of data items in *Data* into the specified file beginning at item *i*, replacing the previous contents of the file at the corresponding position and extending the file if necessary.

It is sometimes necessary to shorten a file; *Truncate* does so. *Create* creates a new, empty file and returns the UFID that is generated. *Delete* removes the specified file.

GetAttributes and *SetAttributes* enable clients to access the attribute record. *GetAttributes* is normally available to any client that is allowed to read the file. Access to the *SetAttributes* operation would normally be restricted to the directory service that provides access to the file. The values of the length and timestamp portions of the

Figure 7.4   Flat file service operations.

Read(File, i, n) → *(Data)* — REPORTS *(BadPosition)*
  If *1* ≤ *i* ≤ *Length(File)*:
    Reads a sequence of up to *n* items in *File* starting at item *i* and returns it in *Data*.
  If *i* > *Length(File)*:
    Returns the empty sequence, reports an error.

Write(File, i, Data) — REPORTS *(BadPosition)*
  If *1* ≤ *i* ≤ *Length(File)+1*:
    Writes a sequence of *Data* to *File*, starting at item *i*, extending the file if necessary.
  If *i* > *Length(File)+1*: null operation, reports an error.

Create() → *File*
  Creates a new file of length 0 and delivers a UFID for it.

Truncate(File, l)
  If *l* < *Length(File)*: shortens the file to length *l*; else does nothing.

Delete(File)
  Removes the file from the file store.

GetAttributes(File) → *Attr*
  Returns the file attributes for the file.

SetAttributes(File, Attr)
  Sets the file attributes (only those attributes that are not shaded in Figure 7.3).

---

attribute record are not affected by *SetAttributes;* they are maintained separately by the flat file service itself.

Comparison with UNIX □ Our interface and the UNIX file system primitives are functionally equivalent. It is a simple matter to construct a client module that emulates the UNIX system calls in terms of our flat file service and the directory service operations described in the next section.

In comparison with the UNIX interface, our flat file service has no *open* and *close* operations – files can be accessed immediately by quoting the appropriate UFID. The *Read* and *Write* requests in our interface include a parameter specifying a starting point within the file for each transfer, whereas the equivalent UNIX operations do not. In UNIX, each *read* or *write* operation starts at the current position of the read-write pointer and the read-write pointer is advanced by the number of bytes transferred after each *read* or *write*.and a *seek* operation is provided to enable the read-write pointer to be explicitly repositioned.

The interface to our flat file service differs from the UNIX file system interface mainly for reasons of fault tolerance:

Repeatable operations: With the exception of *Create*, the operations are *idempotent*, allowing the use of at-least-once RPC semantics – clients may repeat calls to which they receive no reply. Repeated execution of *Create* produces a different new file for each call, causing a *space leak*, but has no other ill-effects. We shall discuss the implications of the space leak in Section 7.5.

Stateless servers: The interface is suitable for implementation by *stateless* servers. Stateless servers can be restarted after a failure and resume operation without any need for clients or the server to restore any state.

The UNIX file operations are neither idempotent nor consistent with the requirement for a stateless implementation. A read-write pointer is generated by the UNIX file system whenever a file is opened and it is retained until the file is closed. The UNIX *read* and *write* operations are not idempotent; if an operation is accidentally repeated, the automatic advance of the read-write pointer results in access to a different portion of the file in the repeated operation. The read-write pointer is a hidden, client-related state variable. To mimic it in a file server, *open* and *close* operations would be needed, and the read-write pointer's value would have to be retained by the server as long as the relevant file is open. By eliminating the read-write pointer we have eliminated the need for the file server to retain any state information on behalf of specific clients.

Using the flat file service □ Service interfaces such as the one defined in Figure 7.4 are designed to be used to construct a client module or user package that provides a different, higher-level interface to application programs. But for the purposes of providing a simple illustration of the use of our file service operations, we shall define and use a Modula-2 module that contains operations similar to those in the flat file service.

The Modula-2 definition module in Figure 7.5 defines such a module. It contains the same functions as the file service interface except that the *GetAttributes* and *SetAttributes* operations are omitted and a *Length* function (which would be implemented in terms of *GetAttributes*) is added, enabling clients to obtain the length of

Figure 7.5 Flat file service interface in Modula-2.

```
DEFINITION MODULE Files;
EXPORT QUALIFIED Read, Write, Length, Truncate, Create, Delete,
    ErrorType, Sequence, Seqptr, MAX, UFID, ErrorReport;

CONST MAX = 2048;
TYPE
    Sequence = RECORD
        l       : CARDINAL;
        s       : ARRAY[1..MAX] OF CHAR;
    END;
    Seqptr = POINTER TO Sequence;
    UFID   = CARDINAL;
    ErrorType = (NONE, READ, WRITE);
VAR
    ErrorReport: ErrorType;
PROCEDURE Read(File : UFID; i, n : CARDINAL) : Seqptr;
PROCEDURE Write(File : UFID; i : CARDINAL; Data : Seqptr);
PROCEDURE Length(File : UFID) : CARDINAL;
            (* Implemented in terms of GetAttributes *)
PROCEDURE Truncate(File : UFID; l : CARDINAL);
PROCEDURE Create() : UFID;
PROCEDURE Delete(File : UFID);
END Files.
```

a file. The module defined in Figure 7.5 can be thought of as a basic client module that provides access to the flat file service and simply adds a *Length* function to it.

The transfers performed by *Read* and *Write* are limited to *MAX* characters. Error reports from the server are passed to the client via a global variable named *ErrorReport*, since Modula-2 lacks an exception-handling mechanism.

As a simple example illustrating the use of these operations, we can construct a procedure *CopyFile* to copy the contents of a file whose UFID is *F1* to a newly created file *F2*. If we suppose for the moment that *F1*, *F2* and *i* are declared and initialized appropriately, the task can be performed by a simple loop of the form:

```
F2 := Create();
FOR i := 1 TO Length(F1) BY MAX DO
    Write(F2, i, Read(F1, i, MAX));
END;
```

Figure 7.6 shows a more complete version of *CopyFile* in which it is assumed that the destination file, supplied as the second argument, already exists when the procedure is called. Note that our *CopyFile* procedure refers to files by their UFID and not by name. It would need to be used in a program that first obtains the UFIDs from the directory service.

Figure 7.6   *CopyFile* using flat file service operations.

```
MODULE CopyFile;
FROM InOut IMPORT WriteString, WriteLn;
FROM Files IMPORT Read, Write, Length, Truncate,
        UFID, ErrorType, MAX, ErrorReport;

PROCEDURE CopyFile(File1, File2 : UFID);
VAR
    i, l : CARDINAL;
BEGIN
    l := Length(File1);
    Truncate(File2, l);
    FOR i := 1 TO l BY MAX DO
        Write(File2, i, Read(File1, i, MAX));
    END;
    IF ErrorReport != NONE THEN
        WriteString("CopyFile failed");
        WriteLn;
    END;
END CopyFile;
END CopyFile.
```

Directory service

Figure 7.7 contains a definition of the RPC interface for the directory service. The primary purpose of the directory service is to provide a service for translating text names to UFIDs. In order to do so, it maintains directory files containing the mappings between text names for files and UFIDs. Each directory is stored as a conventional file with a UFID, so the directory service is a client of the file service.

We define only operations on individual directories. For each operation, a UFID for the file containing the directory is required (in the *Dir* parameter), and the UFID must be one that confers the appropriate permissions (*Read* permission for *Lookup* and *GetNames*; *Write* permission for *AddName*, *UnName* and *ReName*). The *Lookup* operation in the basic directory service performs a single *Name* → *UFID* translation. It is a building block for use in other services or in the client module to perform more complex translations, such as the hierarchic name interpretation found in UNIX. The UFID returned by *Lookup* contains encoded access permissions. The permissions are determined from the file's access control list based on the *UserID* supplied in the *Lookup* request.

There are three operations for altering directories; *AddName*, *ReName* and *UnName*. *AddName* adds an entry to a directory and increments the reference count field in the file's attribute record. If the reference count has become one, *AddName* records *UserID* as the owner of the file and initializes the access control list to a default value. *ReName* changes the name of a file.

Figure 7.7   Directory service operations.

Lookup(Dir, Name, AccessMode, UserID) → (File)
— REPORTS (NotFound, NoAccess)
Locates the text name in the directory and returns the relevant UFID; reports an error
if it cannot be found or if the client making the request is not authorized to access the
file in the manner specified by *AccessMode*.

AddName(Dir, Name, File, UserID) — REPORTS(NameDuplicate)
If *Name* is not in the directory:
 Adds the *(Name, File)* pair to the directory and updates the attribute record
 accordingly.
If *Name* is already in the directory: reports an error.

UnName(Dir, Name) — REPORTS(NotFound)
If *Name* is in the directory:
 The entry containing *Name* is removed from the directory.
If *Name* is not in the directory: reports an error.

ReName(Dir, OldName, NewName) — REPORTS(NotFound)
If *Name* is in the directory:
 The entry containing *Name* gets the new name.
If *Name* is not in the directory: reports an error.

GetNames(Dir, Pattern) → NameSeq
Returns all of the text names in the directory that match the regular expression given
by *Pattern*.

UnName removes an entry from a directory and decrements the reference count.
GetNames is provided to enable clients to examine the contents of directories and to
implement pattern matching operations on file names such as those found in the UNIX
shell. It returns all or a subset of the names stored in a given directory. The names are
selected by pattern matching against a regular expression supplied by the client.

The provision of pattern matching in the *GetNames* operation enables users to
determine the names of one or more file names by giving an incomplete specification of
the characters in the names. A regular expression is a specification for a class of strings
in the form of an expression containing a combination of literal sub-strings and symbols
denoting variable characters or repeated occurrences of characters or sub-strings.

The *reference count*, *owner*, *file type* and *access control list* attributes in Figure
7.3 are managed and used entirely by the directory service. The *reference count* is used
to record the number of directory entries that exist for a file. When it is zero, the
directory service removes the file (using the flat file service *Delete* operation). The
owner is a numerical identifier for the user on whose behalf the file was created or to
whom the file has subsequently been allocated. The *file type* has one of two values: *file*
or *directory*. It is used to enable the directory service to locate references to directories
so that it can periodically validate the directory tree and remove any unreferenced files.
The access control list is a list of users or classes of user (groups) who are authorized to
use the file and the operations that each is permitted to perform.

Constructing a hierarchic file system ☐ A hierarchic file system such as the one that UNIX provides consists of a number of directories arranged in a tree structure. Each directory holds the names of the files and other directories that are accessible from it. Any file or directory can be referenced using a *pathname* – a multi-part name that represent a path through the tree. The root has a distinguished name and each file or directory has a name in a directory. The UNIX file naming scheme is not a strict hierarchy – files can have several names, and they can be in the same or different directories. This is implemented by a *link* operation that adds a new name for a file to a specified directory.

A UNIX-like file naming system can be implemented by the client module using the flat file and directory services that we have defined. A tree-structured network of directories is constructed with files at the leaves and directories at the other nodes of the tree. The root of the tree is a directory with a 'well-known' UFID. Multiple names for files can be supported using the *AddName* operation and the reference count field in the attribute record.

A function can be provided in the client module that gets the UFID of a file given its pathname. The function interprets the pathname starting from the root, using *Lookup* to obtain the UFID of each directory in the path.

In a hierarchic directory service the file attributes associated with files should include a type field that distinguishes between ordinary files and directories. This is used when following a path to ensure that each part of the name, except the last, refers to a directory.

7.5 Implementation techniques

The techniques used for the implementation of file services are an important part of the design of distributed systems. A distributed file system must provide a service that is comparable in performance and reliability with the file systems found in conventional computer systems. It must be convenient to administer, providing operations and tools that enable system administrators to install and operate the system conveniently. In this section we outline techniques that have been developed to achieve these goals and indicate how they can be applied to the implementation of our model file service.

File groups ☐ We intend our flat file service to be implemented by multiple servers. The distribution of files among the servers can be achieved by the introduction of a *file group* construct. The file group construct is designed to ease the task of administering the file service and to simplify the file location algorithm needed in the implementation of the flat file service.

A *file group* is a collection of files mounted on a server computer. A server may hold several file groups, and groups can be moved between servers, but a file cannot change the group to which it belongs. A similar construct (called a *filesystem*) is used in UNIX and in most other conventional operating systems. File groups were originally introduced to support facilities for moving collections of files stored on removable disk cartridges between computers.

In a distributed file service, file groups support the allocation of files to file servers in larger logical units and enable the service to be implemented with files stored on several servers. Our use of the file group construct reflects the use made of similar constructs in many distributed file systems including the Andrew File System described in the next chapter.

In a file system that supports file groups, the representation of UFIDs includes a file group identifier component, enabling the client module in each client computer to take responsibility for despatching requests to the server that holds the relevant file group (see the subsection on *File addressing* on page 217).

File group identifiers must be unique throughout a distributed system. Since file groups can be moved, and distributed systems that are initially separate can be merged to form a single system, the only way to ensure that file group identifiers will always be distinct in a given system is to generate them with an algorithm that ensures global uniqueness. For example, whenever a new file group is created, a unique identifier can be generated by concatenating the 32-bit Internet address of the host creating the new group with a 16-bit integer derived from the date, producing a unique 48-bit integer:

	32 bits	*16 bits*
file group identifier:	Internet address	date

Note that we cannot utilize the Internet address embedded in the identifier for locating the file group, since a file group may be moved to a different host computer, it is simply a convenient method for ensuring uniqueness, since Internet addresses are allocated uniquely. The use of a 16-bit date field would allow each server to create one new file group every day for about 100 years without conflict. Alternatively, to avoid the restriction on the rate of creation of groups, each server can maintain a permanent 16-bit counter that is incremented whenever it creates a new file group, allowing each server to create 2^{16} file groups without duplication.

Space leaks □ A space leak exists in a system if a sequence of events may occur in which memory space becomes permanently inaccessible to the system. A drawback of the separation of file and directory services that we have adopted is that it may lead to the existence of a disk space leak.

In our design, a disk space leak occurs whenever the program responsible for creating a file (or the last program to hold a UFID for the file) terminates without having entered the UFID of the file into any directory and without deleting the file. Such a program might be termed 'delinquent' with respect to the file service, but such delinquency might well be a consequence of an unintentional error in a partially-debugged program.

It is not possible for a directory service to discover the existence of a file that has been lost in this way since the file's UFID is not in any directory. Because of our division of responsibilities between the file service and the directory service, the file service would have difficulty in determining that the file is no longer required since it has no knowledge of the format of directories – they are indistinguishable from any other file as far as the file service is concerned. This is especially so when several directory services, each with a different directory format, coexist in the same system as we have indicated might be desirable above.

A number of views can be taken of this problem. In the Xerox XDFS file server it was ignored on the grounds that it is an infrequent occurrence [Mitchell 1982]. Other servers (for example, CFS, Sun NFS, the Andrew File System) do not encounter the problem because their directory and file access services are integrated. In our basic file service we follow XDFS in ignoring the issue. This approach is likely to be acceptable provided that requests for the flat file service to create files are embedded in a client module that takes care to ensure that an entry is made in a directory whenever a file is created. Thus the client module should include the composite operation:

CreateFile(Name, Dir)
The operation for creating a new file takes the text name to be assigned to the new file and *Dir* – the UFID of a directory into which the file is to be entered. It creates a new file and adds *Name* and the UFID of the new file to *Dir*.

Capabilities and access control   □ Capabilities have been widely used for the protection of resources from unauthorized access in distributed systems [Needham and Herbert 1982, Mullender 1985; Leach *et al.* 1983]. A capability is a 'digital key' – a large integer selected in a manner that makes it difficult to counterfeit. Capabilities are used like conventional physical keys: access to some resource is granted only on presentation of the key. UFIDs can be constructed so that they act as capabilities, conferring permission to access a file. In the next section we describe a method for generating suitable UFIDs – so that they are unique throughout the distributed system and difficult to counterfeit or modify.

In our model, the flat file service maintains capability-based access control: its clients must present an appropriate capability (in the form of a UFID) each time an operation on a file is requested. Clients of the flat file service need not state their identity, since possession of the appropriate capability is taken as proof of the client's authorization to access the file. Capabilities can be used to control individual modes of access to a file (for example, *Read, Write, Delete*), by including a code in each capability to indicate the access modes that are permitted by the capability.

The directory service requires clients to state their identity and uses a conventional identity-based approach for clients' requests for UFIDs. The directory service checks the users' authorizations whenever a client requests a UFID. It does so using an access control list that is stored as a part of the attribute record for each file (see Chapter 6). In this case the access control list is a table identifying the users and groups of users permitted to access the file and their permitted modes of access (a mode of access is associated with each operation or set of operations that is to be controlled such as *Read, Write, Delete*, and so on). Each request to the directory service for a UFID must include the user's identity and the modes of access requested. If the client is authorized to use the file in the modes requested, a capability is supplied in the form of a UFID with the permitted access modes encoded within it.

In the flat file service, the access modes encoded in the UFID are checked; if they are valid for the requested operation, the remainder of the UFID is used to locate the file and the requested operation is performed. This method for controlling access frees the flat file service from concerns about the identity of users and services, file ownership and access control lists, resulting in a simple design with minimal overheads for the majority of file service operations.

Construction of UFIDs □ The flat file service must generate UFIDs in a manner that not only ensures uniqueness but makes them difficult to counterfeit. In general there may be several server computers cooperating to provide a file service, so UFIDs must be unique among all of the computers in a distributed system. Even after the file associated with a given UFID value is deleted, it is important that its UFID is not re-used because clients of the file service may retain obsolete UFIDs. Any attempt to access a deleted file should produce an error rather than allow access to a different file.

The UFID does not act as an address, so it need not contain any information concerning the network address of the server that currently holds the file or the position of the file in storage. In the next section we shall discuss algorithms for mapping UFIDs to disk block addresses using a mapping table maintained by the file service. On page 216 we discuss ways for locating the server that contains a particular file or group of files when the file service is distributed across several servers.

There are a several ways to ensure that a UFID is unique and difficult to forge. All rely on the use of a large, sparsely populated number space. One way to achieve uniqueness is to construct the UFID by concatenating the file group identifier with an integer (the *file number*) that is incremented each time a file is created in that group. File numbers cannot be re-used; the uniqueness of UFIDs would not be ensured if they were. Counterfeiting can be combated by inserting an extra field containing a random number into each UFID, thereby ensuring that the distribution of *valid* UFIDs is sparse and rendering the task of a malicious user wishing to generate any valid UFID so lengthy as to be impractical. The random number is stored with the relevant file (in a location that is inaccessible to clients) so that the flat file service can check the validity of requests to access the file. With this approach the resulting UFIDs might be represented as 112-bit records with a format such as:

48 bits	*32 bits*	*32 bits*
File group identifier	File number	Random number

Access modes □ Access control to files is based upon the fact that a UFID constitutes a 'key' or capability to access a file. In its simplest form, access control is a matter of denying UFIDs to unauthorized clients. But when a file is accessed by several users, the owner of a file needs to hold rights to perform any operation on it, while others may need fewer rights; for example, they may need only to read the file. To provide this, UFIDs are needed that provide selective access to reading, writing and the other file service operations.

This can be achieved by extending the UFIDs to include a *permission field*. The permission field is an encoded representation of the access rights that the UFID confers upon its holder. For example, to control access selectively to writing and deleting, a permission field of two bits would be needed in each UFID:

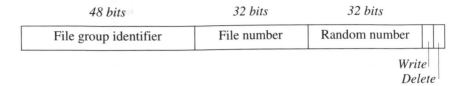

There are seven operations in our flat file service interface, but *Create* does not take a UFID and access to it need not be controlled. We can combine *Truncate* with *Write* for access control purposes, so a 5-bit permission field is sufficient to control access to all of our flat file service operations:

48 bits	32 bits	32 bits	5 bits
File group identifier	File number	Random number	

> Read
> Write/Truncate
> Delete
> GetAttributes
> SetAttributes

When a file is created, a UFID with permissions set for all operations is returned to the owner. But when other clients make *Lookup* requests to the directory service, it returns UFIDs with permissions set only for the operations for which the user is authorized.

Encryption of the permission field □ The use of an unencrypted permission field would be insecure because the possessor of a UFID that confers only some permissions could easily convert it to one with more permissions. To avoid such attempts to penetrate the security of the file service, the permission field and the random number are encrypted to produce a single 37-bit number:

48 bits	32 bits	37 bits	5 bits
File group identifier	File number		

Encrypted permission bits + random number

Unencrypted permission bits

A duplicate, unencrypted permission field is also included so that client and server programs can determine by examination what permissions are included in a UFID, but tampering with the unencrypted permissions field invalidates the UFID. The unencrypted value of the random number associated with each file is stored in the file attributes, in a field that is not accessible via the *GetAttributes* function.

Figure 7.8   Storage structure of a single file.

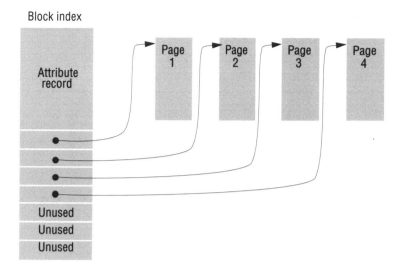

The necessary encryption is performed by the directory service and tampering is detected by the flat file server in one of the following ways. See Section 16.2 for further details on the encryption methods referred to:

- The directory servers and the flat file servers all share a secret key. When a directory server issues a UFID in response to a *Lookup* operation the permissions field and the random part are encrypted with the secret key. When clients present UFIDs for file access, the file server uses the secret key to decrypt them. This method offers poor security because it requires that a secret key is distributed to several servers which must maintain its secrecy.

- The directory server encrypts the two fields to produce the UFID issued to clients using a well-known one-way function. When a client present a UFID to a flat file server the server applies the same one-way function to its copy of the random number for the file and the unencrypted permission bits and compares the result with the encrypted field in the UFID.

File representation ☐ The flat file service is responsible for the storage of files on the disks attached to server computers. We outline here a suitable organisation for file storage. See Tanenbaum [1987] or Silberschatz *et al.* [1993] for a more detailed discussion of file organization.

The data in each file is stored as a non-contiguous collection of blocks. The file is organized by recording the sequence of its block pointers in a separate data structure called the *block index* (similar to the *i-node* structure used in the implementation of the UNIX file system). The block index is organized to support both sequential and random access to the data items in a file. The file attributes are represented as a single fixed-size record that is stored with the block index. The storage structure of a file with a block index is illustrated in Figure 7.8. The structure of the block index is discussed in an accompanying box.

When a new file is created it acquires a block index but contains no pages initially, so no blocks are allocated to it. If a *Write* operation requires the file to be extended to include a new page the file service requests a new block from the block service and stores the block pointer in the file's block index. When a file is deleted or truncated, the blocks are released to the block service.

In the implementation of the *Read* and *Write* operations the argument *i* specifying the position of the first data item is converted to a page number and an offset within the page. The page number is used as an offset for the corresponding block pointer in the block index.

The length of a file cannot be calculated simply by inspection of its index because the last page of the file is in general only partly full. Hence the length must be stored in the attribute record and updated by the flat file service each time it changes.

File location □ In order to satisfy requests for access to files, the flat file service must translate UFIDs to file server locations and file addresses. To ensure location and migration transparency, we have not included file server locations or file addresses in the representation of UFIDs. The flat file service may be implemented by several servers, each holding some file groups, so the first step in satisfying a file service request is to identify the server that holds the required file group. This is done by the client module, with assistance, if necessary, from one of the servers. The second step is to locate the required file's block index. This is done by the server that holds the file.

Group location □ A group location database, giving the current locations of all accessible file groups in the form of *<FileGroupID, PortIdentifier>* pairs is replicated in each participating server. The flat file service interface is extended to provide an additional operation to access the group location database:

Structure of the block index: The block index can occupy one or more disk blocks; the number of blocks required is determined by the number of pages in the file. If a block pointer occupies 4 bytes and there are *b* bytes in each block, an index containing *b*/4 block pointers can be held in a single block and up to $b^2/4$ bytes of data can be referenced from each index block. If, for example, b = 8192 bytes then 2048 block pointers can be held in each index block. But if the attribute record is stored in the first index block, the space available for block pointers is reduced. If the attribute record occupies 1024 bytes there is room for 1792 block pointers in the first index block, allowing for files of up to 1792 × 8192 or some 14 megabytes to be represented with a single index block.

Many files are quite small. For files that are smaller than say 7000 bytes a useful performance optimization can be achieved by storing the file itself in the first block of the index, avoiding the need for one disk access. This technique was used successfully in the Cambridge File Server (CFS) [Needham and Herbert 1982].

Files of lengths greater than 14 megabytes can be accommodated using a block index constructed as a two-level hierarchy. The first index block contains pointers to further index blocks, each of which contains pointers to blocks of the file. With a block size of 8192 bytes and 1792 block pointers in the first index block, the index can refer to 1792 lower-level index blocks, each of which can contain 2048 block pointers. The largest file that can be represented with this index structure is 1792 × 2048 × 8192 bytes or some 30 gigabytes.

GetServerPort(FileGroupID) → PortID — REPORTS(UnknownFileGroup)
   If F*ileGroupID* is known, delivers the port identifier of a server holding the file
   group, else reports an error.

GetServerPort requests can be sent to any server, since all servers hold the group
location database. In order to achieve an application programming interface in each
client that is transparent with respect to the locations of file groups, *GetServerPort*
requests are made by a client module running in the client computer. In order to achieve
acceptable performance, the client module builds a cache containing the results of
GetServerPort requests in the form of a table of *<FileGroupID, PortID>* pairs.

   The client module searches in the local cache for the relevant file group identifier.
If it is in the cache, the corresponding port identifier is used to forward the service
request to the server holding the file. If the file group is not in the local cache, the client
module sends a *GetServerPort* request to a convenient server, which searches its group
location database and returns the corresponding port identifier. The client module adds
the new *<FileGroupID, PortID>* pair to its cache and forwards the original request to
the identified server. Since the file accesses requested by a user-level program are likely
to involve repeated access to a few files, the destinations for the vast majority of file
service requests are likely to be located in the cache.

File addressing □ When a server receives a flat file service request, it uses the file
group identifier and the file number to locate the required file's block index. The *file
number → address of block index* mapping is specific to each file group and is stored
and moved with the group. Since there are 2^{32} file numbers within each group, the entire
map is too large to be represented as a simple indirection table; we must use a condensed
representation and the translation algorithm must involve a search.

   B-trees are an effective method for structuring a set of data for searching. B-trees
were used in XDFS for the translation of UFIDs to file locations and they have since
been used in several other file servers. B-trees were developed as a general-purpose data
structure by Bayer and McCreight [1972] and descriptions of them can be found in
Knuth [1973 pages 473–9] or Ullman [1984].

Server cache □ Access to blocks on disk is performed by a *block transfer* module in
each flat file server node. The block transfer modules provides a *GetBlock* and a
PutBlock operation, each of which takes a block pointer as an argument. The disk block
access system should include a carefully-designed caching system to reduce the cost of
file access by retaining copies of recently-used blocks in the local memory of the server
node. Most file servers include such a caching system; Sturgis *et al.* [1980] reported a
substantial performance gain for XDFS as a result of the use of a disk block cache.

   A disk block cache consists of an area of main memory organized as an array of
blocks that are the same size as the blocks on the disk, together with the block pointer
for each block. On each *GetBlock* operation, the block pointers in the cache are checked.
If the block pointer of the required block is present, the contents of the block are taken
from the cache; otherwise, the contents of the block are loaded from the disk to the cache
and the associated block pointer is updated so that subsequent reads that require the
same block will be able to obtain it from the cache.

To ensure that the copies of blocks in the cache are up-to-date, the cache must be updated whenever a *PutBlock* operation occurs. If a block referenced in the *PutBlock* operation is already in the cache then the new data is stored in the cached block and the block is flagged to show that it has been modified and must later be written to the disk. (This flag is sometimes called a 'dirty' flag).

The area of memory used for the cache will inevitably become full when sufficient *GetBlock* and *PutBlock* operations have been performed. When this occurs one of the blocks in the cache must be released, after storing its contents on the disk if its 'dirty' flag is set. The selection of a block for release may use one of several algorithms. A simple solution is to choose a cache block at random. One of the most effective solutions is to release the *least recently used* block. To achieve this, cached blocks must be timestamped on every read or write operation.

The problem of *cache coherence* arises and has to be addressed in the design of any caching system. A cache is coherent only if the data that it contains is an exact replica of the data in the storage system that it replicates. A cache may lose coherence as a result of an update operation.

We have described a method for caching in which the results of *PutBlock* operations may remain in the main memory for a considerable time – until the cache is 'flushed' or the storage block that it occupies is re-used. If a server crashes the data in its cache is lost. This is not acceptable for the *PutBlock* operations that are involved in atomic transactions. Therefore, *write-through* cache operation should be used – the results of *PutBlock* operations are stored in the cache and immediately written to the disk before any further operations are performed, and the 'dirty' flag can be dispensed with.

File servers are often constructed with several concurrent threads. A server constructed with threads can use shared main memory for its cache. Synchronization is required to ensure the consistency of two simultaneous updates to the same block by different threads. This may be achieved by enclosing the operations that access cache blocks in a monitor.

Client cache □ The use of a server cache avoids repeated access to disk storage for the same disk block and hence enhances the performance of file servers, but it does nothing to reduce delays that clients may experience due to network latency and server loading. The caching of recently-accessed blocks of files, file attributes and directory entries in the client computer is also essential for satisfactory performance. This is implemented in the client module. A cache of file blocks is maintained, indexed by UFID and offset within file. Whenever a *read* request from a user program is processed by the client module, the cache is checked to determine whether it contains the relevant portion of the file. Whenever a *write* is processed, the local client cache is checked and if the relevant block is present, it is updated in the cache and the block is transferred to the server – in other words, the client cache is also uses *write-through*.

Although the RPC interface to the flat file service allows client modules to read or write any portion of a file, if the client module is designed to cache blocks of files in the client node, the transfers actually requested by the client module always constitute the entire block or blocks containing the data requested by the user program. So in the case of a UNIX read request, the value of the offset, i is rounded downward to the nearest block boundary and the length of the sequence of data items to be transferred, n is rounded up to the nearest block. When the client module receives the blocks from the flat file service, it places them in the local cache and then extracts the required sub-sequence and passes it to the user program.

The use of client cache introduces a requirement for the management of updates to files by two or more clients. If several client computers hold copies of the same file block in their caches and one of them updates the block, the copies held at the other clients become out-of-date and must be *invalidated*.

The invalidation of entries in client caches after updates is a key design problem in the implementation of distributed file services. All of the files servers described in Chapter 8 operate client caches and the invalidation methods that they use will provide a representative set of design solutions.

7.6   Summary

We have developed a model for file service with three components, a flat file service, a directory service and a client module. The flat file service manages files that are labelled by large integers (UFIDs), The directory service manages a collection of mappings from text names to UFIDs. The directory mappings are stored in files and are identified by UFIDs, so the directory service is a client of the flat file service. The client module integrates the flat file service and the directory service to produce an emulation of a conventional file service with textual file names.

Our model is based on the characteristics of several practical file services. It is designed to be implemented by stateless servers and to permit at-least-once RPC semantics.

The file names may be hierarchically organized as in UNIX or they may be organized in other structures. Different directory services may co-exist, using the same flat file service, so a single file service may offer emulations of UNIX, MS-DOS and other filing systems, with different directory services and client modules for each.

Our model supports a limited degree of migration transparency. The files managed by the flat file service are organized in file groups. All of the files in a file group are stored at the same server. The client module locates files using information about their groups that is encoded in the UFIDs.

Caching is an essential feature of practical file servers. We have outlined methods for caching file blocks at both the client and the server in the proposed implementation of our model file service. Client caching generates a substantial problem of maintaining consistency between cached copies of the same blocks in different clients. The design of algorithms to maintain cache consistency has been a major concern for the designers of practical file services. Several of the solutions that they have developed are described in Chapter 8.

EXERCISES

7.1   The file service model treats the management of file directories as a separate
      service. What information is stored in directories? What are the advantages
      and drawbacks of the separation?

page 201

7.2   Why are the file attributes stored with files and not in directories? (Hint:
      several directory entries can refer to the same file.)

page 202

7.3   The shading in Figure 7.3 illustrates the division of responsibilities for
      updating the value of each of the file attributes. Explain these decisions.

page 203

7.4   Why is there no *open* or *close* operation in the interface to the flat file
      service or the directory service. What are the differences between our
      directory service *Lookup* operation and the UNIX *open*?

page 206

7.5   Outline the methods by which a client module could emulate the UNIX file
      system interface using our model file service.

page 206

7.6   Define the interface to our model directory service in C, Modula-2 or any
      suitable language.

page 208

7.7   Describe in outline the design of a client module that locates files when they
      may be stored in different file groups located at different servers.

page 210

7.8   Write a procedure *PathLookup(Pathname, Dir)* → *UFID* (in C, Modula-2
      or any suitable language) that implements *Lookup* for UNIX-like pathnames
      based on our model directory service.

7.9   Why should UFIDs be unique across all possible file systems? How is
      uniqueness for UFIDs ensured?

page 213

7.10 List some solutions to the space leak problem for our model file service.
      Discuss the consequences for the model of each of your solutions.

page 211

7.11 Outline a scheme for the use of caching at each server to improve file service
      performance. How does your scheme affect the reliability of the service?

page 217

7.12 Outline a scheme for the use of caching at each client to improve file service
      performance. What problems arise when more than one client updates a
      file?

page 218

8

FILE SERVICE: CASE STUDIES

In this chapter we describe the designs of two distributed file systems that are in widespread use and one experimental system:

- Sun Network File System, NFS
- the Andrew File System, AFS
- the Coda File System

These case studies illustrate a range of design solutions to the emulation of a UNIX file system interface with differing degrees of scalability and fault tolerance. Each solution necessitates a deviation from the strict emulation of UNIX one-copy file update semantics.

8.1   Introduction

In this chapter we describe three practical implementations of distributed file services. The file services discussed in this chapter are second-generation designs, following on from research done during the first half of the 1980s. The characteristics of some important first-generation file services are summarized in Chapter 1.

All of the systems described in this chapter aim to emulate the UNIX file system interface, enabling unchanged UNIX client programs to access files that are stored in a remote file server. This aim has had an important impact on their design. In areas such as the control of access to files and the model of data access, they do not attempt to exceed the capabilities of UNIX.

The emulation of a UNIX file system offers some difficulties to the designer of a distributed file service. The caching of file data in client computers is an essential design feature, but the conventional UNIX file system offers **one-copy update semantics**. This refers to a model for concurrent access to files in which the file contents seen by all of the processes accessing or updating a given file are those that they would see if only single copy of the file contents existed. If this model is strictly followed, any replication or caching that is introduced for performance or fault-tolerance reasons must be totally transparent. When files are replicated or cached at different sites, there is an inevitable delay in the propagation of modifications made at one site to all of the other sites that hold copies, and this may result in some deviation from one-copy semantics.

We shall see that the one-copy model has not been strictly adhered to by any of the distributed file services described in this chapter, but the deviations have been carefully defined to minimize the likelihood that they will be detected with typical UNIX file usage patterns. These usage patterns will be summarized in our discussion of the design of the Andrew file system in Section 8.3.

8.2   The Sun Network File System

Sun Microsystem's *Network File System (NFS)* has been widely adopted in industry and in academic environments since its introduction in 1985. The design and development of NFS were undertaken by staff at Sun Microsystems in 1984 [Sandberg *et al.* 1985; Sandberg 1987]. Although several distributed file services had already been developed and used successfully in universities and research laboratories, NFS was the first file service that was designed as a product. The design and implementation of NFS have achieved considerable success both technically and commercially.

To encourage its adoption as a standard, the definitions of the key interfaces were placed in the public domain [Sun 1989], enabling other vendors to produce implementations, and the source code for a reference implementation was made available to other computer vendors under licence. It is now supported by many vendors and is often taken as the *de facto* standard. It provides a working solution to many requirements for distributed file access, but it does not address some issues whose importance is likely to grow as the size and range of applications for distributed systems increase.

Figure 8.1   Local and remote file systems accessible on an NFS client.

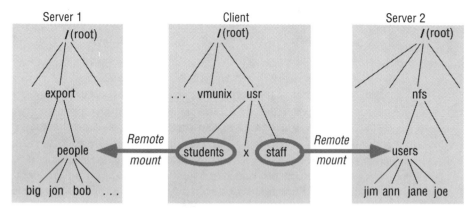

Note: The file system mounted at */usr/students* in the client is actually the sub-tree located at */export/people* in Server 1; the file system mounted at */usr/staff* in the client is actually the sub-tree located at */nfs/users* in Server 1.

NFS provides transparent access to remote files for client programs running on UNIX and other systems. Typically every computer has NFS client and server modules installed in its system kernel, at least in the case of UNIX systems. The client-server relationship is symmetrical: each computer in an NFS network can act as both a client and a server and the files at every machine can be made available for remote access by other machines. A workstation can be a server, exporting some of its files and a client, accessing files on other machines. But it is common practice to configure larger installations with some machines as dedicated servers and others as workstations.

An important goal of NFS was to achieve a high level of support for hardware and operating system heterogeneity. The current version at the time of writing is NFS 4.0. NFS has been implemented and is available for almost every currently available version of UNIX and for Mach. Versions of the client and server modules have been implemented for several other operating systems. Client modules are available for the IBM PC and the Apple Macintosh and server modules for Digital Equipment VMS and Novell Netware.

The other design goals of NFS and the extent to which they have been achieved are described below with reference to the transparency goals described in Chapters 1 and 7:

Access transparency: The NFS client module provides an application programming interface to local processes that is identical to the local operating system's interface. Thus in a UNIX client, accesses to remote files are performed using the normal UNIX system calls. No modifications to existing programs are required to enable them to operate correctly with remote files.

Location transparency: Each client establishes a file name space by adding remote file systems to its local name space. File systems have to be *exported* by the node that holds them and *remote-mounted* by a client before they can be accessed by processes running in the client (see Figure 8.1). The point in a client's name hierarchy at which a remote-mounted file system appears is determined by the client; thus NFS does not enforce a single network-wide file name space – each client sees a set of remote filesystems that is determined locally and remote files may have different pathnames on different clients, but a uniform name space can be established with appropriate configuration tables in each client, achieving the goal of location transparency.

Failure transparency: The NFS service is stateless and most of the operations of the file access protocol are repeatable or *idempotent*. In order to achieve the stateless property for NFS servers, the service operations differ substantially from the UNIX file primitives and resemble closely those of the file service model described in Chapter 7. UNIX file operations are translated into NFS protocol operations by an NFS client module that resides in each client.

The stateless and idempotent nature of the NFS file access protocol ensures that the failure modes observed by clients when accessing remote files are similar to those for local file access. When a server fails, the service that it provides is suspended until the server is restarted, but once it has been restarted user-level client processes proceed from the point at which the service was interrupted, unaware of the failure (except in the case of access to *soft-mounted* remote file systems, which is described below). The failure of a client computer or of a user-level process in a client has no effect on any server that it may be using, since servers hold no state on behalf of their clients.

Performance transparency: Both the client and the server employ caching to achieve satisfactory performance. The extensive use of caching and the installation of the client and server modules in the UNIX kernel result in times to access remote files on lightly-loaded servers within 20 per cent of those for local files on similar storage devices. The caching in the server is straightforward, using the conventional UNIX disk block caching mechanism. The client module maintains a local cache of blocks from remote files, directories and file attribute data. For clients, the maintenance of cache coherence is complex, since several clients may be using and updating the same file. The client cache mechanism is detailed in the next section.

Migration transparency: In addition to the NFS file access service, there is a separate service – the *mount service* – that supports the mounting of remote file systems in the client's local file name space. A mount service process runs in each node and provides an RPC interface to clients for mounting and unmounting local file systems at the client node. The mount service is used mainly in programs responsible for system administration to establish the file name space in client computers at system start-up time. Filesystems (in the UNIX sense, that is, sub-trees of files) may be moved between servers, but the remote mount tables in each client must then be separately updated to enable the clients to access the filesystem in its new location, so migration transparency is not fully achieved by NFS.

The NFS *mount service* operates at system boot time or user login time at each workstation, mounting filesystems wholesale in case they will be used during the login session. This was found too cumbersome for some applications and produces large numbers of unused entries in mount tables. The NFS *Automounter* provides a solution to this and incidentally, a simple method for dynamically selecting one from a number of replicated read-only file stores, allowing the file serving load to be distributed, for example, between several servers that offer identical */usr/lib* filesystems. Automounter runs as a local user-level service in each NFS client and enables pathnames to be used that refer to unmounted remote filesystems. Any reference by a user process to a pathname within a sub-tree managed by Automounter will cause NFS to pass the name to Automounter which resolves it, mounting any filesystems that are needed in order to do so.

Requirements not addressed by NFS include:

Replication transparency: NFS does not support file replication in a general sense. The Sun Network Information Service (NIS, formerly known as Yellow Pages service) is a separate service available for use with NFS that supports the replication of simple databases organized as key-value pairs (for example, the UNIX system files */etc/passwd* and */etc/hosts*). It manages the distribution of updates and accesses to the replicated files based on a simple master-slave replication model (also known as the *primary copy* model, discussed further in Chapter 11) with provision for the replication of part or all of the database at each site. NIS provides a shared repository for system information that changes infrequently and does not require updates to occur simultaneously at all sites.

Concurrency transparency: UNIX file semantics support only rudimentary locking facilities for concurrency control. NFS does not aim to improve upon the UNIX approach to the control of concurrent updates to files. Release 4.0 of NFS has been extended to support remote use of the advisory record-level locks that are a feature of most recent versions of UNIX.

Scalability: The scalability of the NFS service is limited; it was originally designed to allow each server to support approximately 5–10 clients when they rely on NFS servers for all file accesses or a larger number (perhaps as many as 50) when some key files are stored on a local disk at each client. The design limitations of NFS and the absence of support for general-purpose file replication set a practical limit on the scale of NFS-based distributed systems. The number of clients that can simultaneously access a shared file is restricted by the performance of the server that holds the file and this can become a system-wide performance bottleneck for heavily-used files.

Implementation

Figure 8.2 shows the software architecture of NFS clients and servers. The components of NFS concerned with the mounting of remote file systems are not shown. Processes using NFS are referred to here as *user-level client processes* in order to distinguish them from the *NFS client* module which resides in the UNIX kernel on each client computer. The *NFS server* module resides in the kernel on each computer that acts as an NFS server. Requests referring to files in a remote file system are translated by the client module to NFS protocol operations and then passed to the NFS server module at the computer holding the relevant filesytem.

Figure 8.2   NFS software architecture.

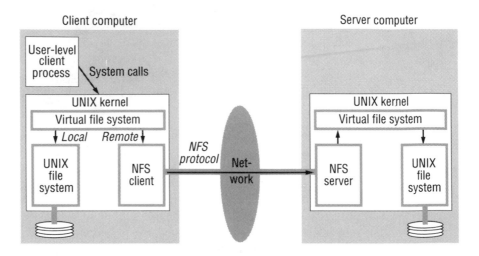

The NFS client and server modules communicate using remote procedure calling. Sun's RPC system, described in Chapter 5, was developed for use in NFS. A port mapper service is included to enable clients to bind to services in a given host by name, although in early releases of NFS, NFS clients accessed the server by quoting a well-known port number. Encryption of the RPC messages can be specified as an optional security feature, but the RPC interface to the NFS server is open. Any process can send requests to an NFS server and if the requests are valid and contain the correct authentication information, they will be acted upon. NFS client and server modules are operating-system independent and have been successfully implemented in several non-UNIX environments, but we shall describe their implementation with reference to UNIX.

The RPC interface provided by the NFS server is shown in Figure 8.3. NFS *file handles* are similar to the UFIDs of Chapter 7. The NFS file access operations *read*, *write*, *getattr* and *setattr* are almost identical to the *Read*, *Write*, *GetAttributes* and *SetAttributes* operations defined for our Flat File Service model in Chapter 7.

Many of the directory operations defined in Figure 8.3 are similar to those in our Directory Service model. The *lookup* operation looks for a single-part name in a given directory and returns the corresponding file handle and the file attributes. When a client uses a multi-part pathname, the NFS client module must parse the name and then look up each part separately, stepping through the name tree. This is done because the pathname may traverse several filesystems which may reside in different servers or in the client itself. It also helps to achieve the goal of operating system heterogeneity, since the parsing of names in the client module may use a name syntax that is specific to the client operating system.

Because the file and directory operations are integrated in a single service, the space leak problem identified in Section 7.5 cannot arise; the creation and insertion of file names in directories is performed by a single *create* operation which takes the text name of the new file and the file handle for the target directory as arguments. The other

Figure 8.3   NFS Server operations.

lookup(dirfh, name) → *fh, attr*
  Returns a file handle and attributes for the file *name* in the directory *dirfh*.

create(dirfh, name, attr) → *newfh, attr*
  Creates a new file *name* in directory *dirfh* with attributes *attr* and returns the new file handle and attributes.

remove(dirfh, name) → *status*
  Removes file *name* from directory *dirfh*.

getattr(fh) → *attr*
  Returns file attributes of file *fh*. (Similar to the UNIX *stat* system call.)

setattr(fh, attr) → *attr*
  Sets the attributes (mode, user id, group id, size, access time and modify time of a file). Setting the size to 0 truncates the file.

read(fh, offset, count) → *attr, data*
  Returns up to *count* bytes of data from a file starting at *offset*. Also returns the latest attributes of the file.

write(fh, offset, count, data) → *attr*
  Writes *count* bytes of data to a file starting at *offset*. Returns the attributes of the file after the write has taken place.

rename(dirfh, name, todirfh, toname) → *status*
  Changes the name of file name in directory dirfh to toname in directory todirfh.

link(newdirfh, newname, dirfh, name) → *status*
  Creates an entry *newname* in the directory *newdirfh* which refers to file *name* in the directory *dirfh*.

symlink(newdirfh, newname, string) → *status*
  Creates an entry *newname* in the directory *newdirfh* of type *symbolic link* with the value *string*. The server does not interpret the *string*, but makes a symbolic link file to hold it.

readlink(fh) → *string*
  Returns the string that is associated with the symbolic link file identified by *fh*.

mkdir(dirfh, name, attr) → *newfh, attr*
  Creates a new directory *name* with attributes *attr* and returns the new file handle and attributes.

rmdir(dirfh, name) → *status*
  Removes the directory empty *name* from the parent directory *dirfh*. Fails if the directory is not empty.

readdir(dirfh, cookie, count) → *entries*
  Returns up to *count* bytes of directory entries from the directory *dirfh*. Each entry contains a file name, file id, and an opaque pointer to the next directory entry, called a *cookie*. The *cookie* is used in subsequent *readdir* calls to start reading from the subsequent entry. A *readdir* with a 0 value for the *cookie* reads from the first entry in the directory.

statfs(fh) → *fsstats*
  Returns file system information (such as block size, number of free blocks, and so on) for the file system containing a file *fh*.

NFS operations on directories are *create*, *remove*, *rename*, *link*, *symlink*, *readlink*, *mkdir*, *rmdir*, *readdir* and *statfs*. They resemble their UNIX counterparts with the exception of *readdir* which provides a representation-independent method for reading the contents of directories and *statfs* which gives the status information on remote file systems.

Virtual file system □ A Virtual File System (VFS) module has been added to the UNIX kernel to distinguish between local and remote files and to translate between the UNIX-independent file identifiers used by NFS and the internal file identifiers normally used in UNIX and other file systems.

The file identifiers used in NFS are called *file handles*. A file handle is opaque to clients and contains whatever information the server needs to distinguish an individual file. In UNIX implementations of NFS, the file handle is derived from the file's *i-node number* by adding two extra fields as follows (the i-node number of a UNIX file is a number that serves to identify and locate the file within the file system in which the file is stored):

File handle:	Filesystem identifier	i-node number of file	i-node generation number

The *filesystem identifier* field is a unique number that is allocated to each filesystem when it is created (and in the UNIX implementation is stored in the superblock of the file system). The *i-node generation number* is needed because in the conventional UNIX file system i-node numbers are reused after a file is removed. In the VFS extensions to the UNIX file system, a generation number is stored with each file and is incremented each time the i-node number is reused (for example, in a *create* system call). The client obtains the first file handle for a remote file system when it mounts it. File handles are passed from server to client in the results of *lookup*, *create* and *mkdir* operations and from client to server in the argument lists of all server operations.

The virtual file system layer has one VFS structure for each mounted file system and one *v-node* per open file. A VFS structure relates a remote file system to the local directory on which it is mounted. The v-node contains an indicator to show whether a file is local or remote. If the file is local, the v-node contains a reference to the index of the local file (an i-node in a UNIX implementation). If the file is remote, it contains the file handle of the remote file.

Client integration □ The NFS client module plays the role described for the client module in Chapter 7, supplying an interface suitable for use by conventional application programs. But unlike our model client module, it emulates the semantics of the standard UNIX file system primitives precisely and is integrated with the UNIX kernel. It is integrated with the kernel and not supplied as a library for loading into client processes so that:

- user programs can access files via UNIX system calls without recompilation or reloading;
- a single client module serves all of the user level processes, with a shared cache of recently-used blocks (described below);

- the encryption key used to protect User IDs passed to the server (see below) can be retained in the kernel.

The NFS client module cooperates with the virtual file system in each client machine. It operates in a similar manner to the conventional UNIX file system, transferring blocks of files to and from the server and caching the blocks in the local memory whenever possible. It shares the same buffer cache that is used by the local input-output system. But since several clients in different host machines may simultaneously access the same remote file, a new and significant cache consistency problem arises. This is discussed below.

Server integration □ The NFS server module is integrated with the UNIX kernel mainly for performance reasons. In fact, a user-level NFS server was implemented at one stage in the NFS development project and achieved approximately 80 per cent of the performance of the kernel version.

Access control and authentication □ Since the NFS server is stateless, it does not keep files open on behalf of its clients, unlike the conventional UNIX file system. So the server must check the user's identity against the file's access permission attributes afresh on each request to see whether the user is permitted to access the file in the manner requested. The Sun RPC protocol requires clients to send user authentication information (for example, the conventional UNIX 16-bit User ID and Group ID) with each request and this is checked against the access permission in the file attributes. These additional parameters are not shown in Figure 8.3; they are supplied automatically by the RPC system.

In its simplest form, there is a security loophole in this access control mechanism. An NFS server provides a conventional RPC interface at a well known port on each host and any process can behave as a client, sending requests to the server to access or update a file. The client can modify the RPC calls to include the User ID of any user, impersonating the user without their knowledge or permission. This security loophole has been closed in NFS 4.0 by the use of an option in the RPC protocol for the DES encryption of the user's authentication information. This, and more comprehensive solutions to the problem of user authentication are described further in Chapter 16.

Path name translation □ UNIX file systems translate multi-part file *pathnames* to i-node references in a step-by-step process whenever the *open*, *creat* or *stat* system calls are used. In NFS, pathnames cannot be translated in the server because the name may cross a 'mount point' at the client. So pathnames are parsed and their translation is controlled by the client. Each part of a name that refers to a remote-mounted directory is translated to a file handle using a separate *lookup* request to the remote server. At each step, the remote mount table in the client is checked to see whether another remote-mounted file store should be accessed. Caching of the results of each step in pathname translations alleviates the apparent inefficiency of this process, taking advantage of locality of reference to files and directories: users and programs typically access files in only one or a small number of directories.

Mount service □ The mounting of remote file stores by clients is supported by a separate *mount service* process that runs at user level on each NFS server computer. On each server there is a file with a well known name (*/etc/exports*) containing the names of local filesystems that are available for remote mounting. An access list is associated with each filesystem name indicating which hosts are permitted to mount the filesystem.

Clients use a modified version of the UNIX *mount* command to request mounting of a remote filesystem, specifying the remote host name, pathname of a directory in the remote filesystem and the local name with which it is to be mounted. The remote directory may be any sub-tree of the required remote file system, enabling clients to mount any part of the remote filesystem. The modified *mount* command communicates with the mount service process on the remote host using a *mount protocol*. This is an RPC protocol and it includes an operation that takes a directory pathname and returns the file handle of the specified directory if the client has access permission for the relevant filesystem. The location of the server and the file handle of the root of the remote file system are passed on to the VFS layer and NFS client.

Normally, mount requests are performed as a part of the system initialization process in the client computer. The required mounts are specified by editing the UNIX startup script (*/etc/rc*). Since the start-up script is executed automatically whenever a UNIX system is initialized, users need not be concerned with the details of the filesystems that are remotely mounted, but if an individual user wants to change the standard configuration this can be done using *mount* explicitly.

Remote filesystems may be *hard mounted* or *soft mounted* in a client computer. When a user-level process accesses a file in a filesystem that is hard mounted, the process is suspended until the request can be completed and if the remote host is unavailable for any reason the NFS client module continues to retry the request until it is satisfied. Thus in the case of a server failure, user-level processes are suspended until the server restarts and then they continue just as though there had been no failure. But if the relevant filesystem is *soft mounted*, the NFS client module returns a failure indication to user-level processes after a small number of retries. Properly-constructed programs will then detect the failure and take appropriate recovery or reporting actions. But many UNIX utilities and applications do not test for the failure of file access operations, and these behave in unpredictable ways in the case of failure of a soft-mounted filesystem.

Automounter □ The Automounter has been added to the UNIX implementation of NFS in order to dynamically mount a file system whenever an 'empty' mount point is referenced by a client. Automounter runs as a user-level UNIX process in each client computer. It maintains a table of mount points (pathnames) with a reference to one or more NFS servers listed against each.

Automounter behaves like a local NFS server at the client machine. When the NFS client module attempts to resolve a pathname that includes one of these mount points, it passes a *lookup( )* request to the local Automounter which locates the required filesystem in its table and sends a 'probe' request to each server listed. The filesystem on the first server to respond is then mounted at the client using the normal mount service. The mounted filesystem is linked to the mount point using a symbolic link, so that accesses to it will not result in further requests to the Automounter. File access then proceeds in the normal way without further reference to Automounter unless there are no references to the symbolic link for several minutes. In the latter case, Automounter unmounts the remote filesystem.

A primitive form of read-only replication can be achieved by listing several servers containing identical filesystems against a name in the Automounter table. This is useful for heavily-used file systems that change infrequently, such as UNIX system binaries. For example, copies of the */usr/lib* directory and its sub-tree might be held on more than one server. On the first occasion that a file in */usr/lib* is opened at a client, all of the servers will be sent probe messages and the first to respond will be mounted at the client. This provides a limited degree of fault-tolerance and load balancing, since the first server to respond will be one that has not failed, and is likely to be one that is not heavily occupied with servicing other requests.

Server caching □ Caching in both the client and the server computer are indispensable features of NFS implementations in order to achieve adequate performance.

In conventional UNIX systems, file pages, directories and file attributes that have been read from disk are retained in a *buffer cache* until the buffer space is required for other pages. If a process then issues a read or a write request for a page that is already in the cache, it can be satisfied without another disk access. *Read-ahead* anticipates read accesses and fetches the pages following those that have most recently been read and *delayed-write* optimizes writes: when a page has been altered (by a write request), its new contents are written to disk only when the buffer page is required for another page. To guard against loss of data in a system crash, the UNIX *sync* operation flushes altered pages to disk every 30 seconds. These caching techniques work in a conventional UNIX environment because all read and write requests issued by user-level processes pass through a single cache that is implemented in the UNIX kernel space. The cache is always kept up-to-date, and file accesses cannot bypass the cache.

NFS servers use the cache at the server machine just as it is used for other file accesses except that the server's write operations are modified to perform *write-through*. The use of the server's cache to hold recently-read disk blocks does not raise any consistency problems; but when a server performs write requests, it must write each modification to disk immediately because a failure of the server might otherwise result in the undetected loss of data by clients. Write-through is not required for conventional UNIX file accesses because failed writes only go undetected when the host computer fails. In that case, the client also fails and such failures can be detected and dealt with by application-level recovery procedures.

Client caching □ The NFS client module caches the results of *read, write, getattr, lookup* and *readdir* operations in order to reduce the number of requests transmitted to servers. Client caching introduces the potential for different versions of files or portions of files to exist in different client nodes. Writes by a client do not result in the immediate updating of cached copies of the file in other clients. A timestamp-based method is used to validate cached blocks whenever they are used in order to minimize such inconsistencies. Whenever a client caches one or more blocks from a file, it also caches a timestamp indicating the time when the file was last modified on the server. To validate all the cached blocks from a given file, a client requests the latest modification time from the server and compares it with its cached timestamp. If the modification time is more recent, all of the cached blocks from that file are invalidated and must be refetched when they are next requested.

The validation check is performed whenever a file is opened and whenever the server is contacted to fetch a new block from a file. But after a check, the cached blocks are assumed to be valid for a fixed time that is specified when the remote filesystem is mounted (normally given as 3 seconds for files and 30 seconds for directories). The first reference to a file after this time has elapsed causes another validation check.

Writes are handled differently. When a cached page is modified it is marked as dirty and is scheduled to be flushed to the server asynchronously. Modified pages are flushed when the file is closed or a *sync* occurs at the client and they are flushed more frequently if bio-daemons are in use (see below).

Since NFS clients cannot determine whether a file is shared on not, the validation procedure must be used for all file accesses. It is a fairly costly procedure (involving a *getattributes* request to the server every 3 seconds for files that are accessed frequently by a client). The validation procedure does not guarantee the same level of consistency of files that is provided in conventional UNIX systems, since recent updates are not always visible to clients sharing a file; there are two sources of time lag, the delay after write before the updated data leaves the cache in the updating client's kernel and the 3-second 'window' for cache validation. Fortunately, most UNIX applications do not depend critically upon the synchronization of file updates and few difficulties have been reported from this source.

To implement read-ahead and delayed-write, the NFS client needs to perform some reads and writes asynchronously. This is achieved in UNIX implementations of NFS by the inclusion of one or more *bio-daemon* processes at each client. (*Bio* stands for block input-output; the term *daemon* is often used to refer to user-level processes that perform system tasks.) The role of the bio-daemons is to perform read-ahead and delayed-write operations. A bio-daemon is notified after each read request and it requests the transfer of the following file block from the server to the client cache. In the case of writing, the bio-daemon will send a block to the server whenever a block has been filled by a client operation. Directory blocks are sent whenever a modification has occurred.

Bio-daemon processes enhance the performance and reduce the chances of inconsistency between caches at different clients but they are not a logical requirement, since in the absence of read-ahead, a *read* operation in a user process will trigger a synchronous request to the relevant server, and the results of *write*s in user processes will be transferred to the server when the relevant file is closed or when the virtual file system at the client performs a *sync* operation.

Other optimizations □ The Sun file system is based on the UNIX BSD 4.2 Fast File System which uses 8 kilobyte disk blocks, resulting in fewer file system calls for sequential file access than previous UNIX systems. The UDP packets used for the implementation of Sun RPC are extended to 9 kilobytes, enabling an RPC call containing an entire block as an argument to be transferred in a single packet and minimizing the effect of network latency when reading files sequentially.

Performance □ The performance figures reported by Sandberg [1987] show that with the caching and other optimizations described above, the use of NFS does not impose a significant performance penalty. He benchmarked NFS using a suite of typical application programs and UNIX system commands. He reported that 'a diskless Sun-3 using a Sun-3 server with a Fujitsu Eagle disk runs the benchmarks faster than the same Sun-3 with a local Fujitsu 2243AS on a SCSI interface'. But he identifies two remaining problem areas:

- the frequent use of the *getattr* call in order to fetch timestamps from servers for cache validation;

- the relatively poor performance of the *write* operation because write-through is used at the server.

He notes that writes are relatively infrequent (about 5 per cent of all calls to the server) and their poor performance is therefore tolerable except when large files are written to the server. His results also show that the *lookup* operation accounts for almost 50 per cent of server calls. This is a consequence of the step-by-step pathname translation method necessitated by UNIX's file naming semantics. Sandberg's measurements were taken with a server dedicated to a single client.

The relatively poor write performance of standard NFS implementations has been addressed by the use of battery-backed *non-volatile RAM* (NVRAM) in the server's disk controller in a project undertaken by Moran et al. [1990]. The use of NVRAM enables the server to report success for write operations before transferring the data to disk, while providing the required guarantee that the data has been recorded in permanent storage.

We shall consider the performance of NFS in multiple-client situations after our discussion of the Andrew File System.

Summary □ Sun NFS closely follows the design model described in Chapter 7 with an additional design goal to enable its implementation in a heterogeneous hardware and operating system environment. The resulting design provides good location and access transparency if the NFS mount service is used properly to produce similar name spaces at all clients. The NFS server implementation is stateless, enabling clients and servers to resume execution after a failure, without the need for any recovery procedures. Migration of files or file volumes is not supported except at the level of manual intervention to reconfigure mount directives after the movement of a filesystem to a new location.

The performance of NFS is much enhanced by the caching of file blocks at each client. This optimization is important for the achievement of satisfactory performance, but results in some deviation from strict UNIX one-copy file update semantics

8.3   The Andrew File System

Andrew is a distributed computing environment developed at Carnegie-Mellon University (CMU) for use as a campus computing and information system [Morris *et al.* 1986]. The Andrew File System is a file service designed to provide an information-sharing mechanism to its users.

The design of the Andrew File System (henceforth abbreviated AFS) reflects an intention to support information-sharing on a large scale. The campus computing network that Andrew serves was expected to grow to include between 5,000 and 10,000 workstations during the lifetime of the system. In 1991 AFS was supporting approximately 800 workstations serviced by approximately 40 servers at CMU, with additional clients and servers at remote sites connected via the Internet. We shall describe AFS-2, the first 'production' implementation, following the descriptions by Satyanarayanan [1989a; 1989b].

AFS is implemented on a network of workstations and servers running BSD 4.3 unix or the Mach operating system (see Section 18.2; but note that Mach supports the same file operations as BSD 4.3 Unix). Like NFS, AFS provides transparent access to remote shared files for UNIX programs running on workstations. Access to AFS files is via the normal UNIX file primitives, enabling existing UNIX programs to access AFS files without modification or recompilation. AFS is compatible with NFS. AFS servers hold 'local' UNIX files, but the filing system in the servers is NFS-based, so files are referenced by NFS-style file handles, rather than i-node numbers, and the files may in fact be remote.

AFS differs markedly from NFS in its design and implementation. The differences are primarily attributable to the identification of *scalability* as the most important design goal. AFS is designed to perform well with larger numbers of active users than other distributed file systems. The key strategy for achieving scalability is the caching of whole files in client nodes. AFS has two unusual design characteristics:

Whole-file serving: The entire contents of files are transmitted to client computers by AFS servers.

Whole-file caching: Once a copy of a file has been transferred to a client computer it is stored in a cache on the local disk. The cache contains several hundred of the files most recently used on that computer. The cache is permanent, surviving reboots of the client computer. Local copies of files are used to satisfy clients' *open* requests in preference to remote copies whenever possible.

Scenario □   Here is a simple scenario illustrating the operation of AFS:

- When a user process in a client computer issues an *open* system call for a file in the shared file space and there is not a current copy of the file in the local cache, the server holding the file is located and is sent a request for a copy of the file.

- The copy is stored in the local UNIX file system in the client computer, the copy is then *open*ed and the resulting UNIX file descriptor is returned to the client.

- Subsequent *read*, *write* and other operations on the file by processes in the client computer are applied to the local copy.

- When the process in the client issues a *close* system call, if the local copy has been updated its contents are sent back to the server. The server updates the file contents and the timestamps on the file. The copy on the client's local disk is retained in case it is needed again by a user-level process on the same workstation.

We shall discuss the observed performance of AFS below, but we can make some general observations and predictions here based on the design characteristics described above:

- For shared files that are infrequently updated (such as those containing the code of UNIX commands and libraries) and for files that are normally accessed by only a single user (such as most of the files in a user's home directory and its sub-tree), locally-cached copies are likely to remain valid for long periods – in the first case because they are not updated and in the second because if they are updated, the updated copy will be in the cache on the owner's workstation. These classes of file account for the overwhelming majority of file accesses.

• The local cache can be allocated a substantial proportion of the disk space on each workstation; say 100 megabytes. This is normally sufficient for the establishment of a working set of the files used by one user. The provision of sufficient cache storage for the establishment of a working set ensures that files in regular use on a given workstation are normally retained in the cache until they are needed again.

• The design strategy is based on some assumptions about average and maximum file size and locality of reference to files in UNIX systems. These assumptions are derived from observations of typical UNIX workloads in academic and other environments [Satyanarayanan 1981; Ousterhout *et al.* 1985; Floyd 1986]. The most important observations are:

   – Files are small; most are less than 10 kilobytes in size.

   – Read operations on files are much more common than writes (about 6 times more common).

   – Sequential access is common and random access is rare.

   – Most files are read and written by only one user. When a file is shared it is usually only one user who modifies it.

   – Files are referenced in bursts. If a file has been referenced recently, there is a high probability that it will referenced again in the near future.

These observations were used to guide the design and optimization of AFS, *not* to restrict the functionality seen by users.

• AFS works best with the classes of file identified in the first point above. There is one important type of file that does not fit into any of these classes – databases are typically shared by many users and are often updated quite frequently. The designers of AFS have explicitly excluded the provision of storage facilities for databases from their design goals, stating that the constraints imposed by different naming structures (that is, content-based access) and the need for fine-grained data access, concurrency control and atomicity of updates make it difficult to design a distributed database system that is also a distributed file system. They argue that the provision of facilities for distributed databases should be addressed separately [Satyanarayanan 1989a].

Implementation

The above scenario illustrates AFS's operation but leaves many questions about its implementation unanswered. Amongst the most important are:

• How does AFS gain control when an *open* or *close* system call referring to a file in the shared file space is issued by a client?

• How is the server holding the required file located?

• What space is allocated for cached files in workstations?

Figure 8.4   Distribution of processes in the Andrew file system.

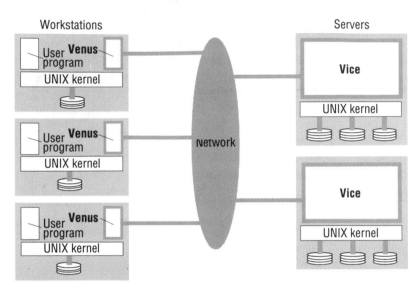

- How does AFS ensure that the cached copies of files are up-to-date when files may be updated by several clients?

We answer these questions below.

AFS is implemented as two software components that exist as UNIX processes called *Vice* and *Venus*. Figure 8.4 shows the distribution of Vice and Venus processes. Vice is the name given to the server software that runs as a user-level UNIX process in each server computer and Venus is a user-level process that runs in each client computer and corresponds to the client module introduced in Chapter 7.

The files available to user processes running on workstations are either *local* or *shared*. Local files are handled as normal UNIX files. They are stored on a workstation's disk and are available only to local user processes. Shared files are stored on servers and copies of them are cached on the local disks of workstations. The name space seen by user processes is illustrated in Figure 8.5. It is a conventional UNIX directory hierarchy, with a specific sub-tree (called *cmu*) containing all of the shared files. This splitting of the file name space into local and shared files leads to some loss of location transparency, but this is hardly noticeable to users other than system administrators. Local files are used only for temporary files (*/tmp*) and processes that are essential for workstation start-up. Other standard UNIX files (such as those normally found in */bin*, */lib*, and so on) are implemented as symbolic links from local directories to files held in the shared space. Users' directories are in the shared space, enabling users to access their files from any workstation.

The UNIX kernel in each workstation and server is a modified version of BSD 4.3 UNIX. The modifications are designed to intercept *open*, *close* and some other file system calls when they refer to files in the shared name space and pass them to the Venus process in the client computer (illustrated in Figure 8.6). One other kernel modification is included for performance reasons and this is described later.

Figure 8.5   File name space seen by clients of the Andrew File System.

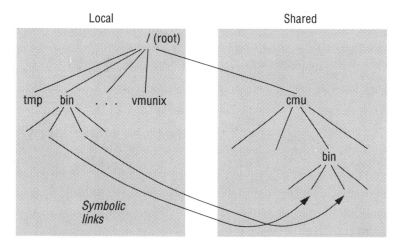

One of the file partitions on the local disk of each workstation is used as a cache, holding the cached copies of files from the shared space. Venus manages the cache, removing the least-recently-used files when a new file is acquired from a server to make the required space if the partition is full. The workstation cache is usually large enough to accommodate several hundred average-sized files, rendering the workstation largely independent of the Vice servers once a working set of the current user's files and frequently-used system files has been cached.

Several features of AFS are similar to the file service model that we have described in Chapter 7:

- Files are grouped into *volumes* for ease of location and movement. AFS volumes are similar to the *file groups* that were introduced in Section 7.5.

Figure 8.6   System call interception in the Andrew file system.

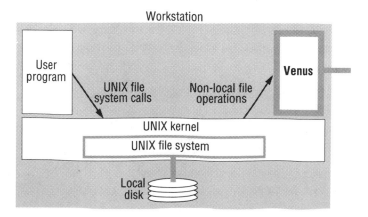

- A flat file service is implemented by the Vice servers and the hierarchic directory structure required by UNIX user programs is implemented by the set of Venus processes in the workstations.

- Each file and directory in the shared file space is identified by a unique, 96-bit file identifier (*fid*) similar to a UFID. The Venus processes translate the pathnames issued by clients to *fid*s.

- The representation of *fid*s is similar to our representation for UFIDs introduced in Section 7.5, but since *fid*s are used only for internal communication between AFS modules (Venus and Vice processes) they need not hold any access control or security codes.

The representation of *fid*s includes the volume number for the volume containing the file (*cf* the *file group identifier* in UFIDs), an NFS file handle identifying the file within the volume (*cf* the *file number* in UFIDs) and a *uniquifier* to ensure that file identifiers are not reused:

32 bits	32 bits	32 bits
Volume number	File handle	Uniquifier

User programs use conventional UNIX pathnames to refer to files, but AFS uses *fid*s in the communication between the Venus and Vice processes. The Vice servers accept requests only in terms of *fid*s. Venus translates the pathnames supplied by clients into *fid*s using a step-by-step lookup to obtain the information from the file directories held in the Vice servers.

Figure 8.7 describes the actions taken by Vice, Venus and the UNIX kernel when a user process issues each of the system calls mentioned in our outline scenario above. The *callback promise* mentioned here is a mechanism for ensuring that cached copies of files are updated when another client closes the same file after updating it. This mechanism is discussed in the next section.

Cache coherence

When Vice supplies a copy of a file to a Venus process it also provides a *callback promise* – a token issued by the Vice server that is the custodian of the file, guaranteeing that it will notify the Venus process when any other client modifies the file. Callback promises are stored with the cached files on the workstation disks and have two states: *valid* or *cancelled*. When a server performs a request to update a file it notifies all of the Venus processes to which it has issued callback promises by sending a *callback* to each – a callback is a remote procedure call from a server to a Venus process. When the Venus process receives a callback, it sets the *callback promise* token for the relevant file to *cancelled*.

Whenever Venus handles an *open* on behalf of a client, it checks the cache. If the required file is found in the cache, then its token is checked. If its value is *cancelled*, then a fresh copy of the file must be fetched from the Vice server, but if the token is *valid*, then the cached copy can be opened and used without reference to Vice.

Figure 8.7   Implementation of file system calls in AFS.

User process	UNIX kernel	Venus	Net	Vice
open(FileName, mode)	If FileName refers to a file in shared file space, pass the request to Venus.	Check list of files in local cache. If not present or there is no valid callback promise, send a request for the file to the Vice server that is custodian of the volume containing the file.		Transfer a copy of the file and a callback promise to the workstation. Log the callback promise.
	Open the local file and return the file descriptor to the application.	Place the copy of the file in the local file system, enter its local name in the local cache list and return the local name to UNIX.		
read(FileDescriptor, Buffer, length)	Perform a normal UNIX read operation on the local copy.			
write(FileDescriptor, Buffer, length)	Perform a normal UNIX write operation on the local copy.			
close(FileDescriptor)	Close the local copy and notify Venus that the file has been closed.	If the local copy has been changed, send a copy to the Vice server that is the custodian of the file.		Replace the file contents and send a callback to all other clients holding callback promises on the file.

When a workstation is restarted after a failure or a shut-down, Venus aims to retain as many as possible of the cached files on the local disk, but it cannot assume that the callback promise tokens are correct, since some callbacks may have been missed. For each file with a valid token, Venus must send a cache validation request containing the file modification timestamp to the server that is the custodian of the file. If the timestamp is current, the server responds with *valid* and the token is reinstated. If the timestamp shows that the file is out-of-date, then the server responds with *cancelled* and the token is set to *cancelled*. Callbacks must be renewed before an *open* if a time T (typically on the order of a few minutes) has elapsed since the file was cached without communication from the server. This is to deal with possible communication failures, which can result in the loss of callback messages.

This callback-based mechanism for maintaining cache coherence was adopted as offering the most scalable approach, following the evaluation in the prototype (AFS-1) of a timestamp-based mechanism similar to that used in NFS. In AFS-1, a Venus process holding a cached copy of a file interrogates the Vice process on each *open*, to determine whether the timestamp on the local copy agrees with that on the server. The callback-based approach is more scalable because it results in communication between client and

Figure 8.8   The main components of the Vice service interface.

Fetch(fid) → attr, data
> Returns the attributes (status) and, optionally, the contents of file identified by the *fid* and records a callback promise on it.

Store(fid, attr, data)
> Returns the attributes and, optionally, the contents of a specified file and records a callback promise on it.

Create() → fid
> Creates a new file and records a callback promise on it.

Remove(fid)
> Deletes the specified file.

SetLock(fid, mode)
> Sets a lock on the specified file or directory. The mode of the lock may be shared or exclusive. Locks that are not removed expire after 30 minutes.

ReleaseLock(fid)
> Unlocks the specified file or directory.

RemoveCallback(fid)
> Informs server that a Venus process has flushed a file from its cache.

BreakCallback(fid)
> This call is made by a Vice server to a Venus process. It cancels the callback promise on the relevant file.

Note: Directory and administrative operations (*Rename, Link, Makedir, Removedir, GetTime, CheckToken*, and so on) are not shown.

---

server and activity in the server only when the file has been updated, whereas the timestamp approach results in a client-server interaction on each *open*, even when there is a valid local copy. Since the majority of files are not accessed concurrently, and *read* operations predominate over *write* in most applications, the *callback* mechanism results in a dramatic reduction in the number of client-server interactions.

The callback mechanism used in AFS-2 and later versions of AFS requires Vice servers to maintain some state on behalf of their Venus clients, unlike AFS-1, NFS and our file service model of Chapter 7. The client-dependent state required consists of list of the Venus processes to which callback promises have been issued for each file. These callback lists must be retained over server failures – they are held on the server disks and are updated using atomic operations.

Figure 8.8 shows the RPC calls provided by AFS servers for operations on files (that is, the interface provided by AFS servers to Venus processes).

Update semantics □ The goal of this cache coherence mechanism is to achieve the best approximation to one-copy file semantics that is practicable without serious performance degradation. A strict implementation of one-copy semantics for UNIX file access primitives would require that the results of each *write* to a file should be distributed to all sites holding the file in their cache before any further accesses can occur. This is not practicable in large-scale systems; instead, the callback promise mechanism maintains a well-defined approximation to one-copy semantics.

For AFS-1, the update semantics can be formally stated in very simple terms. For a client C operating on a file F, whose custodian is a server S the following guarantees of currency for the copies of F are maintained:

after a successful *open*:	*latest(F, S)*
after a failed *open*:	*failure(S)*
after a successful *close*:	*updated(F, S)*
after a failed *close*:	*failure(S)*

Where *latest(F, S)* denotes a guarantee that the current value of F at C is the same as the value at S, *failure(S)* denotes that the *open* or *close* operation has not been performed at S (and the failure can be detected by C), and *updated(F, S)* denotes that C's value of F has been successfully propagated to S.

For AFS-2, the currency guarantee for *open* is slightly weaker and the corresponding formal statement of the guarantee is more complex. This is because a client may open an old copy of a file after it has been updated by another client. This occurs if a *callback* message is lost, for example as a result of a network failure. But there is a maximum time T for which a client can remain unaware of a newer version of a file. Hence we have the following guarantee:

after a successful *open*:	*latest(F, S, 0)*
	or *(lostCallback(S, T) and inCache(F) and*
	latest(F, S, T))

Where *latest(F, S, T)* denotes that the copy of F seen by the client is no more than T seconds out of date, *lostCallback(S, T)* denotes that a callback message from S to C has been lost at some time during the last T seconds, and *inCache(F)* that the file F was in the cache at C before the open operation was attempted. The above formal statement expresses the fact that the cached copy of F at C after an *open* operation is either the most recent version in the system, or a callback message has been lost (due to a communication failure) and the version that was already in the cache has been used; the cached version will be no more that T seconds out of date. (T is a system constant representing the interval at which callback promises must be renewed. At most installations the value of T is set to about 10 minutes.)

In line with its goal – to provide a large-scale, UNIX-compatible distributed file service – AFS does not provide any further mechanism for the control of concurrent updates. The cache coherence algorithm described above comes into action only on *open* and *close* operations. Once a file has been opened, the client may access and update the local copy in any way it chooses without the knowledge of any processes on other workstations. When the file is closed, a copy is returned to the server, replacing the current version.

If clients in different workstations *open*, *write* and *close* the same file concurrently, all but the update resulting from the last *close* will be silently lost (no error report is given). Clients must implement concurrency control independently if they require it. On the other hand, when two client processes in the same workstation open a file, they share the same cached copy and updates are performed in the normal UNIX fashion – block-by-block.

Although the update semantics differ depending on the locations of the concurrent processes accessing a file, and are not precisely the same as those provided by the standard UNIX file system, they are sufficiently close for the vast majority of existing UNIX programs to operate correctly.

Other aspects

UNIX kernel modifications □ We have noted that the Vice server is a user-level process running in the server computer and the server host is dedicated to the provision of an AFS service. The UNIX kernel in AFS hosts is altered so that Vice can perform file operations in terms of file handles instead of the conventional UNIX file descriptors. This is the only kernel modification required by AFS and is necessary if Vice is not to maintain any client state (such as file descriptors).

Location database □ Each server contains a copy of a fully replicated location database giving a mapping of volume names to servers. Temporary inaccuracies in this database may occur when a volume is moved, but they are harmless because forwarding information is left behind in the server from which the volume is moved.

Threads □ The implementations of Vice and Venus make use of a non-preemptive threads package to enable requests to be processed concurrently at both the client (where several user processes may have file access requests in progress concurrently) and at the server. In the client, the tables describing the contents of the cache and the volume database are held in memory that is shared between the Venus threads.

Read-only replicas □ Volumes containing files that are frequently read but rarely modified, such as the UNIX /bin and /usr/bin directories of system commands and /man directory of manual pages can be replicated as read-only volumes at several servers. When this is done, there is only one read-write replica and all updates are directed to it. The propagation of the changes to the read-only replicas is performed after the update by an explicit operational procedure. Entries in the location database for volumes that are replicated in this way are one-to-many, and the server for each client request is selected on the bases of server loads and accessibility.

Bulk transfers □ AFS transfers files between clients and servers in 64 kilobyte chunks. The use of such a large packet size is an important aid to performance, minimizing the effect of network latency. Thus the design of AFS enables the use of the network to be optimized.

Performance □ The primary goal of AFS is scalability, so its performance with large numbers of users is of particular interest. Howard *et al.* [1988] give details of extensive comparative performance measurements that were undertaken on AFS. Not surprisingly, whole-file caching leads to dramatically reduced loads on the servers. Satyanarayanan [1989a] states that a server load of 40 per cent was measured with 18 client nodes running a standard benchmark against a load of 100 per cent for NFS running the same benchmark. This comparison is impressive, especially bearing in mind that NFS is embedded in the system kernel while AFS is entirely at user level.

Satyanarayanan attributes much of the performance advantage of AFS to the reduction in server load deriving from the use of callbacks to notify clients of updates to files, as compared to the time-out mechanism used in NFS for checking the validity of pages cached at clients.

8.4 The Coda File System

The Coda File System is a descendent of AFS that aims to address several new requirements. It has been developed in a research project undertaken by Satyanarayanan and his co-workers at Carnegie-Mellon University [Satyanarayanan *et al.* 1990; Kistler and Satyanarayanan 1992] and was still undergoing refinement in 1992. The design requirements for Coda were derived from experience with AFS at CMU and elsewhere involving its use in large-scale distributed systems on both local and wide-area communication networks.

While the performance and ease of administration of AFS were found to be satisfactory under the conditions of use at CMU, it was felt that the limited form of replication (restricted to read-only volumes) offered by AFS was bound to become a limiting factor at some scale, especially for accessing widely-shared files such as electronic bulletin boards and other system-wide databases.

In addition, there was room for improvement in the fault-tolerance of the service offered by AFS. The most common difficulties experienced by users of AFS arose from the failure (or scheduled interruption) of servers and network components. The scale of the system at CMU was such that a few service failures occurred every day, and they could seriously inconvenience many users for periods ranging from a few minutes to many hours.

Finally, a mode of computer use was emerging that AFS did not cater for – the mobile use of portable computers. This led to a requirement to make all of the files needed for a user to continue their work available while disconnected from the network without resorting to manual methods for managing the locations of files.

Coda aims to meet all three of these requirements under the general heading of *constant data availability*. The aim was to provide users with the benefits of a shared file repository, but to allow them to rely entirely on local resources when the repository is partially or totally inaccessible. In addition to these aims, Coda retains the original goals of AFS with regard to scalability and the emulation of UNIX file semantics.

In contrast to AFS, where read-write volumes are stored on just one server, the design of Coda relies on the replication of file volumes to achieve a higher throughput of file access operations and a greater degree of fault tolerance. In addition, Coda relies on an extension of the mechanism used in AFS for caching copies of files at workstations to enable workstations to operate when they are not connected to the network.

The set of servers holding replicas of a file volume is known as the *volume storage group (VSG)*. At any instant, a client wishing to open a file in such a volume can access some subset of the VSG, known as the *available volume storage group* (AVSG). The membership of the AVSG varies as servers become accessible or are made inaccessible by network or server failures.

Normally, Coda file access proceeds in a similar manner to AFS, with cached copies of files being supplied to the client workstations by any one of the servers in the current AVSG. As in AFS, clients are notified of changes via a *callback promise* mechanism, but this now depends on an additional mechanism for the distribution of updates to each replica. On *close*, copies of modified files are broadcast in parallel to all of the servers in the AVSG.

Disconnected operation occurs when the AVSG is empty. This may be due to network or server failures, or it may be a consequence of the deliberate disconnection of the client workstation, as in the case of a portable workstation. Disconnected operation relies on the presence in the workstation's cache of *all* of the files that are required for the user's work to proceed. To achieve this, the user must cooperate with Coda to generate a list of files that should be cached. A tool is provided that records a historical list of file usage while connected, and this serves as a basis for predicting usage while disconnected.

It is a principle of the design of Coda that the copies of files residing on servers are more reliable than those residing in the caches of workstations. Although it might be possible logically to construct a file system that relies entirely on cached copies of files in workstations, it is unlikely that a satisfactory quality of service would be achieved. The Coda servers exist to provide the necessary quality of service. The copies of files residing in workstation caches are regarded as useful only as long as their currency can be periodically revalidated against the copies residing in servers. In the case of disconnected operation, revalidation occurs when disconnected operation ceases and the cached files are reintegrated with those in the servers. In the worst case, this may require some manual intervention to resolve inconsistencies or conflicts.

The replication strategy used is optimistic – it allows modification of files to proceed when the network is partitioned or during disconnected operation. It relies on the attachment to each version of a file of a *Coda version vector* (CVV) and a timestamp. A CVV is a vector of integers with one element for each server in the relevant VSG. Each element of the CVV is an estimate (a count) of the number of modifications performed on the version of the file that is held at the corresponding server. The purpose of the CVVs is to provide sufficient information about the update history of each file version to enable inconsistencies to be detected and corrected automatically if the updates do not conflict, or with manual intervention if they do.

Inconsistencies can be repaired automatically in the case where the elements of the CVV at one of the sites are all greater than the corresponding elements of the CVVs at the other sites. When this is not the case, the conflict cannot in general be resolved automatically; the file is marked as 'inoperable' and the owner of the file is informed of the conflict. For directories, automatic resolution is possible even in the case of conflicts, since the only changes that can be made to directories are the insertion or deletion of directory entries.

When a modified file is closed, each site in the current AVSG is sent an update message by the Venus process at the client, containing the current CVV and the new contents for the file. The Vice process at each site checks the CVV and if it is consistent with the one currently held, stores the new contents for the file and returns a positive acknowledgement. The Venus process then computes a new CVV with modification counts increased for the servers that responded positively to the update message and distributes the new CVV to the members of the AVSG.

Since the message is sent only to the members of the AVSG and not the VSG, servers that are not in the current AVSG do not receive the new CVV. Any CVV will therefore always contain an accurate modification count for the local server but the counts for non-local servers will in general be lower bounds, since they will be updated only when the server receives an update message.

The box below contains an example illustrating the use of CVVs to manage the updating of a file replicated at three sites. Further details on the use of CVVs for the management of updates can be found in Satyanarayanan *et al.* [1990]. CVVs are based on the replication techniques used in the Locus system [Popek and Walker 1985] and are a variant of the vector timestamp methods that are now widely used in the management of replicas. Vector timestamps and other strategies for the management of replicas are discussed further in Chapter 11.

In normal operation the behaviour of Coda appears similar to AFS. A cache miss is transparent to users and only imposes a performance penalty. The advantages deriving

Example: Consider a sequence of modifications to a file F in a volume that is replicated at 3 servers, S_1, S_2 and S_3. The VSG for F is $\{S_1, S_2, S_3\}$. F is modified at about the same time by two clients C_1, C_2. Because of a network fault, C_1 can access only S_1 and S_2 (C_1's AVSG is $\{S_1, S_2\}$) and C_2 can access only S_3 (C_2's AVSG is $\{S_3\}$).

1. Initially, the CVVs for F at all 3 servers are the same, say $[1,1,1]$.

2. C_1 runs a process that opens F, modifies it and then closes it. The Venus process at C_1 broadcasts an update message to its AVSG, $\{S_1, S_2\}$, finally resulting in new versions of F and a CVV $[2,2,1]$ at S_1 and S_2 but no change at S_3.

3. Meanwhile, C_2 runs two processes each of which opens F, modifies it and then closes it. The Venus process at C_2 broadcasts an update message to its AVSG, $\{S_3\}$ after each modification, finally resulting in a new version of F and a CVV $[1,1,3]$ at S_3.

4. At some later time, the network fault is repaired, and C_2 makes a routine check to see whether the inaccessible members of the VSG have become accessible (the process by which such checks are made is described later) and discovers that S_1 and S_2 are now accessible. It modifies its AVSG to $\{S_1, S_2, S_3\}$ for the volume containing F and requests the CVVs for F from all members of the new AVSG. When they arrive, C_2 discovers that S_1 and S_2 each have CVVs $[2,2,1]$ whereas S_3 has $[1,1,3]$. This represents a *conflict* requiring manual intervention to bring F up-to-date in a manner that minimizes the loss of update information.

On the other hand, consider a similar but simpler scenario that follows the same sequence of events as the one above, but omitting item (3), so that F is not modified by C_2. The CVV at S_3 therefore remains unchanged as $[1,1,1]$, and when the network fault is repaired, C_2 discovers that the CVVs at S_1 and S_2 ($[2,2,1]$) *dominate* that at S_3. The version of the file at S_1 or S_2 should replace that at S_3.

from the replication of some or all file volumes on multiple servers are:

- The files in a replicated volume remain accessible to any client that can access at least one of the replicas.

- The performance of the system can be improved by sharing some of the load of servicing client requests on a replicated volume between all of the servers that hold replicas.

In disconnected operation (when none of the servers for a volume can be accessed by the client) a cache miss prevents further progress and the computation is suspended until the connection is resumed or the user aborts the process. It is therefore important to load the cache before disconnected operation commences so that cache misses can be avoided.

In summary, compared to AFS, Coda enhances availability both by the replication of files across servers and by the ability of clients to operate entirely out of their caches. Both methods depend upon the use of an optimistic strategy for the detection of update conflicts in the presence of network partitions. The mechanisms are complimentary and independent of each other. For example, a user can exploit the benefits of disconnected operation even though the required file volumes are stored on a single server.

Update semantics □   The currency guarantees offered by Coda when a file it is opened at a client are weaker than for AFS, reflecting the optimistic update strategy. The single server S referred to in the currency guarantees for AFS is replaced by a set of servers $\overline{S}$ (the file's VSG) and the client C can access a subset of servers $\overline{s}$ (the AVSG for the file seen by C).

Informally, the guarantee offered by a successful *open* in Coda is that it provides the most recent copy of F from the current AVSG, and if no server is accessible, a locally cached copy of F is used if one is available. A successful *close* guarantees that the file has been propagated to the currently accessible set of servers, or if no server is available, the file has been marked for propagation at the earliest opportunity.

A more precise definition of these guarantees, taking into account the effect of lost callbacks, can be made using an extension of the notation used for AFS. In each definition except the last there are two cases; the first, beginning $\overline{s} \neq \varnothing$, refers to disconnected operation and the second deals with all situations in which the AVSG is not empty:

after a successful *open*:	$\overline{s} \neq \varnothing$ *and (latest($F,\overline{s}$, 0)*
	or (latest($F,\overline{s}$,T) and lostCallback($\overline{s}$, T) and inCache(F)))
	or ($\overline{s} = \varnothing$ and inCache(F))
after a failed open:	$\overline{s} \neq \varnothing$ *and conflict(F, $\overline{s}$)*
	or ($\overline{s} = \varnothing$ and $\neg$ inCache(F))
after a successful close:	$\overline{s} \neq \varnothing$ *and updated(F, $\overline{s}$)*
	or ($\overline{s} = \varnothing$)
after a failed close:	$\overline{s} \neq \varnothing$ *and conflict(F, $\overline{s}$)*

T is the longest time for which a client can remain unaware of an update elsewhere to a file that is in its cache; *latest($F,\overline{s}$, T)* denotes the fact that the current value of F at C was the latest across all the servers in $\overline{s}$ at some instant in the last T seconds and that there were no conflicts among the copies of F at that instant; *lostCallback($\bar{s}$, T)* means that a callback was sent by some member of $\bar{s}$ in the last T seconds and was not received at C and *conflict(F, $\bar{s}$)* means that the values of F at some servers in $\bar{s}$ are currently in conflict.

Accessing replicas □   The strategy used on *open* and *close* to access the replicas of a file is a variant of the *read-one, write-all* approach. On *open*, if a copy of the file is not present in the local cache the client identifies a preferred server from the AVSG for the file. The preferred server may be chosen at random, or on the basis of performance criteria such as physical proximity or server load. The client requests a copy of the file attributes and contents from the preferred server, and on receiving it, it checks with all the other members of the AVSG to verify that the copy is the latest available version. If not, a member of the AVSG with the latest version is made the preferred site, the file contents are refetched and the members of the AVSG are notified that some members have stale replicas. When the fetch has been completed, a callback promise is established at the preferred server.

When a file is closed at a client after modification, its contents and attributes are transmitted in parallel to all the members of the AVSG using a multicast remote procedure calling protocol (see Chapter 4). This maximizes the probability that every replication site for a file has the current version at all times. It doesn't guarantee it because the AVSG does not necessarily include all the members of the VSG. It minimizes the server load by giving clients the responsibility for propagating changes to the replication sites in the normal case (servers are involved only when a stale replica is discovered on *open*).

Since maintaining callback state in all the members of a AVSG would be expensive, the callback promise is only maintained at the preferred server. But this introduces a new problem: the preferred server for one client need not be in the AVSG of another client. If this is the case, an update by the second client will not cause a callback to the first client. The solution adopted to this problem is discussed in the next subsection.

Cache coherence □   The Coda currency guarantees stated above mean that the Venus process at each client must detect the following events within T seconds of their occurrence:

- enlargement of an AVSG (due to the accessibility of a previously inaccessible server);
- shrinking of an AVSG (due to an inaccessible server becoming accessible);
- a lost callback event.

To achieve this, Venus sends a probe message to the all of the servers in VSGs of the files that it has in its cache every T seconds. Responses will be received only from accessible servers. If Venus receives a response from a previously inaccessible server it enlarges the corresponding AVSG and drops the callback promises on any files that it holds from the relevant volume. This is done because the cached copy may no longer be the latest version available in the new AVSG.

If it fails to receive a response from a previously accessible server it shrinks the corresponding AVSG, no callback changes are required unless the shrinkage is caused by the loss of a preferred server, in which case, all callback promises from that server must be dropped. If a response indicates that a callback messages was sent but not received, the callback promise on just one file is dropped.

We are now left with the problem, mentioned above, of updates that are missed by a server because it is not in the AVSG of a different client that performs an update. To deal with this case, Venus is sent a *volume version vector* (*volume CVV*) in response to each probe message. The *volume CVV* contains a summary of the CVVs for all of the files in the volume. If Venus detects any mismatch between the *volume CVVs* then some members of the AVSG must have some file versions that are not up to date. Although the outdated files may not be the ones that are in its local cache, Venus makes a pessimistic assumption and drops the callback promises on all of the files that it holds from the relevant volume.

Note that Venus only probes servers in the VSGs of files for which it holds cached copies, and that a single probe message serves to update the AVSGs and check the callbacks for all of the files in a volume. This, combined with a relatively large value for T (on the order of ten minutes in the experimental implementation), means that the probes are not an obstacle to the scalability of Coda to large numbers of servers and wide-area networks.

Disconnected operation □ During brief disconnections, such as those that may occur because of unexpected service interruptions, the least-recently-used cache replacement policy normally adopted by Venus may be sufficient to avoid cache misses on the disconnected volumes. But it is unlikely that a client could operate disconnected for extended periods without generating references to files or directories that are not in the cache unless a different policy is adopted.

Coda therefore allows users to specify a prioritized list of files and directories that Venus should strive to retain in the cache. Objects at the highest level are identified as *sticky*, and these must be retained in the cache at all times. If the local disk is large enough to accommodate all of them, the user is assured that they will remain accessible. Since it is often difficult to know exactly what file accesses are generated by any sequence of user actions, a tool is provided that enables the user to bracket a sequence of actions; Venus notes the file references generated by the sequence and flags them with a given priority.

When disconnected operation ends, a process of *reintegration* begins. For each cached file or directory that has been modified, created or deleted during disconnected operation, Venus executes a sequence of update operations to make the AVSG replicas identical to the cached copy. Reintegration proceeds top-down from the root of each cached volume.

Conflicts may be detected during reintegration due to updates to AVSG replicas by other clients. When this occurs, the cached copy is stored in a temporary location on the server and the user that initiated the reintegration is informed. This approach is based on the design philosophy adopted in Coda, which assigns priority to server-based replicas over cached copies. The temporary copies are stored in a *covolume* that is associated with each volume on a server. Covolumes resemble the *lost+found* directories found in conventional UNIX systems. They mirror just those parts of the file directory structure needed to hold the temporary data. Little additional storage is required because the covolumes are almost empty.

Performance □   Satyanarayanan *et al.* [1990] compare the performance of Coda with AFS under benchmark loads designed to simulate user populations ranging from 5–50 typical AFS users.

With no replication, there is no significant difference between the performance of AFS and that of Coda. With 3-fold replication, the time for Coda to perform a benchmark load equivalent to 5 typical users exceeds that of AFS without replication by only 5 per cent. However, with 3-fold replication and a load equivalent to 50 users, the time to complete the benchmark is increased by 70 per cent, whereas that for AFS without replication is increased by only 16 per cent. This difference is attributed only in part to the overheads associated with replication – differences in the tuning of the implementation are said to account for a part of the difference in performance.

8.5   Summary

File servers are a standard component of distributed systems. NFS was the first design offered commercially, and its good performance in medium-sized systems with typical UNIX file access patterns, its fault-tolerant design and the flexibility offered by the remote mounting scheme have ensured its success. But its lack of support for replication in a general form and the administrative overheads entailed by the *mount* service limit its scalability and its client caching algorithm is not robust against all sorts of concurrent file access. Its service interface provides access to files at the level of file blocks and the large number of client requests that this leads to is a source of performance problems in heavily-loaded servers.

The Andrew File System was developed as a file service designed to offer better scalability and more consistent performance of file access operations as perceived by clients. The design has been largely successful. AFS supports the replication of read-only file volumes but not writable ones, and its whole-file replication can result in the silent loss of updates when the same file is updated concurrently by different clients.

The Coda File System was developed as a solution to the drawbacks of AFS and to meet the need for disconnected operation of portable workstations. It supports the replication of file volumes, managing the resulting multiple update problem even in the presence of server failures. The replication of file volumes produces a more fault-tolerant service. The same mechanism is used to support disconnected operation, and this has been quite successful. The reintegration of files after a disconnection involves manual intervention in the case of conflicting updates.

Exercises

8.1   To what extent does Sun NFS deviate from one-copy file update semantics? Construct a scenario in which two user-level processes sharing a file would operate correctly in a single UNIX host but would observe inconsistencies when running in different hosts.

pages 222, 231

8.2   Sun NFS aims to support heterogeneous distributed systems by the provision of an operating system-independent file service. What are the key decisions that the implementor of an NFS server for an operating system other than UNIX would have to take? What constraints should an underlying filing system obey to be suitable for the implementation of NFS servers?

pages 228-229

8.3   What data must the NFS client module hold on behalf of each user-level process? Declare a suitable data structure (in C) to hold the data.

pages 228-229

8.4   Outline (in C) client module implementations for the UNIX *open()* and *read()* system calls, using the NFS RPC calls of Figure 8.3, (i) without, and (ii) with a client cache.

pages 228-229

8.5   Explain why the RPC interface to early implementations of NFS is potentially insecure. The security loophole has been closed in NFS 4.0 by the use of encryption. How is the encryption key kept secret? Is the security of the key adequate?

page 229

8.6   After the timeout of an RPC call to access a file on a hard-mounted file system the NFS client module does not return control to the user-level process that originated the call. Why?

pages 224, 229

8.7   How does the NFS Automounter help to improve the performance and scalability of NFS?

page 230

8.8   How many *lookup* calls are needed to resolve a 5-part pathname (for example, */usr/users/jim/code/xyz.c*) for a file that is stored on an NFS server? What is the reason for performing the translation step-by-step?

page 229

8.9   What condition must be fulfilled by the configuration of the mount tables at the client computers for access transparency to be achieved in an NFS-based filing system.

page 223

8.10   How does AFS gain control when an *open* or *close* system call referring to a file in the shared file space is issued by a client?

page 236

8.11   Compare the update semantics of UNIX when accessing local files with those of NFS and AFS. Under what circumstances might clients become aware of the differences?

8.12   How does AFS deal with the risk that callback messages may be lost?

page 241

8.13   Which features of the AFS design make it more scalable than NFS? What are the limits on its scalability, assuming that servers can be added as required?

pages 234-235

8.14   The Coda file system aims to achieve constant data availability through the replication of file volumes in several servers and by allowing the use of files cached in workstations even when the servers are not accessible. Why is it sometimes necessary for users to intervene manually in the process of updating the copies of a file at multiple servers?

page 248

NAME SERVICES

This chapter introduces the name service as a distinct service that is used by client processes to obtain attributes such as the addresses of resources or objects when given their names. The objects named can be of many types and they may be managed by different services. For example, name services are often used to hold the addresses and other details of users, computers, network domains and services.

Basic design issues for name services, such as the structure and management of the space of names recognized by the service and the operations that the name service supports, are outlined and illustrated in the context of a model name service. We also examine how name services are implemented, covering such aspects as navigation through a collection of name servers when resolving a name, caching naming data and replicating naming data to increase performance and availability.

Three case studies of important name servers are included: the Internet Domain Name System (DNS), Global Name Service and X.500 Directory Service.

9.1   Introduction

In a distributed system, names are used to refer to a wide variety of resources such as computers, services, ports and individual information objects, as well as to users. Naming is an issue that is easily overlooked but is nonetheless fundamental in distributed system design. Names are needed in order to communicate and to share resources in a distributed computer system. A name is needed to request a computer system to act upon a given resource chosen out of many. Processes cannot share resources managed by a computer system unless they can name them consistently. Users cannot communicate with one another via a distributed system unless they can name one another.

This chapter motivates the inclusion of name services in distributed systems, which provide clients with data about named objects. It describes approaches to be taken in the design and implementation of name services. We begin by recalling and examining the different types of names that occur and describing general requirements for their management.

Names and attributes ☐ In Chapter 2 we distinguished between human-readable textual names and system identifiers. The former are used to refer to resources when it is important for humans to recognize and memorize their names. System identifiers are chosen for the efficiency with which they can be resolved and stored by software, and are fixed-length bit strings. We shall refer to textual names and system identifiers collectively as *names* henceforth. The following are some types of name which have arisen in this book so far:

Physical network addresses and logical internetwork addresses are described in Chapter 3. Each type of address can be considered to name locations.

Port, process and group identifiers arise in Chapters 4 and 6 as message destinations.

Textual, human-readable service names are introduced in Chapter 5.

Resource identifiers – low-level, location-independent identifiers for resources managed by servers and kernels – were introduced in Chapter 2.

Files, discussed in Chapter 7, are accessed using human-readable textual names.

Figure 9.1 shows how some of these different types of name are composed when an operation is performed upon a resource such as a file with a textual name supplied by a client. The figure shows name mappings in a system such as Amoeba, in which resource identifiers contain port identifiers. Access to a resource involves mapping its textual name onto a resource identifier; mapping this to a port identifier and a service-specific identifier; and mapping the port identifier to a network address, and the service-specific identifier onto the resource in the server concerned.

Many of the names used in a distributed system are specific to some particular service. A client (user or process) uses such a name when requesting a service to perform an operation upon a named object or resource that it manages, as shown in Figure 9.1. If the service manages many objects, then it has to be given a name which, for the sake of efficiency, it can directly map to its representation of the object. For example, a file

Figure 9.1   Composed naming domains are used to access a resource.

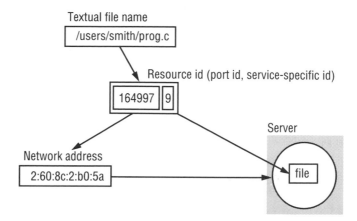

name is given to the file service when requesting that the file be deleted; a process identifier is presented to the process management service when requesting that it be sent a signal. These names are used only in the context of the service that manages the objects named, except when clients communicate about shared objects.

Names are also needed to refer to entities in a distributed system that are beyond the scope of any single service. The major examples of these entities are users (with proper names, login names, user identifiers and electronic mail addresses), computers (with names – *host names* – such as *mac41, jeeves*) and services themselves (such as *file service, printer service*). Note that all of these names must be readable by and meaningful to humans, since users and system administrators need to refer to the major components and configuration of distributed systems; programmers need to refer to services in programs; and users need to communicate with each other via the distributed system and discuss what services are available in different parts of it. Given the connectivity provided by the Internet, these naming requirements are potentially world-wide in scope.

The association between a name and an object is called a *binding*. Names belonging to the first category described above – namely service-specific names – are bound by a service to the actual representation of the object or resource concerned. Names in the second category – which includes users, computers and services – are bound to *attributes* about the objects named. Such objects all have, notably, addresses as attributes. For example, services and computers have physical addresses; users have electronic mail addresses, telephone numbers and personal computer addresses. In addition, users have passwords, home directories; services are associated with version numbers and named protocols used to access them; computers have architecture and operating system types.

In general, attribute values are either primitive values such as integers, or are themselves names, such as the Internet address *230.132.123.112*. Eventually, all names are reduced either to primitive values or *primitive names* – names that cannot be 'looked up' any further such as Ethernet addresses. The attributes stored against names are chosen to be useful not only to users but to other services as well. For example, in electronic mail systems, the Internet Domain Name System (described below), is used to look up mail host addresses from electronic mail addresses, but separate software is used to transmit and store mail messages.

Name services □ A **name service** stores a database of bindings between a set of textual (that is, human-readable) names and attributes for objects such as users and computers that exist outside any specific service. The major operation a name service supports is to **resolve** a name – that is, to look up attributes in the database from a given name. Operations are also required for creating new bindings with new names, deleting bindings and listing bound names. Although we refer to the collection of bindings as a database, it should be noted that names in general are not simple keys, but often consist of several components (for example, *timk@dcs.qmw.ac.uk*) which must be looked up in separate parts of the database, called **contexts**. We describe contexts and a name resolution algorithm in the next section.

Name management is separated from other services largely because of the openness of distributed systems. One of the most striking aspects of this is that services are in general named. For example, an RPC interface name is translated into an appropriate server address. This has no direct counterpart in most centralized systems, where the service invoked by a particular system call is implicit. More specifically, openness brings the following motivations for separating naming from other services:

Unification: It is often convenient for resources managed by different servers – or different services – to appear together under the same naming scheme. In UNIX with NFS, for example, some files are managed on a local disk and others on remote servers; all appear together in a single name space hierarchy. Moreover, some 'file' names refer to local devices, or named pipes.

Integration: It is not always possible to predict the scope of sharing in a distributed system. It may become necessary to share and therefore name resources that were created in different administrative domains. This may be problematic, for example when merging two sets of users, each of which has its own allocation of login names, which may conflict. Worse yet, the two sets of users may use entirely different naming conventions.

General name service requirements □ Name services were originally quite simple, since they were designed only to meet the need to bind names to addresses in a single management domain, corresponding to a single LAN or WAN. The interconnection of networks and the increased scale of distributed systems have produced a much larger name-mapping problem.

Grapevine [Birrell *et al.* 1982] was one of the earliest extensible, multi-domain name services. It was explicitly designed to be scalable over at least two orders of magnitude in the size of the name space and the load of requests that it could handle.

The Global Name Service developed at the Digital Equipment Corporation Systems Research Center [Lampson 1986] is a descendant of Grapevine, with more ambitious goals, including:

To handle an essentially arbitrary number of names and to serve an arbitrary number of administrative organizations: for example, the system should be capable, amongst other things, of handling the electronic mail addresses of all of the computer users in the world.

A long lifetime: many changes will occur in the organization of the name space and in the components that implement the service during its lifetime;

High availability: most other systems depend upon the name service; they can't work when it is broken.

Fault isolation: so that local failures don't cause the entire service to fail.

Tolerance of mistrust: a large open system cannot have any component that is trusted by all of the clients in the system.

The Internet Domain Naming System (DNS), introduced in Chapter 3, is in widespread use. It names objects such as users and computers across the Internet. To provide satisfactory service, it relies heavily upon replication and caching of naming data. The design of DNS and other names services makes the assumption that cache consistency need not be so strictly maintained as in the case of cached copies of files, because updates are less frequent and the use of an out-of-date copy of a name translation can generally be detected by client software. We shall describe the DNS and two other name services as case studies, following the analysis of a simple model of name services set out in the next two sections.

9.2 The SNS – a name service model

This section describes the Simple Name Service (SNS), which is designed for use within the bounds of a single organization; we shall use the example of a university. It is a paper design used to illustrate the general concepts and design points related to name services. It has a number of limitations, but these will be spelled out in the sequel.

The SNS is designed primarily to store attributes of users, computers and services. For users it holds service-specific information such as which computer takes delivery of their electronic mail; information needed for logging in, such as the user's encoded password and home directory; and their telephone number, personal computer name and other administrative information. For computers the SNS holds network addresses and details of computer types. For services, the SNS stores the service address and version number.

The SNS also stores *group names*. Against each group name is held a list of names of individual objects (users or otherwise) and groups. For example, mailing lists appear as group names corresponding to lists of user names. Group names may be nested arbitrarily.

The basic requirements for SNS are as follows:

- the objects named are users, services, computers and groups of these;
- other types of named object may be integrated;
- the names are used only within the organization;
- since name lookups are frequent, they should be carried out efficiently;

- only authorized users may alter data held by the SNS, but all users may read all data stored by it. Controlling access to the SNS database is a topic which is beyond the scope of this chapter. Access control is dealt with in Chapter 16.

SNS names □ A **name space** is the collection of all valid names recognized by a name service such as the SNS. For a name to be valid means that the SNS will attempt to look it up, even though that name may prove not to correspond to any object – to be *unbound*. The SNS undertakes to return attributes for valid names that are bound to objects. Similarly, a client wishing to bind a name to an object must present a valid name.

Name spaces require a syntactic definition. For example, the name *Two* could not possibly be the name of a UNIX process, whereas the integer 2 might be. Similarly, the name '//two' is not acceptable as the name of a UNIX file.

SNS names are strings similar to absolute UNIX file names: they consist of a delimiter '.' followed by a series of one or more **name components** – that is, strings separated by the delimiter. The name components are non-null printable strings not containing '.'. So, for example, *.gene*, *.cs.gene*, *.cs.distrib.gene* and *.phys.gene* are all distinct, valid SNS names, whereas *.gene..parallel* is invalid. Note that, unlike UNIX, the SNS does not consider relative names (such as *distrib.gene*, which is relative to *.cs*) to be valid.

A **prefix** of a name is an initial section of the name which only contains zero or more entire components and does not end with the delimiter. For example, in the SNS *.cs* and *.cs.distrib* are both prefixes of *.cs.distrib.gene*, but *.cs.dist* and *.cs.distrib.* are not.

SNS names can refer either to objects such as computers, or to **directories**, such as *.cs* and *.cs.distrib* in the examples just given. Note that directories are not distinguished from other entities by their names. Any prefix of a valid SNS name identifies a directory. The purpose of partitioning the SNS name space into directories is to render the name space manageable. So-called *flat* name spaces, which do not incorporate distinct directories, do not scale well to large numbers of names. As the numbers increase, a central authority is eventually required for choosing names that do not clash, but it is much more convenient for users to choose their own names.

Directories hold attributes for collections of objects that are related by, for example, their relevance to a particular application. Using directories reduces the scope for conflict when different users might otherwise want to associate the same name with different objects (*gene* in the example above). Furthermore, different directories can conveniently be stored by different servers, and the location of the information in a directory can be looked up from the directory name. The SNS allows an indefinite number of levels of directories, so that the collection of names under each directory is allowed to grow manageably.

Unfortunately, names with more than one or two components are awkward to type and remember. The SNS allows *aliases* (also known as synonyms), which are similar to UNIX-style symbolic links. Aliases save the typing and manipulation of long names. For example, *.gene* could be an alias for *.cs.distrib.gene*. Aliasing works for name prefixes, too, so *.gene.parallel* is an alias for *.cs.distrib.gene.parallel*.

No addresses appear in SNS names – or, rather, if they do then they are not interpreted as addresses by the SNS. Nor do SNS names have any commitment to a particular server used for storing naming information. Names that contain no dependency on the underlying physical configuration are called *pure* [Needham 1993].

By using pure names, the SNS design allows users, services and computers to change their locations while retaining their names; and system administrators can change the server that stores attributes for any particular collection of names.

Terry [1984] uses the term *physically partitioned* to describe name spaces containing names of the form *properName@nameServer*. Such names still appear in some electronic mail addresses. Their advantage is that they can be looked up without having to look up the name server that stores them. But the disadvantage – of having to change names because of a server reorganization – outweighs this advantage. It turns out that by caching and replicating naming data, pure names can be looked up readily in name services such as the DNS (described below) – even on a world-wide basis.

By contrast, the SNS name space is what Terry calls *organizationally partitioned*. This means that names are divided between high-level directories that correspond to different administrative entities within the organization. For example *.cs.gene* and *.phys.gene* could be names assigned by system administrators in the Computer Science and Physics departments of a university, respectively. This is a convenient way of partitioning the name space, but it also reflects underlying divisions between administrative authorities within the university. A convention exists whereby administrators (and privileged users) in any one department are free to bind names with their respective prefixes. However, administrators in the Computer Science department, for example, cannot bind names with the prefix *.phys*, and *vice versa*. If there is distrust between departments, then this convention requires enforcement by suitable protection mechanisms.

A **naming domain** is a name space for which there exists a single overall administrative authority for assigning names within it. This authority is in overall control of which names may be bound within the domain, but it is free to delegate this task. A large domain such as a university may contain domains nested within it, such as departmental naming domains. Such a sub-domain comprises an entire name sub-space (for example, all names with the prefix *.cs* in our example). Responsibility for a naming domain normally goes hand-in-hand with responsibility for implementing the corresponding part of a name service. Naming data belonging to different naming domains are in general stored by distinct name servers managed by the corresponding authorities.

SNS data and operations □   Clients of the SNS perceive it to store attributes of the form *<Type, Value>* against names, where *Type* declares the generic type of the object to which the entry refers, such as *User*, *Service* or *Computer*. In addition, an entry can be a group, alias or directory. The format and content of *Value* depends upon *Type* as shown in Figure 9.2.

The attributes given in Figure 9.2 are the abstract data accessible to clients: an implementation would have to store further, administrative information. The attributes for users and computers shown in the table are examples of the kind of data that might be stored; a real implementation might store different ones. The entry for groups is a list of names, each of which is the name of a group or individual object. An *Alias* entry stores the name to which the alias corresponds (this may be set and examined by clients). A *Directory* entry stores a list of name components of the entities stored in the directory. Entries of type *Alias* and *Directory* have a special significance for the SNS itself, since as we shall see it has to interpret them when looking up names. In general, other types

Figure 9.2   Attributes stored by the SNS.

Type	Value
User	<login name, computer where mail is to be delivered, telephone number, etc.>
Service	<address, version of service>
Computer	<architecture, operating system, network address, owner>
Group	<name1, name2, .. >
Alias	<name>
Directory	<nameComponent1, nameComponent2, .. >

of individual objects may be stored. To avoid confusion, only one set of attributes may be stored by the SNS for a given name.

Sometimes a client will require attributes only of a certain type to be returned by a name lookup. For example, when looking up a computer address it would not be desirable for the SNS to return to it the attributes of a user who happens to have the same name. However, clients that have been handed a name without further information about it may want to look up the name regardless of its type. A client wishing to look up the attributes of a name calls a procedure *Lookup*, supplying the *name*, a buffer *attr* to hold the attributes and the type of object whose name is to be found, *type*. The parameter *type* may take the special value *AnyType*, for clients which do not know the type in advance (Figure 9.3). The attributes returned include the actual type of the named entity. Clients are allowed to look up any valid name, but a name may turn out to be unbound.

Names are bound to attributes by calling the procedure *Bind*, which is supplied with a name *name* and attributes *attr*. This call fails if the caller does not have sufficient privileges, if the name is already bound or if a directory named by a prefix of the name does not exist. Empty directories can be created by calls to *Bind*. Bindings can be destroyed – and empty directories deleted – using the procedure *Unbind*, which requires only the name to be unbound as an argument. *Bind* and *Unbind* are shown in Figure 9.3. Each takes an access identifier as argument, which enables the SNS to determine whether the client has permission to perform the operation. We shall not discuss here a

Figure 9.3   Name service operations in the SNS.

Bind(accessId: Permissions, name: Text, attr: Attributes) → {Success, NotAllowed, AlreadyBound, NoDirectory}
    Creates a binding.

Lookup(name: Text, type: Int, attr: Attributes) → {Success, NotFound}
    Looks up a name and returns attributes if name is bound.

Unbind(accessId: Permissions, name: Text) → {Success, NotFound, NotAllowed, DirectoryNotEmpty}
    Deletes a binding.

mechanism for protecting the SNS name space against unauthorized modifications; Chapter 16 examines the general question of protecting services.

Note that an alternative to the SNS scheme of typed bindings is for administrators to rely upon naming conventions whereby services, users, computers and so on are distinguished by name as in, for example, *.service.cs.printer*, *.users.phys.gene*. On the whole, this is clumsy and of dubious utility, especially as it relies upon adherence to a convention.

Name resolution □ Looking up a name to obtain the associated attributes is technically known as **name resolution**. In general, resolution is an iterative process whereby a name is repeatedly presented to naming contexts. A **naming context** is an abstraction which either maps a given name onto a set of primitive attributes (such as those of a user) directly, or it maps it onto a further naming context and a derived name to be presented to that context. To resolve a name, it is first presented to some initial naming context; resolution iterates as long as further contexts and derived names are output.

The resolution of a name in the SNS is relatively straightforward. The contexts are represented by directories. Take, for example, the SNS name *.cs.distrib.gene*. This name is stripped of its initial '.' and presented to the root directory of the SNS name space as the initial context. On the first iteration, the component *.cs* is found, and since it is a directory it constitutes the next context; the derived name is *distrib.gene*. Now *distrib* is found in the *.cs* context, and again is a directory (*.cs.distrib*). The derived name *gene* is looked up in this context, this time returning a set of attributes of type *User*. Resolution therefore terminates and returns the attributes.

The mapping of an SNS name suffix *n.m....l* in a context (directory) *d* normally maps the first component *n* onto the corresponding context (directory) and produces the derived name *m....l*. However, *n* may be mapped by the context *d* onto an alias *.c.b....a*. In this case, the derived name is *c.b....a.m....l*, and the derived context is the root of the SNS name space. It is in principle possible for cycles to be present in the name space, in which case resolution may never terminate. This is a familiar problem to the designers of file systems with symbolic links. Two solutions are, first, to abandon a resolution process if it traverses a threshold number of (not necessarily distinct) contexts; or, second, to leave system administrators to veto any aliases that would introduce cycles.

Name servers and navigation □ A large organization is highly unlikely to store all of its naming information on a single server. Such a server would be a bottleneck and a critical point of failure. All real name services employ the techniques of replication covered in Chapter 11 to achieve high availability; however, we shall not take up this possibility just yet. The SNS avoids replicating naming data at servers, although it does employ caching. However it does incorporate multiple servers, which store different partitions of the naming database. Some individual departments, at least, will want to administer their own sub-domain on their own computer or computers. That way they can have physical control over the naming data that is entered in their domain; and they can continue to perform name lookups if another department's name server crashes, at least in the case of names that are not within that department's domain.

The logical structure of the SNS name space is, then, mapped onto a number of physical name server sites (Figure 9.4). This is analogous to the partitioning of UNIX file systems between storage at separate computers under NFS (Chapter 8). Each name

Figure 9.4   Name space partitioning between name servers in the SNS.

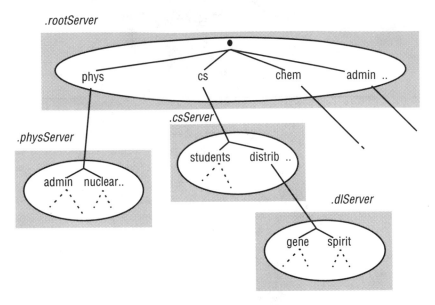

server maintains entire directories; it would be awkward to split directories across sites, since name data would have to be located at the level of individual names rather than directories; and name binding and unbinding would require cooperation between the sites.

Each name server stores naming data for one or more sub-trees of the name space, and records the names of the top-level directories in these trees. So, for example, name server *.physServer* in Figure 9.4 records that it holds the sub-tree rooted at the directory named *.phys*.

The process of locating naming data from among more than one name server in order to resolve a name is called **navigation**. In the case of the SNS, every computer in the organization runs a process called a *user agent* (UA), which carries out navigation on behalf of clients at that computer. The UA checks for a name's validity and communicates with name servers as necessary to resolve a name (Figure 9.5). The UA caches the attributes it receives from the name servers. In general, UAs may appear as user packages linked into individual clients, as in Grapevine [Birrell *et al.* 1982] or as separate processes, as in SNS and X.500. We return to these options after discussing caching.

When a client requests a name lookup, a user package linked into the client code sends the name and required attribute type to the local UA. If the UA does not hold cached attributes from a previous lookup for the name, it sets about finding it. A naive approach would be for the UA always to start with *rootServer*, and to proceed down the name space hierarchy until the required name is resolved. However, rather than repeating its traversal of the upper levels, the UA learns which server stores which sub-trees (identified by their topmost directories), and records their addresses. That is, the UA maintains a list of cached pairs <*topDirectoryName, serverAddress*> from previous lookups. When given a name to resolve for the first time, the UA chooses the longest

Figure 9.5   Iterative navigation.

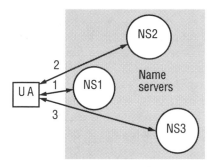

A user agent (UA) iteratively contacts name servers NS1–NS3 in order to resolve a name.

entry from this cache that is a prefix of the required name and forwards the name to the corresponding server. The UA learns the address of the root server by reading a configuration file at boot time.

On receipt of the name, the first server attempts to resolve it. If the server stores the name, then it finds this out by following successive directory entries. A name server stores the physical location of directory contents against directory entries. It returns the attributes (assuming they are of a matching type) when it finds them. However, it may be that the name includes as a prefix a directory that is stored by another server (for example, part of the *.cs* sub-tree shown in Figure 9.4 is stored on *.dlServer*). Instead of a local physical location, the name server stores another server's name under the directory entry, which it returns to the UA.

A name server returns a server name rather than an address, in order to allow server addresses to change. However, this involves an extra lookup for the UA, of the server address. Note that a potential problem arises here, because the server name must not include a prefix stored by that server itself – otherwise the server name could not be looked up. To circumvent this problem in the SNS, server names are stored in the root directory and are cached by UAs.

Equipped with the next server's address, the UA presents it with the name and type to be resolved. Resolution proceeds as before, with further navigation as necessary until attributes are located or the name is discovered to be unbound.

As an example taken from Figure 9.4, suppose that a UA has an address cached for the name *.cs*, and is asked to resolve the name *.cs.distrib.gene*. It will initially request resolution at name server *.csServer*, which will return the name *.dlServer* as storing items under *.cs.distrib*. After looking up an entry for this server to obtain its address, the UA will send the name to *.dlServer*, where resolution will terminate.

Caching □ In the SNS, to summarize the discussion above, UAs cache *<name, attributes>* and *<namePrefix, serverName>* pairs. The former are used to return attributes to the client immediately; the latter are used in navigation to resolve uncached names.

Caching is a key to a name service's performance and assists in maintaining the availability of both the name service and other services despite name server crashes. Its role in enhancing response times by saving communication with name servers is clear. Not only does caching save repeatedly looking up the same name, but time spent looking up new names is also saved by caching name server addresses against the top-level directories stored by them. Moreover, by effectively eliminating high-level name servers – the root server, in particular – from the navigation path, caching allows resolution to proceed despite some server failures. Referring to Figure 9.4, a UA could resolve the name *.cs.distrib.gene* despite the failure of *.rootServer* or *.csServer*, as long as it had cached *.dlServer's* address corresponding to the prefix *.cs.distrib*.

Caching by UAs is widely applied in name services and is particularly successful because naming data are changed relatively rarely. For example, information such as computer or service addresses are liable to remain unchanged for months or years. However, the possibility exists of a name service returning out-of-date attributes or using an out-of-date address during resolution. The SNS relies on stale naming data being detected on use. If, for example, a client attempts to access the printing service using an out-of-date address, then the error will be detected either when the communication software detects that no service is accepting requests on the address, or when a different server that is listening there returns an 'unrecognized' error code. It is assumed that system administrators update naming information promptly at the server concerned, so that stale information is rarely returned.

Note that caching is a reason for using a single separate UA process in each client computer instead of user packages in client processes for resolving names. By sharing a UA process, local clients also share its cache, which potentially increases the number of lookups it saves. On the other hand, the UA does impose extra overheads on client computers compared to a user package, since it is a separate process.

Summary of the SNS □ In summary, the SNS is a name service designed for a university, or any similar large organization which is divided into different administrative domains (for example, departments). The main objects named are users, services, computers and groups of these, although other types of entity can be named. The SNS name space is divided into directories nested arbitrarily deeply. The SNS name space is organizationally partitioned to correspond to the different university departments and administrations. This division is reflected in the partitioning of the naming database between name server computers. Some large departments store sub-trees of their naming domain across several computers. Clients contact user agents (there is one on every computer) to retrieve naming data on their behalf. The navigation model is for user agents to communicate with one or more name servers in order to resolve names. User agents cache the returned values.

9.3   Discussion of the SNS and further design issues

In this section the SNS design is discussed, and design issues that its limited scope did not bring out are described.

The name space □ The SNS name space has several limitations that could make it inconvenient to use in practice, even within an organization the size of a university.

Further limitations arise when we consider extending the SNS to cover a larger distributed system. The limitations are as follows:

Relative names: The SNS requires that all names be absolute, that is, they must be referred to the root directory. Names with multiple components, however, are awkward to remember and use. As users of hierarchical file systems such as that of UNIX will know, relative names assist considerably in this respect. The SNS could be improved by establishing a working context (a directory) for every client. A user could then, for example, type *gene* instead of *.cs.distrib.gene*. Of course, absolute names would still be valid.

Merging: Consider the problem of merging the SNS name spaces of two or more organizations into a single name space. There is a possibility that they will contain the same name, for example, *.phys*. Even if they have distinct names for the same departments, it may be hard to remember which is which, for example, *.phys* in Smith University, and *.physics* in Jones University. A solution to these problems would be to create top-level directories for the universities, which contain the entire corresponding naming domains. So, for example, there would be *.smith.phys* and *.jones.physics*. The problem here is that all absolute names would have to be changed (for example, names beginning *.phys* would all have to be changed to begin with *.smith.phys*). Relative names fare better in that only the working context needs to be redefined for such names as *phys* and *physics*, but this is awkward still and not all names are relative.

Heterogeneity: Smith University may use SNS names, but Jones University uses DNS names, which have a similar syntax but drop the initial '.' and reverse the order of components, such as *gene.distrib.cs*. How can these name spaces still be integrated?

Customization: A user or community of users might wish to customize the organization of a name space – so that, for example, the most-used directories appear near the top of the naming hierarchy. Different users or communities could have private views. This convenience would be traded off against the inconvenience of having to translate names whenever more than one view is involved in a transaction. Aliasing goes some way to providing alternative views. Nonetheless, SNS aliases do not in fact provide different views, since aliases must coexist in the same name space.

Restructuring: If the Astronomy group was to move from under the wing of Mathematical Sciences to be a department in its own right, then presumably all names in the sub-tree *.mathSci.astronomy* should be moved into the sub-tree *.astronomy*. Changing every name would be costly (names are compiled into applications and stored in databases and files). Aliasing *.astronomy* with *.mathSci.astronomy* would leave entries in the Mathematical Sciences naming domain – even though they are stored on a new name server in the Astronomy department. On a smaller scale, if the user *gene* moves from the computer Science department's distributed system laboratory to work in Physics, then the name *.cs.distrib.gene* ceases to be appropriate, and probably should be changed to *.phys.gene*. These examples show how organizationally partitioned name spaces can hinder reorganizations much as can physically partitioned name spaces (that is, ones with names of the form *user@computer*).

Systems that address name space issues □ All of the above problems have been addressed in various designs. The GNS [Lampson 1986], described below, is designed to allow the merging and reorganization of name spaces on a global scale, by manipulation of contexts. It allows heterogeneous name spaces to be merged.

The Univers name server [Bowman *et al.* 1990] allows users to maintain a private alias file, used to impose a private view of the name spaces. Furthermore, Univers allows for individual users to create and manipulate *contexts* (in SNS terms, directories) that are private to them. Indeed, it encourages clients not only to structure the contexts themselves, but also to develop programs for the selection of attributes, that may be downloaded to a Univers name server. Univers, however, is unlike the other name services we have discussed in that it uses attribute-based names, which we now describe.

Attribute-based naming □ We have remarked that name services store a database of <*name, attribute*> pairs. It is natural to go on from this description to consider naming systems in which *attributes* are used as keys instead of, or as well as, textual names. In these services, textual names are just another attribute. For example, it seems reasonable to ask of a name service that stores users' names and telephone numbers: 'What is the name of the user with telephone number 081-695 9980?'. Similarly, it might be asked 'Which computers are Macintoshes running the A/UX operating system?'. X.500 (described in Section 9.4), Profile [Peterson 1988] and Univers [Bowman *et al.* 1990] all provide or define attribute-based name services, that is, ones in which objects are selected by the values of their attributes. All attributes are returned for any objects found to match the attributes supplied. So, for example, the request 'TelephoneNumber = 081-695 9980' might return {Name = John Smith', 'TelephoneNumber = 081-695 9980', ...}. X.500 also provides access to the database by conventional hierarchic textual names.

Attribute-based name services are sometimes called *yellow pages services* and conventional name services are correspondingly called *white pages services*, in an obvious analogy with the different types of telephone directory. Attributes are clearly more powerful than names as designators of objects: programs can be written to select objects according to precise attribute specifications where names might not be known.

Attributes are particularly suitable for the selection of services. For example, a printing service is most usefully selected by the location and type of printer used; and a file system might be selected by the type (for example, UNIX 4.3BSD or MS-DOS) and by whether it contains a particular directory.

Another advantage of attributes is that they do not expose the structure of organizations to the outside world, as do organizationally partitioned names. However, the relative simplicity of use of textual names makes them unlikely to be replaced by attribute-based naming in many applications.

Replication □ The major omission in the SNS implementation is replication of the naming data. Replication is essential for a name service that is to scale to very large numbers of objects and be highly available. We examine the DNS replication scheme in the next section.

Alternative navigation models □ The SNS navigation model, in which the user agent contacts successive name servers as necessary in order to resolve a name, is called

Figure 9.6   Non-recursive and recursive server-controlled navigation.

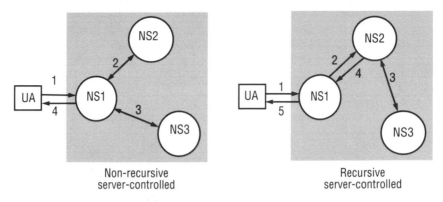

Non-recursive
server-controlled

Recursive
server-controlled

A name server NS1 communicates with other name servers on behalf of a user agent (UA)

iterative navigation: NFS employs iterative navigation in the resolution of a file name, on a component-by-component basis (see Chapter 8). This is because the file service may encounter a symbolic link when resolving a name. A symbolic link must be interpreted in the client's file system name space, because it may point to a file in a directory stored at another server. The client computer must determine which server this is, because only the client knows its mount points.

In a variation of the SNS navigation model, *multicast navigation*, a UA multicasts the name to be resolved and the required object type to the group of name servers. Only the server that holds the named attributes responds to the request. Unfortunately, however, if the name proves to be unbound, then the request is greeted with silence. Cheriton and Mann [1989] describe a multicast-based navigation scheme in which a separate server is included in the group to respond when the required name is unbound. A multicast scheme might improve individual response times over an iterative scheme. We return to the Cheriton and Mann model in a discussion of integrated name management shortly.

Another alternative to the SNS navigation model is one in which a name server coordinates the resolution of the name and passes the result back to the user agent. Ma [1992] distinguishes *non-recursive* and *recursive server-controlled navigation* (Figure 9.6). Under non-recursive server-controlled navigation, any name server may be chosen by the user agent. This server communicates by multicast or iteratively with its peers in the style described above, as though it were a user agent. Under recursive server-controlled navigation the user agent once more contacts a single server. If this server does not store the name, the server contacts a peer storing a (larger) prefix of the name, which in turn attempts to resolve it. This procedure continues recursively until the name is resolved.

If a name service spans distinct administrative domains, then user agents executing in one administrative domain may be prohibited from accessing name servers belonging to another such domain. Moreover, even name servers may be prohibited from discovering the disposition of naming data across name servers in another administrative domain. Then, both UA-controlled and non-recursive server-controlled navigation are inappropriate, and recursive server-controlled navigation must be used. Authorized name servers request name service data from designated name servers managed by different administrations, which return the attributes without revealing where the different parts of the naming database are stored.

UA-controlled navigation frees name server threads from contacting other servers. It is forced upon naming systems that, like NFS, allow clients to possess different name spaces, with different names referring to the same objects.

Integrated name management ☐ In the Cheriton and Mann [1989] naming scheme mentioned above in the discussion of multicast navigation, name serving is integrated with the management of the objects named. The designers point out that for frequently accessed objects such as files, the cost of performing a name lookup separately from the operation upon the corresponding object is prohibitive, and that it is preferable for the two to be combined in a single operation. Their scheme uses multicast navigation (introduced above). Objects are managed by one of a collection of object managers organized as a multicast group. When a name is used for the first time, the request bears the name and is multicast to the members of the group. The object manager that holds the named object performs the operation and returns the manager's address with the result parameters. The client software caches this name against the manager's address for subsequent use. Thus a single round of messages performs the name lookup as well as the object operation; and multicast overheads apply only during the first operation for each name.

9.4   Case studies: DNS, GNS and X.500

The Internet Domain Name System

The Domain Name System (DNS) is a name service design whose principal naming database is used across the Internet. It was devised principally by Mockapetris [1987] to replace the original Internet naming scheme in which all host names and addresses were held in a single central master file and downloaded by FTP to all computers that required them [Harrenstien *et al.* 1985]. This original scheme was soon seen to suffer from three major shortcomings:

- It does not scale to large numbers of computers.

- Local organizations wish to administer their own naming systems.

- A general name service is needed – not one that only serves for looking up computer addresses.

The objects named by the DNS are primarily computers – for which mainly IP addresses are stored as attributes – and what we have referred to in this chapter as naming domains, called simply *domains* in the DNS. In principle, however, any type of object can be named; and its architecture gives scope for a variety of implementations. In common with the SNS, organizations and departments within them can manage their own naming data. The major difference between the requirements met by the DNS and our SNS model is that of scale. Hundreds of thousands of names are bound by the Internet DNS, and lookups are made against it from around the world. Any name can be resolved by any client. This is achieved by hierarchical partitioning of the name database, by replication of the naming data, and by caching.

Domain names □ DNS names are called *domain names*. Some examples of these are *aux786.dcs.qmw.ac.uk* (a computer), *dcs.qmw.ac.uk*, *com*, and *purdue.edu* (the latter three are domains). The name space has a tree structure: a domain name consists of one or more strings called *labels* separated by the delimiter '.'. There is no delimiter at the beginning or end of a domain name, although the root of the DNS name space is sometimes referred to as '.' for administrative purposes.

Domains are collections of domain names; syntactically, a domain's name is the common suffix of the domain names within it, but otherwise it cannot be distinguished from, for example, a computer name. For example, *qmw.ac.uk* is a domain which contains *dcs.qmw.ac.uk*. Note that the term 'domain name' is potentially confusing, since only some domain names identify domains.

The DNS is designed for use in multiple implementations, each of which may have its own name space. In practice, however, only one is in widespread use, and that is the one used for naming across the Internet. The Internet DNS name space is partitioned both organizationally and according to geography. The names are written with the highest-level domain on the right, which is the opposite of SNS names. The top-level organizational domains in use today across the Internet are:

com	–	Commercial organizations
edu	–	Universities and other educational institutions
gov	–	Governmental agencies
mil	–	Military organizations
net	–	Major network support centres
org	–	Organizations not mentioned above
int	–	International organizations.

In addition, countries have their own domains:

us	–	United States
uk	–	United Kingdom
fr	–	France
...	–	...

In practice, the organizational domains mentioned above cover US organizations alone, reflecting the origins of the DNS. Some organizations fall within the geographical domain *us*, such as *nri.reston.va.us*, but these are relatively few. Other countries use their own domain to distinguish their organizations. The UK, for example, has domains *co.uk* and *ac.uk* which correspond to *com* and *edu* respectively (*ac* stands for 'academic community'). Note that, despite its geographical-sounding suffix *uk*, a domain such as *doit.co.uk* could contain objects located in the Spanish office of Doit Ltd, a British company. In other words, domain names are completely independent of their locations.

As in the SNS, the administration of domains may be devolved to sub-domains. The domain *dcs.qmw.ac.uk* – the Department of Computer Science at Queen Mary and Westfield College in the UK – can contain any name the department wishes. But the domain name *dcs.qmw.ac.uk* itself had to be agreed with the College authorities, who manage the domain *qmw.ac.uk*. Similarly, *qmw.ac.uk* had to be agreed with the registered authority for *ac.uk*, and so on.

DNS servers do not recognize relative names: all names are referred to the global root. However in practical implementations, client software keeps a list of domain names that are appended automatically to any single-component name before resolution. For example, the name *aux765* presented in the domain *dcs.qmw.ac.uk* probably refers to *aux765.dcs.qmw.ac.uk*; client software will append the default domain *dcs.qmw.ac.uk* and attempt to resolve this name. If this fails, then further default domain names may be appended; finally, the (absolute) name *aux765* is presented to the root for resolution. Names with more than one component, however, are normally presented intact to the DNS – as absolute names.

DNS queries ☐   The Internet DNS is primarily used for simple host name resolution and for looking up electronic mail hosts, as follows:

> *Host name resolution*: In general, applications use the DNS to resolve host names into IP addresses. For example, the domain name *nic.ddn.mil* might be given to a file transfer program – such as *ftp* on UNIX systems – as the name of a computer which stores files to be transferred. *ftp* makes a DNS enquiry and obtains the IP address of *nic.ddn.mil*, in order to communicate with a file transfer daemon on that computer. As was pointed out in Chapter 3, standard service daemons such as this use well known local port identifiers, so *ftp* can construct the entire transport address from the domain name by using the DNS.

> *Mail host location*: Electronic mail software uses the DNS to resolve domain names into the IP addresses of mail hosts – computers that will accept mail for those domains. For example, when the address *tom@dcs.rnx.ac.uk* is to be resolved, the DNS is queried with the address *dcs.rnx.ac.uk* and the type designation 'mail'. It returns a list of domain names of hosts that can accept mail for *dcs.rnx.ac.uk*, if such exist (and, optionally, the corresponding IP addresses). The DNS may return more than one domain name so that the mail software can try alternatives if the main mail host is unreachable for some reason. The DNS returns an integer preference value for each mail host, indicating the order in which the mail hosts should be tried.

Some other types of query that are implemented in some installations but are considerably less used than those just given are:

> *Reverse resolution*: Some software requires a domain name to be returned given an IP address. This is just the reverse of the normal host name query.

> *Host information*: The DNS can store the machine architecture type and operating system against the domain names of hosts. It has been suggested that this option should not be implemented because it provides useful information for those attempting to gain unauthorized access to computers.

Well known services: A list of the services run by a computer (for example, *telnet*, *ftp*) and the protocol used to obtain them (that is, UDP or TCP on the Internet) can be returned, given the computer's domain name.

In principle, the DNS can be used to store arbitrary attributes. A query is specified by a domain name, class and type. A special domain, *in-addr.arpa*, exists to hold IP network numbers for reverse lookups. The class is used to distinguish, for example, the Internet naming database from other, experimental, DNS naming databases. A set of types is defined for a given database; those for the Internet database are given below.

DNS name servers ☐ The problems of scale are treated by a combination of partitioning the naming database and by replicating and caching parts of it close to the points of need. The DNS database is distributed across a logical network of servers. Each server holds part of the naming database – primarily data for the local domain. Most queries concern computers in the local domain, and are satisfied by servers within that domain. However, each server records the domain names and addresses of other name servers, so that queries pertaining to objects outside the domain or in separately administered sub-domains can be satisfied.

The DNS naming data are divided into *zones*. A zone contains the following data:

- Attribute data for names in a domain, less any sub-domains administered by lower-level authorities. For example, a zone could contain data for Queen Mary and Westfield College – *qmw.ac.uk* – less the Department of Computer Science – *dcs.qmw.ac.uk*.

- The names and addresses of name servers that provide *authoritative* data for the zone. These are versions of zone data that can be relied upon as being reasonably up-to-date.

- The names of name servers that hold authoritative data for delegated sub-zones; and 'glue' data giving the addresses of these servers.

- Zone management parameters, such as those governing the caching and replication of zone data.

A server may hold authoritative data for zero or more zones. In order that naming data are available even when a single server fails, the DNS architecture specifies that each zone must be replicated authoritatively in at least two failure-independent servers.

System administrators enter the data for a zone into a master file, which is the source of authoritative data for the zone. There are two types of server that are considered to provide authoritative data. *Primary* or *master servers* are ones that read zone data directly from a local master file. *Secondary servers* download zone data from a primary server. They communicate periodically with the primary server, to check whether their stored version matches that held by the primary server. If a secondary's copy is out of date, the primary sends it the latest version. The frequency of the secondary's check is set by administrators as a zone parameter, and its value is typically once or twice a day.

Any server is free to cache data from other servers so as to avoid having to contact them when name resolution requires the same data again; it does this on the proviso that clients are told that such data is non-authoritative as supplied. Entries in a zone have a *time-to-live* value – one of the zone parameters just mentioned. When a non-

Figure 9.7   DNS name servers.

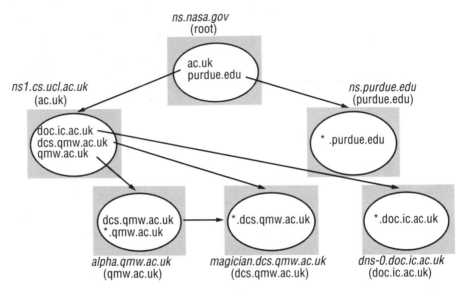

Note: Name server names are in italics and the corresponding zones are in parentheses.
Arrows denote name server entries.

authoritative server obtains data from an authoritative server, it notes the time-to-live. It will only provide its cached data to clients for up to this time; when queried after the time period has expired, it recontacts the authoritative server to check its data. This is a useful feature which minimizes the amount of network traffic while retaining flexibility for system administrators. When attributes are expected to change rarely, they can be given a correspondingly large time-to-live. If an administrator knows that attributes are likely to change soon, then he or she can reduce the time-to-live accordingly.

Figure 9.7 shows the arrangement of some of the DNS database. Note that, in practice, root servers such as *ns.nasa.gov* hold entries for several levels of domain, and do not hold entries for first-level domain names, as might be expected. Similarly, the server *ns1.cs.ucl.ac.uk* maintains entries such as *dcs.qmw.ac.uk*, which are two levels below the top of its zone, *ac.uk*. This is to reduce the number of navigation steps when domain names are resolved. The root domain information is replicated, and all DNS servers store the addresses of one or more copies of the root. They also usually store the address of an authoritative server for the parent domain. Most queries can be satisfied using at worst two navigation steps: one to a root server or other server that stores an appropriate name server entry, and a second to the server whose name is returned.

Referring to Figure 9.7, the domain name *aux768.dcs.qmw.ac.uk* can be looked up from within *dcs.qmw.ac.uk* using the local server *magician.dcs.qmw.ac.uk*. This server does not store an entry for *mac272.doc.ic.ac.uk* at Imperial College's Department of Computing, but it does keep a cached entry for *doc.ic.ac.uk* (*ns1.cs.ucl.ac.uk* is an authorized server for this). The server *dns-0.doc.ic.ac.uk* at Imperial College can be contacted to resolve the full name.

Figure 9.8   DNS resource records.

Record type	Meaning	Main contents
A	A computer address	IP number
NS	An authoritative name server	Domain name for server
CNAME	The canonical name for an alias	Domain name for alias
SOA	Marks the start of data for a zone	Parameters governing the zone
WKS	A well known service description	List of service names and protocols
PTR	Domain name pointer (reverse lookups)	Domain name
HINFO	Host information	Machine architecture and operating system
MX	Mail exchange	List of <*host, preference*> pairs
TXT	Text string	Arbitrary text

Navigation and query processing ☐   In DNS, the user agent is called a *resolver*. It is normally implemented as library software. It accepts queries, formats them into messages expected under the DNS protocol, and communicates with one or more name servers in order to satisfy the queries. A simple request-reply protocol is used, typically using UDP packets on the Internet (DNS servers use a well known port number). The resolver times out and resends its query if necessary. The resolver can be configured to contact a list of initial name servers in order of preference, in case one or more are unavailable.

The DNS architecture allows for both recursive and iterative navigation. The resolver specifies which type of navigation is required when contacting a name server. However, name servers are not bound to implement recursive navigation. As was pointed out above, recursive navigation may tie up server threads, meaning that other requests might be delayed.

In order to save network communication the DNS protocol allows multiple queries to be packed into the same request message, and for name servers correspondingly to send multiple replies in their response messages.

Resource records ☐   Zone data are stored by name servers and in files in one of several fixed types of *resource record*. For the Internet database these include the types given in Figure 9.8. Each record refers to a domain name, which is not shown. The entries in the table refer to items already mentioned, except that *CNAME* entries hold an alias for another domain name; and *TXT* entries are included to allow arbitrary other information to be stored against domain names.

The BIND implementation of the DNS ☐   The Berkeley Internet Name Domain (BIND) is an implementation of the DNS for computers running BSD UNIX. Client programs link in library software as the resolver. DNS name server computers run the *named* daemon.

BIND allows for three categories of name server: primary servers, secondary servers and caching-only servers; the *named* program implements just one of these types according to the contents of a configuration file. The first two categories are as described above. Caching-only servers read in from a configuration file sufficient names and addresses of authoritative servers to resolve any name. Thereafter, they only store this data and data that they learn by resolving names for clients.

A typical organization has one primary server, with one or more secondary servers that provide name serving on different local area networks at the site. Additionally, individual computers often run their own caching-only server, to reduce network traffic and speed up response times still further.

Discussion of the DNS □   The DNS Internet implementation achieves relatively short average response times for lookups, considering the amount of naming data and the scale of the networks involved. We have seen that it achieves this by a combination of partitioning, replicating and caching naming data. The objects named are primarily computers, mail hosts and domains. Computer (host) name-to-IP-address mappings change relatively rarely, as do the identities of mail hosts, so caching and replication occur in a relatively clement environment.

The DNS allows naming data to become inconsistent. That is, if naming data is changed, then other servers may provide clients with stale data for periods in the order of days or months. None of the replication techniques explored in Chapter 11 are applied. However, inconsistency is of no consequence until such time as a client attempts to use stale data. The DNS does not address itself to how staleness of addresses is detected. (We have discussed some ways in which stale address information can be detected in Section 9.2).

Another point regarding consistency is that the DNS has a restrictive, centralized model of entering names into the naming database by adding them to a local file. Ideally, system administrators in different locations within a large organization could update the zone information by accessing different local replicas. But this could lead to inconsistency unless the techniques of Chapter 11 were applied. For example, two users could try to create incompatible entries for the same name.

Apart from computers, the DNS also names one particular type of service: the mail service, on a per-domain basis. DNS assumes there to be only one mail service per addressed domain, so users do not have to include the name of this service explicitly in names. Electronic mail applications transparently select this service by using the appropriate type of query when contacting DNS servers. It would be straightforward to extend this facility to other services that have only one implementation in a given domain and which have been assigned well known port identifiers. Most domains incorporate, for example, an 'anonymous ftp' server, which is used for the dissemination of technical reports and other information produced within a domain. All that would be required to incorporate this as a named services is for a new resource record type to be recognized that corresponds to it. This scheme does not extend, however, to services such as file services of which there may be multiple instances in a domain. These would have to be identified with individual domain names.

In summary, the DNS stores a limited variety of naming data, but this is sufficient in so far as applications such as electronic mail impose their own naming schemes on top of domain names; it could be easily extended to well known services that are unique within domains. It might be argued that the DNS database represents the lowest common denominator of what would be considered useful by the many user communities on the Internet. The DNS was not designed to be the only name service in the Internet; it coexists with local name services that store data most pertinent to local needs (such as Sun's Network Information Service, which stores encoded passwords, for example).

What remains as a potential problem for the DNS design is its rigidity with respect to changes in the structure of the name space. It would not be practical, for example, to put the US on a level footing with other countries by changing the domain *edu* to *edu.us*, *com* to *com.us* and so on. This aspect of naming design is taken up by the next case study, the Global Name Service.

The Global Name Service

A Global Name Service (GNS) was designed and implemented by Lampson and colleagues at the DEC Systems Research Center [Lampson 1986] to provide facilities for resource location, mail addressing and authentication. The design goals of GNS have already been listed in Section 9.1 above; they reflect the fact that a name service for use in an internetwork must support a naming database that may extend to include the names of millions of computers and (eventually) email addresses for billions of users. The designers of GNS also recognized that the naming database is likely to have a long lifetime, that it must continue to operate effectively while it grows from small to large scale and while the network on which it is based evolves. The structure of the name space may change during that time to reflect changes in organizational structures. The service should accommodate changes in the names of the individuals, organizations and groups that it holds; and changes in the naming structure such as those that occur when one company is taken over by another. In this description we shall focus on those features of the design that enable it to accommodate such changes.

The potentially large naming database and the scale of the distributed environment in which GNS is intended to operate makes the use of caching essential and renders it extremely difficult to maintain complete consistency between all copies of a database entry. The cache consistency strategy adopted relies on the assumption that updates to the database will be infrequent and that slow dissemination of updates is acceptable, since clients can detect and recover from the use of out-of-date naming data.

GNS manages a naming database that is composed of a tree of directories holding names and values. Directories are named by multi-part pathnames referred to a root, or relative to a working directory, much like filenames in a UNIX file system. Each directory is also assigned an integer that serves as a unique *directory identifier* (DI). In this section we use names in italics when referring to the DI of a directory, so that *EC* is the identifier of the EC directory. A directory contains a list of names and references. Unlike our SNS model and other naming services, the values stored at the leaves of the directory tree are organized into *value trees*, so that the attributes associated with names can be structured values.

Names in GNS have two parts: *<directory name, value name>*. The first part identifies a directory; the second refers to a value tree, or some portion of a value tree. For example, see Figure 9.9, in which the DIs are illustrated as small integers although they are actually chosen from a range of integers to ensure uniqueness. The attributes of a user Peter.Smith in the directory QMW would be stored in the value tree named *<EC/*

Figure 9.9   GNS directory tree and value tree for user Peter.Smith.

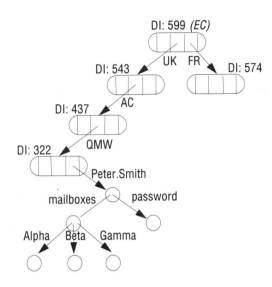

UK/AC/QMW, Peter.Smith>. The value tree includes a password which can be referenced as <*EC*/UK/AC/QMW, Peter.Smith/password>, and several mail addresses, each of which would be listed in the value tree as a single node with the name <*EC*/UK/ AC/QMW, Peter.Smith/mailboxes>.

The directory tree is partitioned and stored in many servers, with each partition replicated in several servers. The consistency of the tree is maintained in the face of two or more concurrent updates – for example, two users may simultaneously attempt to create entries with the same name, and only one should succeed. Replicated directories present a second consistency problem; this is addressed by an asynchronous update distribution algorithm that ensures eventual consistency, but with no guarantee that all copies are always current. This level of consistency is considered satisfactory for the purpose.

Accommodating change □ We now turn to the aspects of the design that are concerned with accommodating growth and change in the structure of the naming database. At the level of clients and administrators, growth is accommodated through extension of the directory tree in the usual manner. But we may wish to integrate the naming trees of two previously separate GNS services. For example, how could we integrate the database rooted at the *EC* directory shown in Figure 9.9 with another database for *NORTH AMERICA*? Figure 9.10 shows a new root *WORLD* introduced above the existing roots of the two trees to be merged. This is a straightforward technique, but how does it affect clients that continue to use names that are referred to what was 'the root' before integration took place? For example, </UK/AC/QMW, Peter.Smith> is a name used by clients before integration. It is an absolute name (since it begins with the symbol for the root '/'), but the root it refers to is *EC*, not *WORLD*. *EC* and *NORTH AMERICA* are *working roots* – initial contexts against which names beginning with the root symbol '/' are to be looked up.

Figure 9.10   Merging trees under a new root.

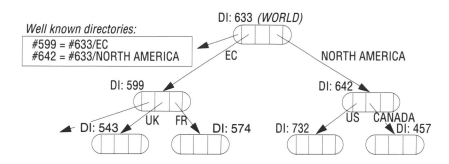

The existence of unique directory identifiers can be used to solve this problem. The working root for each program must be identified as part of its execution environment (much as is done for a program's working directory). When a client in the European Community uses a name of the form </UK/AC/QMW, Peter.Smith>, its local user agent, which is aware of the working root, prefixes the directory identifier *EC* (#599), thus producing the name <#599/UK/AC/QMW, Peter.Smith>. The user agent passes this derived name in the lookup request to a GNS server. The user agent may similarly deal with relative names referred to working directories. Of course, clients that are aware of the new configuration may also supply absolute names to the GNS server that are referred to the conceptual super-root directory containing all directory identifiers, for example, <*WORLD*/EC/UK/AC/QMW, Peter.Smith>, but the design cannot assume that all clients will be updated to take account of such a change.

The technique described above solves the logical problem, allowing users and client programs to continue to use names that are defined relative to an old root, even when a new real root is inserted, but it leaves an implementation problem: in a distributed naming database that may contain millions of directories, how can the GNS service locate a directory given only its identifier, such as #599? The solution adopted by GNS is to list those directories that are used as working roots, such as *EC*, in a table of 'well known directories' held in the current real root directory of the naming database. Whenever the real root of the naming database changes, as it does in Figure 9.10, all GNS servers are informed of the new location of the real root. They can then interpret names of the form *WORLD*/EC/UK/AC/QMW (referred to the real root) in the usual way, and they can interpret names of the form #599/UK/AC/QMW, by use of the table of 'well known directories' to translate them to full pathnames beginning at the real root.

GNS also supports the restructuring of the database to accommodate organizational change. Suppose that the United States becomes part of the European Community(!). Figure 9.11 shows the new directory tree. But if the US sub-tree is simply moved to the EC directory, names beginning *WORLD*/NORTH AMERICA/US will no longer work. The solution adopted by GNS is to insert a 'symbolic link' in place of the original US entry (shown in bold type in Figure 9.11). The GNS directory lookup procedure interprets the link as a redirection to the US directory in its new location.

Figure 9.11   Restructuring the directory.

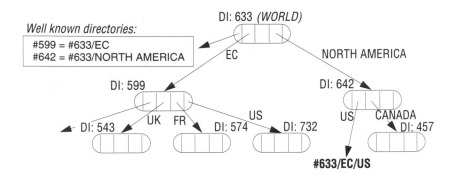

Discussion of GNS □ GNS is descended from Grapevine [Birrell *et al.* 1982] and Clearinghouse [Oppen and Dalal 1983], two successful naming systems developed primarily for the purposes of mail delivery by the Xerox Corporation. GNS successfully addresses needs for scalability and reconfigurability, but the solution adopted for merging and moving directory trees results in a requirement for a database (the table of well known directories) that must be replicated at every node. In a large-scale network reconfigurations may occur at any level and this table could grow to a large size, conflicting with the scalability goal.

The X.500 Directory Service

As the scale of networks and distributed systems grows, users require name services that serve a purpose similar to telephone directories. Users may have a variety of requirements for searching and browsing in a directory of network users, organizations and system resources to obtain information about the entities that the directory contains. The uses for such a service are likely to be quite diverse and may extend well beyond those of telephone directories. They range from enquiries that are directly analogous to the use of telephone directories, such as a simple 'white pages' access to obtain a user's electronic mail address or a 'yellow pages' query aimed, for example, at obtaining the names and telephone numbers of garages specializing in the repair of a particular make of car, to the use of the directory to access personal details such as job roles, dietary habits or even photographic images of the individuals. If the directory contains details of system resources and services it can also fulfil the roles of the name services described in previous sections, offering facilities for programs to identify and locate servers for file transfer, electronic mail and other services.

X.500 is termed a *directory service* to reflect the distinction between it and name services such as DNS and GNS that are intended to be used only to resolve resource names that are known precisely. It is what in Section 9.3 we termed an *attribute-based name service*. A directory service can be used in the same way as a conventional name service, but it can also be used to satisfy imprecise queries, designed to discover the names of other users or system resources. Such queries may originate from users, such as 'yellow pages' uses exemplified by the enquiry about garages mentioned above, or from processes, when they may be used to identify services to meet a functional requirement.

Individuals and organizations can use a directory service to make available a wide range of information about themselves and the resources that they wish to offer for use in the network. Users can search the directory for specific information with only partial knowledge of its name, structure or content.

The CCITT and ISO standards organizations have defined the *X.500 Directory Service* [CCITT 1988] as a network service intended to meet these requirements. The standard refers to it as a service for access to information about 'real-world entities', but it is likely to be used also for access to information about hardware and software services and devices. X.500 is specified as an Application Level service in the Open Systems Interconnection (OSI) set of standards, but its design does not depend to any significant extent on the other OSI standards and it can be viewed as a design for a general-purpose directory service. We shall outline the design of the X.500 Directory Service and its implementation here. Readers interested in a more detailed description of X.500 and methods for its implementation are advised to study Rose's book on the subject [Rose 1992].

The data stored in X.500 servers is organized in a tree structure with named nodes as in the case of the other name servers discussed in this chapter, but in X.500 a wide range of attributes are stored at each node in the tree, and access is not just by name, but also by searching for entries with any required combination of attributes.

The X.500 name tree is called the *Directory Information Tree* (DIT) and the entire directory structure including the data associated with the nodes is called the *Directory Information Base* (DIB). There is intended to be a single integrated DIB containing information provided by organizations throughout the world, with portions of the DIB located in individual X.500 servers. Typically, a medium-sized or large organization would provide at least one server. Clients access the directory by establishing a connection to a server and issuing access requests. Clients can contact any server with an enquiry. If the data required are not in the segment of the DIB held by the contacted server it will either invoke other servers to resolve the query or redirect the client to another server.

In the terminology of the X.500 standard, servers are *Directory Service Agents* (DSAs), and their clients are termed *Directory User Agents* (DUAs). Figure 9.12 shows the software architecture and one of the several possible navigation models, with each DUA client process interacting with a single DSA process which accesses other DSAs as necessary to satisfy requests. The architecture is very similar to that of the SNS model described earlier in this chapter with DUAs in place of user agents and DSAs in place of name servers.

Each entry in the DIB consists of a name and a set of attributes. As in other name servers, the full name of an entry corresponds to a path through the DIT from the root of the tree to the entry. In addition to full or *absolute* names, a DUA can establish a context that includes a base node and then use shorter relative names that give the path from the base node to the named entry.

Figure 9.13 shows the portion of the Directory Information Tree that includes Cambridge University, Great Britain and Figure 9.14 is one of the associated DIB entries. The data structure for the entries in the DIB and the DIT is very flexible. A DIB entry consists of a set of attributes, where an attribute has a *type* and one or more *values*.

Figure 9.12   X.500 service architecture.

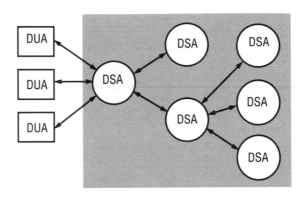

The type of each attribute is denoted by a type name (for example, *countryName, organizationName, commonName, telephoneNumber, mailbox, objectClass*). New attribute types can be defined if they are required. For each distinct type name, there is a corresponding type definition that includes a type description and a syntax definition

Figure 9.13   Part of the X500 Directory Information Tree.

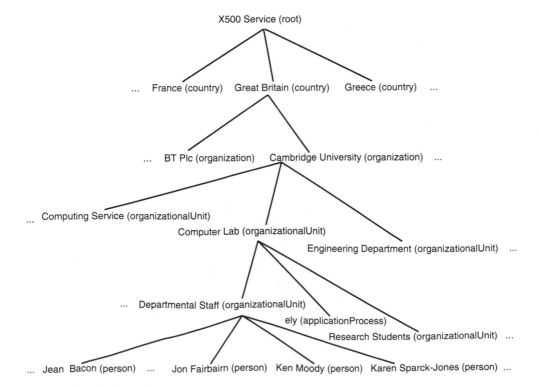

Figure 9.14   An X.500 DIB Entry.

info	
Jean Bacon, Departmental Staff, Computer Lab,	
Cambridge University, GB	

commonName	*uid*
Jean.M.Bacon	*jmb*
Jean.Bacon	*mail*
Jean Bacon	jmb@cl.cam.ac.uk
J. Bacon	Jean.Bacon@cl.cam.ac.uk
surname	*roomNumber*
Bacon	T13
telephoneNumber	*userClass*
+44 223 33 4604	Lecturer

in the ASN.1 Notation (a standard notation for syntax definitions, see Chapter 4) defining representations for all permissible values of the type.

DIB entries are classified in a manner similar to the object class structures found in object-oriented programming languages. Each entry includes an *objectClass* attribute that determines the class (or classes) of the object to which an entry refers. *Organization*, *organizationalPerson*, and *document* are all examples of *objectClass* values. Further classes can be defined as they are required. The definition of a class determines which attributes are mandatory and which are optional for entries of the given class. The definitions of classes are organized in an inheritance hierarchy in which all classes except one (called *topClass*) must contain an *objectClass* attribute, and the value of the *objectClass* attribute must be the name of one or more classes. If there are several *objectClass* values, the object inherits the mandatory and optional attributes of each of the classes.

The name of a DIB entry (the name that determines its position in the DIT tree) is determined by selecting one or more of its attributes as *distinguished attributes*. The attributes selected for this purpose are referred to as the entry's *Distinguished Name* (DN).

Now we can consider the methods by which the directory is accessed. There are two main types of access request:

read: This request resembles the *lookup* access defined in our SNS model. An absolute or relative name (a *Domain Name* in X.500 terminology) for an entry is given together with a list of attributes to be read (or an indication that all attributes are required). The DSA locates the named entry by navigating in the DIT, passing requests to other DSA servers where it does not hold relevant parts of the tree. It retrieves the required attributes and returns them to the client.

search: This is an attribute-based access request as described in Section 9.3 above. A base name and a filter expression are supplied as arguments. The base name specifies the node in the DIT from which the search is to commence; the filter expression is a Boolean expression that is to be evaluated for every node below the base node. The filter specifies a search criterion: a logical combination of tests on the values of any of the attributes in an entry. The *search* command returns a list of names (Domain Names) for all of the entries below the base node for which the filter evaluates to *TRUE*.

For example, a filter might be constructed and applied to find the *commonName*s of members of staff who occupy room T13 in the Computer Lab at Cambridge University (Figure 9.14). A read request could then be used to obtain any or all of the attributes of those DIB entries.

Searching can be quite costly when it is applied to large portions of the directory tree (which may reside in several servers). Additional arguments can be supplied to *search* to restrict the scope of its search, the time for which a search is allowed to continue and the size of the list of entries that is returned.

Administration and updating of the DIB □ The DSA interface includes operations for adding, deleting and modifying entries. Access control is provided for both queries and updating operations, so access to parts of the DIT may be restricted to certain users or classes of users.

The DIB is partitioned, with the expectation that each organization will provide at least one server holding the details of the entities in that organization. Portions of the DIB may be replicated in several servers.

As a standard (or a 'recommendation' in CCITT terminology) X.500 does not address implementation issues. However, it is quite clear that any implementation involving multiple servers in a wide area internetwork must rely on extensive use of replication and caching techniques to avoid too much redirection of queries.

One implementation, described in Rose [1992] is a system developed at University College, London, known as QUIPU [Kille 1991]. In this implementation, both caching and replication are performed at the level of individual DIB entries, and at the level of collections of entries descended from the same node. It is assumed that values may become inconsistent after an update and the time interval in which the consistency is restored may be several minutes. This form of update dissemination is generally considered acceptable for directory service applications.

Discussion of X.500 □ The implementation and application of X.500 is at a pilot stage. Many organizations have installed X.500 directory servers (there were 177 servers, holding a total of about 300,000 entries and serving 370 organizations connected to the Internet in 1992) with databases providing information about individuals and other resources, but the coverage is not yet sufficiently complete to fully determine the effectiveness of X.500 services in the range of potential roles outlined above. Decisions about the scope of the information that will be provided in directories will need to be taken at national and international levels to ensure uniformity for the object classes stored in the DIB.

9.5 Summary

This chapter has described the design and implementation of name services in distributed systems. Name services store attributes of the objects in a distributed system

– in particular, their addresses – and returns these attributes when a textual or attribute-based name is supplied to be looked up. In general, naming is a separate service to object management, since programs and users have certain common generic requirements for referring to objects, and it is useful for the same name to be used by users and a range of services.

The main requirements for the name service are: an ability to handle an arbitrary number of names; for the service to have a long lifetime; high availability; the isolation of faults; and the tolerance of mistrust.

The main design issues are, first, the structure of the name space – for example, whether it is based on textual names or attributes, and the syntactic rules governing names. A related issue is the resolution model: the rules by which a multi-component name is resolved to a set of attributes. The set of bound names must be managed. Most designs consider the name space to be divided into domains – discrete sections of the name space, each of which is associated with a single authority controlling the binding of names within it. Secondly there is the issue of how to manage reconfigurations of naming domains that may occur when organizations merge or change their position in the organizational hierarchy. Finally, there is the question of the interface supported by the service – the operations such as binding names, looking up names and listing directories, and the question of whether or not some of these operations are privileged.

The implementation of the name service may span different organizations and user communities. The naming database, in other words, is stored at multiple name servers, each of which stores at least part of the set of names within a naming domain. The question of navigation therefore arises – of the procedure by which a name is resolved when the necessary information is stored at several sites. The software to which clients submit a name for resolution is called a user agent. The types of navigation that are supported are iterative, multicast, recursive server-controlled and non-recursive server-controlled.

Perhaps the most important aspects of the implementation of a name service is the use of replication and caching. Both of these assist in making the service highly available, and both also reduce the time taken to resolve a name. Inconsistencies may arise in replicated or cached naming data. The name service is responsible for eliminating inconsistencies, but this must be done over a reasonable time frame if good performance is to be maintained. Normally a client is informed that an attribute such as an address supplied by the name service is out of date when it tries to use it.

As well as a model design, the SNS, the chapter has considered three main cases of name service designs and implementations. The Domain Name System is widely used for naming computers and addressing electronic mail across the Internet; it achieves good response times through replication and caching. The Global Name Service is a design that has tackled the issue of reconfiguring the name space as organizational changes occur. X.500 is an attribute-based name service that has been defined as a standard by the CCITT and ISO organizations.

Exercises

9.1   Describe the names (including identifiers) and attributes used in a distributed file service such as NFS (see Chapter 8).

page 254

9.2   What security issues are liable to be relevant to a name service such as the SNS operating within an organization such as a university?

page 258

9.3   Discuss the problems raised by the use of aliases in a name service, and indicate how, if at all, these may be overcome.

page 258

9.4   Suggest possible uses for the *Group* attributes stored by the SNS.

page 259

9.5   SNS *Directory* entries are given, abstractly, as lists of name components. What would an implementation store with these names?

page 259

9.6   i)   Explain why care must be taken when choosing which name server should store which directory forming part of a name server name.

     ii)   Design a rule for the placement of directories that are needed to look up server names. Assume that all clients know how to reach a server storing the root. (Hint: consider the number of components in each server name.)

page 263

9.7   How does caching help a name service's availability?

page 263

9.8   Explain why iterative navigation is necessary in a name service in which different name spaces are partially integrated, such as the file naming scheme provided by NFS.

page 266

9.9   Describe the problem of unbound names in multicast navigation. What is implied by the installation of a server for responding to lookups of unbound names?

page 267

9.10   Discuss the absence of a syntactic distinction (such as use of a final '.') between absolute and relative names in DNS.

page 269

9.11   Investigate your local configuration of DNS domains and servers. You may find a program such as *nslookup* installed on UNIX systems, which enables you to carry out individual name server queries.

page 271

9.12   Why do DNS root servers hold entries for two-level names such as *ac.uk* and *purdue.edu*, rather than one-level names such as *uk*, *edu* and *com*?

page 272

9.13   Which other name server addresses do DNS name servers hold by default, and why?

page 272

9.14 Why might a DNS client choose recursive navigation rather than iterative navigation? What is the relevance of the recursive navigation option to concurrency within a name server?

page 273

9.15 When might a DNS server provide multiple answers to a single name lookup, and why?

page 273

9.16 Investigate the design of the 'name service' that maps IP numbers onto physical machine addresses.

page 90

9.17 GNS does not guarantee that all copies of entries in the naming database are up-to-date. How are clients of GNS likely to become aware that they have been given an out-of-date entry? Under what circumstances might it be harmful?

page 275

9.18 Discuss the potential advantages and drawbacks in the use of a X.500 directory service in place of DNS and the Internet mail delivery programs. Sketch the design of a mail delivery system for an internetwork in which all mail users and mail hosts are registered in an X.500 database.

page 278

10

TIME AND COORDINATION

In this chapter we introduce some topics related to the issue of coordination in distributed systems. We first explore the notion of time in distributed systems. Algorithms for distributed agreement often require a notion of 'happened-before' between events. However the notion of time itself is problematic in distributed systems, since each computer has its own autonomous physical clock, and synchronizing clocks is subject to the constraints imposed by message passing. We go on to explain the notion of logical clocks, which are a tool for ordering events, without knowing precisely when they occurred.

The second half examines briefly some algorithms to achieve distributed coordination. These include algorithms to achieve mutual exclusion among a collection of processes, so as to coordinate their accesses to shared resources. It goes on to examine how an election can be implemented in a distributed system. That is, it describes how a group of processes can agree on a new coordinator of their activities, after the previous coordinator has failed or become unreachable.

10.1 Introduction

This chapter introduces some concepts and algorithms related to the timing and coordination of events occurring in distributed systems. In the first half we examine the notion of time in a distributed system. We examine the problem of how to synchronize clocks in different computers, and so time events occurring at them consistently, and we discuss the related problem of determining the order in which events occurred. In the latter half of the chapter we examine some algorithms whose goal is to confer a privilege upon some unique member of a collection of processes. This can be either to give a process exclusive access to a resource temporarily, or to elect a process that will act as a coordinator of the others' activities. We first turn to the question of time.

Time is an important and interesting issue in distributed systems, for several reasons. First, time is a quantity we often want to measure accurately. In order to know at what time of day a particular event occurred at a particular computer – for example, for accountancy purposes – it is necessary to synchronize its clock with an authoritative, external source of time. This is *external* synchronization. Also, if computer clocks are synchronized with one another to a known degree of accuracy, then we can, within the bounds of this accuracy, measure the interval between two events occurring at different computers, by appealing to their local clocks. This is *internal* synchronization. Two or more computers that are internally synchronized are not necessarily externally synchronized, since they may drift collectively from external time.

Secondly, algorithms that depend upon clock synchronization have been developed for several problems in distribution. These include maintaining the consistency of distributed data (the use of timestamps to serialize transactions is discussed in Chapter 14); checking the authenticity of a request sent to a server (the Kerberos authentication protocol, discussed in Chapter 16, depends on synchronized clocks); and eliminating the processing of duplicate updates (see, for example, [Ladin *et al.* 1992]).

Einstein demonstrated, in his Special Theory of Relativity, the intriguing consequences that follow from the observed premiss that the speed of light is constant for all observers, regardless of their relative velocity. He proved from this assumption, among other things, that two events that are judged to be simultaneous in one frame of reference, are not necessarily simultaneous according to observers in other frames of reference that are moving relative to it. For example, an observer on the earth and an observer travelling away from the earth in a spaceship will disagree on the interval between events, the more so as their relative speed increases.

Moreover, the relative order of two events can even be reversed for two different observers. Fortunately, this cannot happen if one event could have caused the other to occur. In that case, the physical effect follows the physical cause for all observers, although the time elapsed between cause and effect can vary. The timing of physical events was thus proved to be relative to the observer, and Newton's notion of absolute physical time was discredited. There is no special physical clock in the universe to which we can appeal when we want to measure intervals of time.

The notion of physical time is also a problem in a distributed system. This is not due to the effects of special relativity, which are negligible or non-existent for normal computers (unless one counts computers travelling in spaceships!), but the problem is based on a similar limitation concerning our ability to pass information from one computer to another. This is that the clocks belonging to different computers can only be synchronized, at least in the majority of cases, by network communication. Message passing is limited by virtue of the speed at which it can transfer information, but this in itself would not be a problem if we knew how long message transmission took. The problem is that sending a message usually takes an unpredictable amount of time.

In the next section we examine methods whereby computer clocks can be approximately synchronized, using message passing. However, we shall not be able to obtain sufficient accuracy to determine, in many cases, the relative ordering of events occurring at different computers. Fortunately, what we can do is to establish an ordering on some events by appealing to the flow of data between processes in a distributed system. We go on to introduce logical clocks, which are used to define an order on events without measuring the physical time at which they occurred.

10.2 Synchronizing physical clocks

Computers each contain their own physical clock. These clocks are electronic devices that count oscillations occurring in a crystal at a definite frequency, and which typically divide this count and store the result in a counter register. Clock devices can be programmed to generate interrupts at regular intervals in order that, for example, timeslicing can be implemented; however we shall not concern ourselves with this aspect of clock operation. The clock output can be read by software and scaled into a suitable time unit. This value can be used to timestamp any event experienced by any process executing at the host computer. By 'event' we mean an action that appears to occur indivisibly, all at once – such as sending or receiving a message. Note however, that successive events will correspond to different timestamps only if the *clock resolution* – the period between updates of the clock register – is smaller than the rate at which events can occur. The rate at which events occur depends on such factors as the length of the processor instruction cycle.

Applications running at a given computer that are interested only in the order of events, and not in the absolute time at which they occurred, require only the value of the counter to timestamp events. However, the date and time-of-day can be calculated from the counter value, so long as these are known for some earlier value of the counter.

In order to compare timestamps generated by clocks of the same physical construction at different computers, one might think that we need only know the relative offset of one clock's counter from that of the other – for example, that one count had the value 1958 when the other was initialized to 0. Unfortunately, this supposition is based on a false premiss: computer clocks in practice are extremely unlikely to 'tick' at the same rate, whether or not they are of the 'same' physical construction.

Clock drift □   The crystal-based clocks used in computers are, like any other clocks, subject to *clock drift* (Figure 10.1), which means that they count time at different rates, and so diverge. The underlying oscillators are subject to physical variations, with the consequence that their frequencies of oscillation differ. Moreover, even the same clock's frequency varies with temperature. Designs exist that attempt to compensate for this variation but they cannot eliminate it. The difference in the oscillation period

Figure 10.1   Drift between computer clocks in a distributed system.

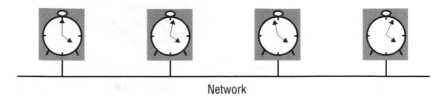

Network

between two clocks might be extremely small, but the difference accumulated over many oscillations leads to an observable difference in the counters registered by two clocks, no matter how accurately they were initialized to the same value. A clock's *drift rate* is the change in the offset (difference in reading) between the clock and a nominal perfect reference clock per unit of time measured by the reference clock. For clocks based on a quartz crystal, this is about 10^{-6} – giving a difference of one second every 1,000,000 seconds, or 11.6 days.

Coordinated universal time □ The most accurate physical clocks known use atomic oscillators, whose accuracy is about one part in 10^{13}. The output of these atomic clocks is used as the standard for elapsed real time, known as *International Atomic Time*. Since 1967 the standard second has been defined as 9,192,631,770 periods of transition between the two hyperfine levels of the ground state of Caesium-133 (Cs^{133}).

Seconds and years and other time units that we use are, of course, rooted in astronomical time. However, they were originally defined in terms of the rotation of the earth on its axis and its rotation about the sun. The period of the earth's rotation about its axis is gradually getting longer, primarily because of tidal friction; atmospheric effects and convection currents within the earth's core also cause short-term increases and decreases in the period. So astronomical time and atomic time have a tendency to get out of step.

Coordinated universal time – abbreviated as *UTC* (*sic*) – is an international standard that is based on atomic time, but a so-called leap second is occasionally inserted or deleted to keep in step with astronomical time. UTC signals are synchronized and broadcast regularly from land-based radio stations and satellites covering many parts of the world. For example, in the US the radio station WWV broadcasts time signals on several shortwave frequencies. Satellite sources include the *Geostationary Operational Environmental Satellites* (GOES) and the *Global Positioning System* (GPS).

Radio waves travel at near the speed of light (3×10^8 metres per second). The time to propagate a radio signal over the length of the UK (about 1000 kilometres), for example, would be only about 3 milliseconds. The propagation delay can be accounted for if the exact speed of propagation of the radio signal and the distance from the source are both known. Unfortunately, the propagation speed varies with atmospheric conditions, and this gives rise to inaccuracy. In general, the accuracy of a received signal is a function of both the accuracy of the source, and its distance from the source through the atmosphere.

Receivers are available commercially. Compared with 'perfect' UTC, the signals received from land-based stations have an accuracy in the order of 0.1–10 milliseconds, depending on the station used. Signals received from GEOS are accurate to about 0.1 millisecond, and signals received from GPS are accurate to about one millisecond. Computers with receivers attached can synchronize their clocks with these timing signals. Unfortunately, receivers are expensive compared to the cost of a workstation; this is particularly so of receivers used for synchronizing with the more accurate satellite-based sources of time.

Note, also, that measuring physical time with an accuracy of 10 milliseconds, for example, is intrinsically too limited to be able to tell the relative order of many events occurring at different computers in a distributed system. In 10 milliseconds, 100,000 instructions can be executed on a processor rated at 10 million instructions per second, and several short messages can be transmitted.

Compensating for clock drift □ If the time provided by a time service, such as Universal Coordinated Time signals, is greater than the time at a computer C, then it may be possible simply to set C's clock to the time service time. Several clock 'ticks' appear to have been missed, but time continues to advance, as expected. We shall shortly describe a way of continuously adjusting the time, if that is what is required.

Now consider what should happen if the time service's time is behind that of C. We cannot set C's time back to the time service time, because this is liable to confuse applications that rely on the assumption that time always advances. For example, the UNIX *make* facility is a tool that is used to compile only those source files that have been modified since they were last compiled. The modification dates of each corresponding pair of source and object files are compared to determine this condition. If a computer set its clock back after compiling a source file but before the file was changed, the source file might appear to have been modified prior to the compilation. Erroneously, *make* will not recompile the source file.

The solution is not to set C's clock back, but to cause it to run slow for a period, until it is in accord with the time server time. It is possible to change the rate at which updates are made to the time as given to applications. This can be achieved in software, without changing the rate at which the hardware clock ticks (an operation which is not always supported by hardware clocks).

Let us call the time given to applications (the software clock's reading) S and the time given by the hardware clock H. Let the compensating factor be δ, so that $S(t) = H(t) + \delta(t)$. The simplest form for δ to make S change continuously is a linear function of the hardware clock: $\delta(t) = aH(t) + b$, where a and b are constants to be found. Substituting for δ in the identity, we have $S(t) = (1 + a)H(t) + b$.

Let the value of the software clock be T_{skew} when $H = h$, and let the actual time at that point be T_{real}. We may have that $T_{skew} > T_{real}$ or $T_{skew} < T_{real}$. If S is to give the actual time after N further ticks, we must have:

$$T_{skew} = (1 + a)h + b, \text{ and } T_{real} + N = (1 + a)(h + N) + b.$$

By solving these equations, we find

$$a = (T_{real} - T_{skew})/N \text{ and } b = T_{skew} - (1 + a)h.$$

Cristian's method for synchronizing clocks □ One way to achieve synchronization between computers in a distributed system is for a central time server process S to supply

Figure 10.2   Clock synchronization using a time server.

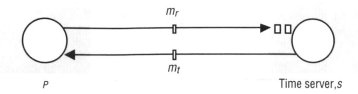

m_r

m_t

P

Time server,s

the time according to its clock upon request, as shown in Figure 10.2. The time server computer can be fitted with a suitable receiver so as to be synchronized with UTC. If a process P requests the time in a message m_r, and receives the time value t in a message m_t, then in principle it could set its clock to the time $t + T_{trans}$, where T_{trans} is the time taken to transmit m_t from S to P (t is inserted in m_t at the last possible point before transmission from S's computer).

Unfortunately, T_{trans} is subject to variation. In general, other processes are competing with S and P for resources at each computer involved, and other messages compete with m_t for the network. These factors are unpredictable and not practically avoidable or accurately measurable in most installations. In general, we may say that $T_{trans} = min + x$, where $x \geq 0$. The minimum value min is the value that would be obtained if no other processes executed and no other network traffic existed; min can be measured or conservatively estimated. The value of x is not known in a particular case, although a distribution of values may be measurable for a particular installation.

Cristian [1989] suggested the use of such a time server, connected to a device that receives signals from a source of UTC, to synchronize computers. Synchronization between the time server and its UTC receiver can be achieved by a method that is similar to the following procedure for synchronization between computers. A process P wishing to learn the time from S can record the total round-trip time T_{round} taken to send the request m_r and receive the reply m_t. It can measure this time with reasonable accuracy if its rate of clock drift is small. For example, the round-trip time should be in the order of 1–10 milliseconds on a LAN, over which time a clock with a drift rate of 10^{-6} varies by at most 10^{-5} milliseconds.

Let the time returned in S's message m_t be t. A simple estimate of the time to which P should set its clock is $t + T_{round}/2$, which assumes that the elapsed time is split equally before and after S placed t in m_t. Let the time between sending and receipt for m_r and m_t be $min + x$ and $min + y$, respectively. If the value of min is known or can be conservatively estimated, then we can determine the accuracy of this result as follows.

The earliest point that S could have placed the time in m_t was min after P dispatched m_r. The latest point at which it could have done this was min before m_t arrived at P. The time by S's clock when the reply message arrives is therefore in the range $[t + min, t + T_{round} - min]$. The width of this range is $T_{round} - 2\,min$, so the accuracy is $\pm (T_{round}/2 - min)$.

Variability can be dealt with to some extent by making several requests to T, and taking the minimum value of T_{round} to give the most accurate estimate. The greater is the accuracy required, the smaller is the probability of achieving it. This is because the most accurate results are those in which both messages are transmitted in a time close to *min* – an unlikely event in a busy network. Full details are given by Cristian [1989].

Discussion of Cristian's algorithm □   As described, Cristian's method suffers from the problem associated with all services implemented by a single-server, that the single time server might fail and thus render synchronization impossible temporarily. Cristian suggested, for this reason, that time should be provided by a group of synchronized time servers, each with a receiver for UTC time signals. For example, a client could multicast its request to all servers, and use only the first reply obtained.

Note that a malfunctioning time server that replied with spurious time values, or an imposter time server that replied with deliberately incorrect times could wreak havoc in a computer system. These problems were beyond the scope of the work described by Cristian [1989], which assumes that sources of external time signals are self-checking. Marzullo [1984] describes a method for distinguishing good servers from those that issue spurious times, as long as the latter are a minority of less than one-third of all servers. The problem of dealing with faulty clocks is addressed partially by the Berkeley algorithm, which is described next. The problem of malicious interference with time synchronization can be dealt with by authentication techniques, which are the subject of Chapter 16. In Section 10.1 we pointed out that some authentication techniques are in turn dependent upon accurate clock synchronization. Chapter 16 discusses the requirement for clock synchronization in the Kerberos authentication system.

The Berkeley algorithm □   Gusella and Zatti [1989] describe an algorithm for internal synchronization which they developed for collections of computers running Berkeley UNIX. In it, a coordinator computer is chosen to act as the *master*. Unlike Cristian's protocol, this computer periodically polls the other computers whose clocks are to be synchronized, called *slaves*. The slaves send back their clock values to it. The master estimates their local clock times by observing the round-trip times (similarly to Cristian's technique), and it averages the values obtained (including its own clock's reading). The balance of probabilities is that this average cancels out the individual clocks' tendencies to run fast or slow. The accuracy of the protocol depends upon a nominal maximum round-trip time between the master and the slaves. The master eliminates any occasional readings associated with larger times than this maximum.

Instead of sending the updated current time back to the other computers – which would introduce further uncertainty due to the message transmission time – the master sends the amount by which each individual slave's clock requires adjustment. This can be a positive or negative value.

The algorithm eliminates readings from clocks that have drifted badly, or that have failed and provide spurious readings. Such clocks could have a significant adverse effect if an ordinary average was taken. The master takes a *fault-tolerant average*. That is, a subset of clocks is chosen that do not differ from one another by more than a specified amount, and the average is taken only of readings from these clocks.

Gusella and Zatti describe an experiment involving 15 computers whose clocks were synchronized to within about 20–25 milliseconds using their protocol. The local clocks' drift rate was measured to be less than 2×10^{-5}, and the maximum round-trip time was taken to be 10 milliseconds.

Should the master fail, then another can be elected to take over and function exactly as its predecessor. Section 10.4 discusses some general-purpose election

Figure 10.3   An example synchronization subnet in an NTP implementation.

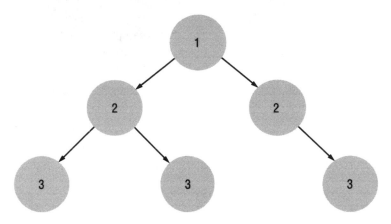

Note: Arrows denote synchronization control, numbers denote strata.

algorithms. Note that these are not guaranteed to elect a new master in bounded time – and so the difference between two clocks would be unbounded if they were used.

The Network Time Protocol □   The Network Time Protocol (NTP) [Mills 1991] defines an architecture for a time service and a protocol to distribute time information over a wide variety of interconnected networks. It has been adopted as a standard for clock synchronization throughout the Internet.

NTP's chief design aims and features are:

To provide a service enabling clients across the Internet to be synchronized accurately to UTC; despite the large and variable message delays encountered in Internet communication. NTP employs statistical techniques for the filtering of timing data and it discriminates between the quality of timing data from different servers.

To provide a reliable service that can survive lengthy losses of connectivity; there are redundant servers and redundant paths between the servers. The servers can reconfigure so as still to provide the service if one of them becomes unreachable.

To enable clients to resynchronize sufficiently frequently; to offset the rates of drift found in most computers. The service is designed to scale to large numbers of clients and servers.

To provide protection against interference with the time service; whether malicious or accidental. The time service uses authentication techniques to check that timing data originate from the claimed trusted sources. It also validates the return addresses of messages sent to it.

The NTP service is provided by a network of servers located across the Internet. *Primary servers* are directly connected to a time source such as a radio clock receiving UTC; *secondary servers* are synchronized, ultimately, to primary servers. The servers are connected in a logical hierarchy called a *synchronization subnet* (see Figure 10.3), whose levels are called *strata*. Primary servers occupy stratum 1: they are at the root. Stratum 2 servers are secondary servers that are synchronized directly to the primary servers; stratum 3 servers are synchronized from stratum 2 servers, and so on. The lowest-level (leaf) servers execute in users' workstations.

The clocks belonging to servers with high stratum numbers are liable to be less accurate than those with low stratum numbers, because errors are introduced at each level of synchronization. NTP also takes into account the total message roundtrip delays to the root, in assessing the quality of timekeeping data held by a particular server.

The synchronization subnet can reconfigure as servers become unreachable or failures occur. If, for example, a primary server's UTC source fails, then it can become a stratum 2 secondary server. If a secondary server's normal source of synchronization fails or becomes unreachable, then it may synchronize with another server.

NTP servers synchronize with one another in one of three modes: multicast, procedure-call and symmetric mode. *Multicast mode* is intended for use on a high-speed LAN. One or more servers periodically multicasts the time to the servers running in other computers connected by the LAN, which set their clocks assuming a small delay. This mode can only achieve relatively low accuracies, but ones which nonetheless are considered sufficient for many purposes.

Procedure-call mode is similar to the operation of Cristian's algorithm, described above. In this mode, one server accepts requests from other computers, which it processes by replying with its timestamp (current clock reading). This mode is suitable where higher accuracies are required than can be achieved with multicast – or where multicast is not supported in hardware. For example, file servers on the same or a neighbouring LAN, which need to keep accurate timing information for file accesses, could contact a local master server in procedure-call mode.

Finally, *symmetric mode* is intended for use by the master servers that supply time information in LANs and by the higher levels (lower strata) of the synchronization subnet, where the highest accuracies are to be achieved. A pair of servers operating in symmetric mode exchange messages bearing timing information. Timing data are retained as part of an association between the servers that is maintained in order to improve the accuracy of their synchronization over time.

In all modes, messages are delivered unreliably, using the standard UDP Internet transport protocol. In procedure-call mode and symmetric mode, messages are exchanged in pairs. Each message bears timestamps of recent message events: the local times when the previous NTP message between the pair was sent and received, and the local time when the current message was transmitted. The recipient of the NTP message notes the local time when it receives the message. The four times T_{i-3}, T_{i-2}, T_{i-1} and T_i are shown in Figure 10.4 for the messages m and m' sent between servers A and B. Note that in symmetric mode, unlike the Cristian algorithm, there can be a non-negligible delay between the arrival of one message and the dispatch of the next. Also, messages may be lost, but the three timestamps carried by each message are nonetheless valid.

For each pair of messages sent between two servers the NTP protocol calculates an *offset* o_i that is an estimate of the actual offset between the two clocks, and a *delay* d_i that is the total transmission time for the two messages. If the true offset of the clock at B relative to that at A is o, and if the actual transmission times for m and m' are t and t' respectively, then we have:

Figure 10.4   Messages exchanged between a pair of NTP peers.

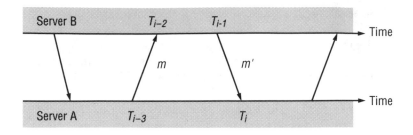

$T_{i-2} = T_{i-3} + t + o,$ and $T_i = T_{i-1} + t' - o$

Defining $a = T_{i-2} - T_{i-3}$ and $b = T_{i-1} - T_i$ this leads to:

$d_i = t + t' = a - b$

Also

$o = o_i + (t' - t)/2$ where $o_i = (a+b)/2$

Using the fact that $t, t' \geq 0$ it can be shown that $o_i - d_i/2 \leq o \leq o_i + d_i/2$. Thus o_i is an estimate of the offset, and d_i is a measure of the accuracy of this estimate.

NTP servers apply a data filtering algorithm to successive pairs $<o_i, d_i>$, which estimates the offset o and calculates the quality of this estimate as a statistical quantity called the *filter dispersion*. A relatively high filter dispersion represents relatively unreliable data. The eight most recent pairs $<o_i, d_i>$ are retained. As with Cristian's algorithm, the value of o_j that corresponds to the minimum value d_j is chosen to estimate o.

The value of the offset derived from communication with a single source is not necessarily used by itself to control the local clock, however. In general, an NTP server engages in message exchanges with several of its peers. In addition to data filtering applied to exchanges with each single peer, NTP applies a peer-selection algorithm. This examines the values obtained from exchanges with each of several peers, looking for relatively unreliable values. The output from this algorithm may cause a server to change the peer that it primarily uses for synchronization.

Peers with lower stratum numbers are more favoured than those at higher strata, because they are 'closer' to the primary time sources. Also, those with the lowest *synchronization dispersion* are relatively favoured. This is the sum of the filter dispersions measured between the server and the root of the synchronization subnet. (Peers exchange synchronization dispersions in messages, allowing this total to be calculated.)

Mills [1991] reports that, in 1991, about 20–30 primary servers and over 2000 secondary servers operated across the Internet, with sites in the US, Canada, UK and Norway. The primary servers frequently exchange messages with most of the other primary servers. The secondary servers communicate frequently with, typically, a single peer at the same stratum and two peers at the next lowest stratum.

Measurements show that the synchronization error is below 30 milliseconds for all but 1 per cent of sample time values taken from servers synchronized by NTP. Furthermore, by using a phase-lock loop mechanism to control the frequency of local clocks in response to offset data, accuracies in the order of one millisecond can be achieved over periods in the order of hours. Nonetheless, no bound can be guaranteed on the difference between two clocks: this is a 'best-effort' service.

The phase-lock loop model is described by Mills [1991]. It involves modification of the local clock's frequency in accordance with observations of its drift rate. To take a simple example, if a clock is discovered always to gain time at the rate of about, say, four seconds per hour, then its frequency can be reduced slightly (in software or hardware) to compensate for this. The clock's drift in the intervals between synchronization is thus reduced.

10.3 Logical time and logical clocks

From the point of view of any single process, events are ordered uniquely by times shown on the local clock. However, as Lamport [1978] pointed out, since we cannot perfectly synchronize clocks across a distributed system, we cannot in general use physical time to find out the order of any arbitrary pair of events occurring within it.

The order of events occurring at different processes can be critical in a distributed application. For example, Chapter 11 shows in detail how systems that replicate data items in order to increase their availability must apply updates in a strict order to the replicas, if they are to remain consistent.

In general, we can use a scheme which is similar to physical causality, but which applies in distributed systems, to order some of the events that occur at different processes. This ordering is based on two simple and intuitively obvious points:

- If two events occurred at the same process, then they occurred in the order in which it observes them.

- Whenever a message is sent between processes, the event of sending the message occurred before the event of receiving the message.

Lamport called the ordering obtained by generalizing these two relationships the **happened-before** relation. It is also sometimes known as the relation of *causal ordering* or *potential causal ordering*.

More formally, we write $x \xrightarrow{p} y$ if two events x and y occurred at a single process p, and x occurred before y. Using this restricted order we can define the *happened-before* relation, denoted by $\rightarrow$, as follows:

HB1:   If $\exists$ process p: $x \xrightarrow{p} y$, then $x \rightarrow y$.

HB2:   For any message m, $send(m) \rightarrow rcv(m)$,
   – where $send(m)$ is the event of sending the message, and $rcv(m)$ is the event of receiving it.

HB3:   If x, y and z are events such that $x \rightarrow y$ and $y \rightarrow z$, then $x \rightarrow z$.

Figure 10.5   Events occurring at three processes.

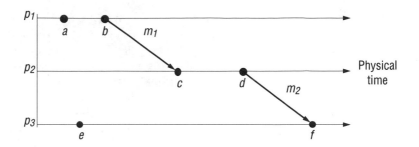

Thus, if $x \to y$, then we can find a series of events $e_1, e_2, e_3, .., e_n$ occurring at one or more processes such that $x = e_1$ and $y = e_n$, and for i = 1, 2, .., n-1, either *HB1* or *HB2* applies between e_i and e_{i+1}: That is, either they occur in succession at the same process, or there is a message m such that $e_i = send(m)$ and $e_{i+1} = rcv(m)$. The sequence of events $e_1, e_2, e_3, .., e_n$ need not be unique.

The relation $\to$ is illustrated for the case of three processes p_1, p_2 and p_3 in Figure 10.5. It can be seen that $a \to b$, since the events occur in this order at process p_1, and similarly $c \to d$; $b \to c$, since these events are the sending and reception of message m_1, and similarly $d \to f$. Combining these relations, we may also say that, for example, $a \to f$.

It can also be observed from Figure 10.5 that not all events are related by the relation $\to$. For example, $a \not\to e$ and $e \not\to a$, since they occur at different processes, and there is no chain of messages intervening between them. We say that events such as a and e that are not ordered by $\to$ are *concurrent*, and write this $a \parallel e.$

The relation $\to$ captures a flow of data intervening between two events. Note, however, that in real life data can flow in ways other than by message passing. For example, if Smith enters a command to his process to send a message, then telephones Jones who commands her process to issue another message, then the issuing of the first message clearly *happened-before* that of the second. Unfortunately, since no network messages were sent between the issuing processes, we cannot model this type of relationship in our system.

Another point to note is that if the *happened-before* relation holds between two events, then the first might or might not actually have caused the second. For example, if a server receives a request message and subsequently sends a reply, then clearly the reply transmission is caused by the request transmission. However, the relation $\to$ captures only *potential* causality, and two events can be related by $\to$ even though there is no real connection between them. A process might, for example, receive a message and subsequently issue another message, but one that it anyway issues every five minutes, and which bears no specific relation to the first message. No actual causality has been involved, but the relation $\to$ would order these events.

Logical clocks ☐ Lamport invented a simple mechanism by which the *happened-before* ordering can be captured numerically, called a **logical clock**. A logical clock is a monotonically increasing software counter, whose value need bear no particular relationship to any physical clock, in general. Each process p keeps its own logical

Figure 10.6   Logical timestamps for the events shown in Figure 10.5.

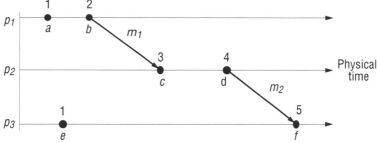

clock, C_p, which it uses to timestamp events. We denote the timestamp of event a at p by $C_p(a)$, and by $C(b)$ we denote the timestamp of event b at whatever process it occurred.

To capture the *happened-before* relation $\rightarrow$, processes update their logical clocks and transmit the values of their logical clocks in messages as follows:

    LC1: C_p is incremented before each event is issued at process p: $C_p := C_p + 1$

    LC2:   a)   When a process p sends a message m, it piggybacks on m the value $t = C_p$.

            b)   On receiving (m, t), a process q computes $C_q := \max(C_q, t)$ and then applies *LC1* before timestamping the event $rcv(m)$.

Although we increment clocks by one, we could have chosen any positive value. It can easily be shown, by induction on the length of any sequence of events relating two events a and b, that $a \rightarrow b \Rightarrow C(a) < C(b)$.

Note that the converse is not true. If $C(a) < C(b)$, then we cannot infer that $a \rightarrow b$. In Figure 10.6 we illustrate the use of logical clocks for the example given in Figure 10.5. Each of the processes p_1, p_2 and p_3 has its logical clock initialized to 0. The clock values given are those immediately after the event to which they are adjacent. Note that, for example, $C(b) > C(e)$ but $b \parallel e$.

Totally ordered logical clocks $\Box$ Logical clocks impose only a partial order on the set of all events, since some pairs of distinct events, generated by different processes, have numerically identical timestamps. However, we can extend this to a total order – that is, one for which all pairs of distinct events are ordered – by taking into account the identifiers of the processes at which events occur. If a is an event occurring at p_a with local timestamp T_a, and b is an event occurring at p_b with local timestamp T_b, we define the global logical timestamps for these events to be (T_a, p_a) and (T_b, p_b) respectively. And we define $(T_a, p_a) < (T_b, p_b)$ if and only if either $T_a < T_b$, or $T_a = T_b$ and $p_a < p_b$.

10.4 Distributed coordination

Distributed processes often need to coordinate their activities. For example, if a collection of processes share a resource or collection of resources managed by a server, then often mutual exclusion is required to prevent interference and ensure consistency when accessing the resources. This is essentially the critical section problem, familiar in the domain of operating systems. In the distributed case, however, neither shared variables nor facilities supplied by a single local kernel can be used to solve it in general.

In Chapter 12 it is described how servers often implement their own locks for synchronizing client accesses to the resources they manage. However, some servers do not have synchronization built in. Consider users who update a common text file. A simple means of ensuring that their updates are consistent is to allow them to access it only one at a time, by requiring the editor to lock the file before updates can be made. This is called file locking. NFS file servers, described in Chapter 8, are designed to be stateless and therefore do not support file locking. For this reason, UNIX systems provide a separate file locking service, implemented by the daemon *lockd*, to handle locking requests from clients.

As another example, consider client processes that access a common window to print output. Each process may be required to display several lines of output consecutively in the window, without interference from other processes' output. Window servers are not normally designed to support synchronized access to windows, so a separate synchronization mechanism must be used.

Chapter 17 describes how processes that access distributed shared memory need to synchronize to maintain consistency. Synchronization may be provided by a separate service from the storage service.

A separate, generic mechanism for **distributed mutual exclusion** is thus required in certain cases – one that is independent of the particular resource management scheme in question. Distributed mutual exclusion involves a single process being given a privilege – the right to access shared resources – temporarily, before another process is granted it. In some other cases, however, the requirement is for a set of processes to choose one of their number to play a privileged, coordinating role over the long term. A method for choosing a unique process to play a particular role is called an **election algorithm**. For example, the previous section described the need for a new time server to be elected if the last one failed.

This section now examines some algorithms for achieving the goals of distributed mutual exclusion and elections.

Distributed mutual exclusion

Our basic requirements for mutual exclusion concerning some resource (or collection of resources) are as follows:

ME1: (safety)   At most one process may execute in the critical section (CS) at a time.

ME2: (liveness)   A process requesting entry to the CS is eventually granted it (so long as any process executing in the CS eventually leaves it).

ME2 implies that the implementation is deadlock-free, and that starvation does not occur. A further requirement which may be made is that of causal ordering:

ME3: (ordering)   Entry to the CS should be granted in *happened-before* order.

A process may continue with other processing while waiting to be granted entry to a critical section. During this time it might send a message to another process, which consequently also tries to enter the critical section. ME3 specifies that the first process should be granted access before the second.

We now discuss some algorithms for achieving these requirements.

The central server algorithm □ The simplest way to achieve mutual exclusion is to employ a server that grants permission to enter a critical section. For the sake of simplicity, we shall assume that there is only one critical section managed by the server. Recall that the protocol for executing a critical section is as follows:

enter()   (* enter critical section – block if necessary *)
.....   (* access shared resources in critical section *)
exit()   (* leave critical section – other processes may now enter *)

Figure 10.7 shows the use of this server. To enter a critical section, a process sends a request message to the server and awaits a reply from it. Conceptually, the reply constitutes a token signifying permission to enter the critical section. If no other process has the token at the time of the request, then the server replies immediately, granting the token. If the token is currently held by another process, then the server does not reply

Figure 10.7   Server managing a mutual exclusion token for a set of processes.

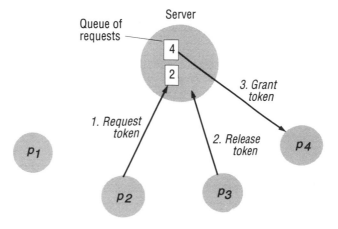

but queues the request. On exiting the critical section, a message is sent to the server, giving it back the token.

If the queue of waiting processes is not empty, then the server chooses the oldest entry in the queue, removes it and replies to the corresponding process. The chosen process then holds the token. In the figure, we show a situation in which p_2's request has been appended to the queue, which already contained p_4's request. p_3 exits the critical section, and the server removes p_4's entry and grants permission to enter to p_4 by replying to it. Process p_1 does not currently require entry to the critical section.

Assuming that no crashes occur and that all messages are sent reliably, it is easy to see that the safety and liveness conditions are met by this algorithm. The reader is invited to consider whether causal ordering is also assured. Entering and exiting the critical section each take just two messages (counting the acknowledgement of a release-token message). But the server might become a performance bottleneck, since all entry requests and exit notifications are sent to it.

The server is also a critical point of failure. What should happen if it fails? The failure of the server will be detected by any process attempting to communicate with it, either to enter or exit the critical section. To recover from a server failure, a new server can be created (or one of the processes requiring mutual exclusion could be picked to play a dual role as a server). Since the server must be unique if it is to guarantee mutual exclusion, an election must be called to choose one of the clients to create or act as the server, and to multicast its address to the others. We shall describe some election algorithms below. When the new server has been chosen, it needs to obtain the state of its clients, so that it can process their requests as the previous server would have done. The ordering of entry requests will be different in the new server from that in the failed one unless precautions are taken, but we shall not address this problem here.

Another problem, which we also shall not address, is how to deal with the failure of one of the client processes – in particular, the failure of a process currently executing within the critical section.

A distributed algorithm using logical clocks □ Ricart and Agrawala [1981] developed an algorithm to implement mutual exclusion that is based upon distributed agreement, instead of using a central server. The basic idea is that processes that require entry to a critical section multicast a request message, and can enter it only when all the other processes have replied to this message. The conditions under which a process replies to a request are designed to ensure that conditions *ME1 – ME3* are met.

Again, we can associate permission to enter a critical section conceptually with possession of a token – although transferring a token in this case takes multiple messages. The assumptions of the algorithm are that the processes $p_1, .., p_n$ know one another's addresses, that all messages sent are eventually delivered, and that each process p_i keeps a logical clock, updated according to the rules *LC1* and *LC2* of the previous section. Messages requesting the token are of the form $<T, p_i>$, where T is the sender's timestamp and p_i is the sender's identifier. For simplicity's sake, we assume that only one critical section is at issue, and so it does not have to be identified.

Each process records its state of having released the token (RELEASED), wanting the token (WANTED) or possessing the token (HELD) in a variable *state*. The protocol is given in Figure 10.8.

Figure 10.8   Ricart and Agrawala's algorithm.

On initialization:
   state := RELEASED;

To obtain the token:
   state := WANTED;
   Multicast request to all processes;   } *Request processing deferred here*
   T := request's timestamp;
   Wait until (number of replies received = $(n-1)$);
   state := HELD;

On receipt of a request <T_i, p_i> *at p_j (i $\neq$ j):*
   if (*state* = HELD *or* (*state* = WANTED *and* $(T, p_j) < (T_i, p_i)$))
   then
                queue request from p_i without replying;
   else
                reply immediately to p_i;
   end if

To release token:
   state := RELEASED;
   reply to any queued requests;

If a process requests the token and the token is RELEASED everywhere else – that is, no other process wants it – then all processes will reply immediately to the request and the requester will obtain the token. If the token is HELD at some process, then that process will not reply to requests until it has finished with the token, and so the requester cannot obtain the token in the meantime. If two or more processes request the token at the same time, then whichever process's request bears the lowest timestamp will be the first to collect $(n - 1)$ replies, granting it the token next. If the requests bear equal timestamps, the process identifiers are compared to order them. Note that, when a process requests the token, it defers processing requests from other processes until its own request has been sent and the timestamp T is known. This is so that processes make consistent decisions when processing requests.

To illustrate the algorithm, consider a situation involving three processes, p_1, p_2 and p_3 shown in Figure 10.9. Let us assume that p_3 is not interested in the token, and that p_1 and p_2 request it concurrently. The timestamp of p_1's request is 41, that of p_2 is 34. When p_3 receives their requests, it replies immediately. When p_2 receives p_1's request, it finds its own request has the lower timestamp, and so does not reply, holding p_1 off. However, p_1 finds that p_2's request has a lower timestamp than that of its own request, and so replies immediately. On receiving this second reply, p_2 possesses the token. When p_2 releases the token, it will reply to p_1's request, and so grant it the token.

Obtaining the token takes $2(n - 1)$ messages in this algorithm: $(n - 1)$ to multicast the request, followed by $(n - 1)$ replies. Or, if there is hardware support for multicast, only one message is required for the request; the total is then n messages. It is thus a

Figure 10.9   Multicast synchronization.

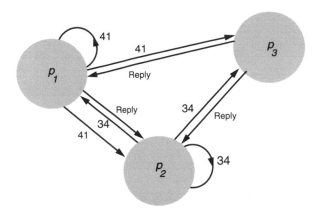

Processes request mutual exclusion by multicasting.

considerably more expensive algorithm, in general, than the central server algorithm just described. Note, also, that while it is a fully distributed algorithm, the failure of any process involved would make progress impossible. And in the distributed algorithm all the processes involved receive and process every request, so no performance gain has been made over the single server bottleneck, which does just the same. Finally, note that a process that wishes to obtain the token and which was the last to possess it still goes through the protocol as described, even though it could simply decide locally to re-allocate it to itself.

Ricart and Agrawala refined this protocol so that it requires n messages to obtain the token in the worst (and common) case, without hardware support for multicast. This is described in [Raynal 1988].

A ring-based algorithm □ One of the simplest ways to arrange mutual exclusion between n processes p_1, ... p_n is to arrange them in a logical ring. The idea is that exclusion is conferred by obtaining a token in the form of a message passed from process to process in a single direction – clockwise, say – round the ring. The ring topology – which is unrelated to the physical interconnections between the underlying computers – is created by giving each process the address of its neighbour in the clockwise direction.

If a process that does not require to enter the critical section receives the token, then it immediately forwards the token to its neighbour. A process that requires the token waits until it receives it, but retains it. To exit the critical section, the process sends the token on to its neighbour.

The arrangement of processes is shown in Figure 10.10. It is straightforward to verify that the conditions *ME1* and *ME2* are met by this algorithm, but that the token is not necessarily obtained in *happened-before* order. It can take from 1 to $(n-1)$ messages to obtain the token, from the point at which the token becomes required. However, messages are sent around the ring even when no process requires the token. If a process fails, then clearly no progress can be made beyond it in transferring the token, until a reconfiguration is applied to extract the failed process from the ring. If the process

Figure 10.10   A ring of processes transferring a mutual exclusion token.

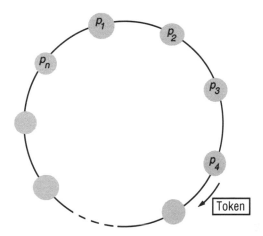

holding the token fails, then an election is required to pick a unique process from the surviving members, which will regenerate the token and transmit it as before.

Care has to be taken, however, in ensuring that the 'failed' process really has failed, and does not later unexpectedly inject the old token into the ring, so that there are two tokens. This situation can arise since process failure can only be ascertained by repeated failure of the process to acknowledge messages sent to it. However, this behaviour can also be manifested by processes that are temporarily disconnected by a network partition.

Discussion of distributed mutual exclusion algorithms □   The three algorithms just described do not seem promising as examples of practical distributed design. None can cope with process or machine failure. The central server algorithm requires the smallest number of messages, on average; but the server may become a bottleneck if a large number of clients transfer the token frequently. The reader may care to analyse how the failure of either the server or of a token-holding client could be dealt with, after reading the description of election algorithms given below.

The beginning of this section gave examples in which the servers that manage resources do not provide locking, so necessitating a separate distributed mutual exclusion service. In general, it is preferable for the server that manages a resource also to provide mutual exclusion between the clients that access it. Clients then only make one operation to access the resource with mutual exclusion, instead of two. Chapter 13 describes servers that implement their own resource locking.

Elections

An election is a procedure carried out to choose a process from a group, for example to take over the role of a process that has failed. The main requirement is for the choice of elected process to be unique, even if several processes call elections concurrently.

The bully algorithm □ The bully algorithm [Silberschatz *et al.* 1993] can be used when the members of the group know the identities and addresses of the other members. The algorithm selects the surviving member with the largest identifier to function as the coordinator. We assume that communication is reliable, but processes can fail during an election. The algorithm proceeds as follows.

There are three types of message in this algorithm. An *election* message is sent to announce an election; an *answer* message is sent in response to an election message; and a *coordinator* message is sent to announce the identity of the new coordinator. A process begins an election when it notices that the coordinator has failed.

To begin an election, a process sends an *election* message to those processes that have a higher identifier. It then awaits an *answer* message in response. If none arrives within a certain time, the process considers itself the coordinator, and sends a *coordinator* message to all processes with lower identifiers announcing this fact. Otherwise, the process waits a further limited period for a *coordinator* message to arrive from the new coordinator. If none arrives, it begins another election.

If a process receives a *coordinator* message, it records the identifier of the coordinator contained within it, and treats that process as the coordinator.

If a process receives an *election* message, it sends back an *answer* message, and begins another election – unless it has begun one already.

When a failed process is restarted, it begins an election. If it has the highest process identifier, then it will decide that it is the coordinator, and announce this to the other processes. Thus it will become the coordinator, even though the current coordinator is functioning. It is for this reason that the algorithm is called the 'bully' algorithm.

The operation of the algorithm is shown in Figure 10.11. There are four processes, $p_1 - p_4$, and an election is called when p_1 detects the failure of the coordinator, p_4, and announces an election (stage 1 in the figure). On receiving an *election* message from p_1, p_2 and p_3 send *answer* messages to p_1 and begin their own elections; p_3 sends an *answer* message to p_2, but p_3 receives no *answer* message from the failed process p_4 (stage 2). It therefore decides that it is the coordinator. But before it can send out the *coordinator* message, it too fails (stage 3). When p_1's timeout period expires (which we assume occurs before p_2's timeout expires), it notices the absence of a *coordinator* message and begins another election. Eventually, p_2 is elected coordinator (stage 4).

In the best case, the process with the second-to-highest identifier notices the coordinator's failure. Then it can immediately elect itself, and send $(n - 2)$ coordinator messages. The bully algorithm requires $O(n^2)$ messages in the worst case, that is, when the process with the least identifier first detects the coordinator's failure. For then $(n - 1)$ processes altogether begin elections, each sending messages to processes with higher identifiers.

A ring-based election algorithm □ We give the algorithm of Chang and Roberts [1979], suitable for a collection of processes that are arranged in a logical ring. We assume that the processes do not know the identities of the others *a priori*, and that each process knows only how to communicate with its neighbour in, say, the clockwise direction. The goal of this algorithm is to elect a single coordinator, which is the process with the largest identifier. The algorithm assumes that all the processes remain functional and reachable during its operation. Tanenbaum [1992] gives a variant in

Figure 10.11   The bully algorithm.

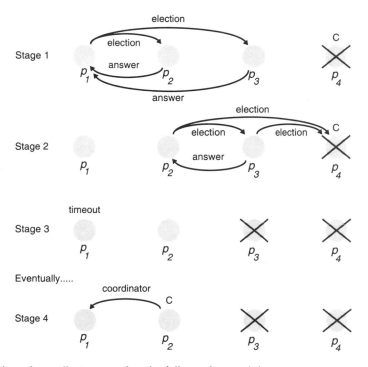

The election of coordinator p_2, after the failure of p_4 and then p_3.

which processes can fail, but which assumes that the processes can communicate directly with any other in the group.

Initially, every process is marked as a *non-participant* in an election. Any process can begin an election. It proceeds by marking itself as a *participant*, placing its identifier in an *election* message and sending it to its neighbour.

When a process receives an *election* message, it compares the identifier in the message with its own. If the arrived identifier is the greater, then it forwards the message to its neighbour. If the arrived identifier is smaller and the receiver is not a *participant* then it substitutes its own identifier in the message and forwards it; but it does not forward the message if it is already a *participant*. On forwarding an *election* message in any case, the process marks itself as a *participant*.

If, however, the received identifier is that of the receiver itself, then this process's identifier must be the greatest, and it becomes the coordinator. The coordinator marks itself as a *non-participant* once more, and sends an *elected* message to its neighbour, announcing its election and enclosing its identity.

When a process other than the coordinator receives an *elected* message, it marks itself as a *non-participant*, and forwards the message to its neighbour.

The point of marking processes as *participant* or *non-participant* is so that messages arising when another process starts an election at the same time are

Figure 10.12 A ring-based election in progress.

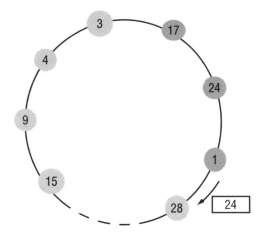

Note: The election was started by process 17. The highest process identifier encountered
so far is 24. Participant processes are shown darkened.

extinguished as soon as possible, and always before the 'winning' election result has
been announced.

If only a single process starts an election, then the worst case is when its anti-
clockwise neighbour has the highest identifier. A total of $n - 1$ messages are then
required to reach this neighbour, which will not announce its election until its identifier
has completed another circuit, taking a further n messages. The *elected* message is then
sent n times, making $3n - 1$ messages in all.

An example of a ring-based election in progress is shown in Figure 10.12. The
election message currently contains 24, but process 28 will replace this with its identifier
when the message reaches it.

10.5 Summary

This chapter began by describing the importance of accurate time-keeping for
distributed systems. It then described algorithms for synchronizing clocks despite the
drift between them and the variability of message delays between computers.

The degree of synchronization accuracy that is practically obtainable fulfils many
requirements, but is nonetheless not sufficient to determine the ordering of an arbitrary
pair of events occurring at different computers. The *happened-before* relationship is a
partial order on events which reflects a flow of information – within a process, or via
messages between processes – between them. Some algorithms require events to be
ordered in *happened-before* order, for example, successive updates made at separate
copies of data. Logical clocks are counters that are updated so as to reflect the *happened-
before* relationship between events.

The chapter then described the need for processes to access shared resources under conditions of mutual exclusion. Locks are not implemented by resource servers in all cases, and a separate distributed mutual exclusion service is then required. Three algorithms were considered which achieve mutual exclusion: the central server, a distributed algorithm using logical clocks, and a ring-based algorithm. These are heavyweight mechanisms that cannot withstand failure, although they can be modified to be fault-tolerant. On the whole, it seems advisable to integrate locking with resource management.

Finally, the chapter considered the bully algorithm and a ring-based algorithm whose common aim is to elect a process uniquely from a given set – even if several elections take place concurrently. These algorithms could be used, for example, to elect a new master time server, or a new lock server, when the previous one fails.

EXERCISES

10.1   Why is computer clock synchronization necessary? Describe the design requirements for a system to synchronize the clocks in a distributed system.

page 288

10.2   A clock is reading 10:27:54.0 (hr:min:sec) when it is discovered to be 4 seconds fast. Explain why it is undesirable to set it back to the right time at that point, and show (numerically) how it should be adjusted so as to be correct after 8 seconds have elapsed.

page 291

10.3   A client attempts to synchronize with a time server. It records the following round-trip times and timestamps returned by the server:

Which of these times should it use to set its clock? To what time should it

Round-trip (ms)	Time (hr:min:sec)
22	10:54:23.674
25	10:54:25.450
20	10:54:28.342

set it? Estimate the accuracy of the setting with respect to the server's clock. If it is known that the time between sending and receiving a message in the system concerned is at least 8 milliseconds, do your answers change?

page 291

10.4   In the system of Exercise 10.3 it is required to synchronize a file server's clock to within ±1 millisecond. Discuss this in relation to Cristian's algorithm.

page 291

10.5   What reconfigurations would you expect to occur in the NTP synchronization subnet?

page 294

10.6   Discuss the factors to be taken into account when deciding to which NTP server a client should synchronize its clock.

page 294

10.7   An NTP server B receives server A's message at 16:34:23.480 bearing a timestamp 16:34:13.430 and replies to it. A receives the message at 16:34:15.725, bearing B's timestamp 16:34:25.7. Estimate the offset between B and A and the accuracy of the estimate.

page 295

10.8   Discuss how it is possible to compensate for clock drift between synchronization points by observing the drift rate over time. Discuss any limitations to your method.

page 297

10.9   Show that $a \rightarrow b \Rightarrow C(a) < C(b)$.

page 299

10.10   Smith is trying to debug a distributed application. To do this, she needs to take a 'snapshot' of the global state of the application, consisting of the states of each of the processes involved. Needless to say, it is impossible to examine these states at precisely the same time. Her approach is for each of the processes concerned to send a message to a central debugger process whenever any event of interest occurs, describing its state.

i)   Discuss and define a notion of *consistent global state* for the application, which can be assembled from messages sent to the debugger process.

ii)   Assuming that messages from different processes may be delivered in a haphazard order at the debugger, how can Smith tell which global states are consistent? (*Hint*: processes should keep a record of other processes' logical clock values as well as their own.)

page 299

10.11   Adapt the central server model for mutual exclusion to handle failure conditions, including: (i) the failure of a token-holding client; (ii) the failure of a client that has requested but not yet received a token; and (iii) the failure of a mutual exclusion server.

page 301

10.12   Give an example to show that the mutual exclusion token is not necessarily obtained in *happened-before* order in the ring-based algorithm.

page 304

10.13   In the Bully algorithm, a recovering process starts an election, and will become the new coordinator if it has a higher identifier than the current incumbent. Is this a necessary feature of the algorithm?

page 306

REPLICATION

Replication is a key to providing good performance, high availability and fault tolerance in distributed systems. In this chapter we describe design issues concerning the replication of data and other resources. The main problem tackled is that of applying operations from clients to multiple replicas in a consistent way, while maintaining reasonable response times and system throughput rates.

The chapter describes two approaches to replication: the gossip approach and the process group approach. In the gossip architecture, updates are lazily propagated between replicas. In the process group approach, updates are multicast to all replicas. Process groups are also more widely applicable, beyond replication. The ISIS programming environment, based on the notions of process groups and virtually synchronous execution, is described.

The chapter deals primarily with the order in which updates are applied, and identifies the main ordering types as causal, total and sync-ordered. Algorithms are given for achieving causal and total ordering, for achieving atomic multicast, and for ordering multicasts with respect to changes in process groups.

11.1 Introduction

Replication is the maintenance of on-line copies of data and other resources. It is a key to the effectiveness of distributed systems, in that it can provide enhanced performance, high availability and fault tolerance. Replication is used widely. For example, the USENET system maintains replicas of items posted to electronic bulletin boards across the Internet, the replicas being held within or close to the various organizations that provide access to it. The DNS naming service, described in Chapter 9, maintains copies of name-to-address mappings for computers and other resources, and is relied on for day-to-day access to services across the Internet. The caching of file and other data from servers in client computers is another form of replication, since the data held in caches and at servers are replicas of one another. In addition, replication is intrinsic to the distributed shared memory implementations discussed in Chapter 17.

The motivations for replication are as follows:

Performance enhancement: The caching of data at clients is by now familiar as a means of performance enhancement, but replication can be applied equally at the level of servers to enhance service response times. Data that are shared between a large client community should not be held at a single server, since this computer will act as a bottleneck that slows down responses and has a limited throughput capacity in terms of requests processed per second. It is preferable to distribute copies of the data to several servers, and to arrange that each provides the data to a smaller community of users which is close to it in network terms. If the servers provide read-only access to data then replication is relatively trivial but this is of limited value, since almost all data are subject to at least occasional modification.

Enhanced availability: If service data are replicated at two or more failure-independent servers running equivalent software and reachable by independent communication links (where these can fail), then client software can in principle access an alternative server should the default server fail or become unreachable. That is, the percentage of time during which the *service* is available can be enhanced by replicating servers. If n servers each have an independent probability p of failing or becoming unreachable, then the availability of a data item stored at each of these servers is:

$$1 - probability(all\ managers\ failed\ or\ unreachable) = 1 - p^n$$

For example, if there is a five per cent probability of any individual failure over a given time period, and if there are two managers, then the availability is $1 - 0.05^2$ $= 1 - 0.0025 = 99.75$ per cent. An important difference between caching systems and server replication is that caches do not necessarily hold collections of data items such as files in their entirety. So caching does not necessarily enhance availability. The Coda file system provides an interesting counter-example in which cached copies of whole files are used as replicas during disconnected operation.

Fault tolerance: If each of a collection of servers processes every request from a client in parallel, then it is possible to provide guarantees of correct request

Figure 11.1 Smith's display from bulletin board reader.

Bulletin board: *os.interesting*		
Item	From	Subject
23	A.Hanlon	Mach
24	G.Joseph	Microkernels
25	A.Hanlon	Re: Microkernels
26	T.L'Heureux	RPC performance
27	M.Walker	Re: Mach
end		

processing, even though one (or more) of the servers should fail. This is a stronger statement than that of high availability, because it can include real-time guarantees, and also guarantees against arbitrary (so-called *Byzantine*) failures rather than simple, so-called *fail-stop* failures in which a component stops after changing to a state in which its failure can be detected. For example, a spaceship engine's thrust and direction could be calculated within a crucial time interval by an on-board computer that continues to function, even though its peer crashes. Furthermore, if one of several replica computers fails in such a way that it does not stop responding but produces random results, then its results can be discarded if two or more of its peers produce the same, majority results.

The chief requirement when data (or other resources) are replicated is for *replication transparency*. That is, clients should not normally be aware that multiple *physical* copies of data exist. As far as clients are concerned, data are organized as individual *logical* data items (or objects), and they name only one item in each case when they request an operation to be performed. Furthermore, under replication transparency operations return only one set of values. This is despite the fact that operations may be performed upon more than one physical copy in concert.

The other general requirement for replicated data – one which can vary in strength between applications – is that of consistency. Consider that clients make requests, and that requests involve updates as well as reads upon a set of logical data items (there is no consistency problem if the data are read-only). It is not normally acceptable for different clients to obtain differing results when they make the same requests affecting the same logical data items. At least, this is not acceptable if the results lead to detectable and significant inconsistencies between different applications or users, or if the results break a constraint within a single application.

Of course, updates are normally eventually applied to all copies of a data item; but it is the order in which operations occur at a given copy which may affect the results of client operations. Note that the problem of identifying and locating all the copies of a data item is itself an interesting issue, but one for which there is little space in this chapter. In Chapter 8 we describe, for example, how Andrew servers keep track of cached file copies held by clients.

The example of a bulletin board is now introduced, which will be used later in this chapter. Figure 11.1 illustrates the information displayed to a client 'Smith' accessing the *os.interesting* bulletin board. The items are numbered, and have sender names and

Figure 11.2   Jones' display from bulletin board reader.

Bulletin board: os.*interesting*		
Item	From	Subject
20	G.Joseph	Microkernels
21	A.Hanlon	Mach
22	A.Sahiner	Re: RPC performance
23	M.Walker	Re: Mach
24	T.L'Heureux	RPC performance
25	A.Hanlon	Re: Microkernels
end		

dates. The user can select any item to view, can post new items, and in particular he or she can respond to a message. In the latter case the subject of the response is automatically given as 'Re: Microkernels', for example, if the subject of the item to which it refers is 'Microkernels'. The bulletin board reader program sends new items to a server, and also fetches items from a server. It automatically requests copies of any new items from the server at regular intervals. Once they are downloaded they are stored locally, but they remain stored at the server, of course.

Suppose that clients at several universities share the same bulletin boards, but that the clients are sufficient in number and the universities sufficiently far apart that the bulletin boards are replicated, with a server at each university holding a replica. A simple *asynchronous model* of replica management is one in which all client requests are processed by the local replica server. The local replica servers communicate updates to all other servers managing replicas of the same data items, in this case bulletin board items. In this asynchronous model each server allows a client operation to return as soon as it has been performed locally, and communicates updates to its peers whenever it is convenient, or perhaps periodically. Servers process updates as they arrive.

Under this replication scheme, the display shown to a client 'Jones' at another university might be as shown in Figure 11.2. Note that the set of items shown is the same except for the item from 'A.Sahiner' on Jones' display, which has arrived at Jones' local server but has not arrived at Smith's local server (or has not yet been retrieved from it). However, the numbering and the ordering of the items differ between the two. Since the propagation of updates is asynchronous and since items are posted from different universities, items may not arrive in the same order at any two universities. This is particularly so where a site fails after it has sent an item to some sites but not others. If the local servers simply number the items as they arrive, then there is similarly no reason why the item numbers should be the same for Smith and Jones. Finally, note in particular items 22 and 24 on Jones' display. Intuitively, an item referring to another item should appear after it. But the variable propagation delays to Jones' university have reversed this natural ordering.

These characteristics are similar to those encountered when using the USENET bulletin board system. That system is used by many people, but the inconsistencies are a nuisance. It would be more convenient if users could refer unambiguously in their items to, for example, 'item number 25 on *os.interesting*'; it would also be more satisfactory if an item whose subject is X could always be read before a response item whose subject is *re:X*. On the other hand, it could be considered a convenient characteristic of this system that a new item marked *Re:X* can be read, even though the *X* item cannot be read currently because all links are down to the university at which it was originally posted.

Now consider by contrast a *totally synchronous model* of replica management, in which all update requests are *totally ordered*. That is, requests are processed at all replicas in the same order. Only after the single current update request has been processed at all servers holding replicas, is control passed back to the client that requested the update, and the next request (from whatever client) handled. This model clearly would maintain strict consistency. In the bulletin board example, all items would be given the same number and therefore appear in the same order. However, it turns out that such a system would give response times and throughput for updates that are worse than that of any single server, because of the extra costs of propagating new items and ordering them.

In general, most replication schemes fall between the simple asynchronous and synchronous models described above. A degree of replica consistency beyond that obtained in the asynchronous model is often required; but the response times provided by the totally synchronous model are sometimes inadequate. Various techniques have been devised to achieve satisfactory trade-offs between consistency, availability and response time. Key among these are two basic approaches.

Quorum-based schemes: Some schemes minimize communication costs and enable a degree of concurrent processing by allowing some but not all managers of replicas to be contacted before a read or update request is allowed to complete.

Causality: There are designs which achieve a degree of concurrent request processing by allowing some requests to be processed in different orders at different replicas – in so far as this cannot produce inconsistencies. An important ordering of this type is *causal ordering* (see Section 10.3). This is missing from our asynchronous bulletin board example, where an item *re:X* can appear before the original item about *X*.

An important general mechanism for keeping replicas consistent is to multicast updates to all processes that manage physical replicas. That is, updates are sent in messages which are delivered to precisely the set of processes that manage replicas of the corresponding data item. **Process groups** are logical destinations for multicast messages, whose membership can be kept transparent to the message sender. The ISIS system [Birman 1993], described below, provides process groups and ordered multicast on top of existing operating systems, particularly UNIX.

Finally, what effect does replication have on performance: the time that elapses between a client issuing a request and values being returned to it, and the number of requests that can be processed per second? If the replicated data are read-only or if consistency is not an issue, then the answer to the first question is surely 'no longer than for a non-replicated implementation'. This is more or less the case for the simple asynchronous model given above (although sending and handling updates in the background would have some impact on response times).

The ratio of read operations to updates performed upon replicated data is an important consideration, especially when designing systems in which the number of replicas is relatively high. The number of replicas varies from the thousands – for example, USENET or the DNS – where the *read/write* ratio is high, to the few replicas used in fault-tolerant systems with relatively small *read/write* ratios.

11.2 Basic architectural model

We now give a basic architectural model for the management of replicated data. For the sake of generality, we describe components by their roles, and do not mean to imply that they are necessarily implemented by distinct processes (or hardware). The model involves replicas of data items held by distinct **replica managers**, which are processes that contain the replicas and perform operations upon them directly. Note that we avoid the term 'replica server' and use 'replica manager' instead, because this general model may be applied to an application rather than a service implementation, and client processes can in that case act as replica managers.

Typically, each replica manager maintains a physical copy of every logical data item, but there is no reason why data items should not be maintained by different sets of replica managers. For example, some data items might be needed mostly by clients on one LAN rather than another, and so there is little to be gained by replicating them at managers on the other LAN.

The general model is shown in Figure 11.3. Clients each make a series of requests. Each request in general involves a combination of reads of logical data items and updates to logical data items. Requests that involve no updates are called *read-only requests*; requests that update at least one data item are called *update requests* (these may also involve reads of data items).

Each client's requests are first handled by a component called a **front end**. The role of the front end is at least to communicate by message passing with one or more of the replica managers, rather than forcing the client to do this itself explicitly. It is the vehicle for implementing replication transparency. A front end may be implemented as a user package executed in each client, or it can be a separate process. The choice involves a trade-off between, on the one hand, the greater efficiency of calling an in-process procedure over communicating with another process; and, on the other hand, possible advantages to sharing information such as server addresses in the front end on behalf of all clients at the same site.

Figure 11.3   A basic architectural model for the management of replicated data.

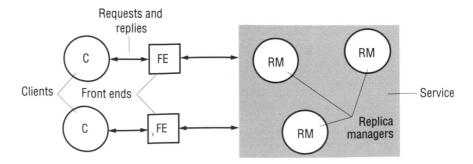

Figure 11.4 The gossip architecture.

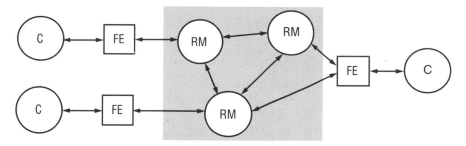

Front ends may communicate with different replica managers.

In different models the front end communicates either with only a single replica manager per operation or with several or all of them. Furthermore, the front end may collate the results of requests performed at more than one replica manager. For example, if a fault tolerant service is being provided, the front end may be used to request values from all replica managers, and to select values returned by a majority to be passed back to the client, in case one or more of them is faulty (see Section 15.3).

If the clients and replica managers are separate processes, the model approximates what we shall call the **gossip architecture** for highly available data [Ladin *et al.* 1992]. We choose this name because the replica managers exchange 'gossip' messages periodically in order to convey the updates (the 'news') they have each received (Figure 11.4). In the gossip architecture, the front end normally communicates with an individual replica manager for each operation (hence the need for exchanging gossip messages); alternatively, it can communicate directly with more than one replica manager per operation. The gossip architecture does not define whether front ends are separate to client processes. Section 11.4 describes the gossip architecture in full.

In the **primary copy** model of data replication for enhanced availability (Figure 11.5), all front ends communicate with the same 'primary' server when updating a particular data item. The primary server propagates the updates to the other servers, called 'slaves'. Front ends may read the item from a slave. If the primary server fails,

Figure 11.5 The primary copy model for replicated data.

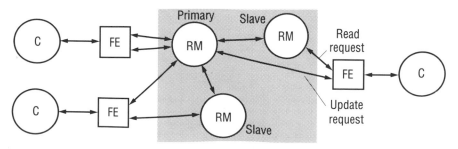

The primary server is accessed for all update requests. It propagates updates to its slaves.

one of the slaves can be promoted to act as the primary. The primary copy model is used in the Harp replicated file system [Liskov *et al*. 1991]. In the Sun Network Information Service (formerly Yellow Pages), information such as password entries which is changed relatively infrequently is updated at a master server and propagated from there to slave servers. Front ends may communicate with either a master or a slave server to retrieve information. In this case, however, front ends may not request updates: updates are made to the master's files.

At the other extreme, an architecture for a shared editor is shown in Figure 11.6. Users at different computers can use the editor to, for example, design a document. (This and other forms of software for multi-user collaboration, called *groupware*, are discussed by Ellis *et al*. [1991].) Each executing instance of the editor program holds a replica of the overall document state. There is only one class of process, and it has to perform the roles of client and replica manager. Additionally, a front end module may be used to hide replication from other modules within the process that access the shared document state.

In between these cases, there lies an architecture in which front ends and replica managers are combined, but are separate from clients. In distributed shared virtual memory implementations, for example, clients read and write data values from and to local variables, and the local kernel acts as a combined front end and replica manager. Processes programmed using the Orca distributed programming language [Bal *et al*. 1990] access shared objects. The Orca run-time system, one copy of which executes at each computer, plays the combined roles of front-end and replica manager.

The role of propagating updates to all replica managers is divided differently between the replica managers and front ends in different architectures. The choice of one pattern of communication rather than another is determined by the requirements for availability, consistency and response times. If high availability is to be achieved, for example, the front end cannot rely upon a particular replica manager since it might fail. For good response times, the front end should contact as few replica managers as are required to ensure consistency before returning a result to the client. In general, the most suitable architecture has to be chosen on the basis of the application requirements.

Figure 11.6   The architecture of a multi-user editor.

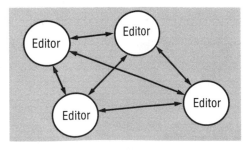

Each circle is a combined client, front end and replica manager (one per user).

11.3 Consistency and request ordering

Section 11.1 described a simple asynchronous communication model in which updates are eventually processed at all replicas, but in no particular order. It also gave a simple synchronous model in which updates are processed at all replica managers, and are processed everywhere in the same, total order. This section motivates some application-level consistency requirements and shows how they lead to ordering constraints for processing requests at different replica managers. The chief orderings considered are total and causal orderings.

It is assumed that a replica manager processes requests one at a time. If it is multi-threaded then it can carry out requests concurrently; but nonetheless we require that their combined execution is equivalent to processing one at a time. (Section 12.4 discusses this concept of *serial equivalence*.) Moreover, each replica manager is assumed to be a *state machine*. That is, the data items managed by a replica have values which are only a function of their initial values and the operations applied to them. Other stimuli, such as the passage of time or the readings of attached sensors, have no bearing on these values [Schneider 1990].

The order in which requests are processed at different replicas is an important issue, not only because it is often necessary that particular ordering constraints are obeyed for correctness, but also because meeting ordering requirements carries certain expenses. First, the processing of a request may be delayed because a 'prior' request has yet to be processed. Secondly, as will be described below, protocols designed to guarantee a particular ordering can be expensive to implement in terms of the number of rounds of messages that have to be transmitted.

Therefore it is advisable to avoid request ordering wherever possible. In general, not all pairs of requests have to be processed in a particular order. Requests r_1 and r_2 whose effect when consecutively processed in the opposite orders $r_1;r_2$ and $r_2;r_1$ is the same are said to *commute*. For example, any two read-only operations commute; and any two operations that do not perform reads but write distinct data commute. A system for managing replicated data may be able to use knowledge of commutativity in order to avoid the expense of request ordering.

Total and causal ordering requirements □ A requirement for total ordering is exemplified by the bulletin board system, where it would be convenient if replica managers could label items with the same numbers so that users could unambiguously refer to them. The cost of achieving total ordering is liable to be prohibitive, however, over a wide area network.

As a second example, consider a multi-user document editor, in which users at different computers may attempt to select an object on the screen such as a word at more or less the same time, in order to change it. The global state of the application is stored and displayed at each computer. The requirement when selecting an object is for total ordering, since one of the conflicting users must be consistently chosen to have selected the item before the other.

Formally, under totally ordered request processing, if r_1 and r_2 are requests then either r_1 is processed before r_2 at all replica managers or r_2 is processed before r_1 at all replica managers. Total ordering is a general relation over events in a distributed system, which Section 4.4 introduced in the case of multicast message delivery.

Figure 11.7   Totally and causally ordered request processing.

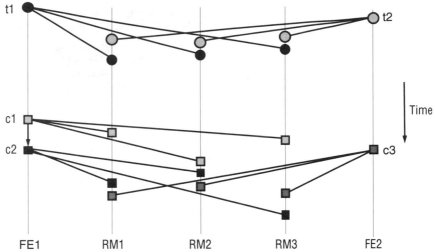

Notice the consistent ordering of *t1* and *t2*, the consistent ordering of the causally related operations *c1* and *c2*, and the arbitrary relative ordering of *c2* and *c3*, which are unrelated.

Causal ordering for request processing is defined according to the general notion of causal ordering – also known as *happened-before* ordering (see Section 10.3). Recall that this ordering captures a potential causal relationship between two events: one event *happened-before* another if information flowed, in part as messages and in part as the sequential actions of individual processes, between the two events. Causal ordering was first applied to request processing by Birman and Joseph [1987]. The bulletin board system exemplifies the requirement for causal ordering, since when an item refers to another item, the posting of the latter clearly *happened-before* the posting of the former, and so should appear before the other. Formally, under causal ordering, if r_1 and r_2 are requests and r_1 *happened-before* r_2, then r_1 is processed before r_2 at all replica managers.

Figure 11.7 illustrates the processing at three replica managers *RM1*, *RM2* and *RM3* of totally ordered requests *t1* and *t2* and causally ordered requests *c1*, *c2* and *c3* originating at two front ends *FE1* and *FE2*. Because *c1 happened-before c2*, the corresponding requests are processed in the same order; but *c3* is unrelated to either *c1* or *c2*, and their relative orderings are mixed.

Note that total ordering is not necessarily also causal ordering. For example, two related items could be consistently ordered across all bulletin board replicas, but in the opposite order to their causal relationship.

Stronger ordering requirements □ Consider a system in which some requests are totally ordered and others are causally ordered. It is sometimes convenient to employ a third, stronger level of ordering which we shall call **sync-ordering**. A sync-ordered request forces the order of requests processed at replica managers to be 'in sync', in the

Figure 11.8   Sync-ordered, totally ordered and causally ordered request processing.

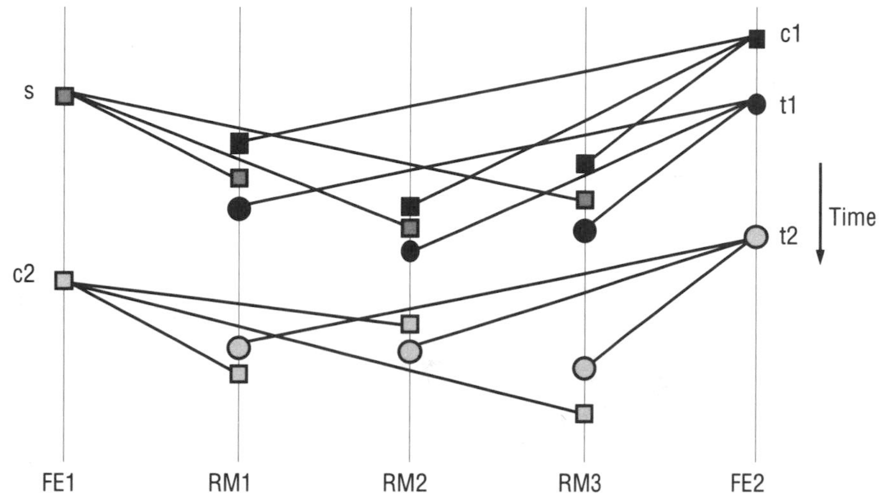

Notice the consistent ordering between *s* and *c1* and *t1*, and the arbitrary relative ordering of *c2* and *t2*.

sense that every other request is consistently processed before it or after it at all of them. Sync-ordering is needed because a causally ordered request and a totally ordered request can be processed in an arbitrary order, unless they are causally related. A sync-ordered request effectively flushes any outstanding requests that have been issued but not yet processed everywhere, so that they are processed before it; all later requests are processed after it. It thus draws a conceptual line across the system, dividing all request processing consistently into a 'past' and a 'future'. Formally, if r_1 and r_2 are requests and r_1 is sync-ordered, then either r_1 is processed before r_2 at all replica managers or r_2 is processed before r_1 at all replica managers *regardless of the declared ordering of r_2* (causal, total or sync).

Figure 11.8 illustrates these ordering properties at replica managers *RM1*, *RM2* and *RM3* for causally ordered requests *c1* and *c2*, totally ordered requests *t1* and *t2*, and sync-ordered request *s*, issued by front ends *FE1* and *FE2*.

Implementing request ordering □ Several algorithms exist for implementing total and causal ordering. Before describing some of these, two remarks about the basic techniques involved are appropriate. The first is that *hold-back* is used. In terms of our general replication model, a received request is not processed by a replica manager until ordering constraints can be met – that is, it is held back. To give the familiar example, a bulletin board item *Re:Microkernels* may be held back until an item concerning *Microkernels* has already appeared.

A request message is said to be *stable at a replica manager* if all prior requests (defined according to the type of ordering) have been processed – that is, if it is ready to be processed next. Schneider defines this concept in [Schneider 1990]. Figure 11.9 shows incoming requests being placed initially on a *hold-back queue*, where they remain

Figure 11.9   Ordering the requests arriving at a replica manager.

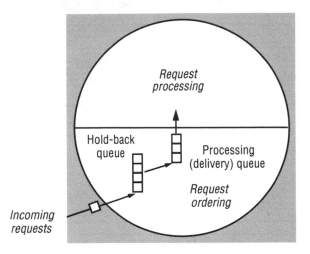

until their order has been determined; when stable, they are placed on a *processing* (or *delivery*) *queue*, from which they are extracted and processed in FIFO order.

Two properties need to be proved, in general, for implementations of request ordering. The *safety* property is that no message will be delivered out of order by being transferred from the hold-back queue to the delivery queue prematurely. That is, the implementation must guarantee that once a request has (potentially) been processed, it is impossible for a 'prior' request to arrive. The *liveness* property is that no message should wait on the hold-back queue indefinitely. An incorrect implementation might await some 'prior' request that will never in fact arrive, and so will never transfer an existing request to the delivery queue.

A second general point concerning the implementation of ordered request processing is that techniques for achieving it are applicable, with appropriate adjustments, to the implementation of ordered multicast. Both the gossip architecture and the ISIS distributed programming toolkit, described below, provide facilities for total and causal request ordering. The basic difference between their approaches is that ISIS provides an ordered multicast facility for delivering requests to replica managers and achieving ordering at the same time, whereas the gossip architecture utilizes unordered point-to-point communication normally, but provides for the replica managers themselves to propagate updates among themselves and to order their processing. This difference is examined in detail below.

Implementing total ordering ☐ Consider the problem of totally ordering requests sent from sites running front ends, 'FE sites', for processing by replica managers at 'RM sites'. The basic approach to implementing total ordering is to assign totally ordered identifiers to requests so that each RM site makes the same ordering decision based upon these identifiers.

We discuss two main methods for assigning identifiers to requests. The first of these is for a process called a **sequencer** to be used to assign them. All requests are sent

Figure 11.10   The ISIS algorithm for total ordering.

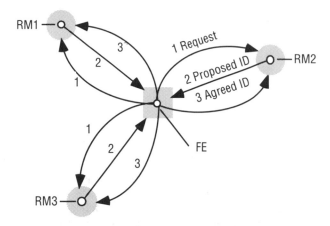

to the sequencer as well as to the RM sites. The sequencer assigns consecutive increasing identifiers to requests as it receives them, and forwards the assigned identifiers to the RM sites. Requests arriving at an RM site are held back until they are next in sequence.

Ideally, the generation of request identifiers is integrated with the transmission of requests to replica managers, to minimize the total number of messages involved. For example, each request can be sent first to the sequencer, which increments its sequence count, attaches this to the request and forwards it to the replica managers. The obvious problem with such a scheme is that the sequencer may become a bottleneck and is a critical point of failure. Nonetheless, practical algorithms exist that address the problem of failure. Chang and Maxemchuk [1984] first suggested a multicast protocol employing a sequencer (which they called a *token site*), and the sequencer-based protocol used in the Amoeba system is discussed in detail in Chapter 18.

The second method for achieving totally ordered request processing avoids the need for a sequencer; it achieves distributed agreement in assigning request identifiers. A simple algorithm – similar to one which was originally developed to implement totally ordered multicast delivery for the ISIS toolkit [Birman and Joseph 1987] – is shown in Figure 11.10. RM sites propose identifiers for requests as they arrive and return these to the corresponding FE sites, which use them to generate final identifiers.

Each RM site stores F_{max}, the largest final identifier agreed so far and P_{max}, its own largest proposed identifier. The algorithm for identifier generation and stability testing proceeds as follows.

1. The FE site sends the request bearing a temporary identifier to all RM sites. The temporary identifier is chosen to be larger than any identifier used previously by the FE site.

2. Each RM site replies; site i responds with a proposal for the request's final identifier of $Max(F_{max}, P_{max}) + 1 + i/N$, where N is the number of RM sites. Each RM site provisionally assigns the proposed identifier to the request and places it on its hold-back queue, which is ordered with the *smallest* request identifier at the

front. The FE site collects all the proposed identifiers and selects the largest one as the next agreed identifier. This is guaranteed to be unique, because of the term i/N in the formula for proposed identifiers.

3. The FE site then notifies all the RM sites of the final identifier. The RM sites attach the final identifier to the request. The request is then reordered on the hold-back queue at sites where the final identifier differs from the proposed identifier assigned in Step 1. When the request at the front of the hold-back queue has been assigned its final identifier, it is stable and is transferred to the tail of the delivery queue. Requests that have been assigned their final identifier but are not at the head of the hold-back queue are not yet transferred, however.

It is easy to see that the liveness property holds for this algorithm, as long as failures do not occur. Every request will eventually be assigned a final identifier and reach the front of the hold-back queue, to be transferred to the delivery queue. (Recall that new requests are assigned increasing proposed identifiers, so a finalized request cannot continually be pre-empted by candidate requests with smaller identifiers.)

To see that the algorithm has the safety property, assume that a request r_1 has been assigned a final identifier and has reached the front of the hold-back queue. Let r_2 be any other request on the same queue that has not yet been assigned its final identifier. We have that:

$$finalId(r_2) \geq proposedId(r_2)$$

by the algorithm just given. Since r_1 is at the front of the queue:

$$proposedId(r_2) > finalId(r_1).$$

Therefore:

$$finalId(r_2) > finalId(r_1),$$

and the safety property is assured.

This algorithm has the advantage that it is relatively straightforward to implement. Unlike a protocol based upon a single sequencer, there is no bottleneck or single point of failure for transmitting messages. Also, the protocol can be adapted so that if an FE site fails while it is engaged in distributing a request, one of the RM sites can detect this and take over co-ordination in its place. But the algorithm is expensive. Three messages are sent between the front end and each replica manager before a request can become stable. Even if hardware broadcast is used to transmit the request initially, the cost can be prohibitive. It is shown below that a sequencer-based protocol can be made cheaper in terms of the numbers of messages sent.

Note that the total ordering chosen by this algorithm is *not* also causal: even if one multicast *happened-before* another, the two messages are delivered in an essentially arbitrary total order, which could conflict with potential causality.

For a third approach to implementing total ordering, see [Garcia-Molina and Spauster 1991].

Implementing causal ordering with vector timestamps □ Consider the example of a bulletin board system with replica managers implemented at three universities. The front ends usually post and receive items by communicating only with their local replica manager, but they are free to communicate with the others. They might do this, for example, if their local replica manager becomes heavily loaded or unavailable for some reason. The consistency problem to be addressed is that no item that refers to another can be posted before the item to which it refers – that is, that items are to be posted in causal order, despite the out-of-order arrival of items from front ends and from peer replica managers.

The problem of achieving causal ordering can be solved through the use of suitable ordered identifiers called *vector timestamps*, which will shortly be defined. The reader may recall the integer logical timestamps introduced in Section 10.3, which are used to timestamp general events in accordance with their causal relationships. At first sight it might seem that these could be used to timestamp the bulletin board replicas and the requests issued by front ends, so as to order request processing causally. Unfortunately these timestamps are unsuitable because no deductions can be made about causal ordering from comparing them. What is required are timestamps (used as identifiers) that carry more information and can be compared to determine causal ordering.

For the sake of simplicity it is assumed that bulletin board items are never removed, and so a bulletin board is updated only by the addition of new items. In fact, however, it is not necessary to consider the details of this application-specific state in order to compare the *versions* or *timestamps* of it held by different replica managers. The timestamp of a bulletin board replica can be represented by counts of the update events that led to the current state. Some update events occur when a front end makes a request directly to the replica manager; other updates are forwarded from its peers. The timestamp of the bulletin board can be represented by a list of counts of update events, one for each of the replica managers. Such an array of event counts is called a **vector timestamp** or a *multipart timestamp*.

Vector timestamps are similar to the Coda version vectors used in the management of replicated data in the Coda file system (see Section 8.4). They were originally used in timestamped database concurrency control [Fischer and Michael 1982, Wuu and Bernstein 1984] and the file system of the Locus distributed operating system [Walker *et al.* 1983]. More recently, their use in event ordering was developed by Fidge [1988], Mattern [1988] and Schiper *et al.* [1989]. Their role in the gossip architecture and in the ISIS causal multicast protocol is described in the next two sections.

For example, suppose that, as shown in Figure 11.11, replica manager *RM1* has processed three new items sent to it directly by front ends, four items forwarded from *RM2* and four from *RM3*. The state of the replica at *RM1* can be represented by the vector timestamp (3,4,4). Similarly, the replica held by *RM2* in the figure has timestamp (2,5,6) and that of *RM3* has timestamp (3,3,7).

In order to maintain causal ordering it is necessary to ensure that each front end reads from a version of the bulletin board that is at least as advanced as the version from which it last read (which may have been from a different replica manager); furthermore, a new item should be added to a replica only when the replica already reflects all causally prior updates. These two goals can be met if the replica managers maintain their

Figure 11.11   The versions of bulletin boards held by three resource managers.

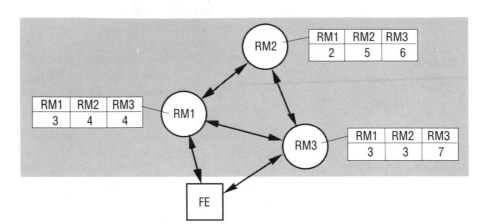

own timestamp representing their version of the bulletin board, and if the front ends maintain vector timestamps reflecting the latest version of the bulletin board they have read.

Let us suppose that the front end in our example has a timestamp (2,3,4), and then reads the latest items from *RM1*. The timestamp of *RM1* is (3,4,4), and the front end's timestamp should be updated to reflect the latest items seen, that is, to (3,4,4). This is a case of *merging* vector timestamps: of choosing the largest values from the two vectors, component-wise. The front end should not be returned data from *RM2* at this stage since by comparing timestamps it can be seen that *RM2* has not seen one of the updates accepted at *RM1* and seen by the front end. Similarly, an update from this front end should not be incorporated at *RM3* at this stage, since the front end has seen four updates originally accepted at *RM2*, whereas *RM3* contains only the first three.

The use of vector timestamps will be fully described in the context of the gossip architecture in the next section. In preparation for that some more formal and general definitions are now given. Let the set of processes (for example, replica managers) being considered be $p_1, p_2, .., p_n$. We shall define, for each p_i, a vector clock whose timestamp reading we denote by VT_i. Each VT_i is a vector of integer values, of length n. The value $VT_i[k]$ represents a count of events (for example, updates to replicas) that have occurred at p_k and that are known at p_i, either because they originate there or because their existence is known about through message passing.

The following is the vector clock update algorithm:

1. All processes p_i initialize VT_i to zeroes.

2. When p_i generates a new event (for example, a new version of its data), it increments $VT_i[i]$ by 1; it piggybacks the value $vt = VT_i$ on the messages it sends.

3. When p_j processes a request bearing a timestamp vt, it updates its vector clock as follows:

$$VT_j := merge(VT_j, vt).$$

The *merge* operation is defined for any pair of vector timestamps u, v as:

$$merge(u, v)[k] = \max(u[k], v[k]), \text{ for } k = 1, 2, .., n.$$

Partial orders '$\leq$' and '$<$' on vector timestamps u, v are defined as follows:

$$u \leq v \; iff \; u[k] \leq v[k], \text{ for } k = 1, 2, .., n. \; u < v \; iff \; u \leq v \text{ and } u \neq v.$$

If e, f are events and u, v are their timestamps, it can be shown that $u \leq v$ if and only if e *happened-before f*. The reader is referred to Raynal [1992] for a general treatment of vector timestamps.

11.4 The gossip architecture

Ladin *et al.* [1992] developed what we have termed the gossip architecture (see Figure 11.4) as a framework for making highly available service implementations through use of replication. It is based upon earlier work on databases by Fischer and Michael [1982] and Wuu and Bernstein [1984]. It has been applied to such areas as distributed garbage detection and deadlock detection, and could be used, for example, to create a highly available electronic mail service or bulletin board service. The presentation given here omits certain aspects of the gossip architecture, in the interests of clarity.

High availability implies that a service remains accessible despite some computer or network failures; it is also desirable to maintain reasonable response times despite heavy load. In the gossip architecture, clients request service operations which are processed initially by a front end (there is a front end for every computer with clients). The front ends normally communicate with only a single replica manager at a time, although they are free to communicate with others. In particular, a front end will communicate with a different replica manager when the one it normally uses fails or becomes unreachable, and it may try one or more others if the normal manager is heavily loaded. The replica managers update one another by exchanging *gossip messages* which contain the most recent updates they have received. They are said to update one another in a *lazy* fashion, in that gossip messages may be exchanged only occasionally, after several updates have been collected, or when a replica manager finds out that it is missing an update sent to one of its peers, which it needs to process a request.

The gossip architecture supports three different strengths of update ordering: *causal, forced* (total and causal) and *immediate* (sync-ordered). The choice of which to use is left to the application designer, and reflects a trade-off between consistency and operation costs. Causal updates are considerably less costly than the others, and are expected to be used whenever possible.

Operations and ordering □ One of the three orderings *causal, forced* or *immediate* has to be specified for each type of update operation, and the system automatically enforces it. Updates are normally applied in a causal (but not total) order. This is the least expensive ordering in terms of latency, and it allows operations to be applied to a replica that is not the most up to date, as long as causality is respected. Forced ordering is causal and total. Immediate ordering is what we have described as sync-ordering: it

Figure 11.12   Query and update operations in gossip.

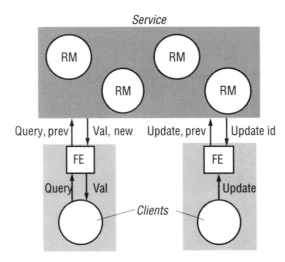

forces an operation to be applied in a consistent order relative to any other operation at all replica managers, whether the other operation be specified as causal, forced or immediate. Note that queries, which can be satisfied by any single replica manager, are always executed in causal order with respect to other operations.

In the electronic bulletin board example, causal ordering could be used for posting items. Forced ordering would be used for adding a new subscriber to a bulletin board, so that if several uncoordinated clients attempt to add the user at more or less the same time, only one will succeed (instead of several entries being created with the same name). Immediate ordering would be used for subtracting a user from a subscription list, so that messages could not be retrieved by that user via some tardy replica manager, once the deletion operation had returned.

The front end in a replicated service is application-specific, since it has to handle client operations. In general, client operations can either read the replicated state, modify it or both. Inside a gossip implementation, however, only two basic types of operation are recognized: *queries* are read-only operations, and *updates* modify but do not read the state (the latter is a more restricted definition than the one we have been using). The front end can convert an operation that both reads and modifies the replicated state into a separate update and query.

Clients are blocked on query operations, since they must wait for a value to be returned to the front end by a replica manager (see Figure 11.12). The default arrangement for update operations, on the other hand, is to return to the client as soon as the operation has been passed to the front end; the front end then propagates the operation in the background. Alternatively, for increased reliability, clients may be prevented from continuing until the update has been delivered to $k+1$ replica managers, and so will be delivered everywhere despite up to k failures.

In order to control the ordering of operation processing, each front end keeps a vector timestamp which reflects the version of the latest values accessed by the front end

Figure 11.13 Front ends propagate their timestamps whenever clients communicate directly.

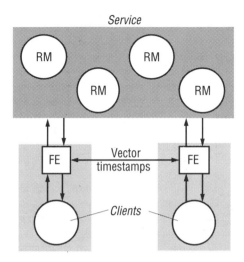

(and therefore accessed by the client). This timestamp, denoted *prev* in Figure 11.12, is sent in every request message from the front end to a replica manager, together with a description of the query or update operation itself. When a value is returned as a result of a query operation, a new timestamp (*new* in Figure 11.12) is also returned, since the replica may have been updated since the last call. Similarly, an update operation returns a vector timestamp (*update id* in Figure 11.12) which is unique to the update. Each returned timestamp is merged with the front end's previous timestamp, to record the version of the replicated data that has been seen by the client.

Clients exchange information in two ways. The first is by accessing the same replicated services. Systems based on the gossip architecture are expected to test for the *happened-before* relationship between operations and respect the ordering implied by this. Secondly, clients are assumed to communicate directly (or via other services). Since this latter communication can also lead to causal relationships between operations applied to the replicated service, it must occur via the clients' front ends. That way, the front ends can piggy-back their vector timestamps on client messages. The recipients merge them with their own timestamps in order that causal relationships can be correctly inferred. The situation is shown in Figure 11.13.

Replica manager state □ Regardless of the application, a replica manager contains the following main state components (Figure 11.14), which are kept in main memory:

Value: This is the value of the application state as maintained by the replica manager. Each replica manager is a state machine, which begins with a specified initial value, which is thereafter solely the result of applying update operations to that state.

Value timestamp: This is the timestamp that represents the updates that are reflected in the value. It is updated whenever an update operation is applied to the value.

Figure 11.14 A gossip replica manager, showing its main state components.

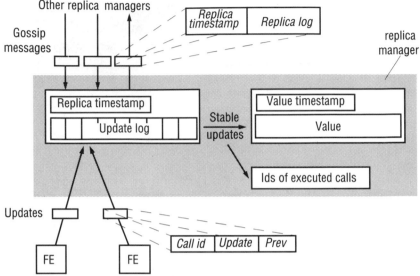

Update log: All update operations are recorded in this log as soon as they are received. A replica manager keeps updates in a log for one of two reasons. The first is that the replica manager cannot yet apply the update because it is not yet stable: that is, it must be held back and not processed yet. The second is that, even though an update has become stable and has been applied to the value, the replica manager has not received confirmation that this update has been received at all other replica managers. In the interests of high availability, it can in the meantime supply the update to those peers that require it.

Replica timestamp: This timestamp represents those updates that have been accepted by the replica manager – that is, placed in the manager's log. It differs from the value timestamp in general, of course, because not all updates in the log are stable.

Identifiers of executed calls: The same update potentially can arrive at a given replica manager from a front end and in gossip messages from other replica managers. To prevent an update from being performed twice, a list is kept of the identifiers of updates that have been applied to the value. The replica managers check this list before executing a stable update.

The replica managers are numbered 1,2,3, .. and the ith element of a vector timestamp held by replica manager i corresponds to the number of updates received from front ends by i; and the jth component ($j \neq i$) equals the number of updates received by j and propagated to i in gossip messages. So, for example, in a three-manager gossip system a value timestamp of (2,4,5) at manager 1 would represent the fact that the value there reflects the first two updates accepted from front ends at manager 1, the first four at manager 2 and the first five at manager 3. The following looks in more detail at how the timestamps are used to effect ordering.

Processing query operations □ The simplest operation to consider is that of a query. Recall that a query request q contains a description of the operation and a timestamp $q.prev$ sent by the front end. The latter reflects the latest version of the value that the front end has read or submitted as an update. Therefore the task of the replica manager is to return a value that is at least as recent as this. If $valueTS$ is the replica's value timestamp, then q can be applied to the replica's value if:

$$q.prev \leq valueTS.$$

The replica manager keeps q on a list of pending query operations (that is, a hold-back queue) until this condition is fulfilled. It can either await the missing updates, which should eventually arrive in gossip messages; or, it can request the updates from the replica managers concerned. For example, if $valueTS$ is (2,5,5) and $q.prev$ is (2,4,6), it can be seen that just one update is missing – from replica manager 3. (The front end that submitted q must have contacted a different replica manager previously for it to have seen this update, which the replica manager has not seen.)

Once the query can be applied, the replica manager returns $valueTS$ to the front end as the timestamp new shown in Figure 11.12. The front end then merges this with its timestamp: $frontEndTS := merge(frontEndTS, new)$. The update at replica manager 2 that can be seen missing in $q.prev$ in the example is reflected in the value returned, and this is shown in the update to $frontEndTS$.

Processing update operations in causal order □ When a replica manager receives an update request it increments its own element in its replica timestamp by one, to keep count of the number of updates it has received directly from front ends. Then the update request u is assigned a unique identifier (a vector timestamp whose derivation is given shortly) and a record for the update is placed in the replica manager's log. If $u.op$ is the update operation, $u.prev$ is the timestamp sent with it by the front end and TS is the unique identifying timestamp assigned to the update, then the log record is constructed as the following tuple:

$$logRecord := <TS, u.op, u.prev>.$$

The identifier TS is derived from $u.prev$ by replacing its ith element by that of the replica timestamp, where i is the replica manager that receives the update from the front end. This action makes TS unique. The remaining elements in TS are copied from $u.prev$, since it is these values sent by the front end which must be used to determine when the update is stable. TS is immediately passed back to the front end, which merges it with its existing timestamp. Note that a front end can submit its update to several replica managers, and receive different unique identifier timestamps in return, all of which have to be merged into its timestamp.

The stability condition for an update u is similar to that for queries:

$$u.prev \leq valueTS.$$

Expressed informally, this condition states that all the updates on which this update depends have already been applied to the value. If this condition is not met at the time the update is submitted, it will be checked again when gossip messages arrive. When the condition has been met for an update record r, the replica manager checks to see whether the call identifier $r.cid$ (contained in $r.op$) appears already in the list of identifiers of executed calls. If not, the update is applied to the value and its timestamp and the executed call list *executed* are updated:

$$value := apply(value, r.op)$$
$$valueTS := merge(valueTS, r.ts)$$
$$executed := executed \cup \{r.cid\}.$$

The first of these three statements represents the application of the update to the value. In the second statement, the update's timestamp is merged with that of the value. In the third, the update's call identifier is added to the set of identifiers of calls that have been executed – which is used to check for repeated operation requests.

Gossip messages □ Gossip messages are sent by replica managers to assist other replica managers to bring their state up to date. Gossip messages normally contain information concerning several updates. The gossip architecture does not specify in general when gossip messages are exchanged. Since gossip travels in both directions between pairs of replica managers there is no need for each message to be separately acknowledged unless timeliness constraints require that missed updates are detected within a certain interval.

A gossip message m consists of two items sent by a replica manager: its log $m.log$ and its replica timestamp $m.ts$ (see Figure 11.14). The replica manager that receives it has three main tasks:

- to merge the arriving log with its own (it may contain updates not seen by the receiver before);

- to apply any updates that have become stable and have not been executed before (stable updates in the arrived log may in turn make pending updates become stable);

- to eliminate records from the log and entries in the list of executed call identifiers when it is known that the updates have been applied everywhere, and for which therefore there is no danger of repeats. Clearing redundant entries from the log and from the list of executed call identifiers is an important task since they would otherwise grow without limit, but there is insufficient space to describe here how this is achieved. Full details are given by Ladin *et al.* [1992].

Merging the log contained in an arrived gossip message with the receiver's log is straightforward. Let *valueTS* denote the recipient's value timestamp. A record r in $m.log$ is added to the receiver's log unless either it is already in it or $r.ts \leq valueTS$. If $r.ts \leq valueTS$, the update is already reflected in the value but the original record has been discarded from the log. The replica manager merges the timestamp of the incoming gossip message with its own replica timestamp *replicaTS*, so that it corresponds to the additions to the log:

$$replicaTS := merge(replicaTS, m.ts).$$

When new update records have been merged into the log, the replica manager collects the set S of any updates in the log that are now stable. These can be applied to the value, but care must be taken over the order in which they are applied, so that the *happened-before* relation is observed. That is, each $r \in S$ is applied only when there is no $s \in S$ such that $s.prev < r.prev$. All updates in the set are applied while following this rule (the set can first be ordered according to the partial order '$\leq$').

Processing forced and immediate update operations □ Forced and immediate updates require special treatment. Recall that forced updates are totally as well as causally ordered. The basic method for ordering forced updates is for a unique sequence number to be appended to the timestamps associated with them, and to process them in order of this sequence number. As explained above, a general method for generating sequence numbers is to use a single sequencer process. But reliance upon a single process is of course inadequate in the context of a highly available service. The solution is to designate a so-called *primary replica manager* as the sequencer at any one time, but to ensure that another replica manager can be elected to take over consistently as the sequencer, should the primary fail. What is required is for a majority of replica managers (including the primary) to record which update is next in sequence before the operation can be applied. Then, as long as a majority of replica managers survive failure, this ordering decision will be honoured by a new primary elected from among the surviving replica managers.

Immediate updates are sync-ordered. They can easily be ordered with respect to forced updates by using the primary replica manager to order them in this sequence. The primary also determines which causal updates are deemed to have preceded an immediate update. It does this by communicating and synchronizing with the other replica managers in order to reach agreement on this. There is insufficient space to cover the details of implementing forced and immediate updates here.

Some optimizations □ Optimizations can be applied to gossip traffic to lessen the size and number of messages. For example, replica managers can note which updates are recorded as having been received by their peers, so as not to send them updates that they have already received.

In addition, communication between the front end and a replica manager can be made more efficient by using a stream connection instead of a request-reply protocol, as long as the replica manager is the one always used by the front end (except when a failure occurs). There is then no need for the front end to receive the identifiers of the updates it sends to the replica manager; the latter merely has to record these for the client. Moreover, unless communication from other clients takes place, there is no need for the front end to send its timestamp to the replica manager. Successive updates can be sent over the stream without blocking, and they can be batched before transmission, in order to save on the number of messages used.

Discussion □ The gossip architecture is aimed at achieving high availability for services. High availability can only be achieved if updates are propagated to more than one failure-independent computer in a timely fashion. For example, a client may cease to be able to obtain the bulletin board service because it depends on an update (that is, a bulletin board item) held by a single replica manager that has failed before sending the update in gossip to another replica manager.

The rate of flow of updates in gossip messages is left unspecified in order to allow this to be tuned to the application. The timeliness of gossip traffic can be important to an application even when no failures occur. Consider, for example, a multi-user document editor. Updates that affect several users should normally be propagated at once. But if a user has the privilege of working alone on some section of the document, then it may be acceptable for her updates to be batched and sent in occasional gossip. Consider, as a second example, our inter-university bulletin board system. It seems unnecessary for every item to be dispatched immediately to all universities. But what if gossip is only exchanged very rarely, say once a day? If only causal updates are used, then it is quite possible for clients at each university to have their own consistent debates over the same bulletin board, oblivious of the discussions at the other universities. Then at, say, midnight, all the debates will be merged; but debates on the same topic will likely be incongruous, when it would have been preferable for them to take account of one another.

The service implementor has the choice of sending requests to one replica manager (as is normally done) or to several of them, depending on load and failure conditions. This reflects different choices of trade-off between different types of latency and also network bandwidth. A request sent to just one replica manager after the previously used replica manager has failed may have to await the arrival of a gossip message before it can be processed. On the other hand, a read request sent to all replica managers may be satisfied by one of them immediately; but the other managers will waste time processing the request redundantly. Extra bandwidth is consumed if the request is sent point-to-point to these managers and extra communication latency is also incurred by the client. The gossip approach to update propagation is compared with the use of multicasts in the next section.

As the number of replica managers grows, so does the size of the timestamps used and the number of gossip messages that have to be transmitted. If a client makes a query, then this normally takes two messages (between front end and replica manager). If a client makes a causal update operation, and if each of the R replica managers normally collects G updates into a gossip message, then the number of messages exchanged is $2 + (R\text{-}1)/G$. The first term represents communication between the front end and replica manager, and the second is the update's share of a gossip message sent to the other replica managers. These expressions assume no piggy-backing of messages, and so are worst cases for the number of packets sent. The network bandwidth taken up by a large update of size U is approximately $U + (R\text{-}1)U$, that is, RU. The first term represents transmission from the front end to a replica manager, and the second represents transmission to the manager's peers.

One approach to making services scalable is to make most of the replicas read-only. In other words, these replicas are updated by gossip messages, but do not receive updates directly from front ends. This arrangement is potentially useful where the *update/query* ratio is small. Read-only replicas can be situated close to client groups, and updates can be serviced by relatively few central replica managers. Gossip traffic is reduced, since read-only replicas have no gossip to propagate. And vector timestamps need only contain entries for the updateable replicas.

11.5 Process groups and ISIS

A process group is a collection of processes that co-operate towards a common goal or that consume one or more common streams of information. Groups can be used to implement replicated services, to collect together clients that subscribe to information published by a service, or to implement self-contained distributed applications. Although the members of a group do not necessarily manage replicated data, the members of a group act together primarily by receiving and processing the same set of messages. Process groups, in other words, are destinations for multicast communication, and transmitting a message to all members of a process group is also known as *group communication*. Chapters 2 and 4 have already discussed multicast communication.

In addition to providing multicast communication, a group service allows process groups to be created and their membership to be changed dynamically. The V system [Cheriton and Zwaenepoel 1985] was the first system to include support for process groups. Currently, the principal example of a group service implementation is ISIS [Birman and Joseph 1987, Birman *et al.* 1991, Birman 1993], which provides a programming interface for process groups on top of UNIX. The following describes the common types of group structure and a simple programming interface for process groups; it goes on to examine the design issues concerning the relationship between multicast and group membership, before describing ISIS.

Group structure

Group structures are defined according to the pattern of communication in which the members of a group are involved. In a *peer group*, all communication is directed from processes within the group to the group. This structure is suitable for a collection of processes implementing a multi-user editor, for example (see Figure 11.6). The processes use the group service to multicast the updates made by users, and to include themselves in the group as users join the editing session. In some peer group models, multicast messages are not delivered to the sender. This is the case, for example, in the model of group communication assumed by the Psync protocol [Peterson *et al.* 1989]. However, in the editor example, delivering a multicast message to the sender may be necessary in order for it to observe the order in which multicasts are delivered.

There are several choices for the group structure when client processes are to make requests that are serviced by a collection of server processes. The simplest method is for the client to make an RPC to some member of a peer group, which uses group communication in implementing the service with its peers, and then replies to the RPC. Alternatively, the client can multicast its requests to a *server group*. All members of the server group receive the request. In simple cases, only one need reply. The process that replies can be chosen on the basis of information known to all members of the group. For example, the oldest surviving member of the group can reply if they are equivalent. Or, if service information is partitioned between the servers, only the server that contains the requisite data processes the request and replies. Alternatively, to achieve rapid response in case a server fails, two or more processes could each process and reply to each request.

Figure 11.15   Two client-server groups.

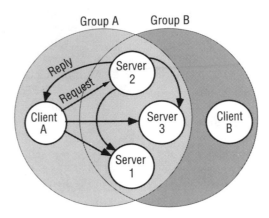

Client A sends a request to Group A, which is processed by Server 2; the reply is multicast to all of the members of the group.

Yet another variation on this model, used in ISIS and shown in Figure 11.15, is the *client-server group*. Here, requests from clients are multicast to all members of a server group, but the server that processes the request from a particular client multicasts the reply to the client-server group, which contains all the server group members plus the client itself. There is one client-server group for each client, so that ISIS has to support many overlapping groups for each service. In this structure, the other servers are able to update their state according to the results returned. In the virtually synchronous execution environment provided by ISIS (described below), if the server that processes requests fails before it can reply, then the other servers in the group will be informed of this and can elect one of their number to reply instead.

A *subscription group* is a group of processes that are sent the same information from an information source. The members of a subscription group do not reply to the messages they receive and they process the published information in their own independent, application-specific ways. For example, brokers dealing on a trading room floor require access to financial information as it arrives from several sources. To realize this, the broker's workstation executes one or more processes that are members of the subscription groups corresponding to the different sources of information required. Central computers gather the data and multicast them to these groups. A set of related servers may also be included in a subscription group, because of dependencies between the information that they each publish. Subscription groups are called *diffusion groups* in ISIS.

To avoid the overheads associated with the management of very large groups, groups can be composed into *hierarchical groups*. For example, a large group can be divided into sub-groups, and one member of each sub-group joins a root group. A process whose information must reach all members multicasts it to the root group, and the members of this group then multicast the information to the sub-groups. This principle can be extended to sub-groups of sub-groups. The advantages gained by

Figure 11.16   Services provided for process groups.

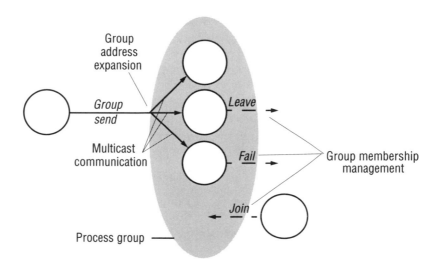

hierarchical groups are the smaller vector timestamps needed for causal ordering, and the fact that communication within separate sub-groups can take place in parallel. Against this there is the increase in latency introduced by causing multicasts to traverse two or more groups.

Finally, group organizations differ as to whether group membership is visible to their members. In a subscription group, group members normally do not need to be aware of their peers. A member process in a server group or peer group, however, often needs to be aware of the membership of the group. For example, if the service provided by a group is reliable, then existing members may need to create a further member when the membership drops below a specified minimum number.

Group services

A system-wide service provides support for process groups. The members of a process group can be distributed across any collection of computers, interconnected by WANs or LANs. As shown in Figure 11.16, an implementation of process groups provides, in general, three main, strongly inter-related, group services: the management of group membership, group address expansion and multicast communication.

Group membership management □ This service provides operations to create and change the membership of groups. Groups, it is assumed, are named by globally unique group identifiers. A group identifier is returned when a new group is created; and the group identifier must be supplied when a process joins or leaves a group. In their simplest form, these group operations are as in Figure 11.17.

Processes may also be removed from a group's membership as a result of failures. The group membership service monitors the group's current membership, recording changes

Figure 11.17   Group operations.

PROCEDURE groupCreate(): groupId
   creates a group consisting of the calling process and returns the group's identifier;

PROCEDURE groupJoin(group: groupId)
   adds the caller to the group membership;

PROCEDURE groupLeave(group: groupId)
   removes the caller from the group.

---

caused either by the above operations or through fail-stop failure. The membership service supplies on request a list of current members for a given group. It also sends messages to interested processes when group membership changes occur, giving them an up-to-date membership list. For example, the members of a group are often interested in changes in their membership.

A process can belong to several groups simultaneously. In a variation on the model described here, processes do not themselves belong to groups. Rather, they possess ports which they insert individually in groups. It is convenient to manage the reception of messages sent to distinct groups, by placing different ports in different groups. The Chorus distributed operating system provides port groups [Rozier *et al.* 1988], although it provides only low-level group communication.

Group address expansion □   A process sending a message to the members of a group does not supply a list of the processes involved. Instead, it supplies a group identifier, which is the same as the group identifier returned by *groupCreate*. The group identifier is mapped onto a current membership list as part of the group communication implementation, which in turn uses the group membership service. This facility hides the group's internal structure from processes that do not need to know it.

The use of group identifiers enables the implementation to synchronize message delivery with changes in the group membership. The expansion of a group identifier into a list of current members could be implemented as a simple request to the group membership service. The resultant list could be passed to the multicast service to transmit the message. But what should happen if a membership change occurs while a multicast is in progress? As the description of virtual synchrony explains below, some applications require that messages are delivered to group members in a consistent order relative to messages informing them about changes in the group state.

If, instead of using a group identifier, processes transmitted messages to a group by explicitly listing the members, then communication would be required with all group senders whenever the membership changed, and synchronization with group membership change notifications would be very awkward to achieve.

Multicast communication □   As explained in Chapter 4, multicast communication semantics vary according to reliability guarantees and also according to message ordering guarantees. To recap, the main reliability guarantees that are found are:

Unreliable multicast: An attempt is made to transmit the message to all members without acknowledgement.

Reliable multicast: One that makes a best effort; however, the message might be delivered to some but not all group members.

Atomic multicast: A reliable multicast which guarantees that either all operational members of the group receive a message, or none of them do.

Reliability and atomicity do not of themselves imply any particular ordering of multicast message delivery. The four ordering semantics that are found in group implementations are: unordered, totally ordered, causally ordered and sync-ordered. Unordered multicast is self-explanatory. Total, causal and sync-ordering are defined similarly to the description of ordered request processing in Section 11.3 above.

Let G_1 and G_2 be groups (not necessarily distinct) with overlapping members (that is, $G_1 \cap G_2$ is non-empty), and let m_1 be a multicast message to G_1 and m_2 be multicast to G_2. Multicast delivery orderings are defined as follows:

Total ordering: Either m_1 is delivered before m_2 at all members of $G_1 \cap G_2$, or m_2 is delivered before m_1 at all members of $G_1 \cap G_2$.

Causal ordering: If the multicast of m_1 *happened-before* the multicast of m_2, then m_1 is delivered before m_2 at all members of $G_1 \cap G_2$.

Sync-ordering: If m_1 is sent with a sync-ordered multicast primitive and m_2 is sent with *any ordered* multicast primitive, then either m_1 is delivered before m_2 at all members of $G_1 \cap G_2$, or m_2 is delivered before m_1 at all members of $G_1 \cap G_2$.

A simple primitive for atomically multicasting a message to a group is as follows. Its first parameter *order* is used to declare the type of ordering required, and is given as *UNORDERED*, *CAUSAL*, *TOTAL* or *SYNC*. As its second argument this procedure takes the identifier *group* of the group to which the message *m* is to be delivered. The sender declares the number of replies *nReplies* that are to be received from members of the group. This can be set to zero, allowing the implementation to multicast the message asynchronously. If it is non-zero, then the implementation collects the stated number of replies and places them in the array of message buffers *replies*.

PROCEDURE multicast(order: orderType, group: groupId, m:msg, nReplies: int,
     replies: ARRAY of msg)
     multicasts a message and optionally obtains replies.

The value of *nReplies* would sensibly be zero when sending to a subscription group, since they will not reply to the message. When a client multicasts to a server group, it would normally be one. Use of a larger value of *nReplies* implies knowledge of the size of the group membership. This might be used, for example, in a peer group, in which a member collates information from its peers. A larger value might also be used where the main goal is fault tolerance. A front end could obtain replies from each of a group of replica managers and choose a value returned by a majority (if such exists), in case some of the replica managers are faulty and can send spurious replies.

ISIS and virtual synchrony

The ISIS system [Birman and Joseph 1987, Birman 1993] is a framework for reliable distributed computing based upon process groups, which has been under development at Cornell University since 1983. ISIS has been fully implemented as a set of library calls on top of UNIX, and is being implemented in a form suitable for integration with Mach and Chorus communication. It is commercially available.

ISIS is a programming toolkit whose most basic facilities consist of process group management calls and ordered multicast primitives for communicating with the members of process groups.

Multicast facilities: ISIS provides unordered multicast (FBCAST), causally ordered multicast (CBCAST), totally ordered multicast (ABCAST) and sync-ordered multicast (GBCAST). All multicasts are reliable; ideally, they would be atomic, but they are not strictly atomic as currently implemented (see the discussion of CBCAST below). A process does not have to be a member of a group in order to communicate with it, and all the types of group structure described above are supported. Indeed, they have come about largely as a result of experience with ISIS.

Group view maintenance: ISIS provides primitives to create, join and leave process groups, which can be referred to by character-string names. Furthermore, ISIS monitors group members so that their fail-stop failure or unreachability is detected. A member is deemed to have left the group through failure when either its local operating system has detected its abnormal termination, or when it fails to respond after repeated attempts are made to communicate with it. ISIS maintains for each group a *group view*, which is a list of the current membership of the group, identified by the members' unique process identifiers. The list is kept ordered according to the order in which the members joined the group. A new group view differs from the last group view by the addition or deletion of one process.

State transfer: Consider a multi-user application such as a shared editor implemented as a peer group of processes, one per user. If a user's workstation crashes, then it ought to be possible for that user to go to a neighbouring workstation, start up the application and recommence work in the same editing session. The state of the application might not be the same as when the user's computer crashed, since the other users may have made updates in the meantime. But the state should at least be consistent with that of the other users, even though they may attempt to update the state while it is being transferred. ISIS provides facilities for the application implementor to arrange that all relevant components of the application state are automatically sent to a newly joining group member; and moreover it guarantees that the state is consistent between all members of the group from the point of joining.

The members of an ISIS group are each conceived of as generating and processing a series of events. Processes generate events visible to other processes when they join or leave groups and when they issue multicasts. The two major types of event that group members *process* (as opposed to generate) are the delivery of a multicast message and the notification of a new group view. Group view notifications can be thought of as the delivery of messages containing the new group view (and indeed they are implemented as a special type of multicast messages).

An ISIS program is constructed as a collection of routines that are declared at run-time to correspond with specific types of incoming events, and which are thereafter called automatically by the ISIS run-time as these events occur. ISIS can be thought of primarily as managing the order of these events on each process's delivery queue and thus scheduling their processing.

Given that multicasts are atomic, all the members of a process group are guaranteed to process the same set of events. The designers of ISIS considered the most useful and efficient relative orderings of event processing between different group members. Two degrees of coupling or *synchrony* between different members are distinguishable.

Closely synchronous execution is similar to the totally synchronous model introduced in Section 11.1. Under closely synchronous execution, all members processing a common set of events (which may pertain to different but overlapping groups) do so in the same order. Moreover:

- this order is consistent with the *happened-before* relation (that is, it is total and causal);

- it *respects failure*: it is guaranteed that no multicast message will be delivered after a view change notifying its sender's failure – since this could lead to inconsistencies;

- it incorporates consistent state transfer. A newly joining process receives state marshalled from the variables of some extant member at the well-defined instant at which the member joins. In other words, the set of incoming events that are subsequently processed on the basis of this state is the same at the new member as it is at the extant members.

The closely synchronous execution model has the advantage of conceptual simplicity, since it automatically enforces complete consistency between members processing the same set of events. An important property is that when the group view changes, the individual members can react consistently without the need for further communication. For example, consider a group of processes that has divided some data equally between the members. They process the data in parallel, and periodically checkpoint completed results by multicasting them to their peers. If one of their number fails, then its work can be re-allocated to one or more extant members. They can all agree at the point of failure notification as to which work has been completed, and the re-allocation can be consistently made without further consultation according to the new group view.

The problems with closely synchronous execution, as was pointed out for the totally synchronous replication model introduced above, are that it does not allow for parallel operation between the members; and it is expensive to implement since it involves totally and causally ordering all events.

Virtually synchronous execution is conceived of in an attempt to retain the virtues of close synchrony while relaxing some of the ordering requirements as far as application consistency constraints will allow. Specifically, the advantageous features retained are the sync-ordered and failure-respecting nature of group view changes, and the associated consistent transfer of state. However, multicast messages do not always have to be totally ordered in their delivery. Causal ordering is cheaper to implement; it allows unrelated messages to be processed in different orders at different group members, thus allowing for a degree of asynchronous operation; and yet it allows consistency constraints to be met in many cases.

Virtual synchrony does not specify the relative ordering of event processing, but it introduces an application-specific choice of causal and total ordering into a framework of sync-ordered group view changes and state transfers. A virtually synchronous execution is *equivalent* to some closely synchronous execution.

The ISIS CBCAST protocol ☐ ISIS uses vector timestamps to implement causally ordered multicasts between the members of a peer group. The method is straightforwardly related to the technique described above for ordering requests in the gossip architecture, and the reader who feels comfortable with the presentation there may safely skip the following description.

It is assumed that all messages are multicast to all members of the group (including the sender). ISIS uses UDP/IP as its basic transport facility, and sends acknowledgements and retransmits packets as necessary to achieve reliability. Messages from a given member are sequenced and delivered in order. There is no assumption that hardware support for broadcast or multicast exists. If IP multicast [Deering and Cheriton 1990] is implemented, then ISIS can exploit it to send a single UDP packet to the appropriate multicast address; IP multicast takes advantage of hardware (for example, Ethernet) multicast facilities. Otherwise packets are sent point-to-point to the individual group members.

Let the members of the peer group be $p_1, p_2, .., p_n$. Once more we shall define, for each p_i, a vector timestamp denoted by VT_i which is used to order multicast delivery. It will turn out that $VT_j[i]$ is the count of multicast messages sent by p_i that causally lead up to the latest message delivered to p_j. The following is the vector timestamp update algorithm:

1. All processes p_i initialize VT_i to zeroes.

2. When p_i multicasts a new message, it first increments $VT_i[i]$ by 1; it piggybacks the value $vt = VT_i$ on the message.

3. When a message bearing a timestamp vt is delivered to p_j, p_j's timestamp is updated as: $VT_j := merge(VT_j, vt)$.

Every multicast message can be delivered to its sender immediately, since it is by definition in causal order with respect to messages already delivered to it. A multicast message arriving at p_j's site from p_i ($p_j \neq p_i$), however, has to be placed on the hold-back queue until it can be delivered in causal order. The incoming message's timestamp vt is examined, and the following criteria are used for transferring the message to p_j's delivery queue:

- The message must be the next in sequence expected from p_i, that is,

  $vt[i] = VT_j[i] + 1$.

- All causally prior messages that have been delivered to p_i when it sent the message, should have been delivered to p_j, that is, $VT_j[k] \geq vt[k]$ for $k \neq i$.

It is straightforward to show that these criteria are necessary and sufficient to satisfy the safety property of causal ordering being assured. Liveness can only be established if:

- all members of the group are destinations for every message, and
- multicast delivery is atomic.

For otherwise, a message delivered to p_i might never be delivered to p_j, and so some messages might indefinitely fail the second of the above criteria.

Atomicity and virtually synchronous group view changes □ Successive group views $view_0$, $view_1$, $view_2$ and so on differ from their immediate predecessors either by the addition of a single new process, or by the removal of a single process that has failed or left the group voluntarily. Messages bearing the view's identifier are delivered to all operational members of that view.

When a view change is to occur, ISIS sends a notification to all member sites, which then must reach a distributed agreement so as to sync-order the view change before passing the notification to the group members. Recall that, under virtually synchronous execution, view changes are delivered to group members consistently with respect to message delivery. This means that all messages sent during a view $view_i$ are guaranteed to be delivered to all operational members of $view_i$ before ISIS delivers notification of $view_{i+1}$. It should be noted, however, that there is an intimate relation between the questions of when a view change is deemed to occur and of which messages are sent in which view.

If some process p has joined the group to produce $view_{i+1}$, then no message originally sent during $view_i$ will be delivered to p; but all messages sent by the members of $view_{i+1}$ after ISIS has delivered notification of $view_{i+1}$ to them will be delivered to the entire new group, that is, including p.

ISIS multicasts are not strictly atomic. Chapter 18 describes a version of the Amoeba multicast protocol that provides guarantees of atomicity despite up to r computer failures. This is a two-phase protocol, and the ISIS designers chose to avoid this expense. Instead, the ISIS guarantee is: as long as at least one member site that stores a message survives, then the message will be delivered to all surviving members despite the failure of the sender and any other sites.

Received messages are stored at each site until they are known to have been delivered to all members of the current view (information about which messages have been received is piggybacked on other traffic in the usual way). We shall call messages that have been delivered to all members of the current view *group-stable* (these are not to be confused with *stable* messages, described in Section 11.3). If ISIS finds that the sender of a message has failed, then some other site that stores the message – if such exists – is elected to send it to all sites not yet known to store it. Such a site can be chosen on a simple basis; for example it could be the oldest surviving member in the group view (which is ordered by age) that holds a copy of the message. Duplicates are of course detected.

If some member q of $view_i$ has failed, producing $view_{i+1}$, then the question arises of whether q's application received all messages delivered during $view_i$; and also whether q sent a message just before it failed which was received at q and perhaps other failed sites. These possibilities may seem awkward, but they are unlikely to lead to inconsistencies since q can no longer communicate and ISIS automatically deletes any tardy messages sent before q failed, which might otherwise be delivered after notification of its failure. Every message bears the identifier of the current view. Messages bearing an earlier view identifier are discarded.

Nonetheless, the failed process may in fact have produced an effect in the external world such as operating a robot arm, which conflicts with the state of the surviving members. The CBCAST multicast primitive may return even before the sent message has been delivered to a single remote destination, if no replies are requested by the sender. If all the sites to which the message has been delivered fail, then no other site will receive the message. For applications requiring greater reliability, ISIS provides a *flush* primitive, which returns only when all sent messages have been delivered to all their destinations.

ISIS combines its multicast protocol and a protocol to agree group view changes in a single algorithm (Figure 11.18). The algorithm starts from $view_i$, when a member is detected as failing or voluntarily leaves the group, or a process joins the group. The next view will be $view_{i+1}$, however it is possible for a member to fail or leave, or for another process to apply to join while the protocol is in operation. The protocol therefore deals with $view_{i+1}$, $view_{i+2}$, and so on, as necessary until it completes without further view changes. On completion the notifications of $view_{i+1}$, $view_{i+2}$, and so on are delivered to the application, followed by any messages sent in those views.

In this protocol a coordinator is elected (see Section 10.4 for a description of some election algorithms). The task of the coordinator is to discover any messages that are not yet group-stable and send them to those members of $view_i$ that are still in the group and that are missing them. Once it is known that all these have been received, they are delivered to the application. This is called *flushing*: messages sent in the previous view must all be delivered before the new group view can be delivered to the application. Messages sent after the protocol was begun but before the new view is delivered can be transmitted while this protocol operates, but they are marked as belonging to the new view and so cannot be delivered until the view itself has been delivered. Note that a sender will find out in which view a multicast occurred when it itself receives the message.

Any failure of any process taking part in this protocol is detected; the protocol moves on to agree $view_{i+2}$, electing a new coordinator if the last one failed. Similarly, members may leave the group and processes may try to join the group while the protocol operates. The protocol iterates indefinitely. Birman *et al.* [1991] have shown how intermediate views can in fact be delivered in case many overlapped view changes occur indefinitely.

The ISIS ABCAST protocol □ The ABCAST (causally and totally ordered multicast) protocol uses a sequencer, which is a member site designated as holding the ABCAST token. In each new group view a token-holder is elected. ABCAST messages carry CBCAST timestamps, but are marked as ABCAST. The token-holder attaches a sequence number to all ABCAST messages it delivers. It causally orders and delivers received ABCAST messages, and sends so-called *sets-order* messages, which contain the sequence numbers of one or more identified ABCAST messages it has received. Other destination sites delay the delivery of a received ABCAST message until:

• they have received a sets-order message referring to it;

Figure 11.18   The ISIS algorithm for view agreement and message delivery.

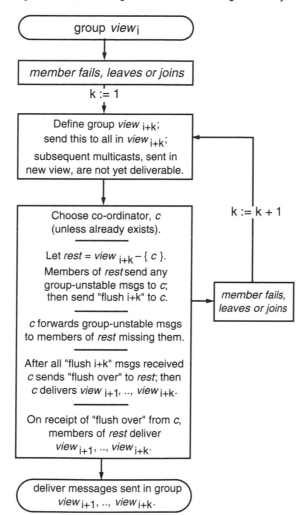

- they have received any prior ABCAST messages referred to in the sets-order message;
- they have delivered any causally prior CBCAST messages.

The token can be transferred between sites. The main advantage of this is that a site that is the sole source of ABCAST messages can be designated as the token holder; separate sets-order messages are unnecessary in this case.

Discussion of the ISIS and gossip approaches

ISIS is a mature product that has been used for a substantial number of real-world applications. It could be used to program the front ends and the group of replica managers in our general replication architecture. It is also applicable outside the domain of replicated data, for example in the propagation of financial and other information to varied clients. The gossip approach has no concept of process groups, is strictly applicable to replicated data and is relatively untested by comparison. But it offers a potentially more lightweight alternative to the use of ISIS for managing replicated data, at least for certain applications. There are two major differences between the approaches: the use of process groups, and the use of multicast as opposed to gossip messages.

Process groups □ Ladin *et al.* [1992] have stated that replica managers can recover after failure, but how this is achieved is not described. In principle, it would involve the consistent transfer of the value, log, timestamps and other administrative information. Moreover, limited attention has been paid to the problem of incorporating a new replica manager into a running gossip-based system. ISIS, by contrast, provides a generic approach to the integration of new process group members through its state transfer and group view maintenance mechanisms. But a process that is deemed to have failed cannot recover: a new process must be created, which must join the group afresh.

In the original ISIS implementation, if a network partitioning occurs then only a majority of group members in a single partition is allowed to continue operation; the rest are automatically killed. This is to obviate the possibility of several collections of processes each continuing under the mistaken assumption that all their peers have failed – a situation that would clearly lead to inconsistencies. In the gossip approach, no manager is killed off when a network partitioning occurs. All replica managers continue to accept updates and satisfy any queries as long they have processed sufficient updates. Replica managers in a majority partition can execute updates. When the partition is repaired, gossip messages and information about forced and immediate operations are exchanged in order to bring all replicas up to date.

To refer once more to our bulletin board example, the difference between the approaches amounts to this. If a university became partitioned from the rest of the country, then under the basic ISIS approach the bulletin board service would be withdrawn altogether from that university until the partition was repaired. Under the gossip design, the users at that university could continue to read items locally, but the set of items would become stale compared to the items posted by those in the other (majority) partition. If posting is implemented as a forced operation, then users at the partitioned university could not continue to post – although users in the majority partition could post. But if posting is a causal operation, then users at the partitioned university could continue to post items. However, as was pointed out for the case of very low rates of gossip exchange, two separate and inconsistent debates might take place about an issue known to users in both partitions.

More recently, the original ISIS restriction on partitioned groups is viewed as tolerable only in the case of a LAN – where partitions are relatively rare. ISIS now incorporates a separate architecture for coping gracefully with WAN partitions – which are more common – and is similar to the gossip approach to partitioning [Birman, private communication, 1993].

Multicast versus gossip □ The choice of ISIS multicast as opposed to the lazy gossip approach to update propagation depends upon the application: it involves a trade-off between the amount of communication and the timeliness of update delivery. ISIS

Figure 11.19 Comparison of ISIS and Gossip.

	ISIS (hardware multicast)	ISIS (point-to-point)	Gossip
Number of messages per query	–	2	2
Bandwidth (large query Q)	–	Q	Q
Number of messages per update	$1 + R$	$2R$	$2 + (R\text{-}1)/G$
Bandwidth (large update U)	U	UR	UR
Number of messages per query-and-update	$1 + R$	$2R$	$4 + (R\text{-}1)/G$

The number of messages and bandwidth utilization for various operations.
R = no. of replica managers; G = no. of updates in gossip message.

multicasts updates to all replica managers immediately; in a gossip-based system, updates are propagated at whatever rate gossip messages are made to occur.

For large numbers of replica managers, an important factor affecting a system's ability to scale is the number of messages that have to be transmitted and processed. The number of messages and bandwidth utilization for various operations are compared in Figure 11.19. The expressions for the gossip architecture are those that were deduced in Section 11.4 above. ISIS can utilize hardware multicast or broadcast over a single LAN that supports this, so entries are given both for the LAN case and for a case in which point-to-point messages must be used. It is very important to note that the figures for the number of messages indicate the worst case. They assume that no piggy-backing takes place, and that each message travels alone in its network packet or packets.

As with the gossip design, a read-only (that is, query) operation can be carried out under ISIS by any single replica manager; this is realized as a multicast to a singleton sub-group of the replica group, and takes just two messages. An update under ISIS requires either a single multicast message or R point-to-point messages (where R is the number of replica managers), followed by R acknowledgements. ISIS directly supports operations that both read and modify the service state, by multicasting requests to the replica group; in the gossip design, such operations have to be realized as two requests: a query and an update.

Of course, the total amount of update processing at each replica manager is the same in either type of system. The expressions given for the number of messages are intended for illustration. They are at best a crude guide to actual performance – that is, client response times and system throughput. This is in part because some ISIS-related messages are received in parallel; and in part because various administrative overheads have not been taken into account. Also, as stated above, the expressions derived are worst cases for the number of packets sent. Both ISIS and the gossip architecture combine multiple requests and acknowledgements in the same network packet wherever possible. For example, a more realistic expression for the number of packets sent per update or query-and-update in the ISIS case is $(1 + R/p)$, where p, the *piggy-back factor*, has been estimated as lying in the range 3–15 in some applications involving small requests and using IP multicast [Birman, personal communication]. A piggy-back factor with similar values can be expected in the gossip architecture.

Timestamp sizes ☐ Another factor affecting a system's ability to scale is the space taken up in messages by vector timestamps. Section 11.4 described the suggestion of maintaining read-only replicas in a gossip-based system, which reduces timestamp information. The size of a timestamp in a gossip-based system is proportional to the number of managers that handle updates directly from clients.

In an ISIS system, by contrast, requests carry timestamps of size proportional to:

number of clients + number of replica managers

These are potentially considerably larger than those of a gossip-based system. To see why there is a timestamp entry for each client, consider that an individual replica manager must order multicast requests arriving from two or more clients that may have communicated with one another. In a gossip-based system, a front end delays communication from one client to another if necessary, until timestamps for all the sending client's outstanding updates have been returned by replica managers. The front ends propagate and merge these timestamps to ensure that ordering is obeyed. But in an ISIS system, the run-time at the replica managers cannot feed back timestamp information to clients in this way (client requests reach replica managers at more or less the same time). Requests must therefore bear timestamps which count the messages sent between the clients in order that the ISIS run-time can order them. (See the ISIS CBCAST protocol, described above.)

In favour of ISIS, client-to-client communication is not delayed by update acknowledgement, as it may be in a gossip-based system. Several techniques for minimizing the amount of transmitted timestamp information in ISIS are described by Birman *et al.* [1991]. A particularly interesting issue addressed there is the problem of dealing with many overlapping groups.

11.6 Summary

Replicating data and other resources is an important means of achieving good performance, high availability and fault tolerance in a distributed system. Clients can access local copies instead of vying for the same resources; and clients can access alternative copies if one copy fails. The attendant problems to be tackled are the achievement of replication transparency, consistency and good response times and system throughput.

Maintaining consistency amounts to ensuring that all replicas process all updates from clients, and that they process these updates in consistent orders. The three types of ordering identified are causal, total and sync-ordered. The choice of which to use depends upon the application semantics.

This chapter has described a general replicated system architecture consisting of clients, front ends and replica managers. Front ends – which may be separate processes or libraries linked into clients – provide replication transparency, and communicate with replica managers on behalf of clients. The chapter has focused on the gossip architecture and the process group model, represented by ISIS.

In the gossip architecture, front ends normally communicate with a single replica manager. Replica managers communicate updates lazily, in so-called gossip messages. This architecture provides primarily for causal update operations, but also provides forced (total and causal) and immediate (sync-ordered) operation orderings.

Process groups are targets for multicast communication. ISIS provides a programming toolkit on top of UNIX for process groups. Its central design concept is virtual synchrony. Processes use CBCAST (causal), ABCAST (total/causal) or GBCAST (sync-ordered) atomic multicasts; ISIS allows processes to leave or join groups, and detects process failures. It manages group views, and sync-orders group view notifications with respect to arriving multicasts. Process groups can be used to implement replica managers. They can also be used, for example, for parallel programs or for publishing information streams.

The process group approach seems preferable where timeliness of update propagation is essential. The gossip approach is lighter in the communication load it imposes, and is an alternative to process groups for applications with less stringent timeliness guarantees.

Replication as applied to fault tolerance is dealt with in Chapter 15. Replication is also relevant to transaction-based systems, which are described in Chapter 14.

EXERCISES

11.1 Three computers together provide a replicated service. The manufacturers claim that each computer has a mean time between failure of five days; a failure typically takes four hours to fix. What is the availability of the replicated service?

page 312

11.2 Describe a scenario in which a message *re:X* can arrive before the original message whose subject is *X*.

page 314

11.3 A multi-user auctioning system displays the current highest bid for an article and allows participants at different workstations to place bids. Discuss the design requirements applying to replication in this case. What is a suitable architecture?

page 316-318

11.4 i) In a multi-user game, players at separate workstations move figures around a common scene. The figures may throw projectiles at one another, and a hit debilitates the unfortunate recipient for a pre-determined interval. What type of ordering is required here?

ii) The game incorporates magic devices which may be picked up by a player to assist him or her. What type of ordering should be applied to the pick-up-device operation?

page 319-321

11.5   What is sync-ordering? Is it necessary in a system that otherwise only supports total ordering?

page 320

11.6   In a bank account service, credits and withdrawals are causally ordered. The service supports lists of users able to perform operations on each particular bank account, and several administrators may attempt to add users to account lists from different points. Explain why adding a user to a list should be totally ordered, and why removing a user from a list should be sync-ordered.

page 319-321

11.7   What is a hold-back queue? In the original ISIS protocol for totally-ordered multicast, can a message that has been assigned a final identifier always be removed immediately from the hold-back queue?

page 321-324

11.8   A front end has vector timestamp (3,5,7) representing the data it has received from members of a group of three replica managers. The three replica managers have vector timestamps (5,2,8), (4,5,6) and (4,5,8), respectively. Which replica manager(s) could immediately satisfy a query from the front end, and what is the resultant time stamp of the front end? Which could incorporate an update from the front end immediately?

page 325

11.9   If VT_i ($i = 1, 2, .., n$) are vector timestamps for a group of replica managers, explain why $VT_i[j] \le VT_j[j]$ for $i, j = 1, 2, .., n$.

page 326

11.10   Could the gossip architecture be used for a distributed auction system as described in Exercise 11.3? A distributed computer game as described in Exercise 11.4? A file service?

page 327

11.11   In the gossip architecture, why does a replica manager need to keep both a 'replica' timestamp and a 'value' timestamp?

page 329

11.12   Explain why making some replica managers read-only may improve the performance of a gossip system.

page 334

11.13   A service is to be replicated for high availability. Compare the use of a server group with a design in which clients send point-to-point requests to a single member picked from a group, and this server multicasts to its peer group.

page 335

11.14   What security implications are raised by process groups?

page 337

11.15 R and S are both members of a group G. The member R multicasts a message m_1 to G, sends a (point-to-point) message m_2 asynchronously to S, then multicasts m_3 to G. On receiving m_1, S multicasts m_4 to G. What delivery guarantees must be met for the messages m_1 to m_4 if delivery is in *causal* order?

page 339

11.16 What is the consistency issue raised by state transfer?

page 340

11.17 Could the ISIS architecture be used for a distributed auction system as described in Exercise 11.3? A distributed computer game as described in Exercise 11.4? A file service?

page 340

11.18 R and S are both members of a group G. If R and S exchange point-to-point messages as well as multicasting to the whole group, does this affect the operation of the CBCAST protocol?

page 342

11.19 How does the ISIS CBCAST protocol fail to be atomic?

page 343

11.20 Compare the ISIS and gossip architectures for implementing a combined update and query operation.

page 347

11.21 Discuss the differences in the size of the vector timestamps required for implementing a replicated service using ISIS and the gossip architecture, respectively.

page 348

12

SHARED DATA AND TRANSACTIONS

This chapter discusses the design of server programs that manage data shared between clients. A server encapsulates resources that are accessed by means of operations invoked by clients. The only way for clients to access a server's resources is by invoking one of the server operations.

The use of threads in a server offers concurrent access to clients. When a server has multiple threads, it must ensure that its operations are atomic in their effect on its data items. Some servers can enhance the cooperation between clients by arranging for one client to wait until another client has provided a resource needed by the first client.

In some cases, such as the transfer of a stream of data items to a client, the interaction between a client and a server is more like a conversation than a simple operation invocation.

When clients need to use a server to store data over a long period of time, the server must be designed to guarantee that the data will survive even when the server process fails.

Many applications require client transactions – a transaction defines a sequence of server operations that is guaranteed by the server to be atomic. The last section of this chapter introduces transactions – which guarantee atomicity in the presence of multiple clients and server failures.

Nesting allows transactions to be structured from sets of other transactions. Nested transactions are particularly useful in distributed systems because they allow additional concurrency.

12.1 Introduction

We have seen in Chapter 2 that a client is a process that initiates an activity, whereas a server is a process that waits for requests from clients and then performs whatever it is asked to do. This chapter and the three following chapters are concerned with issues relating to consistency and reliability in server programs and their clients. We have two contrasting requirements – on the one hand, clients' operations must be prevented from interfering with one another; on the other hand, clients should be able to use servers to share and exchange information. Some servers are required to maintain data on behalf of their clients for long periods of time – such servers should be based on recoverable data – that is data that can be recovered after the server crashes. In some applications, clients need to perform sequences of related server operations as indivisible units known as transactions. A service may be based on several servers with data partitioned between them – for example, a banking service may be based on a set of servers, each of which maintains the accounts for a single branch. A service based on several servers will need to deal with distributed transactions.

This chapter discusses issues of cooperation between clients and maintenance of long lived data in a simple single process server and then introduces transactions. The provision for transactions in a service requires more advanced techniques to prevent interference between clients and to ensure the data is recoverable. Chapter 13 is concerned with concurrency control, Chapter 14 introduces distributed transactions and relates them to issues of concurrency control and replication. The first half of Chapter 15 is concerned with recoverable data in both single server and distributed transactions. The second half of Chapter 15 is concerned with other approaches to the provision of fault tolerant services.

We regard a server as a component of a distributed system that manages a single type of resource, as introduced in Chapter 2. The resources may be application-related, such as email messages or bank-account records or they may be generic, such as files, printers or windows.

A server encapsulates the resources that it manages, allowing them to be created, accessed and manipulated by means of operations that can be invoked by clients. In Chapter 5 we saw that the operations available to clients are defined in the service interface. The only way for clients to access a server's data items is by invoking one of the server's operations. A server process contains within it data items that store the state of its resources. The effect of a request to perform an operation on a service depends on the actual request, its arguments and the current values of the server's data items.

In general, the data items that represent the resources managed by a server may be stored in volatile memory (for example, RAM) or persistent memory (for example, disk). Even if they are stored in volatile memory, the server may use persistent memory to store sufficient information for the state of the resources to be recovered in case the server process fails.

The resources that a server manages are determined by the needs of its clients:

- a directory server might encapsulate the names, addresses and other details of a group of people and provide operations to look up, add or modify names and addresses;

- the resources of the binding service described in Chapter 5 consist of mappings from service names to service ports. When a server starts up it becomes a client of the binder and supplies a new mapping. Clients of a binder access its resources in order to find out the location of services;

- the resources of the Sun NIS service consist of mappings from keys to values. The maps can hold for example, password file information or host names and their internet addresses. Clients of NIS access its resources for example, when users login;

- a server could be defined to provide a diary database that can be viewed and updated interactively by a number of users. A user who wants to make an appointment with someone views that person's diary and writes in an appointment.

We will use a simple directory service called Address to illustrate some of the points made in this chapter. The Address service provides the following operations on a set of resources containing names and addresses:

LookUp(name) → *address*
    returns the address corresponding to the given name.

AddAddress(entry)
    adds a new entry containing a name and address.

ModifyAddress(name, address)
    modifies the address associated with a name.

DeleteAddress(name)
    deletes the entry with the given name.

For example, a client may invoke the *LookUp* operation in a server of the name and address service named *Address* as follows:

    Address$LookUp ("Napoleon");

We now return to the main issue of this chapter which is that unless a server is carefully designed, its operations performed on behalf of different clients may sometimes interfere with one another. Such interference may result in incorrect values in the data items.

Atomic operations at the server □ We have seen in earlier chapters that the use of multiple threads is beneficial to performance in many servers. If a server has more than one thread, it needs to make its operations *atomic* in order to keep its data items consistent. This means that the effect of performing any single operation is free from interference from concurrent operations being performed in other threads.

    For example, in the *Address* service it should be possible to perform two concurrent *ModifyAddress* requests on the same entry in a consistent manner. To perform each operation a thread may read and/or write the values of some of the data items. To ensure that the effect of each operation is atomic, the server must ensure that no other thread can access the same data items until the first thread has finished. This may be achieved by the use of a mutual exclusion mechanism such as the mutex.

Enhancing client cooperation by synchronization of server operations □ Clients may use a server as a means of sharing some resources for example, names and addresses. This is achieved by some clients using operations to update the server's resources and other clients using operations to access the resources. In some services, a situation may arise in which the operation requested by one client cannot be completed until an operation requested by another client has been performed. This can happen when some clients are producers and others are consumers – the consumers may have to wait until a producer has supplied some more of the commodity in question. It can also occur when clients are sharing a resource – clients needing the resource may have to wait for other clients to release it. We shall see in Chapter 13 that a similar situation arises when locks or timestamps are used for concurrency control.

Consider the situation when a consumer client requests a resource that is not currently available. It is unsatisfactory to tell such a client to try again later if the client requires the requested resource to continue. It would involve the client in busy waiting and the server in extra requests (because the client will have to keep trying the request). It is also potentially unfair because other clients may make their requests before the waiting client tries again. A preferable solution is for the server to hold on to the request and the client to wait for a reply until another client has produced a resource. After that, the consumer operation can proceed.

To deal with such situations a server must be able to suspend requests that cannot be executed immediately; to continue to receive other client requests and to resume the suspended requests when they can be executed. To allow for the need to execute more than one client request at a time, a server uses a new thread to execute each request – possibly with some limit on the number of available threads. In some cases a thread will be suspended when it cannot usefully proceed – in our example when a required resource is not available – and later resumed. Chapter 6 discussed the provision of threads, condition variables and synchronization primitives in operating systems. A thread that cannot continue execution requests its own suspension by using the *Wait* operation. Another thread can cause a suspended thread to resume by using the *Signal* operation. For a comprehensive study of these and other issues in concurrent programming see Andrews [1991] and Bacon [1993].

12.2 Conversations between a client and a server

In some applications, a client request may cause a server to perform a lengthy calculation to produce multiple items of output gradually, for example, to request a database server to return all entries matching a particular key. It might be preferable for the server to be able to transmit them one by one to the client, allowing server and client to work concurrently.

As an example, consider the design of an operation in the name and address service for returning the details of all the names and addresses currently stored. If the server has a very large number of names and addresses, it is better for clients to be able to get them one by one or in small batches, rather than receiving them all in a single message. This enables clients to process each name and address when it arrives.

The desired interaction between client and server can be regarded as a *conversation* in which the server keeps track of where a particular client has got to. To support conversations, a service will require two new operations for use by clients:

OpenConversation ( )→ conversationId
   ask to start a conversation with the server – an identifier for the conversation is returned.

CloseConversation (conversationId)
   indicate the end of a conversation.

A conversation is generally about the server resources. In our *Addresses* example, it is about the entries. The role of the server is to give the client each of the name and address entries in turn. It provides an operation for the client to request the next entry or batch:

NextAddress (conversationId)→ entry — REPORTS EndOfSequence
   returns the details of the next name and address; if there are no more entries, returns an error report *EndOfSequence*.

Thus a client might make the following requests to get details of all the names and addresses:

    conversationId := Address$OpenConversation ();
    REPEAT
         entry := Address$NextAddress (conversationId);
         ••• (* process result *)
    UNTIL ErrorReport = EndOfSequence
    Address$CloseConversation(conversationId)

Each conversation has a *conversationId* that is returned by the server when a conversation starts. The name and address service will be extended to hold for each client that is currently conversing with it, a variable containing the *conversationId* and a reference to the next name and address entry whose details are to be returned to that client. Each time *OpenConversation* is executed by the server, such a variable is allocated and when *CloseConversation* is called, the variable used by that conversation is freed.

A threaded server could use one thread for each conversation. This would simplify the programming because each thread would need to remember only its own position in the sequence of data items to be accessed.

Stateful servers □ In the last example the server maintains information on behalf of each of its clients with whom it is currently conversing. The information consists of the conversation identifier and the next entry for each client. It may exhibit the problems associated with stateful servers – in that it is vulnerable to poorly designed or crashing clients – neither of which will close their conversations, with the result that the space allocated for storing conversation information will eventually run out. Servers that hold state on behalf of individual clients generally assume some time limit after which they will no longer hold information on behalf of a particular client. Such issues also arise in the context of transactions. Another problem associated with poorly designed clients is with the use of illegal conversation identifiers with the effect that they might steal or interfere with items from other clients' sequences – this is an issue of security as well as of fault tolerance.

12.3 Fault tolerance and recovery

A fault tolerant server should be able to continue to provide a service in spite of processes crashing and the loss of messages.

In Chapter 4 we showed that a request-reply protocol may be selected to provide the desired level of tolerance to the loss of messages. This level will vary according to the RPC call semantics demanded by the particular server application. Consider our *Address* service: the data items can be arranged as set of entries, each member of which is indexed uniquely by name. The update operations can be designed to be repeatable and at-least-once call semantics are sufficient. In general, the use of idempotent operations in a server reduces the required RPC semantics to at-least-once.

A simple way of designing a server that can tolerate crashing clients is to design it to avoid holding information on behalf of particular clients. Servers designed on this principle are usually called **stateless**. However, simple stateless servers do not meet all application requirements. We saw in the previous section that some servers can benefit from a design that enables them to hold conversations with clients. In Chapter 8 we saw that the Andrew file system uses a call-back mechanism to ensure that clients have up-to-date copies of files in their caches. This involves the servers in retaining state as to which files each client currently has cached. The designers chose this solution in preference to a stateless one because it reduced significantly the number of calls to the servers. The last section of this chapter introduces servers that provide clients with the ability to use transactions – such servers need to hold quite complex information on behalf of their clients.

A fault tolerant server should be able to provide a service even if a server process crashes. To provide an apparently continuous service in the presence of a processor crash, the service will be based on a group of replicas of the service running in different computers. The replicas will monitor one another and will be able to provide a continuous service in the presence of the failure of a limited number of replicas. The use of replicas for fault tolerant services are discussed in Chapter 15 and methods for replication in Chapter 11.

Recoverable data items □ A simple way to provide a service based on a single process that can recover from a crash is to keep the values of the data items representing its resources in a form of storage that will survive a server crash for example, a file on disk – called the recovery file. When such a server is restarted it will recover its data items to the state before the crash by initializing them from the values in the recovery file. This arrangement depends on an external agent to monitor the server and to restart it after any failures. The service should guarantee that after a reply message has been sent to the client the effects of an update operation will remain permanent, even if the server crashes. This requires that after each operation is complete, all the changes to the values of the data items should be written to the recovery file before sending the reply message.

The techniques for organizing a recovery file for a simple server are simplified versions of the techniques used for transactions, which are discussed in Chapter 15.

12.4 Transactions

When we say a server provides **atomic** operations this means that the effect of performing any operation on behalf of one client is free from interference from operations being performed on behalf of other concurrent clients; and either an operation must be completed successfully or it must have no effect at all in the presence of server crashes. In some situations clients require that a sequence of separate requests to a server is atomic in the sense that the combined execution of the corresponding server operations is atomic. A conversation between a client and a server is one example of such a sequence of operations. Returning to our example, the client may wish to retrieve all of the name and address details from the address server without any other clients being allowed to update them (for example, by adding new ones or modifying existing ones) during the retrieval.

We shall use as another example a server that holds data for all of the accounts of a branch of a bank and provides operations to deposit or withdraw money in these accounts. This service called Bank provides the server operations *Deposit*, *Withdraw*, *GetBalance* and *BranchTotal* on a set of bank accounts.

Deposit(Name, Amount)
  deposit amount *Amount* in account *Name*.

Withdraw(Name, Amount)
  withdraw amount *Amount* from account *Name*.

GetBalance (Name)→ Amount
  return the balance of account *Name*.

BranchTotal ()→ total
  return the sum of all the balances.

Each account has a name (*A,B,C...*) used by the client – the server maps account names onto the corresponding data items holding account balances in dollars.

Consider a client that wishes to perform a series of related actions involving bank accounts called A, B, and C. The first action transfers $100 from A to B and the second transfers $200 from C to B. A client achieves a transfer operation by doing a withdrawal followed by a deposit as shown in Figure 12.1.

Transactions originate from the field of databases. In that context a transaction is an execution of a program that accesses a database. Transactions were introduced to

Figure 12.1   A client's banking transaction

> *Transaction:T:*
> *Bank$Withdraw(A, 100);*
> *Bank$Deposit(B, 100);*
> *Bank$Withdraw(C, 200);*
> *Bank$Deposit(B, 200);*

distributed systems in the form of transactional file servers such as XDFS [Mitchell and Dion 1982]. In the context of a transactional file server, a transaction is an execution of a sequence of client requests for file operations. Subsequently transactions have been used in the context of servers of recoverable data as for example in the Argus [Liskov 1988] and Arjuna [Shrivastava *et al.* 1991] systems. In this last context a transaction consists of the execution of a sequence of client requests as for example in Figure 12.1. From the client's point of view, a transaction is a sequence of operations that forms a single step, transforming the server data from one consistent state to another.

In all of these contexts, a transaction applies to recoverable data and is intended to be atomic. It is often called an **atomic transaction.**.(see box labelled ACID properties)

There are two aspects to atomicity:

all-or-nothing: a transaction either completes successfully and the effects of all of its operations are recorded in the data items or (if it fails) it has no effect at all. This all-or-nothing effect has two further aspects of its own;

– *failure atomicity*: the effects are atomic even when the server fails

---

ACID properties: Härder and Reuter [1983] suggest the mnemonic 'ACID' to remember the properties of transactions as follows:

Atomicity: a transaction must be all-or-nothing;

Consistency: a transaction takes the system from one consistent state to another consistent state;

Isolation;

Durability.

We have not included 'consistency' in our list of the properties of transactions because it is generally the responsibility of the programmers of servers and clients to ensure that transactions leave the database consistent.

As an example of consistency, suppose that the Bank service keeps a data item for the total sum of all the account balances and uses its value as the result of *BranchTotal*. Clients can get the total sum of all the account balances either by using *BranchTotal* or by calling *GetBalance* on each of the accounts. For consistency they should get the same result from both methods. To maintain this consistency, the *Deposit* and *Withdraw* operations must update the data item holding the total sum of all the account balances.

– durability: after a transaction has completed successfully all its effects are saved in permanent storage. We use the term permanent storage to refer to files held on disk or another permanent medium. Data saved in a file will survive if the server process crashes

isolation: each transaction must be performed without interference from other transactions, or in other words, the intermediate effects of a transaction must not be visible to other transactions.

 To support the requirement for failure atomicity and durability, the data items must be **recoverable**; when a server halts unexpectedly due to a hardware fault or a software error, the changes due to all completed transactions must be available in permanent storage so that the server can recover its data items to reflect the all-or-nothing effect. By the time the server acknowledges the completion of a client's transaction, all of the transaction's changes to the data items must have been recorded in permanent storage.

A server that supports transactions must synchronize the operations sufficiently to ensure that the isolation requirement is met. One way of doing this is to perform the transactions serially – one at a time in some arbitrary order. Unfortunately this solution would generally be unacceptable for servers whose resources are shared by multiple interactive users. In our banking example, it is desirable to allow several bank clerks to perform on-line banking transactions at the same time as one another.

The aim for any server that supports transactions is to maximise concurrency. Therefore transactions are allowed to execute concurrently if they would have the same effect as a serial execution – that is if they are they are **serially equivalent**.

A *transactional service* is an extension of a service such as the banking service, the name and address service or a file service to provide access to its resources via transactions. An atomic transaction is achieved by cooperation between a client program and a transactional service; the client specifies the sequence of operations that are to comprise a transaction and the transactional service guarantees to preserve the atomic property of the whole sequence. The client specifies a transaction as a sequence of operations, prefacing the sequence with an *OpenTransaction* operation to introduce each new transaction and concluding it with a *CloseTransaction* operation to indicate its end. See Figure 12.2 in which the operations are defined according to our usual notational convention (introduced in Chapter 7) and the following new argument name is used:

Trans: transaction identifiers or TIDs.

The client uses the transaction identifier returned by *OpenTransaction* to indicate which of the subsequent operations (up to the close of the transaction) are to be included in the particular transaction it identifies. See for example, the operations of a transactional file service in Figure 12.2.

Normally, a transactional service notes the start of each new transaction and performs the client's requests until it receives a *CloseTransaction* request. If the transaction has progressed normally the server then reports to the client that the transaction is **committed** – this constitutes an undertaking by the service to the client that all of the changes requested in the transaction are permanently recorded and that any future transactions that access the same data will see the results of all of the changes made during the transaction.

Figure 12.2   Transactional service operations.

OpenTransaction → Trans
>   starts a new transaction and delivers a unique TID *Trans*. This identifier will be used in the other operations in the transaction.

CloseTransaction(Trans) → (Commit, Abort)
>   ends a transaction: a *Commit* returned value indicates that the transaction has committed; an *Abort* returned value indicates that it has aborted.

AbortTransaction(Trans)
>   aborts the transaction.

Alternatively, the transaction may have to **abort** for one of several reasons related to the nature of the transaction itself, to conflicts with another transaction or to the failure of processes or computers. When a transaction is aborted the transactional service must ensure that none of its effects are visible to future transactions, either in the data items or in their copies in permanent storage.

A transaction is either successful or it is aborted in one of two ways – the client aborts it (using an *AbortTransaction* call to the server) or the server aborts it. Figure 12.3 shows these three alternative life histories for transactions.

Service actions related to failures ☐ If a server halts unexpectedly it aborts any uncommitted transactions when it starts up again and uses a recovery procedure to restore the values of the data items to the values produced by the most recently committed transaction. To deal with a client that halts unexpectedly during a transaction, servers can give each transaction an expiry time and abort any transaction that has not completed before its expiry time.

Client actions relating to failures of a server ☐ If a server halts while a transaction is in progress the client will become aware of this when one of the operations returns an error report after a time-out. If a server halts and then restarts during the progress of a

Figure 12.3   Transaction life histories.

Successful	Aborted by client	Aborted by server	
OpenTransaction	*OpenTransaction*		*OpenTransaction*
operation	*operation*		*operation*
operation	*operation*		*operation*
•	•	SERVER	•
•	•	ABORTS→	•
operation	*operation*		*operation ERROR* *reported to client*
CloseTransaction	*AbortTransaction*		

transaction, the transaction will no longer be valid and the client must be informed as a result of the next operation. In either case, the client must then formulate a plan, possibly in consultation with the human user, for the completion or abandonment of the task of which the transaction was a part.

Banking service operations in terms of Read and Write operations □ Many of the techniques for handling transactions have been developed in the context of databases and distributed file services. The *Read* and *Write* operations are used to access and update both database records and portions of files. Servers such as the banking service provide operations such as *Deposit* and *Withdraw* instead of *Read* and *Write* on the data items. However the implementation of such operations can be decomposed in terms of an operation *Read* that accesses the value of a data item and *Write* that replaces it with a new value.

In the discussion of concurrency control and recovery, we use the notation *D.Read* and *D.Write(newValue)* to denote operations within a server that access and update a data item representing the resource D.

For example, we may define informally *Deposit (Name, amount)* as a server operation that reads the balance of account *Name*, increases it by *amount*, in dollars and then writes the balance:

```
Deposit(Name, amount):
    balance := Name.Read ();
    Name.Write (balance + amount)
```

Concurrency control

This section illustrates two well-known problems of concurrent transactions – the 'lost update' problem and the 'inconsistent retrievals' problem in the context of the banking service. This section then shows how both of these problems can be avoided by using serially equivalent executions of transactions.

The lost update problem □ The lost update problem is illustrated by the following pair of transactions on bank accounts A, B and C whose initial balances are $100, $200 and $300 respectively. Transaction T transfers $4 from account A to account B. Transaction U transfers $3 from account C to account B. The net effects of executing the transactions T and U should be to:

- decrease the balance of accounts A by $4 and C by $3;
- increase the balance of account B by $7.

Now consider the effects of allowing the transactions T and U to run concurrently as in Figure 12.4. Both transactions read the balance of B and then write it. The result is incorrect, increasing the balance of account B by $4 instead of $7. This is an illustration of the 'lost update' problem. U's update is lost because T overwrites it without seeing it. Both transactions have read the old value before either writes the new value.

In Figure 12.4 onwards we show the operations that read or write the balance of an account on successive lines down the page, and the reader should assume that an operation on a particular line is executed at a later time than the one on the lines above it.

Figure 12.4   The lost update problem.

Transaction T: Bank$Withdraw(A, 4); Bank$Deposit(B, 4)		Transaction U: Bank$Withdraw(C, 3); Bank$Deposit(B, 3)	
balance := A.Read( )	$100		
A.Write (balance – 4)	$96		
		balance := C.Read( )	$300
		C.Write (balance – 3)	$297
balance := B.Read( )	$200		
		balance := B.Read( )	$200
		B.Write (balance + 3)	$203
B.Write (balance + 4)	$204		

Inconsistent retrievals □ Figure 12.5 shows another example related to a bank account in which transaction T transfers a sum from account A to B and transaction U obtains the sum of the balances of all the accounts in the bank. The balances of the two bank accounts, A and B, are both initially $200. The result includes the sum of A and B as $300. which is wrong. This is an illustration of the 'inconsistent retrievals' problem. U's retrievals are inconsistent because T has performed only the withdrawal part of a transfer at the time the sum is calculated.

Serial equivalence □ If each of several transactions is known to have the correct effect when it is done on its own, then we can infer that if these transactions are done one at a time in some order the combined effect will also be correct. An interleaving of the operations of transactions in which the combined effect is the same as if the transactions had been performed one at a time in some order is a serially equivalent interleaving.

Figure 12.5   The inconsistent retrievals problem.

Transaction T: Bank$Withdraw(A, 100); Bank$Deposit(B, 100)		Transaction U: Bank$BranchTotal( )	
balance := A.Read()	$200		
A.Write (balance - 100)	$100		
		balance := A.Read( )	$100
		balance := balance + B.Read()	$300
		balance := balance + C.Read()	$300+.
balance := B.Read()	$200	•	
B.Write (balance + 100)	$300	•	

Figure 12.6   A serially equivalent interleaving of T and U.

Transaction T: *Bank$Withdraw(A, 4);* *Bank$Deposit(B, 4)*		Transaction U: *Bank$Withdraw(C, 3);* *Bank$Deposit(B, 3)*	
balance := A.Read( )	$100		
A.Write(balance – 4)	$96		
		balance := C.Read( )	$300
		C.Write(balance – 3)	$297
balance := B.Read( )	$200		
B.Write (balance + 4)	$204		
		balance := B.Read( )	$204
		B.Write(balance + 3)	$207

When we say that two different transactions have the *same effect* as one another, we mean that the read operations return the same values and that the data items have the same values at the end.

The use of serial equivalence as a criterion for correct concurrent execution prevents the occurrence of lost updates and inconsistent retrievals.

The lost update problem occurs when two transactions read the old value of a variable and then use it to calculate the new value. This cannot happen if one transaction is performed before the other, because the later transaction will read the value written by the earlier one. As a serially equivalent interleaving of two transactions produces the same effect as a serial one, we can solve the lost update problem by means of serial equivalence. Figure 12.6 shows one such interleaving in which the operations that affect the shared account, B, are actually serial, for transaction T does all its operations on B before transaction U does. Another interleaving of T and U that has this property is one in which transaction U completes its operations on account B before transaction T starts.

We now consider the effect of serial equivalence in relation to the inconsistent retrievals problem in which Transaction T is transferring a sum from account A to B and Transaction U is obtaining the sum of all the balances (see Figure 12.5). The inconsistent retrievals problem can occur when a retrieval transaction runs concurrently with an update transaction. It cannot occur if the retrieval transaction is performed before or after the update transaction. A serially equivalent interleaving of a retrieval transaction and an update transaction (for example, as in Figure 12.7) will also prevent it occurring.

Serial equivalence requires that all of a transaction's accesses to a particular data item should be serialized with respect to accesses by other transactions. All pairs of conflicting operations of two transactions should be executed in the same order.

Serial equivalence is used as a criterion for the derivation of concurrency control protocols. These protocols attempt to serialize transactions in their access to data items. Chapter 13 introduces three approaches to concurrency control:

Figure 12.7   A solution to the problem of inconsistent retrievals

Transaction T: *Bank\$Withdraw(A, 100);* *Bank\$Deposit(B, 100)*		Transaction U: *Bank\$BranchTotal( )*	
balance :=A.Read( )	\$200		
A.Write(balance – 100)	\$100		
balance := B.Read( )	\$200		
B.Write(balance + 100)	\$300		
		balance := A.Read( )	\$100
		balance := balance +B.Read( )	\$400
		balance := balance +C.Read( )	\$400+
		...	

locking: In which each data item is locked by the first transaction that accesses it so that no other transaction may access the item until the first transaction has committed or aborted.

optimistic concurrency control: In which it is hoped that no conflicts of access will occur. Transactions proceed until they are ready to commit, when there is a check. If conflicts with other concurrent transactions have occurred, a transaction is aborted and must be restarted.

timestamps: In which each transaction has a timestamp and data items are timestamped each time they are accessed. Transactions are aborted and restarted when they are too late to perform an operation on a particular item.

Such methods for concurrency control are designed to allow two or more transactions to be executed concurrently while maintaining the serial equivalence property.

Recoverability

A transactional service must record the effects of all committed transactions and none of the effects of aborted transactions. A transactional service must therefore allow for the fact that a transaction may abort by preventing it from affecting other concurrent transactions.

This section illustrates two problems associated with aborting transactions in the context of the banking service. These problems are called 'dirty reads' and 'premature writes' and both of them can occur in the presence of serially equivalent executions of transactions.

Dirty reads □ The isolation property of transactions requires that transactions should not see the uncommitted state of other transactions. The 'dirty read' problem is caused

Figure 12.8   A dirty read when transaction T aborts.

Transaction T: *Bank.$Deposit(A, 3)*		Transaction U: *Bank$Deposit(A, 5)*	
balance :=A.Read( )	$100		
A.Write(balance + 3)	$103		
		balance := A.Read( )	$103
		A.Write (balance + 5)	$108
		Commit transaction	
Abort transaction			

by the interaction between a read operation in one transaction and an earlier write operation in another transaction on the same data item. Consider the executions illustrated in Figure 12.8, in which T reads and writes A and then U reads and writes A and the two executions are serially equivalent. Now suppose that the transaction T aborts after U has committed. Then the transaction U will have seen a value that never existed, since A will be restored to its original value. We say that the transaction U has performed a **dirty read.** As it has committed, it cannot be undone.

Recoverability of transactions □ If a transaction (like U) has committed after it has seen the effects of a transaction that subsequently aborted, the situation is not recoverable. To ensure that such situations will not arise, any transaction (like U) that is in danger of having a dirty read delays its commit operation. The strategy for recoverability is to delay commits until after the commitment of any other transaction whose uncommitted state has been observed. In our example, U delays its commit until after T commits. In the case that T aborts, then U must abort as well.

Cascading aborts □ In Figure 12.8 suppose that the transaction U delays committing until after T aborts. As we have said, U must abort as well. Unfortunately if any other transactions have seen the effects due to U, they too must be aborted. The aborting of these latter transactions may cause still further transactions to be aborted. Such situations are called **cascading aborts**. To avoid cascading aborts, transactions are only allowed to read data items that were written by committed transactions. To ensure that this is the case, any *Read* operation must be delayed until other transactions that applied a *Write* operation to the same data item have committed or aborted. The avoidance of cascading aborts is a stronger condition than recoverability.

Premature writes □ Consider another implication of the possibility that a transaction may abort. This one is related to the interaction between *Write* operations on the same data item belonging to different transactions. For an illustration, we introduce to the Bank service, a new operation *SetBalance(Name, Amount)* which sets the balance of account *Name* to *Amount*. We consider two *SetBalance* transactions T and U on account A, as shown in Figure 12.9. Before the transactions, the balance of account A was $100.

Figure 12.9   Over-writing uncommitted values.

Transaction T: *Bank$SetBalance(A, 3)*		Transaction U: *Bank$SetBalance(A, 5)*	
A.Write(3)	$3		
		A.Write (5)	$5

The two executions are serially equivalent, with T setting the balance to $3 and U setting it to $5. If the transaction U aborts and T commits, the balance should be $3.

Some database systems implement the action of *Abort* by restoring 'before images' of all the *Writes* of a transaction. In our example, A is $100 initially, which is the 'before image' of T's *Write*, similarly $3 is the 'before image' of U's *Write*. Thus if U aborts, we get the correct balance of $3.

Now consider the case when U commits and then T aborts. The balance should be $5 but as the 'before image' of T's *Write* is $100, we get the wrong balance of $100. Similarly if T aborts and then U aborts, the 'before image' of U's *Write* is $3 and we get the wrong balance of $3 – the balance should of course revert to $100.

To ensure correct results, *Write* operations must be delayed until earlier transactions that updated the same data items have either committed or aborted.

Strict executions of transactions □ Generally it is required that transactions should delay both their *Read* and *Write* operations so as to avoid both 'dirty reads' and 'premature writes'. The executions of transactions are called **strict** if the service delays both *Read* and *Write* operations on a data item until all transactions that previously wrote that data item have either committed or aborted. The strict execution of transactions enforces the desired property of isolation.

Tentative versions □ A transactional service must be designed so that any updates of the data items can be removed if and when a transaction aborts. To make this possible, all of the update operations performed during a transaction are done in tentative versions of data items in volatile memory. Each transaction is provided with its own private set of tentative versions of any data items that it has altered. All the update operations of a transaction store values in the transaction's own private set. Access operations in a transaction take values from the transaction's own private set if possible, or failing that, from the data items.

The tentative versions are transferred to the data items only when a transaction commits, by which time they will also have been recorded in permanent storage. This is performed in a single step during which other transactions are excluded from access to the data items that are being altered. When a transaction aborts, its tentative versions are deleted.

Figure 12.10   Transactional file service operations.

TWrite(Trans, File, i, Data) — REPORTS(BadPosition, Aborted)
   has the same effect as *Write(File, i, data)* but records the new data in a tentative form
   pending the completion of the transaction *Trans*.

TRead(Trans, File, i, n) → Data — REPORTS(BadPosition, Aborted)
   delivers the tentative data resulting from the transaction *Trans* if any has been
   recorded, otherwise has the same effect as *Read(File, i, n)*.

TCreate(Trans) → File — REPORTS(Aborted)
   records a tentative *Create* pending the completion of the transaction *Trans*.

TDelete(Trans, File) — REPORTS(Aborted)
   records a tentative *Delete* pending the completion of the transaction *Trans*.

TTruncate(Trans, File) — REPORTS(Aborted)
   records a tentative *Truncate* pending the completion of the transaction *Trans*.

TLength(Trans, File)→ Length — REPORTS(Aborted)
   delivers the tentative new length resulting from the transaction *Trans* if any has been
   recorded, otherwise has the same effect as *Length*.

A transactional file service

A transactional file service is a form of file service that supports atomic transactions on
its files. It supports a construct to allow a client program to group together the file
service operations that comprise an atomic transaction. Figure 12.10 shows the
definitions of the operations in a transactional file service interface. In addition to the
usual file service operations, the operations *OpenTransaction, CloseTransaction* and
AbortTransaction are provided to open, close and abort transactions, see Figure 12.2.
The file operations are similar to those defined in Figure 7.4 but each one has an
additional argument for the transaction identifier.

   When a transaction is opened, the service delivers a unique transaction identifier
(TID) to the client. All of the procedures with the exception of *OpenTransaction* would
report an error for an invalid TID, but these errors are not shown in Figure 12.10. The
client uses the transaction identifier returned by *OpenTransaction* to indicate which of
the subsequent file operations (up to the close of the transaction) are to be included in
the particular transaction it identifies. All of the file service operations defined in
Chapter 7 are included in the transaction service with a modified interface. In this
modified interface, each operation invocation requires an additional argument to specify
the transaction identifier and the procedure names are modified to indicate the
difference: *TRead, TWrite, TCreate, TDelete, TTruncate* and *TLength*.

   Normally, when a client has performed the file operations that comprise the
transaction, it terminates the transaction using *CloseTransaction,* which delivers a
Commit result, indicating that the transaction has committed and that subsequent
transactions by other clients will see the results of all of the changes to files made within

the transaction. If the transaction has been aborted an *Abort* result is delivered from *CloseTransaction* or is reported as an error after an earlier request.

Concurrency control and recovery

Although concurrency control and recovery are essential parts of any transaction system, they also have independent uses. This chapter has shown that concurrency control is required when multiple clients share data and that recovery is required for fault tolerance. When transactions apply to recoverable data that is not shared, concurrency control is not required. For these reasons the design and implementation of mechanisms for concurrency control and recovery should be independent of one another. We therefore present concurrency control and recovery separately in Chapters 13 and 15.

12.5 Nested transactions

A transaction may be structured as a set of **nested transactions**, each of which may itself consist of a set of further nested transactions. For example, a *Transfer* transaction in the banking service could be structured as a pair of nested transactions, one of which is a *Withdraw* operation and the other a *Deposit* operation, as illustrated in Figure 12.11. The atomicity properties stated in Section 12.4 apply to nested transactions — in which the client cannot observe the hierarchic structure.

Nested transactions are useful for two reasons:

1. Nested transactions at one level may run concurrently with other nested transactions at the same level in the hierarchy. This can allow additional concurrency in a transaction. Concurrency control is used to isolate the effects of concurrent nested transactions from one another.

2. Nested transactions can commit or abort independently. In comparison with a single transaction, a nested transaction is more robust. The aborting of a nested transaction does not necessarily imply that its parent must abort. In fact the parent can perform different actions according to whether the child aborts or commits. On the other hand, the committing of a nested transaction is conditional on the committing of its parent.

Consider the *Transfer* transaction. When the two nested transactions (T_1 and T_2) both commit the *Transfer* transaction can also commit. Suppose that a *Withdraw* transaction aborts whenever an account is overdrawn. Now consider the case when the *Withdraw*

Figure 12.11   Nested *Transfer* transaction.

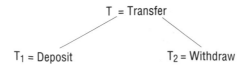

T = Transfer

T_1 = Deposit T_2 = Withdraw

transaction aborts and the *Deposit* transaction commits – and recall that the commitment of a child transaction is conditional on the parent transaction committing. We presume that the parent (*Transfer*) transaction will decide to abort. The aborting of the parent transaction causes the nested transactions to abort – so the *Deposit* transaction is aborted and all its effects are undone.

In some nested transactions the parent transaction may decide to commit in spite of the fact that one or more of its child transactions have aborted. For example, a transaction to deliver a mail message to a list of recipients could be structured as a set of nested transactions, each of which delivers the message to one of the recipients. If one or more of the nested transactions fails, the parent transaction could record the fact and then commit, with the result that all the successful child transactions commit.

Nested transactions are particularly useful in distributed systems because child transactions may be run concurrently in different servers. We return to this issue in Chapter 14.

12.6 Summary

Services provide their clients with operations that enable them to use shared resources, which are represented in the server by data items. The interleaving of threads in a single server due to concurrent clients could cause inconsistencies in these data items. Server operations on shared data must therefore be designed to be atomic.

Conversations between client and server allow the two to work in parallel. Servers that provide conversations cannot be stateless and may require concurrency control at the level of a conversation. The techniques used in transactions can be used for conversations.

Servers need to provide recoverable data if they hold resources that may be used by client processes over a long period of time. This is particularly applicable when a server provides information that users will expect to last for long periods of time.

Transactions provide a means by which clients can specify sequences of operations that are atomic in the presence of other concurrent transactions and server failures. The first aspect of atomicity is achieved by running transactions so that their effects are serially equivalent. Concurrency control protocols are derived from the criterion of serial equivalence. The effects of committed transactions are recorded in permanent storage so that the transaction service can recover from failures. To allow transactions the ability to abort, without having harmful side effects on other transactions, executions must be strict – that is, reads and writes of one transaction must be delayed until other transactions that wrote the same data items have either committed or aborted. To allow transactions the choice of either committing or aborting, their operations are performed in tentative versions that cannot be accessed by other transactions. The tentative versions of data items are copied to the real data items and to permanent storage when a transaction commits.

Nested transactions are formed by structuring transactions from other sub-transactions. Nesting is particularly useful in distributed systems because it allows concurrent execution of sub-transactions in separate servers. Nesting also has the advantage of allowing independent recovery of parts of a transaction.

EXERCISES

12.1   A service called SimpleName manages a set of mappings from *Name* to *Id* and provides the operations:

LookUp(Name) → *Id*
   returns the value corresponding to the given name, *Name*.

Store(Name, Id)
   if there is a mapping with *Name*, replace its *Id*; otherwise add a new mapping from *Name* to *Id*.

Delete(Name)
   delete the mapping with *Name*.

Enumerate( )→ *set of (Name, Id)*
   return all the mappings.

Explain in the context of the SimpleName service: 'The effect of a request to perform an operation on a server depends on the actual request, its arguments and the current values of the server's data items.'

page 354

12.2   The SimpleName service (Exercise 12.1) is to be designed so that its resources can be recovered from a file if the server process fails. Describe the information that must be stored in the recovery file and how it will be arranged, assuming that the service may sometimes hold large amounts of data. When is the recovery file updated? What information is written each time an update takes place? Outline the recovery procedure.

pages 354 and 358

12.3   The TaskBag is a service whose functionality is to provide a repository for 'task descriptions'. It enables clients running in several workstations to carry out parts of a computation in parallel. A *master* process places descriptions of subtasks of a computation in the TaskBag and *worker* processes select tasks from the TaskBag and carry them out, returning descriptions of results to the TaskBag. The *master* then collects the results and combines them to produce the final result.

The TaskBag service provides the following operations:

   SetTask   allows clients to add task descriptions to the bag;

   TakeTask allows clients to take task descriptions out of the bag.

A client makes the request *TakeTask*, when a task is not available, but may be available soon. Discuss the advantages and drawbacks of the following alternatives:

i)   the server can reply immediately, telling the client to try again later;

ii)   make the server operation (and therefore the client) wait until a task becomes available.

page 356

12.4 Explain why server threads are needed for the second alternative in Exercise 12.3. Explain how to use a mutex to prevent the operations of different clients from accessing the data in an inconsistent manner. Describe how to use operations *Wait* and *Signal* to implement this alternative.

page 356

12.5 Consider the *Enumerate* operation of the SimpleName service in Exercise 12.1. Bear in mind that it may return a very large amount of information. Discuss the advantages and drawbacks of the following alternatives:

i)   all the mappings in a set are returned as the result of a single request;

ii)   the server orders the mappings and the arguments of the *Enumerate* operation specify a range of associations;

iii)   the client and server use a 'conversation'.

page 356

12.6 A server manages the data items a_1, a_2, ... a_n. The server provides two operations for its clients:

   Read (i) returns the value of a_i;

   Write(i, Value) assigns *Value* to a_i.

The transactions T and U are defined as follows:

   T: *x:= Read (j); y:= Read (i); Write(j, 44); Write(i, 33);*

   U: *x:= Read(k); Write(i, 55); y := Read (j); Write(k, 66).*

Give three serially equivalent interleavings of the transactions T and U.

page 364

12.7 Give serially equivalent interleaving of T and U in Exercise 12.6 with the following properties: (i) that is strict; (ii) that is not strict but could not produce cascading aborts; (iii) that could produce cascading aborts.

page 366

12.8 Explain the meaning of a 'lost update'. Describe how a client of the service in Exercise 12.6 might experience lost updates.

page 363

12.9 Explain the meaning of 'inconsistent retrievals'. Describe how a client of the service in Exercise 12.6 might experience inconsistent retrievals.

page 363

12.10   An operation for inserting a new account is added to the *Banking Service*:

   Insert(Name, amount) creates a new account called *Name* with initial balance *amount*.

   The transactions T and U are defined as follows:

   T: *Bank$Insert(C, 100)*;

   U: *Bank$Deposit(C, 10); Bank$Deposit(C, 20)*.

   Assume that account B exists and has a balance of $100, but C does not yet exist. Assume also that the *Deposit* operation does nothing if the account given as argument does not exist. Consider the following interleaving of transactions T and U:

T	U
	Bank$Deposit(C, 10);
Bank$Insert(C, 100);	
	Bank$Deposit(C, 20);

   State the balances of B and C after their execution in this order. Are these consistent with serially equivalent executions of T and U?

page 364

12.11   A newly created data item like C in Exercise 12.10 is sometimes called a *phantom*. From the point of view of transaction U, C is not there at first and then appears (like a ghost). Explain with an example, how a phantom could occur when an account is deleted.

12.12   Give an example illustrating how phantoms (see Exercise 12.11) could occur in the use of the transactional file service in Figure 12.10.

12.13   Suppose that the 'Transfer' transactions T and U described in Figure 12.4 are structured as pairs of nested transactions:

   T_1: Bank$Withdraw(A,4); T_2: Bank$Deposit(B,4);

   U_1: Bank$Withdraw(C,3); U_2: Bank$Deposit(B,3).

   Compare the number of serially equivalent interleavings of T1, T2, U1 and U2 with the number of serially equivalent interleavings of T and U. Explain why the use of these nested transactions generally permits a larger number of serially equivalent interleavings than non-nested ones.

pages 364 and 370

12.14 Consider the recovery aspects of the nested transactions defined in Exercise 12.13. Assume that a *Withdraw* transaction will abort if the account will be overdrawn and that in this case the parent transaction will also abort. Describe serially equivalent interleavings of T1, T2, U1 and U2 with the following properties: (i) that is strict; (ii) that is not strict. To what extent does the criterion of strictness reduce the potential concurrency gain of nested transactions?

page 370

13

CONCURRENCY CONTROL

This chapter concentrates on concurrency control for servers whose operations may be modelled in terms of *Read* and *Write* operations on the data items.

All of the concurrency control protocols are based on the criterion of serial equivalence and are derived from rules for conflicts between operations. Three methods are described:

- Locks are used to order transactions that access the same data items according to the order of arrival of their operations at the data items.

- Optimistic concurrency control allows transactions to proceed until they are ready to commit, whereupon a check is made to see whether they have performed conflicting operations on data items.

- Timestamp ordering uses timestamps to order transactions that access the same data items according to their starting times.

13.1 Introduction

In general a server executes operations on behalf of several clients whose requests may be interleaved. Atomic transactions allow clients to specify atomic sequences of operations. Transactions must be scheduled so that their effect on shared data is serially equivalent. A server can achieve serial equivalence of transactions by serializing access to the data items. This chapter discusses methods of concurrency control for transactions whose operations are all addressed to a single server. Chapter 14 discusses how these methods are extended for use with transactions whose operations are addressed to several servers. Figure 12.6 shows an example of how serial equivalence can be achieved with some degree of concurrency – transactions T and U both access account B, but T completes its access before U starts accessing it.

A simple example of a serializing mechanism is the use of exclusive locks. In this locking scheme the server attempts to lock any data item that is about to be used by any operation of a client's transaction. If a client requests access to an item that is already locked due to another client's transaction, the request is suspended and the client must wait until the item is unlocked.

Figure 13.1 illustrates the use of exclusive locks. It shows the same transactions as Figure 12.6, but with an extra column for each transaction showing the locking, waiting and unlocking. In this example, it is assumed that, when transactions T and U start, the data items holding the balances of the accounts A, B and C are not yet locked.

Figure 13.1   Transactions T and U with exclusive locks.

Transaction T: *Bank$Withdraw(A, 4)* *Bank$Deposit(B, 4)*		Transaction U: *Bank$Withdraw(C, 3)* *Bank$Deposit(B, 3)*	
Operations	Locks	Operations	Locks
OpenTransaction			
balance := A.Read( )	locks A		
A.Write(balance – 4)			
		OpenTransaction	
		balance := C.Read( )	locks C
		C.Write(balance – 3)	
balance := B.Read( )	locks B		
		balance := B.Read()	waits for T's lock on B
B.Write(balance + 4)		•	
CloseTransaction	unlocks A, B	•	
		•	locks B
		B.Write(balance + 3)	
		CloseTransaction	unlocks B, C

When transaction T is about to read account B, the server locks it for T. Subsequently, when transaction U is about to read B it is still locked for T, and transaction U waits. When transaction T is committed, B is unlocked whereupon transaction U is resumed. The use of the lock on B effectively serializes the access to B. Note that if for example, T had released the lock on B between its *Read* and *Write* operations, transaction U's *Read* operation on B could be interleaved between them.

Serial equivalence requires that all of a transaction's accesses to a particular data item be serialized with respect to accesses by other transactions. All pairs of conflicting operations of two transactions should be executed in the same order. To ensure this, a transaction is not allowed any new locks after it has released a lock. The first phase of each transaction is a 'growing phase' during which new locks are acquired. In the second phase the locks are released (a 'shrinking phase'). This is called **two-phase locking**.

We saw in Section 12.3 that because transactions may abort, strict executions are needed to prevent dirty reads and premature writes. Under a strict execution regime, a transaction that needs to read or write a data item must be delayed until other transactions that wrote the same data item have committed or aborted. To enforce this rule, any locks applied during the progress of a transaction are held until the transaction commits or aborts. This is called **strict two-phase locking**. The presence of the locks prevents other transactions from reading or writing the data items. When a transaction commits, to ensure recoverability, the locks must be held until all the data items it updated have been written to permanent storage.

A server generally contains a large number of data items and a typical transaction accesses only a few of them and is unlikely to clash with other current transactions. The *granularity* with which concurrency control can be applied to data items is an important issue since the scope for concurrent access to a server will be limited severely if concurrency control (for example, locks) can only be applied to all the data items at once. In our banking example, if locks are applied to all customer accounts at a branch, only one bank clerk could perform an on-line banking transaction at any time – hardly an acceptable constraint!

The portion of the data items to which access must be serialized should be as small as possible, that is, just that part involved in each operation requested by transactions. In our banking example, a branch holds a set of accounts, each of which has a balance. Each banking operation affects one or more account balances – *Deposit* and *Withdraw* affect one account balance and *BranchTotal* affects all of them.

The description of concurrency control schemes given below does not assume any particular granularity.

We discuss concurrency control protocols that are applicable to servers whose operations can be modelled in terms of *Read* and *Write* operations on the data items. For the protocols to work correctly, it is essential that each *Read* and *Write* operation is atomic in its effects on data items.

Concurrency control protocols are designed to cope with **conflicts** between operations in different transactions on the same data item. In this chapter, we use the notion of conflict between operations to explain the protocols. When we say that a pair of operations conflicts we mean that their combined effect depends on the order in which they are executed. The effect of an operation refers to the value of a data item set by a

Figure 13.2   *Read* and *Write* operation conflict rules.

Operations of different transactions		Conflict	Reason
Read	Read	No	Because the effect of a pair of *Read* operations does not depend on the order in which they are executed
Read	Write	Yes	Because the effect of a *Read* and a *Write* operation depends on the order of their execution
Write	Write	Yes	Because the effect of a pair of *Write* operations depends on the order of their execution

Write operation and the result returned by a *Read* operation. The conflict rules for *Read* and *Write* operations are given in Figure 13.2.

Three alternative approaches to concurrency control are commonly used; these are locking, optimistic concurrency control and timestamp ordering. However, most practical systems use locking, which is discussed in Section 13.2. When locking is used, the server sets a lock, labelled with the transaction identifier, on each data item just before it is accessed and removes these locks when the transaction has completed. While a data item is locked, only the transaction that it is locked for can access that item; other transactions must either wait until the item is unlocked or in some cases, share the lock. The use of locks can lead to deadlock with transactions waiting for each other to release locks; as, for example, when a pair of transactions each has a data item locked that the other needs to access. We shall discuss the deadlock problem and some remedies for it in Section 13.2.

Optimistic concurrency control is described in Section 13.3. In optimistic schemes a transaction proceeds until it asks to commit, and before it is allowed to commit the server performs a check to discover whether it has performed operations on any data items that conflict with the operations of other concurrent transactions, in which case the server aborts it and the client may restart it. The aim of the check is to ensure that the data items are all correct.

Timestamp ordering is described in Section 13.4. In timestamp ordering a server records the most recent time of reading and writing each data item and for each operation, the timestamp of the transaction is compared with that of the data item to determine whether it can be done immediately, delayed or rejected. When an operation is delayed, the transaction waits, when it is rejected, the transaction is aborted.

Basically, concurrency control can be achieved either by clients' transactions waiting for one another or by restarting transactions after conflicts between operations have been detected or by a combination of the two.

In all of these methods, we assume that any server of a transactional service provides for each transaction its own private tentative version of the changes it is making and that each transaction is unable to observe the other transactions' tentative versions (see Section 12.4).

13.2 Locks

The operation conflict rules in Figure 13.2 show that pairs of *Read* operations from different transactions on the same data item do not conflict. Therefore, a simple exclusive lock that is used for both *Read* and *Write* operations reduces concurrency more than is necessary.

It is preferable to adopt a locking scheme that controls the access to each data item so that there can be several concurrent transactions reading a data item, or a single transaction writing a data item, but not both. This is commonly referred to as a 'many reader/single writer' scheme. Two types of locks are used: *read locks* and *write locks*. Before a transaction's *Read* operation is performed, the server attempts to set a read lock on the data item. Before a transaction's *Write* operation is performed, the server attempts to set a write lock on the data item. Whenever a server is unable to set a lock immediately it keeps the transaction (and the client) waiting until it is able to do so – it never rejects a client's request.

As pairs of *Read* operations from different transactions do not conflict, an attempt to set a read lock on the data item with a read lock is always successful. All the transactions reading the same data item share its read lock – for this reason, read locks are sometimes called *shared locks*.

The operation conflict rules tell us that:

1. If a transaction T has already performed a *Read* operation on a particular data item, then a concurrent transaction U must not *Write* that data item until T commits or aborts.

2. If a transaction T has already performed a *Write* operation on a particular data item, then a concurrent transaction U must not *Read* or *Write* that data item until T commits or aborts.

To enforce (1) a request for a write lock on a data item is delayed by the presence of a read lock belonging to another transaction. To enforce (2) a request for either a read lock or a write lock on a data item is delayed by the presence of a write lock belonging to another transaction.

The Figure 13.3 shows the compatibility of read locks and write locks on any particular data item. The entries in the first column of the table show the type of lock already set – if any. The entries in the first row show the type of lock requested. The entry in each cell shows the effect on a transaction that requests the type of lock given above when the data item already has the type of lock on the left.

Figure 13.3   Lock compatibility.

For one data item		*Lock requested*	
		Read	*Write*
Lock already set	*None*	OK	OK
	Read	OK	Wait
	Write	Wait	Wait

Figure 13.4   Use of locks in strict two-phase locking.

---

1. When an operation accesses a data item within a transaction:

   a) If the data item is not already locked, the server locks it and the operation proceeds.

   b) If the data item has a conflicting lock set by another transaction, the transaction must wait until it is unlocked.

   c) If the data item has a non-conflicting lock set by another transaction, the lock is shared and the operation proceeds.

   d) If the data item has already been locked in the same transaction, the lock will be promoted if necessary and the operation proceeds. (Where promotion is prevented by a conflicting lock, rule (b) is used.)

2. When a transaction is committed or aborted, the server unlocks all data items it locked for the transaction.

Inconsistent retrievals and lost updates are caused by conflicts between *Read* operations in one transaction and *Write* operations in another. Inconsistent retrievals are prevented by performing the retrieval transaction before or after the update transaction. If the retrieval transaction comes first, its read locks delay the update transaction. If it comes second, its request for read locks causes it to be delayed until the update transaction has completed.

Lost updates occur when two transactions read a value of a data item and then use it to calculate a new value. Lost updates are prevented by making later transactions delay their reads until the earlier ones have completed. This is achieved by each transaction setting a read lock when it reads a data item and then *promoting* it to a write lock when it writes the same data item – when a subsequent transaction requires a read lock it will be delayed until any current transaction has completed.

A transaction with a read lock that is shared with other transactions cannot promote its read lock to a write lock because the latter would conflict with the read locks held by the other transactions. Therefore such a transaction must request a write lock and wait for the other read locks to be released.

Lock promotion refers to the conversion of a lock to a stronger lock - that is a lock that is more exclusive. The lock compatibility table shows which locks are more or less exclusive. The read lock allows other read locks, whereas the write lock does not. Neither allow other write locks. Therefore a write lock is more exclusive than a read lock. Locks may be promoted because the result is a more exclusive lock. It is not safe to demote a lock held by a transaction before it commits because the result will be more permissive than the previous one and may allow executions by other transactions that are inconsistent with serial equivalence.

The rules for the use of locks in a strict two-phase locking implementation are summarized in Figure 13.4. To ensure that these rules are adhered to, the client has no access to operations for locking or unlocking items of data. Locking is performed by the

Figure 13.5   Lock manager functions.

Lock (Trans, DataItem, LockType)
> if there is a conflicting lock, that is, if there is an entry in the table belonging to another transaction that conflicts with *DataItem*, *Wait* on the condition variable associated with the entry.
> if (immediately or after a *Wait*) there are no conflicting locks:
>> if there is no entry for *DataItem*, add an entry to the table of locks
>> else if there is an entry for *DataItem* belonging to a different transaction, add *Trans* to the entry (share the lock)
>> else if there is an entry for *DataItem* belonging to *Trans* and *LockType* is more exclusive than the type in the entry, change entry to *LockType* (promote lock).

UnLock (Trans)
> if there are any entries in the table belonging to transaction *Trans*, for each entry:
>> if there is only one holder (*Trans*) in the entry, remove the entry
>> else (a shared lock) remove *Trans* from the entry and *Signal* the associated condition variable.

---

server when the *Read* and *Write* operations are requested and unlocking by the *Commit* or *Abort* operations of transactional service.

The rules given in Figure 13.4 ensure strictness because the locks are held until a transaction has either committed or aborted. However, it is not necessary to hold read locks to ensure strictness. Read locks must be held until the request to commit or abort to ensure serial equivalence by using two-phase locking.

Lock implementation □ The granting of locks will be implemented by a separate module of the server program that we call the **lock manager**. We discuss the design of a lock manager for use with transactions. A lock manager is responsible for maintaining a table of locks for the data items of a server. Each entry in the table of locks includes:

- the transaction identifiers of the transactions that hold the lock (shared locks can have several holders);

- an identifier for a data item;

- a lock type;

- a condition variable.

The identifier for the data item must be something available to the *Read* or *Write* operation, generally an argument. For example, in our banking example, the identifier would be the name of an account.

In Chapter 12, it is argued that when a client needs to wait to access a shared resource, it is better for the server to suspend the client's request with a *Wait* operation than to tell the client to try again later. To make this possible, each client request runs in a separate server thread. When a lock cannot be granted, the thread running the request

Figure 13.6   Deadlock with read and write locks.

Transaction T		Transaction U	
Operations	Locks	Operations	Locks
balance:= A.Read( )	read locks A		
		balance:= C.Read( )	read locks C
		C.Write(balance – 3)	write locks C
A.Write(balance – 4)	write locks A		
•••			
balance := B.Read( )	read locks B		
		balance := B.Read( )	shares read lock on B
B.Write(balance + 4)	waits for U		
•••		*B.Write(balance + 3)*	waits for T
•••		•••	

Waits on the condition variable and when the server unlocks a data item, the condition variable is *Signalled*.

The lock manager provides the operations *Lock* for requesting locks and *UnLock* for releasing them (as shown in Figure 13.5). The operations on the table of locks must be atomic. The *Lock* operation uses the lock type given as argument and the lock types of entries for the same data item (belonging to other transactions), together with the lock compatibility table to decide whether there is a conflicting entry.

Note that, when several threads *wait* on the same locked item, the semantics of *wait* ensure that each transaction gets its turn. When the queue of waiting threads at a condition variable is headed by several requests for shared locks it is an optimization to allow them all to proceed by signalling more than once.

Deadlocks

The use of locks can lead to deadlock. Consider the use of locks shown in Figure 13.6. This differs from Figure 13.1 in that both transactions now read the balance of account B and share the read lock, but when T wants to write the balance of B it must wait until the other transaction unlocks it. Similarly when U wants to write to the balance of B it must wait until T unlocks the item. This is a deadlock situation – two transactions are waiting and each is dependent on the other to release a lock so it can resume.

The *Deposit* and *Withdraw* operations in our banking service example can easily produce a deadlock. The reason for this is that each operation first requests a read lock on an account and then attempts to promote it to a write lock. Deadlock would be less likely to arise in the banking service if these operations were to request write locks initially.

Figure 13.7   An illustration of Violet showing the union of some diaries.

View: {Smith.qmw, Jones.qmw}				
January 1988				
25 Monday	26 Tuesday	27 Wednesday	28 Thursday	29 Friday
9:00–10:00 Jones unavailable	10:00–12:00 Jones unavailable	9:00–10:00 Jones unavailable	9:00–12:00 Jones Smith unavailable	
13:00–14:00 Jones Smith unavailable	11:00–-12:00 Jones unavailable	14:00–15:00 Jones Smith unavailable		

View: Meetings.qmw				
January 1988				
25 Monday	26 Tuesday	27 Wednesday	28 Thursday	29 Friday
	10:00–12:00 hardware research		9:00–12:00 Equipment planning	
13:00–14:00 Dept. meeting		14:00–15:00 Dr. Visitor Interesting facts		

Deadlock is a particularly common situation when clients are involved in an interactive program, for a transaction in an interactive program may last for a long period of time, resulting in many data items being locked and remaining so, thus preventing other clients from using them. An interesting example of such a program is the Violet system described by Gifford [1979b] and Lampson [1981b]. The Violet system illustrated in Figure 13.7 provides a calendar or diary database that can be viewed and updated interactively by a number of users. It allows users to view pages from other people's diaries before arranging meetings. A user who wants to make an appointment with someone views that person's diary and then writes in an appointment. Another user may have the same idea at the same time and also view a copy of the diary and subsequently attempt to add an appointment for the same day. We can regard one day in a diary as an item of data and viewing it will result in a read lock on it. Adding an entry will require altering the read lock to a write lock. It is permissible for two users to view the same object at the same time and this is implemented by sharing the read lock on the item. However, neither user will be able to write an appointment, as it is not permissible for either client to convert the read lock to a write lock in the presence of the other transaction's shared read lock on the same item.

Note that the locking of sub-items in structured data items can be useful. For example, a day in a diary could be structured as a set of time slots, each of which can be locked independently for updating. On the other hand, the view shown in Figure 13.7

Figure 13.8   The wait-for graph for Figure 13.6.

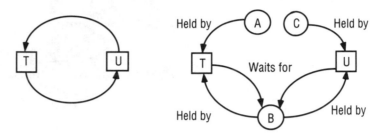

shows a week and for viewing, it may be best to apply a read lock to an entire week. Hierarchic locking schemes are useful if the application requires different granularity locking for different operations.

Deadlock ☐ Deadlock is a state in which each member of a group of transactions is waiting for some other member to release a lock. A wait-for graph can be used to represent the waiting relationships between current transactions at a server. In a *wait-for graph* the nodes represent transactions and the edges represent wait-for relationships between transactions – there is an edge from node T to node U when transaction T is waiting for transaction U to release a lock. See Figure 13.8 which illustrates the wait-for graph corresponding to the deadlock situation illustrated in Figure 13.6. Recall that the deadlock arose because transactions T and U both requested write locks on data item B when they already shared a read lock on B. Therefore T waits for U and U waits for T. The dependency between transactions is indirect – via a dependency on data items. The diagram on the right shows the data items held by and waited for by transactions T and U. As each transaction can wait for only one data item, the data items can be omitted from the wait-for graph – leaving the simple graph on the left.

Suppose that as in Figure 13.9, a wait-for graph contains a cycle T → U → ... → V → T, then each transaction is waiting for the next transaction in the cycle. All of these transactions are blocked waiting for locks. None of the locks can ever be released and the transactions are deadlocked. If one of the transactions in a cycle is aborted, then its locks are released and that cycle is broken. For example if transaction T in Figure 13.9 is aborted, it will release a lock on a data item that V is waiting for – and V will no longer be waiting for T.

Now consider a scenario in which the three transactions T, U and V share a read lock on a data item C, transaction W holds a write lock on data item B on which

Figure 13.9   A cycle in a wait-for graph.

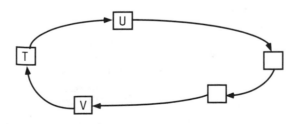

Figure 13.10   Another wait-for graph.

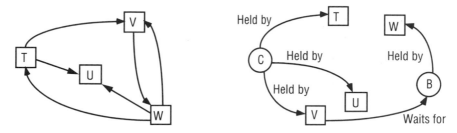

transaction V is waiting to obtain a lock, as shown on the right in Figure 13.10. The transactions T and W then request write locks on data item C and a deadlock situation arises in which T waits for U and V, V waits for W and W waits for T, U and V, as shown on the left in Figure 13.10. This shows that although each transaction can wait for only one data item at a time, it may be involved in several cycles. For example, transaction V is involved in cycles: V → W →T → V and V → W → V.

In this example, suppose that transaction V is aborted, this will release V's lock on C and the two cycles involving V will be broken.

Deadlock prevention □ One solution is to prevent deadlock. An apparently simple, but not very good way to overcome deadlock is to lock all of the data items used by a transaction when it starts. Such a transaction cannot run into deadlock with other transactions, but it unnecessarily restricts access to shared resources. In addition it is sometimes impossible to predict at the start of a transaction which data items will be used. This is generally the case in interactive applications, for example, in the Violet system the user would have to say in advance which weeks of which diaries would be viewed and which days would be updated. Deadlock can also be prevented by requesting locks on data items in a predefined order, but this can result in premature locking and a reduction in concurrency.

Deadlock detection □ Deadlocks may be detected by finding cycles in the wait-for graph. Having detected a deadlock, the server must select a transaction to abort, so as to break the cycle.

The software responsible for deadlock detection can be part of the lock manager. It must hold a representation of the wait-for graph so that it can check it for cycles from time to time. Edges are added to the graph and removed from the graph by the lock manager's *Lock* and *UnLock* operations. At the point illustrated by Figure 13.10 it will have the following information:

Transaction	Waits for transaction
T	U, V
V	W
W	T, U, V

An edge T → U is added whenever the lock manager blocks a request by transaction T for a lock on a data item that is already locked on behalf of transaction U. Note that when a lock is shared, several edges may be added. An edge T → U is deleted whenever U releases a lock that T is waiting for and allows T to proceed. See Exercise 13.7 for a more detailed discussion of the implementation of deadlock detection. If a transaction shares a lock, the lock is not released but the edges leading to a particular transaction are removed.

The presence of cycles may be checked each time an edge is added, or less frequently to avoid server overhead. When a deadlock is detected, one of the transactions in the cycle must be chosen and then be aborted. The corresponding node and the edges involving it must be removed from the wait-for graph. This will happen when the aborted transaction has its locks removed.

The choice of the transaction to abort is not simple. Some factors that may be taken into account are the age of the transaction and the number of cycles it is involved in.

Timeouts □ Lock timeouts are a method for resolution of deadlocks that is commonly used. Each lock is given a limited period in which it is invulnerable. After this time, a lock becomes vulnerable. Provided that no other transaction is competing for the item that is locked, an item with a vulnerable lock remains locked. However, if any other transaction is waiting to access the data item protected by a vulnerable lock, the lock is broken (that is, the data item is unlocked) and the waiting transaction resumes. The transaction whose lock has been broken is normally aborted.

There are many problems with the use of timeouts as a remedy for deadlocks: the worst problem is that transactions are sometimes aborted due to their locks becoming vulnerable when other transactions are waiting for them, but there is actually no deadlock. In an overloaded system, the number of transactions timing out will increase and transactions taking a long time can be penalized. In addition, it is hard to decide on an appropriate length for a timeout. In contrast, if deadlock detection is used, transactions are aborted because deadlocks have occurred and servers can make a choice as to which transaction to abort.

It is possible that the correctness of a transaction does not depend on the value of the data item whose lock is broken and, in that case, it may not be necessary to abort the transaction when a vulnerable lock is broken. In the XDFS file server [Israel *et al*. 1978, Mitchell 1982], the client is notified when a read lock is broken and may voluntarily unlock the item it protects, in which case the transaction may continue and commit successfully. If the client has not unlocked the item after the lock is broken, a commit would fail.

Using lock timeouts, we can resolve the deadlock in Figure 13.6 as shown in Figure 13.11 in which the read lock for T on B becomes vulnerable after its timeout period. Transaction U is waiting to alter it to a write lock. Therefore T is aborted and it releases its share of the read lock on B allowing U to resume, convert its read lock to a write lock and complete the transaction.

Increasing concurrency in locking schemes

Even when locking rules are based on the conflicts between *Read* and *Write* operations and the granularity at which they are applied is as small as possible, there is still some scope for increasing concurrency. We shall discuss two approaches that have been used.

Figure 13.11   Resolution of the deadlock in Figure 13.6.

Transaction T		Transaction U	
Operations	Locks	Operations	Locks
balance:= A.Read( )	read locks *A*		
		balance:= C.Read( )	read locks *C*
		C.Write(balance – 3)	write locks *C*
A.Write(balance – 4)	write locks *A*		
•••		•••	
balance := B.Read( )	read locks *B*		
		balance := B.Read( )	shares read lock on *B*
B.Write(balance + 4)	waits on U's read lock on*B*		
•••		*B.Write(balance + 3)*	waits on T's read lock on *B*
	(timeout elapses) T's lock on *B* becomes vulnerable, unlock *B*, abort T	•••	
		B.Write(balance +3)	write locks *B*
			unlock *B* and *C*

In the first approach (two-version locking), the setting of exclusive locks is delayed until a transaction commits. In the second approach (hierarchic locks), mixed granularity locks are used.

Two-version locking □ This is an optimistic scheme that allows one transaction to write tentative versions of data items while other transactions read from the committed version of the same data items. Read operations only wait if another transaction is currently committing the same data item. This scheme allows more concurrency than read-write locks but writing transactions risk waiting or even rejection when they attempt to commit. Transactions cannot commit their write operations immediately if other uncompleted transactions have read the same data items. Therefore transactions that request to commit in such a situation are made to wait until the reading transactions have completed. Deadlock may occur when transactions are waiting to commit. Therefore transactions may need to be aborted when they are waiting to commit, to resolve deadlocks.

This variation on strict two-phase locking was proposed by Gifford for Violet and implemented in the XDFS file server. It uses three types of locks: a read lock, a write lock and a commit lock. Before a transaction's *Read* operation is performed, the server attempts to set a read lock on the data item – the attempt to set a read lock is successful unless the data item has a commit lock, in which case the transaction waits. Before a

Figure 13.12 Lock compatibility (*read*, *write* and *commit* locks).

For one data item		*Lock to be set*		
		Read	*Write*	*Commit*
Lock already set	*None*	OK	OK	OK
	Read	OK	OK	Wait
	Write	OK	Wait	–
	Commit	Wait	Wait	–

transaction's *Write* operation is performed, the server attempts to set a write lock on the data item - the attempt to set a write lock is successful unless the data item has a write lock or a commit lock, in which case the transaction waits.

When the server receives a request to commit a transaction, it attempts to convert all that transaction's write locks to commit locks. If any of the data items have outstanding read locks, the transaction must wait until the transactions that set these locks have completed and the locks are released. The compatibility of the read, write and commit locks is shown in Figure 13.12.

There are two main differences in performance between the two-version locking scheme and an ordinary read-write locking scheme. On the one hand, *Read* operations in the two-version locking scheme are delayed only during the commitment of transactions rather than during the entire execution of transactions – in most cases the commitment takes only a small fraction of the time required to perform an entire transaction. On the other hand, *Read* operations of one transaction can cause delay in committing other transactions.

Hierarchic locks ☐ In some servers, the granularity suitable for one operation is not appropriate for another operation. In our banking example, the majority of the operations require locking at the granularity of an account. The *BranchTotal* operation is different – it reads the values of all the account balances and would appear to require a read lock on all of them. To reduce locking overhead it would be useful to allow locks of mixed granularity to coexist.

Gray [1978] proposed the use of a hierarchy of locks with different granularities. At each level, the setting of a parent lock has the same effect as setting all the equivalent child locks. This economizes on the number of locks to be set. In our banking example, the branch is the parent and the accounts are children (see Figure 13.13).

Figure 13.13 Lock hierarchy for the Bank Server.

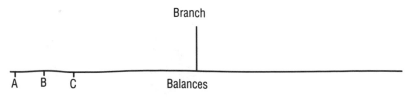

Figure 13.14 Lock hierarchy for Violet.

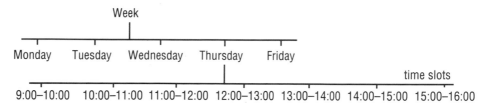

We noted earlier that mixed granularity locks could be useful in the Violet system in which the data could be structured with the diary for a week being composed of a page for each day and the latter subdivided further into a slot for each time of day as shown in Figure 13.14. The operation to view a week would cause a read lock to be set at the top of this hierarchy whereas the operation to enter an appointment would cause a write lock to be set on a time slot. The effect of a read lock on a week would be to prevent write operations on any of the substructures, for example, the time slots for each day in that week.

In Gray's scheme, each node in the hierarchy can be locked – giving the owner of the lock explicit access to the node and implicit access to its children. In our example, a read/write lock on the branch implicitly read/write locks all the accounts. Before a child node is granted a read/write lock, an intention to read/write lock is set on the parent node and its ancestors (if any). The intention lock is compatible with other intention locks but conflicts with read and write locks according to the usual rules. Figure 13.15 gives the compatibility table for hierarchic locks. Gray also proposed a third type of intention lock - that combines the property of a read lock with an intention to write lock.

In our banking example the *BranchTotal* operation requests a read lock on the branch which implicitly sets read locks on all the accounts. A *Deposit* operation needs to set a write lock on a balance, but first it attempts to set an intention to write lock on the branch. These rules prevent these operations from running concurrently.

Hierarchic locks have the advantage of reducing the number of locks when mixed granularity locking is required. The compatibility tables and the rules for promoting locks are more complex. The mixed granularity of locks can increase concurrency when many short transactions are combined with other transactions that take a long time.

Figure 13.15 Lock compatibility table for hierarchic locks.

For one data item		*Lock to be set*			
		Read	*Write*	*I-Read*	*I-Write*
Lock already set	*Read*	OK	Wait	OK	Wait
	Write	Wait	Wait	Wait	Wait
	I-Read	OK	Wait	OK	OK
	I-Write	Wait	Wait	OK	OK

13.3 Optimistic concurrency control

Kung and Robinson [1981] identified a number of inherent disadvantages of locking and proposed an alternative optimistic approach to the serialization of transactions that avoids these drawbacks. We can summarize the drawbacks of locking:

- Lock maintenance represents an overhead that is not present in systems that do not support concurrent access to shared data. Even read-only transactions (queries), which cannot possibly affect the integrity of the data, must, in general, use locking in order to guarantee that the data being read is not modified by other transactions at the same time. But locking may be necessary only in the worst case.

  For example, consider two client processes that are concurrently incrementing the values of n data items. If the client programs start at the same time, and run for about the same amount of time, accessing the data items in two unrelated sequences and using a separate transaction to access and increment each item, the chances that the two programs will attempt to access the same data item at the same time are just one in n on average, so locking is really needed only once in every n transactions.

- The use of locks can result in deadlock. Deadlock prevention reduces concurrency severely and therefore deadlock situations must be resolved either by the use of timeouts or by deadlock detection. Neither of these is wholly satisfactory for use in interactive programs.

- To avoid cascading aborts, locks cannot be released until the end of the transaction. This may reduce significantly the potential for concurrency.

The alternative approach proposed by Kung and Robinson is 'optimistic' because it is based on the observation that, in most applications, the likelihood of two clients' transactions accessing the same data is low. Transactions are allowed to proceed as though there were no possibility of conflict with other transactions until the client completes its task and issues a *CloseTransaction* request. When a conflict arises, some transaction is generally aborted and will need to be restarted by the client.

Each transaction has the following phases:

Read phase: During the read phase, each transaction has a tentative version of each of the data items that it updates. The use of tentative versions allows the transaction to abort (with no effect on the data items), either during the read phase or if it fails validation due to other conflicting transactions. *Read* operations are performed immediately – if a tentative version for that transaction already exists, a *Read* operation accesses it, otherwise it accesses the most recently committed value of the data item. *Write* operations record the new values of the data items as tentative values (which are invisible to other transactions). When there are several concurrent transactions, several different tentative values of the same data item may coexist. In addition two records are kept of the data items accessed within a transaction: a *read set* containing the data items read by the transaction and a *write set* containing the data items written by the transaction. Note that as all *Read* operations are performed on committed versions of the data items, dirty reads cannot occur.

Validation phase: When the *CloseTransaction* request is received, the transaction is validated to establish whether or not its operations on data items conflict with operations of other transactions on the same data items. If the validation is successful, then the transaction can commit. If the validation fails, then some form of conflict resolution must be used and either the current transaction, or in some cases those with which it conflicts, will need to be aborted.

Write phase: If a transaction is validated, all of the changes recorded in its tentative versions are made permanent. Read only transactions can commit immediately after passing validation. Write transactions are ready to commit once the tentative versions of the data items have been recorded in permanent storage.

Validation of transactions ☐ Validation uses the Read/Write conflict rules to ensure that the scheduling of a particular transaction is serially equivalent with respect to all other overlapping transactions – that is any transactions that had not yet committed at the time this transaction started. To assist in performing validation, each transaction is assigned a transaction number when it enters the validation phase (that is, when the client issues a *CloseTransaction*). If the transaction is validated and completes successfully it retains this number; if it fails the validation checks and is aborted, or if the transaction is read only, the number is released for re-assignment. Transaction numbers are integers assigned in ascending sequence; the number of a transaction therefore defines its position in time – a transaction always finishes its read phase after all transactions with lower numbers, that is, a transaction with the number T_i always precedes a transaction with the number T_j if $i < j$. (If the transaction number were to be assigned at the beginning of the read phase, then a transaction that reached the end of the read phase before one with a lower number would have to wait until the earlier one had completed before it could be validated.)

The validation test is based on conflicts between operations in pairs of transaction T_i and T_j. For a transaction T_j to be serializable with respect to an overlapping transaction T_i, their operations must conform to the following rules:

T_i	T_j	Rule	
Read	Write	1.	T_i must not read data items written by T_j
Write	Read	2.	T_j must not read data items written by T_i
Write	Write	3.	T_i must not write data items written by T_j and T_j must not write data items written by T_i.

As the validation and write phases of a transaction are generally short in duration compared with the read phase, a simplification may be achieved by making the rule that only one transaction may be in the validation and write phase at one time. When no two transactions may overlap in the write phase, Rule 3 is satisfied. Note that this restriction on *Write* operations, together with the fact that no dirty reads may occur, produces strict executions. To prevent overlapping, the entire validation and write phases can be implemented as a critical section so that only one client at a time can execute it. In order

Figure 13.16 Validation of transactions.

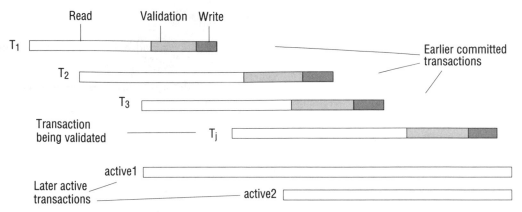

to increase concurrency, part of the validation and writing may be implemented outside the critical section, but it is essential that the assignment of transaction numbers is performed sequentially. We note that at any instant, the current transaction number is like a pseudo-clock that ticks whenever a transaction completes successfully.

The validation of a transaction must ensure that the Rules 1 and 2 are obeyed, by testing for overlaps between the data items of pairs of transactions T_i and T_j. There are two forms of validation – backward and forward [Härder 1984]. Backward validation checks the transaction undergoing validation with other preceding overlapping transactions – those that entered the validation phase before it. Forward validation checks the transaction undergoing validation with other later transactions, which are still active.

Backward validation □ As all the *Read* operations of earlier overlapping transactions were performed before the validation of T_j started, they cannot be affected by the *Writes* of the current transaction (and Rule 1 is satisfied). The validation of transaction T_j checks whether its read set (the data items affected by the *Read* operations of T_j) overlaps with any of the write sets of earlier overlapping transactions T_i. (Rule 2). If there is any overlap, the validation fails.

Let *startTn* be the biggest transaction number assigned (to some other committed transaction) at the time when transaction T_j started its read phase and *finishTn* be the biggest transaction number assigned at the time when T_j entered the validation phase. The following program describes the algorithm for the validation of T_j:

```
Valid := TRUE;
FOR Ti := startTn + 1 TO finishTn DO
        IF read set of Tj intersects write set of Ti THEN
                Valid := FALSE
        END
    END
```

Figure 13.16. shows overlapping transactions that might be considered in the validation of a transaction T_j. Time increases from left to right. The earlier committed transactions are T_1, T_2 and T_3. T_1 committed before T_j started. T_2 and T_3 committed before T_j finished its read phase. *StartTn* + 1 = T_2 and *finishTn* = T_3. In backward validation, the read set of T_j must be compared with the write sets of T_2 and T_3.

In backward validation, the read set of the transaction being validated is compared with the write sets of other transactions that have already committed. Therefore the only way to resolve any conflicts is to abort the transaction that is undergoing validation.

In backward validation, transactions that have no *Read* operations (only *Write* operations) need not be checked.

Optimistic concurrency control with backward validation requires that the write sets of old committed versions of data items corresponding to recently committed transactions are retained until there are no unvalidated overlapping transactions with which they might conflict. Whenever a transaction is successfully validated, its transaction number, *startTn* and write set are recorded in a preceding transactions list that is maintained by the transaction service. Note that this list is ordered by transaction number. In an environment with long transactions, the retention of old write sets of data items may be a problem. For example, in Figure 13.16 the write sets of T_1, T_2, T_3 and T_j must be retained until the active transaction *active1* completes. Note that the although the active transactions have transaction identifiers, they do not yet have transaction numbers.

Forward validation □ In forward validation of the transaction T_j the write set of T_j is compared with the read sets of all overlapping active transactions – those that are in still in their read phase (Rule 1). Rule 2 is automatically fulfilled because the active transactions do not write until after T_j has completed. Let the active transactions have (consecutive) transaction identifiers *active1* to *activeN,* then the following program describes the algorithm for the forward validation of T_j:

```
Valid := TRUE;
FOR Tid := active1 TO activeN DO
        IF write set of Tj intersects read set of Tid THEN
                Valid := FALSE
        END
END
```

In Figure 13.16, the write set of transaction T_j must be compared with the read sets of the transactions with identifiers *active1* and *active2.* (Forward validation should allow for the fact that read sets of active transactions may change during validation and writing.) As the read sets of the transaction being validated are not included in the check, read only transactions always pass the validation check. As the transactions being compared with the validating transaction are still active, we have a choice of whether to abort the validating transaction or to take some alternative way of resolving the conflict. Härder [1984] suggests several alternative strategies:

- Defer the validation until a later time when the conflicting transactions have finished. This is an optimistic approach to validation because there is always the chance that further conflicting active transactions may start before the validation is achieved.

- Abort all the conflicting active transactions and commit the transaction being validated.

- Abort the transaction being validated. This is the simplest strategy, but has the disadvantage that the future conflicting transactions may be going to abort, in which case the transaction under validation has aborted unnecessarily.

Comparison of forward and backward validation □ We have already seen that forward validation allows flexibility in the resolution of conflicts, whereas backward validation allows only one choice – to abort the transaction being validated. In general, the read sets of transactions are much larger than the write sets. Therefore, backward validation compares a possibly large read set against the old write sets, whereas, forward validation checks a small write set against the of read sets of active transactions. We see that backward validation has the overhead of storing old write sets until they are no longer needed. On the other hand, forward validation has to allow for new transactions starting during the validation process.

Starvation □ When a transaction is aborted, it will normally be restarted by the client program. But in schemes that rely on aborting and restarting transactions, there is no guarantee that a particular transaction will ever pass the validation checks, for it may come into conflict with other transactions for the use of data items each time it is restarted. The deprivation of a transaction from ever being able to commit is called starvation.

Occurrences of starvation are likely to be rare, but a server that uses optimistic concurrency control must ensure that a client does not have its transaction aborted repeatedly. Kung and Robinson suggest that this could be done if the server detects a transaction that has been aborted several times. They suggest that when the server detects such a transaction it should be given exclusive access by the use of a critical section protected by a semaphore.

13.4 Timestamp ordering

In concurrency control schemes based on timestamp ordering, each operation in a transaction is validated when it is carried out. If the operation cannot be validated the transaction is aborted immediately and can then be restarted by the client. Each transaction is assigned a unique timestamp value when it starts. The timestamp defines its position in the time sequence of transactions. Using timestamps, requests from transactions can be totally ordered according to their timestamps. The timestamp ordering:basic timestamp ordering rule is based on operation conflicts and is very simple:

> A transaction's request to write a data item is valid only if that data item was last read and written by earlier transactions. A transaction's request to read a data item is valid only if that data item was last written by an earlier transaction.

This rule assumes that there is only one version of each data item and restricts access to one transaction at a time. If each transaction has its own tentative version of each data item it accesses, then multiple concurrent transactions can access the same data item. The timestamp ordering rule is refined to ensure that each transaction accesses a consistent set of versions of the data items. It must also ensure that the tentative versions of each data item are committed in the order determined by the timestamps of the transactions that made them. This is achieved by transactions waiting, when necessary, for earlier transactions to complete their writes. The *Write* operations may be performed after the *CloseTransaction* operation has returned, without making the client wait. But the client must wait when *Read* operations need to wait for earlier transactions to finish. This cannot lead to deadlock since transactions only wait for earlier ones (and no cycle could occur in the wait-for graph).

A server may use its clock to assign timestamps or, as in the previous section, it may use a 'pseudo-time' based on a counter that is incremented whenever a timestamp value is issued. We defer until Chapter 14 the problem of generating timestamps when the transaction service is distributed and several servers are involved in a transaction.

We will now describe a form of timestamp-based concurrency control following the methods adopted in the SDD-1 system [Bernstein *et al.* 1980] and described by Ceri and Pelagatti [1985].

As usual, the *Write* operations are recorded in tentative versions of data items and are invisible to other transactions until a *CloseTransaction* request is issued and the transaction is committed. Every data item has a write timestamp and a set of tentative versions, each of which has a write timestamp associated with it; and a set of read timestamps. The write timestamp of the (committed) data item is earlier than that of any of its tentative versions and the set of read timestamps can be represented by its maximum member. Whenever a transaction's *Write* operation on a data item is accepted, the server creates a new tentative version of the data item with write timestamp set to the transaction timestamp. A transaction's *Read* operation is directed to the version with the maximum write timestamp less than the transaction timestamp. Whenever a transaction's *Read* operation on a data item is accepted, the server adds the timestamp of the transaction to its set of read timestamps. When a transaction is committed, the values of the tentative versions become the values of the data items and the timestamps of the tentative versions become the timestamps of the corresponding data items.

In timestamp ordering, the server checks whether each request by a transaction for a *Read* or *Write* operation on a data item conforms to the conflict rules. A request by the current transaction T_j can conflict with previous operations done by other transactions, T_i whose timestamps indicate that they should be later than T_j. These rules are shown in Figure 13.17, in which $T_i > T_j$ means T_i is later than T_j and $T_i < T_j$ means T_i is earlier than T_j.

Figure 13.17   Transaction conflicts for timestamp ordering.

Rule	T_j	
1.	Write	T_j must not write a data item that has been read by any T_i where $T_i > T_j$ this requires that $T_j \geq$ the maximum read timestamp of the data item
2.	Write	T_j must not write a data item that has been written by any T_i where $T_i > T_j$ this requires that $T_j >$ the maximum write timestamp of the committed data item
3.	Read	T_j must not read a data item that has been written by any T_i where $T_i > T_j$ this implies that T_j cannot read if $T_j <$ write timestamp of the committed version of the data item

Figure 13.18   Write operations and timestamps.

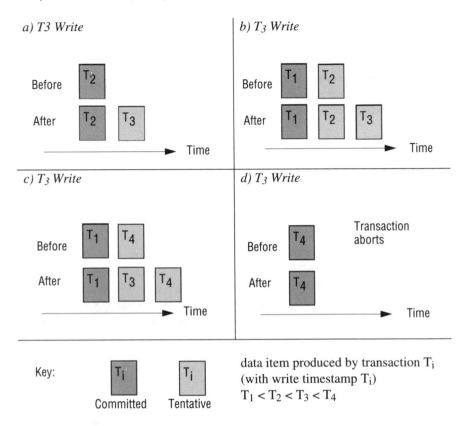

a) T3 Write

Before T_2

After T_2 T_3

→ Time

b) T3 Write

Before T_1 T_2

After T_1 T_2 T_3

→ Time

c) T3 Write

Before T_1 T_4

After T_1 T_3 T_4

→ Time

d) T3 Write

Before T_4 Transaction aborts

After T_4

→ Time

Key: T_i T_i data item produced by transaction T_i (with write timestamp T_i)

Committed   Tentative $T_1 < T_2 < T_3 < T_4$

Timestamp ordering Write rule: By combining Rules 1 and 2 we have the following rule for deciding whether to accept a *Write* operation requested by transaction T_j on data item D:

> *IF* $T_j \geq$ maximum read timestamp on D *AND*
> > $T_j>$ write timestamp on committed version of D *THEN*
> > > perform *Write* operation on tentative version of D with write timestamp T_j
> *ELSE* (* write is too late *)
> > *Abort* transaction T_j
> *END*

If a tentative version with write timestamp T_j already exists, the *Write* operation is addressed to it, otherwise a new tentative version is created and given write timestamp T_j. Note that any *Write* that 'arrives too late' is aborted – it is too late in the sense that a transaction with a later timestamp has already read or written the data item.

Figure 13.18 illustrates the action of a *Write* operation by transaction T_3 in cases where $T_3 \geq$ maximum read timestamp on the data item (the read timestamps are not shown). In cases (a) to (c) $T_3 >$ write timestamp on the committed version of the data item and a tentative version with write timestamp T_3 is inserted at the appropriate place in the list of tentative versions ordered by their transaction timestamps. In case (d) $T_3 <$ write timestamp on the committed version of the data item and the transaction is aborted.

Timestamp ordering Read rule: By using Rule 3 we have the following rule for deciding whether to accept immediately, to wait or to reject a *Read* operation requested by transaction T_j on data item D:

> *IF* T_j > write timestamp on committed version of D *THEN*
> > let $D_{selected}$ be the version of D with the maximum write timestamp $\leq T_j$
> > *IF* $D_{selected}$ is committed *THEN*
> > > perform *Read* operation on the version $D_{selected}$
> > *ELSE*
> > > *Wait* until the transaction that made version $D_{selected}$ commits or aborts
> > > then re-apply the Read rule
> *ELSE*
> > *Abort* transaction *Tj*
> *END*

Note:

- If the transaction T_j has already written its own version of the data item, this will be used.

- A *Read* operation that arrives too early waits for the earlier transaction to complete. If the earlier transaction commits then T_j will read from its committed version. If it aborts then T_j will repeat the Read rule (and select the previous version). This rule prevents dirty reads.

- A *Read* operation that 'arrives too late' is aborted – it is too late in the sense that a transaction with a later timestamp has already written the data item.

The Figure 13.19 illustrates the timestamp ordering read rule. It includes four cases labelled (a) to (d), each of which illustrates the action of a *Read* operation by transaction T_3. In each case, a version whose write timestamp is less than or equal to T_3 is selected. If such a version exists, it is indicated with a line. In cases (a) and (b) the *Read* operation is directed to a committed version – in (a) it is the only version, whereas in (b) there is a tentative version belonging to a later transaction. In case (c) the *Read* operation is directed to a tentative version and must wait until the transaction that made it commits or aborts. In case (d) there is no suitable version to read and the transaction T_3 is aborted.

When a server receives a request to commit a transaction, it will always be able to do so because all the operations of transactions are checked for consistency with those of earlier transactions before being carried out. The committed versions of each data item must be created in timestamp order. Therefore a server sometimes needs to wait for earlier transactions to complete before writing all the committed versions of the data items accessed by a particular transaction but there is no need for the client to wait. In order to make a transaction recoverable after a server crash, the tentative versions of data items and the fact that the transaction has committed must be written to permanent storage before acknowledging the client's request to commit the transaction.

Note that this timestamp ordering algorithm is a strict one – it ensures strict executions of transactions (see Section 12.4). The Timestamp ordering Read rule delays

Figure 13.19 *Read* operations and timestamps.

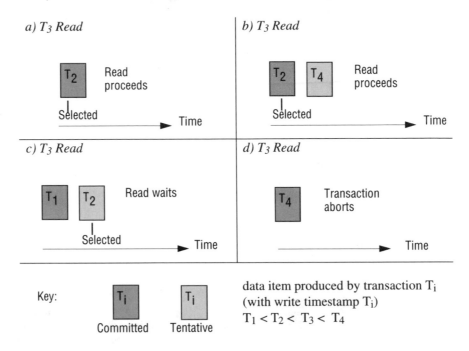

a) T_3 Read

T_2 Read proceeds

Selected   Time

b) T_3 Read

T_2 T_4 Read proceeds

Selected   Time

c) T_3 Read

T_1 T_2 Read waits

Selected   Time

d) T_3 Read

T_4 Transaction aborts

Time

Key:

T_i T_i data item produced by transaction T_i
(with write timestamp T_i)
$T_1 < T_2 < T_3 < T_4$

Committed   Tentative

a transaction's *Read* operation on any data item until all transactions that had previously written that data item have committed or aborted. The arrangement to commit versions in order ensures that the execution of a transaction's *Write* operation on any data item is delayed until all transactions that had previously written that data item have committed or aborted

In Figure 13.20 we return to our illustration concerning the two concurrent banking transactions T and U introduced in Figure 13.1. The columns headed A, B and C refer to information about accounts with those names. Each account has an entry RTS that records the maximum read timestamps and an entry WTS that records the write timestamp of each version – with timestamps of committed versions in bold. Initially all accounts have committed versions written by transaction S and the set of read timestamps is empty. We assume S < T < U. The example shows that when transaction T is ready to write B it will be aborted because the timestamp set by transaction U is more recent. In this example, the outcome is the same as for read and write locks with timeouts to avoid deadlock as shown in Figure 13.11.

The timestamp method just described does avoid deadlock, but is quite prone to restarts. A modification known as 'ignore obsolete write' rule is an improvement. This is a modification to the Timestamp Ordering Write rule:

> If a write is too late it can be ignored instead of aborting the transaction, because if it had arrived in time its effects would have been overwritten anyway. However, if another transaction has read the data item, the transaction with the late write fails due to the read timestamp on the item.

Figure 13.20   Timestamps in transactions T and U.

T	U	Timestamps and versions of data items					
		A		B		C	
		RTS	WTS	RTS	WTS	RTS	WTS
		{}	S	{}	S	{}	S
OpenTransaction							
bal := A.Read ()		{T}					
	OpenTransaction						
	bal := C.Read()					{U}	
A.Write (bal – 4)			S, T				
bal:= B.Read ()				{T}			
	C.Write(bal – 3)						S,U
	bal := B.Read()			{U}			
B.Write(bal + 4)							
Aborts							
	B.Write(bal + 3)				S,U		

Multiversion timestamp ordering □ In this section we have shown how the concurrency provided by basic timestamp ordering is improved by allowing each transaction to write its own tentative versions of data items. In multiversion timestamp ordering, which was introduced by Reed [1983], the server keeps old committed versions as well as tentative versions in its list of versions of data items. This list represents the history of the values of the data item. The benefit of using multiple versions is that *Read* operations that arrive too late need not be rejected.

Each version has a read timestamp recording the largest timestamp of any transaction that has read from it in addition to a write timestamp. As before, whenever a *Write* operation is accepted, it is directed to a tentative version with the write timestamp of the transaction. Whenever a *Read* operation is carried out it is directed to the version with the largest write timestamp less than the transaction timestamp. If the transaction timestamp is larger than the read timestamp of the version being used, the read timestamp of the version is set to the transaction timestamp.

When a read arrives late, the server can allow it to read from an old committed version, so there is no need to abort late *Read* operations. In multiversion timestamp ordering, *Read* operations are always permitted, although they may have to *Wait* for earlier transactions to complete (either commit or abort), which ensures that executions are recoverable. See Exercise 13.15 for a discussion of the possibility of cascading aborts. This deals with Rule 3 in the conflict rules for timestamp ordering.

Figure 13.21 Late *Write* operation would invalidate a *Read*.

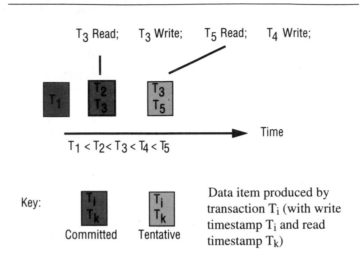

T_3 Read; T_3 Write; T_5 Read; T_4 Write;

$T_1 < T_2 < T_3 < T_4 < T_5$

Time

Key: Committed   Tentative   Data item produced by transaction T_i (with write timestamp T_i and read timestamp T_k)

There is no conflict between *Write* operations of different transactions because each transaction writes its own committed version of the data items it accesses. This removes Rule 2 in the conflict rules for timestamp ordering, leaving us with:

Rule 1.T_j must not write data items that have been read by any T_i where $T_i > T_j$

This rule will be broken if there is any version of the data item with read timestamp $> T_j$; but only if this version has write timestamp less than or equal to T_j. (This write cannot have any effect on later versions.)

Multiversion timestamp ordering Write rule: As any potentially conflicting *Read* operation will have been directed to the most recent version of a data item, the server inspects the version, $D_{maxEarlier}$ with the maximum write timestamp less than or equal to T_j. We have the following rule for performing a Write operation requested by transaction T_j on data item D:

> *IF* read timestamp of $D_{maxEarlier} \leq T_j$ *THEN*
> > perform *Write* operation on a tentative version of D with write timestamp T_j
> *ELSE Abort* transaction T_j
> *END*

Figure 13.21 illustrates an example where a *Write* is rejected. The data item already has committed versions with write timestamps T_1 and T_2. The server receives the following sequence of requests for operations on the data item:

T_3 Read; T_3 Write; T_5 Read; T_4 Write

1. T_3 requests a *Read* operation which puts a read timestamp T_3 on T_2's version;

2. T_3 requests a *Write* operation which makes a new tentative version with write timestamp T_3;

3. T_5 requests a *Read* operation which uses the version with write timestamp T3 (the highest timestamp that is less than T_5);

4. T_4 requests a *Write* operation which is rejected because the read timestamp T_5 of the version with write timestamp T3 is bigger than T_4. (If it were permitted, the write timestamp of the new version would be T_4. If such a version were allowed, then it would invalidate T_5's *Read* operation that should have used the version with timestamp T_4.)

When a transaction is aborted, all the versions that it created are deleted. When a transaction is committed, all the versions that it created are retained, but to control the use of storage space, old versions must be deleted from time to time. Although it has the overhead of storage space, multiversion timestamp ordering does allow considerable concurrency, does not suffer from deadlocks and always permits *Read* operations. For further information about multiversion timestamp ordering, see Bernstein *et al.* [1987].

13.5 Comparison of methods for concurrency control

We have described three separate methods for controlling concurrent access to shared data: strict two-phase locking, optimistic methods and timestamp ordering. All of the methods carry some overheads in the time and space they require and they all limit to some extent the potential for concurrent operation.

The timestamp ordering method is similar to two-phase locking in that both use pessimistic approaches in which the server detects conflicts between transactions as each data item is accessed. On the one hand, timestamp ordering decides the serialization order statically – when a transaction starts. On the other hand, two-phase locking decides the serialization order dynamically – according to the order in which data items are accessed. Timestamp ordering and in particular multiversion timestamp ordering is better than strict two-phase locking for read only transactions. Two-phase locking is better when the operations in transactions are predominantly updates.

Some recent work uses the observation that timestamp ordering is beneficial for transactions with predominantly *Read* operations and that locking is beneficial for transactions with more *Writes* than *Reads* as an argument for allowing hybrid schemes in which some transactions use timestamp ordering and others use locking for concurrency control. Readers who are interested in the use of mixed methods should read Bernstein *et al.* [1987].

The pessimistic methods differ in the strategy used when a conflicting access to a data item is detected. Timestamp ordering aborts the transaction immediately, whereas locking makes the transaction wait – but with a possible later penalty of aborting to avoid deadlock.

When optimistic concurrency control is used all transactions are allowed to proceed, but some are aborted when they attempt to commit, or in forward validation transactions are aborted earlier. This results in relatively efficient operation when there are few conflicts, but a substantial amount of work may have to be repeated when a transaction is aborted.

Locking has been in use for many years in database systems, but timestamp ordering has been used in the SDD-1 database system. Both methods have been used in file servers.

Several recent distributed systems for example, Argus [Liskov 1988] and Arjuna [Shrivastava *et al.* 1991] have explored the use of semantic locks, timestamp ordering and new approaches to long transactions.

Recent work in two application areas has shown that the above concurrency control mechanisms are not always adequate. One of these areas concerns multi-user applications in which all users expect to see common views of data items being updated by any of the users. Such applications require their data to be atomic in the presence of concurrent updates and server failures; and transaction techniques appear to offer an approach to their design. However, these applications have two new requirements relating to concurrency control: (i) users require immediate notification of changes made by other users – which is contrary to the idea of isolation, (ii) users need to be able to access data items before other users have completed their transactions, – which has lead to the development of new types of locks that trigger actions when data items are accessed. Work in this area has suggested many schemes that relax isolation and provide notification of changes. For a review of this work, see Ellis *et al.* [1991]. The second application area concerns what are sometimes described as advanced database applications – such as co-operative CAD/CAM and software development systems. In such applications, transactions last for a long time, and users work on independent versions of data items that are checked out from a common database and checked in when the work is finished. The merging of versions requires co-operation between users. For a review of this work see Barghouti and Kaiser [1991].

13.6 Summary

Operation conflicts form a basis for the derivation of concurrency control protocols. Protocols not only must ensure serializability but also allow for recovery by using strict executions to avoid problems associated with transactions aborting, such as cascading aborts.

When a server receives a request for an operation in a transaction it may choose (i) to execute it immediately, (ii) to delay it, or (iii) to abort it.

Strict two-phase locking uses the first two strategies, resorting to abortion only in the case of deadlock. It ensures serializability by ordering transactions according to when they access common data items. Its main drawback is that deadlocks can occur.

Timestamp ordering uses all three strategies to ensure serializability by ordering transactions' accesses to data items according to the time transactions start. This method cannot suffer from deadlocks and is advantageous for read only transactions. However transactions must be aborted when they arrive too late. Multiversion timestamp ordering is particularly effective.

Optimistic concurrency control allows transactions to proceed without any form of checking until they are completed. Transactions are validated before being allowed to commit. Backward validation requires the maintenance of multiple write sets of committed transactions whereas forward validation must validate against active transactions and has the advantage that it allows alternative strategies for resolving conflicts. Starvation can occur due to repeated aborting of a transaction that fails validation in optimistic concurrency control and even in timestamp ordering.

EXERCISES

13.1 Explain why serial equivalence requires that once a transaction has released a lock on a data item, it is not allowed to obtain any more locks.

A server manages the data items a_1, a_2, ... a_n. The server provides two operations for its clients:

> *Read (i)* returns the value of a_i

> *Write(i, Value)* assigns *Value* to a_i

The transactions T and U are defined as follows:

> T: *x:= Read (i); Write(j, 44);*

> U: *Write(i, 55);Write(j, 66);*

Describe an interleaving of the transactions T and U in which locks are released early with the effect that the interleaving is not serially equivalent.

page 379

13.2 The transactions T and U at the server in Exercise 13.1 are defined as follows:

> T: *x:= Read (i); Write(j, 44);*

> U: *Write(i, 55);Write(j, 66);*

Initial values of a_i and a_j are 10 and 20. Which of the following interleavings are serially equivalent and which could occur with two-phase locking?

(a)

T	U
x:= Read (i);	
	Write(i, 55);
Write(j, 44);	
	Write(j, 66);

(b)

T	U
x:= Read (i);	
Write(j, 44);	
	Write(i, 55);
	Write(j, 66);

(c)

T	U
	Write(i, 55);
	Write(j, 66);
x:= Read (i);	
Write(j, 44);	

(d)

T	U
	Write(i, 55);
x:= Read (i);	
	Write(j, 66);
Write(j, 44);	

page 379 and Chapter 12

13.3   Consider a relaxation of two-phase locks in which read only transactions can release read locks early. Would a read only transaction have consistent retrievals? Would the data items become inconsistent? Illustrate your answer with the following transactions T and U at the server in Exercise 13.1:

    T: *x:= Read (i); y:= Read(j);*

    U: *Write(i, 55);Write(j, 66);*

in which initial values of a_i and a_j are 10 and 20.

page 379 and Chapter 12

13.4   The executions of transactions are strict if *Read* and *Write* operations on a data item are delayed until all transactions that previously wrote that data item have either committed or aborted. Explain how the locking rules in Figure 13.4 ensure strict executions.

page 382 and Chapter 12

13.5   Describe how a non-recoverable situation could arise if write locks are released after the last operation of a transaction but before its commitment.

page 382

13.6   Explain why executions are always strict even if read locks are released after the last operation of a transaction but before its commitment. Give an improved statement of Rule 2 in Figure 13.4.

page 382

13.7   Consider a deadlock detection scheme for a single server. Describe precisely when edges are added to and removed from the wait-for-graph.

Illustrate your answer with respect to the following transactions T, U and V at the server of Exercise 13.1.

T	U	V
	Write(i, 66)	
Write(i, 55)		
		Write(i, 77)
	Commit	

When U releases its write lock on a_i, both T and V are waiting to obtain write locks on it. Does your scheme work correctly if T (first come) is granted the lock before V? If your answer is 'No', then modify your description.

page 387

13.8 Consider hierarchic locks as illustrated in Figure 13.14. What locks must be set when an appointment is assigned to a time-slot in week w, day d, at time, t? In what order should these locks be set? Does the order in which they are released matter?

What locks must be set when the time slots for every day in week w are viewed? Can this be done when the locks for assigning an appointment to a time-slot are already set?

page 390

13.9 Consider optimistic concurrency control as applied to the transactions T and U defined in Exercise 13.2. Suppose that transactions T and U are active at the same time as one another. Describe the outcome in each of the following cases:

i) T's request to commit comes first and backward validation is used;

ii) U's request to commit comes first and backward validation is used;

iii) T's request to commit comes first and forward validation is used;

iv) U's request to commit comes first and forward validation is used.

In each case describe the sequence in which the operations of T and U are performed, remembering that writes are not carried out until after validation.

page 392

13.10 Make a comparison of the sequences of operations of the transactions T and U of Exercise 13.1 that are possible under two-phase locking (Exercise 13.2) and under optimistic concurrency control (Exercise 13.9).

page 392

13.11 Consider the following interleaving of transactions T and U:

T	U
OpenTransaction	*OpenTransaction*
y:= Read(k);	
	Write(i, 55);
	Write(j, 66);
	Commit
x:= Read(i);	
Write(j, 44);	

The outcome of optimistic concurrency control with backward validation is that T will be aborted because its *Read* operation conflicts with U's *Write* operation on a_i, although the interleavings are serially equivalent. Suggest a modification to the algorithm that deals with such cases.

page 392

13.12   Consider the use of timestamp ordering with each of the example
interleavings of transactions T and U in Exercise 13.2. Initial values of a_i
and a_j are 10 and 20 and initial read and write timestamps are t 0. Assume
each transaction opens and obtains a timestamp just before its first
operation, for example, in (a) T and U get timestamps t1 and t2 respectively
where t 0 < t1 < t2. Describe in order of increasing time the effects of each
operation of T and U. For each operation, state the following:

i)   whether the operation may proceed according to the Write or Read
rule;

ii)   timestamps assigned to transactions or data items;

iii)   creation of tentative data items and their values.

What are the final values of the data items and their timestamps?

page 396

13.13   Repeat Exercise 13.12 for the following interleavings of transactions T and U:

T	U	T	U
OpenTransaction		OpenTransaction	
	OpenTransaction		OpenTransaction
	Write(i, 55);		Write(i, 55);
	Write(j, 66);		Write(j, 66);
x:= Read (i);			Commit
Write(j, 44);		x:= Read (i);	
	Commit	Write(j, 44);	

page 396

13.14   Repeat Exercise 13.13 using multiversion timestamp ordering.

page 401

13.15   In multiversion timestamp ordering, *Read* operations can access tentative
versions of data items. Give an example to show how cascading aborts can
happen if all *Read* operations are allowed to proceed immediately.

page 396

13.16   What are the advantages and drawbacks of multiversion timestamp ordering
in comparison with ordinary timestamp ordering.

page 396

14

DISTRIBUTED TRANSACTIONS

This chapter introduces distributed transactions – those that involve more than one server. Distributed transactions may be either flat or nested.

An atomic commit protocol is a cooperative procedure used by a set of servers involved in a distributed transaction. It enables the servers to reach a joint decision as to whether a transaction can be committed or aborted. This chapter describes the two-phase commit protocol which is the most commonly used atomic commit protocol.

The section on concurrency control in distributed transactions discusses how locking, timestamp ordering and optimistic concurrency control may be extended for use with distributed transactions.

The use of locking schemes can lead to distributed deadlocks. Distributed deadlock detection algorithms are discussed.

Transactions with replicated data items must provide replication transparency by ensuring that they are one-copy serializable – that is that clients' transactions appear to have been performed one at a time on single data items.

A simple approach is to read from one copy and to write to all replicas. However, this strategy is not always feasible, for example when servers fail or networks are partitioned.

The chapter ends with a discussion of quorum consensus and other methods for replication in the presence of possible network partitions.

14.1 Introduction

The data items belonging to a service may be distributed among several servers and in general, a client transaction may involve multiple servers. Some client transactions may access more than one service, in which case the transaction is certain to access more than one server. In some other cases, a server accessed by a client transaction may access yet another server. These are examples of transactions whose activities spread into multiple servers either directly by requests made by a client or indirectly via requests made by servers. Any transaction whose activities involve multiple servers is a distributed transaction. Client transactions that involve multiple servers indirectly may be modelled as nested transactions (see Chapter 12).

When a distributed transaction comes to an end, the atomicity property of transactions requires that either all of the servers involved commit the transaction or all of them abort the transaction. To achieve this, one of the servers takes on a coordinator role, which involves ensuring the same outcome at all of the servers. The manner in which the coordinator achieves this depends on the protocol chosen. A protocol known as the 'Two-Phase Commit Protocol' is the most commonly used. This protocol allows the servers to communicate with one another to reach a joint decision as to whether to commit or abort.

Concurrency control in distributed transactions is based on the methods discussed in Chapter 13. Each server applies local concurrency control to its own data items which ensures that transactions are serialized locally. Distributed transactions must be serialized globally. How this is achieved varies as to whether locking, timestamp ordering or optimistic concurrency control is in use. In some cases the transactions may be serialized at the individual servers, but at the same time a cycle of dependencies between the different servers may occur and a distributed deadlock arise.

Transactions may also be applied to services whose data items are replicated at several servers; as in Chapter 11, a goal is to make the replication of data items transparent to clients. This includes an extension of serializability called one-copy serializability in which concurrency control on multiple copies of a data item makes them behave like a single copy. Other issues for replication are concerned with its ability to function correctly when servers have failed or networks are partitioned.

14.2 Simple distributed transactions and nested transactions

A distributed transaction is a client transaction that invokes operations in several different servers. There are two different ways that distributed transactions can be structured: as simple distributed transactions and as nested transactions. In a simple distributed transaction, a client makes requests to more than one server, but each server carries out the client's requests without invoking operations in other servers. For example, in Figure 14.1(a), transaction T is a simple distributed transaction that invokes operations in servers X, Y and Z. A simple (non-nested) client transaction completes each of its requests before going on to the next one. Therefore each transaction accesses servers' data items sequentially. When servers use locking, a transaction can only be waiting for one data item at a time.

Figure 14.1   Distributed transactions.

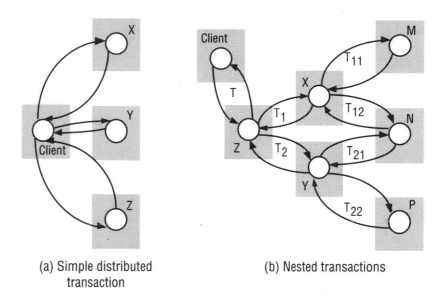

(a) Simple distributed
transaction

(b) Nested transactions

In some cases an operation in a server may invoke an operation in another server
and in general the latter may invoke further operations in yet more servers and so forth.
To deal with this situation, each client transaction is structured as a set of nested
transactions, (see Section 12.5). Figure 14.1(b) shows a client's transaction T at server
Z invoking operations in servers X and Y which form nested transactions T_1 and T_2. The
nested transaction T_1 invokes operations in servers M and N which form further nested
transactions T_{11} and T_{12}. Similarly, T_2 invokes operations in servers N and P which
form further nested transactions T_{21} and T_{22}. In general, a transaction consists of a
hierarchy of nested transactions. Nested transactions at the same level may run
concurrently with one another.

Consider a distributed transaction in which a client transfers $4 from A to C and
then transfers $3 from B to D. The accounts A and B are at separate servers X and Y and
accounts C and D are at server Z. If this transaction is structured as a set of nested
transactions, as shown in Figure 14.2, the four requests (two *Deposit* and two *Withdraw*)
may run in parallel and the overall effect may be achieved with better performance than
a simple transaction in which the four operations are invoked sequentially.

The coordinator of a distributed transaction

Servers that execute requests as part of a distributed transaction need to be able to
communicate with one another to coordinate their actions when the transaction commits.
A client starts a transaction by sending an *OpenTransaction* request to any server. The
server that is contacted carries out the *OpenTransaction* and returns the resulting
transaction identifier to the client. Transaction identifiers for distributed transactions

Figure 14.2   Nested banking transaction.

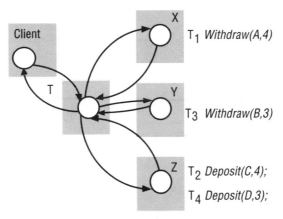

must be unique within a distributed system. A simple way to achieve this is for a TID to contain two parts: the server identifier of the server that created it and a number unique to the server.

The first server in the transaction becomes the *coordinator* for the transaction and is responsible for aborting or committing it and for adding other servers described as *workers*. The coordinator records a list of workers and each worker records the server identifier of the coordinator.

A distributed transaction requires an additional transactional service function:

AddServer(Trans, Server-id of coordinator)
     Informs a server that it is involved in the transaction *Trans*.

AddServer must be used by the client before any operations are requested in a server that has not yet joined the transaction. The *AddServer* call to a new server supplies the transaction identifier and the identifier of the coordinator of the transaction. When a new server receives an *AddServer* request from a client, it initializes a local transaction with the given transaction identifier and sends a *NewServer* request to the coordinator defined as follows:

NewServer(Trans, Server-id of worker)
     Call from a new worker (in *AddServer*) to the coordinator. The coordinator records the server-id of the worker in its worker list.

The *NewServer* request supplies the transaction identifier and the identifier of the server (which is a worker). The coordinator records the latter in its worker list.

The fact that the *coordinator knows all the workers* and *each worker knows the coordinator* will enable them to collect the information that will be needed at commit time.

Figure 14.3   A distributed banking transaction.

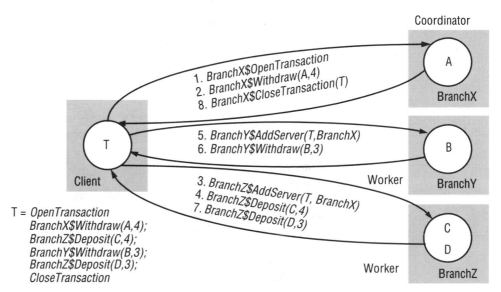

T = OpenTransaction
BranchX$Withdraw(A,4);
BranchZ$Deposit(C,4);
BranchY$Withdraw(B,3);
BranchZ$Deposit(D,3);
CloseTransaction

A user package can be employed to make the distribution of servers in a transaction transparent to user-level programs in the client by recording the identifier of the server that opens the transaction and issuing an *AddServer* call when a new server joins the transaction with the identifier of the coordinator as an argument. When the transaction ends, the user package calls the *CloseTransaction* or *AbortTransaction* in the coordinator.

Figure 14.3 shows a client whose banking transaction involves accounts A, B, C and D at servers BranchX, BranchY and BranchZ. The client's transaction, T transfers $4 from account A to account C and then transfers $3 from account B to account D. The transaction described on the left is expanded to show that *OpenTransaction* and *CloseTransaction* are directed to the server of BranchX and to show the *AddServer* calls. Each client request is numbered to indicate the order in which they are made by the client. The server of BranchX is the coordinator of the transaction and the other two servers are the workers. When the servers BranchY and BranchZ receive their respective *AddServer* requests they make respective requests *NewServer(T, BranchY)* and *NewServer(T, BranchZ)* to the coordinator of the transaction at BranchX.

The following table shows the knowledge held by each of the servers about the other servers in this transaction, T:

Server	Trans	Role	Coordinator	Workers
BranchX	T	Coordinator	(here)	BranchY, BranchZ
BranchY	T	Worker	BranchX	
BranchZ	T	Worker	BranchX	

14.3 Atomic commit protocols

The atomicity of transactions requires that when a distributed transaction comes to an end, either all of its operations are carried out or none of them. In the case of a distributed transaction, the client has requested the operations at more than one server. A transaction comes to an end when the client requests that a transaction should be committed or aborted. A simple way to complete the transaction in an atomic manner is for the coordinator to communicate the commit or abort request to all of the servers in the transaction and to keep on repeating the request until all of them had acknowledged that they had carried it out. This is an example of a **one-phase atomic commit protocol**.

This simple one-phase atomic commitment protocol is inadequate because, in the case when the client requests a commit, it does not allow a server to make a unilateral decision to abort a transaction. Reasons that prevent a server from being able to commit its part of a transaction generally relate to issues of concurrency control. For example, if locking is in use, the resolution of a deadlock can lead to the breaking of locks without the client being aware unless it makes another request to the server. If optimistic concurrency control is in use, the failure of validation at a server would cause it to decide to abort the transaction. The client may not know when a server has failed and restarted during the progress of a distributed transaction – such a server will need to abort the transaction.

The **two-phase commit protocol** is designed to allow any server to abort its part of a transaction. Due to atomicity, if one part of a transaction is aborted, then the whole transaction must also be aborted. In the first phase of the protocol, each server votes for the transaction to be committed or aborted. Once a server has voted to commit a transaction, it is not allowed to abort it. Therefore, before a server votes to commit a transaction, it must ensure that it will eventually be able to carry out its part of the commitment, even if it fails and restarts in the interim. A transaction that can eventually be committed at a server is in a *prepared* state at that server. A server must ensure that the data items altered by any transaction in a prepared state have been saved in permanent storage.

In the second phase of the protocol, every server in the transaction carries out the joint decision. If any one server votes to abort, then the decision must be to abort the transaction. If all the servers vote to commit, then the decision is to commit the transaction.

The problem is to ensure that all of the servers vote and that they all reach the same decision. This is fairly simple if no errors occur, but the protocol must work correctly even when some of the servers fail, messages are lost, or servers are temporarily unable to communicate with one another.

The two-phase commit protocol

During the progress of a transaction there is no communication between the coordinator and the workers apart from the workers informing the coordinator when they join the transaction. A client's request to commit (or abort) a transaction is directed to the coordinator. If the client requests *AbortTransaction*, or if the transaction is aborted by

Figure 14.4 Operations for two-phase commit protocol.

CanCommit?(Trans) → Yes / No
> Call from coordinator to worker to ask whether it can commit a transaction. Worker replies with its vote.

DoCommit(Trans)
> Call from coordinator to worker to tell worker to commit its transaction.

HaveCommitted(Trans, Worker)
> Call from worker to coordinator to confirm that it has committed the transaction.

GetDecision(Trans) → Yes / No
> Call from worker to coordinator to ask for the decision on a transaction after it has voted *Yes*, but has still had no reply after some delay. Used to recover from failure or time out.

---

one of the servers, the coordinator informs the workers immediately. It is when the client asks the coordinator to commit the transaction that two-phase commit protocol comes into use.

In the first phase of the two-phase commit protocol the coordinator asks all the workers if they are prepared to commit and in the second, it tells them to commit (or abort) the transaction. If a server can commit its part of a transaction, it will agree as soon as it is prepared to commit. The coordinator in a distributed transaction communicates with the workers to carry out the two-phase commit protocol by means of server-to-server operations summarized in Figure 14.4.

The two-phase commit protocol consists of a voting phase and a completion phase as shown in Figure 14.5.

By the end of Step (2) the coordinator and all the workers that voted *Yes* are prepared to commit. By the end of Step (3) the transaction is effectively completed. At Step (3a) the coordinator and the workers are committed, so the coordinator can report a decision to commit to the client. At (3b) the coordinator reports a decision to abort to the client.

At Step (4) workers confirm their commitment so that the coordinator knows when the information it has recorded about the transaction is no longer needed.

This apparently straightforward protocol could fail due to one or more of the servers failing or due to a breakdown in communication between the servers. To deal with servers failing, each server saves information relating to the two-phase commit protocol in permanent storage. The recovery aspects of distributed transactions are discussed in Chapter 15. Even when reliable communication is used, the exchange of information between servers can fail when one of the servers fails. To handle this eventuality, some timeout actions are included in the protocol.

Timeouts in the two-phase commit protocol ☐ There are various stages in the protocol at which a server cannot progress its part of the protocol until it receives another request or reply from one of the other servers.

Figure 14.5   The two-phase commit protocol.

Phase 1 (voting phase):

1. The coordinator sends a *CanCommit?* request to each of the workers in the transaction;

2. When a worker receives a *CanCommit?* request it replies with its vote (*Yes* or *No*) to the coordinator. If the vote is *No* the worker aborts immediately;

Phase 2 (completion according to outcome of vote):

3. The coordinator collects the votes (including its own);

   a) If there are no failures and all the votes are *Yes* the coordinator decides to commit the transaction and sends a *DoCommit* request to each of the workers;

   b) Otherwise the coordinator decides to abort the transaction and sends *AbortTransaction* requests to all workers that voted *Yes*;

4. Workers that voted *Yes* are waiting for a DoCommit or AbortTransaction request from the coordinator. When a worker receives one of these messages it acts accordingly and in the case of commit, makes a HaveCommitted call as confirmation to the coordinator.

Consider first the situation where a worker has voted *Yes* and is waiting for the coordinator to report on the outcome of the vote by telling it to commit or abort the transaction. See Step (2) in Figure 14.6. Such a worker is *uncertain* of the outcome and cannot proceed any further until it gets the outcome of the vote from the coordinator. The worker cannot decide unilaterally what to do next and meanwhile the data items used by its transaction cannot be released for use by other transactions. The worker makes a *GetDecision* request to the coordinator to determine the outcome of the transaction. When it gets the reply it continues the protocol at Step (4) in Figure 14.5. If the coordinator has failed, the worker will not be able to get the decision until the coordinator restarts, which can result in extensive delays for workers in the uncertain state.

Figure 14.6   Communication in two-phase commit protocol.

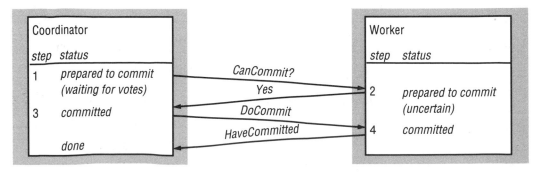

Other alternative strategies are available for the workers to obtain a decision cooperatively instead of contacting the coordinator. These strategies have the advantage that they may be used when the coordinator has failed. See Exercise 14.4 and Bernstein *et al.* [1987] for details. However, even with a cooperative protocol, if all the workers are in the uncertain state, they will be unable to get a decision until the coordinator or a worker with the knowledge restarts.

Another point at which a worker may be delayed is when it has carried out all its client requests in the transaction but has not yet received a *CanCommit?* call from the coordinator. As the client sends the *CloseTransaction* to the coordinator, a worker can only detect such a situation if it notices that it has not had a request in a particular transaction for a long time, for example by a timeout period on a lock. As no decision has been made at this stage, the worker can decide to *Abort* unilaterally after some period of time.

The coordinator may be delayed when it is waiting for votes from the workers. As it has not yet decided the fate of the transaction it may decide to abort the transaction after some period of time. It must then announce *AbortTransaction* to the workers who have already sent their votes. Of course some tardy workers may try to vote *Yes* after this, but their votes will be ignored and they will enter the uncertain state as described above.

Performance of the two-phase commit protocol □ Provided that all goes well – that is, that the coordinator and workers and the communication between them do not fail, the two-phase commit protocol involving N servers can be completed with $(N-1)$ *CanCommit?* messages and replies, followed by $(N-1)$ *DoCommit* messages. That is, the cost in messages is proportional to $3N$ and the cost in time is three rounds of messages. The *HaveCommitted* messages are not counted in the estimated cost of the protocol which can function correctly without them – their role is to enable servers to delete stale coordinator information.

In the worst case, there may be arbitrarily many server and communication failures during the two-phase commit protocol. However, the protocol is designed to tolerate a succession of failures and is guaranteed to complete eventually, although it is not possible to specify a time limit within which it will be completed.

As noted in the section on timeouts, the two-phase commit protocol can cause considerable delays to workers in the uncertain state. These delays occur when the coordinator has failed and cannot reply to *GetDecision* requests from workers. Even if a cooperative protocol allows workers to make *GetDecision* requests to other workers, delays will occur if all the active workers are uncertain.

Three-phase commit protocols have been designed to alleviate such delays. They are more expensive in the number of messages and the number of rounds required for the normal (failure-free case). For a description of three-phase commit protocols, see Exercise 14.2 and Bernstein *et al.* [1987].

Two-phase commit protocol for nested transactions

The outermost transaction in a set of nested transactions is called the *top-level transaction*. Transactions other than the top-level transaction are called *subtransactions*. In Figure 14.1(b), T is the top-level transaction, T_1, T_2, T_{11}, T_{12}, T_{21} and T_{22} are

Figure 14.7   Operations in service for nested transactions.

OpenSubTransaction(Trans) → NewTrans
  Opens a new subtransaction whose parent is *Trans* and returns a unique
  subtransaction identifier *NewTrans*.

GetStatus(Trans) → committed, aborted, tentative
  Asks transaction *Trans* to report on its status.

---

subtransactions. T_1 and T_2 are child transactions of T, which is referred to as their parent. Similarly T_{11} and T_{12} are child transactions of T_1 and T_{21} and T_{22} are child transactions of T_2.

When a subtransaction completes, it makes an independent decision either to commit provisionally or to abort. The final outcome for a provisionally committing subtransaction depends on its parent and eventually on the top-level transaction. When a top-level transaction completes, its server needs to be able to communicate with servers of descendent subtransactions in order to carry out an atomic commit protocol.

A service for nested transactions will provide an operation to open a subtransaction, together with an operation enabling a child transaction to enquire whether its parent has yet committed or aborted, as shown in Figure 14.7.

A client starts a set of nested transactions by opening a top-level transaction by means of an *OpenTransaction* operation, which returns a transaction identifier for the top-level transaction. The top-level transaction starts nested transactions at other servers by means of the *OpenSubTransaction* operation which returns a transaction identifier for a subtransaction. Figure 14.8 shows an example of the use of these operations in some of the nested transactions in Figure 14.1(b).

An identifier for a subtransaction can be created by extending the TID of its parent in such a way that the resulting subtransaction identifier is globally unique. Figure 14.8 shows a client request to server Z to open a top-level transaction. The server returns a transaction identifier, T. The transaction running at server Z requests servers X and Y to open subtransactions of T. To ensure that the subtransaction identifiers are globally unique, servers X and Y generate globally unique extensions to T and server M

Figure 14.8   Nested transactions.

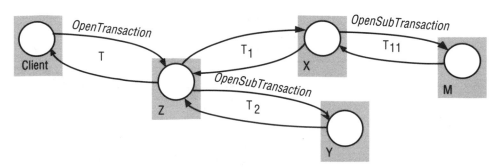

generates a globally unique extension to T_1. A simple way to make a globally unique extension is to use a server-identifier and local number. For example, the transaction identifiers in the figure might be constructed as follows:

TID in example	T	T_1	T_{11}	T_2
actual TID	Z, n_Z	Z, n_Z:X, n_X	Z, n_Z:X, n_X:M, n_m	Z, n_Z:Y, n_Y

where n_Z, n_X, n_Y and n_M are local numbers generated at servers Z, X, Y and M. Note that the ancestors of a subtransaction can be determined from its subtransaction identifier.

The identifier of the parent or top-level transaction of a subtransaction can be determined from its transaction identifier. The terms *ancestors* and *descendants* are used in their usual way to refer to relationships between transactions.

Whenever a subtransaction completes at a server, that server records information as to whether the subtransaction committed provisionally or aborted. Subtransactions will not carry out a real commitment unless the entire nested transaction is committed. Recall from Chapter 12 that a parent transaction – including a top-level transaction – can commit even if one of its child subtransactions has aborted. In such cases the parent transaction will be programmed to take different actions according to whether a child transaction has committed or aborted. For example, consider a banking transaction that is designed to perform all the 'standing orders' at a branch on a particular day. This transaction is expressed as several nested *Transfer* subtransactions, each of which consists of nested *Deposit* and *Withdraw* subtransactions as in Figure 12.11. As in that example, we assume that when an account is overdrawn, *Withdraw* aborts and then the corresponding *Transfer* aborts. But there is no need to abort all the standing orders, just because one *Transfer* subtransaction aborts. Instead of aborting, the top-level transaction will note the *Transfer* subtransactions that aborted and take appropriate actions.

Consider the top-level transaction T and its subtransactions shown in Figure 14.9 which is based on Figure 14.1 (b). Each subtransaction has either provisionally committed or aborted. For example, T_{12} has provisionally committed and T_{11} has aborted, but the fate of T_{12} depends on its parent T_1 and eventually on the top-level transaction, T. Although T_{21} and T_{22} have both provisionally committed, T_2 has aborted and this means that T_{21} and T_{22} must also abort. In this example, T could commit if T_1 commits and T_1 can commit if T_{12} commits.

Figure 14.9 Transaction T decides whether to commit.

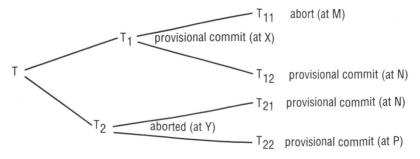

In general, the top-level transaction can commit only if all of its provisionally committed child transactions can commit. The latter can commit only if all of their provisionally committed child transactions can commit and so on until the child transactions without children are reached. When a nested transaction provisionally commits, it reports its status and the status of its descendants to its parent. When a nested transaction aborts, it just reports abort to its parent (all of its descendants must also abort). Eventually the top-level transaction receives a list of all the subtransactions in the tree, together with the status of each. (Descendants of aborted subtransactions are actually omitted from this list. The table below shows the subtransactions T_{21} and T_{22} with strike through because the server of the aborted subtransaction T_2 does not pass on any information about them.) The top-level transaction plays the role of coordinator in the two-phase commit protocol and the worker list consists of the servers of all the subtransactions in the tree that have provisionally committed. In Figure 14.9, the servers X and N of T_1 and T_{12} are workers. It also makes an *AbortList* consisting of the subtransactions that have aborted, in our example T_{11} and T_2.

The information held by each server in the example shown in Figure 14.9 is as follows:

Server	Transaction	Child transactions	Provisional Commit list	Abort List
Z	T	T_1, T_2	$T_1@X, T_{12}@N$	T_{11}, T_2
X	T_1	T_{11}, T_{12}	$T_1, T_{12}@N$	T_{11}
Y	T_2	T_{21}, T_{22}	($T_{21}@N, T_{22}@P$)	T_2
M	T_{11}			T_{11}
N	T_{12}, T_{21}		T_{21}, T_{12}	
P	T_{22}		T_{22}	

It might seem that a one-phase protocol would be sufficient since the workers are just participants that have already provisionally committed. Unfortunately this is not the case because a worker may fail after provisionally committing and before the commit protocol, in which case it will not be able to carry out the commitment. Therefore a two-phase protocol is used to enable such workers to abort unilaterally.

During the protocol, the coordinator and the workers refer to the transaction by its top-level transaction identifier. In the first phase, the coordinator sends a *CanCommit?* request to each of the workers, supplying the transaction identifier of the top-level transaction as argument. Each worker looks for provisionally committed transactions with the given top-level transaction identifier. For example, worker N, on receiving *CanCommit?(T)* finds the transaction T_{12} is provisionally committed and can vote *Yes*.

Unfortunately this does not provide sufficient information to enable correct actions by workers such as N that have a mix of provisionally committed and aborted subtransactions. If N is just asked to commit T it will end up by committing both T_{12} and T_{21}, because, according to its local information, both have provisionally committed. This is wrong in the case of T_{21}, because its parent, T_2, has aborted. To allow for such cases, the *CanCommit?* operation for nested transactions has a second argument that provides a list of aborted subtransactions as shown in Figure 14.10.

Figure 14.10 *CanCommit?* operation of nested transaction service.

CanCommit?(Trans, AbortList) → *Yes / No*
Call from coordinator to worker to ask whether it can commit a transaction. Worker replies with its vote *Yes / No*.

In general a server will have processed several transactions, some of which are descendants of the top-level transaction given as argument to the *CanCommit?* request. It can commit descendants unless they have aborted ancestors.

When a worker receives a *CanCommit?* request, it does the following:

- if the worker has any provisionally committed transactions that are descendants of the top-level transaction, *Trans*:
    - check that they do not have aborted ancestors in the *AbortList*. Then prepare for commitment (by recording the transaction and its data items in permanent storage),
    - those with aborted ancestors are aborted,
    - send a *Yes* vote to the coordinator;
- if the worker does not have a provisionally committed descendent of the top-level transaction, it must have failed since it performed the subtransaction and it sends a *No* vote to the coordinator.

The second phase of the two-phase commit protocol is the same as for the non-nested case. The coordinator collects the votes and then informs the workers as to the outcome. When it is complete, coordinator and workers will have committed or aborted their transactions.

Time out actions □ The two-phase commit protocol for nested transactions can cause the coordinator or a worker to be delayed at the same three steps as in the non-nested version. There is a fourth step at which nested transactions can be delayed. Consider provisionally committed child transactions of aborted subtransactions: they do not get informed of the outcome of the transaction unless they happen to have run at a worker server. In our example, T_{22} is such a subtransaction – it has provisionally committed, but as its parent T_2 has aborted, it does not become a worker. To deal with such potential delays, any child transaction will make an enquiry after a timeout period.

The *GetStatus* operation in Figure 14.7 allows a child transaction to enquire as to whether its parent has committed or aborted. If the parent does not reply, the child can use *GetDecision* operation of Figure 14.4 to ask the coordinator about the fate of the entire transaction.

14.4 Concurrency control in distributed transactions

Each server manages a set of data items and is responsible for ensuring that they remain consistent when accessed by concurrent transactions. Therefore each server is responsible for applying concurrency control to its own data items. The members of a collection of servers of distributed transactions are jointly responsible for ensuring that they are performed in a serially equivalent manner. This implies that if transaction T is before transaction U in the serially equivalent ordering of transactions at one of the servers then they must be in that order at all of the servers whose data items are accessed by both T and U.

Locking in distributed transactions

In a distributed transaction, each server maintains locks for its own data items. The local lock manager can decide whether to grant a lock or make the requesting transaction wait. However it cannot release any locks until it knows that the transaction has been committed or aborted at all the severs involved in the transaction. When locking is used for concurrency control, the data items remain locked and are unavailable for other transactions during the atomic commit protocol.

As servers set their locks independently of one another, it is possible that different servers may impose different orderings on transactions. In some cases, these different orderings can lead to cyclic dependencies between transactions and a distributed deadlock situation arises. The detection and resolution of distributed deadlocks is discussed in the next section of this chapter. When a deadlock is detected, a transaction is aborted to resolve the deadlock. In this case, the coordinator will be informed and will abort the transaction at the workers involved in the transaction.

In nested transactions, parent transactions are not allowed to run concurrently with their child transactions, to prevent potential conflict between levels. Nested transactions inherit locks from their ancestors. For a nested transaction to acquire a read lock on a data item, all the holders of write locks on that data item must be its ancestors. Similarly for a nested transaction to acquire a write lock on a data item, all the holders of read and write locks on that data item must be its ancestors. When a nested transaction commits, its locks are inherited by its parent. When a nested transaction aborts, its locks are removed.

Timestamp ordering concurrency control in distributed transactions

In a single server transaction, the server issues a unique timestamp to each transaction when it starts. Serial equivalence is enforced by committing the versions of data items in the order of the timestamps of transactions that accessed them. In distributed transactions, we require that each server is able to issue globally unique timestamps. A globally unique transaction timestamp is issued to the client by the first server accessed by a transaction. The transaction timestamp is passed to each server that performs an operation in the transaction.

The servers of distributed transactions are jointly responsible for ensuring that they are performed in a serially equivalent manner. For example, if the version of a data item accessed by transaction U commits after the version accessed by T at one server, then if T and U access the same data item as one another at other servers, they must commit them in the same order. To achieve the same ordering at all the servers, the servers must agree as to the ordering of their timestamps. A timestamp consists of a pair *<local timestamp, server-id>*. The agreed ordering of pairs of timestamps is based on a comparison in which the server-id part is less significant.

The same ordering of transactions can be achieved at all the servers even if their local clocks are not synchronized. However for reasons of efficiency it is required that the timestamps issued by one server should be roughly synchronized with those issued by the other servers. When this is the case, the ordering of transactions generally corresponds to the order in which they are started in real time. Timestamps can be kept roughly synchronized by the use of synchronized local physical clocks (see Chapter 10).

When timestamp ordering is used for concurrency control, conflicts are resolved as each operation is performed. If the resolution of a conflict requires a transaction to be aborted, the coordinator will be informed and it will abort the transaction at all the workers. Therefore any transaction that reaches the client request to commit should always be able to commit. Therefore a server involved as a worker in the two-phase commit protocol will normally agree to commit. The only situation in which a worker will not agree to commit is if it had crashed during the transaction.

Optimistic concurrency control in distributed transactions

Recall that with optimistic concurrency control, each transaction is validated before it is allowed to commit. Servers assign transaction numbers at the start of validation and transactions are serialized according to the order of the transaction numbers. A distributed transaction is validated by a collection of independent servers each of which validates transactions that access its own data items. The validation at all of the servers takes place during the first phase of the two-phase commit protocol.

Consider the following interleavings of transactions T and U that access data items A and B at servers X and Y respectively.

T		U	
Read(A)	at X	Read(B)	at Y
Write(A)		Write(B)	
Read(B)	at Y	Read(A)	at X
Write(B)		Write(A)	

The transactions access the data items in the order T before U at server X and in the order U before T at server Y. Now suppose that T and U start validation at about the same time, but server X validates T first and server Y validates U first. Recall that Chapter 13 recommends a simplification of the validation protocol that makes a rule that only one transaction may perform validation and write phases at the same time. Therefore each server will be unable to validate the other transaction until the first one has completed. This is an example of commitment deadlock.

The validation rules in Chapter 13 assume that validation is fast which is true for single server transactions. However in a distributed transaction, the two-phase commit protocol may take some time and will delay other transactions from entering validation until a decision on the current transaction has been obtained. A parallel validation protocol is generally used to increase the concurrency at each individual server. Kung and Robinson [1981] describe parallel validation in their original paper. It must check conflicts between write operations of the transaction being validated against the write operations of other concurrent transactions.

If parallel validation is used, transactions will not suffer from commitment deadlock. However if servers simply perform independent validations, it is possible that different servers of a distributed transaction may serialize the same set of transactions in different orders. For example with T before U at server X and U before T at server Y in our example.

The servers of distributed transactions must prevent this from happening. One approach is that after a local validation by each server, a global validation is carried out [Ceri and Owicki 1982]. The global validation checks that the combination of the orderings at the individual servers is serializable. That is, that the transaction being validated is not involved in a cycle.

Another approach is that all of the servers of a particular transaction use the same globally unique transaction number at the start of the validation [Schlageter 1982]. The coordinator of the two-phase commit protocol is responsible for generating the globally unique transaction number and passes it to the workers in the *CanCommit?* messages. As different servers may coordinate different transactions, the servers must (as in the distributed timestamp ordering protocol) have an agreed order for the transaction numbers they generate.

14.5 Distributed deadlocks

The subsection on deadlocks in Section 13.2 shows that deadlocks can arise within a single server when locking is used for concurrency control. Servers must either prevent or detect and resolve deadlocks. Using timeouts to resolve possible deadlocks is a clumsy approach – it is difficult to choose an appropriate timeout interval and transactions are aborted unnecessarily. With deadlock detection schemes, a transaction is aborted only when it is involved in a deadlock. Most deadlock detection schemes operate by finding cycles in the transaction wait-for graph. In a distributed system involving multiple servers being accessed by multiple transactions, a global wait-for graph can in theory be constructed from the local ones. There can be a cycle in the global wait-for graph that is not in any single local one – that is, there can be a **distributed deadlock**. Recall that the wait-for graph is a directed graph in which nodes represent transactions and data items; and edges represent either a data item held by a transaction or a transaction waiting for a data item. There is a deadlock if and only if there is a cycle in the wait-for graph.

Figure 14.11 shows the interleavings of the transactions U, V and W involving the data items A and B managed by servers X and Y and data items C and D managed by server Z.

Figure 14.11   Interleavings of transactions U, V and W.

U		V		W	
Deposit(D)	lock D				
		Deposit(B)	lock B		
Deposit(A)	lock A				
				Deposit(C)	lock C
Withdraw(B)	wait				
		Withdraw(C)	wait		
				Withdraw(A)	wait

The complete wait-for graph in Figure 14.12 (a) shows that a deadlock cycle consists of alternate edges, which represent a transaction waiting for a data item and a data item held by a transaction. As any transaction can only be waiting for one data item at a time, data items can be left out of wait-for graphs as shown in Figure 14.12 (b).

Detection of a distributed deadlock requires a cycle to be found in the global transaction wait-for graph which is distributed among the servers that were involved in the transactions. Local wait-for graphs can be built by the lock manager at each server

Figure 14.12   Distributed deadlock.

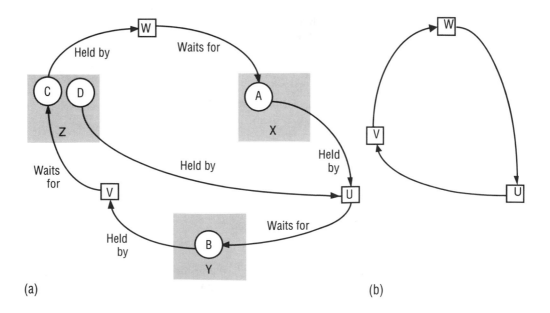

(a)   (b)

as discussed in Chapter 13. In the above example, the local wait-for graphs of the servers are:

server Y: U → V (added when U requests *Withdraw(B)*)
server Z: V → W (added when V requests *Withdraw(C)*)
server X: W → U (added when W requests *Withdraw(A)*)

As the global wait-for graph is held in part by each of the several servers involved, communication between these servers is required to find cycles in the graph.

A simple solution is to use centralized deadlock detection in which one server takes on the role of global deadlock detector. From time to time, each server sends the latest copy of its local wait-for graph to the global deadlock detector, which amalgamates the information in the local graphs in order to construct a global wait-for graph. The global deadlock detector checks for cycles in the global wait-for graph. When it finds a cycle, it makes a decision on how to resolve the deadlock and informs the servers as to the transaction to be aborted to resolve the deadlock.

Centralized deadlock detection is not a good idea because it depends on a single server to carry it out. It suffers from the usual problems associated with centralized solutions in distributed systems – poor availability, lack of fault tolerance and no ability to scale. In addition, the cost of the frequent transmission of local wait-for graphs is high. If the global graph is collected less frequently, deadlocks may take longer to be detected.

Phantom deadlocks □   A deadlock that is 'detected' but is not really a deadlock is called a phantom deadlock. In distributed deadlock detection, information about wait-for relationships between transactions is transmitted from one server to another. If there is a deadlock, the necessary information will eventually be collected in one place and a cycle will be detected. As this procedure will take some time, there is a chance that one of the transactions that holds a lock will meanwhile have released it, in which case the deadlock will no longer exist.

Consider the case of a global deadlock detector that receives local wait-for graphs from servers X and Y as shown in Figure 14.13. Suppose that transaction U then releases a data item at server X and requests the one held by V at server Y. Suppose also that the global detector receives server Y's local graph before server X's. In this case it would detect a cycle T → U → V → T, although the edge T → U no longer exists. This is an example of a phantom deadlock.

The observant reader will have realised that if transactions are using two-phase locks, they cannot release data items and then obtain more data items and phantom

Figure 14.13 Local and global wait-for graphs.

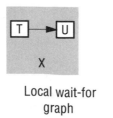

Local wait-for
graph

Local wait-for
graph

Global deadlock detector

deadlock cycles cannot occur in the way suggested above. Consider the situation in which a cycle $T \rightarrow U \rightarrow V \rightarrow T$ is detected: either this represents a deadlock or each of the transactions T, U and V must eventually commit. It is actually impossible for any of them to commit because each of them is waiting for a data item that will never be released.

A phantom deadlock could be detected if a waiting transaction in a deadlock cycle aborts during the deadlock detection procedure. For example, if there is a cycle $T \rightarrow U \rightarrow V \rightarrow T$ and U aborts after the information concerning U has been collected, then the cycle has been broken already and there is no deadlock.

Edge chasing □   A distributed approach to deadlock detection uses a technique called edge chasing or path pushing. In this approach, the global wait-for graph is not constructed, but each of the servers involved has knowledge about some of its edges. The servers attempt to find cycles by forwarding messages called **probes** that follow the edges of the graph throughout the distributed system. A probe message consists of transaction wait-for relationships representing a path in the global wait-for graph.

The question is: when should a server send out a probe? Consider the situation at server X in Figure 14.12. This server has just added the edge $W \rightarrow U$ to its local wait-for graph and at this time, transaction U is waiting to access data item B that transaction V holds at server Y. This edge could possibly be part of a cycle such as $V \rightarrow T_1 \rightarrow T_2 \ldots \rightarrow W \rightarrow U \rightarrow V$ involving transactions using data items at other servers. This indicates that there is a potential distributed deadlock cycle which could be found by sending out a probe to server Y.

Now consider the situation a little earlier when server Z added the edge $V \rightarrow W$ to its local graph: at this point in time, W is not waiting. Therefore there would be no point in sending out a probe.

Each distributed transaction starts at a server (called the coordinator of the transaction) and moves to several other servers (called workers in the transaction), which can communicate with the coordinator. At any point in time, a transaction can be either active or waiting at just one of these servers. The coordinator is responsible for recording whether the transaction is active or is waiting for a particular data item and workers can get this information from their coordinator. Lock managers inform coordinators when transactions start waiting for data items and when transactions acquire data items and become active again. When a transaction is aborted to break a deadlock, its coordinator will inform the workers and all its locks will be removed, with the effect that all edges involving that transaction will be removed from the local wait-for graphs.

Edge-chasing algorithms have three steps – initiation, detection and resolution.

Initiation: When a server notes that a transaction T starts waiting for another transaction U, where U is waiting to access a data item at another server it initiates detection by sending a probe containing the edge $< T \rightarrow U >$ to the server of the data item at which transaction U is blocked. If U is sharing a lock, probes are sent to all the holders of the lock. Sometimes further transactions may start sharing the lock later on, in which case probes can be sent to them too.

Detection: Detection consist of receiving probes and deciding whether deadlock has occurred and whether to forward the probes.

Figure 14.14 Probes transmitted to detect deadlock.

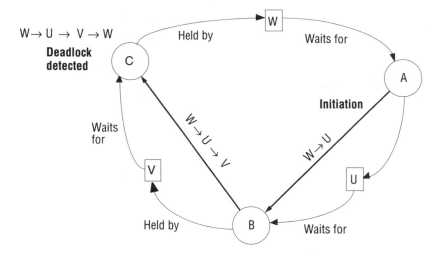

For example, when a server of a data item receives a probe $< T \rightarrow U >$ (indicating that T is waiting for a transaction U that holds a local data item), it checks to see whether U is also waiting. If it is, the transaction it waits for (for example, V) is added to the probe (making it $< T \rightarrow U \rightarrow V >$) and if the new transaction (V) is waiting for another data item elsewhere, the probe is forwarded.

In this way, paths through the global wait-for graph are built one edge at a time. Before forwarding a probe, the server checks to see whether the transaction (for example, T) it has just added has caused the probe to contain a cycle (for example, $< T \rightarrow U \rightarrow V \rightarrow T >$). If this is the case, it has found a cycle in the graph and deadlock has been detected.

Resolution: When a cycle is detected, a transaction in the cycle is aborted to break the deadlock.

In our example, the following steps describe how deadlock detection is initiated and the probes that are forwarded during the corresponding detection phase.

- Server X initiates detection by sending probe $< W \rightarrow U >$ to the server of B (Server Y).

- Server Y receives probe $< W \rightarrow U >$, notes that B is held by V and appends V to the probe to produce $< W \rightarrow U \rightarrow V >$. It notes that V is waiting for C at server Z. This probe is forwarded to server Z.

- Server Z receives probe $< W \rightarrow U \rightarrow V >$ and notes C is held by W and appends W to the probe to produce $< W \rightarrow U \rightarrow V \rightarrow W >$.

This path contains a cycle. The server detects a deadlock.

One of the transactions in the cycle must be aborted to break the deadlock. The transaction to be aborted can be chosen according to transaction priorities, which are described shortly.

Figure 14.14 shows the progress of the probe messages from the initiation by the server of A to the deadlock detection by the server of C. Probes are shown as heavy arrows, data items as circles and transaction coordinators as rectangles. Each probe is shown as going directly from one data item to another. In reality, before a server transmits a probe to another server, it consults the coordinator of the last transaction in the path to find out whether the latter is waiting for another data item elsewhere. For example, before the server of B transmits the probe <W → U → V> it consults the coordinator of V to find out that V is waiting for C. In most of the edge-chasing algorithms, the servers of data items send probes to transaction coordinators which then forward them (if the transaction is waiting) to the server of the data item the transaction is waiting for. In our example, the server of B transmits the probe <W → U → V> to the coordinator of V which then forwards it to the server of C. This shows that when a probe is forwarded, two messages are required.

The above algorithm should find any deadlock that occurs, provided that waiting transactions do not abort and there are no failures such as lost messages or servers crashing. To understand this, consider a deadlock cycle in which the last transaction, W, starts waiting and completes the cycle. When W starts waiting for a data item, the server initiates a probe that goes to the server of the data item held by each transaction that W is waiting for. The recipients extend and forward the probes to the servers of data items requested by all waiting transactions they find. Thus every transaction that W waits for directly or indirectly will be added to the probe unless a deadlock is detected. When there is a deadlock, W is waiting for itself indirectly. Therefore the probe will return to the data item that W holds.

It might appear that large numbers of messages are sent in order to detect deadlock. In the above example, we see two probe messages to detect a cycle involving three transactions. Each of the probe messages is in general two messages (from data item to coordinator and then from coordinator to data item).

A probe that detects a cycle involving N transactions will be forwarded by $(N-1)$ transaction coordinators via $(N-1)$ servers of data items, requiring $2(N-1)$ messages. Fortunately, the majority of deadlocks involve cycles containing only two transactions and there is no need for undue concern about the number of messages involved. This observation has been made from studies of databases. It can also be argued by considering the probability of conflicting access to data items. See Bernstein *et al.* [1987].

Transaction priorities □ In the above algorithm, every transaction involved in a deadlock cycle can cause deadlock detection to be initiated. The effect of several transactions in a cycle initiating deadlock detection is that detection may happen at several different servers in the cycle with the result that more than one transaction in the cycle is aborted.

In Figure 14.15(a), consider transactions, T, U, V and W where U is waiting for W and V is waiting for T. At about the same time, T requests the data item held by U and W requests the data item held by V. Two separate probes < T → U > and < W → V > are initiated by the servers of these data items and are circulated until, deadlock is detected by each of two different servers. See in Figure 14.15(b) where the cycle is < T → U → W → V → T > and (c) where the cycle is < W → V → T → U → W >.

Figure 14.15 Two probes initiated.

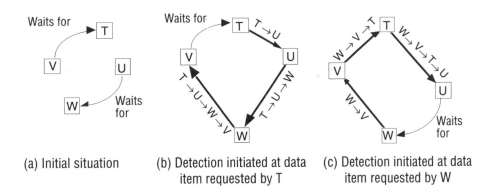

(a) Initial situation (b) Detection initiated at data item requested by T (c) Detection initiated at data item requested by W

In order to ensure that only one transaction in a cycle is aborted, transactions are given *priorities* in such a way that all transactions are totally ordered. Timestamps may for example, be used as priorities. When a deadlock cycle is found, the transaction with the lowest priority is aborted. Even if several different servers detect the same cycle they will all reach the same decision as to which transaction is to be aborted. We write T > U to indicate that T has higher priority than U. In the above example, assume T > U > V > W. Then the transaction W will be aborted when either of the cycles < T → U → W → V → T > and < W → V → T → U → W > is detected.

It might appear that transaction priorities could also be used to reduce the number of situations that cause deadlock detection to be initiated, by using the rule that detection is initiated only when a higher priority transaction starts to wait for a lower priority one. In our example in Figure 14.15, as T > U the initiating probe < T → U > would be sent, but as W < V the initiating probe < W → V > would not be sent. If we assume that when a transaction starts waiting for another transaction it is equally likely that the waiting transaction has higher or lower priority than the waited for transaction, then the use of this rule is likely to reduce the number of probe messages by about half.

Transaction priorities could also be used to reduce the number of probes that are forwarded. The general idea is that probes should travel 'downhill' – that is from transactions with higher priorities to transactions with lower priorities. To do this, servers use the rule that they do not forward any probe to a holder that has higher priority than the initiator. The argument for doing this is that if the holder is waiting for another transaction then it must have initiated detection by sending a probe when it started waiting.

However, there is a pitfall associated with these apparent improvements. In our example in Figure 14.14 transactions U, V and W are executed in an order in which U is waiting for V and V is waiting for W when W starts waiting for U. Without priority rules, detection is initiated when W starts waiting by sending a probe < W → U>. Under the priority rule, this probe will not be sent because W < U and deadlock will not be detected.

The problem is that the order in which transactions start waiting can determine whether or not deadlock will be detected. The above pitfall can be avoided by using a

Figure 14.16   Probes travel downhill.

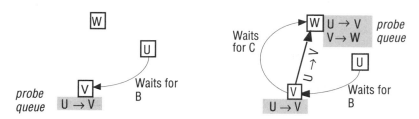

(a) V stores probe when U starts waiting   (b) Probe is forwarded when V starts waiting

scheme in which coordinators save copies of all the probes received on behalf of each transaction in a *probe queue*. When a transaction starts waiting for a data item, it forwards the probes in its queue to the server of the data item which propagates the probes on downhill routes.

In our example in Figure 14.14, when U starts waiting for V, the coordinator of V will save the probe < U → V >. See Figure 14.16(a). Then when V starts waiting for W, the coordinator of W will store < V → W > and V will forward its probe queue < U → V > to W. See Figure 14.16(b) in which W's probe queue has < U → V > and < V → W >. When W starts waiting for A it will forward its probe queue < U → V → W > to the server of A which also notes the new dependency W → U and combines it with the information in the probe received to determine that U → V → W → U. Deadlock is detected.

When an algorithm requires probes to be stored in probe queues, it also requires arrangements to pass on probes to new holders and to discard probes that refer to transactions that have been committed or aborted. This adds much to the complexity of any edge-chasing algorithm. Readers who are interested in the details of such algorithms should see Sinha and Natarajan [1985] and Choudhary *et al.* [1989] who present algorithms for use with exclusive locks. Work by Roesler and Burkhard [1988] is designed for use with semantic locks. An important aspect of shared and semantic locks is that a transaction can wait for two or more other transactions. For example in Figure 14.17, transaction T is waiting for both V and W, Transaction priorities: S < T < V < W < X).

When S starts to wait for T, probes will circulate via two separate routes: < S → T → V → X → S > and < S → T → W → X → S >. One of these probes is

Figure 14.17   Cycles and shared locks.

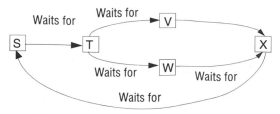

sufficient to detect the deadlock cycle. Roesler and Burkhard's algorithm attempts to eliminate such redundant probe messages.

14.6 Transactions with replicated data

Data items in transactional servers may be replicated to increase both availability and performance. Chapter 11 discusses the potential advantages and drawbacks of replication. To summarize: replication schemes attempt to trade off the desire to enhance the performance and availability of read-only requests which in some cases can be addressed to a single copy, against update requests which are degraded by the need to update multiple copies. We use the term *replicated transactional service* to refer to a transactional service in which a physical copy of each logical data item is replicated at a group of servers which we call replica managers as in Chapter 11.

From a client's viewpoint, a replicated transactional service should appear the same as one with non-replicated data items. In a non-replicated transactional service, transactions appear to be performed one at a time in some order. A transactional service achieves this by ensuring a serially equivalent interleaving of clients' transactions. A replicated transactional service ensures that the effect of transactions performed by various clients on replicated data items are the same as if they had been performed one at a time on single data items. This property is called **one-copy serializability**.

Each replica manager provides concurrency control and recovery of its own data items in the same way as it would for a non-replicated transactional service. In this section we assume that two-phase locking is used for concurrency control.

Recovery is complicated by the fact that a failed server is a member of a group of replica managers and that the other members continue to provide a service during the time that it is unavailable. When a replica manager recovers from a failure, it uses information obtained from the other replica mangers to restore its data items to their current values, taking into account all the changes that have occurred during the time it was unavailable. Replica managers must ensure that during the recovery period, client requests are not served by data items that are out of date.

It is essential that the recovery of a replica of a data item is serialized with respect to transactions. Transactions before the recovery of a data item cannot access it and transactions after the recovery can access it.

A transaction can observe a failure when one of its operations is unable to reach a replica manager. Failures should be serialized with respect to transactions. This means that any failure observed by a transaction must appear to have happened before that transaction started. It is not correct for a transaction to perform some of its operations on a data item at a replica manager that it later observes to have failed.

Therefore, a typical failure event and its recovery must be serially equivalent to a failure event followed by a sequence of complete transactions and then the corresponding recovery event.

This section first introduces the architecture for transactions with replicated data in terms of the model introduced in Chapter 11 in which processes play roles of clients, front ends and replica managers. Architectural questions are: whether a client request can be addressed to any of the replica managers, how many replica managers are required for the successful completion of an operation, whether the replica manager contacted by a client can defer the forwarding of requests until a transaction is committed and how to carry out a two-phase commit protocol.

The implementation of one copy serializability is illustrated by *read one/write all* – a simple replication scheme in which *Read* operations are performed by a single replica manager and *Write* operations are performed by all of them.

The section then discusses the problems of implementing replication schemes in the presence of server failure and recovery. It introduces available copies replication – a variant of the read one/write all replication scheme in which *Read* operations are performed by any single replica manager and *Write* operations are performed by all of those that are available.

A network partition can separate a group of replica managers into subgroups in which the members of each subgroup can communicate with one another, but no communication is possible between the subgroups. Finally, the section presents three replication schemes that work correctly in the presence of network partitions:

- *available copies with validation*: available copies replication is applied in each partition and when a partition is repaired, a validation procedure is applied and any inconsistencies are dealt with.

- *quorum consensus*: a subgroup must have a quorum (meaning that it has sufficient members), in order to be allowed to continue providing a service in the presence of a partition. When a partition is repaired (and when a server restarts after a failure) replica managers get their data items up-to-date by means of recovery procedures.

- *virtual partition*: a combination of quorum consensus and available copies. If a virtual partition has a quorum, it can use available copies replication.

Architecture for replicated transactions

Replication transparency is achieved by means of a front end, which is generally a user package in the client. Each client request may be sent to any one of the group of replica managers of a logical data item. The replica manager that receives a request to perform an operation on a particular data item is responsible for getting the cooperation of the other replica managers in the group that has copies of that data item. On receiving a client request, a replica manager not only executes the request but also communicates with the necessary number of other replica managers in the group before replying to the client.

Different replication schemes have different rules as to how many of the replica managers in a group are required for the successful completion of an operation. For example, in the *read one/write all* scheme, a *Read* request can be performed by a single replica manager, whereas a write request must be performed by all the replica managers in the group as shown in Figure 14.18 (there can be different numbers of replicas of the various data items). Quorum consensus schemes are designed to reduce the number of replica managers that must perform update operations but at the expense of increasing the number of replica managers required to perform *read-only* operations.

Figure 14.18   Replicated transactional service.

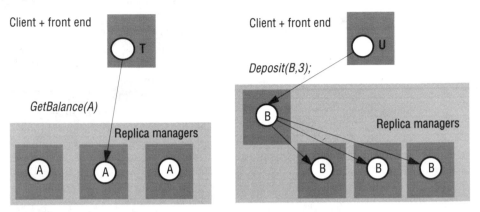

Another issue is whether the replica manager contacted by a client should defer the forwarding of update requests to other replica managers in the group until a transaction commits. At first sight this seems an attractive alternative because it reduces communication between the replicas. However, concurrency control must also be considered. Several different transactions may attempt to access the same data items at different replica managers in a group. To ensure that the transactions are correctly serialized at all the replica managers in the group, each replica manager needs to know about the requests performed by the others. This is the reason that replica managers forward each update request to all the necessary replica managers as soon as it is received.

Read one / write all □ We use this simple replication scheme to illustrate how the use of two-phase locking at each replica manager can be used to achieve one copy serializability. Every *Write* operation must be performed at all of the replica managers, each of which sets a write lock on the data item affected by the operation. Each *Read* operation is performed by a single replica manager which sets a read lock on the data item affected by the operation.

Consider pairs of operations of different transactions on the same data item: any pair of *Write* operations will require conflicting locks at all of the replica managers; a *Read* operation and a *Write* operation will require conflicting locks at a single replica manager. Thus one copy serializability is achieved.

The two-phase commit protocol □ The two-phase commit protocol becomes a two-level nested two-phase commit protocol. As before, the coordinator of a transaction communicates with the workers. But if either the coordinator or a worker is a replica manager it will communicate with the other replica managers to which it passed requests during the transaction.

That is, in the first phase, the coordinator sends the *CanCommit?* to the workers which pass it on to replica managers and collect their replies before replying to the coordinator. In the second phase, the coordinator sends the *DoCommit* or *Abort* request which is passed on to the members of the groups of replica managers.

Figure 14.19   Available copies.

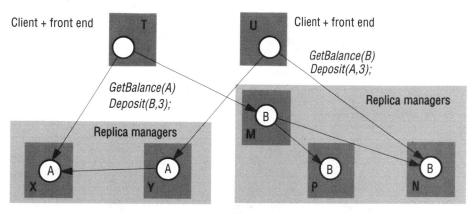

Primary copy replication □ A replicated transaction service can use primary copy replication in which all the client requests are directed to a single primary server (see Figure 11.5). For primary copy replication, concurrency control may be applied at the primary server and it is a good policy to defer sending the update requests to the slave servers until a transaction commits. To commit a transaction, the primary server communicates with the slave servers and then replies to the client. This form of replication allows a slave server to take over if the primary fails.

Note that this differs from the primary copy replication described in Chapter 11 where read requests can be addressed to the slaves and the performance of read requests is thereby enhanced.

Available copies replication

Simple read one/write all replication is not a realistic scheme because it cannot be carried out if some of the replica managers are unavailable, either because they have failed or because of a communication failure. The available copies scheme is designed to allow for some replica managers being temporarily unavailable. The strategy is that a client's *Read* request on a logical data item may be performed by any available replica manager but that a client's update request must be performed by all available replica managers in the group with copies of the data item. The idea of the 'available members of a group of replica managers' is similar to Coda's available volume storage group described in Chapter 8.

In the normal case, client requests are received and performed by a functioning replica manager. *Read* requests can be performed by the replica manager that receives them. *Write* requests are performed by the receiving replica manager and all the other available replica managers in the group. For example in Figure 14.19 the *GetBalance* operation of transaction T is performed by X whereas its *Deposit* operation is performed by M, N and P. Concurrency control at each replica manager affects the operations performed locally. For example, at X, transaction T has read A and therefore transaction U is not allowed to update A with the *Deposit* operation until transaction T has completed. So long as the set of available replica managers does not change, local concurrency control achieves one copy serializability in the same way as in read one/ write all replication. Unfortunately this is not the case if a replica manager fails or recovers during the progress of the conflicting transactions.

Failure case □ When a client makes a request to a replica manager that has failed, the client times out and retries the request at another replica manager in the group. If the request is received by a replica manager at which the data item is out of date because the server has not completely recovered from failure, the replica manager rejects the request and the client retries the request at another replica manager in the group.

One copy serializability requires that failures and recoveries should be serialized with respect to transactions. According to whether it can access a data item or not, a transaction observes that a failure occurs after it finished or before it started. One copy serializability is not achieved when different transactions make conflicting failure observations.

Consider the case in Figure 14.19 where the server X fails just after T has performed *GetBalance* and server N fails just after U has performed *GetBalance*. Assume that both of these servers fail before T and U have performed their *Deposit* operations. This implies that T's *Deposit* will be performed at servers M and P and U's *Deposit* will be performed at server Y. Unfortunately the concurrency control on A at server X does not prevent transaction U from updating A at server Y. Neither does concurrency control on B at server N prevent transaction T from updating B at servers M and P.

This is contrary to the requirement for one-copy serializability. If these operations were to be performed on single copies of the data items, they would be serialized either with transaction T before U or with transaction U before T. This ensures that one of the transactions will read the value set by the other. Local concurrency control on copies of data items is not sufficient to ensure one-copy serializability in the available copies replication scheme.

As *Write* operations are directed to all available copies, local concurrency control does ensure that conflicting writes on a data item are serialized. In contrast, a *Read* by one transaction and a *Write* by another do not necessarily affect the same copy of a data item. Therefore the scheme requires additional concurrency control to prevent the dependencies between a *Read* operation of one transaction and a *Write* operation of another transaction from forming a cycle. Such dependencies cannot arise if the failures and recoveries of replicas of data items are serialized with respect to transactions.

Local validation □ We refer to the additional concurrency control procedure as local validation. The local validation procedure is designed to ensure that any failure or recovery event does not appear to happen during the progress of a transaction. In our example, as T has read from a data item at X, X's failure must be after T. Similarly as T observes the failure of N when it attempts to update the data item, N's failure must be before T. That is:

N fails → T reads data item A at X; T writes data item B at M and P → T commits
→ X fails

It can also be argued for transaction U that:

X fails → U reads data item B at N; U writes data item A at Y → U commits → N fails

Figure 14.20   Network partition.

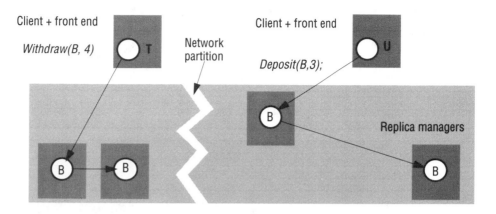

The local validation procedure ensures that two such incompatible sequences cannot both occur. Before a transaction commits it checks for any failures (and recoveries) of replica managers of data items it has accessed. In the example, transaction T would check that N is still unavailable and X, M and P are still available. If this is the case, T can commit. This implies that X fails after T validated and before U validated. In other words, U's validation is after T's validation. U's validation fails because N has already failed.

Whenever a transaction has observed a failure, the local validation procedure attempts to communicate with the failed replica managers to ensure that they have not yet recovered. The other part of the local validation, which is testing that replica managers have not failed since data items were accessed, can be combined with the two-phase commit protocol.

Available copies algorithms cannot be used in environments in which functioning replica managers are unable to communicate with one another.

Network partitions

Replication schemes need to take into account the possibility of network partitions. A network partition separates a group of replica managers into two or more subgroups, in such a way that the members of one subgroup can communicate with one another, but members of different subgroups cannot communicate with one another. For example in Figure 14.20, the replica managers receiving the *Deposit* request cannot send it to the replica managers receiving the *Withdraw* request.

Replication schemes are designed with the assumption that partitions will eventually be repaired. Therefore the replica managers within a single partition must ensure that any requests that they execute during a partition will not make the set of replicas inconsistent when the partition is repaired.

Davidson *et al.* [1985] discuss many different approaches, which they categorize as being either optimistic or pessimistic as to whether inconsistencies are likely to occur.

The optimistic schemes do not limit availability during a partition, whereas pessimistic schemes do.

The optimistic approaches allow updates in all partitions – this can lead to inconsistencies between partitions which must be resolved when the partition is repaired. An example of this approach is a variant of the available copies algorithm in which updates are allowed in partitions and after the partition has been repaired, the updates are validated – any updates that break the one-copy serializability criterion are aborted.

The pessimistic approach limits availability even when there are no partitions but it prevents any inconsistencies from occurring during partitions. When a partition is repaired, all that need be done is to update the copies of the data items. The quorum consensus approach is pessimistic. It allows updates in a partition that has the majority of replica managers and propagates the updates to the other replica managers when the partition is repaired.

Available copies with validation

The available copies algorithm is applied within each partition. This optimistic approach maintains the normal level of availability for *Read* operations even during partitions. When a partition is repaired, the possibly conflicting transactions that took place in the separate partitions are validated. If the validation fails, then some steps must be taken to overcome the inconsistencies. If there had been no partition, one of a pair of transactions with conflicting operations would have been delayed or aborted. Unfortunately as there has been a partition, pairs of conflicting transactions have been allowed to commit in different partitions. The only choice after the event is to abort one of them. This requires making changes in the data items and in some cases, compensating effects in the real world, such as dealing with overdrawn bank accounts. The optimistic approach is only feasible with applications where such compensating actions can be taken.

Version vectors can be used to validate conflicts between pairs of *Write* operations. These are used in the Coda file system and are described in Chapter 8. This approach cannot detect *Read-Write* conflicts but works well in file systems where transactions tend to access a single file and *Read-Write* conflicts are unimportant. It is not suitable for applications such as our banking example where *Read-Write* conflicts are important.

Davidson [1984] uses *precedence graphs* to detect inconsistencies between partitions. Each partition maintains a log of the data items affected by the *Read* and *Write* operations of transactions. This log is used to construct a precedence graph whose nodes are transactions and whose edges represent conflicts between the *Read* and *Write* operations of transactions. Such a graph will not contain any cycles since concurrency control has been applied within the partition. The validation procedure takes the precedence graphs from the partitions and adds edges representing conflicts between transactions in different partitions. If the resulting graph contains cycles, then the validation fails.

Quorum consensus methods

One way of preventing transactions in different partitions from producing inconsistent results is to make a rule that operations can only be carried out within one of the partitions. As the replica managers in different partitions cannot communicate with one another, the subgroup of replica managers within each partition must be able to decide independently whether they are allowed to carry out operations. A quorum is a subgroup of replica managers whose size gives it the right to carry out operations. For example, if having a majority is the criterion, a subgroup that has the majority of the members of a group would form a quorum because no other subgroup could have a majority.

In quorum consensus replication schemes an update operation on a logical data item may be completed successfully by a subgroup of its group of replica managers. The other members of the group will therefore have out of date copies of the data item. Version numbers or timestamps may be used to determine whether copies are up to date. If versions are used, the initial state of a data item is the first version and after each change, we have a new version. Each copy of a data item has a version number; but only the copies that are up to date have the current version number, whereas out of date copies have earlier version numbers. Operations should be applied only to copies with the current version number.

Gifford [1979a] developed a file replication scheme in which a number of votes is assigned to each physical copy at a replica manager of a single logical file. A vote can be regarded as a weighting related to the desirability of using a particular copy. Each *Read* operation must first obtain a read quorum of R votes before it can proceed to read from any up-to-date copy and each *Write* operation must obtain a write quorum of W votes before it can proceed with an update operation. R and W are set for a group of replica managers such that

W > half the total votes;

$R + W$ > total number of votes for the group.

This ensures that any pair, consisting of a read quorum and a write quorum or two write quora, must contain common copies. Therefore if there is a partition, it is not possible to perform conflicting operations on the same copy, but in different partitions.

To perform a *Read* operation a read quorum is collected by making sufficient version number enquiries to find a set of copies, the sum of whose votes is not less than R. Not all of these copies need be up-to-date. Since each read quorum overlaps with every write quorum, every read quorum is certain to include at least one current copy. The read operation may be applied to any up-to-date copy.

To perform a *Write* operation a write quorum is collected by making sufficient version number enquiries to find a set of replica managers with up-to-date copies, the sum of whose votes is not less than W. If there are insufficient up-to-date copies, then a non-current file is replaced with a copy of the current file, to enable the quorum to be established. The updates specified in the *Write* operation are then applied by each replica manager in the write quorum, the version number is incremented and completion of the write is reported to the client.

The files at the remaining available replica managers are then updated by performing the *Write* operation as a background task. Any replica manager whose copy of the file has an older version number than the one used by the write quorum, updates it by replacing the entire file with a copy obtained from a replica manager that is up-to-date.

Two-phase read/write locking may be used for concurrency control in Gifford's replication scheme. The preliminary version number enquiry to obtain the read quorum, R, causes read locks to be set at each replica manager contacted. When a *Write* operation is applied to the write quorum, W, a write lock is set at each replica manager involved. (Locks are applied with the same granularity as version numbers.) The locks ensure one-copy serializability as any read quorum overlaps with any write quorum and any two write quora overlap.

Configurability of groups of replica managers □ An important property of the weighted voting algorithm is that groups of replica managers can be configured to provide different performance or reliability characteristics. Once the general reliability and performance of a group of replica managers is established by its voting configuration, the reliability and performance of *Write* operations may be increased by decreasing W and similarly for *Reads* by decreasing R.

The algorithm can also allow for the use of copies of files on local disks at workstations as well as those at file servers. The copies of files in users' workstations are regarded as *weak representatives* and are always allocated zero votes. This ensures that they are not included in any quorum. A *Read* operation may be performed at any up-to-date copy, once a read quorum has been obtained. Therefore a *Read* operation may be carried out on the local copy of the file if it is up to date. Weak representatives can be used to speed up *Read* operations.

An example from Gifford □ Gifford gives three examples showing the range of properties that can be achieved by allocating weights to the various replica managers in a group and assigning R and W appropriately. We now reproduce Gifford's examples, which are based on the following table:

		Example 1	*Example 2*	*Example 3*
Latency	Replica 1	75	75	75
(milliseconds)	Replica 2	65	100	750
	Replica 3	65	750	750
Voting	Replica 1	1	2	1
configuration	Replica 2	0	1	1
	Replica 3	0	1	1
Quorum	R	1	2	1
sizes	W	1	3	3
Derived performance of file suite:				
Read	Latency	65	75	75
	Blocking probability	0.01	0.0002	0.000001
Write	Latency	75	100	750
	Blocking probability	0.01	0.0101	0.03

The blocking probabilities give an indication of the probability that a quorum cannot be obtained when a *Read* or *Write* request is made. They are calculated assuming that there is a 0.01 probability that any single replica manager will be unavailable at the time of a request.

Example 1 is configured for a file with a high read-to-write ratio in an application with several weak representatives and a single server. Replication is used to enhance the performance of the system, not the reliability. There is one server on the local network that can be accessed in 75 milliseconds. Two clients have chosen to make weak representatives on their local disks which they can access in 65 milliseconds, resulting in lower latency and less network traffic.

Example 2 is configured for a file with a moderate read-to-write ratio which is primarily accessed from one local network. The replica manager on the local network is assigned two votes and the replica managers on the remote networks are assigned one vote apiece. Reads can be satisfied from the local replica manager and writes must access the local replica manager and one remote replica manager. The file will remain available in read-only mode if the local replica manager fails. Clients could create local weak representatives for lower read latency.

Example 3 is configured for a file with a very high read-to-write ratio, such as a system directory in a three server environment. Clients can read from any replica manager and the probability that the file will be unavailable is small. Updates must be applied to all copies. Once again, clients could create weak representatives on their local machines for lower read latency.

The main disadvantage of quorum consensus is that the performance of *Read* operations is degraded by the need to collect a read quorum from R replica managers.

Herlihy [1986] proposes an extension of the quorum consensus method for abstract data types. This method allows the semantics of operations to be taken into account and thereby to increase the availability of data items. Herlihy's method uses timestamps instead of version numbers. This has the advantage that there is no need to make version number enquiries in order to get a new version number before performing a write operation. The main advantage claimed by Herlihy is that the use of semantic knowledge can increase the number of choices for a quorum.

Virtual partition algorithm

This algorithm, which was proposed by El Abbadi *et al.* [1985] combines the quorum consensus approach with the available copies algorithm. Quorum consensus works correctly in the presence of partitions, but available copies is less expensive for *Read* operations. A **virtual partition** is an abstraction of a real partition and contains a set of replica managers. Note that the term 'network partition' refers to the barrier that divides replica managers into several parts, whereas the term, 'virtual partition', refers to the parts themselves. A transaction can operate in a virtual partition if it contains sufficient replica managers to have a read quorum and a write quorum for the data items accessed. In this case the transaction uses the available copies algorithm. This has the advantage that *Read* operations need only ever access a single copy of a data item and may enhance performance by choosing the 'nearest' copy. If a replica manager fails and the virtual partition changes during a transaction, then the transaction is aborted. This ensures one-

Figure 14.21   Two network partitions.

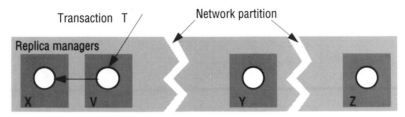

copy serializability of transactions because all transactions that survive see the failures and recoveries of replica managers in the same order.

Whenever a member of a virtual partition detects that it cannot access one of the other members – for example, when a *Write* operation is not acknowledged – it attempts to create a new virtual partition with a view to obtaining a virtual partition with read and write quora.

Suppose for example, that we have four replica managers V, X, Y, and Z, each of which has one vote and that the read and write quora are $R = 2$ and $W = 3$. Initially all the managers can contact one another. So long as they remain in contact, they can use the available copies algorithm. For example, a transaction T consisting of a *Read* followed by a *Write* operation will perform the *Read* at a single replica manager (for example, V) and the *Write* operation at all four of them.

Suppose that transaction T starts by performing its *Read* at V at a time when V is still in contact with X, Y, and Z. Now suppose that a network partition occurs as in Figure 14.21 in which V and X are in one part and Y and Z are in different ones. Then when transaction T attempts to apply its *Write*, V will notice that it cannot contact Y and Z.

When a replica manager cannot contact managers that it could previously contact, it keeps on trying. For example, V will keep on trying to contact Y and Z until one or both of them replies, as for example in Figure 14.22 when Y can be accessed. The group of replica managers V, X and Y comprise a virtual partition because they are sufficient to form read and write quora.

When a new virtual partition is created during a transaction that has performed an operation at one of the replica managers (such as transaction T), the transaction must be aborted. In addition, the replicas within a new virtual partition must be brought up to

Figure 14.22   Virtual partition.

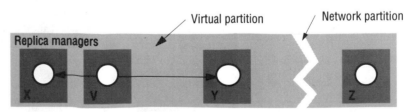

Figure 14.23   Two overlapping virtual partitions.

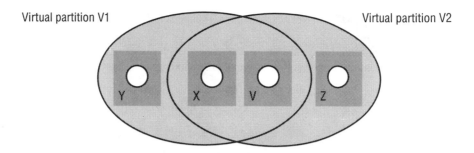

date by copying them from other replicas. Version numbers can be used as in Gifford's algorithm to determine which copies are up to date. It is essential that all replicas are up to date because *Read* operations are performed on any single replica.

Implementation of virtual partitions □   A virtual partition has a creation time, a set of potential members and a set of actual members. Creation times are logical timestamps. The actual members of a particular virtual partition have the same idea as to its creation time and membership (a shared *view* of the replica managers with which they can communicate). For example, in Figure 14.22 the potential members are V, X, Y, Z and the actual members are V, X and Y.

The creation of a new virtual partition is achieved by a cooperative protocol carried out by those of the potential members that can be accessed by the replica managers that initiated it. Several replica managers may attempt to create a new virtual partition simultaneously. For example, suppose that the replica managers Y and Z shown in Figure 14.21 keep making attempts to contact the others and after a while the network partition is partially repaired so that Y cannot communicate with Z, but the two groups V, X, Y and V, X, Z can communicate among themselves. Then there is a danger that two overlapping virtual partitions such as V1 and V2 shown in Figure 14.23 might both be created.

Consider the effect of executing different transactions in the two virtual partitions. The *Read* operation of the transaction in V, X, Y might be applied at the replica manager Y, in which case its read lock will not conflict with write locks set by a *Write* operation of a transaction in the other virtual partition. Overlapping virtual partitions are contrary to one-copy serializability.

The aim of the protocol is to create new virtual partitions consistently, even if real partitions occur during the protocol. The protocol for creating a new virtual partition has two phases as shown in Figure 14.24

A replica manager that replies *Yes* in Phase 1 does not belong to a virtual partition until it receives the corresponding *Confirmation* message in Phase 2.

In our example above, the replica managers Y and Z shown in Figure 14.21 each attempt to create a virtual partition and whichever one has the higher logical timestamp will be the one that is used in the end.

This is an effective method when partitions are not a common occurrence. Each transaction uses the available copies algorithm within a virtual partition.

Figure 14.24 Creating a virtual partition.

Phase 1:

- The initiator sends a *Join* request to each potential member. The argument of *Join* is a proposed logical timestamp for the new virtual partition;

- When a replica manager receives a *Join* request it compares the proposed logical timestamp with that of its current virtual partition;

    - If the proposed logical timestamp is greater it agrees to join and replies *Yes;*

    - If it is less, it refuses to join and replies *No;*

Phase 2:

- If the initiator has received sufficient *Yes* replies to have *Read* and *Write* quora, it may complete the creation of the new virtual partition by sending a *Confirmation* message to the sites that agreed to join. The creation timestamp and list of actual members are sent as arguments;

- Replica managers receiving the *Confirmation* message join the new virtual partition and record its creation timestamp and list of actual members.

14.7 Summary

In the most general case, a client's transaction will request operations on data items in several different servers. A server that carries out a client request may need to request an operation in another server, in which case a nested transaction structure is required. A distributed transaction is any transaction whose activity involves several different servers. A nested transaction structure may be used to allow additional concurrency and independent commitment by the servers in a distributed transaction.

The atomicity property of transactions requires that the servers participating in a distributed transaction should either all commit it or all abort it. Atomic commitment protocols are designed to achieve this effect, even if servers fail during their execution. The two-phase commit protocol allows a server to decide to abort unilaterally. It includes timeout actions to deal with delays due to servers failing. The two-phase atomic commit protocol can take an unbounded amount of time to complete but is guaranteed to complete eventually.

Concurrency control in distributed transactions is modular – each server is responsible for the serializability of transactions that access its own data items. However, additional protocols are required to ensure that transactions are serializable globally. Distributed transactions that use timestamp ordering require a means of generating an agreed timestamp ordering between the multiple servers. Those that use optimistic concurrency control require global validation or a means of forcing a timestamp ordering on committing transactions.

Distributed transactions that use two-phase locking can suffer from distributed deadlocks. The aim of distributed deadlock detection is to look for cycles in the global wait-for graph. If a cycle is found, one or more transactions must be aborted to resolve the deadlock. Edge chasing is a non-centralized approach to the detection of distributed deadlocks.

Transactions can be applied to replicated data. Replication schemes are based on the notion of one-copy serializability. This requires that transactions accessing multiple physical copies of a logical data item should behave as though they are accessing a single copy of the data item in a serially equivalent manner. The simplest replication scheme applies *Read* operations to a single copy and *Write* operations to all copies. Under this scheme, the concurrency control protocols ensure one copy serializability.

The available copies scheme applies *Read* operations to a single copy and *Write* operations to all available copies. It is intended to work in the presence of failed servers. To work correctly, this scheme requires that all failure and recovery events should be serialized with respect to transactions. This scheme does not work in the presence of partitions – when some functioning servers are unable to communicate with other functioning servers.

There are two approaches to the design of replication schemes for use in environments in which partitions may occur. The optimistic approach allows updates to proceed in all partitions independently and when a partition is repaired the effects of conflicting operations are undone. This approach is not practical for use in applications that interact with events in the real world, such as giving out money. The pessimistic approaches allow updates in only one partition and all that has to be done when a partition is repaired is to propagate the updates. The quorum consensus algorithm is an example of the pessimistic approach. Only the partition with the majority consensus may process requests. This algorithm has the disadvantage of having to apply *Read* operations to multiple copies. The virtual partition algorithm is an improvement. Requests may be processed in a virtual partition that has majority consensus. These requests use the available copies algorithm and therefore *Read* operations use single copies. The overheads occur only when a replica manager detects the failure of another replica manager and carries out the protocol to create a new virtual partition.

EXERCISES

14.1   In a decentralized variant of the two-phase commit protocol the workers communicate directly with one another instead of indirectly via the coordinator. In Phase 1, the coordinator sends its vote to all the workers. In Phase 2, if the coordinator's vote is *No*, the workers just abort the transaction; if it is *Yes*, each worker sends its vote to the coordinator and the other workers, each of which decides on the outcome according to the vote and carries it out. Calculate the number of messages and the number of rounds it takes. What are its advantages or disadvantages in comparison with the centralized variant?

page 414

14.2   A three-phase commit protocol has the following parts:

Phase 1: is the same as for two-phase commit.

Phase 2: the coordinator collects the votes and makes a decision; if it is *No*, it *Aborts* and informs workers that voted *Yes*; if the decision is *Yes*, it sends a *PreCommit* request to all the workers. Workers that voted *Yes* wait for a *PreCommit* or *Abort* request. They acknowledge *PreCommit* requests and carry out *Abort* requests.

Phase 3: the coordinator collects the acknowledgments. When all are received, it *Commits* and sends *DoCommit* to the workers. Workers wait for a *DoCommit* request. When it arrives they *Commit*.

Explain how this protocol avoids delay to workers during their 'uncertain' period due to the failure of the coordinator or other workers. Assume that communication does not fail.

page 414

14.3   Suggest two situations related to the failure of processes or communication in which all the workers vote *Yes* in the first phase of the two-phase commit protocol and yet the coordinator decides to abort the transaction.

page 414

14.4   The *GetDecision* procedure defined in Figure 14.4 is provided only by coordinators. Define a new version of *GetDecision* to be provided by workers for use by other workers that need to obtain a decision when the coordinator is unavailable.

Assume that any active worker can make a *GetDecision* request to any other active worker. Does this solve the problem of delay during the 'uncertain' period? Explain your answer.

At what point in the two-phase commit protocol would the coordinator inform the workers of the other workers' identities (to enable this communication)?

page 414

14.5   Explain how the two-phase commit protocol for nested transactions ensures that if the top-level transaction commits, all the right descendents are committed or aborted.

page 417

14.6   Give an example of the interleavings of two transactions that is serially equivalent at each server but is not serially equivalent globally.

page 422

14.7   Extend the definition of two-phase locking to apply to distributed transactions. Explain how this is ensured by distributed transactions using strict two-phase locking locally.

page 422 and Chapter 13

14.8   Assuming that strict two-phase locking is in use, describe how the actions of the two-phase commit protocol relate to the concurrency control actions of each individual server. How does distributed deadlock detection fit in?

pages 414 and 422

14.9 A server uses timestamp ordering for local concurrency control. What changes must be made to adapt it for use with distributed transactions? Under what conditions could it be argued that the two-phase commit protocol is redundant with timestamp ordering?

pages 414 and 422

14.10 Consider distributed optimistic concurrency control in which each server performs local backward validation sequentially (that is, with only one transaction in the validate and write phase at one time), in relation to your answer to Figure 14.6. Describe the possible outcomes when the two transactions attempt to commit. What difference does it make if the servers use parallel validation?

Chapter 13 and page 422

14.11 A centralized global deadlock detector holds the union of local wait-for graphs. Give an example to explain how a phantom deadlock could be detected if a waiting transaction in a deadlock cycle aborts during the deadlock detection procedure.

page 426

14.12 Consider the edge chasing algorithm (without priorities). Give examples to show that it could detect phantom deadlocks.

page 427

14.13 Available copies replication is applied to data items A and B with replicas A_x, A_y and B_m, B_n. The transactions T and U are defined as:

T: *Read(A); Write(B,44). U: Read(B); Write(A, 55).*

Show an interleaving of T and U, assuming that two-phase locks are applied to the replicas. Explain why locks alone cannot ensure one copy serializability if one of the replicas fails during the progress of T and U. Explain with reference to this example, how local validation ensures one copy serializability.

page 435

14.14 Gifford's quorum consensus replication is in use at servers X, Y and Z which all hold replicas of data items A and B. The initial values of all replicas of A and B are 100 and the votes for A and B are 1 at each of X, Y and Z. Also $R = W = 2$ for both A and B. A client reads the value of A and then writes it to B.

  i)   At the time the client performs these operations, a partition separates servers X and Y from server Z. Describe the quora obtained and the operations that take place if the client can access servers X and Y.

  ii)   Describe the quora obtained and the operations that take place if the client can access only server Z.

  iii) The partition is repaired and then another partition occurs so that X and Z are separated from Y. Describe the quora obtained and the operations that take place if the client can access servers X and Z.

page 439

14.15   A group of five replica managers A, B, C, D and E using Gifford's quorum
consensus scheme is configured with the weights A = 3, B = C = 2,
D = E = 1. State the possible values that may be chosen for a write quorum.
Which choices of write quorum allow the service to continue when any one
of the servers is unavailable? Give a choice of read quorum for each of these
write quora. For each read quorum state the ways it may be collected and
the minimum number of servers involved.

page 439

14.16   A group of five replica managers A, B, C, D and E use the virtual partition
algorithm. They are configured with equal weights of 1 and with $R = 3$ and
$W = 3$. Initially all the replica managers are in the same virtual partition. E
is then separated from the others by a network partition. Describe the
forming of the virtual partition when E is separated and the effect of *Read*
and *Write* operations within this virtual partition. Subsequently the replica
managers are separated into two real partitions A, B and C, D, E. Describe
the forming of the new virtual partition, the update of replicas and the effect
of *Read* and *Write* operations within this virtual partition.

page 441

RECOVERY AND FAULT TOLERANCE

The recovery of transactions is concerned with ensuring failure atomicity in the presence of occasional server failures. Servers that provide transactions include a recovery manager whose concern is to ensure that the effects of transactions on a server's data items can be recovered when a server is restarted after a failure. The recovery manager saves the data items in permanent storage together with intentions lists and information about the status of each transaction.

Transactions are not suitable for all applications. Applications with real-time requirements and applications that need to run correctly on faulty hardware need different approaches to fault tolerance.

Fault tolerance has two aspects – the description of the characteristics of faults and the masking of faults. Various types of faults can occur in distributed systems. These include 'fail-stop' and 'Byzantine failure'.

There are two approaches to masking failures in a service: by hierarchic masking and by group masking.

The chapter ends with two case studies:

- stable storage;
- the primary server / backup server arrangement.

15.1 Introduction

There are several approaches to the provision of fault-tolerant services. In general, a fault-tolerant service may occasionally fail temporarily, but it is designed to recover after a failure without loss of data.

Most fault-tolerant applications can be described either as being transaction based or as being concerned with process control. The factor that distinguishes the two is the recovery time. Transactional services can generally accept occasional failures followed by a relatively lengthy recovery procedure.

Process control applications have different requirements [Bacon 1993]. They are characterized by having inputs that are readings taken from sensors and outputs to actuators that are either used to control a process directly or to activate alarms so that humans can intervene in the process. Applications of this type include air traffic control, monitoring patients in hospitals and controlling reactors. They generally have very strict timing requirements. Therefore recovery must be achieved within a very small time limit.

Although transactional services are very suitable for dealing with the maintenance of long-lived shared data, they are not suitable for all distributed applications. A transactional service saves its data items in a recovery file during its normal operation so that they may be recovered when it fails.

Recovering a service by restarting it and restoring its data items from a recovery file may be too slow for some applications. The use of service replicas running in different computers can make recovery much faster. If the replicas are always up-to-date with one another, recovery from a single fault can be instantaneous. The use of several active replicas is expensive in computing resources. A compromise is to have a primary server and some backup servers that lag behind the primary. The primary server deals with clients requests until it fails, at which point a backup server catches up by performing the outstanding operations that it has not yet done and then takes over.

The first section of this chapter discusses the recovery aspects of distributed transactions. The remainder of the chapter is concerned with a more general approach to fault tolerance which includes approaches to the design of services with real time requirements. It introduces the various types of faults that can affect servers or the network, file system or operating system on which the servers depend. These types of faults include 'Fail-stop' and 'Byzantine failure'.

Finally it discusses how a service can mask the faults produced by the components it depends on. The use of groups is a particularly effective way of masking failures. Stable storage and the primary server–backup server arrangement are described as examples of methods for masking faults.

15.2 Transaction recovery

The atomic property of transactions requires that the effects of all committed transactions and none of the effects of incomplete or aborted transactions are reflected in the data items. This property can be described in terms of two aspects: durability and failure atomicity. Durability requires that data items are saved in permanent storage and will be available indefinitely thereafter. Therefore an acknowledgement of a client's commit request implies that all the effects of the transaction have been recorded in permanent storage as well as in the server's (volatile) data items. Failure atomicity requires that effects of transactions are atomic even when the server fails. Recovery is concerned with ensuring that a server's data items are durable and that the service provides failure atomicity.

Although file servers and database servers maintain data in permanent storage, other kinds of servers need not do so except for recovery purposes. In this chapter we assume that when a server is running it keeps all of its data items in its volatile memory and records its committed data in a *recovery file* or files. Therefore recovery consists of restoring the server with the latest committed versions of its data items from permanent storage. Databases need to deal with large volumes of data. They generally hold the data items in stable storage on disk with a cache in volatile memory.

The two requirements for durability and for failure atomicity are not really independent of one another and can be dealt with by a single mechanism – the **recovery manager**. The task of a recovery manager is:

- to save data items in permanent storage (in a recovery file) for committed transactions;

- to restore the server's data items after a crash;

- to reorganize the recovery file to improve the performance of recovery;

- to reclaim storage space (in the recovery file).

In some cases we require the recovery manager to be resilient to media failures – failures of its recovery file. In such cases the recovery file can be replicated using a technique known as *stable storage* which not only has a high probability of surviving media failures but also provides a *Write* operation that is atomic even when the system fails during the write. See Section 15.4 for a description of stable storage.

Intentions list □ Any server that provides transactions needs to keep track of the data items accessed by clients' transactions. Recall from Chapters 12 and 14 that when a client opens a transaction, the server first contacted provides a new transaction identifier and returns it to the client. Each subsequent client request within a transaction up to and including the *Commit* or *Abort* request includes the transaction identifier as an argument. During the progress of a transaction the update operations are applied to a private set of tentative versions of the data items belonging to the transaction.

Each server records an **intentions list** for all of its currently active transactions – an intentions list of a particular transaction contains a list of the names and the values of all the data items that are altered by that transaction. When a transaction is committed, the server uses that transaction's intentions list to identify the data items it affected. The committed version of each data item is replaced by the tentative version made by that transaction and the new value is written to the server's recovery file. When a transaction aborts, the server uses the intentions list to delete all the tentative versions of data items made by that transaction.

Recall also that a distributed transaction must carry out an atomic commitment protocol before it can be committed or aborted. Our discussion of recovery is based on the two-phase commit protocol in which all the servers involved in a transaction first say whether they are prepared to commit and then, later on if all the servers agree, they all carry out the actual commitment. If the servers cannot agree to commit, they must abort the transaction.

At the point when a server says it is prepared to commit a transaction, it must have saved both its intentions list for that transaction and the data items in that intentions list in its recovery file, so that it will be able to carry out the commitment later on, even if it crashes in the interim.

When all the servers involved in a transaction agree to commit it, the coordinator informs the client and then sends messages to the participants to carry out the commitment. Once the client has been informed of the commitment, the recovery files of the participating servers must contain sufficient information to ensure that the transaction is committed by all of the servers, even if some of them crash between preparing to commit and committing.

Entries in recovery file □ To deal with recovery of a server that can be involved in distributed transactions, further information in addition to the data items is stored in the recovery file. This information concerns the *status* of each transaction – whether it is *committed*, *aborted* or *prepared* to commit. In addition, each data item in the recovery file is associated with a particular transaction by saving the intentions list in the recovery file. To summarize, the recovery file includes the following types of entry:

Type of entry	Description of contents of entry
Data item	A value of a data item
Transaction status	Transaction identifier, transaction status (*prepared*, *committed*, *aborted*) – and other status values used for the two-phase commit protocol and for nested transactions (when in use)
Intentions list	Transaction identifier and a sequence of intentions, each of which consists of <identifier of data item>, <position in recovery file of value of data item>

The transaction status values relating to the two-phase commit protocol are discussed in the subsection on recovery of the two-phase commit protocol and the entries relating to nested transactions in the paragraph on the recovery of nested transactions. We shall now describe two approaches to the use of recovery files: logging and shadow versions.

Logging

In the logging technique, the recovery file represents a log containing the history of all the transactions performed by a server. The history consists of values of data items, transaction status entries and intentions lists of transactions. The order of the entries in the log reflects the order in which transactions have prepared, committed and aborted at that server. In practice, the recovery file will contain a recent snapshot of the values of all the data items in the server followed by a history of transactions after the snapshot.

During the normal operation of a server, its recovery manager is called whenever a transaction prepares to commit, commits or aborts a transaction. When the server is prepared to commit a transaction, the recovery manager appends all the data items in its

Figure 15.1   Log for banking service.

P0			P1	P2	P3	P4	P5	P6	P7
Data:A	Data:B	Data:C	Data:A	Data:B	Trans:T	Trans:T	Data:C	Data:B	Trans:U
100	200	300	96	204	prepared	committed	297	207	prepared
					<A, P1>				<C, P5>
					<B, P2>				<B, P6>
					P0	P3			P4

Checkpoint   End of log

intentions list to the recovery file, followed by the current status of that transaction (prepared) together with its intentions list. When a transaction is eventually committed or aborted, the recovery manager appends the corresponding status of the transaction to its recovery file.

It is assumed that the append operation is atomic in the sense that it writes one or more complete entries to the recovery file. If the server fails, only the last write can be incomplete.

The recovery manager associates a unique identifier with each data item so that the successive versions of a data item in the recovery file may be associated with the server's data items. For example, in the banking service (Chapter 12), the bank accounts might be members of an array, and the identifiers of the data items could be their subscripts in the array.

Figure 15.1 illustrates the log mechanism for the banking service transactions T and U in Figure 12.6. The log was recently reorganized and entries to the left of the double line represent a snapshot of the values of A, B and C before transactions T and U started. In this diagram, we use the names A, B and C as unique identifiers for data items. We show the situation when transaction T has committed and transaction U has prepared but not committed. When transaction T prepares to commit, the values of data items A and B are written at positions P1 and P2 in the log, followed by a prepared transaction status entry for T with its intentions list (< A, P1 >, < B, P2 >). When transaction T commits, a committed transaction status entry for T is put at position P4. Then when transaction U prepares to commit, the values of data items C and B are written at positions P5 and P6 in the log, followed by a prepared transaction status entry for U with its intentions list (< C, P5 >, < B, P6 >).

Each transaction status entry contains a pointer to the position in the recovery file of the previous transaction status entry, to enable the recovery manager to follow the transaction status entries in reverse order through the recovery file. The last pointer in the sequence of transaction status entries points to the checkpoint.

Recovery of data items □ When a server is restarted, it first sets default initial values for its data items and then hands over to its recovery manager. The recovery manager is responsible for restoring the server's data items so that they include all the effects of all the committed transactions performed in the correct order and none of the effects of the incomplete or aborted transactions.

The most recent information about transactions is at the end of the log. Therefore a recovery manager will restore a server's data items by 'reading the recovery file backwards'. It uses transactions with committed status to restore those data items that have not yet been restored. It continues until it has restored all of the server's data items.

To recover the effects of a transaction, a recovery manager gets the corresponding intentions list from its recovery file. The intentions list contains the identifiers and positions in the recovery file of values of all the data items affected by the transaction.

If the server fails at the point reached in Figure 15.1 its recovery manager will recover the data items as follows. It starts at the last transaction status entry in the log (at P7) and concludes that transaction U has not committed and its effects should be ignored. It then moves to the previous transaction status entry in the log (at P4) and concludes that transaction T has committed. To recover the data items affected by transaction T it moves to the previous transaction status entry in the log (at P3) and finds the intentions list for T ($<$ A, P1 $>$, $<$ B, P2 $>$). It then restores data items A and B from the values at P1 and P2. As it has not yet restored C, it moves back to P0 which is a data item in a checkpoint and restores C.

To help with subsequent reorganization of the recovery file, the recovery manager notes all the prepared transactions it finds during the process of restoring the server's data items. For each prepared transaction it adds an aborted transaction status to the recovery file.

The server could fail again during the recovery procedures. It is essential that recovery should be idempotent in the sense that it can be done any number of times with the same effect. This is straightforward under our assumption that all the data items are restored to volatile memory. In the case of a database that keeps its data items in permanent storage, with a cache in volatile memory, some of the data items in permanent storage will be out of date when it restarts. Therefore its recovery manager has to restore the data items in permanent storage. If it fails during recovery, the partially restored data items will still be there. This makes idempotence a little harder to achieve.

Reorganizing the recovery file □   A recovery manager is responsible for reorganizing its recovery file so as to make the process of recovery faster and to reduce its use of space. If the recovery file is never reorganized, then the recovery process must search backwards through the recovery file until it has found a value for each of its data items. Conceptually the only information required for recovery is a copy of the committed versions of all the data items in the server. This would be the most compact form for the recovery file. The name **checkpointing** is used to refer the process of writing the current committed values of a server's data items to a new recovery file, together with transaction status entries and intentions lists of transactions that have not yet been fully resolved (including information related to the two-phase commit protocol). The term **checkpoint** is used to refer to the information stored by the checkpointing process. The purpose of making checkpoints is to reduce the number of transactions to be dealt with during recovery and to reclaim file space.

Checkpointing can be done immediately after recovery, but before any new transactions are started. However recovery may not occur very often. Therefore checkpointing may need to be done from time to time during the normal activity of a server. The checkpoint is written to a future recovery file and the current recovery file remains in use until the checkpoint is complete. Checkpointing consists of 'adding a mark' to the recovery file when the checkpointing starts, writing the server's data items to the future recovery file and then copying (i) items before the mark that relate to as yet unresolved transactions and (ii) all items after the mark in the recovery file to the future recovery file. When the checkpoint is complete, the future recovery file becomes the recovery file.

The recovery system can reduce its use of space by discarding the old recovery file. When the recovery manager is carrying out the recovery process it may encounter a checkpoint in the recovery file. When this happens, it can restore immediately all outstanding data items from the checkpoint.

Shadow versions

The **logging** technique records transaction status entries, intentions lists and data items all in the same file – the log. The **shadow versions** technique is an alternative way to organize a recovery file. It uses a *map* to locate versions of the server's data items in a file called a *version store*. The map associates the identifiers of the server's data items with the positions of their current versions in the version store. The versions written by each transaction are shadows of the previous committed versions. The transaction status entries and intentions lists are dealt with separately. Shadow versions are described first.

When a transaction is prepared to commit, any of the data items changed by the transaction are appended to the version store, leaving the corresponding committed versions unchanged. These new as yet tentative versions are called *shadow* versions. When a transaction commits, a new map is made by copying the old map and entering the positions of the shadow versions. To complete the commitment, the new map replaces the old map.

To restore the data items when a server restarts, its recovery manager reads the map and uses the information in the map to locate the data items in the version store.

This technique is illustrated with the same example involving transactions T and U. The first column in the table shows the map before transactions T and U when the balances of the accounts A, B and C are $100, $200 and $300. The second column shows the map after transaction T has committed:

Map at start	Map when T commits
A → P0	A → P3
B → P1	B → P4
C → P2	C → P2

	P0	P1	P2	P3	P4		
Version store	100	200	300 ‖	96	204	297	207

Checkpoint

The version store contains a checkpoint, followed by the versions of A and B at P3 and P4 made by transaction T. It also contains the shadow versions of B and C made by transaction U.

The map must always be written to a well known place (for example at the start of the version store or a separate file) so that it can be found when the system needs to be recovered.

The switch from the old map to the new map must be performed in a single atomic step. To achieve this it is essential that stable storage is used for the map – so that there is guaranteed to be a valid map even when a file write operation fails. The shadow versions method provides faster recovery than logging because the positions of the current committed data items are recorded in the map, whereas recovery from a log requires searching throughout the log for data items. Logging should be faster than shadow versions during the normal activity of the system. This is because logging requires only a sequence of append operations to the same file, whereas shadow versions requires an additional stable storage write (involving two unrelated disk blocks).

Shadow versions on their own are not sufficient for a server that handles distributed transactions. Transaction status entries and intentions lists are saved in a file called the transaction status file. Each intentions list represents the part of the map that will be altered by a transaction when it commits. The transaction status file may for example, be organized as a log.

The figure below shows the map and the transaction status file for our current example when T has committed and U is prepared to commit.

Map	Stable storage	T	T	U
A → P3		prepared	committed	prepared
B → P4		A → P3		B → P6
C → P2	Transaction status file	B → P4		C → P5

There is a chance that a server may crash between the time when a committed status is written to the transaction status file and the time when the map is updated – in which case the client will not have been acknowledged. The recovery manager must allow for this possibility when the server restarts, for example, by checking whether the map includes the effects of the last committed transaction in the transaction status file. If it does not then the latter should be marked as aborted.

The need for transaction status and intentions list entries in a recovery file

It is possible to design a simple recovery file that does not include entries for transaction status items and intentions lists. This sort of recovery file may be suitable when all transactions are directed to a single server. The use of transaction status items and intentions lists in the recovery file is essential for a server that is intended to participate in distributed transactions. This approach can also be useful for servers of non-distributed transactions for various reasons, including the following:

- Some recovery managers are designed to write the data items to the recovery file early – under the assumption that transactions normally commit.

- If transactions use a large number of big data items, the need to write them contiguously to the recovery file may complicate the design of a server.

- In timestamp ordering concurrency control, a server sometimes knows that a transaction will eventually be able to commit and acknowledges the client – at this time the data items are written to the recovery file (see Chapter 13) to ensure their permanence. However, the transaction may have to wait to commit until earlier transactions have committed. In such situations, the corresponding transaction status entries in the recovery file will be *waiting to commit* and then committed to ensure timestamp ordering of committed transactions in the recovery file. On recovery any waiting to commit transactions can be allowed to commit because the ones they were waiting for have either just committed or if not have to be aborted due to failure of the server.

Recovery of the two-phase commit protocol

In a distributed transaction, each server keeps its own recovery file. The recovery management described in the previous section must be extended to deal with any transactions that are performing the two-phase commit protocol at the time when a server fails. The recovery managers use two new status values *done, uncertain*. These status values are shown in Figure 14.6. A coordinator uses committed to indicate that the outcome of the vote is *Yes* and *done* to indicate that the two-phase commit protocol is complete. A worker uses *uncertain* to indicate that it has voted *Yes*, but does not yet know the outcome. Two additional types of entry allow a coordinator to record a list of workers and a worker to record its coordinator:

Type of entry	Description of contents of entry
Coordinator	Transaction identifier, list of workers
Worker	Transaction identifier, coordinator

In Phase 1 of the protocol, when the coordinator is prepared to commit (and has already added a prepared status entry to its recovery file), its recovery manager adds a *coordinator* entry to its recovery file. Before a worker can vote *Yes*, it must have already prepared to commit (and must have already added a prepared status entry to its recovery file). When it votes *Yes*, its recovery manager records a *worker* entry and adds an *uncertain* transaction status to its recovery file. When a worker votes *No* it adds an *abort* transaction status to its recovery file.

In Phase 2 of the protocol, the recovery manager of the coordinator adds either a *committed* or an *aborted* transaction status to its recovery file according to the decision. Recovery managers of workers add a *commit* or *abort* transaction status to their recovery files according to the message received from the coordinator. When a coordinator has received a confirmation from all of its workers its recovery manager adds a *done* transaction status to its recovery file. The *done* status entry is not part of the protocol, but is used when the recovery file is reorganized. Figure 15.2 shows the entries in a log for transaction T in which the server played the coordinator role and for transaction U in which the server played the worker role. For both transactions, the *prepared* transaction status entry comes first. In the case of a coordinator it is followed by a coordinator entry, and a *committed* transaction status entry. The *done* transaction status entry is not shown in Figure 15.2. In the case of a worker the prepared transaction status

Figure 15.2 Log with entries relating to two-phase commit protocol.

Trans:T	Coord'r: T	•	•	Trans:T	Trans:U	•	•	Worker:U	Trans:U	Trans:U
prepared	worker list: . . .			*committed*	*prepared*			Coord'r:...	*uncertain*	*committed*
Intentions list					Intentions list					

entry is followed by a worker entry whose state is uncertain and then a *committed* or *aborted* transaction status entry.

When a server is restarted, the recovery manager has to deal with the two-phase commit protocol in addition to restoring the data items. For any transaction that has played the coordinator role it should find a coordinator entry and a set of transaction status entries. For any transaction that has played the worker role it should find a worker entry and a set of transaction status entries. In both cases the most recent transaction status entry – that is, the one nearest the end of the log – determines the transaction status at the time of failure.

The action of the recovery manager with respect to the two-phase commit protocol depends on whether the server was the coordinator or a worker and on its status at the time of failure as shown in Figure 15.3.

Figure 15.3 Recovery of the two-phase commit protocol.

Role	*Status*	*Action of recovery manager*
Coordinator	*prepared*	No decision had been reached before the server failed. It sends *AbortTransaction* to all the servers in the worker list and adds the transaction status *aborted* in its recovery file. Same action for state *aborted*. If there is no worker list the workers will eventually time-out and abort the transaction.
Coordinator	*committed*	A decision to commit had been reached before the server failed. In case it had not done so before, it sends a *DoCommit* to all of the workers in its worker list and resumes the two-phase protocol at Step 4 (see Figure 14.5).
Worker	*committed*	The worker sends a *HaveCommitted* message to the coordinator in case this was not done before the worker failed. This will allow the coordinator to discard information about this transaction at the next checkpoint.
Worker	*uncertain*	The worker failed before it knew the outcome of the transaction. It cannot determine the status of the transaction until the coordinator informs it of the decision. It will send a *GetDecision* to the coordinator to determine the status of the transaction. When it receives the reply it will commit or abort accordingly.
Worker	*prepared*	The worker has not yet voted and can abort the transaction.
Coordinator	*done*	No action is required.

Reorganization of recovery file □ Care must be taken when performing a checkpoint to ensure that *coordinator* entries of transactions without status *done* are not removed from the recovery file. These entries must be retained until all the workers have confirmed that they have completed their transactions. Entries with status *done* may be discarded. Worker entries with transaction state *uncertain* must also be retained.

Recovery of nested transactions □ The recovery system for nested transactions is designed under the assumption that each subtransaction may run in a separate server.

It was noted in Chapter 13 that several transactions at different levels in the hierarchy can access the same data item. Therefore each subtransaction has its own tentative version of each data item it accesses. All tentative versions are held by the server of the data item.

For example, in Figure 15.4, the transactions T_1, T_{11}, T_{12} and T_2 could all be accessing the same data item, A. However, they access the data item in turn, for example, T and then T_1 and then T_1 and then T_1 and then T, because parent and child transactions cannot run in parallel. To support this, the server of a data item shared by

Figure 15.4   Nested transactions

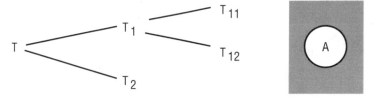

transactions at multiple levels must provide a stack of separate versions – one for each nested transaction to use. Suppose that these versions are called A1, A11, A12 and A2. A1 is based on the committed version of A and A11 is based on A1 and so forth. Each subtransaction bases its tentative version on the tentative version of its parent. When a subtransaction commits, the parent inherits its provisionally committed tentative version. When a subtransaction aborts, its tentative version is discarded. Eventually when the transaction at the top of the hierarchy commits, its version becomes the new committed version. See Moss [1985] and Weikum [1991] for a detailed description of nested transactions.

Provisionally committed tentative versions are written to a server's recovery file on behalf of subtransactions before the top-level transaction commits or aborts. As far as a top-level transaction is concerned, these are early writes of subtransactions that are prepared to commit. A two-phase commit protocol with the top-level transaction as coordinator determines the eventual status of these versions in the recovery file.

Fault model for transactions

Work on transactions originates from the field of databases. An early challenge was to devise an atomic commitment protocol that could tolerate the loss of messages, the failure of servers and even the failure of storage. Atomic transaction commit protocols were devised in the early 1970s and the two-phase commit protocol appeared in Gray [1978]. All the atomic commitment protocols assume that servers stop doing anything when they fail and at all other times they obey the messages they are sent. The completion of an atomic commit protocol (for example, the two-phase commit) can take unbounded time because messages may be lost and servers may fail and restart. On the other hand when the servers are functioning normally and messages are not lost, N servers can perform it with $3N$ messages. In addition it can tolerate the failure of any number of the servers.

Lampson [1981(a)] proposes a fault model for distributed transactions that accounts for failures of disks, servers and communication. In this model, the claim is that the algorithms work correctly in the presence of predictable faults, but no claims are made about their behaviour when a disaster occurs. Although errors may occur, they can be detected and dealt with before any incorrect behaviour occurs. The model states the following:

- Writes to permanent storage may fail – either by writing nothing or by writing a wrong value – for example, writing to the wrong block is a disaster. File storage may also decay. Reads from permanent storage can detect (by a checksum) when a block of data is bad.

- Servers may crash occasionally. When they restart, their volatile memory is reset to a state in which they have forgotten all the values (for example, of data items) from before the crash. When a processor is faulty, it is made to crash so that it is prevented from sending erroneous messages and from writing wrong values to permanent storage. When a processor recovers from a crash it uses information in permanent storage and obtained from other processes to restore the values of data items. Crashes can occur at any time – in particular they may occur during recovery.

- There may be an arbitrary delay before a messages arrives. A message may be lost, duplicated or corrupted. The recipient can detect corrupted messages (by a checksum). Both forged messages and undetected corrupt messages are regarded as disasters.

The fault model for permanent storage, processors and communications was used to design a stable system whose components can survive any single fault and present a simple fault model. In particular, stable storage provides an atomic *Write* operation in the presence of a single fault of the *Write* operation or a failure of the process (see Section 15.4). A *stable processor* uses stable storage to enable it to recover its data items after a crash. Communication errors are masked by using a reliable remote procedure calling mechanism.

In the early 1980s a need for a different fault model arose from process control applications and attempts were made to design systems that would perform correctly even when some of their components are running on faulty hardware. The fault model for transactions has some characteristics that are not acceptable in such applications. These are the following:

- An atomic commit protocol cannot be carried out within a guaranteed time limit, because the number of messages required may be arbitrarily large.

- The recovery of distributed transactions can take more time than is acceptable.

- Atomic commit protocols assume that servers always either behave correctly or crash detectably.

- Atomic commit protocols assume that corrupted messages and faulty data on permanent storage can be detected.

The next section discusses the characteristics of faults and some approaches to fault tolerance that can be applied in other applications.

15.3 Fault tolerance

Each component in a computer system is generally constructed from a collection of other software and hardware components, some of which may fail from time to time. For example, faulty hardware can execute even correct programs in an unpredictable manner. The fact that a distributed system consists of a collection of processes that run concurrently on various computers and communicate via a communication subsystem whose performance is relatively slow and unreliable in comparison to the computers, leads to two important and contrasting points about the construction of correct services in the presence of other faulty components.

1. The operation of a service in a distributed system generally depends on the operation of other services that run on different computers. The latter services sometimes fail to respond, either because a computer has failed or because communication is not entirely reliable. In addition it is hard for a service to detect whether another computer has really failed or is too overloaded for services running on it to respond in a timely manner.

2. A set of servers running in different computers can be combined in such a way that their joint execution is less likely to fail than any one of the individual components. For example, a service may be represented by a set of servers holding replicas of the service's data, to enable the service to continue in the presence of some maximum number of faulty servers.

Point 1 shows that the designers of distributed system services must take into account the fact that the other services they use may fail in a variety of independent ways. Point 2 shows that the designer of a service in a distributed system can take advantage of the availability of multiple computers to mask potential failures in the service being designed.

In both cases, a designer needs to be aware of a range of possible failures that may be exhibited by a service. This implies that the designers of a service must specify not only its correct behaviour but also the different ways in which it may fail. A description of the ways in which a service may fail is called its **failure semantics**. A knowledge of the failure semantics of a service can enable a new service to be designed to mask the faulty behaviour of a service on which it depends. For example, the TCP protocol is constructed to provide a reliable stream communication service from the potentially unreliable datagram service provided by IP.

Chapter 2 states that a fault-tolerant system can detect a fault and either fail predictably or mask the fault from its users. A **fault-tolerant service** operates according to its specification in the presence of faults in other services on which it depends. Note that this definition of fault tolerance still allows a fault-tolerant service to exhibit any faulty behaviour permitted by its failure semantics.

A server **masks** a failure in a service on which it depends, either by hiding it altogether or by converting it to one of the faults it is allowed to exhibit. In the latter case, it generally converts a failure type of a lower level service to a failure type at a higher level.

Characteristics of faults

In order to specify the failure semantics of a service, it is necessary to have a means of describing faults. Cristian [1991] provides a useful classification of failures. A request to a server can change the state of its resources and may produce a result for the client. Cristian's classification assumes that for a service to perform correctly, both the effect on a server's resources and the response to the client must be correct. Part of the classification is given in the following table:

Class of failure	Subclass	Description
Omission failure		A server omits to respond to a request
Response failure		Server responds incorrectly to a request
	Value failure	Returns wrong value
	State transition failure	Has wrong effect on resources (for example, sets wrong values in data items)

Consider the following examples:

- The UDP service has omission failures because it occasionally loses messages, but it does not have value failures because it does not transmit corrupt messages. Thus UDP uses checksums to mask the value failures of the underlying IP by converting them to omission failures.

- RPC call semantics are described in Chapter 5. At-least-once provides a service that masks omission failures of the underlying message passing service by retransmitting request messages. But it sometimes executes a remote procedure more than once. If the service operations are not idempotent, response failures can occur. Thus, at-least-once masks omission failures but may convert them into response failures. At-most-once provides a service without response failures – an example of hiding the omission failures altogether. The latter has more expensive storage requirements. Both at-least-once and at-most-once mask a server crash failure by reporting an exception to the client.

Note that as UDP uses checksums to detect the value failures of IP, there is a very small probability that a value failure may be undetected. Similarly, the RPC protocols use message retransmissions to ensure that request messages are delivered, but there is a very small probability that a request message will not arrive.

A statement about the failure semantics of a server cannot generally be an absolute statement, but instead is a statement of an acceptably low likelihood of a particular type of failure. For example, we might say that UDP has a probability of value failure that is sufficiently low to be discounted.

Timing failures ☐ Cristian's classification also deals with timing failures. These refer to any response that is not available to a client within a specified real-time interval. A timing failure can describe a response that is either too late (that is, performance failures) or too early. For example, an overloaded server may provide responses that arrive too late. Real-time operating systems are designed with a view to avoiding timing failures, but they are more complex to design and may require more hardware resources than an operating system such as UNIX that does not have to meet real-time constraints.

The introduction to this chapter mentions that process control applications require responses from services within a specified time. Services that are used in applications that require timely responses must be able to recover within the time specified. In addition they must not depend on protocols like the atomic commitment protocol that can, in the worse case, require an unbounded time to complete.

Timing is relevant to multimedia workstations with audio and video channels. For example when a server supplies digital audio data containing spoken information, the speech will quickly become incomprehensible if data is not delivered sufficiently rapidly to maintain the speech in real-time. Video information, for example containing images, can require a very high bandwidth. To deliver such information without timing failures can make special demands on both the operating system and the communication system.

Server crash failure ☐ Cristian defines a server crash failure as a repeated omission failure. Most server failures cause a server to stop sending messages, so that it will appear to its clients to have stopped. We have noted elsewhere (for example, in Chapter 4) that clients cannot distinguish for certain between a server failure, a server that is responding very slowly and a breakdown of communication with the server. Timeouts combined with retransmission of request messages are generally used to detect server failures – when a process does not reply after a number of attempts to communicate with it, it is assumed to have failed. This method of detecting a server failure is based on an assumption as to the maximum likely response time of the server and the likelihood of several lost messages. There is therefore a small probability of error.

An important aspect of a server failure is its state after it has been restarted. For example, a transactional service restarts with the effects of all committed transactions reflected in its data items. Cristian gives the following classification of server failures:

Class of failure	Subclass	description
Crash failure		Repeated omission failure: a server repeatedly fails to respond to requests until it is restarted
	Amnesia-crash	A server starts in its initial state, having forgotten its state at the time of the crash
	Pause-crash	A server restarts in the state before the crash
	Halting-crash	Server never restarts

An amnesia crash is actually worse than a repeated omission failure because the server loses its state (for example, the values of its data items). Recovery can be used to ensure that when a server crashes it does not produce amnesia-crash behaviour. The avoidance of amnesia-crash behaviour by the use of recovery adds to the expense of providing a service. Fortunately, amnesia-crash behaviour is adequate for many services. In particular stateless servers can be allowed to exhibit such behaviour.

The provision of a fault-tolerant service can be simplified if it can be assumed that the servers on which it depends crash cleanly. That is, that a server either functions correctly, or else it crashes. A **fail-stop** server is one that, when it is about to fail, changes to a state that permits other servers to detect that a failure has occurred and then stops. The clients of a fail-stop server can assume it will not produce value, omission or timing failures. A failure to respond can only precede a crash. Thus they can detect any crash failure because the server repeatedly fails to respond to requests.

Byzantine failure □ Cristian uses the term *arbitrary* failure semantics to describe a service that exhibits all the above failure semantics – that is: crash, timing, response and omission failures. The term *Byzantine failure behaviour* is commonly used to describe the worst possible failure semantics of a server. Lamport *et al.* [1982] formulated the Byzantine Generals Problem for use in life-critical systems. It models a situation in which most computers work correctly but some faulty computers work as maliciously as possible. Faulty computers can for example, send contradictory messages to different recipients or impersonate one another. The point of considering the worst possible case is so that a system can be made ultra-reliable by allowing for the worst imaginable eventuality that could possibly happen. Byzantine Agreement is intended for use in contexts requiring guaranteed response times and the ability to function correctly in the presence of some faulty hardware (for example, flying an aircraft, monitoring a patient in a hospital, controlling a robot and displaying an image in real-time).

The Byzantine Generals Problem describes a situation in which N divisions of the Byzantine army are camped outside an enemy city. Each division is commanded by a general (that is, a server). The generals communicate with one another only by messenger. Each general has to vote *yes* or *no* to a plan of action. However, some of the generals may be bad and will try to prevent the good generals from reaching agreement. An algorithm solves the Byzantine Generals Problem if it gets all the good generals to agree *yes* or *no* within a bounded time.

It is assumed that the good generals will tend to vote the same way as one another. If they are almost equally divided between *yes* and *no* then the outcome does not matter. This is a realistic assumption for a group of servers performing the same service as one another, because the good servers should produce identical outputs.

Byzantine agreement algorithms send more messages and use more active servers than an atomic commit protocol. Their task is for each server to send the same messages to all of the servers, so that the good servers will all produce the same response within a bounded time. This is equivalent to an atomic multicast (see Chapter 4) that functions correctly even when some of the bad servers exhibit timing faults that cause them to delay their response indefinitely. Each server uses the same method for combining the votes of the other servers, some of which may produce value or omission faults. For example, in Figure 15.5 (a), there are three servers A, B and C (two good servers and one bad server), the good servers vote *yes* and the bad server sends *yes* to one of the good

Figure 15.5   Byzantine Generals.

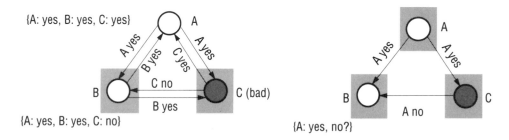

(a) Message originators can be
authenticated by receivers

(b) Message originators cannot be
authenticated by receivers

servers and *no* to the other. One of the good servers (A) will receive {*yes, yes, yes*} and other (B) will receive {*yes, yes, no*}, but in both cases the majority vote is *yes* and the outcome for the good servers is *yes*. This shows that two good servers can compensate for one bad server. If it is assumed (as in this example) that recipients can be sure that messages are not corrupted and that the identity of the sender can be authenticated, then in general $2N + 1$ servers can tolerate N bad servers. This is because the good servers have the majority of the votes. Lamport *et al.* call such messages 'signed messages' because a written message with a signature is regarded as an authentic message from the sender by any recipient that can recognise the signature.

Unfortunately it is possible that a bad Byzantine General may impersonate a good one and thereby add confusion to the outcome for the good generals. Figure 15.5(b) illustrates the situation with unsigned messages in which the good server A votes *yes*, but the bad server C says that A has voted *no*. It is impossible for B to decide what A has voted as it has received two contradictory votes for A. If it is not possible to authenticate the sender of a message, then three good servers are required to compensate for one bad server. The paper by Lamport *et al.* shows that if at least one third of the generals are bad, then the good generals cannot agree reliably, but if less than one third of the generals are bad, then there are solutions which require $O(N^2)$ messages and have constant delay time.

The true Byzantine model requires three good servers to compensate for one bad one. It is more practical to assume that messages are not corrupted and that senders can be authenticated (for example digital signatures described in Chapter 16 can be used to authenticate senders with a very low likelihood of error). The latter model is sometimes called the Authenticated Byzantine Generals model. Its failure semantics include response (value and state transition), omission and timing failures.

For most applications it is sufficient to assume that there is a very high likelihood that a faulty server will crash cleanly rather than exhibit arbitrary behaviour – that is servers are fail-stop. When clients assume fail-stop behaviour in a server, it is regarded as a very unlikely disaster for the server to produce any other types of failure. Clients are not prepared for such disasters, and when they happen, the clients will fail as well.

The fail-stop server assumption is a reasonable one for applications where it is acceptable to have occasional complete failures followed by reasonably fast recovery. The next section shows that this is an attractive choice because the assumption not only simplifies the design of services, but also economizes in the use of hardware.

15.4 Hierarchical and group masking of faults

Cristian describes two approaches to masking faults: *hierarchical failure masking* and *group failure masking*.

Hierarchical masking

Hierarchical failure masking refers to a situation in which a server depends on lower-level services. The server at the higher level attempts to mask the faults at the lower level. In some cases, the faults are entirely hidden, for example a request-reply protocol generally masks omission failures in the message passing service by retransmitting request messages. When a lower-level failure cannot be masked, it is converted to a higher level exception. For example, a request-reply protocol generally masks a server's crash failure by reporting an exception to its client. In general, at each level, failures are either hidden entirely or passed on as exceptions to the level above, where additional masking may take place. Eventually at the level of the user interface, as many faults as possible have been masked, but when this cannot be done, they are reported to the user. Any exceptional conditions should be described to users in terms related to their current task – and not in terms describing the actions of a lower-level server.

Group failure masking

A service can be made fault tolerant by implementing it as a group of servers each of which runs on a different computer. The intention is that if some of the servers fail, the remaining servers can continue to provide the service. Group masking hides the failure of individual members by a group management mechanism. The group output is determined from the outputs of individual members, for example, if the servers do not exhibit value failures, then any one output may be picked. In particular if some of the members exhibit performance failures, the delay to the client can be reduced by choosing the output of the fastest member. On the other hand if the servers do sometimes produce value failures, a majority vote must be used to determine the correct output. For example, a group of two servers is not sufficient to survive a single value failure, because if one server produces the correct value and the other server the wrong value, it is not possible to tell which is the correct value. A group of three servers would be sufficient because two of the servers (a majority) produce the correct value.

A group is *t-fault tolerant* if it performs correctly so long as no more than t of its members fail at the same time as one another. If each member of the group has fail-stop and performance failure semantics, then a group of $t + 1$ servers can mask up to t member failures. However, if each member can have arbitrary failures (or Byzantine failures with authentication of the message sender), a group of $2t + 1$ members is required to mask *t* member failures. In the latter case, a majority vote on the output requires that $t+1$ of the outputs should be the same as one another.

To ensure that each member of a group of servers can provide an equivalent service, each member starts in the same initial state and executes the same requests in the same order, although this can sometimes be relaxed as discussed below. Therefore all the members perform the same operations on their data items and produce identical outputs. There are some requirements on the server's program if this is to work correctly. First, the program must be deterministic – that is the effects of each of its operations are determined entirely by its arguments and the values of the data items. An operation is not deterministic if it uses an external value such as the time of day, a random number, an item in a file or a value obtained from the operating system such as a process identifier. Secondly each operation must be atomic with respect with all the other operations.

A group of servers can be closely synchronized or loosely synchronized. In a **closely synchronized group** of servers, all the members execute all of the requests immediately after receiving them. This approach was suggested by Cooper [1985] in the Circus system in which each server executes a deterministic program and is assumed to be fail-stop. A client request is sent to all the servers in a group by means of a replicated procedure call in such a way that each member executes each procedure at most once. All members execute the procedures in the same order. A service survives so long as one member of the group continues to execute.

Schneider [1990] describes the state machine approach for implementing fault-tolerant services (see Chapter 11). A state machine is an idealised form of server program whose operations are defined to be both deterministic and atomic. A state machine executes its requests according to causal ordering: first, a state machine executes requests from a particular client in the order that the client issued them; secondly if a request made by one client to a state machine causes another client to make another request to the same state machine, then the former is executed before the latter – that is, the causing request is executed before the potentially caused request. A fault-tolerant state machine can be implemented as a closely synchronized group of servers, each of which runs a state machine program on a different computer.

Schneider mentions that the requirement that all of the members of a group of state machines execute the same requests as one another and in the same order as one another can sometimes be relaxed. In particular, read only requests need not be executed by all the members. The number of replies needed by the client depends on the failure semantics of the servers. If the servers are assumed to be fail stop, a single reply will do. If they are assumed to exhibit arbitrary failures, the client needs to collect identical replies from more than half of the members. The requirement that all the members should execute all the requests in the same order as one another can be relaxed if the operations of the servers are commutative.

Schneider discusses approaches for ensuring that all of the members of a group of state machines execute the same requests as one another and in the same order. An atomic multicast can ensure that all the members receive the same requests. A totally-ordered atomic multicast can ensure that they receive them in the same order. To satisfy the state machine's requirement for causality, the multicast must also be causally ordered. If the servers are assumed to exhibit Byzantine failures then the multicast protocol must be designed to function correctly in such an environment.

Closely synchronized groups of servers can be useful in an environment in which a real-time response is required or where it is necessary to assume that servers may display Byzantine failures. In an environment in which it is safe to assume that failures are infrequent and that when they do occur, they exhibit fail-stop behaviour, a loosely synchronized group is an attractive alternative.

In a **loosely synchronized group,** one server (called the primary) is used so long as it performs correctly and other servers (called the backup or stand-by servers) are available to take over when it fails. The primary server deals with all the client requests by executing them and returning replies. One or more backup servers log the requests. If the primary fails, one of the backup servers executes the requests in its log and then takes over. The primary can prevent the backup servers from getting too far behind by occasionally sending them a checkpoint of its state. When a backup receives a checkpoint, it can remove the outstanding requests in its log.

The advantage of a loosely synchronized group is that only the primary server executes all the client requests, whereas all servers in a closely synchronized group do so. Therefore a loosely synchronized group uses less of the available computing resources. On the other hand, recovery takes longer for a loosely synchronized group and would not be acceptable for applications requiring a guaranteed response time.

The primary server/stand-by server arrangement can mask crash failures, but cannot be used for Byzantine failures. This is because the output of the group is the same as the output of the primary server and there is no way to detect when the primary starts producing arbitrary failures – for example, wrong values.

Group masking of faults can be done at the hardware level as well as in software. The hardware is designed to allow components to be added, removed and replaced when they fail, without causing the system to stop. The Tandem system is an example: each component is implemented as a primary/backup pair executing on different processors. Before each request is executed, the primary sends information about its state to the backup in the form of a checkpoint. The checkpoint enables the backup to complete the request if the primary fails. Thus the Tandem system can tolerate the failure of a single hardware unit. For a survey of group masking by means of hardware, see Cristian [1991].

Disks can be made fault-tolerant by replicating them. A recent hardware approach to disk replication is called RAID (redundant arrays of inexpensive disks) [Vaughan-Nichols 1991]. In its simplest form, RAID provides faster disk access. More sophisticated versions of RAID provide fault tolerance by replicating data on pairs of disks.

Stable storage

Stable storage is an example of group masking at the disk block level. It is a generic approach designed by Lampson [1981b] to ensure that any essential permanent data will be recoverable after any single system failure, including system failures during a disk write operation and damage to any single disk block.

The stable storage service uses group masking by duplicating a *careful* storage service. A careful storage service is defined to have only omission failure semantics – that is, the *Read* operation uses a checksum stored with each block to mask value failures by converting them to omission failures. The unit of storage used by stable storage is called a *stable block*. Each stable block is represented by two careful disk blocks that hold the contents of the stable block in duplicate. If possible, the pair of blocks are located in different disk drives to reduce the chances that both will be damaged in a single mechanical failure.

The *Read* operation of the stable storage service reads one of the pair of representative careful blocks. If an omission failure occurs, then it reads the other representative. This enables the stable storage *Read* operation to mask the omission failures of the careful storage service.

A stable storage service guarantees that the following *invariant* is maintained for each pair of blocks:

- Not more than one of the pair is bad.

- If both are good, they both have the most recent data, except during the execution of a *Write* operation.

The stable storage service *Write* operation maintains this invariant by writing the data in each of the two representative careful blocks sequentially, ensuring that the first write is successful before commencing the second.

When a stable storage server is restarted after a crash, a recovery procedure is invoked. At this point, the pair of blocks representing each stable block will be in one of the following states:

1. both good and the same;

2. both good and different;

3. one good, one bad.

The recovery procedure is designed to maintain the above invariant. It inspects the pairs of blocks and does the following in each the above cases:

1. nothing;

2. copies one block of the pair to the other block of the pair;

3. copies the good block to the bad block.

Stable storage operations are more costly in disk space and in time than conventional disk service operations.

Primary and backup servers

This section describes the implementation of services that can survive the failure of any single server computer by means of the primary/backup server arrangement described above.

Some systems (for example, Stratus [Cristian 1991]) are designed to provide fault tolerance by means of duplicated hardware. A service is represented by a pair of servers, each of which has crash failure semantics. Both servers execute all the client requests and the reply of either server may be used. If one of the server computers crashes, the other continues to provide the service. The duplication of hardware enables recovery from a crash to be immediate. If the system will be used for a critical real-time application (for example, controlling a reactor, monitoring a patient's heart beat,

Figure 15.6   Three-way message from A to B.

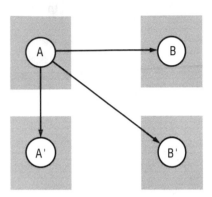

directing an ambulance to its destination) then it is essential that recovery can be done within a specified time limit.

Most applications can tolerate some delay during recovery. If this is the case then it is more appropriate to design the primary/backup pair so that the backup server is relatively inactive during the normal operation of the primary – which is generally most of the time. This enables the backup server computer to be used for other productive work.

Borg *et al.* [1989] describe Auragen, a fault tolerant version of a distributed UNIX based on primary/backup pairs. It is designed for a transaction-processing environment in which occasional delays for recovery are acceptable. Checkpointing is relatively infrequent so that backup servers use only a small fraction of the productive capacity of the computers on which they run. Checkpointing is achieved transparently, enabling any user program to become fault tolerant without recompilation.

In Auragen, each primary process has a backup running on a different computer. The backup process has sufficient information to start executing when its primary fails. When the primary fails, the backup first reads in the checkpoint and then executes the same messages that were executed by the primary and when it catches up it takes over as primary. The receipt of a message by a primary can result in its sending other messages elsewhere. During recovery its backup must avoid resending such messages. To make this possible, a count of the number of messages sent by its primary since the last checkpoint must be available.

A request message from one primary to another is always sent to three destinations: the sender's backup, the receiving primary and its backup. Figure 15.6 shows a message from a primary A to another primary B, which is also transmitted to A's backup A' and B's backup B'.

Each request is a three-way totally ordered atomic multicast. This ensures that primary and backup receive all the same messages in the same order as one another. It also enables the sender's backup to count the number of messages it has sent. Each server performs an appropriate action on receipt of a message. This action is determined by its role as follows:

Role	Action
Primary	Execute the operation requested and return a reply
Backup	Save the message in a log for subsequent use in recovery
Sender's backup	Count the number of messages since the last checkpoint by the sender

A primary server and its backup are synchronized from time to time to prevent the backup from getting too far behind the primary server. Synchronization consists of the following:

- the primary performs a checkpoint by saving the state of its data items for use by its backup;

- the primary informs its backup that it has done the checkpoint, whereupon the backup deletes the messages in its log (because it is now synchronized with the primary) and sets the count of messages sent by the primary since the last checkpoint to zero.

Synchronization is done automatically at specified time intervals and whenever the backup's message log exceeds some maximum length.

When a primary server fails, its backup will initialize the state of its data items from the most recent checkpoint and then execute the outstanding request messages in its log. As the backup server executes each request it will avoid resending messages already sent by the primary by using the count of the number of messages since the last checkpoint.

After this, the backup clears the log of request messages, sets the count of messages since the last checkpoint to zero and takes over as primary.

The system described by Borg *et al.* [1989] is designed to perform checkpoints transparently to user programs. It uses an external pager (see Chapter 6) to enable primary and backup to share checkpoints. An external pager stores and retrieves pages for primary server processes and also holds pages of checkpoints for backup processes. At each checkpoint, any dirty pages are sent to the external pager. During recovery, a backup server demand-pages the address space of the primary at the last synchronization. In this way, transparent checkpointing is achieved.

The paper by Borg *et al.* describes the system running on the special Targon/32 hardware, which provides the atomic three-way multicast in the lowest level of the communication software and in the bus hardware. Babaoglu [1990] proposes that a similar system could be run in an environment running Mach on loosely coupled multiprocessors. User level tasks can be made fault tolerant by backing them up on different computers. The atomic three-way multicast could be implemented in the network servers. Mach's external pagers can be used to enable primary servers to store checkpoints and backup servers to retrieve them.

15.5 Summary

Transaction-based applications have strong requirements for the long-life and integrity of the information stored by transactional services, but they do not usually have requirements for immediate response at all times. Atomic commit protocols are the key to distributed transactions, but they cannot be guaranteed to complete within a particular time limit. A transaction server does not generally have an active backup. It performs its checkpoints and logging in a recovery file which is used for recovery when a server is restarted after a failure. Users of a transaction service would experience some delay during recovery. It is assumed that the servers of distributed transactions are fail-stop and may exhibit performance failures.

Applications with real-time requirements have different requirements for fault tolerance. The existence of real-time requirements rules out both atomic commit protocols and the use of time-consuming recovery techniques. When it can be assumed that servers are fail-stop and may have performance failures, the primary-backup server pair is an attractive solution – the active backup can recover quite quickly when the primary fails, but it does not make heavy processing demands. When a continuous service is required, a closely synchronized group of server replicas may be used – in which a group of $N + 1$ server replicas can mask N servers with crash or performance failures.

A service may be described as fault tolerant if it is designed to function correctly in the presence of specified faults in the other services on which it depends. A service may be described as functioning correctly if it exhibits only the faults described in its failure semantics.

A study of applications that can run correctly even on faulty hardware lead to the Byzantine Generals Model which describes the worst possible behaviour that could be exhibited by a server. Under the sender-authenticated version of this model, a group of $2N + 1$ server replicas can mask N faulty servers.

EXERCISES

15.1 A server manages the data items a_1, a_2, ... a_n. The server provides two operations for its clients:

> *Read (i)* returns the value of a_i
>
> *Write(i, Value)* assigns *Value* to a_i

The transactions T, U and V are defined as follows:

> T: *x:= Read (i); Write(j, 44);*
>
> U: *Write(i, 55);Write(j, 66);*
>
> V: *Write(k, 77);Write(k, 88);*

Describe the information written to the log file on behalf of these three transactions if strict two-phase locking is in use and U acquires a_i and a_j before T. Describe how the recovery manager would use this information to recover the effects of T, U and V when the server restarts after a crash. What is the significance of the order of the commit entries in the log file?

pages 452-453

15.2 The appending of an entry to the log file is atomic, but append operations from different transactions may be interleaved. How does this affect the answer to Exercise 15.1?

pages 452-453

15.3 The transactions T, U and V of Exercise 15.1 use strict two-phase locking and their requests are interleaved as follows:

T	U	V
x := Read(i);		
		Write(k, 77);
	Write(i, 55)	
Write(j, 44)		
		Write(k,88)
	Write(j, 66)	

Assuming that the recovery manager appends the data entry corresponding to each *Write* operation to the log file immediately instead of waiting until the end of the transaction, describe the information written to the log file on behalf of the transactions T, U and V. Does early writing affect the correctness of the recovery procedure? What are the advantages and disadvantages of early writing?

pages 452-453

15.4   The transactions T and U are run with timestamp ordering concurrency control. Describe the information written to the log file on behalf of T and U, allowing for the fact that U has a later timestamp than T and must wait to commit after T. Why is it essential that the commit entries in the log file should be ordered by timestamps? Describe the effect of recovery if the server crashes (i) between the two *Commits* and (ii) after both of them.

T	U
x:= Read(i);	
	Write(i, 55);
	Write(j, 66);
Write(j, 44);	
	Commit
Commit	

What are the advantages and disadvantages of early writing with timestamp ordering?

page 456

15.5   The transactions T and U in Exercise 15.4 are run with optimistic concurrency control using backward validation and restarting any transactions that fail. Describe the information written to the log file on their behalf. Why is it essential that the commit entries in the log file should be ordered by transaction numbers? How are the write sets of committed transactions represented in the log file?

pages 452-453

15.6   Suppose that the coordinator of a transaction crashes after it has recorded the intentions list entry but before it has recorded the worker list or sent out the *CanCommit?* requests. Describe how the workers resolve the situation. What will the coordinator do when it recovers? Would it be any better to record the worker list before the intentions list entry?

page 457

15.7   Consider the distributed transaction T in Figure 14.3. Describe the information concerning transaction T that would be written to the log files at each of the servers if the two-phase commit protocol is completed and T is committed.

Suppose that the server BranchY crashes when it is 'uncertain': will this affect the progress of BranchX and BranchZ? Describe the recovery at BranchY relating to transaction T; what is the responsibility of BranchX with respect to the recovery at BranchY?

Suppose that BranchX crashes after sending out the vote requests, but BranchY and BranchZ are still active: describe the effect on the three logs and describe the recovery of BranchX.

pages 457-458

15.8   In the IP datagram service, packets may be lost, duplicated, delayed or
         delivered out of order and checksums apply only to headers. Describe the
         classes of failures exhibited by this service.

pages 461-462

15.9   In the UDP service, messages can be lost, duplicated, delayed or delivered
         out of order. They can also arrive too fast for the recipient to handle them.
         Describe the classes of failures exhibited by this service.

pages 461-462

15.10   Describe the classes of failure exhibited by a service that uses at-least-once
         RPC call semantics. Which of these failures can be reported to the client?
         How should they be described to the client? Compare this with a service
         using at-most-once call semantics.

pages 461-463

15.11   A request-reply protocol is implemented over a communication service with
         omission failures to provide at-least-once RPC call semantics. In the first
         case the implementor assumes that the service may exhibit performance
         failures. In the second case the implementor assumes that the maximum
         time for the communication and the execution of a server procedure is T. In
         what way does the latter assumption simplify the implementation?

pages 461-462

15.12   A group of N servers needs to reach a common decision. Describe the
         messages passed in a Byzantine agreement protocol. How many messages
         are required? How many replies must each server collect? Is there a limit to
         the time in which a non-faulty processor reaches a decision? Compare this
         with the two-phase commit protocol.

pages 461 and 464

15.13   Describe how the Isis client-server process group can be used to implement
         a t-fault tolerant group of servers, assuming that each member of the group
         has fail-stop and performance failure semantics. Under what circumstances
         would this be a useful service?

page 466 and Chapter 11

15.14   Stable storage assumes that disk reads in careful storage can exhibit
         omission failures. Suppose that disk reads are assumed to exhibit both
         omission and value failures – in other words, the value read can be different
         from the one written. How many blocks must be used to implement a stable
         block? Describe the implementation.

page 468

15.15   Suggest an implementation for a three-way totally ordered multicast for use
         in a primary backup system.

page 469

15.16   Contrast the primary copy or master slave configuration (for example, in
         Sun NIS) with the primary/backup configuration.

Chapter 11 and pages 469-472

16

SECURITY

This chapter describes the threats to security in distributed systems and discusses how they may be addressed. The following requirements are identified:

- Channels of communication should be secure against eavesdropping and tampering with message contents.

- Servers should be able to verify the identity of their clients.

- Clients should be able to verify the authenticity of servers.

- The identity of the originator of a message should be verifiable after the message has been forwarded to a third party – this is analogous to the use of signatures on conventional documents.

Methods available for achieving these goals are based on the use of cryptography to protect messages with a key distribution service to enable a pair of processes to establish a secure communication channel based on an encryption key, together with an authentication service to enable clients, servers and other communication partners to provide each other with convincing evidence of their identities. A digital 'signature' can be associated indelibly with a data item to identity the user or process that originated it.

Protocols to perform these services are defined and a formal method for validating their security is described.

The Kerberos key distribution and authentication service is introduced as a case study and its principles of operation and protocols are described in detail.

16.1 Introduction

Some threats to security in distributed systems are obvious – for example, in most types of local network it is easy to construct a program that obtains copies of the messages transmitted between other parties. Such a program could be executed on a computer that is already attached to the network or on one that is infiltrated into the network through a spare connection point. Other threats are more subtle – a program might install itself as a file server and thereby obtain copies of confidential information stored in the data that clients unwittingly send to it for storage.

To guard against such threats to the security of a distributed system, **security policies** must be adopted that are designed to ensure appropriate levels of security for the activities that are performed in the system and **security mechanisms** must be employed to implement the security policies. Just as the provision of a lock on a door does not ensure the security of a building unless there is a policy for its use, the security mechanisms that we shall describe do not in themselves ensure the security of a system unless policies exist for their use.

The distinction between security policies and mechanisms is useful when designing secure systems, but it is often difficult to be confident that a given set of security mechanisms fully implements the desired security policies. Note that the security policies are independent of the technology used. In the box below we outline a scenario for the preparation of examination papers in a university. This task requires a strong security policy and security mechanisms that are demonstrably sound.

If a distributed system is used to store and transmit the examination papers in our scenario, the testimony of the examiners is likely to be even less convincing. The examination papers are likely to have been stored on a file server, printed on a print server and transmitted through a network to the workstations of examiners. How can it be demonstrated that they have not been exposed to unauthorized access?

We must rely on software security mechanisms to obtain the authentic identities of any users or processes that request access to the examination papers and check them

Scenario: Consider the security requirements for the preparation of examination papers in a university. The security policies might be:

- Examination papers must be seen only by the members of the Board of Examiners.
- Each paper should be altered only by the examiner responsible for that paper.

If the papers are prepared manually, these security policies may be implemented using conventional methods based on mechanisms such as locked filing cabinets, private offices, handwritten amendments and signatures. The Chair of the Board of Examiners may be called upon to certify that the papers have been prepared according to the above policies. They might rely on a signed statement from each examiner to that effect. But even if each member of the Board testifies that the papers have only been worked on in their private office, and that they have always been kept in a locked cabinet when they are not in use, the Chair cannot be totally satisfied that the policies have not been violated, for example, by an unauthorized person using a high-powered telescope or a master key.

against lists of users permitted to access the papers. If the papers are transmitted through a network or left in unprotected storage we must ensure that they are encrypted.

How can the users of a distributed system be sure that the chosen security mechanisms will implement the security policy? A formal proof is required, demonstrating that the security mechanisms and their implementations correctly implement the policy. Proof techniques for computer security systems are the subject of much current research, and the current state of the art does not satisfy all needs. We shall introduce a method for proving the properties of some security mechanisms in Section 16.1. In the absence of a formal proof, we must fall back on informal argument, and this is known to be error-prone.

This chapter defines and classifies the main security threats to distributed systems and describes several software mechanisms and algorithms that can be used to provide protection against them. We do not define specific security policies, since they must be determined by the needs of the users and the owners of the system – the security needs of a bank or a government department are very different from those of a small work group.

The owners and users of security-sensitive computer systems need to be as confident as possible that the security mechanisms that they employ implement the required policies. In addition to the danger of loss or damage to information or resources through direct violations, fraudulent claims may be made against the owner of a system that is not demonstrably secure. To avoid such claims, the owner must be in a position to disprove the claim by showing that the system is proof against such violations or by producing a log of all of the transactions for the period in question. A common instance is the 'phantom withdrawal' problem in automatic cash dispensers (teller machines). The banks routinely claim that there is no possibility of withdrawals being made from customers' accounts by unauthorized third parties because the computer system that supports the machines is secure. They would be likely to find it easier to prove their claim if the security mechanisms on which they rely to protect their communication and computing systems were provably secure.

To demonstrate the validity of the security mechanisms employed in a system, the system's designers must first construct a list of threats – methods by which the security policies might be violated – and show that each of them is prevented by the mechanisms employed. This demonstration may take the form of informal argument, or better, it can take the form of a logical proof. Much attention has been devoted to the construction of formal proofs of the validity of security protocols, and we shall describe the use of one logical formalism that has been developed for this purpose.

No list of threats is likely to be exhaustive, so auditing methods must also be used in security-sensitive applications to detect violations. These are straightforward to implement based on a log of security-sensitive system actions with details of the users performing the actions and their authority.

We shall use the term **principal** to refer to the agents accessing the information or resources that are held in a distributed system. A principal is a person or a process (client, server, group member). In the security model that we shall develop each principal has a *name* which is analogous to the 'user name' found in centralized systems, and a *secret key*, which is analogous to a *password*. Principals are able to obtain access to resources. Their authority to do so rests on their names, and on the ability of each server that is trusted with private or secure resources to test the authenticity of a principal's stated name.

Threats ☐ The purpose of a security system is to restrict access to information and resources to just those principals which are authorized to have access. To produce a system that is demonstrably secure against specific threats it is necessary to classify the threats and the methods by which each of them may be achieved (the method of attack, or *modus operandi*, in criminology terms).

Security threats to computer systems fall into four broad classes:

Leakage: the acquisition of information by unauthorized recipients.

Tampering: the unauthorized alteration of information (including programs).

Resource stealing: the use of facilities without authorization.

Vandalism: interference with the proper operation of a system without gain to the perpetrator.

Methods of attack ☐ To violate a system in any of the above ways, access to the system is necessary. Virtually all computers include communication channels for authorized access to their facilities, and it is through these that unauthorized access must be gained. In distributed systems, computers are attached to a network and their operating systems offer a standard communication interface that enables virtual communication channels to be established.

The methods by which security violations can be perpetrated in distributed systems depend upon obtaining access to existing communication channels or establishing channels that masquerade as connections to a principal with some desired authority. They include:

Eavesdropping: obtaining copies of messages without authority. This may be done by obtaining messages directly from a network or by examining information that is inadequately protected in storage. For example, in the Internet a workstation can set its own network address to that of some other station on the network, enabling it to receive messages addressed to that station.

Masquerading: sending or receiving messages using the identity of another principal without their authority. This may be done by obtaining and using another principal's identity and password or by using an access token or a capability after the authorization to use it has expired.

Message tampering: intercepting messages and altering their contents before passing them on to the intended recipient. This is difficult to achieve in a broadcast medium such as an Ethernet, since the physical communication layer ensures delivery of messages to all stations, but it is relatively simple in store-and-forward networks.

Replaying: storing messages and sending them at a later date, for example, after authorization to use a resource has been revoked. Replaying cannot be defeated by simple encryption, since replaying can be used for resource stealing and vandalism even when the replayed messages cannot be interpreted by the perpetrator.

Infiltration □ To launch such attacks in a distributed system, the attacker must have access to the system in order to run the program that implements the attack. Most attacks are launched by one of the legitimate users of a system. They abuse their authority by running programs that are designed to carry out one of the above forms of attack. If access control lists are correctly set and mechanisms to authenticate principals are in place they will not get far, but it is difficult for system administrators to ensure that this is always the case.

For illegitimate users a simple method of infiltration is by guessing passwords or by the use of 'password cracking' programs to obtain the password of a known user. Such attacks can be prevented by the use of well-chosen passwords of adequate length.

In addition to these direct forms of infiltration, there are several more subtle methods that have become well-known through the publicity that has been given to some successful attacks in which they have featured. These include:

Virus: a program that is attached to a legitimate host program and installs itself in the target environment whenever the host program is run. Once installed it performs its criminal actions whenever it pleases, often using a date as its trigger. As the name implies, one of its acts is to replicate itself by attaching itself to all of the programs that it can find in the target environment. They travel between machines whenever a host program is moved, whether by network communication or by the transport of physical storage. There are many well-known examples in the personal computer environment.

Worm: a program that exploits facilities for running processes remotely in distributed systems. Such facilities may exist accidentally as well as intentionally: the Internet Worm [Spafford 1989] exploited a combination of intentional and accidental features to run programs remotely in BSD UNIX systems.

Trojan horse: a program that is offered to the users of a system as performing a useful function, but has a second ulterior function hidden in it. The most common example is the 'spoof login', a program that presents users with prompts that are indistinguishable from the regular login and password dialogue, but in fact stores the innocent user's input in a convenient file for later illicit use. Such a program is easily insinuated: it can be simply left running on an unattended workstation, where it will simulate the appearance of a machine with no-one logged in.

Their names have achieved some notoriety, but it should be noted that not all programs exhibiting these characteristics are necessarily malicious, and in fact the *worm* has been successfully exploited as a mechanism for the allocation of computing tasks to processors in distributed systems (see the subsection on the use of idle workstations in Section 2.2).

A conclusion from the above discussion of threats and methods of attack is that to produce a secure distributed system, we must design the system components (for example, clients and servers) with the assumption that other parties (people or programs) are untrustworthy until they are demonstrated to be trustworthy.

But there is a potential circularity in this argument. It is impossible to produce a useful system from a base in which no components are trusted. (There is nothing new in this observation; Seneca (4 BC – 65 AD) wrote in his Letters to Lucillius: 'It is a vice to trust all, and equally a vice to trust none'.) The aim therefore must be to produce a system in which a minimum of components are assumed to be trustworthy. Lampson *et al.* [1992] refer to this as the *trusted computing base*.

Given a minimal trusted base of secure computing and storage facilities, we can construct trusted servers. The security of trusted servers can be maintained by a combination of physical control (to prevent interference with the state of the servers, for example, by loading a different operating system) and secure communication channels protected by authentication and encryption.

We can now summarize the above discussion of threats to security in distributed systems:

- The principal threats to security in distributed systems derive from the openness of the communication channels (that is, the ports used for legitimate communication between processes such as clients and servers) and their consequent vulnerability to eavesdropping, masquerading, tampering and replaying. We must assume that every communication channel at all levels of the system's hardware and software is at risk to these threats.

- Potential violators (humans or programs) are not easily identifiable, so we must adopt a view of the world that does not assume trust. But we must start with some trustworthy components in order to build a useful system. An effective design approach is to assume that all communications come from untrustworthy sources until proven otherwise. The trustworthiness of communicating parties must be demonstrated whenever a communication channel is used.

- The mechanisms used for the implementation of security must be validated to a high standard – for example, secure communication protocols and the software that implements them should be demonstrably correct for all possible sequences of messages. The demonstrations should have the rigour of formal proofs.

Scenarios □ Figure 16.1 illustrates a number of scenarios for security violations in client-server interaction. At (a), a communication between a legitimate client and a legitimate server is vulnerable to eavesdropping, which can result in the leakage of private information, and to the copying of messages by eavesdroppers, for subsequent replay.

At (b), a legitimate server is vulnerable to client impostors, who may gain unauthorized access to the server's service functions, and hence alter the server's state or obtain free access to any private information held by the server. A legitimate server is also vulnerable to the replay of messages that were sent earlier by legitimate clients, used by an illegitimate replayer to alter the state of the server's data – for example, to restore the balance in a bank account to yesterday's value, even though withdrawals have been made today – or simply to overload the server, effectively removing its services from the system.

At (c), a legitimate client is vulnerable to server impostors. A server impostor can obtain access to private information in the client's request messages and can dupe the client into believing that requested transactions – for example to debit a charge to a bank account – have been performed when they have not.

Figure 16.1 Threats in client-server communication.

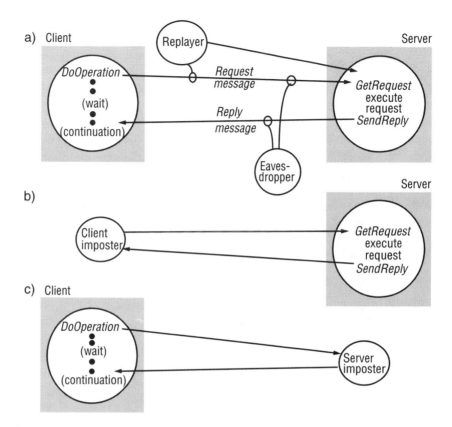

Security requirements for client-server systems □ To prevent security violations of the type discussed above, we must:

- Secure the channels of communication used, to avoid eavesdropping.

- Design clients and servers to view each other with *mutual suspicion*, and to perform appropriate message exchanges (authentication protocol) in order achieve the following states of 'knowledge':

  - servers must be satisfied that clients act on behalf of the principals that they claim to;

  - clients must be satisfied that the servers providing particular services are the authentic servers for those services.

- Ensure that communication is *fresh* in order to avoid security violations through the replay of messages.

Security mechanisms for distributed systems are based on the use of three techniques; cryptography, authentication and access control. The requirement for freshness of messages will be dealt with in our discussion of authentication protocols.

Cryptography ☐ The encryption of messages plays three major roles in the implementation of secure systems:

- It is used to conceal private information where it is exposed in parts of the system, such as physical communication channels, which are vulnerable to eavesdropping and message tampering. This use of cryptography corresponds to its traditional use in military and intelligence activities. It exploits the fact that a message that is encrypted with a particular encryption key can only be decrypted by a recipient that knows the corresponding inverse key.

- It is used in support of mechanisms for authenticating communication between pairs of principals. A principal who decrypts a message successfully using a particular inverse key can assume that the message is authentic if it contains some expected value. It is extremely unlikely to arise from decrypting the received message with any other key and the recipient can therefore infer that the sender of the message possessed the corresponding encryption key. Thus if keys are held in private (or in the case of public-key encryption schemes, if one of a pair of keys is held in private), a successful decryption authenticates the decrypted message as coming from a particular sender.

- It is used to implement a mechanism known as a *digital signature*. This emulates the role of conventional signatures, verifying to a third party that a message is an unaltered copy of one produced by a specified principal. The ability to provide digital signatures depends on there being something that the principal who is the original sender can do that others cannot. This can be achieved by requesting a trusted third party who has proof of the requester's identity, to encrypt the message – or more conveniently, to encrypt a shortened form of the message called a *digest*, analogous to a checksum. The resulting encrypted message or digest acts as a signature that accompanies the message. It can be verified by any recipient by asking the same trusted third party to encrypt the message again. If the results match, the signature is verified.

Authentication mechanisms ☐ In centralized multi-user systems, the authentication mechanisms can be relatively simple – the user's identity can be authenticated by a password check at the start of each interactive session, and the interactive session can then be treated as a domain in which all operations are performed with the authority of the user. This approach relies upon the central control of system resources by the operating system kernel, preventing all attempts to generate new interactive sessions that masquerade as other users. Such a degree of centralized control over the resources in a system is not achievable, or even desirable, in the more open architecture of general-purpose distributed systems.

In distributed systems, authentication is the means by which the identities of servers and clients are reliably established. The mechanism used to achieve this is based on the possession of encryption keys – from the fact that a principal possesses the appropriate secret encryption key, we infer that the principal has the identity that it claims, just as in the secret societies or espionage work, the possession of a secret password is taken to authenticate the possessor's identity.

Authentication mechanisms for distributed systems takes the form of an *authentication service*. Authentication services rely on the use of encryption to

Figure 16.2   Security policy implementation.

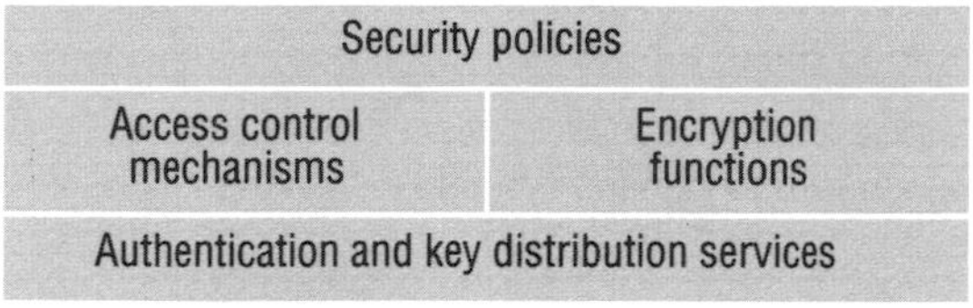

Security policies	
Access control mechanisms	Encryption functions
Authentication and key distribution services	

guarantee security. They require the provision of a secure means for generating, storing and distributing all of the encryption keys needed in a distributed system – known as a *key distribution service*.

In Sections 16.3 and 16.4 we describe the principles on which most authentication and key distribution services are based. We discuss their effectiveness in theory and in practice, taking Kerberos, the most widely-used implementation, as our case study.

Access control mechanisms □ Access control mechanisms are concerned with ensuring that access to information resources (for example, files, processes or communication ports) and hardware resources (for example, printer servers, processor pools or network gateways) is available only to that subset of users that are currently authorized to do so.

Access control mechanisms occur in non-distributed multi-user operating systems. In conventional UNIX and other multi-user systems, files are the most important sharable information resources, and an access control mechanism is provided to allow each user to maintain some private files and to share them in a controlled manner. A well-known mechanism for restricting access to individual files is incorporated in UNIX, based on a version of access control lists. Access control methods are discussed further in Chapter 6.

Figure 16.2 illustrates the ways in which the security mechanisms outlined in the preceding paragraphs are interrelated in the implementation of security policies. The rest of this chapter discusses the design, implementation and validation of security mechanisms.

16.2 Cryptography

To encrypt information we transform it in such a way that it cannot be understood by anyone except the intended recipient, who possesses the means to reverse the transformation. In this section we review the two most commonly-used approaches to computer-based cryptography. Voydock and Kent [1983] give a survey of computer-based cryptographic techniques with critiques of their effectiveness. Readers interested in a more complete treatment of cryptographic methods are also encouraged to examine Kahn [1967] or Denning [1982]. Simmonds [1992] is also a useful source on modern cryptographic methods.

Computer encryption techniques fall into two main classes – *secret-key* and *public-key* encryption methods. Both are useful in the implementation of security, and we shall see that in many cases, either method of encryption can be used without major impact on the methods of authentication and access control used. We use the term *text* in the following to refer to a sequence of items of data of any type.

Transformations and keys □ A message is encrypted by the sender applying some rule to transform it from *plain text* to *cipher text*. The recipient must know the inverse rule in order to transform the cipher text received into the original plain text. Other principals are unable to decipher the message unless they know the inverse rule. The transformations performed by the rules recode data items or transpose data items from one position to another. Such schemes will work, but they are inflexible; the pair of transformation rules must be known to the sender and the recipient; if one sender sends to several recipients, to prevent eavesdropping there must be a different pair of rules for each recipient. The rules must be changed whenever there is a risk that they may have been compromised.

To avoid the need for generating new rules, the encryption and decryption transformations are defined with two parts, a *function* and a *key*. The function defines an *encryption algorithm* that transforms data items in plain text into encrypted data items by combining them with the key and transposing them according to some operations whose results are heavily dependent on the value of the key. We can think of an encryption algorithm as the specification of a large family of functions from which a particular member is selected by any given key.

We denote a text M encrypted with an agreed encryption function and a key K as $\{M\}_K$. The effectiveness of any method for encrypting information depends upon the use of transformation functions that are proof against attacks designed to discover M given $\{M\}_K$, or to discover K given any specific message M and its encrypted form $\{M\}_K$ since the key is likely to be used more than once.

This key-based scheme relies on the secure distribution and storage of keys. Many different keys that are hard to guess are needed to ensure privacy and they must be replaced fairly frequently. In distributed systems the manufacture and distribution of keys is usually the responsibility of a specialized, secure service – a **key distribution service**.

Secret-key encryption □ This is the method of encryption used for the transmission of secret information for centuries before the advent of the computer. When it is implemented in computer systems, larger keys and more complex encryption functions can be used. These improvements are essential, and a key size and encryption function must be selected with care, since attackers should be assumed to have access to computers at least as powerful as the fastest commercially available. As we shall see, these two components have been appropriately selected in the Data Encryption Standard (DES) encryption algorithm and this is currently the most widely-used secret-key encryption method, and plans are in hand for the development of even more secure standards.

A message is encrypted by applying an agreed encryption function to the plain text with a secret key. Decryption is achieved by applying the inverse function to the cipher text using the same key, to produce the original plain text. Since the keys are kept secret, the encryption and decryption functions need not be secret.

Figure 16.3   Secure communication with secret-key encryption.

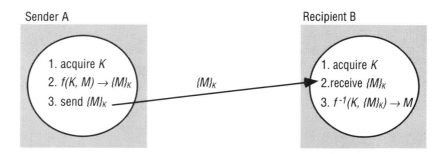

Both sender and recipient must possess the *encryption function* (or its inverse) and a shared secret key. This is illustrated in Figure 16.3, in which a text M is transmitted in encrypted form from the sender to the receiver. Before communication can take place, the secret key K must acquired by both the sender and the receiver through a secure channel. Once a key has been acquired it may be used for several encrypted communications.

In general the encryption function f and its inverse f^{-1} can be different, but since the encryption function need not be a secret, no loss of security occurs if an encryption function is chosen that is its own inverse, and this is what is normally done. The encryption algorithm must be secure against systematic attempts to break it. The most common type of code breaking attack relies on obtaining matching pieces of plain text and cipher text and from these, attempting to discover the key. Cryptographers aim to make the function that defines the rules of substitution and transposition so complex that even if the code breaker is equipped with powerful computers and plenty of corresponding samples of plain text and cipher text, the likelihood of discovering the key is very small.

The Data Encryption Standard (DES) [National Bureau of Standards 1977] was developed by IBM and subsequently adopted as a US national standard for government and business applications. In this standard, the encryption function maps a 64-bit plain text input into a 64-bit encrypted output using a 56-bit key. The algorithm has 16 key-dependent stages known as *rounds*, in which the data to be encrypted is bit-rotated by a number of bits determined by the key and 3 key-independent transpositions. The algorithm would be time consuming to perform on a general-purpose computer, but it has been implemented in fast VLSI hardware and can easily be incorporated into network interface or other communication chips. The DES algorithm is described in detail and its security is discussed by Tanenbaum [1988].

The DES is widely used and there are no known instances of successful attacks against it. It has been criticized on the grounds that a computer-aided attack might crack the code because the size of the key (56 bits) is small enough to yield to a brute-force attempt to find the key given an encrypted message whose contents are known – using a program that enumerates all possible key values and tries each to decrypt the encrypted text until the correct contents are produced, but this would require on average 2^{55} or 3×10^{16} trials.

Figure 16.4 Secure communication with public-key encryption.

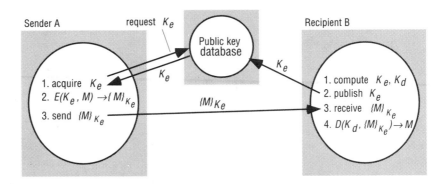

Public-key encryption □ This scheme was first proposed by Diffie and Hellman [1976] as a cryptographic method that eliminates the need for trust between the communicating parties. It is based on the use of the product of two very large prime numbers (greater than 10^{100}), relying on the fact that the determination of the prime factors of such large numbers is so computationally intensive as to be effectively impossible to compute.

Each potential recipient of a message makes a pair of keys, K_e and K_d and keeps the decryption key K_d a secret. The encryption key K_e can be made known publicly for use by anyone who wants to communicate. The method is based on the use of a one-way function to define the relation between the two keys, so that it is very hard to determine K_d from knowledge of K_e. A one-way function is any function $f(X) = Y$ such that given the value of Y, it is very difficult (that is, computationally complex) to determine the corresponding value of X. (One-way functions are a feature of the Amoeba operating system where they are used to protect server capabilities; as described in Chapter 18.)

This is called *public-key encryption* and it avoids the need for the transmission of secret keys between principals. It is based on two separate well-known functions, E and D and two separate keys K_e and K_d for encryption and decryption. For example, if a principal B expects to receive secret information from other principals, B generates a pair of keys, K_e and K_d. B 'publishes' K_e and keeps K_d a secret. It may do this either by sending K_e directly to any principals from which it expects to receive information or by sending K_e to a public-key distribution service that maintains a database of public keys. A public-key distribution service supplies keys in response to requests from any client of the form 'what is B's public key'.

Any principal wishing to send secret information to B acquires B's public key K_e and uses $E(K_e, M)$ to produce $\{M\}_{K_e}$ before sending it to B. Only B knows K_d and can apply $D(K_d, \{M\}_{K_e})$ to decrypt the message. The idea is illustrated in Figure 16.4, in which A transmits a secret message to B after obtaining B's public key from a key distribution service.

Several algorithms have been suggested for the generation and use of key pairs in public-key encryption. The Rivest, Shamir and Adelman (RSA) design for a public-key cipher [Rivest *et al.* 1978] is based on the difficulty of finding factors of large numbers.

Despite extensive investigations no flaws have been found in it, and it is now quite widely used. An outline of the method follows.

To find a key pair *e, d*:

1. Choose two large prime numbers, *P* and *Q* (each greater than 10^{100}), and form $N = P \times Q$ and $Z = (P–1) \times (Q–1)$.

2. For *d* choose any number that is relatively prime with Z (that is, such that *d* has no common factors with Z).

> We illustrate the computations involved using much smaller integer values for *P* and *Q*:
>
> $P = 13$ and $Q = 17$;
> $N = 221$
> $Z = 192$
> $d = 5$

3. To find *e* solve the equation:
$e \times d = 1 \ mod \ Z$
That is, e ×d is the smallest element in the series Z+1, 2Z+1, 3Z+1, ... that is divisible by *d*.

> $e \times d = 1 \ mod \ 192$
> $= 1, 193, 385, ...$
> 385 is divisible by *d*
> $e = 385/5 = 77$

To encrypt text using the RSA method, the plain text is divided into equal blocks of length *k* bits where $2^k < N$ (that is, such that the numerical value of a block is always less than *N*; in practical applications, *k* is usually in the range 256 to 512).

> $k = 7$
> so blocks will be of size $2^7 = 128$

The function for encrypting a single block of plain text *M* is:

$E'(e,N,M) = M^e \ mod \ N.$

> for a message *M*,
> the cipher text is $M^{77} \ mod \ 221$

The function for decrypting a block of encrypted text *c* to produce the original plain text block is:
$D'(d,N,c) = c^d \ mod \ N$

Rivest *et al.* have proved that E' and D' are mutual inverses (that is $E'(D'(x)) = D'(E'(x)) = x$) for all values of *P* in the range $0 \leq P \leq N$.

The two parameters *e,N* can be regarded as a key for the encryption function, and similarly *d,N* represent a key for the decryption function. So we can write $K_e = <e,N>$ and $K_d = <d,N>$ and we get the functions E and D used in Figure 16.4.

In terms of our earlier description and the diagram, an intending recipient of secret information must publish or otherwise distribute the pair $<e,N>$ while keeping d secret. The publication of $<e,N>$ does not compromise the secrecy of d because any attempt to determine d requires knowledge of the original prime numbers P and Q, and these can only be obtained by the factorization of N. Factorization of large numbers (we recall that P and Q were chosen to be $> 10^{100}$, so $N > 10^{200}$) is extremely time-consuming, even on very high performance computers. In 1978 Rivest *et al.* [1978] concluded that factoring a number as large as 10^{200} would take more than four billion years with the best known algorithm on a computer that performs one million instructions per second. Faster computers and better factorization methods have been developed since then, but the computational complexity remains sufficiently great to ensure the security of the method.

Key distribution □ In the secret-key case, before communication can occur both the sender and the recipient must possess a shared key and each must be convinced that the key is a secret known only to the other (and possibly to a trusted third party), The same key is used for both encryption and decryption.

The transmission of encryption keys to the relevant principals raises a security problem since the channels through which the keys are communicated must be secure. In traditional cryptography this problem was resolved by transmitting the key through a different physical communication channel, but that is not a convenient solution for use in a computer network. In the next section we discuss the design of authentication servers that are suitable for this purpose. Their design requires only that each principal is initially supplied with a single secret key that is known to the authentication server.

For public keys, there is a need for the recipients of public keys to be sure that the keys they receive are authentic, that is, that they are the public key part of a pair of keys for which the secret key is known only to the intended communication partner. Otherwise an impostor could gain access to the information by impersonating another principal and publishing a false public key. This need can be met in two ways. A key distribution server of similar design to those used in secret-key cryptography can be used, or the public keys can be distributed freely using conventional database methods, but each key is distributed with a 'certificate' produced when the key is generated. A key is certified by attaching the name of the key's originator and the digital signature (see Section 16.2) of an accepted authority. The signature verifies that the key has not been replaced by an impostor's public key.

Comparison of secret- and public-key cryptography □ We can summarize the advantages and drawbacks of the two major techniques for encryption as follows:

Security: With suitable keys and encryption algorithms both methods are secure enough for all normal purposes. There are no known cases of successful attacks on either.

Convenience: Public-key encryption can be more convenient to implement because a secret channel is not required to distribute the keys (but authenticated communication is required, see above). When a key distribution server is available, public-key encryption can be used to establish initial contact between each new principal and the server and to transmit a secret key that is used for all subsequent transactions.

Figure 16.5   The performance of encryption methods compared.

Algorithm		Software implementation (bits per second)	Hardware implementation (bits per second)
RSA public-key	encrypt:	0.5×10^3	220×10^3
	decrypt:	32×10^3	N/A
DES secret-key	encrypt/decrypt:	400×10^3	1.2×10^9

Performance: Secret-key encryption algorithms are much faster, see Figure 16.5 for details. The software figures in Figure 16.5 are based on a hardware performance of 0.5 MIPS (the measurements were made on an 8 megaHertz Intel 286 processor). The public-key implementation is based on 500-bit blocks. The secret-key implementation requires a 64 kilobyte table for each key. (The table is from Lampson *et al.* [1992]. They urge caution in reliance on the figures because many variables can affect performance. The original sources are Comba [1990] for the software figures, Shand *et al.* [1990] and Eberle and Thacker [1992] for the hardware figures.)

Current practice □ Computer cryptography and methods for applying it are the subject of much current research and development. The cryptographic techniques described in this section have been developed recently and are now beginning to appear in distributed operating systems and applications. Some earlier applications of computer cryptography are described in Meyer and Matyas [1982].

Amoeba and Mach both provide for the encryption of interprocess communication (see Chapter 18). An example of the use of cryptography at the application level is the Privacy Enhanced Mail (PEM) scheme proposed for adding privacy to Internet mail applications.

The PEM scheme is described in a series of Internet RFCs [Linn *et al.* 1993]. It uses both public and secret-key encryption – mail users obtain a public/private key pair from a local PEM program and publish the public key with their mail address. To send a secret message, the PEM program generates a one-shot secret key and encrypts the message in it using the DES algorithm. The secret key is encrypted in the recipient's public key and appended to the encrypted message.

This scheme retains the efficiency of secret-key cryptography for the bulk encryption but avoids the need for a secure key distribution server – each user relies on a local PEM program that maintains a small database of their keys. PEM is available as an application program called RIPEM that uses a public-key-encryption library called RSAREF produced by RSA Data Security Inc, under licence from PKP (Public Key Partners), a firm that owns a patent covering the RSA public-key encryption method. The licences covering RSAREF and RIPEM allow them to be used for non-commercial purposes without fee.

PEM can also be used to produce 'signed' messages (see Section 16.2, below). To do so, a digest (also called a 'fingerprint') of the message is produced; the digest is encrypted in the sender's private key and appended to the message as the signature. The recipient can check this digital signature by decrypting it using the sender's public key and comparing it with the result of applying the digest function to the message received.

Another example of the widening use of cryptography is a program called PGP (Pretty Good Privacy) [Wallach 1993], originally developed by Philip Zimmermann and carried forward by him and others. This is part of a technical and political campaign to ensure that the availability of cryptographic methods is not controlled by the US government. PGP has been developed and distributed with the aim of enabling all computer users to enjoy the level of privacy afforded by the use of public-key cryptography in their communications.

Like PEM, PGP generates and manages secret keys on behalf of a user and uses public-key encryption only to transmit secret keys to the intended communication partner. However it uses the IDEA secret-key encryption algorithm to encrypt mail messages because the use of the DES algorithm is controlled by the US government.

There are legal and political overtones; PGP uses a non-proprietary implementation of the RSA algorithm, but because it uses the RSA *method*, PKP claim that the use of PGP in the US or Canada is an infringement. The IDEA secret-key algorithm is also protected by a patent. Also, the US government seeks to control the export of RSA, DES and other US-developed cryptographic software for security reasons.

Despite these complications, implementations of both PEM and PGP for personal computers and UNIX workstations are effectively in the public domain and are widely available both within the US and outside it. It is to be hoped that such useful applications of cryptography will eventually be commercially available to all who need to use them, but government action may yet impede this development.

16.3 Authentication and key distribution

The two problems of authentication and of secure distribution of keys are best addressed by a single service, which is discussed in this section.

Considerable progress has been made in recent years on the theory and practice of authentication. In this section we describe Needham and Schroeder's model for an authentication server. In the next section we describe the Kerberos authentication service that has been developed at MIT using the Needham and Schroeder model as its basis.

Needham and Schroeder [1978] first suggested a solution to authentication and key distribution based on an **authentication server** that supplies secret keys to clients. The job of the authentication server is to provide a secure way for pairs of processes to obtain keys. To do this, it must communicate with its clients using encrypted messages. Needham and Schroeder describe two protocols for a secure authentication server, the first using secret keys and the second using public keys.

Needham and Schroeder with secret keys □ In their model, a process acting on behalf of a principal A that wishes to initiate secure communication with another process acting on behalf of a principal B can obtain a key for the purpose. The protocol is described for two arbitrary processes A and B, but in client server systems, A is likely to be a client initiating a sequence of requests to some server B. The key is supplied to

A in two forms, one that A can use to encrypt the messages that it sends to B and one that it can transmit securely to B. (The latter is encrypted in a key that is known to B but not to A, so that B can decrypt it and the key is not compromised during transmission.)

The authentication server S maintains a table containing a *name* and a *secret key* for each principal known to the system. The secret key is used only to authenticate client processes to the authentication server and to transmit messages securely between client processes and the authentication server. It is never disclosed to third parties and it is transmitted across the network at most once, when it is generated. (Ideally, a key should always be transmitted by some other means, such as on paper or in a verbal message, avoiding any exposure on the network.) A secret key is the equivalent of the password used to authenticate users in centralized systems. For human principals the name held by the authentication service is their 'user name' and the secret key is their password. Both are supplied by the user on request to client processes acting on the user's behalf.

We tabulate the messages in the Needham and Schroeder secret-key protocol in Figure 16.6, using the $\{\}_K$ notation introduced earlier to denote encryption with key K. The authentication server is S.

Figure 16.6   The Needham – Schroeder secret-key authentication protocol.

Header	*Message*	*Notes*
1. A → S:	A, B, N_A	A requests S to supply a key for communication with B.
2. S → A:	$\{N_A, B, K_{AB}, \{K_{AB}, A\}_{K_B}\}_{K_A}$	S returns a message encrypted in A's secret key, containing a newly-generated key K_{AB}, and a 'ticket' encrypted in B's secret key. The nonce N_A demonstrates that the message was sent in response to the preceding one. A believes that S sent the message because only S knows A's secret key.
3. A → B:	$\{K_{AB}, A\}_{K_B}$	A sends the 'ticket' to B.
4. B → A:	$\{N_B\}_{K_{AB}}$	B decrypts the ticket and uses the new key K_{AB} to encrypt another nonce N_B.
5. A → B:	$\{N_B - 1\}_{K_{AB}}$	A demonstrates to B that it was the sender of the previous message by returning an agreed transformation of N_B.

Notation:

A	Name of principal for the process initiating communication.
B	Name of principal for A's communication partner.
K_A	A's secret key (password).
K_B	B's secret key (password).
K_{AB}	Secret key for communication between A and B.
N_A	A nonce generated by A.
$\{M\}_K$	Message M encrypted in key K

The protocol is based on the generation and transmission of 'tickets' by the authentication server. A ticket is an encrypted message containing a secret key for use in communication between A and B.

A nonce is an integer value that is introduced into a message to demonstrate its freshness. Nonces are used only once and are generated on demand. For example, the nonces may be generated as a sequence of integer values or by reading the clock at the sending machine.

If the protocol is successfully completed, both A and B can be sure that any message encrypted in K_{AB} that they receive comes from the other, and that any message encrypted in K_{AB} that they send can be understood only by the other or by S (and S is assumed to be trustworthy). This is so because the only messages that have been sent containing K_{AB} were encrypted in A's secret key or B's secret key.

There is a weakness in this protocol in that B has no reason to believe that Message 3 is fresh. An intruder that manages to obtain the key K_{AB} and make a copy of the ticket

Figure 16.7 The Needham – Schroeder public-key authentication protocol.

Header	Message	Notes
1. A → S:	A, B	A requests B's public key from S.
2. S → A:	$\{PK_B, B\}_{SK_S}$	S sends B's public key to A, encrypted using its secret key. The message is encrypted to ensure that it is not tampered with. A (and everyone else) is able to decrypt the message using the server's public key, PK_S.
3. A → B:	$\{N_A, A\}_{PK_B}$	A sends a message containing a nonce to B, encrypted in B's public key. Only B can decrypt it to get A's name.
4. B → S:	B, A	B requests A's public key from S.
5. S → B:	$\{PK_A, A\}_{SK_S}$	S sends A's public key to B, encrypted using its secret key.
6. B → A:	$\{N_A, N_B\}_{PK_A}$	B sends A a pair of nonces encrypted in A's public key.
7. A → B:	$\{N_B\}_{PK_B}$	A sends B the nonce it has just received encrypted in B's public key, proving that the communication is fresh, and that it is indeed A that is communicating (since only A could decrypt Message 6).

Additional notation:
PK_A A's public key.
PK_B B's public key.
PK_S Server's public key.
SK_S Server's secret key.

and authenticator $\{K_{AB}, A\}_{K_B}$, (both of which might have been left in an exposed storage location by a careless or a failed client program running under A's authority), can use them to initiate a subsequent exchange with B, impersonating A. For this attack to occur an old value of K_{AB} has to be compromised; in today's terminology, Needham and Schroeder did not include this possibility on their threat list, and the consensus of opinion is that one should do so. The weakness can be remedied by adding a timestamp to Message 3, so that it becomes: $\{K_{AB}, A, t\}_{K_B}$. B decrypts this message and checks that t is recent. This is the solution adopted in Kerberos.

Needham and Schroeder with public keys □ Public keys must be distributed by a trusted key distribution server in order to avoid intrusions by impostors. When obtaining a public key for use in communicating with B, A wishes to be sure that it really is obtaining B's public key and not some other public key sent to it by an impostor purporting to be B.

The Needham and Schroeder authentication protocol for public-key encryption is given in Figure 16.7.

A weakness was subsequently detected in this protocol by Burrows, Abadi and Needham using the logic (described in Section 16.5) that they have developed especially for analysing the properties of authentication protocols [Burrows, Abadi and Needham 1990]. The weakness is that A and B must believe that the public keys they receive from S are fresh. There is no protection against the replay of old messages. This can be remedied by adding timestamps to Messages 2 and 5.

16.4 Case study: Kerberos

Kerberos is an authentication protocol based on the Needham and Schroeder secret-key protocol. It was developed at MIT [Steiner *et al.* 1988] to provide a range of authentication and security facilities for use in the Athena campus computing network and other open systems. The Kerberos protocol has undergone a number of revisions and enhancements in the light of experience and feedback from user organizations and the most recent version, which we shall describe here is known as Version 5. An implementation of Kerberos version 5 for UNIX is available from MIT [1994]; it is widely used at MIT and elsewhere to provide secure access to NFS, the Andrew File System and many other services. The Open Software Foundation's Distributed Computing Environment and recent releases of the Andrew File System (Version 3 and later) include an integrated implementation of Kerberos.

Figure 16.8 shows the process architecture. Kerberos deals with three kinds of security objects:

> *Ticket*: a token issued to a client by the Kerberos ticket-granting service for presentation to a particular server, verifying that the sender has been recently authenticated by Kerberos. Tickets include an expiry time and a newly-generated session key for use by the client and the server.
>
> *Authenticator*: a token constructed by a client and sent to a server to prove the identity of the user and the currency of any communication with a server. An

Figure 16.8   System architecture of Kerberos.

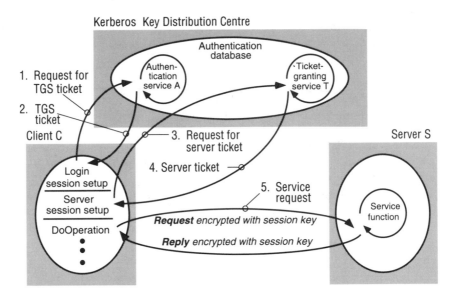

authenticator can be used only once. It contains the client's name and a timestamp and is encrypted in the appropriate session key.

Session key: a secret key randomly generated by Kerberos and issued to a client for use when communicating with a particular server. Encryption is not mandatory for all communication with servers; the session key is used for encrypting communication with those servers that demand it and for encrypting all authenticators (see above).

Client processes must possess a ticket and a session key for each server that they use. It would be impractical to supply a new ticket and key for each client-server interaction, so most tickets are granted to clients with a lifetime of several hours so that they can be used for interaction with a particular a server until they expire.

A Kerberos server is known as a Key Distribution Centre (KDC). Each KDC offers an Authentication Service (AS) and a Ticket Granting Service (TGS). On login, users are authenticated by the Authentication Service, using a network-secure variation of the password method, and the client process acting on behalf of the user is supplied with a *ticket-granting ticket* and a session key for communicating with the TGS. Subsequently, the original client process and its descendants can use the ticket-granting ticket to obtain tickets and session keys for specific services from the TGS.

The Needham and Schroeder protocol is followed quite closely in Kerberos, with time values (integers representing a date and time) used as nonces. This serves two purposes:

• to guard against replay of old messages intercepted in the network or the reuse of old tickets found lying in the memory of machines from which the authorized user has logged-out (nonces were used to achieve this purpose in Needham and Schroeder);

- to apply a lifetime to tickets, enabling the system to revoke users' rights when, for example, they cease to be authorized users of the system.

Below we describe the Kerberos protocols in detail, using the notation defined at the bottom of the page. First, we describe the protocol by which the client obtains a ticket and a session key for access to the TGS.

A Kerberos ticket has a fixed period of validity starting at time t_1 and ending at time t_2. A ticket for a client C to access a server S takes the form:

$$\{C, S, t_1, t_2, K_{CS}\}_{K_S}$$

which we shall denote as:

$$\{ticket(C,S)\}_{K_S}$$

The client's name is included in the ticket to avoid possible use by impostors, as we shall see later. The message numbers below correspond to those in Figure 16.8. Note that Message 1 is not encrypted and does not include C's password. It contains a nonce that is used to check the validity of the reply.

Header	Message	Notes
1. C → A: Request for TGS ticket	C, T, n	Client C requests the Kerberos authentication server A to supply a ticket for communication with the ticket granting service T.
2. A → C: TGS session key and ticket	$\{K_{CT}, n\}_{K_C}, \{ticket(C,T)\}_{K_T}$ containing C, T, t_1, t_2, K_{CT}	A returns a message containing a ticket encrypted in its secret key and a session key for C to use with T. The inclusion of the nonce n encrypted in K_C shows that the message comes from the recipient of Message 1, who must know K_C.

Message 2 is sometimes called a 'challenge' because it presents the requester with information that is only useful if it knows C's secret key, K_C. An impostor who attempts to impersonate C by sending Message 1 can get no further, since they cannot decrypt

Notation:

A	Name of Kerberos authentication service.
T	Name of Kerberos ticket granting service.
C	Name of client.
n	A nonce.
t	A timestamp.
t_1	Starting time for validity of ticket.
t_2	Ending time for validity of ticket.

Message 2. For principals that are users, K_C is a scrambled version of the user's password. The client process will prompt the user to type their password and will attempt to decrypt Message 2 with it. If the user gave the right password, the client process obtains the session key K_{CT} and a valid ticket for the ticket-granting service, if not, it obtains gibberish. Servers have secret keys of their own, known only to the relevant server process and to the authentication server.

When a valid ticket has been obtained from the authentication service, the client C can use it to communicate with the ticket granting service to obtain tickets for other servers any number of times until the ticket expires. Thus to obtain a ticket for any server S, C constructs an authenticator encrypted in K_{CT} of the form:

$$\{C, t\}_{K_{CT}}$$

which we shall denote as:

$$\{auth(C)\}_{K_{CT}}$$

and sends a request to T:

3. C →T: Request ticket for service S	$\{auth(C)\}_{K_{CT}}$, $\{ticket(C,T)\}_{K_T}$, S, n	C requests the ticket-granting server T to supply a ticket for communication with another server S.
4. T →C: Service ticket	$\{K_{CS}, n\}_{K_{CT}}$, $\{ticket(C,S)\}_{K_S}$	T checks the ticket. If it is valid T generates a new random session key K_{CS} and returns it with a ticket for S (encrypted in the server's secret key K_S).

C is then ready to issue request messages to the server, S:

5. C → S: Service request	$\{auth(C)\}_{K_{CS}}$, $\{ticket(C,S)\}_{K_S}$, request, n	C sends the ticket to S with a newly-generated authenticator for C and a request. The request would be encrypted in K_{CS} if secrecy of the data is required.

For the client to be sure of the server's authenticity, S should return the nonce n to C. (To reduce the number of messages required this could be included in the messages that contains the server's reply to the *request*):

6. S →C: Server auth- entication	$\{n\}_{K_{CS}}$	(Optional): S sends the nonce to C, encrypted in K_{CS}.

Figure 16.9 Diagrammatic view of the Kerberos protocol.

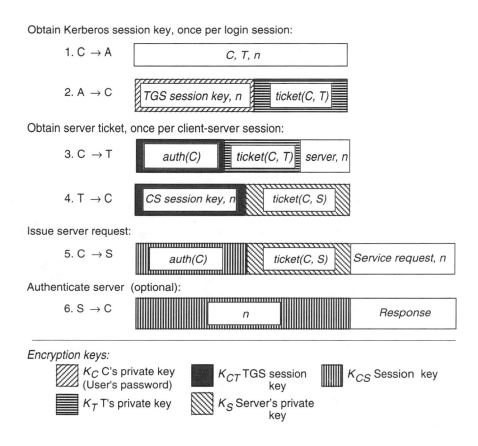

Obtain Kerberos session key, once per login session:

1. C → A   C, T, n

2. A → C   TGS session key, n   ticket(C, T)

Obtain server ticket, once per client-server session:

3. C → T   auth(C)   ticket(C, T)   server, n

4. T → C   CS session key, n   ticket(C, S)

Issue server request:

5. C → S   auth(C)   ticket(C, S)   Service request, n

Authenticate server (optional):

6. S → C   n   Response

Encryption keys:

K_C C's private key (User's password) K_{CT} TGS session key K_{CS} Session key

K_T T's private key K_S Server's private key

C is the client, A refers to the Kerberos authentication server and T refers to the Kerberos TGS. S is any service with which C requires secure communication. The different shadings indicate the encryption keys used in each message. (We are grateful to William Roberts for the original version of this graphical presentation.)

In Figure 16.9 we illustrate the protocol graphically using shaded boxes to indicate the encryption keys used.

Application of Kerberos □ Kerberos was developed for use in Project Athena at MIT – a campus-wide networked computing facility for undergraduate education with many workstations and servers providing a service to more than 5000 users. The environment is such that neither the trustworthiness of clients nor the security of the network and the machines that offer network services can be assumed – for example, workstations are not protected against the installation of user-developed system software and server machines (other than the Kerberos server) are not necessarily secured against physical interference with their software configuration.

Kerberos provides virtually all of the security in the Athena system. It is used to authenticate users and other principals. Most of the servers running on the network have been extended to require a ticket from each client at the start of every client-server interaction. These include file storage (NFS and Andrew File System), electronic mail, remote login and printing. Users' passwords are known only to the user and to the Kerberos authentication service. Services have secret keys that are known only to Kerberos and the servers that provide the service.

We will describe the way in which Kerberos is applied to the authentication of users on login and its use to enhance the security of the NFS service.

Login with Kerberos □ When a user logs in to a workstation, the login program sends the user's name to the Kerberos authentication service. If the user is known to the authentication service it replies with a session key and a nonce encrypted in the user's password and a ticket for the TGS. The login program then attempts to decrypt the session key and the nonce using the password that the user typed in response to the password prompt. If the password is correct, the login program obtains the session key and the nonce. It checks the nonce and stores the session key with the ticket for subsequent use when communicating with the TGS. At this point, the login program can erase the user's password from its memory, since the ticket now serves to authenticate the user. A login session is then started for the user on the workstation. Note that the user's password is never exposed to eavesdropping on the network – it is retained in the workstation and is erased from memory soon after it is entered.

Accessing typical servers with Kerberos □ Whenever a program running on a workstation needs to access a new service, it requests a ticket for the service from the ticket granting service. For example, when a user wishes to login to a remote computer, the *rlogin* command program on the user's workstation obtains a ticket from the Kerberos ticket granting service for access to the *rlogind* network service. The *rlogin* command program sends the ticket, together with a new authenticator in a request to the *rlogind* process on the computer where the user wishes to login. The *rlogind* program decrypts the ticket with the *rlogin* service's secret key and checks the validity of the ticket (that is, that the ticket's lifetime has not expired). Server machines must take care to store their secret keys in storage that is inaccessible to intruders.

The *rlogind* program then uses the session key included in the ticket to decrypt the authenticator and checks that the authenticator is fresh (authenticators can be used only once). Once the *rlogind* program is satisfied that the ticket and authenticator are valid, there is no need for it to check the user's name and password, the user's identity is known to the *rlogind* program and a login session is established for that user on the remote machine.

NFS with Kerberos □ Workstations are not trusted, and all permanent system and user files are accessed from a file server. When a user has logged in to a workstation, their home directory is located and the relevant filesystem is mounted using NFS. Similarly, a filesystem root ('/') is mounted on the workstation from a remote file server. This enables the user to invoke programs to operate on any files in the file hierarchies accessible from the mount points. Of course, NFS applies the usual UNIX permission checks before allowing access, but these checks depend upon a knowledge of the user's identity.

In the original standard implementation of NFS, the user's identity is included in each request in the form of an unencrypted numeric identifier. (The identifier is encrypted in later versions of NFS.) NFS does not take any further steps to check the authenticity of the identifier supplied. This implies a high degree of trust in the integrity of the workstation and its software by NFS, whereas the aim of Kerberos and other authentication-based security systems is to reduce to a minimum the range of components in which trust is assumed. Essentially, when NFS is used in a 'Kerberized' environment it should accept requests only from clients whose identity can be shown to have been authenticated by Kerberos.

One obvious solution considered by the Kerberos developers was to change the nature of the credentials required by NFS to be a full-blown Kerberos ticket and authenticator. But because NFS is implemented as a stateless server each individual file access request is handled on its face value and the authentication data would have be included in each request. This was considered unacceptably expensive in time required to perform the necessary encryptions and would have entailed adding the Kerberos client library to the kernel of all workstations.

Instead, a hybrid approach was adopted in which the NFS *mount server* is supplied with full Kerberos authentication data for the user when their home and root filesystems are mounted. The results of this authentication, including the user's conventional numerical identifier and the address of the workstation is retained by the server with the mount information for each filestore. (Although the NFS server does not retain state relating to individual client processes it does retain the current mounts at each workstation.)

On each file access request, the NFS server checks the user identifier and the sender's address and only grants access if they match those stored at the server for the relevant workstation at mount time. This hybrid approach involves only minimal additional cost and is safe against most forms of attack provided that only one user at a time can log in to each workstation. At MIT, the system is configured so that this is the case.

Note, however, that the requests and responses transferred between NFS servers and clients are not protected by encryption, and that replay could be used to cause an NFS server to send data to a third party who is legitimately logged in and has been authenticated, though not to the replayer.

Implementation of Kerberos □ Kerberos is implemented as a server that runs on a secure machine. A set of libraries is provided for use by client applications and services. The DES encryption algorithm is used, but this is implemented as a separate module that can be easily replaced.

The Kerberos service is scalable – the world is divided into separate domains of authentication authority, called *realms*, each with its own Kerberos server. Most principals are registered in just one realm, but the Kerberos ticket-granting servers are registered in all of the realms. Principals can authenticate themselves to servers in other realms through their local ticket-granting server.

Within a single realm, there can be several authentication servers, all of which have copies of the same authentication database. The authentication database is replicated by a simple master-slave technique. Updates are applied to the master copy by a single Kerberos Database Management service (KDBM) that runs only on the master machine. The KDBM handles requests from users to change their passwords and requests from system administrators to add or delete principals and to change their passwords.

To make this scheme transparent to users, the lifetime of TGS tickets ought to be as long as the longest possible login session, since the use of an expired ticket will result in the rejection of service requests, and the only remedy is for the user to reauthenticate the login session and then request new server tickets for all of the services in use. In practice, ticket lifetimes in the region of 12 hours are used.

Critiques of Kerberos □ The protocol for Kerberos Version 5 described above contains several improvements designed to deal with criticisms of earlier versions [Bellovin and Merritt 1990, Burrows, Abadi and Needham 1990]. Some of the criticisms of Bellovin and Merritt address operational aspects that do not directly affect the security of Kerberos when it is used in the environment for which it is intended. Their most important criticism is that in Version 4 of Kerberos the nonces used in authenticators are implemented as timestamps and protection against the replay of authenticators depends upon at least loose synchronization of clients' and servers' clocks. Furthermore, if a synchronization protocol is used to bring client and server clocks into loose synchrony, the synchronization protocol must itself be secure against security attacks.

The protocol definition for Version 5 allows the nonces in authenticators to be implemented as timestamps or as sequence numbers. In both cases, it requires that they be unique, and that servers should hold a list of recently-received nonces from each client to check that they are not replayed. This is an inconvenient implementation requirement and is difficult for servers to guarantee in case of failures. Kehne *et al.* [1992] have published a proposed improvement to the Kerberos protocol that does not rely on sychronized clocks.

Burrows, Abadi and Needham's criticisms are derived from their analysis of the earlier Kerberos Version 4 protocol using their *logic of authentication*. We describe their logic of authentication in the next section. Their conclusions about the Version 4 protocol included a criticism of the requirement for clock synchronization between clients and servers similar to the one mentioned above, and a comment that the use of double encryption in some messages served no useful purpose and could be expensive when encryption is performed by software. The latter criticism has been addressed in the Version 5 protocol which does not entail any double encryption.

Finally, we note that the security of Kerberos depends on limited session lifetimes – the period of validity of TGS tickets is generally limited to a few hours; the period must be chosen to be long enough to avoid inconvenient interruptions of service, but short enough to ensure that users who have been de-registered or downgraded do not continue to use the resources for more than a short period. This might cause difficulties in commercial environments, because the consequent requirement for the user to supply a new set of authentication details at an arbitrary point in the interaction might intrude on the application.

16.5 Logics of authentication

Computer security is a complex subject, and informal arguments made in an attempt to show the correctness of authentication protocols are prone to errors. Our intuition can help us understand roughly how a protocol works, but it is not normally sufficient to expose clearly all the conditions under which the protocol in fact meets the goals of authentication. When a security loophole exists, it is only a matter of time before an attacker will discover and exploit it.

The descriptions of the Needham-Schroeder and Kerberos protocols include informal arguments to the effect that the protocols achieve their stated security goals. On close examination, it can be seen, first, that the protocols are based on certain assumptions (such as: a server that knows my password is to be trusted). Secondly, it can be seen that each principal involved implicitly makes certain deductions based on the assumptions and on information it has received in messages.

Ideally, it should be possible to make explicit all the assumptions involved in a protocol, and to transform each protocol step into the application of one or more of a few general deduction rules allowing further conclusions to be drawn. To formalize an argument is to account rigorously for all the steps and assumptions made, expressing them in a symbolic way so that checking becomes a mechanical process. A logical calculus based on an agreed set of deduction rules for formally reasoning about authentication protocols is called a **logic of authentication**. The following main benefits can be derived from such a logic:

> *Correctness*: It should be possible to prove that a protocol does or does not meet its security goals. If it does not achieve the stated goals, the logic of authentication should show what it does in fact achieve.

> *Efficiency*: If it can be shown that the security goals can be achieved without some of the messages, contents of messages or encryptions of message contents which are part of a protocol, then the protocol can be made more efficient by eliminating them.

> *Applicability*: In order to judge whether a protocol can be used in a practical situation, it helps to clarify the protocol's assumptions by formally stating them. Moreover, it can be ascertained whether any of the stated assumptions are not in fact needed to achieve the authentication goals.

Burrows, Abadi and Needham describe a logic of authentication [Burrows, Abadi and Needham 1990], which is referred to henceforth as BAN logic, for the sake of brevity. BAN logic has been applied to analyse both the Needham-Schroeder and Kerberos protocols, amongst others [Burrows, Abadi and Needham 1989, Burrows, Abadi and Needham 1990]. We now introduce BAN logic, and reproduce an argument given by Burrows, Abadi and Needham [1989] that the Needham-Schroeder protocol contains an assumption that was not made explicit, but upon which the security conclusions in fact rest.

The method and formalism of BAN logic

There are three main stages to the analysis of a protocol using BAN logic. The first step is to express the assumptions and goals as *formulas* (also known as *statements*) in a symbolic notation, so that the logic can proceed from a known state so as to be able to ascertain whether the goals are in fact reached. The second stage is to transform the protocol steps also into formulas in symbolic notation. Lastly, a set of deduction rules called *postulates* are applied. The postulates should lead from the assumptions, via intermediate formulas, to the authentication goals.

A protocol is analysed from the point of view of each particular principal P that participates in it. Each message received by P is considered in relation to previous messages received by P and sent by P. The question is what a principal should believe, on the basis of the messages it has sent and received. The assumptions of BAN logic are similar to those of the authentication protocols for whose analysis it is intended: that authentication is carried out between trustworthy principals (it will be explained below what is meant by 'trustworthy'), although attackers can attempt to foil a protocol by eavesdropping, replaying messages, or by sending malicious messages.

Belief □ When a principal is persuaded of the truth of a formula – or is entitled to conclude that it is true – we say that the principal **believes** it. (Bold-face words such as **believes**, **sees** and **controls** are used as predicates in the BAN formalism.) If the principal is P and the formula is X, we write P **believes** X. Note that this sense is rather different from the colloquial sense of 'believe', which does not necessarily connote 'with justification'. Thus only beliefs which are justified in terms of BAN logic are of interest. Some of these beliefs are introduced as assumptions; the others are deduced in the logic using the postulates.

We assume that trusted (trustworthy) principals do not lie about their beliefs to other principals. In other words, if P is trusted, and if a formula X is received in a message known to have been sent by P as part of the current run of the protocol, then it can be deduced that P **believes** X.

A principal is assumed to participate in a number of non-overlapping runs of a protocol throughout its lifetime, perhaps with different principals over time. It is important to note that, as far as time is concerned, BAN logic only has the notions of present and past, and does not assume that messages are timestamped. A principal of course knows which messages it sends during to the present run of a protocol. However, past messages – belonging to previous runs of the protocol – can be replayed any time. And what a principal **believe**d in the past is not necessarily valid in the present. For example, a server may have believed in the past that a key K was a secret key for use between two principals. The key might have been discovered by another principal since then.

The formulas and notation of BAN logic □ In order to apply the logic, the messages and the actions of the principals are transformed into formulas. P **believes** X is only one type of formula. The other types of formula we shall consider are as follows:

> P **sees** X: The principal P receives a message containing X. P might need to perform a decryption to extract X from the message. P is in a position to repeat X in messages to other principals. X can be a statement or a simple item of data such as a nonce (or a combination of both types). The term 'sees' is meant to convey

the fact that the receiving principal observes X, but does not necessarily believe it if X is a statement. (In BAN logic, **see**-ing is not necessarily **believe**-ing!) Of course, messages belonging to a correct protocol should ultimately entitle principals to new beliefs, otherwise they are useless from the point of view of authentication.

P **said** X: At some point in the past, P is known to have sent a message including X. This implies that, if P is trusted, P **believe**d X when it sent the message.

P **controls** X (*P has jurisdiction over X*): P is trusted as an authority on X. For example, an authentication server is trusted as an authority on statements about the key that is allocated as a shared secret between two principals.

fresh(X): X has not been sent in a message belonging to a previous run of the protocol. Thus nonces are values which, by definition, are constructed to be fresh.

$P \overset{K}{\leftrightarrow} Q$: P and Q are entitled to use the secret key K. K is a secret between P and Q and possibly other principals trusted by P or Q (such as an authentication server).

The notation of BAN logic also includes the encryption notation used previously in this chapter: if K is a key, then $\{X\}_K$ means X encrypted with the key K. Finally, if X and Y are statements, then X,Y means X and Y. For the sake of brevity, other constructs described by Burrows, Abadi and Needham [1990] will not be introduced here.

The postulates of BAN logic □ First, a point about notation. To express that the statement Z follows from a conjunction of statements X and Y, say, we write:

$$\frac{X,Y}{Z}$$

The main postulates – deduction rules – of BAN logic are as follows:

The message meaning rule:

$$\frac{P \text{ believes } P \overset{K}{\leftrightarrow} Q, P \text{ sees } \{X\}_K}{P \text{ believes } (Q \text{ said } X)}$$

We can interpret this postulate as follows: if P believes that it shares a secret key K with Q, and if P receives a message containing X encrypted with K, then P is entitled to believe that Q once said X (that is, that Q believed X and included X in a message). Note that this rule is valid only under two important assumptions. First, X must contain a recognisable datum to prove that the key K was used for encryption (and not some other key). Second, P must be able to tell that the message is not a replay of a message sent previously by itself, nor of one sent by any trusted principal which also knows K.

The nonce-verification rule:

$$\frac{P \text{ believes fresh}(X), P \text{ believes } (Q \text{ said } X)}{P \text{ believes } (Q \text{ believes } X)}$$

If P believes that Q once said X, then P believes that Q once believed X, by definition. But does Q **believe** X currently? The nonce-verification rule says that, if we have the additional assertion that P **believes** X is fresh, then P must **believe** that Q currently **believes** X. Note that X must not be encrypted – otherwise Q could merely have echoed an encrypted statement in which it does not necessarily believe.

The jurisdiction rule:

$$\frac{P \text{ believes } (Q \text{ controls } X), P \text{ believes } (Q \text{ believes } X)}{P \text{ believes } X}$$

This rule formalizes the notion of what it means for a principal to have jurisdiction over a statement: if P **believes** that Q has jurisdiction over whether or not X is true, and if P **believes** that Q **believes** it to be true, then P must **believe** in it also, since Q is an authority on the matter as far as P is concerned.

There are also various postulates for decomposing messages and for judging their freshness, for example:

(a) $\dfrac{P \text{ sees } (X, Y)}{P \text{ sees } X}$, (b) $\dfrac{P \text{ believes fresh}(X)}{P \text{ believes fresh}(X,Y)}$, (c) $\dfrac{P \text{ believes } (Q \text{ believes}(X,Y))}{P \text{ believes } (Q \text{ believes } X)}$

Informally, (a) states that a principal can observe each component of a message if it observes all of it; (b) states that a combination of components of a message is fresh if one of the components is fresh and (c) rests on our intuition that belief in a combination of several message components implies belief in them individually.

Further important postulates are given by Burrows, Abadi and Needham [1990], concerning public keys and shared secrets; but these are not necessary for this outline of the application of BAN logic to the Needham-Schroeder protocol, and they are omitted for brevity.

Applying BAN logic to the Needham-Schroeder protocol □ The explicit assumptions of the Needham-Schroeder protocol are as follows. These assumptions are explicit in the sense that they are mentioned or implied in the explication given in [Needham and Schroeder 1978]. However, it will shortly be seen that an extra assumption must be made in order to meet the security goals. The same notation is used for keys and nonces as in the description of the protocol given above; in particular, principals A and B obtain a secret key through an authentication server S.

Needham-Schroeder assumptions (explicit)		
A believes:	*B believes*:	*S believes*:
$A \overset{K_A}{\leftrightarrow} S$	$B \overset{K_B}{\leftrightarrow} S$	$A \overset{K_A}{\leftrightarrow} S, B \overset{K_B}{\leftrightarrow} S$
S controls $A \overset{K_{AB}}{\leftrightarrow} B$	S controls $A \overset{K_{AB}}{\leftrightarrow} B$	$A \overset{K_{AB}}{\leftrightarrow} B$
S controls fresh($A \overset{K_{AB}}{\leftrightarrow} B$)		fresh($A \overset{K_{AB}}{\leftrightarrow} B$)
fresh(N_A)	fresh(N_B)	

The goals of the Needham-Schroeder protocol are that A and B each believe they share the secret key K_{AB}, and that moreover they each believe that the other believes it:

| | Authentication goals | |
A believes:		B believes:
$A \overset{K_{AB}}{\leftrightarrow} B$		$A \overset{K_{AB}}{\leftrightarrow} B$
B believes $A \overset{K_{AB}}{\leftrightarrow} B$		A believes $A \overset{K_{AB}}{\leftrightarrow} B$

The main goals A **believes** $A \overset{K_{AB}}{\leftrightarrow} B$ and B **believes** $A \overset{K_{AB}}{\leftrightarrow} B$ are to allow A and B to communicate in private subsequently. The subsidiary goals in the last row are not general authentication goals, however, and indeed whether they are ever required is debatable. Informally, they amount to no more than that A and B each believe that the other is present, by virtue of the fact that it has used the secret key. But presence is itself a very limited notion, since it applies only to a single point in any protocol. Nothing follows from the other's presence in terms of future messages – which must all be treated with fresh skepticism.

The authentication protocol is analysed by first transforming each message into an *idealized message*, which contain only nonces and statements that are implicitly asserted by the sender of the message (if the sender is genuine, then it **believes** the statements). Note that only encrypted message contents are relevant to this analysis; clear text can provide no security and is only included in actual messages for convenience.

Message	Idealized Message
1. $A \rightarrow$ S: A, B, N_A	
2. $S \rightarrow$ A: $\{N_A, B, K_{AB}, \{K_{AB}, A\}_{K_B}\}_{K_A}$	$\{N_A, A \overset{K_{AB}}{\leftrightarrow} B, \textbf{fresh}(A \overset{K_{AB}}{\leftrightarrow} B),$ $\{A \overset{K_{AB}}{\leftrightarrow} B\}_{K_B}\}_{K_A}$
3. $A \rightarrow$ B: $\{K_{AB}, A\}_{K_B}$	$\{A \overset{K_{AB}}{\leftrightarrow} B\}_{K_B}$

The idealized version of Message 2 contains the statements $A \overset{K_{AB}}{\leftrightarrow} B$, $\textbf{fresh}(A \overset{K_{AB}}{\leftrightarrow} B)$ and $\{A \overset{K_{AB}}{\leftrightarrow} B\}_{K_B}$. Although these statements do not appear explicitly, S implicitly asserts them by sending the message in the context of the protocol. The message-meaning rule can now be applied using the first of these statements:

$$\frac{A \textbf{ believes} A \overset{K_A}{\leftrightarrow} S, A \textbf{ sees } \{M\}_{K_A}}{A \textbf{ believes } (S \textbf{ said } M)}$$

where $\qquad M = (N_A, A \overset{K_{AB}}{\leftrightarrow} B, \textbf{fresh}(A \overset{K_{AB}}{\leftrightarrow} B))$

Since M contains N_A, applying postulate (b) above gives:

$$A \textbf{ believes fresh}(M)$$

By the nonce-verification rule:

$$\frac{A \textbf{ believes fresh } (M), A \textbf{ believes } (S \textbf{ said } M)}{A \textbf{ believes } (S \textbf{ believes } M)}$$

We expand M and apply postulate (c) to obtain:

$$\frac{A \textbf{ believes } (S \textbf{ believes } (N_A, A \overset{K_{AB}}{\leftrightarrow} B, \textbf{fresh}(A \overset{K_{AB}}{\leftrightarrow} B)))}{A \textbf{ believes } (S \textbf{ believes } A \overset{K_{AB}}{\leftrightarrow} B)}$$

We deduce similarly that A **believes** (S **believes fresh** ($A \overset{K_{AB}}{\leftrightarrow} B$)). Now the jurisdiction rule can be applied using the assumption that A **believes** (S **controls** $A \overset{K_{AB}}{\leftrightarrow} B$):

$$\frac{A \textbf{ believes } (S \textbf{ controls } A \overset{K_{AB}}{\leftrightarrow} B), A \textbf{ believes } (S \textbf{ believes } A \overset{K_{AB}}{\leftrightarrow} B)}{A \textbf{ believes } A \overset{K_{AB}}{\leftrightarrow} B}$$

And similarly:

$$\frac{A \textbf{ believes } (S \textbf{ controls fresh}(A \overset{K_{AB}}{\leftrightarrow} B)), A \textbf{ believes } (S \textbf{ believes fresh}(A \overset{K_{AB}}{\leftrightarrow} B))}{A \textbf{ believes fresh}(A \overset{K_{AB}}{\leftrightarrow} B)}$$

In summary, A **believes** $A \overset{K_{AB}}{\leftrightarrow} B$ and A **believes fresh**($A \overset{K_{AB}}{\leftrightarrow} B$). What of B? By the message-meaning rule applied to Message 3, B **believes** (S **said** $A \overset{K_{AB}}{\leftrightarrow} B$). But it cannot be deduced that B **believes** (S **believes** $A \overset{K_{AB}}{\leftrightarrow} B$) since B has no evidence that **fresh**($A \overset{K_{AB}}{\leftrightarrow} B$). Message 3 could be a replay of one sent by S in a previous run of the protocol. It is necessary to make the additional *assumption*: B **believes fresh**($A \overset{K_{AB}}{\leftrightarrow} B$). Only then can the nonce-verification and jurisdiction rules be used to deduce that B **believes** $A \overset{K_{AB}}{\leftrightarrow} B$.

Now for the remainder of the protocol. According to Burrows, Abadi and Needham [1989], the idealized messages are as follows:

Message	Idealized Message
4. B → A: $\{N_B\}_{K_{AB}}$	$\{N_B, A \overset{K_{AB}}{\leftrightarrow} B\}_{K_{AB}}$
5. A → B: $\{N_B - 1\}_{K_{AB}}$	$\{N_B, A \overset{K_{AB}}{\leftrightarrow} B\}_{K_{AB}}$

At Step 4, by the message meaning rule we have that A **believes** (B **said** $A \overset{K_{AB}}{\leftrightarrow} B$); and the above analysis of Steps 1–3 showed that A **believes fresh**($A \overset{K_{AB}}{\leftrightarrow} B$). By the nonce-verification rule, it can be deduced that A **believes** (B **believes** $A \overset{K_{AB}}{\leftrightarrow} B$). At Step 5 it can similarly be deduced that B **believes** (A **believes** $A \overset{K_{AB}}{\leftrightarrow} B$); the only difference is that B **believes fresh**($A \overset{K_{AB}}{\leftrightarrow} B$) is deduced from the presence of the nonce N_B.

However, it can be argued that the idealization given in Burrows, Abadi and Needham [1989] of the message at Step 4 is incorrect. This is because the message contains no recognisable text for checking that it was encrypted with the key K_{AB} as opposed to any other key. The message that A receives is merely a bit string, which could in principle represent any value N' encrypted by some key K', for which $\{N'\}_{K'} = \{N_B\}_{K_{AB}}$. The message at step 4 has no idealized form. It cannot, therefore, be deduced that A **believes** (B **believes** $A \overset{K_{AB}}{\leftrightarrow} B$). Note that this argument does not affect the idealization of Step 5: the deduction that B **believes** (A **believes** $A \overset{K_{AB}}{\leftrightarrow} B$) stands.

The foregoing illustrates the point that idealizing messages is an activity which leaves room for argument. This is an important point, since an analysis carried out using BAN logic is only as good as the informal protocol idealization upon which it rests.

Applying the BAN logic postulates can itself be tedious and is not immune to error. The postulates have been encoded for the Jape proof editor [Bornat and Sufrin 1993], which assists in the interactive construction of proofs. In addition to automatically applying the postulates as directed by the user, Jape can suggest applications that lead to given statements. The user can therefore work back towards the assumptions from the statement to be proved, which is sometimes easier than forward reasoning.

Other formal theories of security □ BAN logic is not the only formal system for reasoning about security and authentication. The need for formal methods to validate the design of security systems is now widely recognized and this is an active area of research. The goal of the research is to produce methods for demonstrating that a given set of protocols and security mechanisms satisfy a required security policy, addressing the need that users have for security validation mentioned in Section 16.1.

For example, Lampson et al. [1992] have developed an extensive theory of authentication and trust , based on the notion of a minimal trusted computing base (TCB), in which the trustworthiness of each resource that is not included in the TCB is formally derivable. The simple notion of principal is extended to include communication channels and a **speaks for** (written $\Rightarrow$) relation between principals is introduced. A **hand-off** rule is postulated:

$$(A \text{ says } (B \Rightarrow A)) \supset (B \Rightarrow A)$$

enabling a principal to allow another principal to **speak for** it. This is necessary, for example, since the TCB does not include all of the communication channels required to implement any system, and it would be very inconvenient for each channel to have to be separately known to, and authenticated by, the authentication server. It is also useful when a server is required to perform an operation on behalf of a particular client (eliminating the need which might otherwise arise for the server to assume privileges greater than those of all of its clients).

A formal system called Security Logic (SL) is described by Glasgow et al. [1992] for reasoning about security policies – as opposed to the authentication mechanisms formalized by BAN logic. Security policies are taken to concern secrecy and integrity in a distributed system. Secrecy is formally translated into propositions about subjects (principals), and what they have permission to know; integrity is translated into propositions about what these subjects are obligated to know. An example of a proposition related to secrecy is 'Jones has permission to know the contents of Smith's files'. An example related to integrity is for a server to be obligated to know certain information as it was supplied by a set of clients.

Knowledge, permission and obligation have all been formalized in modal logics [Hughes and Cresswell 1972], and SL is in part based upon this work. Moreover, SL incorporates temporal logic [Rescher and Urquhart 1971] to describe the security properties of a system as it develops over time. Permission is similar to a safety property, and obligation is similar to a liveness property. An example of a secrecy property which a security policy might stipulate is that whenever a subject s knows a formula f, then s

has permission to know *f*. An example of an integrity policy is that if *s* is obliged to know *f*, then *s* will eventually know *f*. Further examples are given by Glasgow *et al.* [1992].

16.6 Digital signatures

Documents such as contracts and cheques are signed in handwriting and then transmitted to other parties. Handwritten signatures are intended to enable any person who receives a signed document to verify that the document was originally produced by the signatory and that it has not subsequently been altered. A handwritten signature also commits the signatory – a person who has signed a document cannot subsequently repudiate it.

Handwritten signatures provide only an imperfect solution to these requirements:

- Forged signatures are hard to detect without genuine samples to compare them with and even then they may go undetected.

- A handwritten signature does little to prevent the alteration of a document, although the use of a pen does serve to distinguish the original document from photocopies of it.

- The signatory may accidentally or deliberately be deceived into signing or be forced to sign a document and under those conditions, the signatory may well be able to repudiate their signature subsequently.

- Witnesses' signatures are often added to a document to authenticate the main signature, but they may suffer from similar weaknesses.

Despite these imperfections, handwritten signatures are widely used as an authentication technique for conventional documents. A handwritten signature testifies that the document was produced with the knowledge of the signatory and that it was not subsequently altered. Handwritten signatures are not applicable to computer-based documents. (The attachment of digital images of handwritten signatures has no merit, since a digital image of a signature can be copied and appended to any computer-based document at any time.) Let us see whether the ideal properties of signatures outlined in the first paragraph of this section can be achieved for computer-based documents.

In computer systems, documents or messages may be originated under the authority of one principal, transmitted to another and subsequently retransmitted to others. It is often important that each of the recipients should be able to verify that the claimed originator of a document is the real originator, that the document has not subsequently been altered, and that the originator will not be able to repudiate the document subsequently.

In short, a digital signature that has the same authentication and legally binding functions as a handwritten signature is required. The requirement differs from that for an authentication and key distribution service in that once a signature is attached to an electronic document, it should be possible for any principal that receives a copy of the message from any source to verify that the document was originally sent by the signatory, and that it has not been altered in transit.

An electronic document or message M can be 'signed' by a principal A by encrypting a copy of M in a key K_A and attaching it to a plain-text copy of M and A's identifier. The signed document then consists of $<M,A,\{M\}_{K_A}>$. The purpose of appending a signature to a document is to enable any principal that subsequently receives the document to verify that it was indeed originated by A and that its contents, M, have not been altered subsequently.

The verification of the signature proceeds differently depending on whether secret-key or public-key encryption was used to produce the signature. We describe the two cases below.

To reduce the size of digital signatures for potentially large documents a *digest function D* is used to produce a characteristic value that uniquely identifies the message to be signed. The characteristic value is a fixed-length binary string derived from the message in a manner similar to a checksum or hash function. Digest functions are sometimes also called secure hash functions. They must be carefully designed to ensure that $D(M)$ is different from $D(M')$ for all likely pairs of messages M and M'. (If there are any pairs of different messages M and M' such $D(M) = D(M')$, then a duplicitous principal could send a signed copy of M, but when confronted with it, claim that M' was originally sent, and that it must have been altered in transit.) A message digest function known as MD5 has been specifically designed to meet this requirement and is proposed by Rivest [1992] for use in secure mail and other applications in the Internet. Mitchell *et al.* [1992] survey digital signature techniques in depth, with a useful discussion of message digest functions.

Digital signatures with public keys □ It is very simple to produce the required result using public-key encryption techniques. The originator A of a message M can sign it by attaching a copy of $D(M)$ encrypted in A's secret key $K_{Aprivate}$ and sending it to any other principal. The recipient, and any principal that may subsequently receive a copy of the message, can verify the signature by using A's public key $K_{Apublic}$ to decrypt the signature to get $D(M)$ and comparing it with its own computation of $D(M)$. Thus in the public-key case, no server is involved, except a key distribution server to supply a copy of A's public key to any principal that does not already have it. The protocol for A to send a signed document to B and for B to validate the signature would be:

Header	Message	Notes
1. A → B:	$M, A,$ $\{D(M)\}_{KAprivate}$	A sends the original message and the signature to B.
2. B → S:	A	B requests A's public key from S.
3. S → B:	$A, K_{Apublic}$	S supplies A's public key $K_{Apublic}$. B uses it to decrypt the signature received in Message 1 and compare it with a newly-computed value for $D(M)$.

Digital signatures with secret keys □ Needham and Schroeder [1978] have described a digital signature service that is based on the authentication service described in the same paper and already discussed in Section 16.3 above. We shall now describe their proposed protocol steps by which a principal A sends a signed message M to another principal B using secret keys:

Header	Message	Notes
1. A → S:	A, {D(M)}$_{K_A}$	A computes $D(M)$, the digest of the message and encrypts $D(M)$ with A's secret key and sends it to the authentication server.
2. S → A:	{A, D(M), t}$_{K_S}$	The server makes a signed and dated certification of A's signature on the document. It does this by making a composite text containing A's name, $D(M)$ and a timestamp t and encrypts it with its secret key. It sends the resulting certificate back to A.
3. A → B:	M, {A, D(M), t}$_{K_S}$	A sends the original message and the certificate in a message to B.
4. B → S:	B, {A, D(M), t}$_{K_S}$	B saves a copy of the message and the certificate and then sends the certificate to the authentication server for decrypting.
5. S → B:	{A, D(M), t}$_{K_B}$	The server decrypts the certificate. It then uses B's secret key to encrypt the resulting plain text and sends it to B, where it is decrypted.

By this stage, B has two things – the message that it received from A, containing the name of A and the message text; and the plain text certificate, A, $D(M)$. It uses the digest function to compute the value of $D(M)$ from the message text and compares it with the value that it received from the authentication server. If they match then B can be confident that the message is the one that A originally produced and that A will not repudiate it because:

- The authentication server verifies A's signature at Step 2. User B trusts the authentication server and has a message from the server stating that A's signature has been verified.

- It would be difficult for A to claim that the signature was forged, for B has a copy of a certificate that can be checked with the authentication server. A could not claim that B had forged the certificate, for B does not know the server's secret key.

16.7 Summary

The openness of distributed systems exposes them to security threats that are well-known in other contexts: leakage of information, tampering with information, stealing of resources and vandalism. The methods by which these threats are realized (known as the *modus operandi* in criminology) are based on illicit intervention on communication channels. They include eavesdropping, masquerading, tampering with messages and replaying old messages.

Most attacks are perpetrated by legitimate users. Communication channels such as local area networks are open to all of the computer users in an organization. Attackers who are not legitimate users of a network or of the host computer that is the subject of an attack may attempt to infiltrate it in several ways including the use of viruses, network worms and Trojan horse programs.

There is now a well-developed body of knowledge about techniques for the protection of distributed systems against such threats and a full theoretical basis for reasoning about their efficacy is in the process of development. The techniques are based upon the use of cryptography, not only to conceal information but also to authenticate it.

Methods for encrypting data fall into two classes, secret-key cryptography, such as the DES algorithm, in which a secret key is required which is known only to the two principals engaged in a private communication; and public-key cryptography, in which a pair of keys $K_{Apublic}$ and $K_{Aprivate}$ are assigned to a principal A with the property that each is the inverse of the other with respect to the encryption function, but a knowledge of $K_{Apublic}$ provides no help in obtaining $K_{Aprivate}$. $K_{Aprivate}$ is kept as a secret by A and is used to decrypt all the encrypted messages that A receives. $K_{Apublic}$ is published and can be used by any principal wishing to communicate privately with A. Public-key encryption is convenient because it avoids the need to transmit secret keys across a network, but its performance is significantly worse than secret-key encryption and if used to encrypt all client-server or group communication it would seriously degrade the performance of distributed systems. Hence public-key encryption is often used only to transmit secret keys which are then used in secret-key algorithms such as DES to encrypt the remainder of the conversation.

The authentication of principals depends upon the existence of a trusted third party. In distributed systems this takes the form of an authentication service. An authentication service is implemented by a server holding the passwords of the users that it authenticates. When a user has been authenticated the authentication service supplies 'tickets' to the client module acting on their behalf. When the tickets are passed to other services they enable other services to check the authenticity of the sender. Kerberos is a service designed to implement this idea in a practical form. It has been implemented successfully and is now used widely for the purpose.

A logic of authentication has been developed that may be used to verify the security properties of authentication protocols. The logic can be used to prove statements such as 'A believes that K_{AB} is a good key for its communication with B' where 'is a good key' has a precisely defined meaning. Further research on security logics is in hand, and these may eventually be adequate to provide convincing proofs of other aspects of privacy and integrity for distributed systems.

Digital signatures can be constructed in order to authenticate the origins of electronic documents. Digital signatures may be based on public keys or secret keys. When public keys are used the method is very straightforward: the signature for a document is simply a 'digest' of the document encrypted in the secret key of the document's originator. Any principal wishing to check the authenticity of the signature simply has to obtain the originator's public key, use it to decrypt the signature and compare the result with another application of the digest function to the document.

Exercises

16.1   Define these types of attack: *eavesdropping*, *masquerading*, *message tampering* and *replaying*. Give an example of a security violation that might be produced by each in the examination paper scenario outlined on page 478.

pages 478, 480

16.2   Which of the above types of attack are not prevented simply by the encryption of client-server communication using a session key?

pages 480, 496

16.3   Define the terms: *encryption function*, *encryption key*, *session key*, *one-way function*, *plain text*, *cipher text*. Can data in formats other than text be encrypted?

page 485

16.4   Estimate the computing time required to crack a DES key by a brute-force attack using a 100 MIPS (million instruction per second) workstation and 10,000 MIPS parallel processor.

page 487

16.5   Explain the need for a secure key distribution service:

i)   when secret key encryption is used;

ii)   when public key encryption is used.

page 490

16.6   Define the terms: *principal*, *authenticator*, *capability*.

pages 479, 495

16.7   In the Needham and Shroeder authentication protocol with secret keys, explain why the Message 2 includes the identity of B.

page 492

16.8   In the Needham and Shroeder authentication protocol with secret keys, explain why the following version of Message 5 is not secure:

$$A \rightarrow B: \quad \{N_B\}_{K_{AB}}$$

page 492

16.9   What is a *nonce*? Explain why each of the nonces used in the Needham and Shroeder protocol is included, giving an example of the type of attack by an intruder against which each is designed to guard and the type of security breach that could result if they were not included.

page 492

16.10 The Kerberos system requires a highly-secure Kerberos server. What information does this server hold and how is that information used to establish a session key known only to the Kerberos server and the user?

page 495

16.11 Outline the sequence of messages exchanged between a user's workstation, the Kerberos server, and a secure file server, for the user to gain access to his or her secured files.

page 496

16.12 Explain why the Kerberos system can be confident of the user's identity without the user sending any password-related information over the network.

page 497

16.13 How can a user change his or her password in the Kerberos system?

page 497

16.14 Suggest a mechanism by which the user can test the authenticity of a server (for example, a file server), and show the messages that would be exchanged.

page 497

16.15 Explain how a Kerberos ticket is intended to be used and how it achieves its security goals. What risks are inherent in the use of a timestamp and how could they be addressed?

page 497

16.16 Explain the assumptions under which the message meaning rule can be validly applied, and discuss how these can be ensured in practice.

page 505

16.17 Discuss whether the following should be considered valid postulates:

i)
$$\frac{P \; \mathbf{believes} \, (X, \, Y)}{P \; \mathbf{believes} \, X}$$

ii)
$$\frac{P \; \mathbf{believes} \, P \overset{K}{\leftrightarrow} Q, \, P \; \mathbf{sees} \, \{X\}_K}{P \; \mathbf{sees} \, X}$$

iii)
$$\frac{P \; \mathbf{sees} \, X, \, P \; \mathbf{sees} \, Y}{P \; \mathbf{sees} \, (X, \, Y)}$$

page 507

16.18 We introduce the notation P **hasPublic** K to mean that the principal P has a public key K. The corresponding secret key K^{-1} is known to P and will never be discovered by a principal other than one trusted by P. Is the following postulate reasonable?

$$\frac{P \; \mathbf{believes} \, (P \; \mathbf{hasPublic} \; K), \, P \; \mathbf{sees} \, \{X\}_K}{P \; \mathbf{sees} \, X}$$

page 507

16.19   What is wrong with the following? Suggest a correct version.

$$\frac{P \textbf{ believes } (Q \textbf{ hasPublic } K),\ P \textbf{ sees } \{X\}_K}{P \textbf{ believes } (Q \textbf{ said } X)}$$

page 507

16.20   Produce an analysis of the Kerberos authentication protocol using BAN logic.

page 508

DISTRIBUTED SHARED MEMORY

This chapter describes distributed shared memory (DSM), an abstraction used for sharing data between processes in computers that do not share physical memory. The motivation for DSM is that it allows a shared memory programming model to be employed, which has some advantages over message-based models. For example, programmers do not have to marshal data items in DSM.

A central problem in implementing DSM is how to achieve good performance that is retained as systems scale to large numbers of computers. Accesses to DSM involve potential underlying network communication. Processes competing for the same or neighbouring data items may cause large amounts of communication to occur. The amount of communication is strongly related to the consistency model of a DSM – the model that determines which, of possibly many, written values will be returned when a process reads from a DSM location.

The chapter discusses DSM design issues such as the consistency model and implementation issues such as whether copies of the same data item are invalidated or updated when one copy is written. It goes on to discuss invalidation protocols in more detail. Finally, it describes release consistency – a relatively weak consistency model which is adequate for many purposes and relatively cheap to implement.

17.1 Introduction

Distributed shared memory (DSM) is an abstraction used for sharing data between computers that do not share physical memory. Processes access DSM by reads and updates to what appears to be ordinary memory within their address space. However, an underlying run-time system ensures transparently that processes executing at different computers observe the updates made by one another. It is as though the processes access a single shared memory, but in fact the physical memory is distributed (see Figure 17.1).

The main point of DSM is that it spares the programmer the concerns of message passing when writing applications that might otherwise have to use it. DSM is primarily a tool for parallel applications or for any distributed application or group of applications in which individual shared data items can be accessed directly. DSM is in general less appropriate in client-server systems, where clients normally view server-held resources as abstract data and access them by request (for reasons of modularity and protection). However, servers can provide DSM that is shared between clients. For example, memory-mapped files that are shared and for which some degree of consistency is maintained are a form of DSM. (Mapped files were introduced with the MULTICS operating system [Organick 1972].)

Message passing cannot be avoided altogether, of course, in a distributed system: in the absence of physically shared memory, the DSM run-time support has to send updates in messages between computers. DSM systems manage replicated data: each computer has a local copy of recently accessed data items stored in DSM, for speed of access. The problems of implementing DSM are in this respect related to those discussed in Chapter 11, as well as those of caching shared files discussed in Chapter 7.

DSM has been an active area of research since the early 1980s. One of the first notable examples of a DSM implementation was the Apollo Domain file system [Leach *et al.* 1983], in which processes hosted by different workstations share files by mapping them simultaneously into their address spaces. This example shows that distributed shared memory can be persistent. That is, it may outlast the execution of any process or group of processes that accesses it, and be shared by different groups of processes over time.

Figure 17.1   The distributed shared memory abstraction.

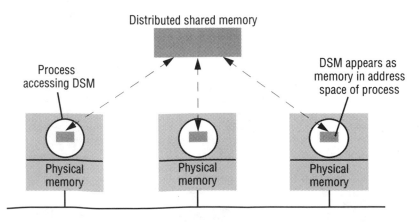

The significance of DSM has grown alongside the development of shared-memory multiprocessors (see the subsection on them in Section 2.2 for a brief description). Much research has gone into investigating algorithms suitable for parallel computation on these multiprocessors, and into the use of hardware caching for maximizing the number of processors that can be sustained by them [Dubois *et al.* 1988]. However, the practical limit stands at about 10 or 20 processors, where these are connected to memory modules over a common bus; after this the benefit of adding extra processors tails off rapidly.

Distributed memory multiprocessors and networked distributed systems, on the other hand, scale to far greater numbers of processors or computers. Emerging shared-memory multiprocessor designs employ memory modules that are interconnected by high-speed networks, although processors see a single address space. A central question that has been pursued by the DSM and multiprocessor research communities is whether the investment in knowledge of shared memory algorithms and the associated software can be directly transferred to a more scalable distributed memory architecture.

Message passing versus DSM □ As a communication mechanism, DSM is comparable to message passing rather than to request-reply-based communication, since its application to parallel processing, in particular, entails the use of asynchronous communication. The DSM and message passing approaches to programming can be contrasted as follows:

Programming model: Under the message passing model, variables have to be marshalled from one process, transmitted and unmarshalled into other variables at the receiving process. By contrast, with shared memory the processes involved share variables directly, so no marshalling is necessary – even of pointers to shared variables – and of course no separate communication operations are necessary. Most implementations allow variables stored in DSM to be named and accessed similarly to ordinary unshared variables. In favour of message passing, on the other hand, is that it allows processes to communicate while being protected from one another by having private address spaces, whereas processes sharing DSM can, for example, cause one another to fail by erroneously altering data. Furthermore, when message passing is used between heterogeneous computers, marshalling takes care of differences in data representation; but how can memory be shared between computers with, for example, different integer representations?

Synchronization between processes is achieved in the message model through message passing primitives themselves, using techniques such as the lock server implementation discussed in Chapter 10. In the case of DSM, synchronization is via normal constructs for shared memory programming such as locks and semaphores (although these require different implementations in the distributed memory environment). Chapter 6 discussed briefly such synchronization objects in the context of programming with threads.

Finally, since DSM can be made persistent, processes communicating via DSM may execute with non-overlapping lifetimes. A process can leave information in an agreed location for the other to examine when it runs. By contrast, processes communicating via message passing must execute at the same time.

Efficiency: Experiments show that certain parallel programs developed for DSM can be made to perform about as well as functionally equivalent programs written for message passing platforms on the same hardware [Carter *et al.* 1991] – at least in the case of relatively small numbers of computers (ten or so). However, this result cannot be generalized. The performance of a program based on DSM depends upon many factors, as we shall discuss below – particularly the pattern of data sharing (such as whether an item is updated by several processes).

There is a difference in the visibility of costs associated with the two types of programming. In message passing, all remote data accesses are explicit, and therefore the programmer is always aware of whether a particular operation is in-process or involves the expense of communication. Using DSM, however, any particular read or update may or may not involve communication by the underlying run-time support. Whether it does or not depends upon such factors as whether the data have been accessed before, and the sharing pattern between processes at different computers.

There is no definitive answer as to whether DSM is preferable to message passing for any particular application. DSM is a promising tool whose ultimate status depends upon the efficiency with which it can be implemented.

Main approaches to DSM □   There are three main approaches to the implementation of distributed shared memory, which respectively involve the use of hardware, virtual memory or library support. Note that they are not necessarily mutually exclusive:

Hardware-based: Some multiprocessor architectures (for example, Dash [Lenoski *et al.* 1992], PLUS [Bisiani and Ravishankar 1990]) rely on specialized hardware to handle load and store instructions applied to addresses in DSM, and to communicate with remote memory modules as necessary in order to implement them. These hierarchical designs, in which clusters of processors and memory modules are connected via a high-speed network, are aimed at orders of magnitude more processors than the limit of 10 or so that can be accommodated over a common bus: the prototype Dash multiprocessor has 64 nodes.

Page-based: Ivy [Li and Hudak 1989], Munin [Carter *et al.* 1991], Mirage [Fleisch and Popek 1989], Clouds [Dasgupta *et al.* 1991], Choices [Sane *et al.* 1990], COOL [Lea *et al.* 1993] and Mether [Minnich and Farber 1989] all implement DSM as a region of virtual memory occupying the same address range in the address space of every participating process. (A case study of Clouds is given in Chapter 18.) In each case the kernel maintains the consistency of data within DSM regions as part of page fault handling.

Library-based: Some languages or language extensions such as Orca [Bal *et al.* 1990] and Linda [Carriero and Gelernter 1989] support forms of DSM. In this type of implementation sharing is not implemented through the virtual memory system but by communication between instances of the language run-time. Processes make library calls inserted by a compiler when they access data items in DSM. The libraries access local data items and communicate as necessary to maintain consistency. Processes may also execute threads to handle incoming messages requesting operations related to DSM.

Figure 17.2 Mether system program

```
#include "world.h"
struct shared {
      int   a,b;
};
Program Writer:
main()
{
      struct shared *p;
      methersetup();                         /* Initialize the Mether run-time */
      p = (struct shared *)METHERBASE;
                                             /* overlay structure on METHER segment */
      p->a = p->b = 0;                       /* initialize fields to zero */
      while(TRUE){                           /* continuously update structure fields */
            p ->a = p ->a + 1;
            p ->b = p ->b - 1;
      }

}
Program Reader:
main()
{
      struct shared *p;
      methersetup();
      p = (struct shared *)METHERBASE;
      while(TRUE){                           /* read the fields once every second */
            printf("a = %d, b = %d\n", p ->a, p ->b);
            sleep(1);
      }

}
```

The requirement for specialized hardware makes the first approach currently suitable only for multiprocessors; this chapter concentrates on the use of software to implement DSM on standard computers. (Even with hardware support, high-level software techniques may be used to minimize the amount of communication between components of a DSM implementation.) Of the other two, the page-based approach is receiving the most attention. This is primarily because it imposes no particular structure on the DSM, which appears as a sequence of bytes; and it avoids the user-level overheads associated with libraries. Modern microkernels such as Mach and Chorus provide virtual memory facilities which support DSM (and other memory abstractions – the Mach virtual memory facilities are described in Chapter 18). The advent of microprocessors such as the MIPS R4000 and DEC Alpha with their 64-bit address spaces widens the scope for this form of DSM by relaxing constraints on address space management [Bartoli *et al.* 1993]. In object-based systems such as Clouds, Choices and

COOL, page-based DSM allows threads to execute in parallel in objects that are replicated at multiple computers.

The example in Figure 17.2 is of two C programs, *Reader* and *Writer*, which communicate via the page-based DSM provided by the Mether system [Minnich and Farber 1989]. *Writer* updates two fields in a structure overlaid upon the beginning of the Mether DSM segment (beginning at address *METHERBASE*), and *Reader* periodically prints out the values it reads from these fields.

The two programs contain no special operations; they are compiled into machine instructions that access a common range of virtual memory addresses (starting at *METHERBASE*). Mether runs over conventional Sun workstation and network hardware.

17.2 Design and implementation issues

This section discusses design and implementation options concerning the main features that characterize a DSM system. These are: the structure of data held in DSM; the synchronization model used to access DSM consistently at the application level; the DSM consistency model, which governs the consistency of data values accessed from different computers; the update options for communicating written values between computers; the granularity of sharing in a DSM implementation; and the problem of thrashing.

Structure

What is the application programmer's view of the contents of DSM? Three main approaches have been implemented, which view DSM as being composed respectively of bytes, shared objects or immutable data items.

Byte-oriented: This is the view illustrated above by the Mether system. It is also the view of, for example, the Ivy system. It allows applications (and language implementations) to impose whatever data structures they want on the shared memory. Byte-oriented DSM is accessed as ordinary virtual memory.

Shared objects: An advantage of viewing shared memory as a collection of objects is that synchronization can be applied at the level of the object operation. Orca views DSM as a collection of shared objects, and automatically serializes operations upon any given object.

Immutable data: Both Agora [Bisiani and Forin 1988] and Linda view DSM as a collection of immutable data items that all processes can read. Processes have to replace data items in the DSM in lieu of modifying them. For example, Linda uses the tuple model. This comprises the notion of tuple space – a collection of immutable tuples with typed data items in their fields – and a set of primitives for accessing tuple space that can be added to any base language. Processes may place tuples in tuple space, and read or extract them from tuple space. Processes select tuples by specifying the number of their fields and their values or types.

The byte-oriented view allows the data types of any language to be superimposed relatively straightforwardly (as long as the DSM is shared between computers of homogeneous architecture – Exercise 17.2 explores the problem of heterogeneous computer architectures).

Synchronization model

Many applications apply constraints concerning the values stored in shared memory. This is as true of applications based on DSM as it is of applications written for shared memory multiprocessors (or indeed for any concurrent programs that share data, such as operating system kernels and multi-threaded servers). For example, if a and b are two variables stored in DSM, then a constraint might be that $a = b$ always. If two or more processes execute the following code:

$a := a + 1;$
$b := b + 1;$

then an inconsistency may arise. Suppose a and b are initially zero, and that Process 1 gets as far as setting a to 1. Before it can increment b, Process 2 sets a to 2 and b to 1. The constraint has been broken. The solution is to make this code fragment into a critical section: to synchronize processes to ensure that only one may execute it at a time [Bacon 1993].

In order to use DSM, then, a distributed synchronization service needs to be provided, which includes familiar constructs such as locks and semaphores. Even when DSM is structured as a set of objects, the implementors of the objects have to be concerned with synchronization. Synchronization constructs are implemented using message passing (see Chapter 10 for a description of a distributed lock server). Special machine instructions such as *test-and-set*, which are used for synchronization in shared memory multiprocessors, are in principle applicable to page-based DSM, but their operation in the distributed case is very inefficient. The most recent DSM implementations, discussed in Section 17.4, take advantage of application synchronization to reduce the amount of update transmission. The DSM then includes synchronization as an integrated component.

Consistency model

DSM implementations employ caching for enhanced performance. In the terminology of Chapter 11, each process has a local replica manager, which holds replicas of some DSM data items. In most implementations, data items are read using local values for efficiency, but updates have to be propagated to the other replica managers. In a page-based DSM implementation, the kernels are replica managers: they cache DSM pages, which they map into the address spaces of local processes sharing DSM. In the Orca implementation, the processes themselves act as replica managers (when they execute library code). If DSM segments are persistent, then one or more storage servers (for example, file servers) will also act as replica managers.

In addition to caching, a DSM implementation could in principle buffer write accesses, and thus amortize communication costs by spreading them over multiple writes. Given that these techniques are available, the question arises of whether DSM

Figure 17.3   Two processes accessing shared variables.

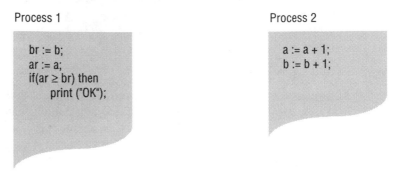

Process 1

```
br := b;
ar := a;
if(ar ≥ br) then
     print ("OK");
```

Process 2

```
a := a + 1;
b := b + 1;
```

memory itself is consistent when they are used. Note that this aspect of consistency, called *memory consistency* [Mosberger 1993], is different from that discussed under the heading of application synchronization above.

Cheriton [1985] describes how forms of DSM can be envisaged for which some degree of inconsistency is acceptable. For example, DSM might be used to store the loads of computers on a network, in order that clients can select the least-loaded computers for running applications. Since such information is by its nature liable to become inaccurate on relatively small time scales, it would be a waste of effort to keep it consistent at all times.

Most applications do, however, have stronger consistency requirements. Care must be taken to give programmers a model that conforms to reasonable expectations of the way memory should behave. Before describing memory consistency requirements in more detail, it is helpful first to look at an example.

Consider an application in which two processes access two variables, a and b (Figure 17.3), which are initialized to zero. Process 2 increments a and b, in that order. Process 1 reads the values of b and a into auxiliary variables br and ar, in that order. Note that there is no application-level synchronization. Intuitively, Process 1 should expect to see one of the following combinations of values, depending upon the points at which the read operations applied to a and b (implied in the statements $br := b$ and $ar := a$) occur with respect to process 2's execution: $ar = 0$, $br = 0$; $ar = 1$, $br = 0$; $ar = 1$, $br = 1$. In other words, the condition $ar \geq br$ should always be satisfied, and Process 1 should print 'OK'. However, a DSM implementation might deliver the updates to a and b out of order to the replica manager for Process 1, in which case the combination $ar = 0$, $br = 1$ could occur.

The reader's immediate reaction to the example just given is probably that the DSM implementation, which reverses the order of two updates, is incorrect. If Process 1 and Process 2 execute together at a single-processor computer, we would assume that the memory subsystem was malfunctioning. However, it may be a correct implementation, in the distributed case, of a consistency model that is weaker than what many of us would intuitively expect, but which nonetheless can be useful and is relatively efficient.

The literature can only be described as inconsistent on the matter of the terms used to describe types of memory consistency model. However, Mosberger [1993] delineates a range of models that have been devised for shared-memory multiprocessors and software DSM systems. The main consistency models that can be practically realized in DSM implementations are sequential consistency and models that are based on weak consistency.

Sequential consistency □ The central question to be asked in order to characterize a particular memory consistency model is this: when a read access is made to a memory location, which write accesses to the location are candidates whose values could be supplied to the read? At the weakest extreme, the answer is: any write that was issued before the read. This model would be obtained if replica managers could delay propagating updates to their peers indefinitely. It is too weak to be useful.

At the strongest extreme, all written values are instantaneously available to all processes: a read returns the most recent write at the time that the read takes place. Unfortunately, this definition is problematic in two respects. First, neither writes nor reads take place at a single point in time, so the meaning of 'most recent' is not always clear. Each type of access has a well-defined point of issue, but they complete at some later time (for example, after message passing has taken place). Secondly, Chapter 10 showed that clocks cannot be synchronized sufficiently accurately in a distributed system to resolve events at this level of granularity. So the relation 'before' (in absolute time) is not a useful one for these events. A model called atomic consistency has been formulated to remove these ambiguities, but it remains impractical for a DSM system; it is described by Mosberger.

Fortunately, it is possible to define useful and practical memory consistency models logically, so that they can be reasoned about and compared with what programmers intuitively expect from memories. The strongest and most important such model is **sequential consistency** [Lamport 1979]. Sequential consistency is similar to one-copy serializability (see Chapter 14) – but it applies to memory systems at the granularity of individual memory operations, rather than transactions. Under it, the result of any execution is equivalent to one in which the following conditions obtain:

• all the reads and writes issued by the individual processes concerned are satisfied in program order – as the programmers of those processes surely expect, and

• the memory operations belonging to different processes occur in some serial order.

The condition can be restated more concretely as follows: no process may read values that conflict with its program order or that of any other participating process. In an actual execution, memory operations may be overlapped and some updates may be ordered differently at different processes, as long as the definition's constraints are not thereby broken. Note that memory operations upon the entire DSM have to be serializable to satisfy the conditions of sequential consistency – and not just the operations on each individual location.

The combination $ar = 0$, $br = 1$ in the above example could not occur under sequential consistency, because Process 1 would be reading values that conflict with Process 2's program order. An example interleaving of the processes' memory accesses is shown in Figure 17.4.

Figure 17.4   An example serialization under sequential consistency.

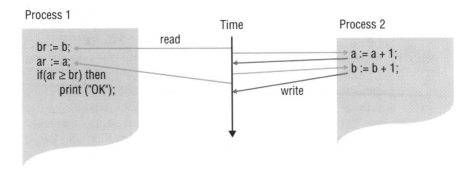

Sequentially consistent DSM could be implemented by using a single server to hold all the shared data, and by making all processes perform reads or writes by sending requests to the server, which globally orders them. This architecture is of course too inefficient for a DSM implementation, and practical means of achieving sequential consistency are described below.

Weak consistency ☐ Dubois *et al.* [1988] developed the weak consistency model in an attempt to avoid the costs of sequential consistency on multiprocessors. This model exploits knowledge of synchronization operations in order to relax memory consistency, while appearing to the programmer to implement sequential consistency (at least, under certain conditions that are beyond the scope of this book). For example, if the programmer uses a lock to implement a critical section, then a DSM system can assume that no other process may access the data items accessed under mutual exclusion within it. It is therefore redundant for the DSM system to propagate updates to these items until the process leaves the critical section. While items are left with 'inconsistent' values some of the time, they are not accessed at those points; the execution appears to be sequentially consistent. Adve and Hill [1990] describe a generalization of this notion called weak ordering: '(A DSM system) is weakly ordered with respect to a synchronization model if and only if it appears sequentially consistent to all software that obeys the synchronization model'. Release consistency, which is a form of weak ordering, will be described in Section 17.4 below; Section 17.5 outlines some other consistency models.

Update options

Two main implementation choices have been devised for propagating updates made by one process to the others: write-update and write-invalidate. These are applicable to a variety of DSM consistency models, including sequential consistency. In outline, the options are as follows:

> *Write-update*: The updates made by a process are made locally and multicast to all other replica managers possessing a copy of the data item, which immediately

Figure 17.5 DSM using write-update.

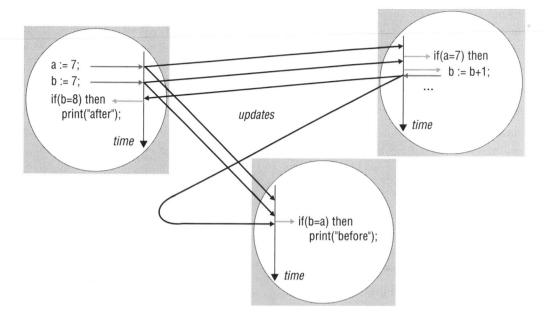

modify the data read by local processes (Figure 17.5). Processes read the local copies of data items, without the need for communication. In addition to allowing multiple readers, several processes may write the same data item at the same time; this is known as *multiple-reader-multiple-writer sharing*.

The memory consistency model that is implemented with write-update depends on several factors, mainly the multicast ordering property. Sequential consistency can be achieved by using multicasts that are totally ordered (see Chapter 11 for a definition of totally ordered multicast), which do not return until the update message has been delivered locally. All processes then agree on the order of updates. The set of reads that take place between any two consecutive updates is well-defined, and their ordering is immaterial to sequential consistency.

Reads are cheap in the write-update option. However, Chapter 11 showed that ordered multicast protocols are relatively expensive to implement in software. Orca uses write-update, and employs the Amoeba multicast protocol described in Chapter 18, which uses hardware support for multicast. Munin supports write-update as an option. A write-update protocol is used with specialized hardware support in the PLUS multiprocessor architecture.

Write-invalidate: This is commonly implemented in the form of multiple-reader-single-writer sharing. At any time, a data item may either be accessed in read-only mode by one or more processes, or it may be read and written by a single process. An item that is currently accessed in read-only mode can be copied indefinitely to other processes. When a process attempts to write to it, a multicast message is first sent to all other copies to invalidate them, and this is acknowledged before the write can take place; the other processes are thereby prevented from reading stale data (that is, data that are not up-to-date). Any processes attempting to access the data item are blocked if a writer exists. Eventually, control is transferred from the writing process and other accesses may take place once the update has been sent. The effect is to process all accesses to the item on a first-come-first-served basis. By the proof given by Lamport [1979], this scheme achieves sequential consistency. We shall see in Section 17.4 that invalidations may be delayed under release consistency.

Under the invalidation scheme, updates are only propagated when data are read, and several updates can take place before communication is necessary. Against this must be placed the cost of invalidating read-only copies before a write can occur. In the multiple-reader-single-writer scheme described, this is potentially expensive. But if the read/write ratio is sufficiently high, then the parallelism obtained by allowing multiple simultaneous readers offsets this cost. Where the read/write ratio is relatively small, a single-reader-single-writer scheme can be more appropriate: that is, one in which at most one process may be granted read-only access at a time.

Granularity

An issue that is related to the structure of DSM is the granularity of sharing. Conceptually, all processes share the entire contents of a DSM. As programs sharing DSM execute, however, only certain parts of the data are actually shared, and then only for certain times during the execution. It would clearly be very wasteful for the DSM implementation always to transmit the entire contents of DSM as processes access and update it. What should be the unit of sharing in a DSM implementation? That is, when a process has written to DSM, which data does the DSM run-time send in order to provide consistent values elsewhere?

We focus here on page-based implementations, although the granularity issue does arise in library-based implementations (see Exercise 17.7 at the end of this chapter). In a page-based DSM, the hardware supports alterations to an address space efficiently in units of pages – essentially by the placement of a new page frame pointer in the page table (see Chapter 6 and, for example, Bacon [1993] for a description of paging). Page sizes can typically range up to 8 kilobytes, so this is an appreciable amount of data that must be transmitted over a network to keep remote copies consistent when an update occurs. By default, the price of the whole page transfer must be paid whether the entire page has been updated, or just one byte of it.

Using a smaller page size – say 512 bytes or 1 kilobyte – does not necessarily lead to an improvement in overall performance. First, in cases where processes do update large amounts of contiguous data, it is better to send one large page rather than several smaller pages in separate updates, because of the fixed software overheads per network packet. Secondly, using a small page as the unit of distribution leads to a large number of units that must be separately administered by the DSM implementation.

To complicate matters further, processes tend to contend more for pages when the page size is large, because the likelihood that the data they access will lie within the same page increases with the page size. Consider, for example, two processes, one of which accesses only data item A and the other accesses only data item B, which lie within the same page (Figure 17.6). For the sake of concreteness, let us assume that one

Figure 17.6   Data items laid out over pages.

process reads A and the other updates B. There is no contention at the application level. However, the entire page must be transmitted between the processes, since the DSM run-time does not by default know which locations in the page have been altered. This phenomenon is known as *false sharing*: two or more processes share parts of a page, but only one in fact accesses each part. In write-invalidate protocols, false sharing can lead to unnecessary invalidations. In write-update protocols, when several writers falsely share data items they may cause them to be overwritten with older versions.

In practice, the choice of the unit of sharing has to be made based on the physical page sizes available, although a unit of several contiguous pages may be taken if the page size is small. The layout of data with respect to page boundaries is an important factor in determining the number of page transfers made when a program executes.

Thrashing

A potential problem with write-invalidate protocols is thrashing. Thrashing is said to occur where the DSM run-time spends an inordinate amount of time invalidating and transferring shared data, compared to the time spent by application processes doing useful work. It occurs when several processes compete for the same data item, or for falsely shared data items. If, for example, one process repeatedly reads a data item that another is regularly updating, then this item will be constantly transferred from the writer and invalidated at the reader. This is an example of a sharing pattern for which write-invalidate is inappropriate, and write-update would be better. The next section describes the Mirage approach to thrashing, in which computers 'own' pages for a minimum period; Section 17.4 describes how Munin allows the programmer to declare access patterns to the DSM system, so it can choose appropriate update options for each data item and avoid thrashing.

17.3 Sequential consistency and Ivy

This section describes methods for implementing sequentially consistent, page-based DSM. It draws upon Ivy [Li and Hudak 1989] as a case study.

The system model □   The basic model to be considered is one in which a collection of processes share a segment of DSM (Figure 17.7). The segment is mapped to the same range of addresses in each process, so that meaningful pointer values can be stored in the segment. The processes execute at computers equipped with a paged memory management unit. We shall assume that there is only one process per computer that accesses the DSM segment. There may in reality be several such processes at a computer. However, these could then share DSM pages directly (the same page frame

Figure 17.7   System model for page-based DSM.

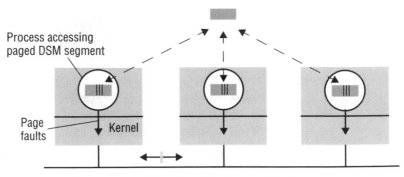

Pages transferred over network

can be used in the page tables used by the different processes). The only complication would be to coordinate fetching and propagating updates to a page when two or more local processes access it. This description ignores such details.

Paging is transparent to the processes; they can logically both read and write any data in DSM. However, the DSM run-time restricts page access permissions in order to maintain consistency when processing reads and writes. Paged memory management units allow the access permissions to a data page to be set to *none*, *read-only* or *read-write*. If a process attempts to exceed the current access permissions, then it takes a read or write page fault, according to the type of access. The page fault handler – which normally runs entirely in the kernel – processes the fault in a special way, to be described below, when it determines that the page belongs to DSM, before returning control to the user process.

This description will ignore the page fault processing that takes place as part of the normal virtual memory implementation. Apart from the fact that DSM segments compete with other segments for page frames, the implementations are independent.

The problem of write-update □ The previous section outlined the general implementation alternatives of write-update and write-invalidation. In practice, invalidation is normally the only option when DSM is page-based. This is because standard kernel-level page fault handling is unsuited to the task of processing updates in the way that the write-update option requires.

To see this, consider that in the write-update case every update has to be multicast to the remaining replicas. Suppose that a page has been write-protected. When a process attempts to write upon the page, it takes a page fault and a handler routine is called. This handler could, in principle, examine the faulting instruction to determine the value and address being written, and multicast the update before restoring write access and returning to complete the faulting instruction.

But now that write access has been restored, subsequent updates to the page will not cause a page fault! To circumvent this, it would be necessary for the page fault handler to set the process into TRACE mode, whereby the processor generates a TRACE exception after each instruction. The TRACE exception handler would turn off write permissions to the page and turn off TRACE mode once more. The whole exercise would be repeated when a write fault next occurred.

Figure 17.8   State transitions under write-invalidation.

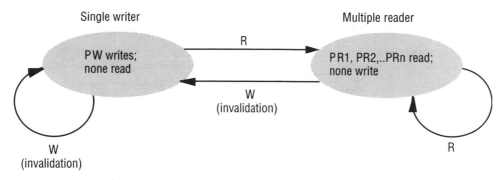

Note: R = read fault occurs; W = write fault occurs.

It is clear that this method is liable to be very expensive. There would be many exceptions caused during the execution of a process. Page fault and TRACE exception handling each involve a context switch to the kernel. In addition, every write carries the expense of a totally ordered multicast.

Write-invalidation ☐ Invalidation-based algorithms use page protection to enforce consistent data sharing. When a process is updating a page, it has read and write permissions locally; all other processes have no access permissions to the page. When one or more processes are reading the page, they have read-only permission; all other processes have no access permissions (although they may acquire read permissions). No other combinations are possible. A process with the most up-to-date version of a page p is designated as its *owner* – referred to as *owner(p)*. This is either the single writer, or one of the readers. The set of processes that have a copy of a page p is called its *copy set* – referred to as *copyset(p)*.

The possible state transitions are shown in Figure 17.8. When a process P_W attempts to write a page p to which it has no-access or read-only access, a page fault takes place. The page fault handling procedure is as follows:

- The page is transferred to P_W's kernel, if it does not already have an up-to-date read-only copy.

- All other copies are invalidated: the page permissions are set to no-access at all members of *copyset(p)*.

- *copyset(p)* := {P_W}.

- *owner(p)* := P_W.

- The kernel maps the page with read-write permissions into P_W's address space, and P_W is restarted.

Note that two or more processes with read-only copies may take write faults at more or less the same time. A read-only copy of a page may be out-of-date when ownership is eventually granted. To detect whether a current read-only copy of a page is out-of-date, each page can be associated with a sequence number, which is incremented whenever ownership is transferred. A kernel requiring write access encloses the sequence number of its read-only copy, if it possesses one. The current owner can then tell whether the page has been modified and therefore needs to be sent. This scheme is described by Kessler and Livny [1989] as the 'shrewd algorithm'.

When a process P_R attempts to read a page p for which it has no access permissions, a read page fault takes place. The page fault handling procedure is as follows:

- The page is copied from $owner(p)$ to P_R's kernel.

- If the current owner is a single writer, then it remains as p's owner and its access permission for p is set to read-only access. Retaining read access is desirable in case the process attempts to read the page subsequently – it will have retained an up-to-date version of the page. However, as the owner it will have to process subsequent requests for the page even if it does not access the page again. So it might turn out to have been more appropriate to reduce permission to no-access and transfer ownership to P_R.

- $copyset(p) := copyset(p) \cup \{P_R\}$.

- P_R's kernel maps the page with read-only permissions into P_R's address space, and P_R continues.

It is possible for a second page fault to occur during the transition algorithms just described. In order that transitions take place consistently, any new request for the page is not processed until after the current transition has completed.

The description just given has only explained *what* must be done. The problem of *how* to implement page fault handling efficiently is now addressed.

Invalidation protocols □ Two important problems remain to be addressed in a protocol to implement the invalidation scheme:

1. How to locate $owner(p)$ for a given page p.

2. Where to store $copyset(p)$.

For Ivy, Li and Hudak [1989] describe several architectures and protocols that take varying approaches to these problems. The simplest we shall describe is their improved centralized manager algorithm. In it, a single server called a manager is used to store the location (transport address) of $owner(p)$ for every page p. The manager could be one of the kernels, or it could be any separate process. In this algorithm, the set $copyset(p)$ is stored in the kernel of $owner(p)$. That is, the identifiers and transport addresses of the members of $copyset(p)$ are stored.

As shown in Figure 17.9, when a page fault occurs the local kernel (which we shall refer to as the *client*) sends a message to the manager containing the page number and the type of access required (read or read-write). The client awaits a reply. The manager handles the request by looking up the address of $owner(p)$ and forwarding the request to the owner. In the case of a write fault, the manager sets the new owner to be the client. Subsequent requests are thus queued at the client until it has completed the transfer of ownership to itself.

The previous owner sends the page to the client. In the case of a write fault, it also sends the page's copy set. The client performs the invalidation when it receives the copy

Figure 17.9   Central manager and associated messages.

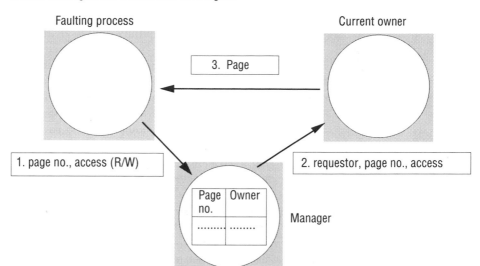

set. It sends a multicast request to the members of the copy set, awaiting acknowledgement from all the kernels concerned that invalidation has taken place. The multicast need not be ordered. The former owner need not be included in the list of destinations, since it invalidates itself. The details of copy set management are left to the reader, who should consult the general invalidation algorithms given above.

The manager is a performance bottleneck and a critical point of failure. Li and Hudak suggested three alternatives that allow the load of page management to be divided between computers: fixed distributed page management, multicast-based distributed management and dynamic distributed management. In the first, multiple managers are used, each functionally equivalent to the central manager just described; but the pages are divided statically between them. For example, each manager could manage just those pages whose page numbers hash to a certain range of values. Clients calculate the hash number for the needed page, and use a predetermined configuration table to look up the address of the corresponding manager.

This scheme would ameliorate the problem of load in general, but it has the disadvantage that a fixed mapping of pages to managers may not be suitable. When processes do not access the pages equally, some managers will incur more load than others. We now describe multicast-based and dynamic distributed management.

Using multicast to locate the owner □ Multicast can be used to eliminate the manager completely. When a process faults, its kernel multicasts its page request to all the other kernels. Only the kernel that owns the page replies. Care must be taken to ensure correct behaviour if two clients request the same page at more or less the same time: each client must obtain the page eventually, even if its request is multicast during transfer of ownership.

Consider two clients C_1 and C_2, which use multicast to locate a page owned by O. Suppose that O receives C_1's request first, and transfers ownership to it. Before the page arrives, C_2's request arrives at O and at C_1. O will discard C_2's request because it no longer owns the page. Li and Hudak pointed out that C_1 should defer processing C_2's request until after it has obtained the page – otherwise it would discard the request because it is not the owner, and C_2's request would be altogether lost. However, a problem still remains. C_1's request has been queued at C_2 meanwhile. After C_1 has eventually given C_2 the page, C_2 will receive and process C_1's request – which is now obsolete!

One solution is to use totally ordered multicast, so that clients can safely discard requests that arrive before their own (requests are delivered to themselves as well as to other kernels). Another solution, which uses a cheaper unordered multicast but which consumes more bandwidth, is to associate each page with a vector timestamp, with one entry per kernel (see Chapter 11 for a description of vector timestamps). When page ownership is transferred, so is the timestamp. When a kernel obtains ownership, it increments its entry in the timestamp. When a kernel requests ownership, it encloses the last timestamp it held for the page. In our example, C_2 could discard C_1's request, because C_1's entry in the request's timestamp is lower than that which arrived with the page.

Whether an ordered multicast or unordered multicast is used, this scheme has the usual disadvantage of multicast schemes: kernels that are not the owners of a page are interrupted by irrelevant messages, wasting processing time.

A dynamic distributed manager algorithm □ Li and Hudak suggested the dynamic distributed manager algorithm, which allows page ownership to be transferred between kernels, but uses an alternative to multicast as its method of locating a page's owner. The idea is to divide the overheads of locating pages between those computers that access them. Every kernel keeps, for every page p, a hint as to the page's current owner – the probable owner of p, or *probOwner(p)*. Initially, every kernel is supplied with accurate page locations. In general, however, these values are *hints*, because pages can be transferred elsewhere at any time. As in previous algorithms, ownership is only transferred when a write fault occurs.

The owner of a page is located by following chains of hints that are set up as ownership of the page is transferred from computer to computer. The length of the chain – that is, the number of forwarding messages necessary to locate the owner – threatens to increase indefinitely. The algorithm overcomes this by updating the hints as more up-to-date values become available. Hints are updated and requests are forwarded as follows:

- When a kernel transfers ownership of page p to another kernel, it updates *probOwner(p)* to be the recipient.

- When a kernel handles an invalidation request for a page p, it updates *probOwner(p)* to be the requester.

- When a kernel that has requested read access to a page p receives it, it updates *probOwner(p)* to be the provider.

- When a kernel receives a request for a page p that it does not own, it forwards the request to *probOwner(p)*, and resets *probOwner(p)* to be the requester.

The first three updates follow simply from the protocol for transferring page ownership and providing read-only copies. The rationale for the update when forwarding requests

Figure 17.10   Updating *probOwner* pointers.

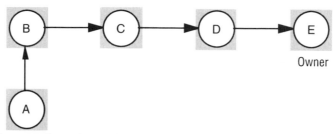

(a) *probOwner* pointers just before process A takes a page fault for a page owned by E.

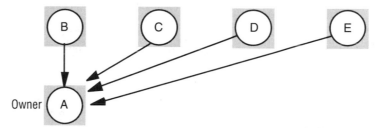

(b) Write fault: *probOwner* pointers after A's write request is forwarded.

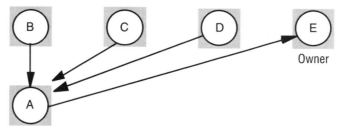

(c) Read fault: *probOwner* pointers after A's read request is forwarded.

is that, for write requests, the requester will soon be the owner, even though it is not currently. In fact, in Li and Hudak's algorithm, assumed here, the *probOwner* update is made whether the request is for read access or write access. We return to this point shortly.

Figure 17.10 (parts (a) and (b)) illustrates *probOwner* pointers before and after process *A* takes a write page fault. *A*'s *probOwner* pointer for the page initially points to *B*. Processes *B*, *C* and *D* forward the request to *E* by following their own *probOwner* pointers; thereafter, all are set to point to *A*, as a result of the update rules just described. The arrangement after fault handling is clearly better than that which preceded it: the chain of pointers has collapsed.

If, however, *A* takes a read fault, then process B is better off (two steps instead of three to E), C's situation is the same as it was before (two steps), but D is worse off, with two steps instead of one (Figure 17.10 (c)). Simulations are required to investigate the overall effect of this tactic on performance.

The average length of pointer chains can further be controlled by periodically broadcasting the current owner's location to all kernels. This has the effect of collapsing all chains to length one.

Li and Hudak describe the results of simulations that they carried out to investigate the efficacy of their pointer updates. With faulting processes chosen at random, for 1,024 processors they found that the average number of messages taken to reach the owner of a page was 2.34 if broadcasts announcing the owner's location are made every 256 faults, and 3.64 if broadcasts are made every 1,024 faults. These figures are given only as illustrations: a complete set of results is given by Li and Hudak [1989]. Note that a DSM system that uses a central manager requires two messages to reach the owner of a page.

Finally, Li and Hudak describe an optimization that potentially both makes invalidation more efficient and reduces the number of messages required to handle a read page fault. Instead of having to obtain a page copy from the owner of a page, a client can obtain a copy from any kernel with a valid copy. There is a chance that a client attempting to locate the owner will encounter such a kernel before the owner on the pointer chain.

This is done with the proviso that kernels keep a record of clients that have obtained a copy of a page from them. The set of kernels that possess read-only copies of a page thus form a tree rooted at the owner, with each node pointing to the child nodes below, which obtained copies from it. The invalidation of a page begins at the owner and works down through the tree. On receiving an invalidation message, a node forwards it to its children in addition to invalidating its own copy. The overall effect is that some invalidations occur in parallel. This can reduce the overall time taken to invalidate a page – especially in an environment without hardware support for multicast.

Thrashing ☐ It can be argued that it is the programmer's responsibility to avoid thrashing. The programmer could annotate data items in order to assist the DSM run-time in minimizing page copying and ownership transfers. The latter approach is discussed in the next section in the context of the Munin DSM system.

Mirage [Fleisch and Popek 1989] takes an approach to thrashing which is intended to be transparent to programmers. Mirage associates each page with a small time interval. Once a process has access to a page, it is allowed to retain access for the given interval, which serves as a type of timeslice. Other requests for the page are held off in the meantime. An obvious disadvantage of this scheme is that it is very difficult to choose the length of the timeslice. If the system uses a statically chosen length of time, it is liable to be inappropriate in many cases. A process might, for example, write a page only once and thereafter not access it; nonetheless, other processes are prevented from accessing it. Equally, the system might grant another process access to the page before it has finished using it.

A DSM system could choose the length of the timeslice dynamically. A possible basis for this is observation of accesses to the page (using the memory management unit's *referenced* bits). Another factor that could be taken into account is the length of the queue of processes waiting for the page.

17.4 Release consistency and Munin

The algorithms in the previous section were designed to achieve sequentially consistent DSM. The advantage of sequential consistency is that DSM behaves in the way that programmers expect shared memory to behave. Its disadvantage is that it is costly to implement. DSM systems require the use of multicasts in their implementations whether they are implemented using write-update or write-invalidation – although unordered multicast suffices for invalidation. Locating the owner of a page tends to be expensive: a central manager that knows the location of every page's owner acts as a bottleneck; following pointers involves more messages, on average. In addition, invalidation-based algorithms may give rise to thrashing.

The Munin DSM design [Carter *et al.* 1991] attempts to improve the efficiency of DSM by implementing the release consistency model, which is weaker than sequential consistency. Furthermore, Munin allows programmers to annotate their data items according to the way in which they are shared, so that optimizations can be made in the update options selected for maintaining consistency. It is implemented upon the V kernel [Cheriton and Zwaenepoel 1985], which allows user-level threads to handle page faults and manipulate page tables.

Release consistency

Release consistency was introduced with the Dash multiprocessor, which implements DSM in hardware, primarily using a write-invalidation protocol [Lenoski *et al.* 1992]. Munin has adopted a software implementation of it. Release consistency is weaker than sequential consistency and cheaper to implement, but it has reasonable semantics that are tractable to programmers.

The idea of release consistency is to reduce DSM overheads by exploiting the fact that programmers use synchronization objects. An implementation can use knowledge of accesses to these objects to allow memory to become inconsistent at certain points, while the use of synchronization objects nonetheless preserves application-level consistency. The operations executed by processes can be divided into ordinary accesses (to DSM) and synchronization accesses, for example, operations upon locks. Synchronization accesses are in turn divided into acquire accesses and release accesses, corresponding, for example, to the acquisition and release of a lock used to guard a critical section. (A more complete categorization of accesses is given by Gharachorloo *et al.* [1990].)

The main guarantee provided by release-consistent DSM is the following:

> All ordinary memory accesses issued prior to a release have taken effect at all other processes before the release completes – including those accesses issued prior to the preceding acquire.

That is, when a release has taken place, no other process can read stale versions of data modified by the process that performs the release. This is consistent with the programmer's expectation that a release of a lock, for example, signifies that a process has finished modifying data within a critical section. Gharachorloo *et al.* give a formal definition of release consistency. There are two other conditions that must be satisfied by a DSM for it to be release consistent. These are trivially satisfied by a DSM system that uses message passing rather than access to shared variables to implement synchronization, and they are not described here.

The DSM run-time can only enforce the release consistency guarantee if it is aware of synchronization accesses. In Munin, for example, the programmer is forced to use Munin's own *acquireLock*, *releaseLock* and *waitAtBarrier* primitives. (A barrier is a synchronization object which blocks each of a set of processes until all have waited on it; all processes then continue.)

Gharachorloo *et al.* show that release-consistent DSM gives equivalent results to executions on sequentially consistent DSM, as long as the processes concerned use appropriate synchronization accesses. Note that a program must use synchronization to ensure that updates are made visible to other processes. Two processes that share DSM but never use synchronization objects may never see one another's updates, if the implementation strictly applies the sole guarantee given above.

The release consistency model allows an implementation to avoid some blocking of processes and to delay some communication until a release occurs. For example, a process need not be blocked when it makes updates within a critical section. Nor do its updates have to be propagated until it leaves the critical section by releasing a lock. Furthermore, updates can then be collected and sent in a single message. Only the final update to each data item need be sent.

Consider the following processes, which acquire and release a lock in order to access a pair of variables *a* and *b* (*a* and *b* are initialized to zero):

Process 1:
  acquireLock();(* enter critical section *)
  a := a + 1;
  b := b + 1;
  releaseLock();(* leave critical section *)

Process 2:
  acquireLock();(* enter critical section *)
  print ("The values of a and b are: ", a, b);
  releaseLock();(* leave critical section *)

Process 1 updates *a* and *b* under conditions of mutual exclusion, so that Process 2 cannot read *a* and *b* at the same time and so will find $a = b = 0$ or $a = b = 1$. The critical sections enforce consistency – equality of *a* and *b* – *at the application level*. It is therefore redundant to maintain sequential consistency for the variables affected during the critical section. If Process 2 tried to access *a*, say, outside a critical section, then it might find an inconsistent value. That is a matter for the application writer.

Let us assume that Process 1 acquires the lock first. Process 2 will block and not cause any activity related to DSM until it has acquired the lock and attempts to access *a* and *b*. If the two processes were to execute under sequential consistency, then Process 1 would block when it updates *a* and *b*. Under a write-update protocol it would block while all versions of the data are updated; under a write-invalidation protocol, it would block while all copies are invalidated.

Under release consistency, Process 1 will not block when it accesses *a* and *b*. The DSM run-time system notes which data (pages) have been updated, but need take no further action at that time. It is only when Process 1 has released the lock that communication is required. Under a write-update protocol, the updates to *a* and *b* will be sent to all replicas; under a write-invalidation protocol, the invalidations should be sent.

Munin

The following points apply to Munin's implementation of release consistency:

- Munin uses library code to monitor the pages that are updated. The V kernel allows a process's page tables to be altered from user-level, to set and remove write protection. Munin write-protects each newly acquired page, and notes the page's identity in a user-level handler called on a subsequent page fault.

- Munin sends update or invalidation information as soon as a lock is released.

- The programmer can make annotations that associate a lock with particular data items. In this case, the DSM run-time can propagate relevant updates in the same message that transfers the lock to a waiting process – ensuring that the lock's recipient has copies of the data it needs before it accesses them.

Keleher *et al.* [1992] describe an alternative to Munin's *eager* approach of sending update or invalidation information at the time of a release. Instead, this *lazy* implementation does so only when the lock in question is next acquired. Furthermore, it sends this information only to the process acquiring the lock, and piggy-backs it onto the message granting the lock. It is unnecessary to make the updates visible to other processes until they in turn acquire the lock.

Sharing annotations □ Munin implements a variety of consistency protocols, which are applied at the granularity of individual data items. The protocols are parameterized according to the following options:

- whether to use a write-update or write-invalidate protocol;

- whether several replicas of a modifiable data item may exist simultaneously;

- whether or not to delay updates or invalidations (for example, under release consistency);

- whether the item has a fixed owner, to which all updates must be sent;

- whether the same data item may be modified concurrently by several writers;

- whether the data item is shared by a fixed set of processes;

- whether the data item may be modified.

These options are chosen according to the nature of the data item, and the pattern of its sharing between processes. The programmer can make an explicit choice of which parameter options to use for each data item. However, Munin supplies a small, standard set of annotations for the programmer to apply to data items, each of which implies a convenient choice of the parameters, suitable for a variety of applications and data items. These are as follows:

Read-only: No updates may be made after initialization, and the item may be freely copied.

Migratory: Processes typically take turns in making several accesses to the item, at least one of which is an update. For example, the item might be accessed within a critical section. Munin always gives both read and write access together to such an object, even when a process takes a read-fault. This saves subsequent write-fault processing.

Write-shared: Several processes update the same data item (for example, an array) concurrently, but this annotation is a declaration from the programmer that the processes do not update the same parts of it. This means that Munin can avoid false sharing, but must propagate only those words in the data item that are actually updated at each process. To do this, Munin makes a copy of a page (inside a write-fault handler) just before it is locally updated. Only the differences between the two versions are sent in an update.

Producer-consumer: The data object is shared by a fixed set of processes, only one of which updates it. As we explained when discussing thrashing above, a write-update protocol is most suitable here. Moreover, updates may be delayed under the model of release consistency, assuming that the processes use locks to synchronize their accesses.

Reduction: The data item is always modified by being locked, read, updated and unlocked. An example of this is a global minimum in a parallel computation, which must be atomically fetched and modified if it is greater than the local minimum. These items are stored at a fixed owner. Updates are sent to the owner, which propagates them.

Result: Several processes update different words within the data item; a single process reads the whole item. For example, different 'worker' processes might fill in different elements of an array, which is then processed by a 'master' process. The point here is that the updates need only be propagated to the master, and not to the workers (as would occur under the 'write-shared' annotation just described).

Conventional: The data item is managed under an invalidation protocol similar to that described in the previous section. No process may therefore read a stale version of the data item.

Carter *et al.* [1991] detail the parameter options used for each of the annotations we have given. Of course, this set of annotations is not fixed. Others may be created, as sharing patterns that require different parameter options are encountered.

17.5 Other consistency models

Models of memory consistency can be divided into *uniform models*, which do not distinguish between types of memory accesses, and *hybrid models* which do distinguish between ordinary and synchronization accesses (as well as other types of access).

Several uniform models exist that are weaker than sequential consistency. These include:

Causal consistency: Reads and writes may be related by the *happened-before* relationship (see Chapter 10). This is defined to hold between memory operations when either (a) they are made by the same process, (b) a process reads a value written by another process, or (c) there exists a sequence of such operations linking the two operations. The model's constraint is that the value returned by a read must be consistent with the *happened-before* relationship. This is described by Hutto and Ahamad [1990].

Processor consistency: The memory is both coherent and adheres to the pipelined RAM model (see the following). This was first defined informally by Goodman [1989] and later formally defined by Ahamad *et al.* [1992].

Cache consistency (coherence): The memory is sequentially consistent on a location-by-location basis. Processors agree on the order of writes from any processor to a given location; but they may differ on the order of writes from different processors to different locations [Goodman 1989, Gharachorloo *et al.* 1990].

Pipelined RAM: All processors agree on the order of writes issued by any given processor [Lipton and Sandberg 1988].

Considerable research is under way into the applicability of these models. For example, Ahamad *et al.* show that, under processor consistency, one common algorithm developed for sequentially consistent memories works correctly under processor consistency, but not all do. Goodman conjectures that most do work correctly under processor consistency.

Release consistency is a hybrid model. As mentioned in Section 17.2, release consistency is a relaxation of weak consistency. Weak consistency does not distinguish between acquire and release synchronization accesses. One of its guarantees is that all previous ordinary accesses complete before *either* type of synchronization access completes.

Discussion □ Release consistency, and some of the other consistency models weaker than sequential consistency, seem promising for DSM. It does not appear to be a significant disadvantage of the release consistency model that synchronization operations need to be known to the DSM run-time – as long as those supplied by the system are sufficiently powerful to meet the needs of programmers.

It is important to realise that, under the hybrid models, most programmers are not forced to consider the particular memory consistency semantics used, as long as they synchronize their data accesses appropriately. But there is a general danger in DSM designs of asking the programmer to perform many annotations to his or her program in order to make its execution efficient. This includes both annotations identifying data items with synchronization objects, and the sharing annotations such as those of Munin. One of the advantages of shared memory programming over message passing is supposed to be its relative convenience.

The investigation of consistency models is a lively area of current research, particularly in the multiprocessor research community. The reader is referred to Mosberger [1993] for an overview.

17.6 Summary

This chapter has described and motivated the concept of distributed shared memory as an abstraction of shared memory that is an alternative to message-based communication in a distributed system. DSM is primarily intended for parallel processing and data sharing. It has been shown to perform as well as message passing for certain parallel applications, but it is difficult to implement efficiently and its performance varies with applications.

The chapter has concentrated on software implementations of DSM – particularly those using the virtual memory subsystem – but it has been implemented with hardware support.

The main design and implementation issues are the DSM structure, the means by which applications synchronize, the memory consistency model, the use of write-update or write-invalidation protocols, the granularity of sharing and thrashing.

The DSM is structured either as a series of bytes, a collection of language-specific data structures, a collection of shared objects, or a collection of immutable data items.

Applications using DSM require synchronization in order to meet application-specific consistency constraints. They use objects such as locks for this purpose, implemented using message passing for efficiency.

The most common and strictest type of memory consistency implemented in DSM systems is sequential consistency. An emerging weaker level of consistency is release consistency, which requires integration of the synchronization mechanism with the DSM mechanism.

Write-update protocols are those in which updates are propagated to all copies as data items are updated. These are implemented usually in hardware, although software implementations using totally ordered multicast exist. Write-invalidation protocols prevent stale data from being read by invalidating copies as data items are updated. These are more suited to page-based DSM, for which write-update may be an expensive option.

The granularity of DSM affects the likelihood of contention between processes that falsely share data items because they are contained in the same unit of sharing (for example, page). It also affects the cost per byte of transferring updates between computers.

Thrashing may occur when write-invalidation is used. This is the repeated transfer of data between competing processes, at the expense of application progress. This may be reduced by application-level synchronization, by allowing computers to retain a page for a minimum time, or by labelling data items so that both read and write access are always granted together.

The chapter has described Ivy's three main write-invalidate protocols for page-based DSM, which address the problems of managing the copy set and locating the owner of a page. These were: the central manager protocol, in which a single process stores the current owner's address for each page; the protocol which uses multicast to locate the current owner of a page; and the dynamic distributed manager protocol, which uses forwarding pointers to locate the current owner of a page.

The final section discussed release consistency and applied it to an example. Release consistency enables the implementation to exploit the use of synchronization objects to achieve greater efficiency, without breaking application-level consistency constraints. This and other consistency models that are weaker than sequential consistency are the subject of current research. Munin implements release consistency. It also allows programmers to annotate their data items in order to select the protocol options that are best suited to them, given the way in which they are shared.

EXERCISES

17.1 Discuss whether message passing or DSM is preferable for fault-tolerant applications.

page 519

17.2 How would you deal with the problem of differing data representations for a library-based implementation of DSM on heterogeneous computers? How would you tackle the problem in a page-based implementation? Does your solution extend to pointers?

page 520

17.3 We use the notation $W(x)v$ to denote a write operation to the variable x with the value v, and $R(x)v$ to denote a read operation on the variable x that returns the value v.

Initially, all variables are set to zero. Is the memory underlying the following two processes sequentially consistent?:

P1: $R(x)1; R(x)2; W(y)1$

P2: $W(x)1; R(y)1; W(x)2$

page 525

17.4 In write-update, show that sequential consistency could be broken if each update was made locally before asynchronously multicasting it to other replica managers, even though the multicast is totally ordered. Discuss whether an asynchronous multicast can be used to achieve sequential consistency. (Hint: consider whether to block subsequent operations.)

page 526

17.5 Construct an argument to prove that sequential consistency is guaranteed when write-invalidate is used.

page 526

17.6 Explain why, under a write-update protocol, care is needed to propagate only those words within a data item that have been updated locally.

Devise an algorithm for representing the differences between a page and an updated version of it. Discuss the performance of this algorithm.

page 526

17.7 Explain why granularity is an important issue in DSM systems. Compare the issue of granularity between a DSM implementation using libraries to access mutable data, and a page-based implementation.

Why is granularity relevant when DSM is structured as a collection of immutable data items?

page 528

17.8 What are the implications of DSM for page replacement policies (that is, the choice of which page to purge from main memory in order to bring a new page in)?

page 529

17.9 In Ivy's dynamic distributed manager algorithm, what steps are taken to minimize the number of lookups necessary to find a page?

page 534

17.10 Why, under release consistency, is it desirable to use an interface to associate data items with synchronization objects?

page 537

17.11 Why is thrashing an important issue in DSM systems, and what methods are available for dealing with it?

pages 529, 536, 540

17.12 (See Exercise 17.3 for an explanation of the notation.) Is the memory underlying the following execution coherent (cache consistent)? Is it sequentially consistent?

P1: $W(x)1; R(y)0$

P2: $W(y)1; R(x)0$

Sequentially consistent memory can be implemented using a write-update protocol employing a synchronous, totally-ordered multicast. Discuss what multicast ordering requirements would be necessary to implement coherent memory.

page 541

18

DISTRIBUTED OPERATING SYSTEMS: CASE STUDIES

This chapter contains case studies of four distributed operating system kernels which are related to the framework in Chapter 6 and used to discuss further design principles:

Mach: a state-of-the-art system with a highly flexible virtual memory design in which memory objects can be backed up by external pagers;

Chorus: another state-of-the-art commercial system that illustrates alternative approaches to design and implementation;

UNIX emulation: over Mach and Chorus;

Amoeba: a research system in which all objects are protected by capabilities;

Clouds: a distributed operating system whose aim is to support distributed objects.

Two further case studies give examples of an RPC implementation and a multicast protocol:

Firefly RPC: which has examined and implemented several approaches to making RPC more efficient;

Amoeba multicast protocol: a sequencer-based totally ordered multicast protocol.

18.1 Introduction

Earlier chapters in this book gave the principles behind the design of basic distributed operating system features, remote procedure calling and multicast communication.

This chapter looks at particular features of several case studies in order to make those design considerations concrete, and also to introduce some design points not covered in Chapter 6 that are better dealt with in the context of particular designs.

The section on Mach can be read alone. It is intended for readers who want to know about the current state-of-the-art in distributed operating systems and microkernel design. Most of this section can be read with a knowledge of Chapters 1 and 2, together with parts of the chapters on Interprocess Communication and Remote Procedure Calling. In particular, it assumes a knowledge of ports, marshalling, interface definitions, stubs and stub compilers. An understanding of UNIX processes and interprocess communication is also useful. Where more advanced concepts are mentioned, reference is made to the relevant parts of Chapter 6.

The writers of research papers and other documentation of the Mach and Chorus microkernels have coined their own words for some of the concepts introduced in Chapter 6. In particular, Mach refers to tasks and Chorus to actors, both of which correspond to the execution environment part of what we call processes. We use the terms task and actor in the sections on Mach and Chorus. Otherwise we use the terminology introduced in Chapter 6.

We include Amoeba because of its long history, and because its design is based upon just a few, simple principles. It is useful for educational purposes because it illustrates the application of concepts such as capabilities in a real working framework.

The study on Chorus should be read after the section on Mach. It shows an alternative approach to some of the design and implementation choices.

Mach and Chorus have long pedigrees, and are each the subject of considerable current interest, in particular because they are geared towards the emulation of UNIX and other existing, conventional operating systems. These operating systems appear in commercial forms.

The study of UNIX emulation discusses the design alternatives and compares the approaches used by Mach and Chorus.

Clouds is designed to cater for the requirements of distributed objects, as opposed to communicating processes. Clouds is an important example of the object-thread paradigm which is used by several experimental systems in which objects located in different computers in a distributed system are able to invoke one another's operations, enabling distributed programs to be written in object-oriented programming languages. The discussion of Clouds assumes some familiarity with distributed shared memory (Chapter 17).

Firefly RPC provides a model for the performance of RPC and shows how the overall performance of RPC can be enhanced by improving the performance of each of the mechanisms it subsumes.

The totally ordered multicast protocol of Kaashoek and Tanenbaum [1991] is a design that achieves very high performance on a local area network by exploiting hardware support for multicast.

18.2 Mach

History and architectural overview

The Mach project [Acetta *et al.* 1986], [Boykin *et al.* 1993], [Loepere 1991] is based at Carnegie-Mellon University in the US. It is the successor to two previous projects, RIG [Rashid 1986] and Accent [Rashid and Robertson 1981, Rashid 1985, Fitzgerald and Rashid 1986]. RIG was developed at the University of Rochester in the 1970s, and Accent was developed at Carnegie-Mellon during the first half of the 1980s. In contrast to its RIG and Accent predecessors and to Amoeba, the Mach project never set out to develop a complete distributed operating system. Instead, the Mach kernel was developed to provide direct compatibility with BSD UNIX. It was designed to provide advanced kernel facilities which would complement those of UNIX and allow a UNIX implementation to be spread across a network of multiprocessor and single-processor computers. From the beginning, the designers' intention was for much of UNIX to be implemented as user-level processes.

Despite these intentions, version 2.5 Mach, the first of the two major releases, includes all the UNIX compatibility code inside the kernel itself. It runs on SUN-3s, the IBM RT PC, multiprocessor and uniprocessor VAX systems and the Encore Multimax and Sequent multiprocessors, among other computers. From 1989 Mach 2.5 was incorporated as the base technology for OSF/1, the Open Software Foundation's rival to System V Release 4 as the industry standard version of UNIX. An older version of Mach was used as a basis for the operating system for the NeXT workstation.

The UNIX code was removed from the version 3.0 Mach kernel, however, and it is this version which we describe. The version 3 Mach kernel runs on Intel 386- and 486-based PCs, the DECstation 3100 and 5000 series computers, some Motorola 88000-based computers and SUN SPARCStations. Ports to the Macintosh and the following processors are also available or under development: IBM's RS6000, Hewlett Packard's Precision Architecture and Digital Equipment Corporation's Alpha. Version 3 Mach is a basis for building user-level emulations of operating systems, database systems, language run-time systems and other items of system software that we call subsystems (Figure 18.1). Operating system emulations that have been produced, or which are being implemented or planned at the time of writing include UNIX (BSD4.3, System V.4 and IBM's AIX), OS/2, MS-DOS and VMS.

The emulation of conventional operating systems makes it possible to run existing binaries developed for them. In addition, new applications for these conventional operating systems can be developed. At the same time, distributed operating systems and applications that take advantage of the benefits of distribution can be developed; and the implementations of the conventional operating systems can also be distributed. Two important issues arise for operating system emulations. First, distributed emulations cannot be entirely accurate, because of the new failure modes that arise with distribution. Secondly, the question arises of whether acceptable performance levels can be achieved.

It is too early to say whether subsystems such as UNIX emulation on top of Mach will be successful, in terms of their general acceptance by the user community. But

Figure 18.1   Mach supports operating systems, databases and other subsystems.

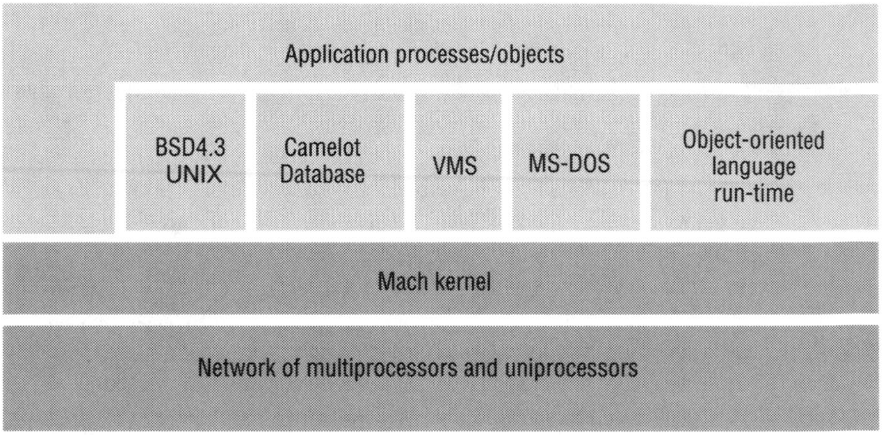

results reported for the user-level BSD4.3 UNIX server suggest that a comparable performance to monolithic implementations can be attained in at least some respects.

Design goals and chief design features

The main Mach design goals and features are as follows:

Multiprocessor operation: Mach was designed to execute on a shared memory multiprocessor, so that both kernel threads and user-mode threads could be executed by any processor. Mach provides a multi-threaded model of user processes, with execution environments called *tasks*. Threads are pre-emptively scheduled, whether they belong to the same tasks or to different tasks, to allow for parallel execution on a shared memory multiprocessor.

Transparent extension to network operation: In order to allow for distributed programs that extend transparently between uniprocessors and multiprocessors across a network, Mach has adopted a location-independent communication model involving ports as destinations. The Mach kernel, however, is designed to be 100 per cent unaware of networks. The Mach design relies totally on user-level network server processes to ferry messages transparently across the network (Figure 18.2). This is a controversial design decision, given the costs of context switching that we examined in Chapter 6. However, it allows for absolute flexibility in the control of network communication policy.

User-level servers: Mach supports an object-based model in which resources are managed either by the kernel or by user-level servers. As we have mentioned, a primary aim is for most UNIX facilities to be implemented at user-level, while providing binary compatibility with existing UNIX. With the exception of some kernel-managed resources, resources are accessed uniformly by message passing, however they are managed. To every resource, there corresponds a port managed by a server. The *Mach Interface Generator* (MiG) was developed to generate RPC

Figure 18.2   Mach tasks, threads and communication.

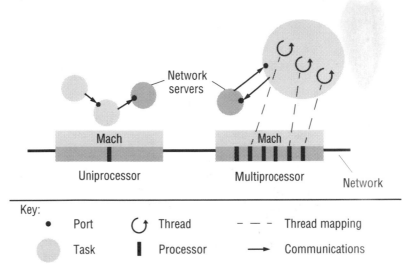

stubs used to hide message-based accesses at the language level [Draves *et al*. 1989].

Operating system emulation: To support the binary-level emulation of UNIX and other operating systems, Mach allows for the transparent redirection of operating system calls to emulation library calls and thence to user-level operating system servers. It also includes a facility that allows exceptions such as address space violations arising in application tasks to be handled by user-level operating system servers.

Flexible virtual memory implementation: Much effort was put into providing virtual memory enhancements that would equip Mach for UNIX emulation and for supporting other subsystems. This included taking a flexible approach to the layout of a process' address space. Mach supports a large, sparse process address space, possibly containing many regions. Both messages and open files, for example, can appear as virtual memory regions. Regions can be private to a task, shared between tasks or copied from regions in other tasks. The design includes the use of memory mapping techniques, notably copy-on-write, to avoid copying data when, for example, messages are passed between tasks. Finally, Mach was designed to allow user-level servers to implement backing storage for virtual memory pages. Regions can be mapped to data managed by external pagers. Mapped data can reside in any generalized abstraction of a memory resource such as distributed shared memory, as well as in files. Chapter 6 for a discussion of copy-on-write and external pagers.

Portability: Mach was designed to be portable to a variety of hardware platforms. For this reason, machine-dependent code has been isolated as far as possible. In particular, the virtual memory code has been divided between machine-independent and machine-dependent parts [Rashid *et al*. 1988].

Summary of the main Mach abstractions

We can summarize the abstractions provided by the Mach kernel as follows (these will be described in detail later in this section):

Tasks: A Mach task is an execution environment. This consists primarily of a protected address space, and a collection of *kernel-managed* capabilities used for accessing ports.

Threads: Tasks can contain multiple threads. The threads belonging to a single task can execute in parallel at different processors in a shared memory multiprocessor.

Ports: A port in Mach is a unicast, unidirectional communication channel with an associated message queue. Ports are not accessed directly by the Mach programmer and are not part of a task. Rather, the programmer is given handles to *port rights*. These are capabilities to send messages to a port or receive messages from a port.

Port sets: A port set is a collection of port receive rights local to a task. It is used to receive a message from any one of a collection of ports. Port sets should not be confused with port *groups*, which are multicast destinations but are not implemented in Mach.

Messages: A message in Mach can contain port rights in addition to pure data. The kernel employs memory management techniques to transfer message data efficiently between tasks.

Devices: Servers such as file servers running at user-level must access devices. The kernel exports a low-level interface to the underlying devices for this purpose.

Memory object: Each region of the virtual address space of a Mach task corresponds to a memory object. This is an object which in general is implemented outside the kernel itself, but is accessed by the kernel when it performs virtual memory paging operations. A memory object is an instance of an abstract data type that includes operations to fetch and store data that are accessed when threads give rise to page-faults in attempting to reference addresses in the corresponding region.

Memory cache object: For every mapped memory object, there is a kernel-managed object that contains a cache of pages for the corresponding region that are resident in main memory. This is called a memory cache object. It supports operations needed by the external pager that implements the memory object.

We shall now consider the main abstractions. The abstraction of devices is omitted in the interests of brevity.

Ports, naming and protection

Mach identifies individual resources with ports. To access a resource, a message is sent to the corresponding port. The Mach assumption is that servers will in general manage

Figure 18.3   A task's port name space.

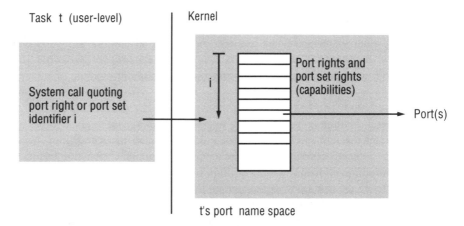

t's port name space

many ports: one for every resource. A single server UNIX system uses about 2000 ports [Draves 1990]. Ports therefore have to be cheap to create and manage.

The problem of protecting a resource from illegal accesses amounts to that of protecting the corresponding port against illegal sends. This is achieved in Mach by kernel control over the acquisition of capabilities for the port, and also by network server control over messages that arrive over the network.

The capability to a port has a field specifying the port access rights belonging to the task that holds it. There are three different types of port rights. *Send rights* allow the threads in the task that possesses them to send messages to the corresponding port. A restricted form of these, *send-once rights*, allow at most one message to be sent, after which the rights are automatically destroyed by the kernel. This restricted form allows, for example, a client to obtain a reply from a server in the knowledge that the server can no longer send a message to it (thus protecting it from buggy servers); in addition, the server is spared the expense of garbage-collecting send rights received from clients. Finally, *receive rights* allow a task's threads to receive messages from the port's message queue. At most one task may possess receive rights at any one time, whereas any number of tasks may possess send rights or send-once rights. Mach only supports N-to-one communication: multicast is not supported directly by the kernel.

At creation, a task is given a *bootstrap port right*, which is a send right it uses to obtain the services of other tasks. After creation, the threads belonging to the task acquire further port rights either by creating ports, or by receiving port rights sent to them in messages.

Mach's port rights are stored inside the kernel and protected by it (Figure 18.3). Tasks refer to port rights by local identifiers which are only valid in the task's local *port name space*. This allows the kernel's implementors to choose efficient representations for these capabilities (such as pointers to message queues), and to choose integer local names that are convenient for the kernel in looking up the capability from the name. In fact, like UNIX file descriptors, local identifiers are integers used to index a kernel table containing the task's capabilities.

The Mach naming and protection scheme thus allows rapid access to local message queues from a given user-level identifier. Against this advantage, we must set the expense of kernel processing whenever rights are transmitted in messages between tasks. At the very least, send rights have to be allocated a local name in the recipient task's name space, and space in its kernel tables. And we note that, in a secure environment, the transmission of port rights by the network servers requires encryption of those rights, to guard against forms of security attack such as eavesdropping [Sansom *et al.* 1986].

Tasks and threads

A task is an execution environment: tasks themselves cannot perform any actions, only the threads within them can. However, for convenience we shall sometimes refer to a task performing actions when we mean a thread within the task. The major resources associated directly with a task are its address space, its threads, its port rights, port sets and the local name space in which port rights and port sets are looked up. We shall now examine the mechanism for creating a new task, and the features related to the management of tasks and the execution of their constituent threads.

Creating a new task □ The UNIX *fork* command creates a new process by copying an existing one. Mach's model of process creation is a generalization of the UNIX model. Tasks are created with reference to what we shall call a *blueprint task* (which need not be the creator). The new task resides at the same computer as the blueprint task. Since Mach does not provide a task migration facility, the only way to establish a task at a remote computer is via a task that already resides there. The new task's bootstrap port right is inherited from its blueprint, and its address space is either empty or is inherited from its blueprint (address space inheritance is discussed in the subsection on Mach virtual memory below). A newly created task has no threads. Instead, the task's creator requests the creation of a thread within the child task. Thereafter, further threads can be created by existing threads within the task. See Figure 18.4 for some of the Mach calls related to task and thread creation.

Invoking kernel operations □ When a Mach task or thread is created, it is assigned a so-called *kernel port*. Mach 'system calls' are divided into those implemented directly as kernel traps, and those implemented by message passing to kernel ports. The latter method has the advantage of allowing network-transparent operations on remote tasks and threads as well as local ones. A kernel service manages kernel resources in the same way that a user-level server manages other resources. Each task has send rights to its kernel port, which enables it to invoke operations upon itself (such as to create a new thread). Each of the kernel services accessed by message passing has an interface definition. Tasks access these services via stub procedures, which are generated from their interface definitions by the Mach Interface Generator.

Exception handling □ In addition to a kernel port, tasks and (optionally) threads can possess an *exception port*. When certain types of exception occur, the kernel responds by attempting to send a message describing the exception to an associated exception port. If there is no exception port for the thread, the kernel looks for one for the task. The thread that receives this message can attempt to fix the problem (it might, for example,

Figure 18.4   Task and thread creation.

---

task_create(parent_task, inherit_memory, child_task)
> *parent_task* is the task used as a blueprint in the creation of the new task, *inherit_memory* specifies whether the child should inherit the address space of its parent or be assigned an empty address space, *child_task* is the identifier of the new task.

thread_create(parent_task, child_thread)
> *parent_task* is the task in which the new thread is to be created, *child_thread* is the identifier of the new thread. The new thread has no execution state and is suspended.

thread_set_state(thread, flavour, new_state, count)
> *thread* is the thread to be supplied with execution state, *flavour* specifies the machine architecture, *new_state* specifies the state (such as the program counter and stack pointer), *count* is the size of the state.

thread_resume(thread)
> This is used to resume the suspended thread identified by *thread*.

---

grow the thread's stack in response to an address space violation), and it then returns a status value in a reply message. If the kernel finds an exception port and receives a reply indicating success, it then restarts the thread that raised the exception. Otherwise, the kernel terminates it.

For example, the kernel sends a message to an exception port when a task attempts an address space access violation or to divide-by-zero. The owner of the exception port could be a debugging task, which could execute anywhere in the network by virtue of Mach's location-independent communication. Page faults are handled by external pagers. Section 18.4 describes how Mach handles system calls directed to an emulated operating system.

Task and thread management □ About 40 procedures in the kernel interface are concerned with the creation and management of tasks and threads. The first argument of each procedure is a send right to the corresponding kernel port, and message passing system calls are used to request the operation of the target kernel. Some of these task and thread calls are shown in Figure 18.4. In summary, thread scheduling priorities can be set individually, threads and tasks can be suspended, resumed and terminated, and the execution state of threads can be externally set, read and modified. The latter facility is important for debugging, and also for setting up software interrupts. Yet more kernel interface calls are concerned with the allocation of a task's threads to particular *processor sets*. A processor set is a subset of processors in a multiprocessor. By assigning threads to processor sets, the available computational resources can be crudely divided between different types of activity. The reader is referred to Loepere [1991] for details of kernel support for task and thread management and processor allocation. Tokuda *et al.* [1990] describe a set of extensions to Mach for real-time thread scheduling and synchronization.

Figure 18.5   A Mach message containing port rights and out-of-line data.

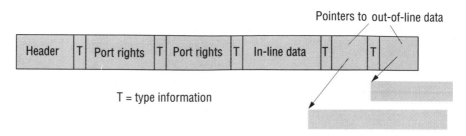

T = type information

Communication model

Mach provides a single system call for message passing: *mach_msg*. Before describing this, we shall say more about messages, ports and port sets in Mach.

Messages □ A message consists of a fixed-size header followed by a variable-length list of data items (Figure 18.5).

The fixed-size header contains:

The destination port: For simplicity, this is part of the message rather than being specified as a separate parameter to the *mach_msg* system call. It is specified by the local identifier of the appropriate send rights.

A reply port: If a reply is required, then send rights to a local port (that is, one for which the sending thread has receive rights) are enclosed in the message for this purpose.

An operation identifier: This identifies an operation (procedure) in the service interface and is meaningful only to applications.

Extra data size: Following the header (that is, contiguous with it) there is, in general, a variable-sized list of typed items. There is no length limit to this, except the number of bits in this field and the total address space size.

Each item in the list after the message header is one of the following (which can occur in any order in the message):

Typed message data: individual, in-line type-tagged data items;

Port rights: referred to by their local identifiers;

Pointers to out-of-line data: data held in a separate non-contiguous block of memory.

Mach messages consist of a fixed-size header and multiple data blocks of variable sizes, some of which may be *out-of-line* (that is, non-contiguous). However, when out-of-line message data are sent, the kernel – not the receiving task – chooses the location in the receiving task's address space of the received data. This is a side-effect of the copy-on-write technique used to transfer this data. Extra virtual memory regions received in a message must be de-allocated explicitly by the receiving task, if they are no longer required. Since the costs of virtual memory operations outweigh those of data copying for small amounts of data, it is intended that only reasonably large amounts of data are sent out-of-line.

The advantage of allowing several data components in messages is that this allows the programmer to allocate memory separately for data and for metadata. For example, a file server might locate a requested disk block from its cache. Instead of copying the block into a message buffer, contiguously with header information, the data can be fetched directly from where they reside, by providing an appropriate pointer in the reply message. This is a form of what is known as *scatter-gather I/O*, wherein data is written to or read from multiple areas of the caller's address space in one system call. The UNIX *readv* and *writev* system calls also provide for this [Leffler *et al.* 1989].

The type of each data item in a Mach message is specified by the sender (as for example, in ASN.1). This enables user-level network servers to marshal the data into a standard format when they are transmitted across a network. However, this marshalling scheme has performance disadvantages compared to marshalling and unmarshalling performed by stub procedures generated from interface definitions. Stub procedures have common knowledge of the data types concerned, need not include these types in the messages, and may marshal data directly into the message (See Section 4.2). A network server may have to copy the sender's typed data into another message as it marshals them.

Ports □   A Mach port has a message queue whose size can be set dynamically by the task with receive rights. This facility enables receivers to implement a form of flow control. When a normal send right is used, a thread attempting to send a message to a port whose message queue is full will be blocked until room becomes available. When a thread uses a send-once right, the recipient always queues the message, even if the message queue is full. Since a send-once right is used, it is known that no further messages can be sent from that source. Server threads can avoid blocking by using send-once rights when replying to clients.

Sending port rights □   When port send rights are enclosed in a message, the receiver acquires send rights to the same port. When receive rights are transmitted, they are automatically de-allocated in the sending task. This is because receive rights cannot be possessed by more than one task at a time. All messages queued at the port and all subsequently transmitted messages can be received by the new owner of receive rights, in a manner that is transparent to tasks sending to the port. The transparent transfer of receive rights is relatively straightforward to achieve when the rights are transferred within a single computer. The acquired capability is simply a pointer to the local message queue. In the inter-computer case, however, a number of more complex design issues arise. These are discussed below.

Monitoring connectivity □   The kernel is designed to inform senders and receivers when conditions arise under which sending or receiving messages would be futile. For this purpose, it keeps information about the number of send and receive rights referring to a given port. If no task holds receive rights for a particular port (for example, because the task holding these rights failed), then all send rights in local tasks' port name spaces become *dead names*. When a sender attempts to use a name referring to a port for which receive rights no longer exist, the kernel turns the name into a dead name and returns an error indication. Similarly, tasks can request the kernel to notify them asynchronously of the condition that no send rights exist for a specified port. The kernel performs this notification by sending the requesting thread a message, using send rights given to it by the thread for this purpose. The condition of no send rights can be ascertained by keeping a reference count that is incremented whenever a send right is created, and decremented when one is destroyed.

It should be stressed that the conditions of no senders/no receiver are tackled within the domain of a single kernel at relatively little cost. Checking for these conditions in a distributed system is, by contrast, a complex and expensive operation. Given that rights can be sent in messages, the send or receive rights for a given port could be held by any task, or even be in a message, queued at a port or in transit between computers.

Port sets ☐ Port sets are locally-managed collections of ports that are created within a single task. When a thread issues a receive from a port set, the kernel returns a message that was delivered to some member of the set. It also returns the identifier of this port's receive rights, so that the thread can process the message accordingly.

Ports sets are useful because a server typically is required to service client messages at all of its ports at all times. Receiving a message from a port whose message queue is empty blocks a thread, even if a message that it could process arrives on another port first. Assigning a thread to each port overcomes this problem but is not feasible for servers with large numbers of ports because a thread is a more expensive resource than a port. By collecting ports into a port set, a single thread can be used to service incoming messages without fear of missing any. Furthermore, this thread will block if no messages are available on any port in the set, so avoiding a busy-waiting solution in which the thread polls until a message arrives on one of the ports.

Mach_msg ☐ The *Mach_msg* system call provides for both asynchronous message passing and Request-Reply-style interactions, which makes it extremely complicated. We shall give only an overview of its semantics. The complete call is as follows:

---

mach_msg(msg_header, option, snd_siz, rcv_siz, rcv_name, timeout, notify)
>   *msg_header* points to a common message header for the sent and received messages, *option* specifies send, receive or both, *snd_siz* and *rcv_siz* give the sizes of the sent and received message buffers, *rcv_name* specifies the port or port set receive rights (if a message is received) *timeout* sets a limit to the total time to send and/or receive a message, *notify* supplies port rights which the kernel is to use to send notification messages under exceptional conditions.

Mach_msg either sends a message, receives a message, or both. It is a single system call that clients use to send a request message and receive a reply, and servers use to reply to the last client and receive the next request message. Another benefit of using a combined send/receive call is that in the case of a client and server executing at the same computer the implementation can employ an optimization called *handoff scheduling*. This is where a task about to block after sending a message to another task 'donates' the rest of its timeslice to the other task's thread. This is cheaper than going through the queue of RUNNABLE threads to select the next thread to run.

Figure 18.6   Network communication in Mach.

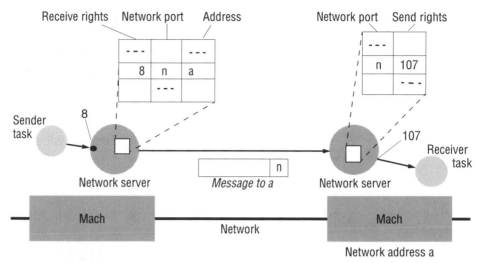

Messages sent by the same thread are delivered in sending order and message delivery is reliable. At least, this is guaranteed where messages are sent between tasks hosted by a common kernel – even in the face of lack of buffer space. When messages are transmitted across a network to a failure-independent computer, at-most-once delivery semantics are provided.

The timeout is useful for situations in which it is undesirable for a thread to be tied up indefinitely, for example awaiting a message that might never arrive, or waiting for queue space at what turns out to be a buggy server's port.

Communication implementation

One of the most interesting aspects of the Mach communication implementation is the use of user-level network servers. The network servers (called *netmsgservers* in the Mach literature), one per computer, are collectively responsible for extending the semantics of local communication across the network. This includes preserving, as far as possible, delivery guarantees and making network communication transparent. It also includes effecting and monitoring the transfer of port rights. In particular, the network servers are responsible for protecting ports against illegal access, and for maintaining the privacy of message data across the network. Full details of Mach's treatment of protection issues are available in Sansom *et al*. [1986].

Transparent message delivery □ Since ports are always local to a Mach kernel, it is necessary to add an externally imposed abstraction of *network port*, to which messages can be addressed across the network. A network port is a globally unique channel identifier that is handled only by the network servers, and is associated by them with a single Mach port at any one time. Network servers possess send and receive rights to network ports, in the same way that tasks possess send and receive rights to Mach ports.

The transmission of a message between tasks located at different computers is shown in Figure 18.6. The rights held by the sender task are to a local port, for which receive rights are held by the local network server. In the figure, the network server's local identifier for the receive rights is 8. The network server at the sender's computer looks up an entry for the rights identifier in a table of network ports for which it has send rights. This yields a network port and a network address hint. It sends the message, with the network port attached, to the network server at the address indicated in the table. There, the local network server extracts the network port and looks this up in a table of network ports for which it has receive rights. If it finds a valid entry there (the network port might have been relocated to another kernel), then this entry contains the identifier of send rights to a local Mach port. This network server forwards the message using these rights, and the message is thus delivered to the appropriate port. The whole process of handling by the network servers is transparent to both the sender and the receiver.

How are the tables shown in Figure 18.6 set up? The network server of a newly booted computer engages in an initialization protocol, whereby send rights are obtained to network-wide services. Consider what happens thereafter, when a message containing port rights is transferred between network servers. These rights are typed, and therefore can be tracked by the network servers. If a task sends a local port's send rights, the local network server creates a network port identifier and a table entry for the local port – if none exists – and attaches the identifier to the message it forwards. The receiving network server also sets up a table entry if none exists.

When receive rights are transmitted, the situation is a little more complicated. This is an example in which migration transparency is required: clients must be able to send messages to the port while it migrates. First, the network server local to the sender acquires the receive rights. All messages destined for the port, local and remote, start arriving at this server. It then engages in a protocol whereby the receive rights are consistently transferred to the destination network server.

The main issue concerning this transfer of rights is how to arrange that messages sent to the port now arrive at the computer to which receive rights have been transferred. One possibility would be for Mach to keep track of all network servers possessing send rights to a given network port, and to notify these servers directly when receive rights were transferred. This scheme was rejected as being too expensive to manage. A cheaper alternative would have been to use a hardware broadcast facility to broadcast the change of location to all network servers. However, such a broadcast service is not reliable, and hardware broadcast is not available on all networks. Instead, responsibility for locating a network port was placed upon the network servers that hold send rights to the port.

Recall that a network server uses a location hint when it forwards a message to another network server. The possible responses are:

port here: the destination holds receive rights;

port dead: the port is known to have been destroyed;

port not here, transferred: receive rights were transferred to a specified address;

port not here, unknown: there is no record of the network port;

no response: the destination computer is dead.

If a forwarding address is returned, the sending network server forwards the message; but this in turn is only a hint and might be inaccurate. If at some point the sender runs out of forwarding addresses, then it resorts to broadcasting. How to manage chains of forwarding addresses and what to do when a computer holding a forwarding address crashes are both major design issues for this type of location algorithm, particularly over a WAN. Use of forwarding addresses over a WAN is described in Black and Artsy [1990].

A second issue in achieving migration transparency is how to synchronize message delivery. Mach guarantees that two messages sent by the same thread are delivered in the same order. How can this be guaranteed while receive rights are being transmitted? If care is not taken, a message could be delivered by the new network server before a prior message queued at the original computer was forwarded. The network server can achieve this, by holding off delivery of all messages at the original computer until any queued messages have been transferred to the destination computer. Message delivery can thereafter be rerouted safely, and the forwarding address returned to senders.

Transport protocols □ Despite the intention that a range of transport protocols should be accommodated by running the network servers in user space, at the time of writing, Mach's network servers in widespread use employ only TCP/IP as the transport protocol. This was prompted in part by UNIX compatibility, and in part it was selected by Carnegie-Mellon University because of its complex network containing over 1700 computers, about 500 of which run Mach. TCP/IP is tuned to achieve robustness fairly efficiently in the face of such a network. However, this is not necessarily suitable on LANs when request-reply interactions predominate, for performance reasons. We discuss the performance of Mach communication in Section 18.6 below.

User-level network drivers □ Some network servers provide their own, user-level network device driver. The aim of this is to speed up network accesses. Apart from achieving flexibility in relation to using a range of hardware, placing device drivers at user-level is largely a means of compensating for the performance degradation due to using a user-level network server. The kernel exports an abstraction of each device, which includes an operation to map the device controller's registers into user space. In the case of an Ethernet, both the registers and the packet buffers used by the controller can be mapped into the network server's address space. In addition, special code is run in the kernel to wake up a user-level thread (belonging, in this case, to the network server), when an interrupt occurs. This thread is thus able to handle the interrupt by transferring data to or from the buffers used by the controller, and resetting the controller for the next operation.

Memory management

Mach is notable not only for its use of large, sparse address spaces, but also for its virtual memory techniques allowing for memory sharing between tasks. Not only can memory be shared physically between tasks executing on the same Mach kernel, but Mach's support for external pagers (called *memory managers* in the Mach literature) allows for the contents of virtual memory to be shared between tasks, even when they reside at different computers. Lastly, the Mach virtual memory implementation is notable for being divided into machine-independent and machine-dependent layers, to aid in porting the kernel [Rashid *et al.* 1988].

Address space structure □ In Chapter 6 we introduced a generic model of an address space consisting of regions. Each region is a range of contiguous logical addresses with a common set of properties. These properties include access permissions (read/write/ execute), and also extensibility. Stack regions, for example, are allowed to grow towards decreasing addresses; and heaps can grow upwards. The model used by Mach is similar.

However, the Mach view of address spaces is that of a collection of contiguous groups of pages named by their addresses, rather than of regions which are separately identifiable. Thus, protection in Mach is applied to pages rather than regions. Mach system calls refer to addresses and extents rather than to region identifiers. For example, Mach would not 'grow the stack region'. Instead, it would allocate some more pages just below those which are currently used for the stack. However, for the most part this distinction is not too important.

We shall refer to a contiguous collection of pages with common properties as a region. As we have seen, Mach supports large numbers of regions, which can be used for varying purposes such as message data or mapped files.

Regions can be created in any of four ways:

- They can be allocated explicitly by a call to *vm_allocate*. A region newly created with *vm_allocate* is, by default, zero-filled.

- A region can be created in association with a *memory object*, using *vm_map* (memory objects are described in Chapter 6).

- Regions can be assigned in a brand new task by declaring them (or rather them and their contents) to be inherited from a blueprint task, using *vm_inherit* applied to the blueprint's region.

- Regions can be allocated automatically in a task's address space as a side-effect of message passing.

All regions can have their read/write/execute permissions set, using *vm_protect*. Regions can be copied within tasks using *vm_copy*, and their contents can be read or written by other tasks using *vm_read* and *vm_write*. Any previously allocated region can be de-allocated, using *vm_deallocate*.

We shall now describe Mach's approach to the implementation of the UNIX *fork* operation, and the virtual memory aspects of message passing, which are incorporated in Mach so as to enable memory sharing to take place wherever convenient.

Memory sharing: inheritance and message passing □ Mach allows for a generalization of UNIX *fork* semantics through the mechanism of *memory inheritance*. We have seen that a task is created from another task which acts as a blueprint. A region that is inherited from the blueprint task contains the same address range, and its memory is either:

shared: backed by the same memory; or

copied: backed by memory that is a copy of the blueprint's memory at the time the child region was created;

it is also possible, in case a region is not required in the child, to set it to be non-inherited.

In the case of a UNIX *fork*, the program text of the blueprint task is set to be inherited for sharing by the child task. The same would be true of a region containing shared library code. The program heap and stack, however, would be inherited as copies of the blueprint's regions. In addition, if the blueprint is required to share a data region with its child (as is allowed by System V UNIX), then it could set up this region to be inherited for sharing.

Out-of-line message data is transferred between tasks in a way that is somewhat similar to copy-inheritance (see Chapter 6). A region is created by Mach in the receiver's address space, and its initial contents are a copy of the region passed as out-of-line data by the sender. Unlike inheritance, the received region does not in general occupy the same address range as the sent region. The address range of the sent region might already be used by an existing region in the receiver.

Chapter 6 described implementation techniques for both memory sharing and copying. Mach uses copy-on-write for both copy-inheritance and message passing. Mach thus makes an optimistic assumption: that some or all the memory that is copy-inherited or passed as out-of-line message data will not be written by either task, even when write permissions exist.

To justify this optimistic assumption, consider once again, for example, the UNIX *fork* system call. It is common for a *fork* operation to be followed soon by an *exec* call, over-writing the address space contents, including the writeable heap and stack. If memory had been physically copied at the time of the fork, then most of this copying would have been wasted: few pages are modified between the two calls.

As a second important example, consider a message sent to the local network server for transmission. This message might be very large. If, however, the sending task does not modify the message, or modifies only parts of it, in the time taken to transmit the message, then much memory copying can be saved. Of course, the network server has no reason to modify the message. The copy-on-write optimization helps to offset the context switching costs incurred in transmitting via the network server.

Evaluation of copy-on-write □ While copy-on-write assists in passing message data between tasks and the network server, copy-on-write cannot be used to facilitate transmission across a network. This is because the computers involved do not, of course, share physical memory.

Copy-on-write is normally efficient as long as sufficient data are involved. The advantage of avoiding physical copying has to outweigh the costs of page table manipulations (and cache manipulations, if the cache is virtually mapped – see Section 6.3). Figures for a Mach implementation on a SUN 3/60 are given by Abrossimov *et al.* [1989], and we reproduce some of them in Figure 18.7. The figures are given for illustration only, and do not necessarily represent the most up-to-date performance of Mach.

Times for regions of two sizes, 8 kilobytes (1 page) and 256 kilobytes (32 pages), are given. The first two columns are for reference only. The column 'Simple copy' shows the time it would take simply to copy all the data involved between two pre-existing regions (that is, without using copy-on-write). The column 'Create region' gives the time required to create a zero-filled region (but one which is not accessed). The remaining columns give measured times taken from experiments in which a pre-existing region was copied into another region using copy-on-write. The figures include the time for creating the copy region, copying data on modification, and destroying the copy

Figure 18.7   Copy-on-write overheads.

Region size	Simple copy	Create region	Amount of data copied (on writing)		
			0 kilobytes (0 pages)	8 kilobytes (1 page)	256 kilobytes (32 pages)
8 kilobytes	1.4	1.57	2.7	4.82	–
256 kilobytes	44.8	1.81	2.9	5.12	66.4

Note: all times are in milliseconds.

region. For each region size, figures are given for cases of different amounts of data modified in the source region.

If we compare the times for a one page region, there is an overhead of $4.82 - 2.7 = 2.12$ milliseconds due to the page being written. 1.4 milliseconds of this can be ascribed to copying the page; the remaining 0.72 milliseconds is taken up by write-fault handling and modification of internal virtual memory management data structures. For sending a message of size 8 kilobytes between two local tasks, sending the data out-of-line (that is, using copy-on-write) seems to be of dubious advantage over sending it in-line, when it will be simply copied. In-line transfer would involve two copies (user-kernel and kernel-user), and therefore would take somewhat more than 2.8 milliseconds in all. But the worst out-of-line case is significantly more expensive. On the other hand, transmitting a 256 kilobyte message out-of-line is far less expensive than in-line transmission if the optimistic assumption holds; and even in the worst case, 66.4 milliseconds is less than the 2×44.8 milliseconds required to copy 256 kilobytes of in-line data into and out of the kernel.

As a final point regarding virtual memory techniques for copying and sharing data, note that care has to be taken over specifying the data involved. Although we did not state this above, a user can specify regions as address ranges that do not begin and end on a page boundary. Mach, however, is forced to apply memory sharing at the granularity of a page. Any data that are within the pages concerned but were not specified by the user will nonetheless be copied between the tasks. This is an example of what is known as *false sharing* (see also the discussion of the granularity of shared data items in Chapter 17).

External pagers

In keeping with the microkernel philosophy, the Mach kernel does not support files or any other abstraction of external storage directly. Instead, it assumes that these resources are implemented by external pagers. Following Multics [Organick 1972], Mach has chosen the mapped access model for memory objects, which we introduced in Section 6.6. Instead of accessing stored data using explicit *read* and *write* operations, the programmer is required only to access corresponding virtual memory locations directly. An advantage of mapped access is its uniformity: the programmer is presented with one model for access to data, not two. However, the question of whether mapped access is

Figure 18.8   External pager.

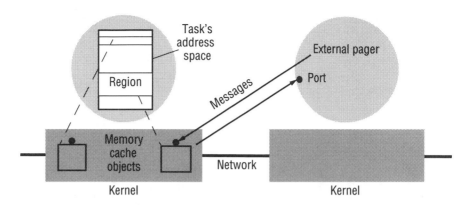

preferable to using explicit operations is complex in its ramifications, especially as regards performance, and we shall not attempt to deal with it here. We shall concentrate now on the distributed aspects of the Mach virtual memory implementation. This consists primarily of the protocol between the kernel and an external pager that is necessary to manage the mapping of data stored by the latter.

Mach allows a region to be associated with contiguous data from a specified offset in a memory object, using a call to *vm_map*. This association means that read accesses to addresses in the region are satisfied by data backed by the memory object, and data in the region modified by write accesses are propagated back to the memory object. In general, the memory object is managed by an external pager, although a default pager may be supplied, implemented by the kernel itself. The memory object is represented by send rights to a port used by the external pager, which satisfies requests from the kernel concerning the memory object.

For each memory object mapped by it, the kernel keeps a local resource called a *memory cache object* (Figure 18.8). This essentially is a list of pages containing data backed by the corresponding memory object.

Recall from Section 6.6 that the roles of an external pager are (i) to store data that have been purged by a kernel from its cache of pages, (ii) to supply page data as required by a kernel, and (iii) to impose consistency constraints pertaining to the underlying memory resource abstraction, in the case where the memory resource is shared and several kernels can hold memory cache objects for the same memory object simultaneously.

The main components of the message passing protocol between the kernel (K) and external pager (EP) are summarized in Figure 18.9. When *vm_map* is called, the local kernel contacts the external pager using the memory object port send right supplied to it in the *vm_map* call, sending it a message *memory_object_init*. The kernel supplies send rights in this message, which the external pager is to use to control the memory cache object. It also declares the size and offset of the required data in the memory object, and the type of access required (read/write). The external pager responds with a message *memory_object_set_attributes*, which tells the kernel whether the pager is yet ready to handle data requests, and supplies further information about the pager's requirements in relation to the memory object. When an external pager receives a *memory_object_init*

Figure 18.9   External pager messages.

Event	Sender	Message
vm_map called by task	K → EP	*memory_object_init*
	EP → K	*memory_object_set_attributes*, or
	EP → K	*memory_object_data_error*
Task page-faults when no data	K → EP	*memory_object_data_request*
frame exists	EP → K	*memory_object_data_provided*, or
	EP → K	*memory_object_data_unavailable*
Kernel writes modified page to persistent store	K → EP	*memory_object_data_write*
External pager directs kernel to	EP → K	*memory_object_lock_request*
write page/set access permissions	K → EP	*memory_object_lock_completed*
Task page-faults when insufficient	K → EP	*memory_object_data_unlock*
page access	EP → K	*memory_object_lock_request*
Memory object no longer mapped	K → EP	*memory_object_terminate*
External pager withdraws memory	EP → K	*memory_object_destroy*
object	K → EP	*memory_object_terminate*

message, it is able to determine whether it needs to implement a consistency protocol, since all kernels wishing to access the corresponding memory object have to send this message.

Supporting non-shared access to a memory object □ We begin by considering the case in which just one computer maps a particular memory object. For the sake of concreteness, we can think of the memory object as a file. Assuming no pre-fetching of file data from the external pager, all pages in the mapped region corresponding to this file are initially hardware-protected against all accesses, since no file data is resident. When a thread attempts to read one of the region's pages, a page fault occurs. The kernel looks up the memory object port send right corresponding to the mapped region, and sends a *memory_object_data_request* message to the external pager (which is, in our example, a file server). If all is well, the external pager responds with the page data, in a *memory_object_data_provided* message.

If the file data is modified by the computer that has mapped it, then sometimes the kernel needs to write the page from its memory cache object. To do this, it sends a message *memory_object_data_write* to the external pager, containing the page data. Modified pages are transmitted to the external pager as a side-effect of page replacement (when the kernel needs to find space for another page). In addition, the kernel can decide to write the page to backing store (but leave it in the memory cache object) in order to meet persistence guarantees. Implementations of UNIX, for example, write modified data to disk normally at least every 30 seconds, in case of a system crash. Some operating systems allow programs to control the safety of their data by issuing a *flush* command on an open file, which causes all modified file pages to be written to disk by the time the call returns.

Different types of memory resource can have differing persistence guarantees. The external pager can itself request, in a *memory_object_lock_request* message to a kernel, that modified data in a specified range should be sent back to the pager for commitment to permanent storage in accordance with these guarantees. When the kernel has completed the requested actions, it sends a *memory_object_lock_completed* message to the external pager. (The external pager requires this, because it cannot know which pages have been modified, and so need to be written back to it.)

Note that all the messages we are describing are sent asynchronously, even if they sometimes occur in request-reply combinations. This is, first, so that threads are not suspended, but can get on with other work after issuing requests. Moreover, a thread is not tied up when it has issued a request to an external pager or kernel that turns out to have crashed (or when the kernel sends a request to an ill-behaved external pager that does not reply). Lastly, an external pager can use the asynchronous message-based protocol to implement a page pre-fetching policy. It can send page data in *memory_object_data_provided* messages to memory cache objects in anticipation of the data's use, instead of waiting for a page-fault to occur and for the data then to be requested.

Supporting shared access to a memory object □ Let us now suppose, following our example, that several tasks residing at different computers map a common file. If the file is mapped read-only in every region used to access it, then there is no consistency problem and requests for file pages can be satisfied immediately. If, however, at least one task maps the file for writing, then the external pager (that is, the file server) has to implement a protocol to ensure that tasks do not read inconsistent versions of the same page.

The reader is invited to translate the write-invalidate protocol for achieving sequential consistency, as discussed in Chapter 17, into messages sent between the Mach kernel and external pagers.

Discussion of Mach's main features

In summary, the Mach kernel runs on both multiprocessor and uniprocessor computers connected by networks. It is designed for an extremely ambitious enterprise: to allow new distributed systems to evolve while maintaining UNIX compatibility. Mach is a relatively stable design. A working emulation of 4.3BSD UNIX runs on version 3 with a range of high performance servers such as gateways.

Due to the sophistication of some of the facilities Mach is designed to emulate, the kernel itself is complex. The kernel's interface includes several hundreds of calls, although many of these are stubs which make only *mach_msg* system call traps. An operating system such as UNIX cannot be emulated using message passing alone. Sophisticated virtual memory facilities are required, and Mach provides these. Mach's model of tasks and threads and the integration of virtual memory management with communication, all represent a considerable improvement over basic UNIX facilities, incorporating lessons learned in attempting to implement UNIX servers, in particular. Its model of inter-task communication is functionally rich, and extremely complex in its semantics. However, it should be borne in mind that only a few system programmers should ever have to use it in its raw form: for example, simple UNIX pipes and remote procedure call are both provided on top of it.

Although the Mach kernel is often referred to as a microkernel, it is of the order of 500 kilobytes of code and initialized data (including a substantial proportion of device driver code). Even though its size belies this term, Mach is wedded to the microkernel philosophy. The kernel is a fixed platform that includes no management of files or other high-level resources; many operating system facilities are left to be implemented by user-level servers.

Apart from the success or otherwise of its UNIX emulation (see Section 18.4), there are two aspects of Mach which we note as being controversial, both of which stem from its adherence to user-level servers. The first is the decision for network communication to be implemented outside the kernel, as in Accent, rather than providing some support for this in the kernel, and leaving other protocols to be implemented outside it. This decision has a performance penalty in comparison with supporting network communication in the kernel. The advantages are the gain in flexibility in design of the network servers and their protocols.

The second point of controversy is the decision that servers should always run at user-level. Chorus, which is similar to Mach in many ways, diverges from Mach on this point, and we shall take up the issue as we discuss the Chorus design.

18.3 Chorus

History and architectural overview

Chorus began life in 1979 as a research project on distributed systems at the Institut National de Recherche en Informatique et Automatique (INRIA) in France. The goal of the project was to develop a message-based computational model for constructing a modular distributed operating system. Chorus went through three design phases at INRIA, and three corresponding versions of the distributed operating system emerged. In version 0 a model of communicating processes called *actors* was developed and a prototype implementation was made using a small kernel. In version 1 the previous design was ported from a LAN-based system to a distributed memory multiprocessor. For version 2 a team that had been working on implementing UNIX joined the project, and an attempt was begun to emulate UNIX using the Chorus kernel and re-using some of the code written by the UNIX team. When the project ceased at INRIA, a company, Chorus Systèmes, was set up to continue the development of Chorus on both LANs and multiprocessors. The Chorus kernel (version 3), also called the *nucleus*, and a UNIX emulation built on top of it, Chorus/MiX, are now being produced and developed by Chorus Systèmes [Rozier *et al.* 1988, 1990]. We describe Chorus version 3.3 in this section.

A Chorus system consists of uniprocessor or multiprocessor computers connected by a network. Chorus is architecturally similar to Mach in many ways. The Chorus kernel is a microkernel aimed at supporting subsystems. A Chorus subsystem is a collection of servers which provide a binary emulation of an operating system (UNIX in particular), or which provide some other major service to applications, such as the run-time support for a language. Generic run-time support for object-oriented languages on top of the Chorus kernel is the subject of research [Lea *et al.* 1993]. At the time of writing, the kernel has been implemented on the Intel 80386, Motorola 68030 and 88000 microprocessors, and Transputers, among others. A binary emulation of System V Release 4 UNIX exists for Intel 80386-based and Motorola 88000-based computers, and a BSD 4.3 UNIX emulation is being implemented.

Chorus has been implemented as a basis for real-time process control systems running on embedded distributed memory multiprocessors based on 68020, 80386 and Transputer microprocessors.

Design goals and chief design features

Chorus has the following design goals in common with Mach (see Section 18.2):

- microkernel support for open system services, accessed by message passing;
- support for binary-level operating system emulation (in particular the emulation of UNIX) and other subsystems;
- transparent extensibility of kernel facilities to network operation;
- flexible virtual memory implementation;
- portability (the Chorus kernel is written in C++ and designed to be modular and split into machine-dependent and machine-independent parts);
- exploitation of shared memory multiprocessors.

Chorus also has the following goals and features:

Dynamically loadable servers: Chorus aims to achieve the same degree of modularity and openness as does Mach. However, Chorus has not equated these goals with the use of user-level servers. Instead, Chorus supports dynamically loadable servers which may execute either at user-level or within the kernel address space.

Enhancement of UNIX: The Chorus design anticipates that users of the UNIX emulation might want to use enhanced facilities provided by the underlying kernel from within UNIX processes, such as multiple threads and the ability to create a new process at a remote computer.

Support for server groups and server reconfiguration: Chorus provides support for server groups in the form of group addressing modes for sending messages, including multicast. Port migration can be used to transfer management of a resource or collection of resources dynamically between servers, and is similar to the transfer of port receive rights in Mach.

Distributed memory multiprocessor operation: Chorus has been implemented on several distributed memory multiprocessors. Processors used in embedded multiprocessor systems may have relatively primitive hardware support for memory management. This has constrained the provision of features that assume the existence of sophisticated MMU hardware.

Figure 18.10   The main Chorus abstractions (messages and local caches not shown).

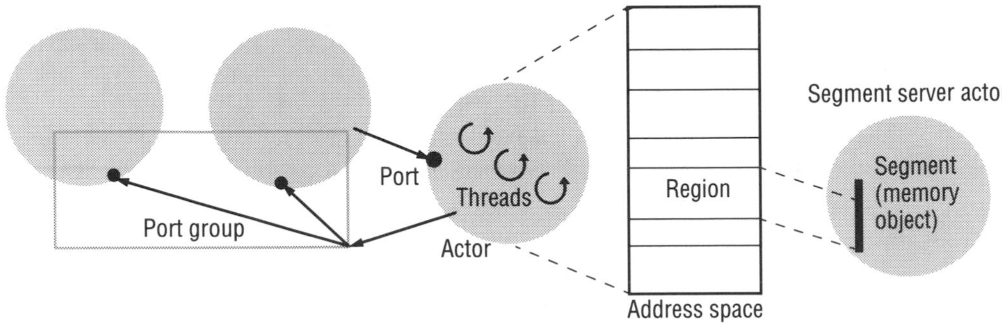

Real-time operation: The Chorus design aims to support real-time subsystems on the kernel. To this end, Chorus provides for flexible allocation of thread priorities and allows for customized thread scheduling policies; threads executing within the kernel can be scheduled pre-emptively.

Summary of the main Chorus abstractions

The main abstractions provided by the Chorus kernel (Figure 18.10) are as follows:

Actors: A Chorus actor is an execution environment equivalent to a Mach task. An actor can have one or more threads.

Ports: A port is a unidirectional communication channel with an associated message queue. Ports can be migrated between actors.

Port groups: Ports can be made members of port groups. A port group is a destination for messages, and there are several addressing modes for sending messages to a port group. Port groups should not be confused with the port *sets* of Mach.

Messages: A Chorus message consists of a variable length body (limited to 64 kilobytes), and optionally a fixed-size (64-byte) header.

Regions, segments and local caches: An actor's address space is divided into regions, which are as we defined them in Chapter 6. A region can be mapped onto a portion of a *segment*, which is the equivalent of a Mach memory object. For each mapped segment the kernel keeps a *local cache*, similar to a Mach cache object.

The virtual memory design in Chorus is very similar to that of Mach and we shall not pursue this further even though its implementation is interesting [Abrossimov *et al.* 1989]. We now turn to the main design features that do differ from Mach.

Process management model

The basic processing building blocks in Chorus are *actors* and threads. An *actor* is similar to a Mach task and the chief components of its execution environment are an

Figure 18.11   Chorus servers.

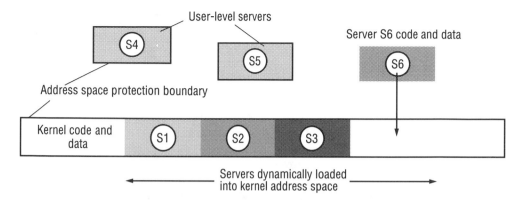

Note: The figure shows the code and data for a server being dynamically loaded into the kernel address space, where it will execute. It also shows some user-level servers, which execute within private address spaces.

address space and a collection of ports used to receive messages. Where Chorus differs chiefly from Mach is that actors can be dynamically loaded into the kernel address space, and their threads can execute in the kernel protection domain.

Servers are loaded dynamically at those computers where they are needed and are accessed by message-based communication. Servers are generally run as user-level processes to ensure mutual protection between the kernel and the servers it runs.

The price paid for this, however, is that of the extra context switches that occur in accessing user-level servers, compared to kernel-provided services. The Chorus designers decided that, in the case of some servers, the extra context switches incurred were too high a price to pay. They opted instead for an architecture in which:

• server code and data can be loaded dynamically at a computer as needed, and accessed via message passing, but

• a separate decision can be taken for each server as to whether the server program is added to the contents of the kernel's address space, or run in a private protection domain (Figure 18.11).

With this scheme, clients are unaware of whether a server with which they communicate is a user-level actor or is executing within the kernel. Clients and servers use the same message passing interface in either case. Moreover, the message passing interfaces can still be used between servers that reside in the same kernel address space. Inside the kernel, the implementation of message passing is designed to be efficient by taking advantage of shared memory to reduce data copying. This illustrates the fact that these servers use the message passing interface only as a convention. They can perform arbitrary accesses to one another's data if they so choose, or if they contain bugs. Note, however, that actors can be debugged at user-level. If their performance at user-level is deemed unsatisfactory, they can be run later in the kernel, without altering the source code, to gain the performance advantage this brings.

Figure 18.12 Types of actor, showing address spaces and allowable threads.

Actor type	Private address space	User threads	Supervisor threads
User actor	Yes	Yes	Yes (created externally)
System actor	Yes	Yes (system privilege)	Yes
Supervisor actor	No: shares kernel's	No	Yes

Chorus supports three different levels of privilege for threads accessing local resources. Privilege is sometimes nominally ascribed to actors, but since only threads can take actions with respect to resources, privilege really resides with threads. The three level of privilege are:

user privilege: no direct access to machine resources; cannot invoke certain system calls;

system privilege: no direct access to machine resources, but can invoke all system calls – similar to the level of privilege of a UNIX process bearing the 'root' user identifier;

supervisor privilege: complete access to machine resources.

We now describe these privileges in more detail, in the context of actors and threads.

Actors □ Every actor is either a *user actor*, a *system actor* or a *supervisor actor*. System actors and user actors have their own separate address spaces, and may not access that of the kernel. However, the threads belonging to a system actor may make privileged system calls not available to those of user actors. For example, unlike a user actor, a system actor's thread can insert a port into a port group used to provide a system service. System actors can be created only by threads belonging to existing system actors, or by threads with supervisor privilege. At system initialization, one or more system actors are created at each computer, which may create further system actors. The kernel can check whether an actor is a system actor: its status is held securely in a table in the kernel address space.

Supervisor actors differ from the other two types in that their code and data reside in the kernel address space. Any program tested as a user-level actor can be run without source-level alteration as a supervisor actor. However, in order to execute within the kernel, the binary code has to be link-edited dynamically. There are two aspects to this. First it is necessary for kernel system calls to be replaced by calls to kernel procedures. Since threads belonging to supervisor actors execute in the kernel, they should take advantage of the cheapest available invocation mechanism. Second, space has to be found in the kernel address space where the supervisor actor's code and data will reside. Neither the server program's address space location, nor the addresses of the kernel procedures that it calls are known in advance. Therefore all absolute program addresses used in the server program must be set dynamically using load-time location information.

Note that not all supervisor actors can be run at user-level – even as system actors. This is because the code for a supervisor actor can, for example, contain privileged machine instructions for manipulating hardware registers. Attempting to execute these instructions at user-level would result in a hardware exception. The three types of actor and their main properties are shown in Figure 18.12.

Creating actors □ All actors are created with only one port – the so-called *default port*, to which operations upon the actor are sent. A brand new actor consists of very little state: it has no threads and, unlike a Mach task, it always has an empty address space. However, some initial characteristics are defined: actors are created as children of existing actors, from which they inherit, for example, their scheduling priority.

The system call to create an actor is *actorCreate*:

---

actorCreate(actorInit, actorCap, type, status)
>   creates a new actor as a child of *actorInit*, with type *type* (*USER*, *SYSTEM* or *SUPERVISOR*). A capability for the new *actor* is returned via *actorCap*; *status* specifies whether or not all new threads in the new actor are to be suspended initially.

(The structure of capabilities in Chorus is described below.) A new actor always resides at the same computer as its parent, so there is no need to specify a computer. The creation of actors at remote computers is left to subsystems to implement.

User and supervisor threads □ The threads belonging to system actors are privileged in that they may make certain system calls. This does not imply any special privileges with respect to direct access to hardware resources such as physical memory and device registers. However, threads belonging to any type of actor may execute as *supervisor threads*, which execute in the address space of the kernel, and with the processor in supervisor mode (see Section 6.2). They therefore have unlimited access to hardware resources. Note that all the threads belonging to a supervisor actor have to be supervisor threads, since their code is mapped into the kernel.

The system call *threadCreate*, which follows, is used to create a thread in an actor:

---

threadCreate(actorCap, privilege, status, priority, entry, stackPointer)
>   creates a new thread in an actor specified with the capability *actorCap*, with privilege *privilege* (*USER* or *SUPERVISOR*) and with scheduling priority *priority* relative to the process. The initial program counter and stack pointer are *entry* and *stackPointer*.

If *privilege* has the value *USER*, then *entry* and *stackPointer* are addresses in the address space of the given actor, which must be a user actor or system actor. If *privilege* is *SUPERVISOR*, then *entry* must be an address of an instruction in the kernel address space (normally the address of a kernel procedure).

System actors can create supervisor threads. How can a user-level actor come to know the address of a kernel procedure? The address has to be looked up from the procedure's name in the symbol table of the kernel. However, the stack pointer for a supervisor thread is allocated by the kernel, and the value given in *stackPointer* is ignored in this case.

Figure 18.13 A Chorus capability.

UI (64 bits)	Key (64 bits)

Threads are scheduled pre-emptively by the kernel according to individual thread priorities, but these priorities can be set dynamically by actors. Chorus supports two-level scheduling. Thread priorities are set relative to their actor's priority, and actors are assigned absolute priorities. A thread's absolute priority is the sum of these two priorities. Even supervisor threads can be scheduled pre-emptively, in order to meet real-time demands. By contrast, conventional implementations of UNIX schedule processes executing kernel code without pre-emption.

Naming and protection

Chorus uses *capabilities*, *unique identifiers* and *local identifiers* as basic names for resources.

Capabilities: These are the most general type of resource identifier in Chorus. They are used for identifying and restricting access to resources such as segments managed by servers, and also some resources managed by the kernel itself, notably actors and port groups. A capability consists of a unique identifier, which is normally the identifier of a port, and an additional 64-bit structure called a *key* (Figure 18.13). The key can be used to identify a resource from among multiple resources accessed via the same port. Servers choose the key so it is hard to guess, and thus provides a degree of protection against illegal accesses to resources.

Unique identifiers: Ports and other resources managed by the kernel are assigned 64-bit *unique identifiers*. Unique identifiers (UIs) are guaranteed to be unique within a network of Chorus computers, over its lifetime. They are fabricated as bit strings with three components: the type of the kernel resource identified by them (for example, port, actor or port group), the identifier of the computer that created it and a local timestamp guaranteed to be unique over the lifetime of the computer.

Local identifiers: Local identifiers are used to name the threads and ports belonging to an actor. They are 32-bit integers which are valid only within the actor which uses them. An actor's port can have aliases: its local identifier and its (globally valid) UI. Using the local identifier is the most efficient, however: local identifiers are generated by the kernel for fast access to the resources named. They are similar in this respect to Mach's identifiers.

Identifying resources managed by groups □ In order that a service can be provided by different servers at different times, or so that a service can be implemented at any one time by several servers, the ports that processes use to receive requests can be collected in groups. Messages can be addressed to port groups as well as ports, in one of several group-addressing modes.

The system calls for creating and manipulating port groups are as follows:

grpAllocate
Allocate a capability for a port group.

grpPortInsert
Insert a port into a port group.

grpPortRemove
Remove a port from a port group.

In order to manipulate the membership of a port group, an actor needs a capability for it. Capabilities are allocated dynamically for port groups, via calls to *grpAllocate*. This call can be used either to obtain a capability for a well-known port group, or to allocate a capability for a brand new group. Any actor that knows the group capability can insert a port into the group, using *grpPortInsert*, or remove a port, using *grpPortRemove*.

For sending purposes, only a port group's UI is required, and not the capability. Group identifiers provide a level of indirection, so that an actor using a group identifier does not need to know which ports belong to the group. When a message is sent using a group identifier, the sender selects one of the following addressing modes:

Multicast mode: An attempt is made to deliver the message, unreliably, to all members of the group (this is also known as *Broadcast mode*).

Functional mode: The message is delivered to at most one member of the group, but the member chosen is undefined in advance.

Selective functional mode: In this mode, the sender has to include a UI as well as the group capability. The message is delivered to at most one member of the group, one which exists at the same computer as the resource with the given UI.

We now provide illustrations of how these addressing modes are used to access resources managed by groups of servers.

Multicast mode □ Consider the problem of requesting an operation upon a resource that is managed by some member of a group of servers, but it is not known which. The request can be multicast in a message containing a service-specific identifier of the resource. This can be a low-level system identifier, or, for example, a file pathname. Upon receipt of the message, only the server that manages the resource will perform the operation; the other servers can ignore the request (Figure 18.14).

A significant disadvantage of this scheme is that all processes in the group have to receive the message, even if it is not relevant to them. This arrangement would be impractical for the processing of all operations on resources managed by the group. It is preferable for clients to request a capability for the resource initially, using multicast. The capability returned by the server that manages the resource will contain the identifier of a port, and all the client's subsequent requests can be sent directly to the server that owns this port. The initial multicast is effectively a name lookup: a capability is returned when the client presents a resource name to the group.

Note that the Chorus multicast service is primitive in that it is unreliable and provides no ordering guarantees. This is a reasonable choice for a microkernel, considering that higher-level requirements are liable to vary, and can be implemented

Figure 18.14 A message multicast to a group.

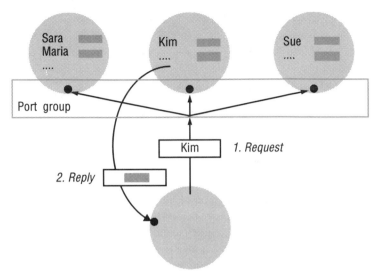

on top of the Chorus mechanism. In Chapter 11 we described the use and implementation of reliable and ordered multicast facilities.

Functional mode □ To illustrate the use of functional addressing, we now consider the problem of replacing a single server that provides a given service – for example, to replace a server with an upgrade. One solution to this problem is for the service to be provided via a group of server ports, which normally has only one member. All requests are sent to this group of servers, using functional mode addressing. This addressing mode delivers the request messages to one member of the group – and there is only one member. The replacement server can join this group by inserting its port using *grpPortInsert*; the server to be replaced can leave the group by using *grpPortRemove* to remove its port from the group (Figure 18.15). For reconfiguration transparency to be achieved, care has to be taken to synchronize message processing so that client requests are processed consistently.

Note that message delivery under functional mode group addressing can be implemented as efficiently as unicast message delivery. Once a port belonging to the group has been located, messages can be sent using a unicast protocol to that port until such time as the port leaves the group. At that point, computers sending to the group will receive a negative acknowledgement notifying them that they need to search for another port in the group.

Selective functional mode □ The *selective functional* group addressing mode is useful for identifying a particular server from a group of servers. For example, a service that provides information about computer loads could be implemented using an actor at each computer, which monitors activity at that computer. Each such actor places a port in a common group. To find the load at a particular computer, a request can be sent to this 'load monitoring' group, using selective functional addressing with the UI of the required computer included in the address.

Figure 18.15 Functional mode addressing.

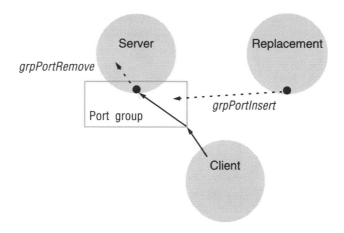

Each computer manages a database of UIs which is searched when attempting to deliver a message using selective functional addressing. Chorus includes in this database, by default, the UIs of the computer, all local actors and all local ports. In addition, an actor can declare a UI of its choice as belonging to its local database using *uiDeclare*, and it can remove it later using *uiForget*. This allows servers to declare themselves as being associated with particular resources for the purposes of selective functional addressing.

Transferring resources between servers □ We have already described how port groups are used to implement reconfigurable servers. There is in addition a *port migration mechanism* whereby a port can be removed from one Chorus actor and inserted in another. This transfers from one actor to another the ability to receive messages sent to the port. Using this mechanism, management of an individual resource – or a group of resources – can be transferred from one server actor to another. After a port migrates, all requests sent to it become queued for reception by the new actor. This is so, whether the senders of these requests use capabilities that contain the port's UI, or use the identifier of a group of which it is a member. As one would expect, ports remain members of port groups when they migrate.

This mechanism is equivalent in its effects to the transfer of port receive rights in Mach; it differs only in the fact that the actor at which the port initially resides is not required to take part in the migration. Note that port migration seems at first sight to be equivalent to placing one actor's port in a port group and removing the other actor's port. However, the group mechanism, unlike port migration, can be used even if the original port becomes unavailable due to a crash of its host computer. Under those circumstances, the original port is deemed automatically to have left the group. In favour of port migration, however, note that managing ports requires less memory overheads than managing port groups. Furthermore, the port migration mechanism offers control over continuity of request handling, which cannot be guaranteed using the group mechanism. Messages sent using functional mode addressing that were previously delivered to the original port may be delivered to *any* port in the group after this port is removed – and not necessarily the one intended as the replacement port.

Protection □ Chorus port identifiers and capabilities can be propagated freely in messages between processes, without intervention by the kernel. Port identifiers exist in a sufficiently large name space (they are 64-bit UIs) that guessing a port identifier that has been chosen at random is not practically feasible. Capabilities can be made hard to forge through the choice of their keys, and so resource protection can be applied even against actors that know the relevant port identifier.

However, capabilities cannot be used as the sole basis for a scheme to emulate UNIX *user-group-other* protection semantics (see Section 18.5). For this reason, Chorus undertakes a form of authentication on behalf of service implementors. That is, Chorus is able to identify securely the source of a message to a server that receives it. For example, in order to emulate UNIX, actors implementing UNIX processes can be associated with the equivalent of UNIX user identifiers.

To enable authentication to take place, a *protection identifier* is associated with each actor. An actor's protection identifier (PI) is by default that of the actor that created it; but it can be changed by supervisor threads or system actor threads. When an actor receives a message, it can request the kernel to specify the PI of the actor that sent it. A service could use this mechanism to implement access control for the resources it manages.

Of course, this mechanism provides security only if the association between actors and PIs is itself securely applied. At a single computer, the kernel can easily transmit PIs securely. An authentication protocol is required, however, to provide secure authentication across a network, in the face of possible eavesdropping, tampering and replaying. We discussed authentication protocols in Chapter 16.

The Chorus approach to ensuring that only legitimate servers can provide a service is to make port group membership secure. An actor may only add a port to a group if it possesses a capability for it. Although the capability may contain a well known group UI, the key part is chosen dynamically to be hard to guess. As long as port group capabilities are kept secret, actors cannot masquerade as system servers through the port group mechanism.

Communication model and implementation

Communication system calls □ Chorus provides the following main system calls related to communication:

---

ipcCall
    Send a request and receive a reply.

ipcSend
    Asynchronously send a message.

ipcReceive
    Receive a message.

ipcReply
    Reply to a message.

ipcSave, ipcRestore
Save/restore current message.

ipcGetData
Receive body of message.

ipcSysInfo
Return information about current message.

portCreate, portDelete
Create/delete a port.

portEnable, portDisable
Enable/disable a port.

portLi, portUi
Translate port's UI to/from local identifier.

Like Mach, Chorus provides primitives for asynchronous message passing as well as for request-reply interactions. *IpcSend* is used to send a message asynchronously. It can be given either a port UI as a destination, or a group identifier with any addressing mode. *IpcCall* sends a request message and awaits a reply. It can be given any type of destination as an argument except a group addressed in multicast mode. The exception is because *ipcCall* cannot support the processing of multiple copies of a request, or the multiple reply messages that may ensue.

Threads receive requests using *ipcReceive*, which can be given either a local identifier of a port as the reception interface, or a special flag signifying that a message is to be received only from a member of a set of local ports. After receiving a message, a thread can additionally call *ipcSysInfo* to find out information about the message such as the protection identifiers associated with it, before deciding whether to process and reply to it.

When a port is created, using *portCreate*, the kernel allocates and returns a UI for the port. *PortLi* is used to convert the port's UI into a local identifier which can be used with *ipcReceive*. As we explained above, the local identifier is used to gain rapid access to the internal port data structure. Chorus is inconsistent in not allowing the UIs of ports belonging to other actors to be converted to LIs, as might be done for the purposes of efficient message sending. However, the identifiers of these ports may be sent in messages, and only UIs will do for this purpose, since LIs are only valid in the context of a single actor.

By setting an appropriate collection of ports into the *enabled* state, a thread can receive a message from what is the equivalent of a Mach port set. However, there can be only one 'port set' per actor – that is, for all the threads within the actor. To be a member of this set, a port has to be *enabled*. Every port is either *enabled* or *disabled*, and actors can change the state of their ports at will, using *portEnable* and *portDisable*.

Threads reply to requests using *ipcReply*. Normally, the reply is to the last message received by the thread. However, if they are able to request input-output without blocking, threads can postpone replying to a request until the input-output has been performed, and meanwhile respond to other requests. This is useful when, for example, a request arrives for some data that must be fetched from a disk, but when the following request, from a different client, can be serviced without a disk access. Replying out of order is achieved using the concept of *current message*. There is at most one current message per actor at any one time. By default, the current message is the last one received. A thread can save the current message using *ipcSave*, and then receive and reply to further messages. When the thread is ready to reply to the saved request, it can restore it to be the current message, by using *ipcRestore* and quoting a message identifier supplied by the kernel at the time it was saved. *IpcReply* is then used to reply to this message.

Messages □ Chorus, unlike Mach, uses simple messages consisting of at most a fixed-size *header* and a variable-sized body. A thread can use *ipcGetData* to extract the body of a message after receiving its header and determining from the data within it the reception buffer to use.

Chorus uses copy-on-write to transfer large message bodies efficiently when *ipcSend* is used, if MMU support for this is available. Unlike Mach, however, Chorus does not generate a new address space region in the receiver as a by-product, but always uses the address range specified by the receiver. There is also an option that can be used with *ipcSend* that causes the pages used to implement the body of a message to be transferred to the receiving actor's address space (assumed to reside at the same computer) – and removed from the sender's address space. This allows the message to be transmitted entirely by page table manipulations. Moving rather than copying data between address spaces in this way is particularly useful where, for example, a message is being forwarded and the sender has no further need for the message body.

The network manager □ The Network Manager is an actor that extends the communication facilities of the kernel transparently across a network, and is in this respect similar to Mach's network server. The Network Manager is responsible both for message transport and for port location. When a thread presents a port UI to the kernel to send a message, this UI is looked up on a list of ports known to be local. If it is not found there, then the port's UI is automatically forwarded by the kernel to the Network Manager, which attempts to locate the port by communicating with other network managers. Once the port has been located, messages sent to the port thereafter are delivered directly to a port belonging to the Network Manager, which forwards them transparently. Similarly, the Network Manager is responsible for locating members of port groups residing at computers across a network from the sending computer.

Discussion of main Chorus features

In summary, the Chorus microkernel is aimed at the support of open services, operating system emulation – particularly System V UNIX – and other subsystems in a distributed system. It runs on network-based distributed systems and on distributed memory multiprocessors. Its scheduling architecture is designed to support real-time systems.

The Chorus kernel provides: multi-threaded processes called actors; communication using ports and groups of ports as destinations; and sophisticated use of virtual memory allowing regions to be backed by external pagers.

The port group and port migration facilities allow for services to be implemented by server groups. However, the level of support for groups is limited to services in which resources are partitioned between servers. Stronger multicast semantics are required when resources are replicated between servers to achieve high availability. A resource or group of resources can be migrated dynamically from one server to another using port migration or port group manipulations. However, although we did not mention this earlier, achieving resource migration transparently in practice involves considerable extra work in transferring resource state between the two servers involved, and synchronizing them.

The communication facilities of Chorus are less dependent than those of Mach upon the existence of sophisticated MMU hardware, and are, by the same token, less flexible in terms of message structure.

The Chorus facility for allowing dynamically loaded servers to execute in the kernel address space is an attempt to improve performance, at the expense of losing hardware protection boundaries between such servers and the kernel. The facility has been utilized in the Chorus/MiX UNIX emulation subsystem, as will be seen in the following section.

18.4 UNIX emulation in Mach and Chorus

Section Chapter 2.3 and Section 18.2 above have motivated the requirement for emulating operating systems at the binary level on top of distributed operating system kernels. Mach and Chorus are designed to emulate operating systems, notably UNIX; UNIX emulation has also been implemented on the V kernel.

Strict binary compatibility requires that all binary files compiled to run on a conventional implementation of a version of UNIX (for example, 4.3BSD or SVR4) should run correctly and without modification on the emulation, for the same machine architecture. This implies that the following list of requirements should be met:

Address space layout: The emulation must provide the regions expected by the program. If the code is non-relocatable, the machine instructions assume that regions such as the program text and heap occupy certain expected address ranges. Address space regions such as the stack must be grown as necessary.

System call processing: Whenever a program executes a system call with a valid set of arguments, the emulation must handle this correctly according to the defined call semantics; it must handle the associated *TRAP* instruction and obey the parameter-passing conventions expected by the program.

Error semantics: Whenever a program presents invalid arguments to a system call, the emulation must reproduce correctly the error semantics defined for the system call. In particular, if the user program provides an invalid memory address, the emulation should simply return an error status, and not raise a hardware exception at user-level.

Failure semantics: The emulation should not introduce new system call failure modes. An example of a failure mode applicable to a conventional UNIX implementation is the inability to complete a call due to lack of system resources such as table space (for example, *fork* may fail in this way).

Protection: User data and the UNIX emulation system itself must not be compromised.

Signals: Signals must be generated and user-level handlers called as appropriate when a UNIX program causes an exception such as an address space violation.

Emulation software is required at every computer that can run UNIX processes. One of the aims when emulating UNIX in a distributed system is to implement a single UNIX image across several computers, so that, for example, UNIX processes have globally unique process identifiers, and signals can be transmitted transparently between computers. It becomes difficult or impossible to meet the requirement of reproducing UNIX failure semantics – in so far as they are defined – in these circumstances. Effectively, many UNIX system calls would have to be implemented as transactions, because of the independent failure modes of computers and networks. Moreover, suitable protection mechanisms are required, strictly speaking, when user data are transferred across a network.

The Mach emulation

A UNIX process is implemented using a Mach task with a single thread. 4.3BSD UNIX services are provided by two software components: an *emulation library* and a *4.3BSD server*. The emulation library is linked as a distinct region into every task emulating a UNIX process. This region is inherited from */etc/init* by all UNIX processes. There is one 4.3BSD server (that is, one such task) for every computer running the emulation. This server both handles requests sent by clients and acts as an external pager when clients fault on mapped UNIX files, as we shall discuss.

Applications do not invoke the code in the emulation library directly. Mach provides a call *task_set_emulation*, which assigns the address of a handler in the emulation library to a given system call number; this is called for each UNIX system call when the emulation is initialized. When a UNIX process executes a system call, the *TRAP* instruction causes the Mach kernel to transfer control back to the thread in the UNIX task, so that this same thread executes the corresponding emulation library handler (Figure 18.16). The handler then either sends a message requesting the required service to the 4.3BSD server task and awaits a reply or, in some cases, performs the UNIX system service using data accessible to the emulation library itself.

Each UNIX process and its local 4.3BSD server share two regions, of size one page. One of these is read-only for the process, and it contains information such as the process's identifier, user identifier and group identifier. If a process calls *getpid*, for example, then the emulation library may read the process identifier directly from this page and return it without communicating with the 4.3BSD server. The other shared region can be written by the UNIX process; it contains signal-related information and an array of data structures relating to the process's open files.

When a UNIX process opens a file it is mapped into a region of its address space, with the 4.3BSD server acting as the external pager. The emulation assigns a region of 64 kilobytes for each file; if the file is larger, then the region is used as a movable window onto the file. When the process calls *read* or *write* on the file, the corresponding emulation library procedure copies the data between the mapped region and the user's buffer and updates the file pointer. The data copying requires no explicit communication with the 4.3BSD server. However, the library may generate page faults as it accesses the file region, which will result in the kernel communicating with the 4.3BSD server.

Figure 18.16   UNIX emulation under Mach.

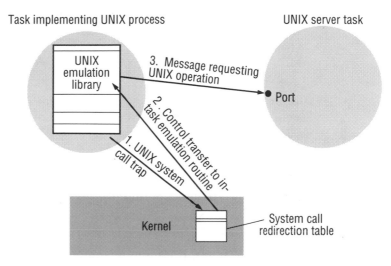

The emulation library has to synchronize with the 4.3BSD server before it accesses the file data if it needs the file window to be moved, or if the open file is shared (for example, with a child or parent process). In the latter case, the file's read-write pointer must be consistently updated. A token is used to obtain mutual exclusion over its use. The emulation library is responsible for requesting the token from the 4.3BSD server and releasing it. (See the subsection on distributed mutiual exclusion in Section 10.4 for a description of centralized token management.)

The Mach exception handling scheme facilitates the implementation of UNIX signals arising from exceptional conditions. A thread belonging to a 4.3BSD server can arrange to be sent messages pertaining to exceptions, and it can respond to these by adjusting the victim task's state so as to call a signal handler, before replying to the kernel. The exception handling scheme also facilitates automatic stack growth and task debugging.

The 4.3BSD server requires internal concurrency in order to handle the calls made upon it efficiently. Recall that UNIX processes undergo a context switch and execute within the kernel to handle their system calls in a conventional implementation; there is thus a process in the kernel for every system call. The 4.3BSD server uses many C threads (see Section 6.3) to receive requests and process them. Most of the threads are kept in a pool and assigned dynamically to requests from emulation library calls. There are also a few dedicated threads: the *Device reply* thread requests device activity from the kernel; the *Softclock* thread implements timeouts; the *Netinput* thread handles network device interactions with the kernel; and the *Inode pager* thread implements an external pager corresponding to mapped UNIX files.

The Chorus emulation

In Chorus, any operating system emulation subsystem consists of two types of component: a *subsystem process manager* and zero or more other server actors. A subsystem process manager is a supervisor actor that operates at the 'front-line' of operating system emulation: it handles system call traps to its subsystem. A process manager runs at each site where the subsystem is implemented. In some cases, the process manager can service a system call itself. In other cases, it communicates by message passing with other, specialized subsystem actors to service the system call. Chorus/MiX, the UNIX SVR4 UNIX emulation subsystem, consists primarily of the following actors:

> *Process manager*: This provides process creation and destruction and signal handling, and communicates with the other, specialized subsystem actors as necessary to handle system calls.

> *File (Object) manager*: Performs file management and acts as the external pager for mapped files.

> *Device managers*: Control particular devices such as the disk.

> *Streams manager*: Manages pipes, networking, System V IPC and pseudo-terminals.

Apart from the Process Manager, the managers are run at each computer only as necessary: for example, a diskless node does not run the File Manager.

A supervisor or system actor can dynamically 'connect' a table of *TRAP* handler routines to be called by the kernel when an actor executes a corresponding *TRAP* instruction. The table contains the address of a routine for each emulated system call. When an actor implementing a UNIX process executes a *TRAP* instruction, the thread executing the call enters the kernel's protection domain. In other words, it becomes temporarily a supervisor thread. The kernel automatically switches the thread context so that it executes the corresponding *TRAP* handler previously installed by the Chorus/MiX process manager (Figure 18.17). This thread may be able to complete the system call itself using its own data – for example, it might achieve a file *read* or *write* by copying data between pages in the cache and the user address space. More generally, this thread will communicate by message passing with one of the other Chorus/MiX subsystem servers. For example, it will communicate with the File Manager if there is no cached data to satisfy a *read*. The File Manager will then communicate with the Disk Manager to fetch the data.

Since they are accessed by message passing, any of the other subsystem servers may provide system-wide facilities – unlike the process managers, which only handle local *TRAP*s.

The process manager establishes, in each actor representing a local UNIX process, a supervisor thread and a control port for it. This thread is used to handle operations upon the process resulting from system calls made by other UNIX processes. For example, if a process is sent a signal, a message is delivered to the process's control port and handled by the corresponding supervisor thread. This thread can then, as appropriate, terminate the UNIX process or modify its state so that a signal handler is called within it.

Comparison

When a Mach task executes a UNIX system call *TRAP* the kernel passes control to a handler in the emulation library, whose code and data reside in the address space of the

Figure 18.17   The emulation of UNIX in Chorus.

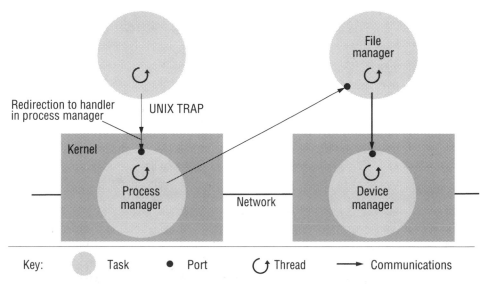

Key: ⬤ Task   • Port   ↻ Thread   ⟶ Communications

Note: Only some subsystem servers shown.

task. This has the disadvantage compared to the Chorus scheme, of allowing buggy code within the task to interfere with the data in the emulation library, and thus to give rise to non-standard failure modes. The Chorus scheme preserves complete isolation of system data structures from UNIX processes.

In Mach, all UNIX facilities are provided by the single UNIX (4.3BSD) server, as opposed to several servers in Chorus. The advantage of the Chorus design is its modularity. Since the separate servers communicate by message passing, any server can be re-implemented independently of the others, as long as the interfaces are adhered to. However, the consequence of this is that the system state relevant to a single emulated UNIX process is distributed across several servers – and perhaps several computers. The exact apportionment of state between subsystem servers is a difficult design issue. Extra communication can be required to maintain this state consistently if it is replicated, and functionality can be affected by a decision to split state without replication between servers. Mach, on the other hand, need concern itself only with the process state in the emulation library's data and that of the single UNIX server.

Subsystem servers require access to devices. Chorus differs from Mach in its approach to device access: in Mach, devices are normally managed by the kernel, and a message-based interface is provided to privileged tasks such as UNIX servers. In Chorus, by contrast, actors may dynamically introduce device drivers into the executing kernel, and take complete control over devices:

• Actors may dynamically connect interrupt handler routines to device interrupts. Whenever an interrupt occurs, the kernel calls the associated routine, which is part of the code of a supervisor actor. This routine can either handle the interrupt itself, or, for example, it can send a message to a pre-arranged port, so that a thread can handle it.

- System or supervisor actors can establish supervisor threads to control devices. These threads can handle requests for the device sent as messages to them, and they have direct access to device registers in handling the requests.

The Chorus approach to device management appears to offer a performance advantage over the Mach scheme, and it is flexible with respect to how much device processing is performed at kernel level and how much at user level. However, it is debatable whether a particular subsystem should gain complete access over a device, since this would normally be to the exclusion of other subsystems. If device accesses are multiplexed through the kernel, on the other hand, then in principle several subsystems can coexist at a single site. An example of this is Mach's use of a programmable *packet filter* installed in the kernel, which multiplexes incoming packets to different subsystem servers according to data in their headers. For example, all incoming NFS packets could be handled by a UNIX subsystem server, whereas Appletalk packets could be handled by a MacOS emulation server. These packets can be identified by simple programs provided by the respective servers.

Golub *et al*. [1990] and Armand *et al*. [1989] describe UNIX emulation on Mach and Chorus respectively; Dean and Armand [1992] describe UNIX emulation on Mach and Chorus in more detail, and give performance figures. Cheriton *et al*. [1990] describe UNIX emulation on the V kernel.

18.5 Amoeba

History and architectural overview

Amoeba is a complete distributed operating system design, including all the basic facilities that one would expect from a conventional operating system. It is currently being developed at the Vrije Universiteit in Amsterdam, where its design and implementation were begun in 1981, and it was previously developed jointly with the Centrum voor Wiskunde, also in Amsterdam. The version of Amoeba we shall discuss is version 5 [Tanenbaum *et al*. 1990, Tanenbaum 1992]. We have already met the Amoeba system model in Chapter 2, as an example of the *processor pool model*. The hardware architecture is shown in Figure 2.6. The main components making up the architecture are the processor pool, workstations (SUN-3s and VAXstations are supported), X-terminals, servers and gateways. The gateways are used for connecting Amoeba sites over WANs; we do not have space to cover this aspect of Amoeba.

The assumptions behind this architecture are that memory and processors will become sufficiently cheap that each user will be allocated multiple processors, and each processor will have plenty of memory to run applications, without the need for backing store. Rather than allocating a multiprocessor to each user, processing power is largely concentrated in the processor pool, where it can be shared more flexibly among users and more economically housed and interconnected.

Design goals and chief design features

Three central design goals were set for the Amoeba distributed operating system, as follows.

Network transparency: All resource accesses were to be network transparent. In particular, there was to be a seamless system-wide file system, and processes were to execute at a processor of the system's choosing, without the user's knowledge.

Object-based resource management: The system was designed to be *object-based*, in the sense defined in Chapter 2. Each resource is regarded as an object and all objects, irrespective of their type, are accessed by a uniform naming scheme. Objects are managed by servers, where they can be accessed only by sending messages to the servers. Even when an object resides locally, it will be accessed by request to a server.

User-level servers: The system software was to be constructed as far as possible as a collection of servers executing at user-level, on top of a standard microkernel that was to run at all computers in the system, regardless of their role. An issue that follows from the last two goals, and to which the Amoeba designers paid particular attention, is that of protection. The Amoeba microkernel supports a uniform model for accessing resources using capabilities.

The basic abstractions supported by the microkernel are processes and threads, and ports for communication, whose main characteristics are all as we have defined them in preceding chapters. Each server is a multi-threaded, protected process. Server processes can occur singly, or in groups, as we shall discuss. Communication between processes at distinct computers running Amoeba on a network is normally via an RPC protocol developed by the Amoeba designers. This protocol is implemented directly by the kernel. Servers that have been constructed include several file servers and a directory server, which stores mappings of path-name components to capabilities for files and other resources.

All three goals, familiar from Chapter 6, have been achieved. They took precedence over any issues of compatibility with existing operating systems. In particular, while a UNIX emulation library exists, the emulation is at the source level and is not accurate.

Protection and capabilities

Chapter 7 introduced the use of capabilities to protect files.

In Amoeba all resource identifiers are capabilities, implemented in the form shown in Figure 18.18. A capability is 128 bits long. It contains an identifier that is mapped at run-time onto a *server port*, and the *object number* is used to identify the object within that server. The two additional fields, the *permissions field* and *check field*, are used respectively to identify the types of accesses that the possessor of the capability is allowed to make, and to protect against forgery of the capability.

Recall from Chapter 7 that the permissions field requires integrity checks, to prevent users from forging capabilities or tampering with the permissions. Amoeba uses the check field for this purpose as follows.

Figure 18.18 An Amoeba capability.

48	24	8	48
Server port	Object number	Permi-ssions	Check field

Field sizes are shown in bits.

When a client requests the creation of a new object, the server supplies a capability with all permissions set – an *owner capability* (the creator of an object can do with it what it likes). This capability contains: the identifier of the server port for receiving request messages; a new object number; a permissions field allowing all operations on the object; and a 48-bit random number in the check field. The server stores the owner capability with the new object's data.

Now, consider a client that attempts to forge a capability with all the permissions bits set. It can copy the server port identifier from another capability and guess an object number. However the client is unlikely to be able to guess the check field. There are 2^{48} – about 10^{14} – combinations of 48-bit wide fields. Generating and testing all these combinations by brute force would involve passing each guess in a message to the server, at about 2 milliseconds for each guess. That is about 2×10^{11} seconds, or about 6,300 years. The same argument can be applied to the 48-bit server port identifier, to show that a process not knowing the target process's port identifier is highly unlikely to succeed in guessing it using brute force.

Reduced capabilities □ Clients with owner capabilities often want to allow others to access their resources, but they do not necessarily want other clients to be able to perform all operations upon the resource. The client must be able to acquire *reduced capabilities* – legitimate capabilities with restricted rights – and the server must be able to test them for validity. An obvious solution is for the server to generate and store a different check field for each combination of rights for each object. This has two disadvantages: first it introduces further storage requirements at the server, and second, clients must request the creation of new capabilities by the server.

In the Amoeba algorithm, a client can use one-way function (see Chapter 16) to create a reduced capability from an owner capability. The client creates the reduced capability by using a one-way function f and the exclusive-or binary operator XOR, as follows:

s	o	r	c	$\rightarrow$	s	o	r'	$f(r'$ XOR $c)$

The new capability thus has the same server port (s) and object number (o) fields, rights field set to the reduced rights r', and check field equal to $f(r'$ XOR *original-check-field*). In order to check a capability with reduced rights, the server performs the same computation to calculate the check field as the client, using the stored check field, the rights in the capability being checked and the same one-way function. If the capability is not a forgery, then its check field will match the result of this computation. The computation can be avoided by caching the results after the first time it is made. This avoids subsequent calculations for the same rights combination, when a direct comparison can be made of the check field with the cached value.

A client with a reduced capability cannot increase its rights using this method, since it does not know and cannot determine the original check field (because a one-way function was used). Note that only a client possessing an owner capability can fabricate a reduced capability. Clients possessing a reduced capability have to request the server (or another client with an owner capability) to fabricate a capability with yet fewer rights.

If servers use access control lists, an authentication protocol (see Chapter 16) would be required for each access. Capabilities avoid this (although authentication is required at some point in order to obtain existing capabilities in the first place).

Capabilities do not solve the problems of eavesdropping and replaying: an intruder can examine messages being sent over the network, and copy capabilities (or encrypted capabilities) out of them, to be used in malicious accesses to the corresponding resource.

A final disadvantage of capabilities in general, compared to access control lists, is that they cannot easily be retracted. If Smith and Jones have each been given capabilities to access a certain file, how is it possible to retract Jones's rights to access the file, but not Smith's? The only way is for the server to associate a different set of capabilities with the file, and to give a new capability to Smith, but to ensure that it is not given to Jones. However, if Smith decides to grant access to the file to Jones, then she has only to pass the capability to Jones, thus thwarting the owner's wishes.

Processing and communication

An Amoeba process consists of an execution environment together with one or more pre-emptively scheduled threads. An Amoeba address space consists of an arbitrary number of regions, which may be mapped into the address space of more than one process, enabling sharing.

Each process is associated with some threads, some ports and some memory segments. An Amoeba memory segment is an array of bytes, which can be mapped into a region. It might be stored, for example, in a file or in main memory.

Amoeba does not provide demand paging, swapping or any other scheme whereby mapped data can be non-memory-resident. The designers claim that workstations in the near future will have sufficient memory to enable most large programs to fit into it. Performance is enhanced and the kernel is simplified by the assumption that all mapped data is in memory.

A *process descriptor* is a data structure that describes a process: the layout of its address space, capabilities for the corresponding memory segments, the ports and the states of its threads (including state of execution, program counter, stack pointer and other registers). Given a process descriptor, a process can be created. The address space, threads and ports can be created as kernel-managed resources; the data in the memory segments can be copied or mapped into the address space.

An executing process can be sent a signal that causes it to be suspended, and causes a process descriptor to be constructed. In principle, this can be used to recreate the process at another host computer, and free the resources at the original computer. This is a means of achieving process migration.

Most servers run at user-level, although some, such as the memory server, execute in the kernel for efficiency. Processes that execute at user-level but which have to access hardware resources such as device controllers do so through a message passing interface exported by the kernel. Of course, only processes in possession of the requisite capabilities can access these resources.

The kernel provides just three major system calls, which are similar to *DoOperation*, *GetRequest* and *PutReply* introduced in Chapter 4, and are used in the same way. The equivalent of *DoOperation* is called *trans*, and has at-most-once semantics (see the subsection on delivery guarantees in Section 5.2). There is no asynchronous message *send* call in Amoeba. Those wishing to avoid the synchronous behaviour of *trans* must create a separate thread to make the call.

The definitions of the Amoeba communication calls are given in the ANSI C language. All three calls use a *Msg* data structure, which is a 32-byte header with several fields to hold capabilities and other items. Note that each request or reply message can consist of just a header or a header and an additional component.

---

trans(Msg *requestHeader, char *requestBuffer, int requestSize, Msg *replyHeader,
    char *replyBuffer, int replySize)
    Client sends a request message and receives a reply; the header contains a capability
    for the object upon which an operation is being requested.

get_request(Msg *requestHeader, char *requestBuffer, int requestSize)
    Server gets a request from the port specified in the message header.

put_reply(Msg *replyHeader, char *replyBuffer, int replySize)
    Server replies.

Several threads may receive messages from the same port. Amoeba automatically routes the message sent using *put_reply* to the sender of the corresponding call to *trans*. A thread cannot reply out of order to messages it has received, and must follow every call to *get_request* with a call to *put_reply*.

The advantage of Amoeba's message format is that many requests or replies consist of only a few bytes of data, which can be packed in the header alone, without an extra message component being necessary. The kernel is optimized to pre-allocate buffers of the right size to hold message header data, and to provide a fast path to the network or another local process's message queue for this data. Otherwise, the kernel has to be prepared to allocate a buffer for an arbitrary amount of data on each call.

The Amoeba kernel finds out that a given port is being used when it handles a call to *get_request* that contains the port's identifier. Several servers, for example, several instances of the same service, are allowed to use the same port. A client using the port identifier will reach at most one such server, but there is no explicit means given to the programmer to control which one. However, a server connected to the same LAN as the client will be chosen in preference to any that reside on a neighbouring LAN.

Port identifiers for system services are allocated to servers under the control of system administrators. Where capabilities refer to persistent objects – ones that can

Figure 18.19 Putports and getports.

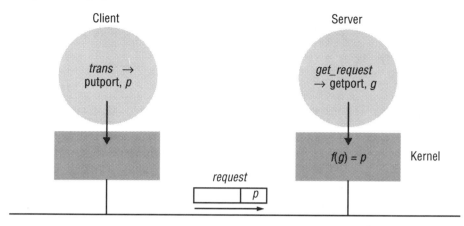

outlive the execution of any particular server process that manages them – the same port identifier is used each time a server runs. Otherwise, clients would have to rebuild their capabilities according to the latest server port. For short-term or private communication, however, processes can generate random port identifiers and pass them in messages to the processes with which they need to communicate.

A security problem addressed by Amoeba is the possibility of malicious processes being able to masquerade as legitimate servers. Amoeba provides a mechanism to guarantee the authenticity of the server listening on a port.

Amoeba distinguishes between *putports* and *getports* (Figure 18.19). Clients use ordinary port identifiers called putports. Servers use a related secret identifier called a getport when they call *get_request*. The Amoeba kernel passes this getport through a one-way function, *f*. The result is matched with the putports being used by clients attempting to reach the server. Therefore, only processes that know the getport *g* such that $f(g) = p$ can service requests sent to putport *p*. The putport *p* can be made public but because *f* is a one-way function, *g* cannot be determined from knowledge of *p*: *g* is a secret which the system administrators will reveal only to those server processes that should know it.

In addition to RPC, version 5 Amoeba added the notion of process groups, and included a reliable multicast delivery service to these groups. This is described in Section 18.9. This form of communication is designed only for communication between members of a group of servers in order, for example, to implement a fault-tolerant service. Clients are expected to continue to use RPC communication with one of the servers, so that replication is transparent.

Communication implementation

The Amoeba designers decided to include network communication in the kernel as a basic service. They considered the extra context-switching costs that would be incurred through use of a separate, user-level network manager process to be prohibitive.

Figure 18.20 Amoeba multi-packet protocol.

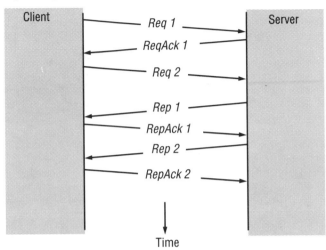

The kernel is responsible for implementing network communication only over what is described as a *local internet*. This consists of a few LANs interconnected by gateways or bridges. Amoeba RPC has been implemented with considerable attention to its performance, and exhibits some of the best null RPC delay and RPC bandwidth figures that have been measured [van Renesse *et al.* 1989].

Amoeba relies upon additional protocols implemented externally to Amoeba for message transmission over WANs. The request-reply protocol is implemented in two layers: the RPC layer, which implements a Request-Reply protocol that provides at-most-once RPC and the FLIP (Fast Local Internet Protocol) layer (see the subsection on FLIP in Section 3.5).The reason for this division is that, while RPC is intrinsic to the Amoeba design, some additional general communication services were felt to be needed, including group communication, security, support for process migration and operation over connected networks.

The FLIP protocol □ The FLIP layer provides a datagram service that transmits messages of up to a gigabyte to destinations called FLIP ports, and deals with the location of FLIP ports. FLIP ports are intermediaries between Amoeba ports and physical addresses. Each process is associated with a unique FLIP port identifier. Even if two servers use the same port, they will each possess a unique FLIP port.

If a service has several instances and one of them migrates, its clients will attempt to relocate it. Amoeba guarantees that the same instance of the service is located. not one of its peers. This is assured because the FLIP port is specified in the search algorithm. Even though the peer implements the same service, the original server could possess state relevant to its clients' operations, so it is important that the original server continues to service the same clients. Also, it is important that retransmissions of client requests are not picked up at a different server and treated as if they are fresh, when they could have been executed already at a peer that had failed or was migrating.

Request-Reply protocol □ The RPC layer implements at-most-once call semantics over FLIP, using the RRA protocol, introduced in the subsection on RPC exchange

Figure 18.21 Sending a packet group in VMTP.

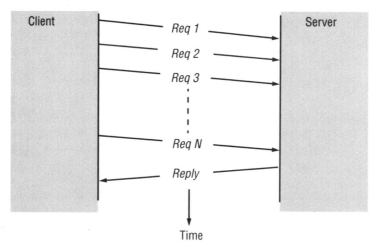

protocols in Section 4.3. It retries request messages and filters duplicate requests. The RRA protocol acknowledges the reply message, so that the server's data does not need to be retained.

When the user-level request or reply data is too big to fit into a single packet, FLIP uses a multipacket protocol. The service is not reliable, although the protocol does acknowledge all the packets in a multipacket message, except the last. Figure 18.20 shows a multipacket request message in packets *Req1* and *Req2* and a multipacket reply message in packets *Rep1* and *Rep2*. FLIP sends the client's first request packet *Req1*, then waits for an acknowledgement *ReqAck1* from the server before sending the next request packet, *Req2*. Similarly FLIP sends the server's first reply packet *Rep1*, then waits for an acknowledgement *RepAck1* from the client before sending the next reply packet, *Rep2*.

As in the case when both the request message and the reply message fits into a single packet, it is the responsibility of the RPC layer to provide at-most-once call semantics over FLIP's multipacket datagrams.

The overall effect of the RPC layer over FLIP multipackets is very similar to Birrel and Nelson's multipacket protocol, except that Amoeba acknowledges the last reply packet whereas Birrel and Nelson [1984] assume that the next request message will do as an acknowledgement.

Flow control □ We turn now to considerations of flow control, by comparing FLIP with another protocol, VMTP. FLIP is an example of a *stop-and-go* protocol: it does not transmit a next packet until the previous one has been acknowledged. By contrast, the VMTP protocol [Cheriton 1986] (developed by David Cheriton, the V system's principal designer, also for request-reply exchanges) is a *burst protocol*: it allows for data belonging to long messages to be sent in bursts of packets called *packet groups* (Figure 18.21). Instead of acknowledging each packet, VMTP acknowledges packet groups, which can contain up to 16 kilobytes of data.

The advantage of a burst protocol over a stop-and-go protocol is that greater throughput can be achieved, because data can be transmitted concurrently with acknowledgements. The disadvantage is that packets transmitted *back-to-back* – that is, as fast as the sending operating system can send them through its network controller – can sometimes result in the receiving computer dropping packets, necessitating a recovery action. Packets are dropped either because the receiving network controller fails to respond sufficiently quickly after the previous packet to be able to accept a new one, or because the kernel runs out of buffer space for incoming packets. At worst, every other packet might be dropped by a network controller.

There are two ways to alleviate this situation. First, VMTP acknowledges packet groups with a small bit map describing which packets, if any, were not received. Only these packets have to be retransmitted, instead of retransmitting the whole group. This is known as *selective retransmission*. Second, it is possible for the sender to introduce a small delay called an *inter-packet gap* between packets, reducing the tendency to overrun the receiver. The value of this delay can be adjusted dynamically. A sender could increase the delay until acknowledgements tell it that all packets are arriving at the receiver, or until the rate at which packets are dropped has reached an acceptable level.

Timer management ☐ Protocols normally include actions to be taken when timers expire, in order to cope with the non-arrival of expected messages. A timeout has to be arranged for every message that is sent reliably. Setting up a timeout can occur at the beginning of the wait for an acknowledgement, and so does not add directly to client latency; but it does represent a cost to the system as a whole. Additionally, the timeout has to be cancelled in the common case in which an acknowledgement arrives before the timer expires. The kernel therefore has to provide efficient facilities for this purpose.

Amoeba optimizes timeout handling by placing the responsibility for it with a single kernel thread. This thread periodically sweeps a list of protocol data structures, of which there is one for every transaction in progress. If it notices that nothing has occurred since its last sweep, then it initiates a timeout action (that is, usually it retransmits a message). The sweeper thread is run with a low priority to minimize its interference with other system operations, and the times at which timeout actions occur are not very accurate. This is of little significance in general, since the values of timeout periods are only guesses anyway.

Locating ports and FLIP ports ☐ As the Amoeba kernel does not monitor the passage of capabilities in messages, when a client first attempts to use a capability, the port it refers to might not have been seen before at that computer. It is the responsibility of the Amoeba kernel to locate the port. Whenever a process makes a first attempt to receive a message, the Amoeba kernel generates a new FLIP port and associates it with the process at that computer. When a client calls *trans*, the RPC layer looks up a mapping from a port identifier to a FLIP port identifier, in a cache of entries of the following form:

Port	FLIP port	Network address

The network address field is a hint as to the current FLIP port's location (and therefore the port's location).

We shall refer temporarily to ports as 'RPC ports', to distinguish them from FLIP ports. Recall that different client computers may use different servers which employ the same RPC port identifier. The associations between RPC ports and FLIP ports can thus differ between computers. However, the association between FLIP ports and network addresses is unique. If no entry is found for the given RPC port identifier, then a location algorithm is run.

The RPC port location algorithm broadcasts a location message containing the RPC port identifier. The RPC layer in any kernel that hosts a process using the given RPC port identifier will know a FLIP port identifier for a corresponding local process, and will respond with this identifier and the network address. This response packet is used to set up a cache entry for the port at the sender. If several kernels respond with FLIP ports for the given RPC port identifier, then responses after the first are ignored, thus retaining an entry for the computer that responded most quickly.

FLIP broadcasts a message to all destinations within a distance called a *hop count*. The hop count is transmitted in the broadcast message but decremented by one at every gateway computer the message encounters, and not propagated beyond that computer if the hop count reaches zero.

The port location algorithm broadcasts the location message with a hop count of one, which reaches the local internet where hardware broadcast can be used. If there is no response, the hop count is incremented by one and the broadcast attempted again. This is repeated if necessary until either the RPC port is found or the entire local internet has been traversed.

Amoeba does not piggy-back the request data in the port location packet, so the request message has then to be sent to the known address. Piggy-backing the request data would be more efficient, but then the request could be executed at more than one server, which might have undesirable effects.

The RPC layer passes the FLIP port as the address of the datagram it is sending. The FLIP layer consults the cache to determine what network address to use. If the cache entry proves stale, then this is detected on use: the receiving computer will send a negative acknowledgement, telling the sending computer that no such FLIP port is known there. The FLIP layer then has to resort to broadcasting to locate the FLIP port afresh. If the FLIP port is relocated, then the cache is automatically updated.

Discussion of main Amoeba features

In summary, the design of the Amoeba kernel is based on an object-based client-server model, in which as many system services as possible are implemented by user-level processes or groups of these. Amoeba supports this model with a few key abstractions: multi-threaded processes and RPC communication using ports and process groups. Amoeba implements protection by uniformly supporting capabilities for protected access to resources. It has achieved its goal of network transparency, and the majority of its servers execute at user-level. Its optimized RPC implementation is fast by present-day standards. However, implementing RPC in the kernel means that it is provided whether it is required or not; and providing a particular RPC protocol as the only directly supported communication protocol is restrictive.

We have studied Amoeba because it is a consistently designed system based on just a few design principles and goals. However, Amoeba has limitations which might inhibit its general acceptance. First, its assumption that memory will become sufficiently cheap to avoid the need for demand-paged virtual memory seems questionable. The memory requirements of applications (and, equally importantly, useful combinations of applications) are not to be underestimated. The main advantages of virtual memory in the face of these requirements are that it provides a graceful degradation when memory capacity is exceeded, and it allows the programmer to be relatively unconcerned with physical memory limitations. As an example of virtual memory being perceived as a requirement in the 1990s, Windows NT is the operating system kernel developed by Microsoft for workstations and servers to support MS-DOS and other operating environments such as Windows [Custer 1992]. Windows NT includes virtual memory as a distinctive feature that its predecessors lacked.

Secondly, Amoeba does not support binary-level compatibility with any generally-used operating system such as UNIX or DOS, and provides only a partial, library-level emulation of UNIX. This limits severely the current utility of Amoeba. Users are reluctant to give up their software base, unless improved functionality or quality of service justify the migration costs.

One of the problems in emulating UNIX on Amoeba – even at the source code level – is the difficulty that arises when trying to implement UNIX-style *user/group/ other* semantics for file permissions using capabilities alone. These semantics, deriving from access control lists, are administratively much more convenient than having to distribute capabilities. We have already pointed out, for example, that preventing a user Smith from accessing a particular file while continuing to allow Jones to access it is awkward in a capability-based system. Amoeba stores capabilities for files in directories managed by directory servers. How is a directory server to decide which capability (that is, what rights), if any, is to be granted to a particular client when the client presents the file pathname? It would need to know to which of the *user/group/other* categories the client belonged for the particular file concerned. But this is impossible to determine without proof of the client's user and group identities. Since Amoeba capabilities can be copied freely between processes (and are subject to eavesdropping), they cannot fulfil this purpose by themselves.

The moral of this is that some servers must be free to implement access control lists and to require authentication of clients. Capabilities are not generally applicable. Nor do they provide security unless messages are encrypted and replays are detected, because of eavesdropping (see Chapter 16).

On the other hand, Amoeba has been successful in reminding us of the advantages of simplicity that originally inspired the designers of UNIX. Amoeba's simple microkernel interface is maintainable and relatively easy to understand and conform to.

18.6 A comparison of Mach, Amoeba and Chorus

Amoeba is a complete and novel distributed operating system constructed as a collection of user-level servers supported by the microkernel. Mach and Chorus are primarily microkernel designs geared towards the emulation of existing operating systems, notably UNIX, in a distributed system.

Mach, Chorus and Amoeba have many common general goals, including the support of network transparency, encapsulated resource management and user-level servers. In Mach and Chorus, some objects are managed by the kernel and others by user-level servers, whereas all Amoeba objects are managed outside the kernel. Chorus allows user-level servers to be loaded dynamically in the kernel address space.

Mach, Chorus and Amoeba all provide separate abstractions of processes and threads. Mach and Chorus can take advantage of a multiprocessor.

The Amoeba kernel interface is very simple, because of its simple communication model and lack of support for virtual memory. The Mach and Chorus kernels offer many more calls due to their more complex communication models and the desire to emulate UNIX.

Naming and protecting resources □ Resources are named and protected by capabilities in Amoeba and Chorus and by ports in Mach. Resources identified by capabilities in Amoeba and in Chorus are accessed by sending a message to the appropriate server port and the server accesses the particular resource identified in the capability. In Mach, servers generally manage many ports, one for every resource. Resources are accessed by sending messages to the corresponding ports.

Capabilities alone are not suitable for implementing the sort of identity-based access control required in UNIX file systems. The Chorus kernel provides protection identifiers to enable user-level services to authenticate the actor that sent a message and the port used by that actor.

Mach's port rights are capabilities that confer send or receive rights on the process that possesses them. However, unlike Amoeba's capabilities and Chorus's port identifiers, which can be freely constructed and manipulated at user-level, Mach's port rights are stored inside the kernel and protected by it, allowing efficient representations and rapid access. But the Mach kernel has the additional expense of processing port rights in messages.

For local communication, the Mach approach eliminates the need for random number generators and one-way functions, which are associated with Amoeba capabilities. However, in a secure environment, the Mach network servers must encrypt port rights transmitted in messages.

Amoeba capabilities and Chorus capabilities can persist beyond the execution of any process that uses them. An Amoeba capability for a persistent resource such as a file can be stored in a directory. Each component of the capability, in particular the port identifier, remains valid as long as the file exists and the check field has not been changed at the server. By contrast, Mach capabilities for send rights are volatile. To access a resource, a Mach client requires a higher-level, persistent identifier to obtain the current identifier of the appropriate send rights; this higher-level identifier must be resolved by the service concerned before access can be obtained.

There does not seem to be a clear winner between Mach's scheme of kernel-managed port capability transfers, and the Chorus and Amoeba scheme of user-controlled capability transfers. In Amoeba, processes are obliged to generate port identifiers themselves, and then test for their uniqueness. The Chorus port naming scheme improves upon this since the kernel generates UIs for port identifiers, thus avoiding clashes.

Both Amoeba and Chorus allow for groups of servers to manage resources. In Amoeba the processes form groups, but in Chorus processes effectively become members of groups by making their ports join port groups.

Interprocess communication □ The Mach, Chorus and Amoeba kernels all provide a synchronous request-reply protocol. Chorus and Mach also provide for asynchronous message passing. Mach packages all forms of message passing in a single system call, whereas Chorus provides alternative calls.

Amoeba and Chorus provide for group communication. In the case of Amoeba this is a reliable, totally ordered multicast to be used by the members of a process group. Chorus provides an unreliable multicast to all the members of a group of ports or to selected members. Chorus services can be reconfigured by servers adding or removing their ports from a group.

Messages □ Amoeba messages consist of a fixed-size header and an optional out-of-line block of data of variable size. But Mach is more flexible in that it allows multiple out-of-line blocks in a single message. Mach and Chorus employ their virtual memory management techniques to the passing of large messages between processes in the same computer.

The contents of Mach messages are typed – enabling port rights to be transmitted. Messages in Chorus and Amoeba are just contiguous sequences of bytes.

Network communication □ Communication between processes in different computers is performed in Mach and Chorus by user-level network servers running at every computer. The network servers are also responsible for locating ports.

The Amoeba kernel supports network communication directly, and is highly tuned to achieve rapid request-reply interactions over a LAN. The Amoeba designers considered that the extra context switching costs that would be incurred through use of a separate, user-level network manager process would be prohibitive,

Mach, Chorus and Amoeba use similar schemes for locating ports. Location hints are used first but if those fail they resort to broadcasting.

The use of user-level network servers should allow for a variety of protocols. However, Mach's network servers primarily use TCP/IP as the transport protocol. Chorus also sticks to international standards, providing Internet and OSI protocols. However, this is not necessarily suitable on LANs when request-reply interactions predominate.

The Amoeba kernel supports an RPC protocol based upon the FLIP datagram protocol, which is optimized for performance on small sets of connected LANs.

A figure of 11 milliseconds for a null RPC in Mach on a Sun-3/60 is quoted by Peterson *et al.* [1990]; for a DECStation 5000/200 the figure is 6.3 milliseconds [Orman *et al.* 1993]. The poorness of these figures compared to, say, Amoeba's of 1.4 milliseconds on a 68020-based computer is in part due to the transport protocol used. It is not totally due to this factor: a conventional UNIX implementation on a Sun-3/75 takes 6.1 milliseconds using TCP [Peterson *et al.* 1990]. (All figures are for a 10 megabits-per-second Ethernet.) Recently, Mach IPC has been re-implemented using the x-kernel, with the transport protocols placed in the kernel to improve performance. Orman *et al.* [1993] quote an improved null RPC figure of 4.8 milliseconds.

Memory management □ Amoeba has very simple memory management scheme without virtual memory. In contrast Mach and Chorus provide similar very powerful and flexible virtual memory management schemes allowing a variety of different ways of sharing between processes, including copy-on-write.

Mach and Chorus both make use of external pagers and local caches, which allow virtual memory to be shared between processes, even when they run in different computers.

UNIX emulation □ Amoeba does not provide binary compatibility with UNIX. Chorus and Mach both provide emulation of UNIX as subsystems. Section 18.4 compares them.

18.7 Clouds

History and architectural overview

Clouds [Dasgupta *et al.* 1991] is an operating system for the support of distributed objects, developed at the Georgia Institute of Technology, US. The first version of Clouds was implemented in 1986. We describe version 2, which has been developed since 1987. This version is based upon a microkernel, called *Ra*, that has been designed to support a variety of distributed object programming models. Clouds incorporates a complete set of system-level facilities, including storage and input-output. It is based on an object-thread paradigm, which is a distributed operating system version of the object-oriented programming paradigm. Objects are heavyweight, passive entities, each with its own address space that encapsulates code and data. Threads are activities that execute the methods within objects, invoking operations on further objects as they do so.

Each Clouds object is represented by one persistent replica held at a server computer, and possibly several volatile replicas at computers where operations upon the object are being executed. Distributed shared memory techniques are employed so that the memory inside a single object being shared at different computers is rendered consistent (see Chapter 17).

In the Mach, Chorus and Amoeba distributed operating systems, shared resources are managed by servers. These systems are object-based in the sense that clients can refer to all resources in a uniform manner.

Clouds distinguishes itself from Amoeba, Mach and Chorus in its object-oriented style of invocations and the type of threads it supports.

As we shall see, Clouds does not provide message passing; and although objects are akin to the execution environments found in process-based operating systems, objects are not associated with their own threads. Threads in Clouds are activities that can move from object to object and thus from computer to computer.

Clouds is designed to support a range of languages based on the object-thread paradigm. As currently implemented, it incorporates language support for an extension of C++ [Stroustrup 1986] called DC++, and an extension of Eiffel [Meyer 1988] called Distributed Eiffel. Programmers can create and compile classes using these languages, and create *instances* – that is, objects with private state – from these classes. Interactive users can create threads implicitly by specifying object invocations from the command line. Clouds executes threads and carries out invocations in a network-transparent fashion.

The Clouds system architecture (Figure 18.22) consists of three classes of computer: workstations, data servers and compute servers.

Figure 18.22   The Clouds system architecture.

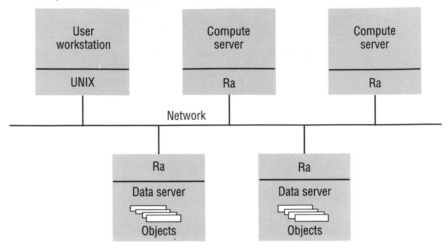

Workstations are used for interaction by the users, and these run the UNIX operating system. UNIX provides a file service and user interaction service to the rest of the Clouds implementation.

Data servers manage secondary storage for the code and data belonging to objects. Data servers run the Ra kernel. No file service is presented to programmers in Clouds, which has no special file concept. Instead, all objects in Clouds are themselves persistent. Objects, like files, outlive any threads that perform invocations upon them, until they are explicitly deleted. We shall explore this notion further, below.

Compute servers are, taken together, functionally similar to the processor pool in Amoeba, although they need not be rack-based and can be entire computers. Clouds threads execute operations on objects at compute servers that are dynamically chosen on an invocation-by-invocation basis. The compute server computers are homogeneous, and do not need any secondary store. They run the Ra kernel.

The data server and compute server roles are logical. In principle, a single computer with secondary storage attached could play both roles.

Design goals and chief design features

Clouds has the following major design goals and features:

Support for object-thread computational model: Clouds objects are abstractions of protected, passive storage, and threads are activity abstractions which exist independently of objects. Since Clouds objects are heavyweight (they include a virtual address space), it is envisaged that language run-time support software can implement many fine-grained objects (of size in the order of tens or hundreds of bytes) inside a single Clouds object. These small objects have language-specific semantics, which may differ from the basic Clouds object model. The clustering of objects inside host Clouds objects reduces the average object creation and deletion costs. Since some invocations in general will be between objects within the same Clouds object, clustering can also reduce the number of context switches consequent upon invocations.

Network-transparent object invocation: Direct access to the code or data within an object is prevented by memory management hardware. The only mechanism to access the state of an object is that of invocation. An invocation specifies a target object, the method to be called within it, and the input and output parameters. A thread making an invocation is blocked until the corresponding method has been executed and any result parameters sent back. All data transfer between objects occurs, from the programmer's point of view, by invocation parameter passing, and not by message passing such as that provided by say, Amoeba and Mach. Invocation is network transparent, and a thread can execute an object invocation at any compute server – regardless of where the object is stored.

Persistent, single-level storage: To the programmer, there is only a single level of storage instead of the usual primary/secondary storage hierarchy. Changes made to an object's data are, with certain exceptions, automatically reflected in a version held on secondary store at a data server. This mechanism is akin to mapped files. Objects do not have to be explicitly saved, or marshalled to any special form (such as a sequence of bytes) in order to be stored. Of course, for an object operation to be executed, Clouds must fetch the object's code and data into a compute server's primary memory.

Sharing via objects: All sharing in Clouds takes place by performing invocations upon common objects – just as sharing occurs through files in other systems. Threads executing methods inside the same object share the object's code and data. Clouds therefore provides low-level concurrency control mechanisms such as semaphores. However, to complicate matters further from the implementation point of view, threads executing at separate computers can execute concurrently within the same object (this is transparent to the programmer). The threads access the same code and data at the same virtual addresses, even though the computers at which they execute do not share physical memory. Memory can indeed be *logically* shared between threads that execute at different computers without *physical* shared memory, through the abstraction of distributed shared memory. Techniques for implementing distributed shared memory are described in Chapter 17.

Automatic load balancing: Clouds enables a system-supported load balancing policy to be exercised whenever an invocation is made, to choose the compute server to execute the method on the target object. Alternatively, the programmer may specify locations for invocation execution.

Objects, threads and invocations

An object's virtual address space consists of regions that are mapped to memory resources called *segments*. An object contains persistent segments for code, data and a

Figure 18.23   Invocations upon a rectangle object.

```
clouds_class rectangle;
int x,y;                            // persistent data for rect.
entry rectangle;                    // constructor
entry size (int x,y);               // set size of rect.
entry int area();                   // return area of rect.
end_class


rectangle_ref rect;                 // 'rect' is a variable that holds
                                    // an instance of a class that refers
                                    // to an object of type rectangle


rect.bind("RectA");                 // call to name server, which returns
                                    // sysname for existing object "RectA"
rect.size(5,10);                    // invocation of RectA
printf("%d\n", rect.area());        // will print 50
```

heap. In fact, an object typically contains two heaps. The persistent heap is used for dynamically allocated memory that persists with the object. An object can also contain a volatile segment for temporary heap data. The contents of a volatile segment can be discarded by the system as long as no thread executes within the object that contains them. All segments are accessed by direct memory references: it is the responsibility of the virtual memory implementation to read or write the corresponding data from or to secondary storage as appropriate.

Objects are referenced by globally unique, location-independent identifiers called *sysnames*. A thread performing an invocation must supply the target object's sysname. It obtains the sysnames of shared objects through a name server, which stores a mapping of textual names to sysnames. An invocation specifies a method identifier which is used to look up an *entry point* in the target object – an address from which the system continues the execution of the invoking thread when it enters the invoked object. Clouds assumes static (compile-time) type checking is used to ensure that only legitimate entry points in legitimate objects are accessed by threads.

Figure 18.23 (adapted from Dasgupta *et al.* [1991]) shows some example DC++ code for manipulating a rectangle object which is an instance of the class *rectangle*. After looking up the named instance "RectA" from the name server, the code makes two further invocations upon this rectangle, to set its size and determine its area. Note that, corresponding to the *rectangle* class, the language automatically provides the *rectangle_ref* class of references to rectangle instances. This provides the *bind* method, which makes a call to the name server to look up the sysname from a textual name, as well as inheriting the methods of the underlying *rectangle* class.

Figure 18.24 shows a thread invoking operations upon a succession of objects, and returning after each invocation has been executed, eventually to the original invoking object. Invocation is synchronous. If a thread is required to continue executing in an object while another invocation is performed, it can create a second thread to perform the invocation while the original thread continues.

Figure 18.24   A single thread performs invocations on three objects.

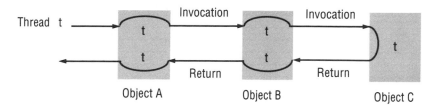

The movement of a single thread between objects in separate address spaces is known as *thread diffusion*. Of course, this view is an abstraction: thread diffusion is implemented using familiar activity and communication abstractions provided by the underlying Ra kernels. However, what does differ fundamentally from the previous computational models we have considered is that Clouds programmers do not control the number of threads within an object. Whereas, for example, a Mach programmer explicitly creates the threads assigned to receiving incoming RPCs arriving at a task, threads in Clouds enter an object 'from outside'. Potentially as many threads execute within an object as there are invocations to be executed. Of course, there is a physical resource limit on the number of threads that can execute at the same compute server, imposed by the Ra kernel.

Objects do not contain their own stacks. Instead, each thread is associated with a single stack, and this stack is installed in an object's address space when the thread performs an invocation upon the object. We now look at the implementation of the invocation mechanism and the single-level store model in more detail.

Implementation of the computational model

The Ra microkernel provides three basic abstractions:

> *isibas* are the activity abstractions, which execute either in user mode or supervisor mode but which are confined, unlike the higher-level threads, to a single computer;
>
> *segments* are mapped memory resources;
>
> *virtual spaces* consist of collections of regions mapped to segments.

Virtual spaces are not themselves entire address spaces. Each isiba can be associated with up to three distinct virtual spaces: *O space* contains the object code and data for the current user-level invocation; *P space* contains thread-specific, private data such as a stack and a parameter-passing area; and *K space* contains an image of the kernel itself and is common to all isibas.

In addition to the kernel, K space also contains system objects. These are objects that perform some higher-level service function than the standard kernel. System objects are the servers of the Clouds system. System objects execute in the kernel's address space for the sake of efficiency. They are separately compiled, and loaded into the kernel at configuration time. They, like the kernel itself, are written in the C++ language. They inherit operations from the kernel's classes, and thus can invoke its services directly (whereas user-level isibas must make system call traps). Unlike Chorus servers, there is no facility for loading system objects dynamically.

System objects are used to implement network communication, and to control input-output between Ra nodes and the users' workstations. The main system objects of relevance here, however, are the *thread manager* and *user object manager*.

Performing an invocation □   First, unless the programmer has specified a target node, a compute server is chosen to execute an invocation upon a given object. If the chosen server differs from the one where the thread currently resides, then an RPC is made to the destination, requesting it to perform the invocation. The user object manager at the compute server creates the object's virtual space, O space, if it does not already exist there. It is able to do this using the object's virtual space descriptor segment, stored on a data server. It adds a P space containing the invoking thread's stack, copied from the invoking computer, and a parameter-passing area. The thread manager, a system object that records information about threads as they execute across the distributed system, is notified of the thread's new location. The thread manager also stores information concerning the workstation from which the thread was launched, and the windows on that workstation to which the thread's output is to be directed.

After it has established the object's address space at a compute server, the user object manager then looks up the appropriate entry point in the object and creates an isiba to execute from that address. As the isiba executes the method, it page-faults on the pages not already resident and these are brought in from a data server.

Clouds summary and discussion

In summary, Clouds is a microkernel-based operating system for distributed objects. It is designed to support the object-thread paradigm, in which passive objects containing protected code and data are invoked by independent threads that can cross computer boundaries. Data is passed between objects only in the form of invocation parameters. Clouds provides a persistent, single-level store, so that object data is automatically saved to secondary storage and fetched from secondary storage without the programmer's intervention. Consequently, there is no requirement for a separate file construct, and objects do not require marshalling before they can be copied to secondary storage.

The Clouds system architecture consists of: workstations for users; data servers for storing the code and data segments from which objects are composed, and compute servers that execute object methods. Load balancing is carried out automatically across the compute servers as invocations take place. Since threads can execute within the same object at compute servers that do not share physical memory, the distributed shared memory abstraction is required, and support for this is allowed in the form of DSM client and server system objects, which can be configured to execute in the Ra microkernel's address space. All high-level service provision in Clouds (including network communication) is provided by the UNIX workstations and by Ra system objects.

All of the Clouds features that we have mentioned have been implemented on Sun 3/50 and Sun 3/60 computers. Null invocation timings have been measured from 8 milliseconds to 103 milliseconds, depending on whether the invoked object's data are in memory or requires transport from a data server [Dasgupta *et al.* 1991].

The Clouds invocation mechanism is interesting by virtue of its contrast with our other distributed operating system case studies. However, support for fine-grained objects is limited and the efficiency of the invocation mechanism seems questionable, since it requires virtual memory manipulations regardless of the amount of data which is required to be transferred by an invocation.

The Clouds DSM-based invocation mechanism belongs to one of three main models, the other two of which are *RPC-based invocation* and *proxies*. In RPC-based invocation, objects are implemented inside execution environments such as Mach tasks. An invoker performs a remote procedure call to a port representing the target object. A thread in the target object's host execution environment executes the method and returns any results. By migrating the object's port, the object itself can be transparently migrated between execution environments. The COOL system, constructed over the Chorus kernel sometimes uses this invocation style and sometimes uses distributed shared memory techniques similar to Clouds. COOL chooses the mechanism according to efficiency considerations.

In the third style of implementing invocations, based on so-called proxies, objects are again implemented behind ports in execution environments. However, when an invocation is performed upon a remote object, the invocation is issued transparently firstly to a local object called a proxy [Shapiro 1986]. The proxy can forward the invocation identifier and parameters in a message to the remote object's port. But, since the proxy is an object, it may alternatively use specialized techniques to implement the invocation. For example, it could satisfy the invocation with data cached locally. Or, as another example, it could multicast the invocation message to a collection of remote objects, in a scheme that uses object replication to achieve high availability. A comparison of these three techniques is given by Blair and Lea [1992].

The brief description we have given of Clouds omits some notable features that are necessary to construct full support for distributed objects in general. Some of these features are being investigated by the Clouds project. They include: object location algorithms; garbage collection; dynamically loading persistent objects into existing execution environments; object migration policies for load balancing and network traffic reduction; and the details of the DSM implementation and its interaction with concurrency control mechanisms such as locks. For further information about system support for distributed objects, the reader is referred to COOL [Lea *et al.* 1993], SOR [Shapiro 1989], Emerald [Jul *et al.* 1988] and Amber [Chase *et al.* 1989].

18.8 Firefly RPC

Firefly RPC was designed as a vital component of the new software developed for the Firefly multiprocessor at the DEC Systems Research Centre. It was intended that RPC would be the primary means of communication between processes in the same or different computers and also for system calls. The designers took an approach in which the performance of an RPC was optimized for the 'fast path' – the path taken by the vast majority of RPCs. This implies that minority activities such as dealing with multipackets and retransmissions should not intrude on the fast path, so that the implementation is optimized for the normal case.

Schroeder and Burrows [1990] describe the steps in the fast path, giving times for each of those steps. They provide a model of how time is spent in an average RPC. The emphasis is on the performance of RPCs between different computers. Section 6.5 introduced the main costs involved in an RPC; this section extends that analysis.

Firefly RPC makes use of client and server stub procedures generated from an interface definition written in Modula2+, an extension to Modula2 designed for use in distributed systems. The steps in the Firefly RPC fast path are as follows:

- the client program calls a remote procedure and control passes to a client stub procedure which (1) obtains a packet buffer with a partially filled-in header, (2) marshals the call parameters into a message, (3) sends the request message, and (4) receives and unmarshals the reply;

- at the server, generic RPC run-time code receives the incoming request and looks up and calls the appropriate server stub;

- the server stub (1) unmarshals the request message, but keeps the message buffer, (2) calls the designated procedure, and (3) marshals the reply into the saved message buffer and sends the reply to the client.

Note that although Firefly RPC deals with message retransmissions, acknowledgments, multipacket request and reply messages and server threads, these mechanisms do not belong to the 'fast path' and need not be considered as part of the model for a normal RPC.

Marshalling □ Marshalling (and unmarshalling) is normally carried out by Modula2+ stub procedures, which copy arguments to request messages and results from reply messages. Complex types can be marshalled by calling marshalling procedures in a library. Measurements of marshalling overheads were taken for the Firefly RPC implementation, by subtracting the time taken for a null RPC to a separate local address space from the time taken for a similar RPC but with given arguments. The Firefly implementation is such that the difference is accounted for only by the costs of both marshalling and unmarshalling.

The marshalling times for a variable length array passed by reference as a return parameter are given as 115 microseconds for a one-byte array, and 550 microseconds for a 1440-byte array. These figures are for a microVAX II. The increase in marshalling time with size was found to be linear for the case of arrays given, as long as they were shorter than the maximum that would fit in a single packet.

Firefly RPC reduces marshalling costs, by not marshalling data unnecessarily, and by eliminating copying steps. In particular, most parameters are passed in one direction only. Modula2+ interface definitions distinguish between parameters that are passed in both directions, *IN* parameters, which are transmitted from client to server and *OUT* parameters, which are transmitted from server to client. *IN* parameters are not marshalled in the reply message and similarly, *OUT* parameters are not marshalled in the request message.

If an RPC takes place between computers with the same architecture, then data types need not be converted. Firefly monitors when data conversion is not required. If the size of a result parameter is known and is small enough, Firefly reserves space for it in the reply packet, and a pointer to this is passed by the server stub to the server procedure. The procedure can then write the value directly into the message.

Figure 18.25   The component costs of Firefly remote procedure calls.

Procedure	Action	Time in microseconds
Null( )	Stubs and RPC run-time	606
	Send+receive 74-byte call packet	954
	Send+receive 74-byte result packet	954
	TOTAL	2514
MaxResult(buffer)	Stubs and RPC run-time	606
	Marshal 1440-byte result packet	550
	Send+receive 74-byte call packet	954
	Send+receive 1514-byte result packet	4414
	TOTAL	6524

Packet initialization □ Network packet headers have to be initialized with appropriate values for fields such as the destination address and port number. A multi-layer protocol stack, such as RPC/UDP/IP/Ethernet, requires several headers to be initialized. To some extent, initialization costs can be amortized by using packet headers with pre-initialized values in those fields that remain constant for every packet sent by the process. The Firefly designers suggest that implementing RPC directly over Ethernet packets would save about 100 microseconds per RPC.

In addition to headers, a cost arises from checksum calculations. Each protocol layer may calculate a checksum, which is transmitted with the data for checking at the receiving end. The cost of calculating a checksum increases with the packet size. Figures of 45 microseconds to calculate the checksum for a 74-byte UDP packet, and 440 microseconds for a 1514-byte packet are quoted for the microVAX II.

Shared packet buffers □ In the Firefly RPC design, packet buffers are mapped simultaneously and permanently in both the kernel's address space and those of all user processes. Stubs use these buffers as the targets of their marshalling operations, so that no user-to-kernel data copying is necessary. Furthermore, these buffers are accessible by DMA from the network controller, and no copying is required inside the kernel for the data to reach the network controller.

The Firefly RPC buffer pool is shared between all user processes because of the difficulty in answering the following question for any communication design: When an incoming packet arrives, where should the data be placed? The identity of the destination process cannot be ascertained until the packet has been stored and examined. In Firefly RPC, since the buffers are shared between all processes, the kernel can choose any buffer and the problem is avoided. However, this scheme is of limited applicability. Since user processes must be able to allocate and de-allocate buffers from what is a shared pool, this scheme implies trust that no user process will interfere with the buffers or copy private data. The risk is acceptable or non-existent in the case of a single-user workstation or dedicated server computer, but not acceptable for a multi-user computer.

Firefly RPC performance □ In order to summarize the relative costs for the actions that go to make up an RPC, we now report the results described by Schroeder and Burrows. These are in fact a mixture of measured and calculated component times, but

Figure 18.26 The costs, in microseconds, of sending and receiving a packet.

Action	74-byte packet	1514-byte packet
	– Send–	
Initialize packet headers and checksum	104	499
User-kernel context switch	37	37
Set up message transfer	147	147
DMA transfer to controller	70	815
Ethernet transmission	60	1230
	– Receive –	
DMA transfer to/from controller	80	835
Handle receive interrupt	191	191
calculate UDP checksum	45	440
Wake up RPC thread	220	220
TOTAL	954	4414

they are sufficiently accurate when totalled to provide for comparisons between the costs of the components. Two remote procedure calls are considered: *Null*() is a null remote procedure call, and *MaxResult(buf)*, transfers 1440 bytes of data from the server to the caller's buffer, which is given as the argument *buf*. The Firefly RPCs we shall consider are implemented by an exchange of two packets: the call packet and result packet. The RPCs are between MicroVax-based Firefly multiprocessors over a 10 megabits-per-second Ethernet. We shall not concern ourselves with the multiprocessor nature of the Firefly, and assume a single processor is used at both client and server.

The designers of Firefly RPC went to great pains to optimize their implementation. This included hand-coding critical parts of the code in assembler. The total time for an RPC is made up of three main components:

- the time spent in the client and server stubs to construct the two packets for transmission; this includes buffer allocation and local procedure calling within the RPC run-time software;

- the time to send and receive the call packet; and

- the time to send and receive the result packet.

Figure 18.25 gives the calculated times, which differ slightly from the measured times. The marshalling of the reply packet is carried out by a stub, but is listed separately for clarity.

The costs for sending and receiving the packets are as shown in Figure 18.26. The items in this table are self-explanatory, except that the item 'set up message transfer' involves enqueuing the message for transmission, and communicating with the network controller via a dedicated Firefly processor. Figure 18.27 summarizes the division between hardware and software costs. Note that the single most costly component of message transmission in the *Null*() case is the time taken to wake up the RPC thread

Figure 18.27   Relative hardware and software costs when sending and receiving a packet.

74 bytes

1514 bytes

Sending   Hardware   Receiving
software   software

Note: 'Hardware' includes DMA and Ethernet transfer times. 'Software' includes times to
communicate with network controllers.

awaiting a packet. The Firefly implementation did not use the optimization of *spinning*, whereby an idle processor remains in the context of the last thread to execute, in case this same thread is the next to be scheduled. This optimization would have reduced this cost considerably.

Considering remote procedure calls overall, we can see that the ratio of software costs to hardware costs varies considerably according to the size of the packets required for the call, and is very high in the case of *Null* (see Figure 18.28). The hardware costs (DMA and network transmission times taken together) make up about 17 per cent of the overall costs for *Null*, but about 47 per cent of the overall costs for *MaxResult(buffer)*.

The remainder of the time taken by these calls is accounted for by actions taken directly by the processor. Increasing the network bandwidth by a factor of 10, from 10 megabits per second to 100 megabits per second, would reduce the time for *Null* by only about 110 microseconds – just a 4 per cent improvement. On the other hand, increasing the speed of the CPU by a factor of 10 would give a saving for a call to *Null* of about 75 per cent.

As a final point it should be noted that, apart from marshalling, data copying is avoided in the Firefly implementation. As explained above, the shared buffer pool implementation used to achieve this is not applicable to a multi-user environment. Most RPC implementations carry additional memory-to-memory copying overheads.

Summary

The Firefly RPC implementation concentrates upon remote procedure calls between processes residing at different computers. It has been optimized for the common case in

Figure 18.28   Relative hardware and software costs for remote procedure calls.

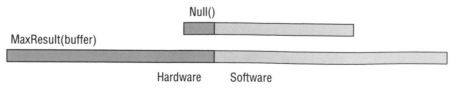

Null()

MaxResult(buffer)

Hardware   Software

Note:'Hardware' includes DMA and Ethernet transfer times. 'Software' includes times to
communicate with network controllers.

which arguments and results are sent in single packets. Data type conversion is omitted except between heterogeneous computers; packet headers are partially pre-initialized; and packet buffers are shared between the kernel and user processes. The resulting performance is good, but not demonstrably better than others (faster implementations exist, but on different processors). Performance would be worse on a multi-user computer, because packet buffers could not be shared. Nonetheless, the implementors took pains to account for the time spent in an RPC. The results confirm the assertion of Chapter 6, that a large proportion of RPC delay is accounted for by the operations of the operating system and RPC run-time, rather than hardware. Scheduling costs, which are a large proportion of the null RPC delay, could have been improved by the technique of spinning.

18.9 The Amoeba multicast protocol

This section describes the reliable multicast protocol developed by Kaashoek and Tanenbaum for group communication in Amoeba. This is a totally ordered multicast protocol that can be configured to provide a range of degrees of reliability [Kaashoek *et al.* 1989]. It employs a sequencer to order multicasts totally, and it uses the FLIP layer (see Section 18.5), which employs hardware multicast to minimize the number of messages transmitted when multicasting over a local area network. The main achievement of this protocol is that in the normal case where no messages are lost, a multicast requires only two messages. We first describe the simplest version of the protocol, and then show how it can be extended to recover from computer failure.

If all multicast messages are funnelled through a single member of a process group, that member can assign message identifiers from a sequence. The funnelling process is called the *sequencer*. Figure 18.29 illustrates the role of the sequencer in the transmission of a multicast message. The originator of a multicast message sends it to the sequencer which adds a sequence number and then relays it to the other members

Figure 18.29   Multicast with a sequencer.

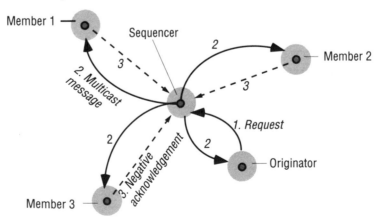

Note: the dashed arrows indicate (infrequent) requests for missing messages.

using a single broadcast message. The sequence numbers are used to ensure that multicast messages are delivered in the same order to all members.

The components that take part in the protocol are the members of a process group and the communication kernels that reside at each computer hosting a group member. The kernels implement multicast. At any one time, just one of the kernels acts as the sequencer. Several members of a group may run on the same computer. It is a straightforward matter to distribute a multicast message arriving at a computer to all the local group members. We therefore concentrate on multicasting a message to a set of destinations, where by 'destination' is meant computer.

In the simplest version of the protocol, the sequencer keeps the following information:

A *list of destinations* for the multicast messages (we assume that there is only one group and therefore one such set of destinations, but there could be more);

A *sequence number* that is incremented by one for every new multicast message. The sequence numbers are used to ensure that request messages are delivered in the same order to all the multicast destinations;

A *history buffer*, which holds a list of messages already sent to the destinations, together with their sequence numbers.

The originator of a multicast attaches a unique identifier to the message and transmits it point-to-point to the sequencer. The sequencer increments the sequence number and appends it to the message, which it stores in the history buffer. Then it transmits the message to all of the destinations. Hardware broadcast or multicast is used by the sequencer, assuming it is available, allowing the same network packet to be used to reach the multicast destinations and to acknowledge the originator's message. Otherwise, point-to-point messages would have to be used.

The originator times out and retransmits the message as necessary until it receives an acknowledgement. The sequencer checks for repeated messages against its history buffer, and merely sends an acknowledgement to the originator if the message is found there.

By contrast, the communication between the sequencer and the destinations uses a negative acknowledgment scheme in which the destinations request retransmission of lost messages from the sequencer. Lost messages are detected when a message arrives with a higher sequence number than is expected by the recipient. This is an example of a protocol designed to perform best under the normal conditions for local area networks – that is the loss of messages is infrequent. On the other hand, if a message does not arrive at a member that has stopped multicasting, then it won't find out that the message is missing until it sends a 'heartbeat' message to the sequencer, as discussed below.

Unless precautions are taken, the number of messages stored at the sequencer will grow indefinitely. The protocol takes the following steps to ensure that the history buffer capacity is not exceeded:

1. The highest sequence number received by the originator is piggy-backed on all the multicast messages. This enables the sequencer to record the highest message identifier seen by each member. Messages are removed from the history buffer after they have been acknowledged by all members of the group.

2. To ensure that there are regular acknowledgments even when members are not originating multicasts, each member is expected to send periodic 'heartbeat' acknowledgments of the highest sequence number received.

3. If the space occupied in the history buffer exceeds a pre-defined limit, the sequencer enters a synchronization phase during which no multicasts are done and the sequencer requests and ensures that all the members fetch any outstanding messages. After that the sequencer deletes the history buffer's contents and resumes its normal role.

Consider the case of a single group member multicasting repeatedly, with no other communication by group members. This is a worst-case scenario from the point of view of deleting messages from the history buffer. If the history buffer can hold h messages and if there are N group members, then after h messages are sent each of $N-1$ members will have sent a heartbeat message, as mentioned above, in order that the history buffer is not filled. Assuming hardware multicast or broadcast is used, the number of packets required for h messages is $2h + N - 1$, and the number of packets per message is therefore $2 + (N-1)/h$. This number is liable to be close to 2, for a reasonably-sized history buffer.

One potential problem with this protocol is that the sequencer may become a bottleneck when the number of group members becomes large and multicasting is frequent. The results of a theoretical analysis are quoted by Kaashoek and Tanenbaum [1991] who suggest that this would be a problem at around 400 nodes for the most multicast-intensive applications they tried, although they do not specify what this is.

The most serious deficiency of this protocol as described is that its behaviour is unsatisfactory for many applications under conditions of failure.

Reliability measure □   Kaashoek and Tanenbaum [1991] describe two ways in which the protocol described above is extended to take account of computer failures. First, the application is offered a chance to reconstitute the group and continue execution after computer failure is detected, even if the sequencer has failed. Secondly, multicast messages are guaranteed to be delivered to all surviving group members, despite up to r simultaneous computer failures, where the value of r is chosen by the user. If r is less than the number of members in the group, then multicast is not atomic. But the user can trade off this 'degree' of atomicity against what turns out, not surprisingly, to be the increased expense of the protocol as r increases.

When a computer fails in a fail-stop mode, one or more kernels notice this by virtue of its failure to respond. From that point, all group-related primitives are caused to fail. It is left up to the application to notice this and to respond. Any member can reconstitute the group by calling a special primitive, *resetGroup*. The effect of this primitive is to reestablish and report the group membership, and to once more enable multicasts to take place – so long as the group population exceeds a minimum number specified by the user.

When a group member fails, it is necessary to agree a new group membership list, agree on the kernel which is to act as the sequencer and to agree a new *incarnation number*. The incarnation number is effectively a group view identifier. Messages bearing an old incarnation number will be rejected by the sequencer.

To recover from the failure of the sequencer, the history buffer is replicated at all member sites. Each site retains copies of the messages it receives, and only deletes them

Figure 18.30 Fault-tolerant multicast with a sequencer.

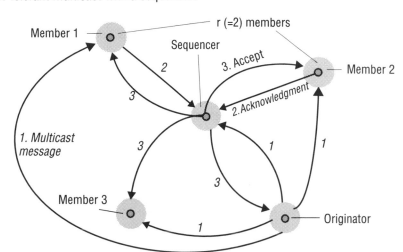

when informed by the sequencer that they have been received everywhere (this information can be piggy-backed on normal message traffic). When a computer failure occurs, all computers at which *resetGroup* has been called send an *invitation* message to all other members of the group. In response, they send the highest sequence number received. Repeated attempts are made to gain a response from each computer, if necessary. The coordinator with the highest sequence number is elected as the final coordinator (the one with, say, the highest computer identifier is chosen in the case of a draw). The coordinator then fetches any missing messages (remember that not all computers contend to be the coordinator) and sends a *result* message containing the new incarnation identifier, the group membership and the highest sequence number to all members.

On receipt of the *result* message, the other kernels collect any missing messages from the coordinator. Once this is done, they send an *acknowledgement* message to the coordinator and resume normal operation. The coordinator resumes normal operation and acts as the new sequencer after it has received all *acknowledgement* messages. If it is discovered after the result message is sent that another process has failed, the protocol starts again from the beginning.

Finally, there is the problem of atomicity. Under the protocol so far described, a message could be delivered to some proper subset of the group, all of which then fail. The remaining members will never receive the message. There is a version of the protocol that guarantees atomic delivery despite up to a specified number *r* of computer failures. In this version of the protocol (shown in Figure 18.30), the exchange of messages is different.

The originator multicasts the message. The recipients regard the message as unstable (that is, as not yet eligible for delivery) and keep it on a hold-back queue until they receive an *accept* message from the sequencer containing the sequence number. Control is not returned to the message's sender until the *accept* message is received. On receiving a message, a member records it and then sends an acknowledgment to the sequencer. After the sequencer has received the message, it waits for r acknowledgments and then broadcasts an *accept* message containing the next sequence number. At that point, $r+1$ kernels hold the message; any r of them can fail, and the message will still be delivered to the remaining kernels. The price paid for this guarantee is a two-phase protocol, which introduces considerable extra latency.

Summary

The Amoeba multicast protocol employs a sequencer, which labels multicast messages with sequence numbers in order to totally order the messages. Where hardware multicast is used, the basic protocol involves little more than two messages for each multicast. The protocol relies on a negative acknowledgement scheme, so that a process that has missed a message may not discover this until a subsequent 'heartbeat' message is sent to the sequencer. This delay may not be acceptable for some applications. The implementors report that the sequencer does not appear to be a bottleneck for the applications that they tried. However, it is not clear whether a sequencer-based protocol can be used to implement an efficient multicast service that could be used simultaneously by many applications.

A version of the protocol exists that allows the programmer to select the degree of reliability of the multicast: that is, the number of computers that may fail before delivery to the remaining computers cannot be guaranteed. This protocol relies on replication of the history buffer, which stores a record of all messages received by the sequencer.

EXERCISES

18.1   Why are the contents of Mach messages typed?

page 554

18.2   i)   A server in Mach manages many *thingumajig* resources. Discuss the advantages and disadvantages of associating:

      a)   a single port with all the thingumajigs;

      b)   a single port per thingumajig;

      c)   a port per client.

   ii)   What is a port set in Mach, and what is its purpose?

  iii)   A client supplies a thingumajig identifier to the server, which replies with a port right. What type of port right should the server send back to the client? Explain why the server's identifier for the port right and that of the client may differ.

  iv)   A thingumajig client resides at a different computer from the server. Explain how the client comes to possess a port right that enables it to communicate with the server, even though the Mach kernel can only transmit port rights between local tasks.

page 555-557

18.3 Discuss whether the Mach kernel's ability to monitor the number of send rights for a particular port should be extended to the network.

page 555

18.4 i) Is it necessary that a received message's address range is chosen by the kernel when copy-on-write is used?

ii) Is copy-on-write of use for sending messages to remote destinations in Mach?

iii) A task sends a 16 kilobyte message asynchronously to a local task on a 10 MIPS, 32-bit machine with an 8 kilobyte page size. Compare the costs of 1) simply copying the message data (without using copy-on-write) 2) best-case copy-on-write and 3) worst-case copy-on-write. You can assume that:

- creating an empty region of size 16 kilobytes takes 1000 instructions;

- handling a page fault and allocating a new page in the region takes 100 instructions.

page 554,561

18.5 A file is opened and mapped at the same time by two tasks residing at machines without shared physical memory. Discuss the problem of consistency this raises. Design a protocol using Mach external pager messages which ensures sequential consistency for the file contents (see Chapter 17).

page 565

18.6 Explain the advantages and disadvantages of the Chorus approach of allowing servers to reside in either the shared kernel address space or in private user-level address spaces.

page 568

18.7 An electronic mail service is to be provided by many servers. A mail message may be created at one such server, but may migrate to another server when being delivered. As the designer of such a system, would you prefer to associate a Mach port, a Chorus port or a Chorus port group with a mail message?

page 572

18.8 i) Can an operating system be emulated on a monolithic kernel, and would this be worthwhile?

ii) Explain the steps taken to reduce communication with the UNIX server in Mach's UNIX emulation. Does file mapping eliminate message passing? Can the same techniques be applied in the Chorus emulation?

iii) How many threads should a UNIX server have?

page 579

18.9   i)   Joe is an Amoeba user who has a legitimate capability for a thingumajig. He adds 1 to the object identifier in the capability, on the (correct) assumption that the thingumajig server keeps an array of information indexed by object id. Can he succeed in obtaining access to another thingumajig?

       ii)   Files can in general be readable, writeable and executable. A client with only read and execute permissions for a file wishes to give another client read permission only. Explain how this must be achieved.

      iii) Describe a form of security attack that undermines the use of capabilities in Amoeba (or, for that matter, Mach and Chorus).

page 585

18.10 Discuss the approach of storing the entire contents of a process's address space on disk and then reloading it at another computer to achieve process migration.

page 587

18.11 i)   When an Amoeba server wishes to communicate separately with a client it generates a random port identifier and sends it back to the client. Compare this method of generating port identifiers with the Chorus approach of asking the kernel to generate a port identifier.

       ii)   Explain how Amoeba locates a port when a port identifier is used to send a request for the first time from a particular computer. Explain the relevance of process migration to your protocol.

page 592

18.12 i)   Explain how operating system requirements for supporting distributed objects differ from those for supporting communicating processes.

       ii)   Outline how you would provide support for distributed objects on top of Mach or Chorus, without the use of distributed shared memory.

page 598

18.13 i)   Why does Clouds provide distributed shared memory?

       ii)   Why does Clouds support persistent objects, rather than files?

      iii) How does a Clouds thread differ from a Mach thread?

page 599

18.14 i)   When should COOL use RPC-based invocation, and when should it use distributed-shared-memory-based invocation?

       ii)   What is object migration and why is it required?

      iii) Does Clouds support object migration? Does the model you described in Exercise 18.12 support object migration? Justify your answers, and make any distinctions necessary between language-level objects and operating system objects.

page 602

18.15   By what percentage would the performance of a null Firefly RPC improve
        if the 10 megabits-per-second Ethernet was replaced by a 500 megabits-per-
        second ATM network?

page 607

18.16   i)   Is Amoeba multicast causally ordered as well as totally ordered? Does
              your answer change if processes could send multicasts
              asynchronously, instead of being blocked until an acknowledgement
              is received from the sequencer?

        ii)   Why do kernels send 'heartbeat' messages in the Amoeba multicast
              protocol?

        iii) In a development of the Amoeba protocol, several groups may exist
              and individual processes may belong to more than one group. Is it
              possible to implement this design using several sequencers?

        iv)   In the reliable form of the Amoeba protocol that withstands the failure
              of up to r computers, is it necessary that the sender is blocked until it
              receives an *accept* message?

page 608

REFERENCES

[Abrossimov *et al.* 1989]   Abrossimov, V., Rozier, M. and Shapiro, M. (1989). Generic Virtual Memory Management for operating system kernels. *Proc. of 12th ACM Sym. on Operating System Principles,* pp. 123-136, December.

[Acetta *et al.* 1986]   Accetta, M., Baron, R., Golub, D., Rashid, R., Tevanian, A. and Young, M. (1986). Mach: A New Kernel Foundation for UNIX Development. *Proc. Summer 1986 USENIX Conf.* pp. 93-112.

[Adve and Hill 1990]   Adve, S. and Hill, M. (1990). Weak Ordering – A New Definition. *Proc. 17th. Annual Sym. on Computer Architecture*, IEEE, pp. 2-14.

[Ahamad *et al.* 1992]   Ahamad, M., Bazzi, R., John, R., Kohli, P. and Neiger, G. (1992). The Power of Processor Consistency. *Tech. report GIT-CC-92/34*, Georgia Institute of Technology, Atlanta GA.

[Anderson *et al.* 1992]   Anderson, D., Osawa, Y. and Govindan, R. (1992). A File System for Continuous Media. *ACM Trans. Computer Systems,* vol. 10, no. 4, pp. 311-37.

[Anderson *et al.* 1991]   Anderson, T., Bershad, B., Lazowska, E. and Levy, H. (1991). Scheduler Activations: Efficient Kernel Support for the User-level Management of Parallelism. *Proc. 13th ACM Sym. on Operating System Principles*, pp. 95–109.

[Andrews 1991]   Andrews, G.R. (1991). *Concurrent Programming Principles and Practice*. Redwood City CA: Benjamin Cummings.

[ANSA 1989]   ANSA (1989). *The Advanced Network Systems Architecture (ANSA) Reference Manual*. Castle Hill, Cambridge England: Architecture Project Management.

[Armand *et al.* 1989]   Armand, F., Gien, M., Herrman, F. and Rozier, M. (1989). Distributing UNIX brings it back to its original virtues. *Proc. Workshop on Experiences with Building Distributed and Multiprocessor Systems*, pp. 153-174, October.

[Babaoglu 1990]   Babaoglu, O. (1990). Fault-tolerant computing based on Mach. *ACM Operating Systems Review*, vol. 24, no. 1, pp. 27-39.

[Bacon 1993]   Bacon, J. (1993). *Concurrent Systems*. Wokingham: Addison-Wesley, 1993.

[Bacon *et al.* 1991]   Bacon, J.M., Moody, K., Thompson, S.E. and Wilson, T.D. (1991). A Multi-Service Storage Architecture. *ACM Operating Systems Review*, vol. 25, no. 4.

[Bal *et al.* 1990]   Bal, H.E., Kaashoek, M.F. and Tanenbaum, A.S. (1990). Experience with Distributed Programming in Orca. *Proc. Int. Conf. on Computer Languages '90*, IEEE, pp. 79-89.

[Barghouti and Kaiser 1991]   Barghouti, N.S. and Kaiser G.E. (1991). Concurrency Control in Advanced Database Applications. *Computing Surveys*, vol. 23, no. 3, pp. 269-318.

[Bartoli *et al.* 1993]   Bartoli, A., Mullender, S.J. and van der Valk, M. (1993). Wide-Address Spaces – Exploring the Design Space. *ACM Operating Systems Review*, vol. 27, no. 1, pp. 11-17.

[Bayer and McCreight 1972]   Bayer, R. and McCreight, E. (1972). Organization and maintenance of large ordered indexes. *Acta Informatica*, vol. 1, pp. 173–89.

[Bellovin and Merritt 1990]   Bellovin, S.M. and Merritt, M., Limitations of the Kerberos Authentication System. ACM Computer Communications Review, vol. 20, no. 5, pp. 119-132.

[Ben Ari 1990]   Ben-Ari, M. (1990). *Principles of Concurrent and Distributed Programming*. Englewood Cliffs NJ: Prentice-Hall.

[Berners-Lee *et al.* 1992a]   Berners-Lee, T.J. Cailliau, R., Groff, J.-F., Pollermann, B. (1992). World-Wide Web: The Information Universe. In *Electronic Networking: Research, Applications and Policy*, vol. 2 no. 1, pp. 52-58, Westport CT: Meckler Publishing.

[Berners-Lee *et al.* 1992b]   Berners-Lee, T.J., R. Cailliau and Groff, J.-F. (1992). The World-Wide Web. *Computer Networks and ISDN Systems,* 25, pp. 454-459. Amsterdam: North-Holland.

[Bernstein *et al.* 1980]   Bernstein, P.A., Shipman, D.W. and Rothnie, J. B. (1980). Concurrency control in a system for distributed databases (SDD-1). *ACM Trans. Database Systems*, vol. 5, no. 1, pp. 18–51.

[Bernstein *et al.* 1987]   Bernstein, P., Hadzilacos, V. and Goodman, N. (1987). *Concurrency control and Recovery in Database Systems*. Reading MA: Addison-Wesley.

[Bershad *et al.* 1990]   Bershad, B., Anderson, T., Lazowska, E. and Levy, H. (1990). Lightweight Remote Procedure Call. *ACM Trans. Computer Systems*, vol. 8, no. 1, pp. 37-55.

[Bershad *et al.* 1991]   Bershad, B., Anderson, T., Lazowska, E. and Levy, H. (1991). User-level Interprocess Communication for Shared Memory Multiprocessors. *ACM Trans. Computer Systems*, vol. 9, no. 2, pp. 175-198.

[Birman 1993]   Birman, K.P. (1993). The Process Group Approach to Reliable Distributed Computing. *Comms. ACM*, vol. 36, no. 12, pp. 36–53.

[Birman and Joseph 1987]   Birman, K.P. and Joseph, T.A. (1987). Reliable Communication in the Presence of Failures. *ACM Trans. Computer Systems*, vol. 5, no. 1, pp. 47–76.

[Birman *et al.* 1991]   Birman, K.P., Schiper, A. and Stephenson, P. (1991). Lightweight Causal and Atomic Group Multicast. *ACM Trans. Computer Systems*, vol. 9, no. 3, pp. 272–314.

[Birrell and Needham 1980]   Birrell, A.D. and Needham, R.M. (1980). A universal file server. *IEEE Trans. Software Engineering*, vol. SE-6, no. 5, pp. 450–3.

[Birrell and Nelson 1984]   Birrell, A.D. and Nelson, B.J. (1984). Implementing remote procedure calls. *ACM Trans. Computer Systems*, vol. 2, pp. 39–59.

[Birrell *et al.* 1982]   Birrell, A.D., Levin, R., Needham, R.M. and Schroeder, M.D. (1982). Grapevine: an exercise in distributed computing. *Comms. ACM*, vol. 25, no. 4, pp. 260–73.

[Bisiani and Forin 1988]   Bisiani, R. and Forin, A. (1988). Multilanguage Parallel Programming of Heterogeneous Machines. *IEEE Trans. Computers*, vol. 37, no. 8, pp. 930-945.

[Bisiani and Ravishankar 1990]   Bisiani, R. and Ravishankar, M. (1990). Plus: a Distributed Shared Memory System. *Proc. 17th Int. Sym. on Computer Architecture*, pp.115-124.

[Black 1990]   Black, D. (1990). Scheduling Support for Concurrency and Parallelism in the Mach Operating System, *IEEE Computer*, vol. 23, no. 5, pp. 35–43.

[Black and Artsy 1990]   Black, A. and Artsy, Y. (1990). Implementing Location Independent Invocation, *IEEE Trans. Parallel and Distributed Systems*, vol. 1, no. 1.

[Black *et al.* 1987]   Black, A. Hutchinson, N., Jul, E., Levy, H. and Carter L. (1987). Distribution and Abstract Types in Emerald. *IEEE Trans. Software Engineering, vol. SE-13*, no. 1, pp. 65-76.

[Blair and Lea 1992]   Blair, G.S. and Lea, R. (1992). The Impact of Distribution on the Object-Oriented Approach to Software Development, *IEE/BCS Software Engineering Journal*, vol. 7, no. 2.

[Borg *et al.* 1989]   Borg, A., Blau, W. Graetsch, W., Hermann, F. and Oberle, W. (1989). Fault-tolerance under Unix. *ACM Trans. Computer Systems*, vol. 5, no. 1, pp. 1-24.

[Bornat and Sufrin 1993]   Bornat, R. and Sufrin, B.A. (1993). The Gist of Jape, *Tech. Report*, Oxford University Computing Laboratory.

[Bowman *et al.* 1990]   Bowman, M., Peterson, L. and Yeatts, A., Univers: an Attribute-based Name Server. *Software–Practice and Experience*, vol. 20, no. 4, pp. 403–24.

[Boykin *et al.* 1993]   Boykin, J., Kirschen, D., Langerman, A. and LoVerso, S. (1993). *Programming under Mach*. Reading MA: Addison-Wesley.

[Brinch Hansen 1978]   Brinch Hansen, P. (1978). Distributed Processes: a Concurrent Programming Concept. *Comms. ACM*, vol. 21, no. 11, pp. 934-41.

[Brownbridge *et al.* 1982]   Brownbridge, D.R., Marshall, L.F. and Randell, B. (1982). The Newcastle connection, or UNIXes of the world unite! *Software–Practice and Experience*, vol. 12, pp. 1147–62.

[Burrows, Abadi and Needham 1989]   Burrows, M., Abadi, M. and Needham, R. (1989). A Logic of Authentication. *Tech. Report 39*, Palo Alto CA: Digital Equipment Corporation Systems Research Center.

[Burrows, Abadi and Needham 1990]   Burrows, M., Abadi, M. and Needham, R. (1990). A Logic of Authentication. *ACM Trans. Computer Systems*, vol. 8, pp. 18-36, February 1990.

[Campbell *et al.* 1993]   Campbell, R., Islam, N., Raila, D. and Madany, P. (1993). Designing and implementing Choices: an object-oriented system in C++. *Comms. ACM*, vol. 36, no. 9, pp. 117-26.

[Carriero and Gelernter 1989]   Carriero, N. and Gelernter, D. (1989). Linda in Context. *Comms. ACM*, vol. 32, no. 4, pp. 444-58.

[Carter *et al.* 1991]   Carter, J.B., Bennett, J.K. and Zwaenepoel, W. (1991). Implementation and Performance of Munin. *Proc. 13th ACM Sym. on Operating System Principles*, pp. 152-64, 1991.

[CCITT 1985]   CCITT (1985). *Recommendation X.409*: Presentation Transfer Syntax and Notation. Red Book, vol. VIII, International Telecommunications Union, Place des Nations, 1211 Geneva, Switzerland.

[CCITT 1988]   CCITT (1988). *Recommendation X.500*: The Directory – Overview of Concepts, Models and Service. International Telecommunications Union, Place des Nations, 1211 Geneva, Switzerland.

[CCITT 1990]   CCITT (1990). *Recommendation I.150*: B-ISDN ATM Functional Characteristics. International Telecommunications Union, Place des Nations, 1211 Geneva, Switzerland.

[Ceri and Owicki 1982]   Ceri, S. and Owicki, S. (1982). On the use of Optimistic Methods for Concurrency Control in Distributed Databases. *Proc. 6th Berkeley Workshop on Distributed Data Management and Computer Networks*, Berkeley, pp. 117-30.

[Ceri and Pelagatti 1985]   Ceri, S. and Pelagatti, G. (1985). *Distributed Databases – Principles and Systems*. McGraw-Hill.

[Chang and Roberts 1979]   Chang, E.G. and Roberts, R. (1979). An improved algorithm for decentralized extrema-finding in circular configurations of processors. *Comms. ACM*, vol. 22, no. 5, pp. 281-3.

[Chase *et al.* 1989]   Chase, J.S., Amador, F.G., Lazowska, E.D., Levy, H.M. and Littlefield, R.J. (1989). The Amber System: Parallel Programming on a Network of Multiprocessors. *Proc. 12th. ACM Sym. on Operating System Principles*, pp. 147-58, December.

[Cheriton 1984]   Cheriton, D.R. (1984). The V kernel: a software base for distributed systems. *IEEE Software*, vol. 1 no. 2, pp. 19–42.

[Cheriton 1985] Cheriton, D.R. (1985). Preliminary Thoughts on Problem-oriented Shared Memory: a Decentralized Approach to Distributed Systems. *ACM Operating Systems Review*, vol. 19, no. 4, pp. 26-33.

[Cheriton 1986] Cheriton, D. R. (1986). VMTP: A Protocol for the Next Generation of Communication Systems. *Proc. SIGCOMM '86 Sym. on Communication Architectures and Protocols,* ACM, pp. 406-15.

[Cheriton and Mann 1989] Cheriton, D. and Mann, T. (1989). Decentralizing a Global Naming Service for Improved Performance and Fault Tolerance. *ACM Trans. Computer Systems*, vol. 7, no. 2, pp. 147–83.

[Cheriton and Zwaenepoel 1985] Cheriton, D.R. and Zwaenepoel, W. (1985). Distributed process groups in the V kernel. *ACM Trans. Computer Systems*, vol. 3, no. 2, pp. 77–107.

[Cheriton et al. 1990] Cheriton, D., Whitehead, G. and Sznyter, E. (1990). Binary emulation of Unix using the V kernel, *Proc. USENIX Summer Conference*, pp. 73-85.

[Choudhary et al. 1989] Choudhary, A., Kohler, W., Stankovic, J. and Towsley, D. (1989). A Modified Priority Based Probe Algorithm for Distributed Deadlock Detection and Resolution. *IEEE Trans. Software Engineering,* vol. 15, no. 1.

[Comba 1990] Comba, P. (1990). Exponentiation Cryptosystems on the IBM PC. *IBM Systems Journal*, vol. 28, pp. 525-38.

[Comer 1991] Comer, D.E. (1991). *Internetworking with TCP/IP, Volume 1; Principles, protocols and architecture.* (Second Edition), Englewood Cliffs NJ: Prentice-Hall.

[Cooper 1985] Cooper, E. (1985). Replicated distributed programs. *Proc. 10th Sym. on Operating Systems Principles*, ACM, pp. 63-78.

[Cooper 1988] Cooper, E. (1988). C Threads, *Tech. Report CMU-CS-99-154*, Carnegie-Mellon University, USA.

[Cristian 1989] Cristian, F. (1989). Probabilistic clock synchronization. *Distributed Computing*, vol. 3, pp. 146-158, 1989.

[Cristian 1991] Cristian, F. (1991). Understanding Fault-Tolerant Distributed Systems. *Comms. ACM*, vol. 34, no. 2.

[Custer 1992] Custer, H., *Inside Windows NT*. Microsoft Press, 1992.

[Dasgupta et al. 1991] Dasgupta, P., LeBlanc Jr., R. J. Ahamad, M. and Ramachandran, U. (1991). The Clouds Distributed Operating System. *IEEE Computer*, vol. 24, no. 11, pp. 34-44.

[Davidson 1984] Davidson, S. B. (1984). Optimism and Consistency in Partitioned Database Systems. *ACM Trans. Database Systems*, vol. 9, no. 3, pp. 456-81.

[Davidson et al. 1985] Davidson, S. B., Garcia-Molina, H. and Skeen, D. (1985). Consistency in Partitioned Networks. *Computing Surveys*, vol. 17, no.3, pp. 341-70.

[Davison *et al.* 1992]   Davison, A., Drake, K., Roberts, W. and Slater, M. (1992). *Distributed Window Systems, a Practical Guide to X11 and OpenWindows.* Wokingham: Addison-Wesley.

[Dean and Armand 1992]   Dean, R. and Armand, F. (1992). Data movement in kernelized systems. *Proc. USENIX Workshop on Microkernels.*

[Deering and Cheriton 1990]   Deering, S.E. and Cheriton, D.R. (1990). Multicast Routing in Datagram Internetworks and Extended LANs, *ACM Trans. Computer Systems*, vol. 8, no. 2.

[Denning 1982]   Denning, D. (1982). *Cryptography and Data Security*, Reading MA: Addison-Wesley.

[Diffie and Hellman 1976]   Diffie, W. and Hellman, M.E. (1976). New Directions in Cryptography. *IEEE Trans. Information Theory*, vol. IT-22, pp. 644-54.

[Donahue 1985]   Donahue, J. (1985). Integration mechanisms in Cedar, *Proc ACM SIGPLAN 85 Sym. on Programming Languages and Environments.*

[Draves 1990]   Draves, R. (1990). A Revised IPC Interface, *Proc. USENIX Mach Workshop*, pp. 101-21, October 1990.

[Draves *et al.* 1989]   Draves, R.P., Jones, M.B., Thompson, M.R. (1989). MIG - the Mach Interface Generator. *Tech. Report,* Dept. of Computer Science, Carnegie Mellon University.

[Dubois *et al.* 1988]   Dubois, M., Scheurich, C. and Briggs, F.A. (1988). Synchronization, Coherence and Event Ordering in Multiprocessors. *IEEE Computer*, vol. 21, no. 2, pp. 9-21.

[Eberle and Thacker 1992]   Eberle, H. and Thacker, C.A. (1992). 1 Gbit/second GaAs DES chip. In *Proc. IEEE 1992 Custom Integrated Circuit Conference*, Boston MA, pp. 19.7.1-4.

[El Abbadi *et al.* 1985]   El Abbadi, A., Skeen, D. and Cristian, C. (1985). An Efficient Fault-Tolerant Protocol for Replicated Data Management. *4th Annual ACM SIGACT/SIGMOD Sym. on Principles of Data Base Systems*, Portland OR.

[Ellis *et al.* 1991]   Ellis, C., Gibbs, S. and Rein, G. (1991). Groupware – Some Issues and Experiences, *Comms. ACM*, vol. 34, no. 1, pp. 38–58.

[Farber and Larson 1972]   Farber, D.J. and Larson, K.C. (1972). The system architecture of the distributed computer system – the communications network. *Proc. Sym. on Computer Networks*, Polytechnic Institute of Brooklyn.

[Farmer and Newhall 1969]   Farmer, W.D. and Newhall, E.E. (1969). An experimental distributed switching system to handle bursty computer traffic. *Proc. ACM Sym. on Problems in Optimization of Data Communication Systems*, ACM, pp. 1–33.

[Fidge 1988]   Fidge, L. (1988). Timestamps in Message Passing Systems that Preserve the Partial Ordering. *Proc. 11th Australian Computer Science Conference*, pp. 56–66.

[Fischer and Michael 1982] Fischer, M.J. and Michael, A. (1982). Sacrificing Serializability to Attain High Availability of Data in an Unreliable Network. *Proc. Sym. on Principles of Database Systems*, ACM, pp. 70–75.

[Fitzgerald and Rashid 1986] Fitzgerald, R. and Rashid, R.F. (1986). The integration of virtual memory management and interprocess communication in Accent. *ACM Trans. Computer Systems*, vol. 4, no. 2, pp. 147–77.

[Fleisch and Popek 1989] Fleisch, B. and Popek, G. (1989). Mirage: a coherent distributed shared memory design. *Proc. 12th ACM Sym. on Operating System Principles*, December, pp. 211-23.

[Floyd 1986] Floyd, R. (1986). Short term file reference patterns in a UNIX environment. *Tech. Rep. TR 177*, Rochester NY: Dept. of Computer Science, University of Rochester.

[Garcia-Molina and Spauster 1991] Garcia-Molina, H. and Spauster, A. (1991). Ordered and Reliable Multicast Communication. *ACM Trans. Computer Systems*, vol. 9, no. 3, pp. 242–71.

[Gharachorloo *et al.* 1990] Gharachorloo, K., Lenoski, D., Laudon, J., Gibbons, P., Gupta, A. and Hennessy, J. (1990). Memory Consistency and Event Ordering in Scalable Shared-Memory Multiprocessors. *Proc. 17th. Annual International Sym. on Computer Architecture*, May, pp. 15–26.

[Gifford 1979a] Gifford, D.K. (1979). Weighted voting for replicated data. *Proc. 7th Sym. on Operating Systems Principles*, ACM, pp. 150–62.

[Gifford 1979b] Gifford, D.K. (1979). Violet: an experimental decentralized system, *ACM Operating Systems Review*, vol. 13, no. 5.

[Glasgow et al. 1992] Glasgow, J., MacEwan, G. and Pananageden, P. (1992). A Logic for Reasoning about Security. *ACM Trans. Computer Systems*. vol. 10, no. 3. pp. 265-310.

[Goldberg 1988] Goldberg, A., Ed. (1988). *A History of Personal Workstations*. New York: ACM Press/Addison-Wesley.

[Golub *et al.* 1990] Golub, D., Dean, R., Forin, A. and Rashid, R. (1990). UNIX as an application program. *Proc. USENIX Summer Conference*, pp. 87-96.

[Goodman 1989] Goodman, J. (1989). Cache Consistency and Sequential Consistency. *Tech. Report 61*, SCI Committee.

[Govindan and Anderson 1991] Govindan, R. and Anderson, D. (1991). Scheduling and IPC Mechanisms for Continuous Media. *Proc. 13th Sym. on Operating System Principles*, ACM, pp. 68-80.

[Gray 1978] Gray, J. (1978). Notes on database operating systems. In *Operating Systems: an Advanced Course*. (Ed. Bayer, R., Graham, R.M. and Seegmuller, G.) Lecture Notes in Computer Science, vol. 60, pp. 394–481, Springer-Verlag.

[Gusella and Zatti 1989] Gusella, R. and Zatti, S. (1989). The accuracy of clock synchronization achieved by TEMPO in Berkeley UNIX 4.3BSD. *IEEE Trans. Software Engineering*, vol. 15, pp. 847-53.

[Harbison 1992] Harbison, S.P. (1992). *Modula-3*. Englewood Cliffs NJ: Prentice-Hall.

[Härder 1984]   Härder, T. (1984). Observations on Optimistic Concurrency Control Schemes. *Information Systems*, vol. 9, no. 2, pp. 111-20.

[Härder and Reuter 1983] Härder, T. and Reuter, A. (1983). Principles of Transaction-Oriented Database Recovery. *Computing Surveys*, vol.15, no. 4.

[Harrenstien *et al.* 1985] Harrenstien, K., Stahl, M. and Feinler, E. (1985). HOSTNAME Server, *Tech. Report RFC 953*, file available for anonymous file transfer from the Internet Network Information Center, Internet host: nic.ddn.mil, directory: /usr/pub/RFC.

[Herlihy 1986]   Herlihy, M. (1986). A Quorum-Consensus Replication Method for Abstract Data Types. *ACM Trans. Computer Systems*, vol. 4, no. 1, pp. 32-53.

[Hoare 1978]   Hoare, C.A.R. (1978). Communicating sequential processes. *Comms. ACM, vol. 21, pp. 667–77.*

[Howard *et al.* 1988]   Howard, J.H., Kazar, M.L., Menees, S.G, Nichols, D.A., Satyanarayanan, M., Sidebotham, R.N. and West, M.J. (1988). Scale and Performance in a Distributed File System. *ACM Trans. Computer Systems*, vol. 6, no. 1, pp. 51-81.

[Hughes and Cresswell 1972] Hughes, G.E. and Cresswell, M.J. (1972). *An Introduction to Modal Logic*, University Paperbacks.

[Hutchinson *et al.* 1989] Hutchinson, N., Peterson, L., Abbott, M., O'Malley, S. (1989). RPC in the x-Kernel: Evaluating New Design Techniques. *Proc 12th ACM Sym. on Operating System Principles,* pp. 91-101.

[Hutto and Ahamad 1990] Hutto, P. and Ahamad, M. (1990). Slow memory: weakening consistency to enhance concurrency in distributed shared memories. *Proc. 10th Int. Conf. on Distributed Computer Systems*, IEEE, pp. 302-311.

[IEEE 1983]   Institute of Electrical and Electronic Engineers (1983). Special issue on local area networks. *IEEE Journal on Selected areas in Communications (SAC)*, vol. 1, no. 5.

[IEEE 1985a]   Institute of Electrical and Electronic Engineers (1985). *Local Area Network – CSMA/CD Access Method and Physical Layer Specifications*. American National Standard ANSI/IEEE 802.3, IEEE Computer Society.

[IEEE 1985b]   Institute of Electrical and Electronic Engineers (1985). *Local Area Network – Token Ring Access Method and Physical Layer Specifications*. American National Standard ANSI/IEEE 802.5, IEEE Computer Society.

[IEEE 1985c]   Institute of Electrical and Electronic Engineers (1985). *Local Area Network – Logical Link Control*. American National Standard, ANSI/ IEEE 802.2, IEEE Computer Society.

[IEEE 1985d]   Institute of Electrical and Electronic Engineers (1985). *Draft IEEE Standard 802.1 (Part A): Overview and Architecture*. IEEE Computer Society.

[IEEE 1990]   Institute of Electrical and Electronic Engineers (1990). *IEEE Standard 802: Overview and Architecture.* American National Standard ANSI/ IEEE 802, IEEE Computer Society.

[ISO 1992]   International Standards Organization (1992). *Basic Reference Model of Open Distributed Processing, Part 1: Overview and guide to use.* ISO/ IEC JTC1/SC212/WG7 CD 10746-1, International Standards Organization, 1992.

[Israel *et al.* 1978]   Israel, J.E., Mitchell, J.G. and Sturgis, H.E. (1978). Separating data from function in a distributed file system. In *Operating Systems: Theory and Practice.* (Ed. Lanciaux, D.), pp. 17–27, Amsterdam: North-Holland.

[Jeffay 1989]   Jeffay, K. (1989). The real-time producer/consumer paradigm: Towards verifiable real-time computations. *PhD Thesis, Tech. report 89-09-15,* Dept. of Computer Science, University of Washington.

[Jones and Hopper 1993] Jones A. and Hopper, A. (1993). Handling Audio and Digital Streams in a Distributed Environment, *ACM Operating Systems Review*, vol. 27, no. 5, pp. 231-243.

[Jones and Rashid 1986] Jones, M.B. and Rashid, R.T. (1986). Mach and Matchmaker: kernel and language support for object-oriented distributed systems, *ACM Sigplan Notices*, vol. 21, no. 11, pp. 67–77.

[Jul *et al.* 1988]   Jul, E., Levy, H., Hutchinson, N. and Black, A. (1988). Fine-grained Mobility in the Emerald System. *ACM Trans. Computer Systems*, vol. 6, no. 1, pp. 109-33.

[Kaashoek and Tanenbaum 1991]   Kaashoek, F. and Tanenbaum, A. (1991). Group Communication in the Amoeba Distributed Operating System. *Proc. 11th International Conference on Distributed Computer Systems*, pp. 222-230.

[Kaashoek *et al.* 1989]   Kaashoek, F., Tanenbaum, A., Flynn Hummel, S. and Bal, H. (1989). An Efficient Reliable Broadcast Protocol. *Operating Systems Review*, vol. 23, no. 4, pp. 5-20.

[Kaashoek *et al.* 1993]   Kaashoek, M.F., van Renesse, R., van Staveren, H. and Tanenbaum, A. (1993). FLIP: An Internetwork Protocol for Supporting Distributed Systems. *ACM Trans. Computer Systems*, vol. 11, no. 1, pp. 73-106.

[Kehne *et al.* 1992]   Kehne, A., Schonwalder, J. and Langendorfer, H. (1992). A Nonce-based Protocol for Multiple Authentications. *ACM Operating Systems Review*, vol. 26, no. 4, pp. 84-89.

[Keleher *et al.* 1992]   Keleher, P., Cox, A. and Zwaenepoel, W. (1992). Lazy consistency for software distributed shared memory. *Proc. 19th Annual International Sym. on Computer Architecture.* pp. 13-21, May 1992.

[Kessler and Livny 1989] Kessler, R.E. and Livny, M. (1989). An Analysis of Distributed Shared Memory Algorithms, *Proc. 9th Int. Conf. Distributed Computing Systems.* IEEE, pp. 98–104.

[Kille 1992]   Kille, S. (1992). *Implementing X.400 and X.500: The PP and QUIPU systems.* Artech House.

[Kindberg 1990]   Kindberg, T. (1990). *Reconfiguring Distributed Computations. PhD thesis*. University of Westminster, England.

[Kistler and Satyanarayanan   Kistler, J.J. and Satyanarayanan, M. (1992). Disconnected
1992]   Operation in the Coda File System. *ACM Trans. on Computer Systems*, vol 10, no. 1, pp. 3–25.

[Knuth 1973]   Knuth, D.E. (1973). *The Art of Computer Programming, Vol. 3: Sorting and Searching*. Reading MA: Addison-Wesley.

[Kung and Robinson 1981]   Kung, H.T. and Robinson, J.T. (1981). Optimistic methods for concurrency control. *ACM Trans. on Database Systems*, vol. 6, no. 2, pp. 213–26.

[Ladin *et al.* 1992]   Ladin, R., Liskov, B., Shrira, L. and Ghemawat, S. (1992). Providing Availability Using Lazy Replication. *ACM Trans. on Computer Systems*, vol. 10, no. 4, pp. 360–391.

[Lamport 1978]   Lamport, L. (1978). Time, clocks and the ordering of events in a distributed system. Comms. ACM, vol. 21, no. 7, pp. 558–65.

[Lamport 1979]   Lamport, L. (1979). How to Make a Multiprocessor Computer that Correctly Executes Multiprocess Programs. *IEEE Trans. Computers*, vol. C-28, no. 9, pp. 690–1.

[Lamport *et al.* 1982]   Lamport, L., Shostak, R. and Paese, M. (1982). Byzantine Generals Problem. *ACM Trans. Programming Languages and Systems*. vol. 4, no. 3, pp. 382–401.

[Lampson 1986]   Lampson, B.W. (1986). Designing a Global Name Service. *Proc. 5th ACM Sym. Principles of Distributed Computing*, pp. 1–10, August.

[Lampson 1981a]   Lampson, B.W. (1981). Atomic Transactions. In *Distributed systems: Architecture and Implementation. Lecture Notes in Computer Science 105,* pp. 254–9. Berlin: Springer-Verlag.

[Lampson 1981b]   Lampson, B.W. (1981). Ethernet, Pup and Violet. In *Distributed systems: Architecture and Implementation. Lecture Notes in Computer Science 105*, pp. 265–73. Berlin: Springer-Verlag.

[Lampson 1983]   Lampson, B.W. (1983). Hints for computer system design. *ACM Operating Systems Review, vol. 17, no. 5*, pp. 33–48.

[Lampson *et al.* 1992]   Lampson, B.W., Abadi, M., Burrows, M. and Wobber, E. (1992). Authentication in Distributed Systems: Theory and Practice. *ACM Trans. on Computer Systems*, vol. 10, no. 4, pp. 265–310.

[Lea *et al.* 1993]   Lea, R., Jacquemot, C. and Pillevesse, E. (1993). COOL: system support for distributed programming. *Comms. ACM*, vol. 36, no. 9, pp.37–46.

[Leach *et al.* 1983]   Leach, P.J., Levine, P. H., Douros, B.P., Hamilton, J.A., Nelson, D.L. and Stumpf, B.L. (1983). The architecture of an integrated local network. *IEEE J. Selected Areas in Communications*, vol. SAC-1, no. 5, pp. 842–56.

[Leffler *et al*. 1989]   Leffler, S., McKusick, M., Karels, M. and Quartermain J. (1989). *The Design and Implementation of the 4.3 BSD UNIX Operating System.* Reading MA: Addison-Wesley.

[Lenoski *et al*. 1992]   Lenoski, D., Laudon, J., Gharachorloo, K., Weber, W.D., Gupta, A., Hennessy, J., Horowitz, M. and Lam, M.S. (1992). The Stanford Dash multiprocessor. *IEEE Computer*, vol. 25, no. 3, pp. 63–79.

[Li and Hudak 1989]   Li, K. and Hudak, P. (1989). Memory Coherence in Shared Virtual Memory Systems. *ACM Trans. on Computer Systems*, vol. 7, no. 4, pp. 321–359.

[Linn *et al*. 1993]   Linn, J., Kent, S., Balenson, D., Kaliski, B. (1993). Privacy Enhancement for Internet Electronic Mail: Parts I – IV. *Tech. Reports RFC 1421 – 1424*, files available for anonymous file transfer from the Internet Network Information Center, Internet host: nic.ddn.mil, directory: /usr/pub/RFC.

[Lipton and Sandberg 1988]   Lipton, R. and Sandberg, J. (1988). PRAM: A scalable shared memory. *Tech. Report CS-TR-180-88*, Princeton University.

[Liskov 1988]   Liskov, B. (1988). Distributed programming in Argus. *Comms. ACM, vol 31, no.3*, pp. 300–12.

[Liskov and Guttag 1986]   Liskov, B. and Guttag, J. (1986). *Abstraction and Specification in Program Development.* MIT Press/McGraw-Hill.

[Liskov and Scheifler 1982]   Liskov, B. and Scheifler, R.W. (1982). Guardians and actions: linguistic support for robust, distributed programs. *ACM Trans. Programming Languages and Systems*, vol. 5, no. 3, pp. 381–404.

[Liskov and Shrira 1988]   Liskov, B. and Shrira, L. (1988). Promises: Linguistic Support for Efficient Asynchronous Procedure Calls in Distributed Systems. *Proc SIGPLAN '88 Conf. Programming Language Design and Implementation.* Atlanta, Georgia.

[Liskov *et al*. 1981]   Liskov, B., Moss, E., Schaffert, C., Sheifler, R. and Snyder, A. (1981). CLU Reference Manual. In *Lecture Notes in Computer Science* 114, Berlin: Springer-Verlag.

[Liskov *et al*. 1991]   Liskov, B., Ghemawat, S., Gruber, R., Johnson, P., Shrira, L., Williams, M. (1991). Replication in the Harp File System. *Proc. 13th ACM Sym. on OS Principles*, pp. 226–38.

[Loepere 1991]   Loepere, K. (1991). *Mach 3 Kernel Principles.* Open Software Foundation and Carnegie-Mellon University.

[Ma 1992]   Ma, C. (1992). Designing a Universal Name Service. *Tech. Report 270*, University of Cambridge.

[Marsh *et al*. 1991]   Marsh, B., Scott, M., LeBlanc, T. and Markatos, E. (1991). First-class User-level Threads. *Proc.13th ACM Sym. Operating System Principles*, pp. 110–21.

[Martin 1993]   Martin, J.L. (1993). Travels with Gopher. *IEEE Computer*, vol.26, no.5, pp. 84–7.

[Marzullo 1984]   Marzullo, K. (1984). Maintaining the Time in a Distributed System. *Tech. Report OSD-T8401*, Xerox Corporation.

[Mattern 1988]   Mattern, F.(1989). Virtual time and global states of distributed systems. In *Parallel and Distributed Algorithms* (Ed. M. Cosnard *et al*), North-Holland, Amsterdam, pp. 215-226.

[Metcalfe and Boggs 1976] Metcalfe, R.M. and Boggs, D. R. (1976). Ethernet: distributed packet switching for local computer networks. *Comms. ACM*, vol. 19, pp. 395–403.

[Meyer 1988]   Meyer, B. (1988). *Object-Oriented Software Construction*. Englewood Cliffs NJ: Prentice-Hall.

[Meyer and Matyas 1982]   Meyer, C.H. and Matyas, H. (1982). *Cryptography: a New Dimension in Computer Data Security*. Wiley.

[Mills 1991]   Mills, D. L. (1991). Internet Time Synchronization: the Network Time Protocol. *IEEE Trans. on Comms*, vol. 39, no. 10, pp. 1482–93.

[Minnich and Farber 1989] Minnich, R. and Farber, D. (1989). The Mether System: a Distributed Shared Memory for SunOS 4.0. *Proc. Summer* 1989 *Usenix Conf.*

[MIT 1994]   Massachusetts Institute of Technology (1994). Documentation and source code for the current implementation of Kerberos. *Files available for anonymous file transfer from MIT,* Internet host: athena-dist.mit.edu, directory: /pub/kerberos.

[Mitchell 1982]   Mitchell, J.G. (1982). File servers for local area networks. In *Lecture notes for course on Local Area Networks*. Kent University, England, pp. 83–114.

[Mitchell 1985]   Mitchell, J.G. (1985). File servers. In *Local Area Networks: an Advanced Course, Lecture Notes in Computer Science*, 184, Springer-Verlag, pp. 221–59.

[Mitchell and Dion 1982]   Mitchell, J.G. and Dion, J. (1982). A comparison of two network-based file servers. *Comms. ACM*, vol. 25, no. 4, pp. 233–45.

[Mitchell *et al.* 1979]   Mitchell, J.G., Maybury, W. and Sweet, R. (1979). Mesa Language Reference Manual (Version 5.0). *Tech. Report CSL-79-3*, Xerox PARC, Palo Alto, CA.

[Mitchell *et al.* 1992]   Mitchell, C.J., F. Piper, F. and Wild, P. (1992). Digital Signatures. In *Contemporary Cryptology* (Ed. Simmons, G.J.) New York: IEEE Press.

[Mockapetris 1987]   Mockapetris, P. (1987). Domain Names – Concepts and Facilities. *Tech. Report RFC 1034*, file available for anonymous file transfer from the Internet Network Information Center, Internet host: nic.ddn.mil, directory: /usr/pub/RFC.

[Moran *et al.* 1990]   Moran, J., Sandberg, R., Coleman. D., Kepecs, J. and Lyon, B. (1990). Breaking the NFS Performance Barrier. *Proc. European Unix Users' Group (EUUG)*, pp. 199–206.

[Morris *et al.* 1986]   Morris, J., Satyanarayanan, M., Conner, M.H., Howard, J.H., Rosenthal, D.S., Smith, F.D. (1986). Andrew: a distributed personal computing environment. *Comms. ACM*, vol. 29, no. 3, pp. 184–201.

[Mosberger 1993]   Mosberger, D. (1993). Memory Consistency Models. *Tech. Report 93/11*, University of Arizona.

[Moss 1985]   Moss, E. (1985). *Nested Transactions, An Approach to Reliable Distributed Computing*. MIT Press.

[Mullender 1985]   Mullender, S.J. (1985). *Principles of Distributed Operating System Design*, Mathematisch Centrum, Amsterdam (Doctoral Thesis)

[Myer 1988]   Myer, B. (1988). *Object-oriented Software Construction*. New York: Prentice Hall.

[National Bureau of Standards 1977]   National Bureau of Standards (1977). *Data Encryption Standard (DES)*. Federal Information Processing Standards No. 46, Washington DC: US National Bureau of Standards.

[Needham 1993]   Needham, R. (1993). Names. In *Distributed Systems, an Advanced Course*. (Ed. Mullender, S.), Second Edition, Wokingham: ACM Press/Addison-Wesley. pp. 315-26.

[Needham and Herbert 1982]   Needham, R.M. and Herbert, A.J. (1982). *The Cambridge Distributed Computing System*. Wokingham: Addison-Wesley.

[Needham and Schroeder 1978]   Needham, R.M. and Schroeder, M.D. (1978). Using encryption for authentication in large networks of computers. *Comms. ACM*, vol. 21, pp. 993–9.

[Nelson 1991]   Nelson, G. Ed. (1991). *Systems Programming with Modula-3*. Prentice Hall.

[Nichols 1987]   Nichols, D. (1987), Using Idle Workstations in a Shared Computing Environment, *Proc. 11th. Symposium on Operating System Principles*, ACM, pp. 5–12.

[Organick 1972]   Organick, E.I. (1972). *The MULTICS System: an Examination of its Structure*. Cambridge, MA: MIT Press.

[Orman *et al.* 1993]   Orman, H., Menze, E., O'Malley, S. and Peterson, L. (1993). A fast and general implementation of Mach IPC in a Network. *Proc. Third USENIX Mach Conference*, April.

[OSF 1990]   Open Software Foundation (1990). *OSF Distributed Computing Environment Rationale*. Cambridge MA: Open Software Foundation.

[Ousterhout *et al.* 1985]   Ousterhout, J., Da Costa, H., Harrison, D., Kunze, J., Kupfer, M., Thompson, J. (1985). A Trace-driven analysis of the UNIX 4.2 BSD file system. *10th ACM Sym. Operating System Principles*.

[Ousterhout *et al.* 1988]   Ousterhout, J., Cherenson, A., Douglis, F., Nelson, M. and Welch, B. (1988). The Sprite Network Operating System. *IEEE Computer, vol. 21, no. 2*, pp. 23–36.

[Parker 1992]   Parker, B. (1992). The PPP AppleTalk Control Protocol (ATCP). *Tech. Report RFC 1378*, file available for anonymous file transfer from the Internet Network Information Center, Internet host: nic.ddn.mil, directory: /usr/pub/RFC.

[Peterson 1988]   Peterson, L. (1988). The Profile Naming Service. *ACM Trans. Computer Systems*, vol. 6, no. 4, pp. 341–64.

[Peterson *et al.* 1989]   Peterson, L.L., Buchholz, N.C. and Schlichting, R.D. (1989). Preserving and Using Context Information in Interprocess Communication. *ACM Trans. on Computer Systems*, vol. 7, no. 3, pp. 217–46.

[Peterson *et al.* 1990]   Peterson, L., Hutchinson, N., O'Malley, S. and Rao, H. (1990). The x-kernel: A Platform for Accessing Internet Resources. *IEEE Computer*, vol. 23, no. 5, pp. 23–33.

[Pierce 1972]   Pierce, J., (1972). How far can data loops go? *IEEE Trans. Communications*, vol. COM-20, pp. 527–30.

[Pike *et al.* 1990]   Pike, R., Presotto, K., Thompson, K. and Trickey, H. (1990). Plan 9 from Bell Labs. *Proc. UK Unix Users Group Summer 1990 Conference*, London.

[Popek and Walker 1985]   Popek, G. and Walker, B. (Eds.). (1985). *The LOCUS Distributed System Architecture*. Cambridge MA: MIT Press.

[Postel 1981a]   Postel, J. (1981). Internet Protocol. *Tech. Report RFC 791*, file available for anonymous file transfer from the Internet Network Information Center, Internet host: nic.ddn.mil, directory: /usr/pub/RFC.

[Postel 1981b]   Postel, J. (1981). Transmission Control Protocol. *Tech. Report RFC 793*, file available for anonymous file transfer from the Internet Network Information Center, Internet host: nic.ddn.mil, directory: /usr/pub/RFC.

[Rashid 1985]   Rashid, R.F. (1985). Network operating systems. In *Local Area Networks: an Advanced Course, Lecture Notes in Computer Science*. 184, Springer-Verlag, pp. 314–40.

[Rashid 1986]   Rashid, R.F. (1986). From RIG to Accent to Mach: the evolution of a network operating system. *Proceedings of the ACM/IEEE Computer Society Fall Joint Conference*, ACM, November.

[Rashid and Robertson 1981]   Rashid, R. and Robertson, G. (1981). Accent: a communications oriented network operating system kernel. *ACM Operating Systems Review*, vol. 15, no. 5, pp. 64–75.

[Rashid *et al.* 1988]   Rashid, R., Tevanian Jr., A., Young, M., Golub, D., Baron, R., Black, D., Bolosky, W. J. and Chew, J. (1988). Machine-Independent Virtual Memory Management for Paged Uniprocessor and Multiprocessor Architectures. *IEEE Trans. Computers*, vol. 37, no. 8, pp. 896–907.

[Raynal 1988]   Raynal, M. (1988). *Distributed Algorithms and Protocols*. Wiley.

[Raynal 1992]   Raynal, M. (1992). About Logical Clocks for Distributed Systems. *ACM Operating Systems Review*, vol. 26, no. 1, pp. 41–8.

[Reed 1983]   Reed, D.P. (1983). Implementing atomic actions on decentralized data. *ACM Trans. on Computer Systems*, vol. 1, no.1, pp. 3–23.

[Rescher and Urquhart 1971]   Rescher, N. and Urquhart, A. (1971). *Temporal Logic*. Springer-Verlag.

[Ricart and Agrawala 1981]   Ricart, G. and Agrawala, A.K. (1981). An optimal algorithm for mutual exclusion in computer networks. *Comms. ACM*, vol. 24, no. 1, pp. 9–17.

[Ritchie 1984]   Ritchie, D. (1984). A Stream Input Output System. *AT&T Bell Laboratories Technical Journal*, vol. 63, no. 8, pt. 2, pp. 1897–910.

[Ritchie and Thompson 1974]   Ritchie, D.M. and Thompson, K. (1974). The UNIX time-sharing system. *Comms. ACM*, vol. 17, no. 7, pp. 365–75.

[Rivest 1992]   Rivest, R. (1992). The MD5 Message-Digest Algorithm. *Tech. Report RFC 1321*, file available for anonymous file transfer from the Internet Network Information Center, Internet host: nic.ddn.mil, directory: /usr/pub/RFC.

[Rivest *et al*. 1978]   Rivest, R.L., Shamir, A. and Adelman, L. (1978). A method of obtaining digital signatures and public key cryptosystems. *Comms. ACM*, vol. 21, no. 2, pp. 120–6.

[Roesler and Burkhard 1988]   Roesler, M. and Burkhard, W. (1988). Deadlock Resolution And Semantic Lock Models in Object-Oriented Distributed Systems. *ACM SIGMOD Proc.* vol. 17, no 3.

[Romkey 1988]   Romkey, J. (1988). Nonstandard for transmission of IP datagrams over serial lines: SLIP. *Tech. Report RFC 1055*, file available for anonymous file transfer from the Internet Network Information Center, Internet host: nic.ddn.mil, directory: /usr/pub/RFC.

[Rose 1992]   Rose, Marshall T. (1992). *The Little Black Book: Mail Bonding with OSI Directory Services*. Prentice-Hall, Englewood Cliffs NJ.

[Rozier *et al*. 1988]   Rozier, M., Abrossimov, V., Armand, F., Boule, I., Gien, M., Guillemont, M., Herrman, F., Kaiser, C., Langlois, S., Leonard, P. and Neuhauser, W. (1988). Chorus Distributed Operating Systems. *Computing Systems Journal*, vol. 1, no. 4, pp. 305–70.

[Rozier *et al*. 1990]   Rozier, M., Abrossimov, V., Armand, F., Boule, I., Gien, M., Guillemont, M., Herrman, F., Kaiser, C., Langlois, S., Leonard, P. and Neuhauser, W. (1990). Overview of the Chorus Distributed Operating System. *Tech. Report CS/TR-90-25.1*, Chorus Systèmes, France.

[Saltzer *et al*. 1984]   Saltzer, J.H., Reed, D.P. and Clarke, D. (1984). End-to-end arguments in system design. *ACM Trans. on Computer Systems*, vol. 2, no. 1, pp. 3–21.

[Sandberg 1987]   Sandberg, R. (1987). The Sun Network File System: Design, Implementation and Experience. *Tech. Report*. Mountain View CA: Sun Microsystems.

[Sandberg *et al*. 1985]   Sandberg, R., Goldberg, D., Kleiman, S., Walsh, D., Lyon, B. (1985). The Design and Implementation of the Sun Network File System. *Proc. Usenix Conf.*, Portland OR.

[Sane *et al*. 1990]   Sane, A., MacGregor, K. and Campbell, R. (1990). Distributed Virtual Memory Consistency Protocols: Design and Performance. *Second IEEE Workshop on Experimental Distributed Systems*, pp. 91–6, October.

[Sansom *et al*. 1986]   Sansom, R.D., Julin, D.P. and Rashid, R.F. (1986). Extending a capability based system into a network environment. *Tech. Report CMU-CS-86-116*, Carnegie-Mellon University.

[Santifaller 1991]   Santifaller. M. (1991). *TCP/IP and NFS, Internetworking in a Unix Environment*. Reading MA: Addison-Wesley.

[Satyanarayanan 1981]   Satyanarayanan, M. (1981). A study of file sizes and functional lifetimes. *Proc. 8th ACM Sym. Operating System Principles*, Asilomar CA.

[Satyanarayanan 1989a]   Satyanarayanan, M. (1989). Distributed File Systems. In *Distributed Systems, an Advanced Course*. (Mullender, S. Ed.), Second Edition, Wokingham: ACM Press/Addison-Wesley. pp 353–83.

[Satyanarayanan 1989b]   Satyanarayanan, M. (1989). Integrating Security in a Large Distributed System. *ACM Trans. on Computer Systems*, vol. 7, no. 3, pp. 247–80.

[Satyanarayanan *et al.* 1990] Satyanarayanan, M., Kistler, J.J., Kumar, P., Okasaki, M.E., Siegel, E.H. and Steere, D.C. (1990). Coda: A Highly Available File System for a Distributed Workstation Environment. *IEEE Trans. on Computers*, vol. 39, no. 4, pp. 447–59.

[Scheifler and Gettys 1986] Scheifler, R.W. and Gettys, J. (1986). The X window system. *ACM Trans. on Computer Graphics*, vol. 5, no. 2, pp. 76–109.

[Schiper *et al.* 1989]   Schiper, A., Eggli, J. and Sandoz, A. (1989). A New Algorithm to Implement Causal Ordering. *Proc. Third Int. Workshop on Distributed Algorithms*. In *Lecture Notes on Computer Science 392*, Springer-Verlag, New York, pp. 219–32.

[Schlageter 1982]   Schlageter, G. (1982). Problems of Optimistic Concurrency Control in Distributed Database Systems. *SigMOD Record,* vol. 13, no. 3, pp. 62–6.

[Schneider 1990]   Schneider, F.B. (1990). Implementing Fault-tolerant Services Using the State Machine Approach: A Tutorial. *ACM Computing Surveys*, vol. 22, no. 4, pp. 300–19.

[Schroeder and Burrows 1990] Schroeder, M. and Burrows, M. (1990). The Performance of Firefly RPC. *ACM Trans. Computer Systems*, vol. 8, no. 1. pp. 1–17.

[Shand *et al.* 1990]   Shand, M., Bertin, P. and Vuillemin, J. (1990). Resource tradeoffs in fast long integer multiplication. *Second ACM Sym. on Parallel Algorithms and Architectures*, Crete.

[Shapiro 1986]   Shapiro, M. (1986). Structure and encapsulation in distributed systems: the proxy principle. *Proc. 6th IEEE Int. Conf. on Distributed Computing Systems*, Cambridge MA, pp.198–204.

[Shapiro 1989]   Shapiro, M. and Gautron, P. (1989). Persistence and migration for C++ Objects. *Proc. Third European Conference on Object-Oriented Programming*, Nottingham, pp. 191–203.

[Shoch and Hupp 1980]   Shoch, J.F. and Hupp, J.A. (1980). Measured performance of an Ethernet local network. *Comms. ACM*, vol. 23, no. 12, pp. 711–21.

[Shoch and Hupp 1982]   Shoch, J.F. and Hupp, J.A. (1982). The 'Worm' programs – early experience with a distributed computation. *Comms. ACM*, vol. 25, no. 3, pp. 172–80.

[Shoch *et al.* 1982]   Shoch, J.F., Dalal, Y.K. and Redell, D.D. (1982). The evolution of the Ethernet local area network. *IEEE Computer*, vol. 15, no. 8, pp. 10–28.

[Shoch *et al.* 1985]   Shoch, J.F., Dalal, Y.K., Redell, D.D. and Crane, R.C. (1985). The Ethernet. In *Local Area Networks: an Advanced Course,* Lecture Notes in Computer Science No. 184, Springer-Verlag, pp. 1–33.

[Shrivastava *et al.* 1989]   Shrivastava, S.K., Dixon, G., Parrington, G.D., Hedayati, F., Wheater, S. and Little, M. (1989). The Design and Implementation of Arjuna. *Proc. Third Conference on Object-Oriented Programming*, Nottingham.

[Shrivastava *et al.* 1991]   Shrivastava, S., Dixon, G.N. and Parrington, G.D. (1991). An Overview of the Arjuna Distributed Programming System. *IEEE Software*, January 1991. pp. 66–73.

[Siewiorek *et al.* 1981]   Siewiorek, D., Bell, C.G. and Newell, A. (Eds), (1981). *Computer Structures: Readings and Examples.* (Second edition), New York: McGraw-Hill.

[Silberschatz *et al.* 1993]   Siberschatz, A., Peterson, J. and Galvin, P. (1993). *Operating Systems Concepts. (*Fourth edition), Reading MA: Addison-Wesley.

[Simmonds 1992]   Simmons, G.J. (ed.). (1992). *Contemporary Cryptology.* New York: IEEE Press.

[Sinha and Natarajan 1985]   Sinha, M. and Natarajan, N. (1985). A Priority Based Distributed Deadlock Detection Algorithm. *IEEE Trans. on Soft. Engineering,* vol. 11, no. 1, pp. 67-80.

[Spafford 1989]   Spafford, E.H. (1989). The Internet Worm: Crisis and Aftermath. *Comms. ACM*, vol. 32, no. 6, pp. 678–87.

[Spector 1982]   Spector, A.Z. (1982). Performing remote operations efficiently on a local computer network. *Comms. ACM*, vol. 25, no. 4, pp. 246–60.

[Steiner *et al.* 1988]   Steiner, J., Neuman, C. and Schiller, J. (1988). Kerberos: an authentication service for open network systems. *Proc. Usenix Winter Conf.* Berkeley.

[Stroustrup 1986]   Stroustrup, B. (1986). *The C++ Programming Language.* Reading MA: Addison-Wesley.

[Sturgis *et al.* 1980]   Sturgis, H.E., Mitchell, J.G. and Israel, J. (1980). Issues in the design and use of a distributed file system. *ACM Operating Systems Review*, vol. 14, no. 3, pp. 55–69.

[Sun 1989]   Sun Microsystems Inc. (1989). NFS: Network File System Protocol Specification. *Tech. Report RFC 1094*, file available for anonymous file transfer from the Internet Network Information Center, Internet host: nic.ddn.mil, directory: /usr/pub/RFC.

[Sun 1990]   Sun Microsystems Inc. (1990). *Network Programming.* Sun Microsystems, Mountain View, CA. March.

[Tanenbaum 1987]   Tanenbaum, A.S. (1987). *Operating Systems: Design and Implementation.* Englewood Cliffs NJ: Prentice-Hall.

[Tanenbaum 1988]   Tanenbaum, A.S. (1988). *Computer Networks. Second edition*, Englewood Cliffs NJ: Prentice-Hall.

[Tanenbaum 1992]   Tanenbaum, A.S. (1992). *Modern Operating Systems*. Englewood Cliffs NJ: Prentice Hall.

[Tanenbaum *et al*. 1990]   Tanenbaum, A.S., van Renesse, R., van Staveren, H., Sharp, G., Mullender, S., Jansen, J. and van Rossum, G. (1990). Experiences with the Amoeba Distributed Operating System. *Comms. ACM*, vol. 33, no. 12, pp. 46–63.

[Teitelman 1984]   Teitelman, W. (1984). A tour through Cedar. *IEEE Software*, vol. 1, no. 2, pp. 44–73.

[Terry 1984]   Terry, D. (1984). An Analysis of Naming Conventions for Distributed Computer Systems. *Proc. SIGCOMM 84, Tutorial and Sym. on Communication Architectures and Protocols*, pp. 218–24, June.

[Tokuda *et al*. 1990]   Tokuda, H., Nakajima, T. and Rao, P. (1990). Real-time Mach: towards a predictable real-time system. *Proceedings USENIX Mach Workshop*, pp. 73–82, October.

[Ullman 1984]   Ullman, J.D. (1984). *Principles of Database Systems*. Computer Science Press.

[van Renesse *et al*. 1989]   van Renesse, R., van Staveran, H. and Tanenbaum, A. (1989). The Performance of the Amoeba Distributed Operating System. *Software – Practice and Experience*, vol. 19, no. 3, pp. 223–34.

[Vaughan-Nichols 1991]   Vaughan-Nichols, S.J. (1991). Disk Insurance, *Byte*, August, pp. 195–202.

[Voydock and Kent 1983]   Voydock, V.L. and Kent, S.T. (1983). Security Mechanisms in High-level Network Protocols. *Computing Surveys* vol. 15, no.2, pp. 135–71.

[Walker *et al*. 1983]   Walker, B., Popek, G., English, R., Kline, C. and Theil, G.H. (1983). The Locus distributed operating system. *Proc. 9th. ACM Sym. Operating System Principles*, October, pp. 49–70.

[Wallach 1993]   Wallach, P. (1993). Electronic Envelopes. *Scientific American*, February, pp. 30–2.

[Wegner 1984]   Wegner, P. (1984). Capital-intensive Software Technology. *IEEE Software*, vol. 1, no. 3.

[Weikum 1991]   Weikum, G. (1991). Principles and Realization Strategies of Multilevel Transaction Management. *ACM Trans. Database Systems*, vol. 16, no. 1, pp. 132–40.

[Wuu and Bernstein 1984] Wuu, G.T. and Bernstein, A.J. (1984). Efficient Solutions to the Replicated Log and Dictionary Problems. *Proc. Third Annual Sym. Principles of Distributed Computing, ACM*, pp. 233–42.

[Xerox 1981]   Xerox Corporation (1981). *Courier: the remote procedure call protocol. Xerox Systems Integration Standards*. Stamford CT: Xerox Corporation.

INDEX